Revisioning Gender

Editors
Myra Marx Ferree
Judith Lorber
Beth B. Hess

SAGE PUBLICATIONS
Thousand Oaks ■ London ■ New Delhi

For information:

SAGE Publications, Inc.
2455 Teller Road
Thousand Oaks, California 91320
E-mail: order@sagepub.com

SAGE Publications Ltd.
6 Bonhill Street
London EC2A 4PU
United Kingdom

SAGE Publications India Pvt. Ltd.
M-32 Market
Greater Kailash I
New Delhi 110 048 India

Printed in the United States of America

Library of Congress Cataloging-in-Publication Data

Main entry under title:

　　Revisioning gender / edited by Myra Marx Ferree, Judith Lorber,
and Beth B. Hess
　　　　p.　　cm. — (The gender lens; v. 5)
　　Includes bibliographical references and index.
　　ISBN 0-7619-0616-9 (cloth: acid-free paper).
　　ISBN 0-7619-0617-7 (pbk.: acid-free paper)
　　　1. Feminist theory.　2. Women—Social conditions.　3. Sex role.
4. Sex differences.　I. Ferree, Myra Marx.　II. Lorber, Judith.
III. Hess, Beth B., 1928-　IV. Series.
HQ1190.R483　1998
305.3—ddc21　　　　　　　　　　　　　　　　98-25488

This book is printed on acid-free paper that meets Environmental Protection Agency standards for recycled paper.

99　00　01　02　03　04　05　7　6　5　4　3　2　1

Acquisition Editor:	Peter Labella
Production Editor:	Astrid Virding
Editorial Assistant:	Stephanie Allen
Typesetter/Designer:	Rose Tylak
Cover Designer:	Ravi Balasuriya

In Memory of Jessie Bernard
June 8, 1903–October 6, 1996

Jessie was a mother/sister/mentor/friend to so many of us. Her work inspired the entire field. Her outspoken feminism cleared a path for many younger and less well-known female scholars to move toward an unabashed feminism. Her incredible intellectual breadth, wisdom, and generosity to other scholars, as well as her personal sweetness and kindness to everyone who crossed her path, will not be forgotten by those of us who were fortunate enough to have known her. To know Jessie was to admire and love her, to be enriched by her wisdom and spirit.

—*Jean Lipman-Blumen*

CONTENTS

It is now more than 20 years since feminist sociologists identified gender as an important analytic dimension in sociology. In the intervening decades, theory and research on gender have grown exponentially. With this series, we intend to further this scholarship, as well as ensure that theory and research on gender become fully integrated into the discipline as a whole.

In a classic edited collection, the precursor to this volume, Beth Hess and Myra Marx Ferree (1987) identify three stages in the study of women and men since 1970. Initially, the emphasis was on sex differences and the extent to which such differences might be based in biological properties of individuals. In the second stage, the focus shifted to individual-level sex roles and socialization, exposing gender as the product of specific social arrangements, although still conceptualizing it as an individual trait. The hallmark of the third stage is the recognition of the centrality of gender as an organizing principle in all social systems, including work, politics, everyday interaction, families, economic development, law, education, and a host of other social domains. As our understanding of gender has become more social, so has our awareness that gender is experienced and organized in race- and class-specific ways.

In the summer of 1992, the American Sociological Association (ASA) funded a small conference, organized by Barbara Risman and Joey Sprague, to discuss the evolution of gender in these distinctly sociological frameworks. The conference brought together a sampling of gender scholars working in a wide range of substantive areas with a diversity of methods to focus on gender as a principle of social organization. The discussions of the state of feminist scholarship made it clear that gender is pervasive in society and operates at multiple levels. Gender shapes identities and perception, interactional practices, and the very forms of social institutions and it does so in race- and class-specific ways. If we did not see gender in social phenomena, we were not seeing clearly.

The participants in this ASA-sponsored seminar recognized that although these developing ideas about gender were widely accepted by feminist sociologists and many others who study social inequalities, they were relatively unfamiliar to many who work within other sociological paradigms. This book series was conceived at that conference as a means of introducing these ideas to sociological colleagues and students, and of helping to develop gender scholarship further.

As series editors, we feel it is time for gender scholars to speak to our colleagues and to the general education of students. There are many sociologists and scholars in other social sciences who want to incorporate scholarship on gender and its intersections with race, class, and sexuality in their teaching and research, but lack the tools to do so. For those who have not worked in this area, the prospect of the bibliographic research necessary to develop supplementary units, or to transform their own teaching and scholarship, is daunting. Moreover, the publications necessary to penetrate a curriculum resistant to change and encumbered by inertia have simply not been available. We conceptualize this book series as a way of meeting the needs of these scholars, and thereby also encouraging the development of the sociological understanding of gender by offering a "gender lens."

What do we mean by a *gender lens*? We mean working to make gender visible in social phenomena, asking if, how, and why social processes, standards, and opportunities differ systematically for women and men. We also mean recognizing that gender inequality is inextricably intertwined with other systems of inequity. Looking at the world through a gendered lens thus implies two seemingly contradictory tasks. First, it means unpacking the taken-for-granted assumptions about gender that pervade sociological research, and social life more generally. At the same time, looking through a gender lens means showing just how central assumptions about gender continue to be to the organization of the social world, regardless of their empirical reality. We show how our often unquestioned ideas about gender affect the worlds we see, the questions we ask, the answers we can envision. The **Gender Lens** series is committed to social change directed toward eradicating these inequalities. Our goals are consistent with initiatives at colleges and universities across the United States that are encouraging the development of more diverse scholarship and teaching.

The books in the **Gender Lens** series are aimed at different audiences and have been written for a variety of uses, from assigned readings in introductory undergraduate courses to graduate seminars, and as professional resources for our colleagues. The series includes several different styles of books that address these goals in distinct ways. We are excited about this series and anticipate that it will have an enduring impact on the direction of both pedagogy and scholarship in sociology and other related social sciences. We invite you, the reader, to join us in thinking through these difficult but exciting issues by offering feedback or developing your own project and proposing it to us for the series.

About This Volume

The authors and editors of this unique collection of articles help us once again to re-vision gender with ever more sophisticated lenses. This revised understanding takes gender seriously as both process and structure, from the individual to societal levels of analysis. This volume differs from many in the **Gender Lens** series because it is not exclusively sociological. Rather, this volume goes beyond disciplinary issues and structures. The editors—Myra Marx Ferree, Beth B. Hess, and Judith Lorber—argue that one of the components of a feminist agenda for the social sciences includes calling disciplinary distinctions into question. The focus of this collection of feminist theory and research is to no longer take dichotomous gender for granted but to begin to explain the meaning of gender itself. To do this, the authors look at both structure and process, at both the reproduction of inequality and the reality of human agency. The editors show us that deconstructing gender as a category is not an occasion to fall into a morass of relativism and apolitical apologies for all kinds of diversity. Rather, it is an invitation to understand "*how* and *what* is being produced in the active construction of gender . . . to ask *why*." Each of the authors in this volume writes at the cutting edge of her or his field, and we offer this volume to readers of the **Gender Lens** series with delight.

Judith A. Howard
Barbara Risman
Mary Romero
Joey Sprague
Gender Lens Series Editors

Reference

Hess, Beth B. and Myra Marx Ferree, eds. 1987. *Analyzing Gender: A Handbook of Social Science Research.* Newbury Park, CA: Sage.

Over the past 25 years, the expansion of research on gender has been nothing less than explosive. The social scientific community can scarcely have failed to notice the sheer quantitative growth in the number of studies that make gender a part of their central problematic (not to mention the many more that routinely take some account of gender while focusing on another issue). Yet the question of how profoundly the concern with gender has infiltrated and changed the basic agenda of the social sciences remains. As Marx Ferree and Hall (1996) note, most introductory sociology textbooks still treat gender as an individual attribute and gender inequality as an outcome of childhood socialization. In contrast, current feminist thinking stresses the far greater input of the division of labor, power, social control, violence, and ideology as structural and interactional bases of inequality, not only between women and men, but among women and men of diverse social classes and racial ethnic groups.

In the early 1970s, influential collections such as Moss Kantor and Millman's *Another Voice* (1975) set out the nature of the challenge by documenting and critiquing the invisibility of women in social science theory as well in as specific subject areas. Such early challenges set an agenda for inclusion by exploring the biases in the concepts and methods that defined the various disciplines. Arguing that research designs were based on men's experiences, feminist social scientists demanded a fundamental transformation in how questions are asked and what criteria are employed to define an answer as acceptable. Deeply dissatisfied with how "normal science" marginalized women and gender, they argued for a transformation of epistemology and methodology (e.g., Harding 1986; Nielson 1990; Stanley and Wise 1983). The inclusion of women could not happen, many concluded, without the sort of paradigm shift that Kuhn (1970) has called a scientific revolution. By bringing gender in as a crucial concept, fields of study would have to change in multiple ways. Numerous interdisciplinary volumes in the late 1970s and the 1980s attempted to track and describe such transformations by field or topic (e.g., Aiken et al. 1988; Hess and Ferree 1987; Sherman and Beck 1979).

This volume builds on these earlier overviews and attempts to move beyond them, not only by focusing on the research done in the past decade but by encouraging thinking about how the questions we ourselves ask have changed. In that sense, it adopts the reflexive stance suggested by the emergent field of feminist methodology: The transformations we seek in the disciplines are also transformations of our own ways of thinking (Belenkey et al. 1986; Goldberger et al. 1996). As such changes have begun to take place, it has become evident to many feminist scholars that it will not be possible to understand gender without also altering the customary social science understandings of race and class. Thus this collection critiques both feminist and mainstream modes of studying gender in isolation from other social processes and begins to suggest what the outlines of an alternative might look like.

The alternative mode of thinking the contributors are developing attends to the structures of inequality, especially the intersectionality of the genders with social class positions, racial ethnic groupings, and the diversity of sexual orientations. It also pays great attention to the standpoints and perspectives of different groups, as these affect the production of knowledge and culture. The third element in the new feminist epistemology is *agency*—how rebellious individuals and collective social movements reform, resist, and transform the social order.

In the 1980s, it was also becoming clear that this feminist scientific revolution, like those that Kuhn had studied, would not take place without resistance. As Kuhn has noted, scientific disciplines are aptly named—they discipline thought by making some ideas seem natural and others almost unthinkable. The practices of science involve commitments to such disciplines, and the commitments of the scholarly community to certain ideas and ways of thinking seem to stand in the way of new theories, however useful they might prove to be in the long run. Within the disciplines, the anomalies increasingly produced by feminist scholarship's effort to "bring women in" were causing an intellectual ferment that was variously viewed as exciting or disturbing. Increasingly, feminist scholars have been attempting to identify what it was about the theories and practice of specific social sciences that made for resistance or openness to seeing gender as a significant social force.

Stacey and Thorne (1985) offered an influential analysis of why and how the feminist revolution was "missing" in sociology relative to anthropology (and why other disciplines such as economics and political science were even less transformed). One difference among the disciplines was the relative centrality in anthropology of kinship relations, seen as ordering society as a whole. In sociology, when gender was similarly seen primarily as an organizing principle of the family, the other areas of social life were falsely conceptualized as "ungendered." The borders between the disciplines, as well as the separations between subareas such as "family" and "work and organizations" within disciplines, reflect and reify a division between the supposedly ungendered "public" and the gendered "private" that is ideological and misleading (Gerson and Peiss 1985; Scott 1986).

Stacey and Thorne also criticized the disciplines as wedded to a functionalist and static view of gender that neglected the role of agency and change. Acker (1989) extended their analysis to point out the resistance to transformation that emerges from understanding society from the vantage point of those engaged in what Smith (1990a, 1990b) has called the "relations of ruling." In traditional sociology, the questions asked and the categories constructed often reflect the needs of the many administrations and bureaucracies that structure our lives. When scholarship is produced by or for the privileged, the issues and problems of the disadvantaged are ignored (Collins 1990). By developing social scientific theory from the diverse specific positions of women as knowers, "standpoint theories" have begun to transform the way gender is studied by feminist scholars. As a result, the conventional disciplinary distinctions become less relevant to the kinds of questions asked, and more focused and active interdisciplinary subareas are emerging within the broad scope of women's studies and social science. For example, gender and development research involves economics, health sciences, political science, history, and anthropology. Feminist studies of schools involve social psychologists, sociologists, educators, and organizational researchers who are looking critically at relations of power and interpersonal relations and asking questions about the gender, class, and racial ethnic processes involved in coeducation, dating, sports, and sexual harassment (e.g., Thorne 1993; Holland and Eisenhardt 1990).

This interdisciplinary approach has helped to shift the focus away from gender as the static dichotomy that sex role theory assumed (Hess and Ferree 1987). Feminist research now recognizes the diversity of gender statuses in the social order, statuses that intersect with social class, race, and ethnicity and so are imbued with enormous differences in economic opportunity and political power. Gender is not seen as a permanent result of childhood socialization, but as a lifelong "work in progress." Nor is gender construed only as a confining set of norms and expectations; feminists now credit the significance of agency and analyze how and why some people reconstruct and modify the structural and cultural systems that make gender divisions so pervasive and why those with different interests and positions in the social order support the status quo. These questions of agency and power challenge the "disciplined" division of research topics favored in academic institutions (Smith 1990a).

The present volume therefore does not follow the discipline-by-discipline structure that made sense a decade ago. Rather than transforming the separate disciplines, the feminist agenda for the social sciences seems increasingly to us to call such disciplinary distinctiveness into question. The issues posed here touch on all of the social sciences, but not as discrete entities. The focus of this collection of feminist theory and research has shifted toward conceptualizing that is "outside the box" of any specific disciplinary agenda in order to ask questions that focus on the very boundaries and points of intersection. For example, gender is intertwined with political processes at many levels when state policies favor certain kinds of families or control procreation choices. Gender, race, ethnicity, and class combine to create certain formal organizations of interests, histories of policy making, and popularized ideologies that influence the allocation of resources and benefits, as can be seen in the origins of social security, AFDC, and other pension programs in the United States (Skocpol 1992; Gordon 1994). A close look at these gendered struggles makes it obvious that women and men both played active roles, and highlights the many divisions within these overdichotomized categories.

The organization of this book reflects the advances in gender scholarship of the past decade in its emphasis on all levels of social structure, from the most macro to the most individual. *Analyzing Gender* (Hess and Ferree 1987), the predecessor to this volume, pointed out the significance of the emergence of gender as a paradigm distinct from either the sex differences or sex roles approaches of previous work. Whereas sex differences debates took the form of feminist-antifeminist struggles to define the extent (small versus large) and nature (insignificant and changeable versus fixed and important) of those differences, sex role debates shifted the questions to those of origin (biological versus social factors) and purpose (functionality and adjustment versus relations of dominance and oppression). Both of these debates were seen by advocates of the new gender paradigm, among whom we count ourselves, as missing the point, because they both started from the self-evident nature of "men" and "women" as social groupings. Given the variety and multiplicity of human differences and the many similarities among people regardless of what gender categories they might be assigned to, what creates the categories of "men" and "women" and makes them socially meaningful? When the dichotomy is no longer taken for granted as obvious and natural, gender itself needs to be explained.

Such an explanation, as Wallach Scott (1986) has pointed out, needs to be specific and contextual, for the categories of gender are both empty and overflowing: "Empty because they have no ultimate, transcendent meaning. Overflowing because even when they appear to be fixed, they still contain within them alternative, denied or suppressed definitions" (p. 1074). Constructing "men" and "women" is a social process at all levels—the intrapsychic, the interactional, and the organizational, institutional, and cultural practices of entire societies. Gender is itself now understood as a dynamic *process,* one that West and Zimmerman (1987) have called "doing gender" and others have referred to as "gendering." It is also understood simultaneously as a *structure,* that is, a latticework of institutionalized social relationships that, by creating and manipulating the categories of gender, organize and signify power at levels above the individual, from cultural meanings to government policies (Lorber 1994).

By *revisioning gender,* we mean taking seriously this understanding of gender as a process and structure, and using it to illuminate the workings of society (rather than merely of the social sciences). Thus the organization of this book deliberately emphasizes the continuum from macro to micro levels of analysis at which gender is relevant rather than the disciplinary boundaries that have been historically constructed around the levels.

As sociologists, we come from a discipline that has claimed the full range of society, from the most macro to the most micro, as its legitimate field of interest. Yet sociology's practices and its understandings of gender have typically failed to reach across these levels. In macro-level analysis, when looking at entire societies taken as a whole or the interrelations among such societies, sociologists have tended to make gender relatively invisible and instead to see only class or economic relations (Ferree and Hall 1996). Similarly, in political science, international relations remains one of the areas least widely understood as gendered, despite important contributions by feminist scholars to such analysis (e.g., Peterson 1992). At the meso level of interactions among groups, our discipline has been able to see and analyze race and ethnicity, but not gender. Instead, gender (but not race or class) is often treated only as a micro-level phenomenon, as a matter of individuals and the interactions among them (Ferree and Hall 1996).

We do not doubt the significance and importance of gender at this individual level, but we also see the identification of gender with the traits, attitudes, behaviors, and interactions of individuals alone as a means of containing and deflecting the more fundamental critical impetus of gender analysis for the revisioning of society. To take a gender perspective seriously means to question the categories used for analysis at all levels, including but not limited to the categories of "women" and "men." The categories of political and nonpolitical, of public and private, of dependent and independent, of production and consumption, of races, nations, states, ethnicities, families, and communities, all begin to fall apart in our hands as we take up the problem of gender. We do not see gender categories as homogeneous wholes; rather, we see gendering as a process of creating and using such categories to order our social world. But deconstructing static categories of gender is not, as it may be in the humanities, an occasion to relax into relativism and disorganized "diversity"; rather, it is an invitation to the social sciences to begin to understand *how* and *what* is being produced in the active construction of gender. Furthermore, we have to ask *why*. It is in the historically varying, politically contested, economically significant, geographically situated, and psychologically meaningful relations of gender that the social sciences most truly apply, even when the older social science models constructed on the paradigm of static categories fail. They fail repeatedly and conspicuously when they envision their other concepts—be they "the individual" or "production" or "independence" or "aggression"—as ungendered rather than constructed with a covert masculinity that varies by specific context.

This volume is also a step, however tentative, toward constructing a new analytic approach for the social sciences, one that explores the historical and geographic construction of and changes in many of the categories of analysis long assumed to be unproblematic and static. The authors we have invited to participate in this rethinking argue for and model by example a perspective that queries the underlying assumptions of many conventional categories of analysis, not only those of mainstream social science, but also those of recent feminist scholarship.

Reconceptualizing Gender

The three chapters in Part I lay out the accomplishments and the dilemmas in recent reconceptualizations of gender in feminist theory and research, making it clear that there is by no means a unified gender theory or gender constructs. In Chapters 1 and 2, Evelyn Nakano Glenn and Joan Acker tackle one of the most important conceptual issues in current feminist thought: how to integrate gender with the other main organizing constructs of social life. Although Nakano Glenn concentrates on race and Acker on class, both call for a framework that sees gender, race, and social class as simultaneous social processes. Gender cannot be understood outside of racial ethnic and class hierarchies, and the meaning and structural effects of race, ethnicity, and class are always gendered. According to Nakano Glenn, these processes operate at meso, micro, and macro levels. These levels are (a) *representation* through the use of symbols and images, (b) *micro-interaction* involving the rules of etiquette and spatial segregation that govern face-to-face behavior, and (c) *social structure*, or the allocation of power and material resources. She argues that the intertwined representational, relational, and social structural processes constitute power and produce inequality, yet also incorporate possibilities for change.

In Nakano Glenn's framework, race and gender are socially constructed, historically specific outcomes of the actions of and conflicts among dominant and subordinate groups, and they organize and permeate all the institutions of contemporary society in the United States. As applications of her framework, she examines how public and private reproductive labor are simultaneously raced and gendered and, similarly, how the political and legal systems use race and gender in the construction of citizenship. She concludes by calling for critical and analytic studies of the "unmarked" (e.g., White men), of the gendered aspects of "hybridity" (mixed categories), and of heterogeneity (differences within categories). Other areas that need further study are relations among subordinated groups and transnational race-gender formations, especially in the global economy.

Acker notes that a global concept of class as raced and gendered would lead to a better understanding of the interrelationships and standpoints of differently located people as they are affected by international capitalist processes, such as restructuring and development. The concept of class is rooted in nineteenth-century capitalist development, in which women's subordination, colonialism, and slavery were integral. To be a viable concept today, class must similarly include the different effects of a broad notion of the "economic" on subordinate and dominant women and men. In order to reflect the reality of people's lives, the economic must include all kinds of market and nonmarket survival strategies, and class must include the hidden as well as evident networks of exploitation and expropriation of women's and men's labor.

In Chapter 3, Joan Wallach Scott takes on the concept of gender itself, noting that the sex/gender distinction, although useful in principle, is by no means widely observed, even among feminists. (Our arguments among ourselves and our struggles for consistency among our authors are ample testimony to this question!) Her own contention is that, conceptually, gender is grounded in sex because bodies cannot be represented as entirely social. The common conflation of sex and gender is therefore "an accurate representation of the lack of sharp distinction between the two terms." If we see gender as "the social rules that attempt to organize the relationships of men and women in societies," then "both sex and gender are expressions of certain beliefs about sexual difference; they are organizations of perception rather than transparent descriptions or reflections of nature." A "gender analysis," then, is an examination of the rules, laws, and institutional arrangements of social groups that organize and maintain the differences between women and men. These differences are not only bodily and social, they are also, quite significantly, sexual and psychological. "From a psychoanalytic perspective, the psychological, the social, and the physical do not exist independent of one another; they are instead inextricably combined, constituted in and by psychic processes that are crucially informed by the unconscious." Politics, then, is often imbued with sexual fantasies; challenges to established authority become breaches of sexual boundaries.

Furthermore, political maneuvering often makes sexual differences salient for its own purposes. In the French Revolution, Wallach Scott points out, men defined themselves as equal to each other and different—by virtue of bodies and sexual reproduction—from women, and then used that politically created difference to reserve the rights of citizens only to those with a penis (or, in the psychoanalytic interpretation, a phallus). A similar process has masculinized politics in twentieth-century postcommunist Poland. The erasure of sexual difference has been the opposite aim of feminist politics, especially around the call for universal human rights. But here, too, a careful analysis is needed to ensure that *universal* and *human* are not masked terms for *masculine* and *male*. And where a claim for human rights for women (sexual autonomy or procreative choice) clashes with men's traditional or patriarchal rights, the notion of universality is split once more by issues of sexual difference. These issues are, in Wallach Scott's view, at the heart of gender and of politics.

The Macrosocial Organization of Gender

The chapters in Part II address the macrostructures that organize gender. In Chapter 4, Anette Borchorst raises fundamental questions about the role of the state and political authority. As she points out, feminist analyses of the extent to which the state is good or bad for women often reflect the analysts' particular national experiences with their own states. Thus Anglo-American scholars have tended to see the state as patriarchal in its very essence, whereas Scandinavian feminists have been more ambivalent. As feminist theorizing on the state expanded and became cross-national and comparative, the focus shifted from making claims about "the" state to trying to classify the variety of state approaches to institutionalizing gender relations in law and policy. Borchorst reviews the classifications developed on the basis of male experience that were adapted to women; they were ultimately unable to encompass women's experiences both as policy makers and as clients and consumers, that is, as "policy takers."

Borchorst then points to recent efforts to understand which policies benefit specific groups of women and why. This approach, she notes, moves away from a single, categorical view of women. She also suggests that these theories rightly focus on single mothers as a litmus test of state policy toward women, because the state must translate into concrete policies its understanding of the value of both caregiving and the production of material goods. However, all the policies of the welfare state, such as income support, pensions, child care, and tax subsidies for various individuals and enterprises, reflect gendered values.

In Chapter 5, Valentine M. Moghadam extends the gendered perspective on the state to encompass not only the relatively affluent welfare states on which Borchorst focuses, but the world-system as a whole. Thus she analyzes how gender is institutionalized in economic restructuring and globalization, two macro-level processes in which governments, transnational corporations, and international organizations like the World Bank are the main actors. Moghadam places the advances some women have made into better jobs and more secure circumstances into the context of trends that are "feminizing" all labor—that is, making it more temporary and part-time, more poorly paid, more informal, and less organized in collective forms of interest representation, such as unions. Moreover, the simultaneous need to produce income and to provide care, which Borchorst identifies as the crux of state policies for single mothers, Moghadam also points to as the conundrum for women in the countries that have been undergoing "structural adjustment."

On the one hand, globalization has drawn women into cash-producing employment on an unprecedented scale. Manufactured goods exported from developing countries, such as textiles and electronics, are disproportionately produced by women, making modern industrialization a process that is "female led" as much as export led. The world trade in services also favors women's labor migration, especially as nurses, domestics, and clerical workers. On the other hand, the demand for women as non-cash-producing labor—whether in agriculture or domestic caregiving for the young, the old, and the sick—has not abated. Indeed, as government's role in providing public care is reduced in the name of "privatization," more and more of the burden falls on women, the historical providers of private care. Thus, as Moghadam shows, economic restructuring policies are gendered in part because they heighten the contradictory demands being placed on women around the world. Yet she also points to women's responses to globalization as a hopeful sign, particularly the emergence of women's labor organizing initiatives and transnational feminist networks.

In Chapter 6, Lisa D. Brush brings Moghadam's analysis "home," as she examines the distinction between and intersection of production and reproduction in constructing gender relations in the economies of industrialized societies. Brush exposes as reciprocal myths the definitions of men as "workers" and women as "mothers" and of making things as "what men do" and caring for people as "what women do." Yet these gender dichotomies, unstable and political as they are in practice, still provide the lens through which most societies understand the organization of labor and thus the policies they pursue. Using the economic problem of deindustrialization as her focus, Brush deconstructs the ways in which nongendered theories and gendered labor practices together serve to hide the nature of the impact of macro-level change in the lives of ordinary women and men. Enterprises and households, she argues, are not separate "sectors" of society, but deeply interconnected sites in a single process that is simultaneously transforming both jobs and families.

Thus the crises of deindustrialization that are conventionally viewed separately as job loss and wage decline (affecting men), the rise in single parenthood and the impoverishment of single mothers (affecting women), and the privatization of public services and cutbacks in benefits (affecting welfare states) are brought together into a revised account of economic transformation that does not respect the boundaries of public and private, states and households. Brush's integrated account of how work, families, and communities are parts of a single gendered system makes clear that what deindustrialization means depends on the standpoint from which one is examining it. Feminist rethinking of "work" and "workers" has not only made women visible in the paid labor force, it has also revealed "the enduring importance of gender in the organization of production," as Brush puts it, and the equally gendered organization of unpaid work, those "activities that not only sustain but also add value to individual and community life." But those feminist theories that treat production and reproduction as two separate, parallel, and gendered tracks ignore the actual struggles men and women go through to combine them, hide the transformative effect of each on the other, and fail to recognize how the linked changes in both are already transforming gender relations. Seeing deindustrialization as one unitary gendered process may also help us to understand society's ongoing responses to these interconnected transformations— be it in fundamentalist reassertions of male privilege or in feminist visions of enhanced equality.

Gender, Discourse, and Culture

Although we are familiar with thinking of states and economies as macro-level factors in society, we may tend to overlook cultural institutions as similarly broad forces. The contributors to Part III take up the issue of gender, discourse, and culture at this macrosocietal level. The idea that cultural institutions convey gender meanings is a familiar one, but both authors in this section go further and assert that gender as a process is integral to the construction of cultural practices in general.

In Chapter 7, Susan Starr Sered takes up the question of the interrelation of gender and religion at a global level. She confronts the contradictory trends evident in the dramatic expansion of feminist emancipatory claims in society and fundamentalist restrictive demands in a variety of world religions. Her analysis rests on a distinction between "women" as actual people with a certain degree of agency and "Woman" as a symbolic construct conflating gender, sex, and sexuality. Because symbols are the currency of religion, the significance of Woman and the tensions between women and their symbolic representation are particularly pronounced in this domain. Much social control, Starr Sered argues, occurs at the meeting point of symbol and agency, where cultures attempt to override women's sense of their own agency by modifying their bodies or appearance and restricting their behavior in ways that make them view themselves as symbols. When women have the resources to do so, they also struggle over their own symbolic representation.

The gendered processes of globalization that Brush and Moghadam explore at a structural level in Part II provide the backdrop for Starr Sered's understanding of the cultural struggle between symbol and actor in religion. Because certain local male institutions are often strengthened by colonial states and corporate investors, women may lose ground in controlling their own traditions, be they midwifery or woman-centered religious rituals. Men who are threatened by globalization in turn tend to take up fundamentalist discourses that reassert the legitimacy of local male authorities. As a highly charged symbolic category, Woman becomes the battlefield on which political interpretations of past and future are contested. In this fray, different women may come to view themselves as the guardians of ancient tradition or as the defenders of modernity, secularization, and religious change.

In a variety of religions, more empowered women are venturing into roles once reserved for men. Thus, as Mapuche men are drawn into wage labor in Chile, village women have more control over the local subsistence economy and are increasingly replacing men as shamans as well. Starr Sered sees these changes as not unlike the challenges that feminists are posing to Jewish, Christian, and Islamic traditions. The complexity of the interplay between abstract symbol and real people's lives is the focus of her analysis of these gender transformations in religions.

In Chapter 8, Suzanna Danuta Walters examines the cultural meanings of various forms of media that integrate the symbolic with the personal. Looking at how cultural studies has approached the issue of gender, she argues for an understanding of media users both as "spectators" in the abstract and as concrete "audiences." The models developed in the humanities for analyzing texts tend to posit spectators in an idealized and often highly gender-stereotypical relation to books, movies, TV shows, and other "texts." By recognizing the textual characteristics that define "the gaze" as male, such analyses show how women become objectified and marginalized in the text itself. But real viewers, or audiences, are not necessarily as constrained by the text as these models assume. Readers or viewers can appropriate texts for their own, potentially subversive purposes, "against the grain" of the producer's intent.

Social scientists face a real challenge, however, in trying to discover the uses to which specific audiences put texts. Because meanings are contextual and interactively produced, it would be as fallacious to assume that all people in audiences always resist as to posit them as spectators who are necessarily at the mercy of the properties of the texts themselves. Danuta Walters looks to ethnographic research on media use and users for explorations of this complex domain. She sees feminist research as making progress in understanding culture by using ethnography to reveal the interplay of power relations embedded in the structures that produce representations and in the acts of selecting and using cultural representations for one's own pleasure. By emphasizing reception and agency as part of what makes cultures "mean" things, Danuta Walters brings out the negotiations between competing frames of reference and the uses of gender as a category of both oppression and resistance.

Gender in Social Institutions

The interplay between institutions making gender and gender shaping institutional forms is the focus of Part IV. The essays in this section expand on feminist ideas of the social construction of gender by the sciences, the workplace, the family, and sports. The contributors show how these areas of social life are socially constructed by gender, or, more precisely, genders, because they call our attention to issues of race, class, and sexuality as well.

Using an *intersectional* approach, Patricia Hill Collins argues in Chapter 9 that although feminist critiques of science have documented the male biases in the production of scientific knowledge, especially in the area of biology and putative sex differences, they have neglected the equally invidious effects of Eurocentrism. According to Hill Collins, "The construct of intersectionality references two types of relationships: the interconnectedness of ideas and the social structures in which they occur, and the intersecting hierarchies of gender, race, economic class, sexuality, and ethnicity. Viewing gender within a logic of intersectionality redefines it as a constellation of ideas and social practices that are historically situated within and that mutually construct multiple systems of oppression." The intersection of social constructs, especially gender and race, underpins two further intersecting areas of inquiry— scientific knowledge and political power, and theoretical assumptions and practices in scientific research. The challenges that a woman's perspective brings to scientific thinking and practice (research priorities, questions, subjects, design) are enhanced by racial ethnic and class diversity.

In a particularly provocative analysis, Hill Collins links science and modernity, and shows how both are simultaneously raced and gendered. Scientific thinking is the essence of modern thought—rational, objective, universal, and abstract. This way of thinking was developed as a contrast and challenge to the emotional, subjective, particularistic, and concrete ways of thinking that were openly claimed to be characteristic of women and "primitives." White women and African peoples were relegated to being the inferior Other by the Enlightenment and colonialism. The progress claimed by scientific, "modern" thought was the basis for the justificatory ideology of subordination and conquest by White European men in the eighteenth and nineteenth centuries, and still imbues the relations of ruling in the so-called First World.

In order to address adequately the power politics implicit in science and modernism, White feminists must recognize their complicity in this hierarchy of power. It is not enough to develop a feminist science or postmodern critique of received wisdom. The underlying, intersected raced and gendered basis of Western (Eurocentric) thinking must be made visible.

In Chapter 10, Patricia Yancey Martin and David L. Collinson examine the impact on organizational theories and research of the introduction of the feminist concepts of gendering and sexuality. For 20 years now, there has been extensive research on the persistence and effects of the inequality built into the gendered composition of job descriptions, pay scales, and authority ladders. Yet, despite this research and the everyday experience of men and women workers that workplaces are organized by gender, much organizational theory and research has proceeded on the assumption they are gender neutral and universalistic. The insistence of feminist researchers that hierarchical organizations are deeply gendered made evident the deliberate and unconscious practices that produced and maintained gender inequality in most postindustrial workplaces.

Current studies investigate how organizational practices use gender to create workers' identities as women and men, which are then invoked in justification of the continuance of inequality in job assignments, promotions, and wages. Recent work also examines the ways that organizations sexualize workers—presenting authority and physical labor as testaments of heterosexual masculinity, and good looks, "service with a smile," and covert sexiness as evidence of heterosexual femininity. These norms and expectations are maintained by open and hidden harassment and subtle and blunt sanctions by workers of each other and by bosses of the workers under them. However, because gender and sexuality are socially constructed by organizational practices, Yancey Martin and Collinson argue that they are potential sites of resistance and change. Racial ethnic and sexual diversity and the recognition of different styles of management among men as well as women are having an impact on organizations. Finally, feminist organizations, whose practices are egalitarian and nonhierarchical, have provided data on the possibilities of deliberately structuring a workplace for diversity and equality.

In Chapter 11, Anne R. Roschelle reviews the theoretical perspectives usually used to analyze the economic problems of racial ethnic families in the United States. Concentrating on African Americans, Chicanos, and Puerto Ricans, Roschelle claims that the focus on culture—as detrimental or as a source of strength—minimizes the effects of historical events and structural patterns, such as immigration and job markets, on the lives of the members of these families. In contrast, "structural models focus on how macroeconomic forces have produced high rates of family poverty among particular subgroups, resulting in the reliance on extended family networks and the proliferation of female-headed households." The classical structural model, however, is limited by its economic focus on the problems facing nuclear families. A gender analysis within this approach reveals that while lack of jobs because of the shift of manufacturing out of urban areas penalizes the men in these families, the low wages and intermittent work of traditional women's jobs, plus lack of child care, make it almost impossible for women to provide an adequate level of economic support without government supplements. This model also neglects cultural variations in family networks.

An integrative model would allow for analysis of how gender, culture, racial ethnic discrimination, and structural forces—encouragement of and constraints on immigration, education, and job opportunities—affect one another. This model is, of course, reflective of the intersectionality that Hill Collins discusses in Chapter 9. It takes us beyond poor racial ethnic families to theories and politics of family and work. The experiences of women and men in these and poor White families call into question the conceptual validity and the ideological narrowness of the work-family split and child-centered parenting modeled on more prosperous White nuclear families.

In Chapter 12, the final one in Part IV, Shari L. Dworkin and Michael A. Messner ask an ironic question: "Just do . . . what?" Thanks to the feminist movement, women and girls have burst onto the sports scene in a big way. But have any of the traditional ideas about women's and men's bodies and physical capabilities really been changed as a result? Sport, a ubiquitous site of moneymaking, is also a prime source of the social construction of gender within racial ethnic and class-based stratification systems. As Dworkin and Messner put it, "Sport, as a cultural and commercial production, constructs and markets gender; besides making money, making gender may be sport's chief function."

In men's sports, the glorification of athletes' powerful bodies, sexuality, and violence reproduces race, class, and gender relations of power. Sport presents an interlocked reinforcement of superiority and inferiority—men over women, White men (the power brokers and audience) over men of color, and those whose upward mobility is based on education over the few who make it to the top as athletes. In women's sports, greater equality has resulted in adoption of masculine attitudes, in part due to an increase in men coaches attracted by growing financial resources. At the same time, the popularity of more feminized sports—gymnastics and ice-skating—has reinscribed and exaggerated physical femininity and conventionalized gender displays.

Women's sports have also been co-opted by corporate capitalism. In commercial endorsements and in ads touting women's physical fitness and sports success, Dworkin and Messner note, "corporations have found peace and profit with liberal feminism by co-opting a genuine quest by women for bodily agency and empowerment and channeling it toward a goal of physical achievement severely limited by its consumerist context." An invisible subtext is that the expensive products being sold are made mostly by women in the developing countries working for low wages in sweatshop factories.

Just as the resistant and transformative possibilities of men's sports as a way out of racial ethnic ghettos have been reduced to a few highly paid and publicized career athletes who exemplify physical prowess and heterosexual masculinity, the potential for gender rebellion in women's sports has encouraged women athletes to emulate men commercially, while carefully keeping their bodies and "look" clearly female and "heterosexy." In sum, an analysis that integrates race and ethnicity, class, and gender shows that sport and physical activity have empowered some women and men from disadvantaged groups, but have done little to empower or change the structural position of the majority of members of those groups.

Gendering the Person

The chapters that make up Part V deal with "gendering the person," by which we mean those interactive processes at the micro level through which gender is constituted, performed, and re-created daily. In Chapter 13, social psychologists Peter Glick and Susan T. Fiske examine how a person's sex activates gender stereotypes that in turn affect judgments of social worth as well as overt behavior. Such stereotypes may be a necessary and universal "cognitive energy-saving device," but they also reflect a deeply gendered social structure, namely, a sex-segregated division of labor, patriarchal power relationships, and heterosexuality. In this view, contrary to much previous psychological theorizing, stereotypes are not a "cause" of prejudice and discrimination as much as reflections of the basic inequality built into the settings of interaction—home, school, work, voluntary associations. Thus the psychological variables of cognition and prejudice are linked to discriminatory behavioral outcomes that are both product and reproducer of macrostructural systems.

In their discussion of the ideological supports for the differential evaluation and treatment of women, Glick and Fiske make an important distinction between what they call "benevolent" sexism and the more commonly recognized "hostile" variety. Benevolent sexism imputes positive motives and values to women, but with equally constraining results—paternalism and chivalry being no less limiting than blunter displays of dominance. But it is in the dyads of heterosexual relationships, often viewed as the wellspring of gender inequality, that Glick and Fiske find possibilities for resistance and change. Because male dominance coexists with dependency on a female partner in the search for intimacy, a certain ambivalence suffuses the relationship, providing an opportunity for women to claim a degree of independence and dyadic power.

In Chapter 14, Barbara Katz Rothman expands on the implications of a crucial aspect of women's claims to independence: "choice." One of the rallying cries of the emergent women's movement of the late 1960s, "choice" evoked a range of freedoms hitherto denied many women, before becoming almost exclusively focused on procreative issues. It was and is a cardinal tenet of feminism that equality for women is impossible without the ability to control the number and spacing of one's children. But, as Katz Rothman notes, choice is a good place to start, but it is only that—an abstract right may not be able to be exercised. What of the many American women who lack the appropriate resources—information, money, and access to family planning services—to avail themselves of procreative choices?

The major concern of this chapter, however, is with another dimension of choice: the expanding range of *what* can be chosen. Choices are no longer simply a matter of if and when and how we choose to enter motherhood, but increasingly questions of what kind of child to bear (or even to have someone else do it for you). The technological imperative that has generated so many new techniques for predicting and intervening in pregnancy outcomes has also produced a new range of choices—to terminate a pregnancy in the case of severe fetal deformity, to "harvest" superfluous fertilized ova after the use of fertility drugs, to abort selectively in cases of multiple fetuses, to select for given traits through in vitro fertilization, and, most recently, to choose the sex of the baby. How curious, Katz Rothman notes, that abortions for "genetic problems" are generally condoned, whereas those for sex selection, surely also a genetic condition, fall outside the ethical pale. Furthermore, because it is not so much a girl or boy, but a daughter or son that the parents have in mind, the selection is really for gender rather than for sex. And what happens to the child, so specially chosen, who does not live up to the parents' gender expectations? Finally, once the Human

Genome Project has unlocked even more mysteries of genetic transmission, how much information and control could or should we have over what kinds of children we bear? The ultimate in choice—a "designer gene" offspring—is no longer unthinkable, but is it desirable? What then would be left to the child to become on her or his own?

In Chapter 15, Judith Lorber takes up an area of feminist scholarship where there has been so much controversy that the term *sex wars* has been used to sum it up. The arguments have raged over men's domination and sexual violence in heterosexual relationships, pornography, and prostitution, with one side taking a stand that focuses on women's subordination and victimization and the other insisting on at least the potentiality of women's sexual autonomy. These debates are still pertinent, imbuing both scholarly research and interchanges in the mass media.

An emerging area of work has presented questions of the origins and stability of heterosexuality and homosexuality and the significance of bisexuality. Feminism's encounters with queer theory have led, as a 1994 issue of *Differences* (summer-fall) put it, to more "gender trouble," because queer theory deconstructs and explodes the binary categories of female/male, homosexual/heterosexual, and woman/man. Research on transgendering, Lorber shows, has turned up even more ambiguities and paradoxes of sex, sexuality, and gender. Conformity and transgression blur and shift in a complex web of self-presentation and identity politics. Lorber ends with some thoughts on what feminist theories of gender and sexuality can take away from queer theory.

Bodies are the central focus of Chapter 16 by R. W. Connell—bodies as "players" in social life, as agents and objects of gender practices. That is, in contrast to many postmodernists who see the body as something upon which culture is written, and to sociobiologists, for whom the body is a vehicle for evolutionary forces, Connell places the material body at the nexus of sexuality, identity formation, and gender practices, none of which is reducible to the other(s). As Connell puts it: "The practices that construct femininity and masculinity are formative of reality. As body-reflexive practices, they constitute a world that has a bodily dimension, but is not bodily determined." In this view, masculinity and femininity are "gender projects," products of gender practices, the ways in which behavior is organized by individuals and collectivities. In turn, these projects and practices constitute gender structures, mutually transformed and transforming through time.

Connell takes us on a delightfully learned tour of contemporary debates over the nature of sex, gender, identities, and sexualities, pointing out the difficulties in attempts to reduce complex phenomena to simple processes or even a limited number of categories. Bodies come in all sizes and shapes, and undergo change historically. Nor can sexuality or gender be so easily captured in neat schemata; rather, "the outcomes of human development, indeed, seem curiously undichotomous." Yet Connell also finds that the social constructionist position runs the risks of floating free of the bodily processes and products that constitute sexual experience. Thus Connell brings us full circle to contemplate the links between intimate relations and large-scale institutions, the ways in which decisions at the level of the collectivity affect expressions of sexuality, the formation of identities, and the practices of gender. Less obvious but nonetheless important to the gender perspective are the ways in which practices, projects, and processes can become sites of resistance and redefinition.

Conclusion

We hope that this book shows how the use of gender by scholars in different and overlapping fields of study has shifted concepts and research designs. Such a wide incorporation of theories of gender as a mode of analysis in so many areas may mean that the influence of feminist ideas in academic scholarship is deep and permanent. We suggest that without a grounding in the multiple social locations of gender, class, race, and ethnicity, as well as bodies and sexualities, research and theories will seem thin and unreal. However, as all of the contributors to this volume make amply clear, the very categories of research and theory—gender, sex, sexuality, class, race, ethnicity, culture, bodies, psyches, and identities—are no longer self-evident concepts. They are all under debate as intertwined social constructions, at the same time constraining and resistible, persistent and fluid. The feminist examination of these concepts, as is evident from this book, is forcing a rethinking of social science categories and concepts (e.g., class and social stratification, identity and perception, culture and representation). It also in many ways goes back to old debates—structure and agency, objectivity and values, research and politics. Our intent in this volume is to encourage the continuation of all these debates with a fresh perspective.

References

Acker, Joan. 1989. "Making Gender Visible." Pp. 65-81 in *Feminism and Sociological Theory*, edited by Ruth A. Wallace. Newbury Park, CA: Sage.

Aiken, Susan Hardy, Karen Anderson, Myra Dinnerstein, Judy Nolte Lensink, and Patricia MacCorquodale, eds. 1988. *Changing Our Minds: Feminist Transformations of Knowledge.* Albany: State University of New York Press.

Belenkey, Mary Field, Blythe M. Clinchy, Nancy Rule Goldberger, and Jill M. Tarule, eds. 1986. *Women's Ways of Knowing: The Development of Self, Voice, and Mind.* New York: Basic Books.

Collins, Patricia Hill. 1990. *Black Feminist Thought: Knowledge, Consciousness, and the Politics of Empowerment.* New York: Routledge, Chapman & Hall.

Ferree, Myra Marx and Elaine J. Hall. 1996. "Rethinking Stratification from a Feminist Perspective: Gender, Race, and Class in Mainstream Textbooks." *American Sociological Review* 61:929-50.

Gerson, Judith M. and Kathy Peiss. 1985. "Boundaries, Negotiation, Consciousness: Reconceptualizing Gender Relations." *Social Problems* 32:317-31.

Goldberger, Nancy Rule, Jill M. Tarule, Blythe M. Clinchy, and Mary Field Belenkey, eds. 1996. *Knowledge, Difference, and Power: Essays Inspired by Women's Ways of Knowing.* New York: Basic Books.

Gordon, Linda. 1994. *Pitied but Not Entitled: Single Mothers and the History of Welfare 1890-1935.* New York: Free Press.

Harding, Sandra. 1986. *The Science Question in Feminism.* Ithaca, NY: Cornell University Press.

Hess, Beth B. and Myra Marx Ferree, eds. 1987. *Analyzing Gender: A Handbook of Social Science Research.* Newbury Park, CA: Sage.

Holland, Dorothy and Margaret Eisenhardt. 1990. *Educated in Romance.* Chicago: University of Chicago Press.

Kanter, Rosabeth Moss and Marcia Millman, eds. 1975. *Another Voice: Feminist Perspectives on Social Life and Social Science.* Garden City, NY: Doubleday Anchor.

Kuhn, Thomas S. 1970. *The Structure of Scientific Revolutions.* 2d ed. Chicago: University of Chicago Press.

Lorber, Judith. 1994. *Paradoxes of Gender.* New Haven, CT: Yale University Press.

Nielson, Joyce. 1990. *Feminist Research Methods: Exemplary Readings in the Social Sciences.* Boulder, CO: Westview.

Peterson, V. Spike, ed. 1992. *Gendered States: Feminist (Re)Visions of International Relations Theory.* Boulder, CO: Lynne Rienner.

Scott, Joan Wallach. 1986. "Gender: A Useful Category of Historical Analysis." *American Historical Review* 91:1053-75.

Sherman, Julia and Evelyn Torton Beck, eds. 1979. *The Prism of Sex: Essays in the Sociology of Knowledge*. Madison: University of Wisconsin Press.

Skocpol, Theda. 1992. *Protecting Soldiers and Mothers: The Political Origins of Social Policy in the United States*. Cambridge, MA: Belknap University Press.

Smith, Dorothy E. 1990a. *The Conceptual Practices of Power: A Feminist Sociology of Knowledge*. Toronto: University of Toronto Press.

———. 1990b. *Texts, Facts, and Femininity: Exploring the Relations of Ruling*. New York: Routledge.

Stacey, Judith and Barrie Thorne. 1985. "The Missing Feminist Revolution in Sociology." *Social Problems* 32:301-16.

Stanley, Liz and Sue Wise. 1983. *Breaking Out: Feminist Consciousness and Feminist Research*. London: Routledge.

Thorne, Barrie. 1993. *Gender Play: Girls and Boys in School*. New Brunswick, NJ: Rutgers University Press.

West, Candace and Don Zimmerman. 1987. "Doing Gender." *Gender & Society* 1:125-51.

PART I

RECONCEPTUALIZING GENDER

CHAPTER 1

The Social Construction and Institutionalization of Gender and Race

An Integrative Framework

EVELYN NAKANO GLENN

Toward a Social Constructionist Approach to Gender and Race

Historically, gender and race have constituted separate fields of scholarly inquiry. By studying each in isolation, however, each field marginalized major segments of the communities it claimed to represent. In studies of "race," men of color stood as the universal racial subject, whereas in studies of "gender," White women were positioned as the universal female subject. Women of color were left out of both narratives, rendered invisible both as racial and as gendered subjects.[1]

In the 1980s, women of color began to address this omission through detailed historical and ethnographic studies of Black, Latina, and Asian American women in relation to work, family, and community (e.g., Cheng 1984; Dill 1980; Gilkes 1985; Glenn 1986; Ruiz 1987; Zavella 1987). These studies not only uncovered overlooked dimensions of experience, they exposed flaws in theorizing from a narrow social base. For example, explanations for gender inequality based on middle-class White women's experience focused on women's encapsulation in the domestic sphere and economic dependence on men. These concepts did not apply to Black women and therefore could not account for their subordination.

Initial attempts to bring race into the same frame as gender treated the two as independent axes. The bracketing of gender was in some sense deliberate, because the concern of early feminism was to uncover what women had in common that would unite them politically. However, if we begin with gender separated out, we have to "add" race in order to account for the situation of women of color. This leads to an

3

additive model in which women of color are described as suffering from "double" jeopardy (or "triple" oppression, if class is included). Women of color expressed dissatisfaction with this model, which they said did not correspond to the subjective experiences of African American, Latina, Asian American, and Native American women. These women did not experience race and gender as separate or additive, but as simultaneous and linked. They offered concepts such as "intersectionality," "multiple consciousness," "interlocking systems of oppression," and "racialized gender" to express this simultaneity (Crenshaw 1989, 1992; Harris 1990; Collins 1990; Glenn 1992).

Yet, despite increased recognition of the interconnectedness of gender and race, race remained undertheorized even in the writings of women of color. In the absence of a "theory" of race comparable to a "theory" of gender, building a comprehensive theory has proven elusive. Especially needed is a theory that neither subordinates race and gender to some broader (presumably more primary) set of relations, such as class, nor substantially flattens the complexity of these concepts.[2] Lacking a comprehensive theory, can we do analyses that recognize and account for the simultaneity of gender and race? In this chapter, following on the valuable work of such scholars as Liu (1991), Brooks Higginbotham (1992), Kaminsky (1994), and Stoler (1996), I argue that a synthesis of social constructionist streams within critical race and feminist studies offers a framework for integrated analysis. Social constructionism provides a useful "mid-level" framework, a common vocabulary and set of concepts for looking at how gender and race are mutually constituted—at the ways gender is racialized and race is gendered.

Gender

Social constructionism has had a somewhat different trajectory with respect to gender and race. In both fields, social constructionism arose as an alternative to biological and essentialist conceptions that rendered gender and race static and ahistorical, but it achieved centrality earlier and has been elaborated in greater detail in feminist scholarship on women and gender than in race studies. This is so even though—or perhaps because—gender seems to be rooted more firmly than race in biology: in bodies, reproduction, and sexuality. Indeed, feminist scholars adopted the term *gender* precisely to free our thinking from the constrictions of naturalness and biological inevitability attached to the concept of sex. Rubin (1975) has proposed the term *sex-gender system* to capture the idea of societal arrangements by which biological sexuality is transformed into socially significant gender.

Since its introduction, gender has emerged as the closest thing we have to a unifying concept in feminist studies, cutting across the various disciplines and theoretical schools that make up the field. Many feminist historians and sociologists use gender as an analytic concept to refer to socially created meanings, relationships, and identities organized around reproductive differences (Connell 1989; Laslett and Brenner 1989; Scott 1986). Others focus on gender as a social status and organizing principle of social institutions detached from and going far beyond reproductive differences (Acker 1990; Lorber 1994). Still others see gender as an ongoing product of everyday social practice (Thorne 1993; West and Zimmerman 1987). The concept of gender thus provides an overarching rubric for looking at historical, cultural, and situational variability in definitions of womanhood and manhood, in meanings of masculinity and femininity, in relationships between men and women, and in the extent of their relative power and political status. If one accepts gender as variable, then one must acknowledge that it is never fixed, but rather is continually constituted and reconstituted.

By loosening the connection to concrete bodies, the notion of socially constructed gender freed us from thinking of sex/gender as solely, or even primarily, a characteristic of individuals. By examining gender as a constitutive feature and organizing principle of collectivities, social institutions, historical processes, and social practices, feminist scholars have demonstrated that major areas of life—including sexuality, family, education, economy, and state—are organized according to gender principles and shot through with conflicting interests and hierarchies of power and privilege. As an organizing principle, gender involves both cultural meanings and material relations. That is, gender is constituted simultaneously through deployment of gendered rhetoric, symbols, and images and through allocation of resources and power along gender lines. Thus an adequate account of any particular gender phenomenon requires an examination of both structure and meaning. For example, an understanding of the persistent gender gap in wages involves an analysis of divisions of labor in the home, occupational segregation and other forms of labor market stratification, cultural evaluations of gendered work, such as caring, and gendered meanings of concepts such as "skill."

The most recent theoretical work is moving toward imploding the sex-gender distinction itself. The distinction assumes the prior existence of "something real" out of which social relationships and cultural meanings are elaborated. A variety of poststructuralist feminist critics have problematized the distinction by pointing out that sex and sexual meanings are themselves culturally constructed (e.g., Butler 1990). Lorber (1994), a sociologist, carefully unpacks the concepts of biological sex (which refers to either genetic or morphological characteristics), sexuality (which refers to desire and orientation), and gender (which refers to social status and identity), and shows that they are all equally socially constructed concepts. One result of this kind of work is the undermining of the idea that there are "really" two sexes or two genders or two sexual orientations. At present, the conceptual distinctions among sex, sexuality, and gender are still being debated, and new work on the body is revealing the intertwining and complexity of these concepts (e.g., Butler 1993).

Race

Scholars of race have been slower to abandon the idea of race as rooted in biological markers, even though they recognize that social attitudes and arrangements, not biology, maintain White dominance.[3] Fields (1982) notes the reluctance of historians to digest fully the conclusion reached by biologists early in the twentieth century that race does not correspond to any biological referent and that racial categories are so arbitrary as to be meaningless. Race had thus been exposed as a social creation—a fiction that divides and categorizes individuals by phenotypic markers, such as skin color, that supposedly signify underlying differences. Nonetheless, as Pascoe (1991) notes, historians continued well into the 1980s to study "races" as immutable categories, to speak of race as a force in history, and to view racism as a psychological product rather than a product of social history. Pascoe suggests that the lack of a separate term, like *gender*, to refer to "socially significant race" may have retarded full recognition of race as a social construct. In sociology, liberal scholarship took the form of the study of "race relations"—that is, the examination of relations among groups that were already constituted as distinct entities. Quantitative researchers treated race as a preexisting "fact" of social life, an independent variable to be correlated with or regressed against other variables. How categories such as Black and White were historically created and maintained was not interrogated.

Only in the late 1980s did historians and social scientists begin to study systematically variations and changes in the drawing of racial categories and boundaries. The greatest attention has been paid to the construction of Blackness. In an influential pair of essays, Fields (1982, 1990) examines how the definition and concept of Blackness shifted over the course of slavery, Reconstruction, and the Jim Crow era. Slave owners created the category "Black" from disparate African groups, and then maintained the category by incorporating growing numbers of those of "mixed" parentage. Concerned with maximizing the number of slaves, slave owners settled on the principle that a child's status followed that of the mother, in violation of the customary patriarchal principle of inheritance. Exploring the origins of the principle of hypodescent and the "one-drop rule" for defining Blackness in the United States, Davis (1991) has shown it to be peculiar in light of the wide range of variation among Latin American, Caribbean, and North American societies in the status of people of mixed ancestry. In her study of "Creole" identity in Louisiana, Dominguez (1986) found that competing understandings of racial categories may coexist in the same society. The Creole designation was claimed both by people of mixed Black-White ancestry (to distinguish themselves from darker "Blacks") and by White descendants of original French settlers (to distinguish themselves from later Anglo in-migrants). By the 1970s, however, White "Creoles" had ceded the label to the mixed population and relabeled themselves "French."

"Whiteness" has also been problematized. Historians have looked at the shift from an emphasis on "Anglo-Saxon" identity to a more inclusive "White" identity and the assimilation of groups that had been considered separate races in an earlier period, such as the Irish, Jews, and Mexicans, into the White category (Almaguer 1994; Ignatiev 1995; Roediger 1991; Sacks 1994). These groups achieved "Whiteness" through a combination of external circumstances and their own agency. State and social policies organized along a Black-White binary required individuals and groups to be placed in one category or the other. Individuals and groups also actively claimed Whiteness in order to attain the rights and privileges enjoyed by already established White Americans. Because of the association of Whiteness with full legal rights, scholars in the field of critical legal studies have scrutinized the concept of Whiteness in the law (e.g., Haney Lopez 1996; Harris 1993). Harris (1993) argues that courts have protected racial privilege by interpreting Whiteness as property, including the right to exclude others.

Only a few studies have looked beyond the Black-White binary that dominates conceptions of race. For example, Espiritu (1992) examined the forging of a pan-Asian American identity in the late 1960s, when Chinese, Japanese, and Filipino student activists came together to organize in "Third World" solidarity with Black and Latino students. Activists asserted both essentialist grounds (similarities in culture and appearance) and instrumental grounds (a common history of discrimination and stereotyping) as the basis for the new identity. In contrast to the notion that Asian groups experience similar treatment that leads to pan-Asian identity, Ong (1996) argues that among new Asian immigrants, rich and poor groups are being differentially "racialized" within the Black-White binary in the United States. Well-educated professional and managerial Chinese immigrants are "Whitened" and assimilated into the American middle class, whereas poor Khmer, dependent on welfare, are "Blackened."

Many of the studies of shifting racial categories and meanings have been influenced by the pathbreaking theoretical work of Omi and Winant (1986, 1994). Their racial formation model is rooted in neo-Marxist conceptions of class formation, but they specifically position themselves against existing models that subsume race under some presumably broader category, such as class or nation. They firmly assert that "race is a fundamental axis of social organization in the U.S.," not an epiphenomenon of some other category (1994:13). At the same time, they see race not as fixed, but as "an unstable and 'decentered' complex of social meaning constantly being transformed by political struggle" (1994:55). The terrain on which struggle is waged has varied historically. Just as social constructionism arose as an alternative to biologism or essentialism in the twentieth century, the concept of biological race arose in the eighteenth and nineteenth centuries to replace religious paradigms for viewing differences between Europeans (Christians) and (non-Christian) "others" encountered in the age of conquest. With the waning of religious beliefs in a God-given social order, race differences and the superiority of White Europeans to "others" came to be justified and legitimated by "science." As Omi and Winant (1994) note, the "invocation of scientific criteria to demonstrate the natural basis of racial hierarchy was both a logical consequence of the rise of [scientific] knowledge and an attempt to provide a subtle and more nuanced account of human complexity in the new 'enlightened' age" (p. 63).

After World War II, liberal politics emphasized equality under the law and an assumption of sameness in daily encounters. In the 1960s and 1970s, identity politics among civil rights activists emphasized differences, but valorized them in such ideas as Black power and *la raza.*

The 1980s and 1990s saw a questioning of the essentialism and solidity of racial and sex/gender categories and a focus on structural concepts of racial and patriarchal social orders. Paralleling the structural approach to gender, Omi and Winant assert that race is a central organizing principle of social institutions, focusing especially on the "racial state" as a central arena for creating, maintaining, and contesting racial boundaries and meanings. Their concept of the racial state is akin to MacKinnon's (1989) concept of the patriarchal state.

An Integrative Framework

There are important points of congruence between the concept of racial formation and the concept of socially constructed gender. These convergences point the way toward an integrative framework in which race and gender are defined as mutually constituted systems of relationships—including norms, symbols, and practices—organized around perceived differences. This definition focuses attention on the *processes* through which racialization and engendering take place, rather than on the elucidation of characteristics of fixed race-gender categories. These processes take place at multiple levels, including *representation,* or the deployment of symbols, language, and images to express and convey race/gender meanings; *micro-interaction,* or the application of race/gender norms, etiquette, and spatial rules to orchestrate interaction within and across race/gender boundaries; and *social structure,* or the allocation of power and material resources along race/gender lines.

Within this integrated framework, race and gender share three key features as analytic concepts: They are *relational* concepts whose construction involves *both representational and social structural processes* in which *power* is a constitutive element. Each of these features is important in terms of building a framework that both analyzes inequality and incorporates a politics of change.

Relationality

By *relational* I mean that race-gender categories (e.g., Black/White, woman/man) are positioned and therefore gain meaning in relation to each other. According to poststructural analysis, meaning within Western epistemology is constructed in terms of dichotomous oppositions or contrasts. Oppositional categories require the suppression of variability within each category and the exaggeration of differences between categories. Moreover, because the dichotomy is imposed over a complex "reality," it is inherently unstable. Stability is achieved when the dichotomy is made hierarchical—that is, one term is accorded primacy over the other. In race and gender dichotomies, the dominant category is rendered "normal" and therefore "transparent," whereas the other is the variant and therefore "problematic." Thus White appears to be raceless (Dyer 1988) and man appears to be genderless. The opposition also disguises the extent to which the categories are actually interdependent.

One can accept the notion of meaning being constructed through contrast without assuming that such contrasts take the form of fixed dichotomies. In the United States "White" has been primarily constructed against "Black," but it has also been positioned in relation to varying "others," and therefore has varying meanings. The category "Anglo" in the Southwest, which is constructed in contrast to "Mexican," and the category "haole" in Hawaii, which is constructed in contrast to both Native Hawaiians and Asian plantation workers, both have meanings that are similar to and different from those of the category "White" in the South and Northeast. For example, haole was originally a simultaneous race-class designation for Europeans and Anglo-Americans of the planter-manager class; European groups, such as the Portuguese, who were plantation laborers and supervisors were not considered haole (Fuchs 1983). Similarly, the meanings of dominant masculinity have varied by time and place by way of contrast to historically and regionally differing subordinate masculinities and femininities.

The concept of relationality is important for several reasons. First, as in the above example, it helps to problematize the dominant categories of Whiteness and masculinity, which depend on contrast. The importance of contrast is illustrated by the formation of "linked identities" in the cases of housewives and their domestic employees (Palmer 1989), reformers and the targets of reform (Pascoe 1990), and colonizers and colonized peoples (Ware 1992). In each of these cases, the dominant group's self-identity (e.g., as moral, rational, and benevolent) depends on the casting of complementary qualities (e.g., immoral, irrational, and needy) onto the subordinate "other."

Second, relationality helps to point out the ways in which "differences" among groups are systematically related. Too often, "difference" is understood simply as experiential diversity, as in some versions of multiculturalism (Barrett 1987). The concept of relationality suggests that the lives of different groups are interconnected, even without face-to-face relations. Thus, for example, a White person in the United States enjoys privileges and a higher standard of living by virtue of the subordination and lower standard of living of people of color, even if she or he is not personally exploiting or taking advantage of any persons of color.

Third, relationality helps to address the critique that social constructionism, by rejecting the fixity of categories, fosters the postmodern notion that race and gender categories and meanings are free-floating and can mean anything we want them to mean. Viewing race and gender categories and meanings as relational partly addresses this critique by providing "anchor" points that are not, however, static.

Structure and Representation

The social construction of race/gender is a matter of *both* social structure and cultural representation. This point is important because, by virtue of its eschewal of biology and essentialism, a social constructionist approach could be interpreted as concerned solely with representation. This is particularly tempting in the case of race, where it can be argued that there is no objective referent. Indeed, Fields (1990), an eminent historian, has argued that race is a category without content; having no rooting in material reality, race is pure ideology, a lens through which people view and make sense of their experiences. However, Fields seems to be conflating biology and material reality. It is one thing to say that race and gender are not biological givens, but quite another to say that they exist only in the realm of representation or signification. As noted above, race and gender are features of social structures. Social structural arrangements, such as labor market segmentation, residential segregation, and stratification of government benefits, produce race and gender "differences" in ways that cannot be understood purely in representational terms. For this reason, I find neoliberal attacks on affirmative action and other measures aimed at redressing race and gender disadvantage to be either perverse or disingenuous. Proponents of this view argue that these measures falsely reify race and gender and that therefore social policy ought to be race- and gender-blind. Unfortunately, not paying attention to race and gender does not make gender-race inequalities go away, precisely because these inequalities are institutionalized and not just ideas in people's heads.

Conversely, other theorists view meaning systems as epiphenomena and maintain that race and gender inequalities can be understood through structural analysis alone. However, historical evidence suggests that a structural approach alone is not sufficient either. As historians of working-class formation have pointed out, one cannot make a direct connection between particular structural conditions and specific forms of consciousness, identity, and political activity. Rather, they have found that race, gender, and class consciousness draws on the available rhetoric of race, gender, and class. In nineteenth-century England, skilled artisan men experiencing changes in their conditions due to industrialization were able to organize and articulate their class rights by drawing on available concepts of manhood—the dignity of skilled labor and family headship (Rose 1995). Symbols of masculinity were thus constitutive of class identity. Their counterparts in the United States drew on symbols of race, claiming rights on the basis of their status as "free" labor, in contrast to Black slaves, Chinese contract workers, and other figures symbolizing "unfree labor" (Roediger 1994). Class formation in the United States was then and continues to be infused with racial as well as gender meanings.

In the contemporary United States, the paucity of culturally available class discourse seems to play a role in damping down class consciousness. Breslow Rubin (1994) found that White working-class men and women, whose economic circumstances were becoming more perilous due to stagnating or declining income, were strikingly silent about class. Instead, they drew on a long tradition of racial rhetoric, blaming immigrants and Blacks, not corporations or capitalists, for their economic anxieties. By constructing immigrants and Blacks as unworthy beneficiaries of welfare and affirmative action, they articulated their own identities as Whites, rather than as members of an economic class.

The preceding examples suggest a dialectical relation between material and structural conditions and cultural representation. The language of race, gender, and class formation draws on historical legacy, but also grows out of political struggle. Omi and Winant's concept of rearticulation—the investment of already present ideas and knowledge with new meanings—is relevant here. For example, the Black civil rights and women's liberation movements in the 1960s and 1970s drew on existing symbols and language about human rights, but combined them in new ways and gave them new meanings (e.g.,

"The personal is political," "Black power") that fostered mass political organizing.

Power

The organization and signification of power are central to the constructionist framework, despite the frequent charge that this approach elides issues of power and inequality. Yet power is a central element in the formulations of Scott (1986) and Connell (1989). For Scott, gender is a primary way of signifying relations of power; for Connell, gender is constituted by power, labor, and cathexis. Power and politics are also integral to Omi and Winant's (1994) definitions of race and racism, when they describe race as constantly being transformed by political struggle and racism as aimed at creating and maintaining structures of domination based on essentialist conceptions of race.

The concept of power as constitutive of race and gender draws on an expanded notion of politics coming from three sources. First has been the feminist movement, whose most widely publicized slogan was "The personal is political" (Echols 1989). Feminist activists and scholars have exposed the power and domination, conflict and struggle that saturate areas of social life thought to be private or personal: sexuality, family, love, dress, art. Second has been Gramsci's (1971) concept of hegemony, the taken-for-granted practices and assumptions that make domination seem natural and inevitable to both the dominant and the subordinate. Social relations outside the realm of formal politics establish and reinforce power—art, literature, ritual, custom, and everyday interaction; for this reason, oppositional struggle also takes place outside the formal realm of politics, in forms such as artistic and cultural production. Third has been Foucault's (1977, 1978) work on sexuality and scientific knowledge. Power in these loci is often not recognized because it is exercised not through formal domination but through disciplinary complexes and modes of knowledge.

In all of these formulations, power is seen as simultaneously pervasive and dispersed in social relations of all kinds, not just those conventionally thought of as political. This point is particularly relevant to an examination of race and gender, where power is lodged in taken-for-granted assumptions and practices, takes forms that do not involve force or threat of force, and occurs in dispersed locations. Thus, contestation of race and gender hierarchies may involve challenging everyday assumptions and practices, may take forms that do not involve direct confrontation, and may occur in locations not considered political.

Applications

The framework I have laid out above makes race and gender amenable to historical analysis, so that they can be seen as mutually constitutive. If race and gender are socially constructed, they must arise at specific moments under particular circumstances and will change as these circumstances change. One can examine how gender and race differences arise, change over time, and vary within different social and geographic locations and institutional domains. Race and gender are not predetermined, but are the products of men's and women's actions in specific historical contexts. An understanding of race and gender requires us to examine not only how dominant groups and institutions attempt to impose particular race/gender meanings, but also how subordinate groups contest dominant conceptions and construct alternative meanings.

All institutions in the contemporary United States are organized and permeated by race and gender. The most central of these are the economy, the state, the family, and cultural production. In each of these areas, racialized engendering and gendered racialization occur through processes taking place at the levels of representation, interaction, and social structure. In the following pages, I examine these processes in two institutional areas that are particularly central to the formation of race and gender relations: the labor system (through the race and gender construction of reproductive labor) and the political and legal system (through the race and gender construction of citizenship).

The Race and Gender Construction of Reproductive Labor

Feminist sociologists and historians have revolutionized labor studies by making gender a central part of the analysis of work.[4] One of their most significant contributions has been to expand the concept of labor to include activities that were not previously recognized as forms of work, especially unpaid work in the household. In this discussion I will focus on the analysis of nonmarket work, particularly the labor of social reproduction, which has been extensively explored as a form of gendered labor, but not as labor that is simultaneously racialized.

Gender and Reproductive Labor. The term *social reproduction* was coined by feminist scholars to refer to the array of activities and relationships involved in maintaining people both on a daily basis and intergenerationally (Laslett and Brenner 1989). Reproductive labor includes such activities as purchasing household goods, preparing meals, washing and repairing clothing, maintaining furnishings and appliances, socializing children, providing emotional support for adults, and maintaining kin and community ties. Marxist feminists in the 1970s and 1980s placed the gendered construction of reproductive labor at the center of women's oppression (Barrett 1980; Bose, Feldberg, and Sokoloff 1987; Hartmann 1976). They pointed out that this labor is performed disproportionately by women and is essential to the industrial economy. Yet because it takes place mostly outside the market, it is invisible, not recognized as real work. Men benefit directly and indirectly from this arrangement—directly in that they contribute less labor in the home while enjoying the services that women provide as wives and mothers, and indirectly in that, freed of domestic labor, they can concentrate their efforts in paid employment and attain primacy in that area. Thus, the gender division of reproductive labor in the home interacts with and reinforces the gender division in paid work.

These analyses drew attention to the way the gender construction of reproductive labor helped to create and maintain inequality between men and women and, conversely, how unequal power has enabled men to avoid doing reproductive labor and hampered women's ability to shift the burden. When feminist scholars represent gender as the sole basis for assigning reproductive labor, they imply that all women have the same relationship to it and that it is therefore a universal female experience. And although feminists increasingly are aware of the interaction of race and gender in stratifying the labor market, they have rarely considered whether race might interact with gender in shaping reproductive labor; thus, they have failed to examine differences across racial, ethnic, and class groups in women's relationship to that labor.

The Racial Construction of Labor. Because scholarship on race and labor has been, consciously or unconsciously, male-centered, it has focused exclusively on the paid labor market and especially on male-dominated areas of production. U.S. historians have documented the ways in which race has been integral to the structure of labor markets since the beginnings of the nation. In the 1970s, several writers seeking to explain the historic subordination of peoples of color pointed to dualism in the labor market—its division into distinct markets for White workers and for racial ethnic workers—as a major vehicle for maintaining White domination (e.g., Barrera 1979; Blauner 1972). According to these formulations, labor systems have been organized to ensure that racial ethnic workers are relegated to the low tier of low-wage, dead-end, marginal jobs; institutional barriers, including restrictions on legal and political rights, prevent workers from moving out of that tier.

Writers have differed in their views about the relative agency of capitalists and White workers in the creation and maintenance of color lines. Some have interpreted the color line as a divide-and-conquer strategy of capital to prevent workers from organizing (e.g., Reich 1981); others have depicted White workers as active agents in drawing color lines in order to secure a privileged position in the market (e.g., Bonacich 1972, 1976). Both camps see class conflict as generating race conflict. Whatever the ultimate cause of the conflict, labor struggles in the United States have often taken the form of racial exclusion movements. Forbath (1996) describes how European American men workers in the nineteenth century constructed their identities as Whites and claimed their rights in contrast to Blacks around racialized notions of work: "skilled" versus "unskilled," "free" versus "unfree," and "dirty" versus "clean" work. These studies draw attention to the material and ideological advantages Whites gain from the racial division of labor. However, these studies either take for granted or ignore women's paid and unpaid household labor and fail to consider whether this work might also be "racially divided."

In short, the analysis of the race construction of reproductive labor has been a missing piece of the picture in both literatures. The omission stems from a focus on race alone or gender alone. Only by viewing reproductive labor as simultaneously raced and gendered can we grasp the distinct exploitation of women of color. Using a race-gender lens reveals that reproductive labor is divided along racial as well as gender lines, with White and racial ethnic women having distinctly different responsibilities for social reproduction, not just in their own households but in other work settings. The specific characteristics of the division have varied regionally and changed over time as capitalist economic structures have reorganized reproductive labor, shifting parts of it from the household to the market. Before World War II, racial ethnic women were employed as servants to perform reproductive labor in White households, relieving White middle-class women of more onerous aspects of that work. Since that time, with the expansion of commodified services (services turned into commercial products or activities), racial ethnic women are disproportionately employed as service workers in institutional settings to carry out lower-level "public" reproductive labor, while cleaner white-collar supervisory, as well as lower professional, positions are filled by White women. In both periods, less desirable or more onerous aspects of reproductive labor have devolved on women of color, "freeing" White women for higher-level pursuits. Thus the organization of reproductive labor is as much a source of division and hierarchy as it is of unity and commonality among women.

The Race and Gender Division of Private Reproductive Labor. From the late nineteenth century to the mid-twentieth century, poor and working-class women not only did reproductive labor in their own homes, they also performed it for middle-class families. The division between White women and women of color grew in the latter half of the nineteenth century, when the demand for household help and the number of women employed as servants expanded rapidly (Chaplin 1978). Rising standards of cleanliness, larger and more ornately furnished homes, the sentimentalization of the home as a "haven in a heartless world," and the new emphasis on childhood and mother's role in nurturing children all served to enlarge middle-class women's responsibilities for reproduction at a time when technology had done little to reduce the sheer physical drudgery of housework (Cowan 1983; Degler 1980; Strasser 1982).

By all accounts, middle-class women did not challenge the gender-based division of labor or the enlargement of their reproductive responsibilities. To the contrary, as readers and writers of literature, and as members and leaders of clubs, charitable organizations, associations, reform movements, religious revivals, and the cause of abolition, they helped to elaborate and refine the domestic code (Epstein 1981; Ryan 1981). Instead of questioning the inequitable gender division of labor, they sought to slough off the burdensome tasks onto more oppressed groups of women (see Kaplan 1987).

In the United States, the particular groups hired for private reproductive work varied by region. In the Northeast, European immigrant women, especially Irish, were the primary servant class. In regions with a substantial racial minority population, the servant caste consisted almost exclusively of women of color. In the early years of the twentieth century, 90 percent of non-agriculturally employed Black women in the South were servants or laundresses, constituting more than 80 percent of female servants (Katzman 1978:55). In cities of the Southwest, such as El Paso and Denver, where the main division was between Anglos and Mexicans, approximately half of all employed Mexican women were domestic or laundry workers (Deutsch 1987; Garcia 1981). In the San Francisco Bay Area and in Honolulu, where there were substantial numbers of Asian immigrants, a quarter to half of all employed Japanese women were private household workers (Glenn 1986; Lind 1951, table 1:74).

Women of color shouldered not only the burdens of household maintenance, but also those of family nurturing for White middle-class women. They did both the dirty, heavy manual labor of cleaning and laundering and the emotional work of caring for children. By performing the dirty work and time-consuming tasks, they freed their mistresses for supervisory tasks, for leisure and cultural activities, or, more rarely during this period, for careers. Ironically, then, many White women were able to fulfill White society's expectation of feminine domesticity only through the domestic labor of women of color.

For the domestic worker, the other side of doing reproductive labor for White families was not being able to perform reproductive labor for their own families. Unlike European immigrant domestics, who were mainly single young women, racial ethnic servants were usually wives and mothers (Stigler 1946; Watson 1937). Yet the code that sanctified White women's domesticity did not extend to them. In many cases, servants had to leave their own children in the care of relatives in order to "mother" their employers' children. A 6½-day workweek was typical. A Black children's nurse reported in 1912 that she worked 14 to 16 hours a day caring for her mistress' four children. Describing her existence as a "treadmill life," she said she was allowed to go home

> only once in every two weeks, every other Sunday afternoon—even then I'm not permitted to stay all night. I see my own children only when they happen to see me on the streets when I am out with the children [of her mistress], or when my children come to the "yard" to see me, which isn't often, because my white folks don't like to see their servants' children hanging around their premises. (quoted in Katzman 1982:179)

The dominant group ideology naturalized the mistress-servant relationship by portraying women of color as particularly suited for service. These racialized gender constructions ranged from the view of African American and Mexican American women as incapable of governing their own lives and requiring White supervision to the view of Asian women as naturally subservient and accustomed to a low standard of living. Although racial stereotypes undoubtedly preceded their entry into domestic work, household workers were also induced to enact the role of race-gender inferiors in daily interactions with employers. Domestic workers interviewed by Rollins (1985) and Romero (1992) described a variety of rituals that affirmed their subordination and dependence; for example, employers addressed the household workers by their first names and required them to enter by the back door, eat in the kitchen, wear uniforms, and accept with gratitude "gifts" of discarded clothing and leftover food.

The lack of respect for racial ethnic women's family roles stood in marked contrast to the situation of White middle-class women in the late nineteenth and early twentieth centuries, when the cult of domesticity defined White womanhood primarily in terms of wifehood and motherhood. While the domestic code constrained White women, it placed racial ethnic women in an untenable position. Forced to work outside the home, they were considered deviant according to the dominant gender ideology. On the one hand, they were denied the buffer of a protected private sphere; on the other, they were judged deficient as wives and mothers compared with White middle-class women who could devote themselves to domesticity full-time (Pascoe 1990). Women of color had to construct their own definitions of self-worth and womanhood outside the standards of the dominant culture. Their efforts to maintain kin ties, organize family celebrations, cook traditional foods, and keep households together were crucial to the survival of ethnic communities.

The Race and Gender Construction of Public Reproductive Labor. Due to the expansion of capital into new areas for profit making, the fragmentation of families and breakdown of extended kin and community ties, and the squeeze on women's time as they moved into the labor market, the post-World War II era saw the expansion of commodified services to replace the reproductive labor formerly performed in the home (Braverman 1974:276). Among the fastest-growing occupations in the economy in the 1980s and 1990s were lower-level service jobs in health care, food service, and personal services (U.S. Department of Labor 1993). Women constitute the main labor force in these occupations. Within this new realm of "public reproductive labor," we find a clear race-gender division of labor. Women of color are disproportionately assigned to do the dirty work, as nurse's aides in hospitals, kitchen workers in restaurants and cafeterias, maids in hotels, and cleaners in office buildings. In these same institutional settings, White women are disproportionately employed as supervisors, professionals, and administrative support staff. This division parallels the earlier division between the domestic servant and the housewife. And just as in the household, dirty work is considered menial and unskilled, and the women who do it are too; moreover, White women benefit by being able to do higher-level work.

With the shift of reproductive labor from the household to market, face-to-face race and gender hierarchies have been replaced by structural hierarchies. In institutional settings, race and gender stratification is built into organizational structures, including lines of authority, job descriptions, rules, and spatial and temporal segregation. Distance between higher and lower orders is ensured by structural segregation. Much routine service work is organized to be out of sight. It takes place behind institutional walls, where outsiders rarely penetrate (nursing homes, chronic care facilities), in back rooms (restaurant kitchens), or at night or other times when occupants are gone (office buildings and hotels). Although workers may appreciate this time and space segregation, which allows them some autonomy and freedom from demeaning interactions, it also makes them and their work invisible. In this situation, more privileged women do not have to acknowledge the workers or confront any contradiction between shared womanhood and inequality by race and class.

Implications. Both historically and in the contemporary United States, the racial construction of gendered labor has created divisions between White and racial ethnic women that go beyond differences in experience and standpoint. Their situations have been interdependent: The higher status and living standards of White women have depended on the subordination and lower standards of living of women of color. Moreover, White women have been able to meet more closely the hegemonic standards of womanhood because of the devaluation of the womanhood of racial ethnic women. This analysis suggests that if these special forms of exploitation were to cease, White women as well as men would give up certain privileges and benefits. Thus, social policies to improve the lot of racial ethnic women may entail loss of privilege or status for White women and may therefore engender resistance from them as well as from men.

The Race and Gender Construction of Citizenship

The second institutional domain that often has been looked at as either gendered or raced, but rarely as both, is the state. Because the topic of the state is vast, I will focus this discussion on one aspect, namely, the construction of who is a citizen and what rights and responsibilities go with that status.

Gender and Citizenship. The denial of first-class citizenship has been a central issue for feminist political theorists. Pateman (1988, 1989), Young (1989), and Okin (1979) have analyzed the conception of citizenship in Hobbes, Locke, Rousseau, and other canonical writings and have found that the "universal citizen" defined in these writings is male. Pateman (1988, 1989), for example, traces women's exclusion to the construction of a public/private binary and other oppositions in liberal political thought. The "public" and the "private" are constructed in opposition; the public is the realm of citizenship, rights, and generality, whereas sexuality, feeling, and specificity—and women—are relegated to the private. Citizenship thus is defined in opposition to womanhood.

Recently there has been a growing interest in social citizenship, a key concept in analyses of the modern welfare state (Marshall 1950). Some feminist critics have characterized the state as patriarchal in its provision of welfare, in that it both supports the male-headed household and exerts authority over women by regulating their conduct (e.g., Abramovitz 1996; Sapiro 1986). Other critics have pointed out that from the 1890s on, the United States institutionalized a two-tiered system of social rights (e.g., Gordon 1994; Michel 1996; Nelson 1990): The upper level, consisting of entitlements such as unemployment benefits, old-age insurance, and disability payments, disproportionately goes to men by virtue of their record of regular employment; the lower level, consisting of various forms of stigmatized "welfare," such as AFDC, is what women disproportionately are forced to turn to because of need.

Race and Citizenship. Historians and sociologists looking at race and citizenship have generally been animated by Myrdal's *An American Dilemma* (1944), the disjunction between a professed belief in equal rights existing alongside the denial of fundamental civil and political rights to major segments of the population. In his monumental study, *We the People and Others,* Ringer (1983) argues that this exclusion was not a "flaw," but an inherent feature of the American political system from its very inception. According to Ringer, the United States established a dual legal political system based on colonialist principles. The "people's domain," made up of those considered full members of the national community, "among whom principles of equality and democracy might prevail despite unequal distribution of wealth, power and privilege," exists alongside a second level of those excluded from the national community, "who become the objects of control and exploitation and who are subject to the repressive powers of the state without the basic protection of citizenship" (Ringer and Lawless 1989:86).

Horsman (1981) notes that republican discourse tied the idea of Whiteness to notions of independence and self-control necessary for self-governance. This conception emerged in concert with European and Anglo-American conquest and colonization of non-Western societies. Understanding non-European others as dependent and lacking the capacity for self-governance rationalized the extermination and forced removal of Native Americans, the enslavement of Blacks, and the takeover of land from Mexicans in the Southwest. Smith (1988) notes, "From the revolution era on, many American leaders deliberately promoted the popular notion that Americans had a distinctive character, born of their freedom-loving Anglo-Saxon ancestors and heightened by the favorable conditions of the new world," that "set them above Blacks and truly Native Americans, and later Mexicans, Chinese, Filipinos, and others who were labeled unfit for self-government" (p. 233).

Citizenship as Raced and Gendered. The problem with looking at citizenship as only gendered or only raced is the familiar one: Women of color fall through the cracks. According to existing accounts, White women were not accorded full adult citizenship by dint of having their identities subsumed by their husbands and fathers. White women were "virtual citizens" because men were assumed to represent their wives' and children's interests along with their own. Men of color were deemed noncitizens by virtue of their being "unfree labor," lacking the cultural traits of "freedom," and being "servile." The question remains: Where do women of color fit? In what follows, I attempt to synthesize the largely separate literatures on gendered citizenship and raced citizenship to trace the racialized gender construction of American citizenship. Although necessarily sketchy, this account may suggest some directions for future analyses.

At its most general level, *citizenship* refers to the status of being a full member of the community in which one lives (Hall and Held 1989). Citizenship in Western societies always has had a dual aspect as a system of equality and as a major axis of inequality. On the one hand, citizenship is defined as a universal status in which all who are included have identical rights and responsibilities, irrespective of their individual characteristics. This conception emerged out of the political and intellectual revolutions of the seventeenth and eighteenth centuries, as the older concept of society organized as a hierarchy of status, expressed by differential rights, gave way to the notion of a political order established through social contract. The concept of social contract implied free and equal status among those party to it. On the other hand, the process of defining membership and rights of citizenship entailed drawing boundaries that created "noncitizens." Rhetorically, the citizen was defined and gained meaning through its contrast with the "noncitizen" as one who lacked the essential qualities of a citizen. Materially, the autonomy and freedom of the citizen were made possible by the often involuntary labor of noncitizen wives, slaves, children, servants, and employees.

Given this heritage, the disjunction in American citizenship between the ideal of universality (the so-called American Creed) and the reality of exclusion should not be surprising. The major groups left out by the nation's founders—women, the poor, slaves, Native Americans, and other racialized minorities—were deemed dependent in one way or another. Women of all classes were presumed to be members of a dependent class. Upon marriage, a woman's legal identity was subsumed by her husband's; she could not bring suit in a court of law, make contracts, own property, or pursue independent occupations. As chattel, enslaved Blacks did not have any independent legal identity and could not own property, even their own persons. The exclusion of racialized minorities became national policy with the passage of the 1790 Naturalization Act, which limited the right to become citizens to "Whites." Later interpretations of the act in cases involving Asian immigrant applicants for naturalization placed them in the category of "aliens ineligible for citizenship" (Haney Lopez 1996).

The conventional view is that over the course of the nineteenth and twentieth centuries, "defects" in the American Creed were gradually repaired as formal civil and political rights were won by previously excluded groups. Still, as the previous discussion of the two-tiered welfare system suggests, race and gender hierarchies remain central in the construction of citizenship and rights. However, there has been a shift in the way race and gender are deployed: Until the late nineteenth and early twentieth centuries, White women and people of color were explicitly and categorically excluded. Justifications for their exclusion drew on ideologies that posited essential, natural differences between men and women and between Whites and people of color. More recently, as formal citizenship rights were demanded and gradually won on the basis of universalistic principles of personhood, rights associated with citizenship have become stratified into superior and inferior grades. Allocation to these grades and their differential rights are justified by seemingly universalistic criteria, such as economic productivity and civic virtue. These criteria are, however, infused by race and gender assumptions, including elements of earlier ideologies that supported categorical exclusion, in particular, the public/private and independence/dependence dichotomies.

These dichotomies have been central elements in the conception of the "ideal citizen" since classical times (Pocock 1985). In the Aristotelian model, citizens, free from their individual, concrete, material interests, came together to make decisions on behalf of the general welfare. This formula depended on strict separation of *polis* from *oikos*—the private, material realm of people and things, where women and slaves took care of the citizen's material needs and left him free to engage in politics. The dichotomies were also central in the writings of Locke, Rousseau, and other Enlightenment philosophers who shaped American political thought. Additionally, the colonial experience and the subsequent war to establish an independent nation significantly affected American conceptions of independence. Under British citizenship, all who were born in British jurisdictions were subjects of the crown. In this context, dependence was viewed not as involuntary subjugation, but as a reciprocal relationship involving a web of obligations in which rights and duties flowed in both directions. Independence was thought of primarily in economic terms, as a condition made possible by owning property, which negated the necessity of having to work for or under someone else (Fraser and Gordon 1994; Gunderson 1987).

The meanings of independence and dependence underwent transformation as American Revolutionary rhetoric sought to replace the concept of subjectship with that of voluntary citizenship. Voluntary citizenship required independence, not only in the sense of having property, but in the sense of personal freedom. Revolutionary-era debates over issues of loyalty and suffrage reveal considerable anxiety about dependence. Roediger (1991) connects this anxiety to the proximity of chattel slavery. For White workingmen, independence was what distinguished them from despised slaves and protected them from the possibility of "White enslavement." Whereas previously dependence had been accepted as a status shared by many, it came to be viewed as incompatible with White masculinity. Independence became race and gender specific: All White men were independent and all women and Blacks were dependent. When the United States was established, all state constitutions, with one exception, limited suffrage to White men, cutting out even property-owning White women, who, as *femmes seules*, had been allowed to vote in many colonial jurisdictions. In most states, free Blacks were also excluded from the franchise and prohibited from serving on juries and testifying in court.

From Categorical Exclusion to Stratified Rights. During the course of the nineteenth century, contestations over rights and protections escalated as organized movements sought civil and political citizenship for propertyless White men, African American men, and women. The first of these, universal White manhood suffrage, was achieved by the early nineteenth century. The terms of inclusion, however, were linked to the exclusion of women and racialized minorities (Litwak 1961). By the beginning of the nineteenth century, the growth of industrial capital and urbanization was eroding the position of small farmers, self-employed artisans, and craftsmen and increasing the proportion of men reliant on wage labor. In a society in which the small producer was viewed as the backbone of a democratic polity and in which masculinity was equated with independence, the transition to wage labor created a crisis for White male identity. Earlier, White working-class organizations had condemned what they called wage slavery. This stance expressed the conviction that forms of dependence acceptable for women, Blacks, and "lower races" were unacceptable for White men. However, once wage labor became more common, the term *wage slavery* itself came to be seen as demeaning. According to Roediger (1991), a new working-class rhetoric emerged that valorized wage labor and denied that it compromised the worker's freedom and independence. In the new vocabulary, "masters" became "bosses" and "servants" became "hired men." The dependence inherent in wage work was transmuted into "independence" through its contrast with slavery and indentured servitude.

The linking of race, gender, and citizenship served to mediate conflicting class interests. Working-class European American men, through labor organizations, constructed their own identities as men, as Whites, and as citizens around the concept of themselves as "free, productive, independent" workers, in opposition to people of color as "unfree, unproductive, dependent" labor. Litwak (1961) notes that the extension of universal White manhood suffrage was usually coupled with disfranchisement of Blacks. From 1819, when Maine was admitted to the Union, until the end of the Civil War, all new states guaranteed suffrage to White males irrespective of property and denied the vote to Blacks. Legislatures in several states lacking such provisions in their original constitutions passed restrictive legislation.

Neither Litwak (1961) nor Roediger (1991) sufficiently stresses that White men's rhetoric of "independence" was gendered as well as racialized. It has been left to feminist historians to identify gender as a theme running through wage-earning men's claims for full manhood and citizenship in nineteenth-century America and England (Rose, 1986; Seccombe 1986). Artisanal men staked their claim to suffrage and to a family wage on their positions as fathers and heads of household and on their independence through honorable labor and membership in skilled trades. In short, White working-class men's claim of independence (and therefore of full rights of citizenship) was premised on the dependence of women and the subordination of people of color. Various forms of dependence—political, civil-legal, and social—not acceptable or congruent with White male status were mapped onto these others (Rose 1995).

Two other major movements for civil and political citizenship were waged by African Americans and women during the late nineteenth and early twentieth centuries. In both cases, formal suffrage and civil rights were won through constitutional amendments. However, citizenship remained incomplete. In the South, land redistribution was never accomplished under Reconstruction, foreclosing the possibility of Black economic independence (Du Bois 1935). When Reconstruction ended, the White planter class was able to retake political control. Whites disenfranchised African Americans through poll taxes and tests of "understanding," curtailed their civil rights, and constrained their mobility through Jim Crow laws buttressed by extralegal violence. Blacks challenged state and local segregation laws, but federal courts upheld laws that nullified 14th Amendment protections by manipulating public/private boundaries. The courts carved out vast areas of activity as "private conduct" exempt from equal protection by the state (Ringer 1983).

For women, passage of the 19th Amendment did little to alter the common law and myriad statutes that assumed women's dependence and husbands' prerogatives over wives' labor and income. Women had to challenge laws piecemeal, with change coming slowly and painfully.

For example, as recently as 1965, only 21 states had made women eligible for jury duty on the same basis as men. The others either excluded women or granted them exemptions (Freeman 1995:372).

Nonetheless, as categorical exclusion of whole groups gave way to stratification among citizens, discourses on citizenship, race, and gender also changed. Justifications for categorical exclusion had rested on claims of essential, natural differences between men and women and between Whites and non-Whites. The rationale for stratified rights used seemingly universalistic criteria, such as economic productivity. These criteria, however, incorporated the same conceptual dichotomies that had justified categorical exclusion. In both periods, independence and activity in the public sphere were linked to the capacity to exercise citizenship and to entitlement to full rights, whereas dependence and activity in the private sphere were deemed outside the realm of citizenship and rights.

Consideration of the simultaneous race and gender construction of citizenship reveals further layers of stratification. With regard to social citizenship, for example, women of color were shut out of both secondary rights based on "dependence" (welfare) and primary rights based on economic contribution (entitlements). Mink (1994) and Gordon (1994) have documented the exclusion of Black and Mexican single mothers from Progressive Era and New Deal assistance programs on the grounds that they did not meet the criterion of worthy motherhood. These women were viewed as "employable" long before the cutting of welfare assistance for single mothers and the institution of work requirements in the 1990s.

Implications. This brief history of contestation over citizenship reveals deep-seated race, gender, and class tensions in U.S. society that continue to the present day. The vision of a democracy rooted in the freedom, equality, and independence of individual citizens clashes with the vision of a social order based on a homogeneous citizenry. In the 1990s this contestation has continued, with attempts to restrict immigrant women's and children's access to social and health services, the reinstatement of the use of prison chain gangs made up of Black male prisoners, and demands by some members of Congress to redraw the boundaries of citizenship to exclude American-born children of noncitizen residents. Citizenship is still being deployed to create and maintain race and gender hierarchies.

Emerging Trends and Future Directions

Race and gender studies are becoming increasingly sophisticated in their recognition of multiple axes of difference. The appreciation of multiplicity is in part due to cross-fertilization among ethnic and African American studies, women's studies, gay-lesbian studies, and postcolonial cultural studies, and in part due to the globalization of capital that has brought about rapid and bewildering movements of people, goods, cultural symbols, and ideas across national borders. In this final section, I identify some emerging areas of scholarship that are advancing social constructionist thinking. As work in these areas expands, it too will benefit from more sustained attention to a simultaneous race-gender analysis.

Studying the Unmarked

Studies of the "unmarked" but normative categories of Whiteness and masculinity have burgeoned. Men's studies emerged as a counterpart to women's studies more than two decades ago, drawing on psychoanalytic theory, role theory, and other approaches prevalent in women's studies. In the past decade, the social constructionist approach has emerged as the main paradigm in sociological studies of masculinity (e.g., Klein 1993; Messner 1992). According to Connell (1995), these studies emphasize themes similar to those on the social construction of womanhood: "the construction of masculinity in everyday life, the importance of economic and institutional structures, the significance of differences among masculinities and the contradictory and dynamic character of gender" (p. 35). This approach stresses diversity and the presence of subordinated or oppositional masculinities. The concept of hegemonic masculinity was developed to express the idea that recognizing diversity is not enough, that relations of domination and subordination among different masculinities must also be analyzed. A significant number of studies have examined the construction of class-gender identities (e.g., Cockburn 1983; Connell 1995; Messerschmidt 1993), but relatively few have explored race-gender masculinity (Mesner 1992; Staples 1982).

The growth of scholarly interest in Whiteness has been more recent, pioneered by Roediger (1991, 1994) and Frankenberg (1993).[5] Since the mid-1990s there has been a veritable explosion of conferences, papers, monographs, and anthologies on Whiteness (e.g., Frankenberg 1997; Wray and Newitz 1997). With few exceptions, gender has not been incorporated integrally into studies of Whiteness. Those works that have undertaken integrated analysis have focused only on the discursive level (e.g., Bederman 1995; Frankenberg 1993, 1994; Ware 1992). For example, Frankenberg's *White Women, Race Matters* (1993), based on interviews of White women, examines these women's concepts of self in relation to White and racial ethnic masculinities. Although she notes at the beginning of the book that Whiteness is importantly a location of structural advantage, in my opinion, Frankenberg does not offer an integrated analysis of gendered Whiteness as structural location.

Studying Hybridity

An increasingly active area for research and writing is that concerning so-called mixed-race people (Root 1992, 1995; Spickard 1989). American scholars of race have become interested in the concept of "mixed race" because this status disrupts the neatly ordered, mutually exclusive categories on which racial stratification is based. Because the United States has historically been a "racial dictatorship," in Omi and Winant's (1994) words, the maintenance of racial boundaries has been critical. The majority of states had antimiscegenation laws in force at one time or another, prohibiting marriage between Whites and various "others" (Pascoe 1991, 1996). Not until 1967 were the last 15 of these state laws invalidated by the U.S. Supreme Court. Such law was buttressed by widespread "scientific" and commonsense beliefs about the biological inferiority, moral degeneracy, and sociocultural maladjustment of racial "hybrids" (Nakashima 1992). Despite taboos and prohibitions, extensive mixing has always gone on, but the presence of "mixed-race" people was disguised by the legal fiction that "White" is a pure category. Thus, in the case of mixed parentage, children were placed in the category of the subordinate-race parent.

The gender dimension of interracial relations is just beginning to be explored. Now and in the past, interracial unions have not been gender-symmetrical. In the case of Blacks after the period of slavery, the preponderance of voluntary unions occurred between Black men and White women. For most other groups, the predominant pattern has involved White men and women of color. For example, contemporary Asian-White interracial unions disproportionately involve White men and Asian women (Shinagawa and Pang 1996). Pascoe (1991) found that miscegenation laws were most prevalent in areas where unions between men of color and White women were most likely; she infers that these laws were designed to prevent men of color from having access to White women, but not to bar White men's access to women of color. In the context of definitions of Whiteness hinging on "purity" of blood, White women are literally the reproducers of Whiteness. Thus White women's bodies are controlled to maintain racial boundaries (Liu 1991; Stoler 1996). Where barriers have been erected against White men, it has taken the form of laws to bar them from passing property to children from interracial unions (Pascoe 1996).

Other mixed-race issues that cry out for a racialized gender analysis include the relationship of mixed-race masculinity/femininity to hegemonic masculinity/femininity and the relationships of mixed-race men and women to cultural nationalism. Women of color have pointed out that male activists are quick to suspect them of being disloyal (Cheung 1990; Garcia 1989; Moraga 1986; Wong 1995), especially if they are lesbian, feminist, and/or mixed race.

Studying Heterogeneity

Recognizing and studying differences within gender and race categories is also an important new direction. Bounded categories, such as Black, Hispanic, and Asian American, when posed in contrast to White or European American, appear monolithic, but in fact are variegated. Members of a racial category differ along lines of class, generation, ethnicity, and culture, as well as gender. Even the Black category, which appears to be ethnically homogeneous, is in fact heterogeneous, including not only native-born Blacks, but also West Indian, Haitian, Puerto Rican and other Latino, and Cape Verdean, many of whom become racialized as Black when they settle in the United States (Levins Morales 1989). The federally defined category of Hispanic—which is an ethnic, not racial, designation—consists of four groupings that vary considerably not only in class, but also in "race" composition. Mexicans are defined as White for legal purposes, but popular understanding casts them as "Brown" (Almaguer 1994). The majority of Cubans in America are considered "White" in part because lighter-skinned upper- and middle-class persons were more likely to flee Cuba after the Cuban Revolution (Kaminsky 1994:22). In contrast, three-fifths of Puerto Rican migrants are perceived as Black in the United States, even though most were known either as White or as one of many other color designations recognized in Puerto Rico (Davis 1991:104).

The category Asian Pacific American, which is a very recent formation, continues to undergo rapid change in composition because of large-scale immigration, high rates of out-marriage, and economic mobility. The two groups of immigrants that Ong (1996) compares, wealthy Chinese investors and professionals and impoverished Khmer refugees, represent one example of heterogeneity among Asian Americans. In general, the ethnic and class composition of more recent immigrant groups differs radically from the composition of groups that immigrated prior to 1965. As a result, the meaning of *Asian American* is subject to constant reexamination and a continuing tension between specific ethnic identity and general Asian American identity.

For both Latinos and Asian Americans, the larger grouping is important in terms of aggregate numbers needed for political clout. However, lumping groups together hides important differences in the characteristics and needs of different communities. It has frequently been pointed out that statistics indicating the socioeconomic success of Asian Americans hide the fact that some groups within this larger category are not doing well. The same point could be made about differences in the social and economic situations of various Latino groups. The need to have the situations of particular groups monitored led Asian American political groups to fight U.S. Census Bureau plans to stop collecting and tabulating data on specific ethnicities of Asian Americans (Wright 1994).

A racialized gender analysis would contribute to the study of heterogeneity within categories by examining differences in gender within various communities. For example, rather than assuming a monolithic "Asian" gender system that can be contrasted with an "American" or "White" gender system, researchers need to do more work to document gender in specific social and historical contexts. Class, ethnicity, generation, and other axes of difference interact to shape heterogeneous genders.

Studying Relations among Subordinate Groups

Some writers on race have pointed to the need to decenter Whiteness as the reference by looking at multigroup relations and relations among racial minorities. Popular awareness of the "browning" of America and the new multiracial, multiethnic configuration of U.S. cities grew in the wake of the violent upheaval in Los Angeles following the acquittal of four White police officers in the beating of Rodney King. Mass audiences were mesmerized by television and other media images of rainbow crowds attacking the shops of Asian, Latino, African American, and European American owners. What got the most attention, however, was the targeting of Korean-owned businesses by Blacks. In Kim's (1993) and Palumbo-Liu's (1994) views, White racism shaped media coverage of the Korean-Black conflict by posing Koreans either as model Americans defending their property against Black/Brown hordes or as ruthless shopkeepers enriching themselves at the expense of impoverished inner-city residents.

Although the multiracial aspects of the violence have been widely analyzed, their simultaneously gendered features have not. Whereas the majority of Black and Latino attackers were male, the gender composition of the Korean shopkeepers was more even. Because Korean business owners rely on pooled family labor, Korean women are often the ones who interact with customers. In a prior incident that fueled Black resentment, a Korean woman shop owner had shot and killed an African American customer whom she said she believed was attempting to shoplift, and had been acquitted. The cross-race, cross-gender dynamics reinforce the importance of considering not only clear-cut dominance and subordination, but also relative privilege and power in relations among subordinate groups.

Another example of this point can be found in Hawaii, where fault lines have opened up between Native Hawaiians and Asian Americans as a result of the rearticulation of Hawaiian identity within the Hawaiian sovereignty movement. The term *local* had long been used to designate both Hawaiians and groups from plantation worker backgrounds, such as Chinese, Japanese, Filipino, and Portuguese. This designation emphasized not only the unique culture that emerged from the mixture of peoples on the plantations, but also a shared history of discrimination and exploitation by the haole establishment. This "local" identity is being challenged by movement leaders, who emphasize the singular status of Hawaiians as indigenous people displaced from their land and culture by outsiders, White colonizers, and immigrant laborers alike. Some Asian American leaders have balked at accepting group responsibility for the displacement of Hawaiians, but there is increasing recognition that the concept of interracial justice requires accountability among subordinate groups, not just White responsibility (Yamamoto 1995). In this instance also, gender needs to be included in the analysis; for example, many of the most militant leaders of the Hawaiian sovereignty movement are women, whereas the state and local officials with whom they negotiate are often Asian men.

Studying Transnational Race-Gender Formations

Globalization has meant dismantling borders to facilitate the flow of capital, goods, labor, and cultural products. One result has been the internationalization of the race and gender division of labor. A striking instance is the swelling migration of women from the Third World to fill the demand for reproductive labor in the metropolitan centers of Europe, Asia, and North America. The debt-ridden economies of many Third World countries have become reliant on remittances sent by migrants working abroad (Chang 1997). The Philippines alone was sending 700,000 contract workers abroad each year in the late 1990s, 55 percent of whom were women. More than two-thirds of these women were employed as nannies, housekeepers, or maids in middle- or upper-middle-class homes in the United States, Europe, the Middle East, Japan, Hong Kong, and other parts of Asia. Typically these workers have left their own children behind; because of the lower standard of living in the Philippines, a Filipina maid in Los Angeles or Rome can afford to pay poorer Filipina women to care for her family back home. According to Parrenas (1998), the racial division of female reproductive labor has been transformed by globalization into what amounts to an "international transference of mothering."

The expanding flow of peoples across national borders is also creating the phenomenon of transnational identities. An increasing number of people move back and forth, oscillating between being part of the majority in one nation and being members of an ethnic minority in another. Transnationalism is not a new condition for many Latinos. Mexican Americans in the Southwest and Mexicans in northern Mexico have long inhabited a "borderland" both literally and culturally in that national boundaries were drawn across what had been continuous Mexican territory. Twin cities such as Ciudad Juarez and El Paso span each side of the border, and people cross back and forth both legally and illegally as part of their daily routine to shop, work, and visit. Historically, many Mexicanos have maintained bilateral ties and been drawn back and forth by economic swings and fluctuations in U.S. policy. During periods of labor demand, the U.S. government has recruited "temporary" Mexican workers, as under the Bracero Program; during periods of recession, it has expelled them, as in the repatriation programs of the 1930s and 1940s and in Operation Wetback in the early 1950s (Gutierrez 1995).

Because of the growing power of Asian economies, the loosening of borders, and the telecommunications revolution, the maintenance of bilateral ties is now possible even when distances are vast, as in the case of Asia and North America. Affluent Taiwanese and Hong Kong families are splitting members to get the best of both worlds: an economic and cultural base in Asia and the political stability and educational opportunities in North America. Children—so-called parachute kids—are sent to attend school and establish permanent residency in the United States while the breadwinner stays in Asia to tend to business. Family ties are maintained by phone, e-mail, and frequent visits in both directions. This growing phenomenon of transnational identities in turn forces a rethinking of the term *Asian American* (Lowe 1996).

While the phenomena noted above illustrate the ways in which globalization is heightening race, gender, and national inequalities, globalization is also spurring movements for race and gender justice to organize across borders. Subordinated groups within one nation can link up with groups in other countries and gain visibility and leverage. For example, indigenous peoples around the globe have forged bonds that support efforts within particular nations to organize to fight for land rights; maintenance of native languages, cultures, and religions; and political self-determination. Ties with other indigenous peoples, particularly in the Pacific Rim, gave the Hawaiian sovereignty movement the impetus to revive the Hawaiian language as a living tongue through state-sponsored Hawaiian-language immersion schools. Similarly, in 1995 women from around the globe gathered in China for a U.N.-sponsored conference of nongovernmental organizations. In that forum, women shared their experiences of how the structural adjustment programs imposed by the International Monetary Fund on Third World economies had affected their livelihoods. Participants were able to see the "big picture" of the devastating impacts of cuts in social welfare benefits and of the relationship between structural adjustment programs and migration, as women were forced to seek ways to support their families abroad (Chang 1997).

A Closing Thought

This review of several areas of thinking and research that have recently emerged and that will constitute central themes in the future underscores the importance of race and gender to an understanding of the most critical social and political issues in the twenty-first century. In particular, the changes now occurring in the organization and functioning of the international economy will have dramatic and profound effects on how race and gender relations are constituted, and, conversely, the way race and gender relations are constructed in response to the new globalization can have powerful impacts on the pace and direction of economic and social change. For those concerned with social justice, it will be more important than ever to be alert to the shifting and dynamic constructions of race and gender within the new international economy.

Notes

1. The title of a collection on African American women edited by Hull, Scott, and Smith (1982) puts it this way: *All the Women Are White, All the Blacks Are Men, but Some of Us Are Brave.*

2. Some preliminary attempts, including those of West and Fenstermaker (1995), Bonacich (1994), and Brodkin Sacks (1989), have nonetheless been illuminating.

3. In this regard, see, for example, Jordan's (1968) "Note on the Concept of Race" at the end of his monumental study of the history of White American attitudes toward Blacks, in which he attempts to clarify the latest scientific understanding of race as directed toward the study of genetics and evolution.

4. Much of the material in this section is drawn from Glenn (1992).

5. It would be more accurate to say that interest on the part of White scholars is recent. There has been a long tradition of Black writings on Whiteness (see Du Bois [1903] 1989; hooks 1992).

References

Abramovitz, Mimi. 1996. *Regulating the Lives of Women.* Rev. ed. Boston: South End.

Acker, Joan. 1990. "Hierarchies, Jobs, and Bodies: A Theory of Gendered Organizations." *Gender & Society* 4:139-58.

Almaguer, Tomas. 1994. *Racial Faultlines: The Historical Origins of White Supremacy in California.* Berkeley: University of California Press.

Barrera, Mario. 1979. *Race and Class in the Southwest.* Notre Dame, IN: University of Notre Dame Press.

Barrett, Michèle. 1980. *Women's Oppression Today: Problems in Marxist Feminist Analysis.* London: Verso.

———. 1987. "The Concept of 'Difference.' " *Feminist Review* 26 (July):29-41.

Bederman, Gail. 1995. *Manliness and Civilization.* Chicago: University of Chicago Press.

Blauner, Robert. 1972. *Racial Oppression in America.* New York: Harper & Row.

Bonacich, Edna. 1972. "A Theory of Ethnic Antagonism: The Split Labor Market." *American Sociological Review* 37:547-59.

———. 1976. "Advanced Capitalism and Black/White Relations in the United States: A Split Labor Market Interpretation." *American Sociological Review* 41:34-51.

———. 1994. "Race, Class and Gender: A Tentative Theoretical Exploration." Presented at the Honors Colloquium, University of Rhode Island.

Bose, Chris, Roslyn Feldberg, and Natalie Sokoloff, with the Women and Work Research Group, eds. 1987. *Hidden Aspects of Women's Work.* New York: Praeger.

Braverman, Harry L. 1974. *Labor and Monopoly Capital.* New York: Monthly Review Press.

Butler, Judith. 1990. *Gender Trouble: Feminism and the Subversion of Identity.* New York: Routledge.

———. 1993. *Bodies That Matter: On the Discursive Limits of "Sex."* New York: Routledge.

Chang, Grace. 1997. "The Global Trade in Filipina Workers." Pp. 132-52 in *Dragon Ladies: Asian American Feminists Breathe Fire,* edited by Sonia Shah. Boston: South End.

Chaplin, David. 1978. "Domestic Service and Industrialization." *Comparative Studies in Sociology* 1:97-127.

Cheng, Lucie. 1984. "Free, Indentured, Enslaved: Chinese Prostitutes in Nineteenth Century America." Pp. 402-34 in *Labor Immigration under Capitalism: Asian Immigrant Workers in the United States before World War II,* edited by Lucie Cheng and Edna Bonacich. Berkeley: University of California Press.

Cheung, King-kok. 1990. "The Woman Warrior versus the Chinaman Pacific: Must a Chinese American Critic Choose between Feminism and Heroism?" Pp. 234-51 in *Conflicts in Feminism,* edited by Evelyn Fox Keller and Marianne Hirsch. New York: Routledge.

Cockburn, Cynthia. 1983. *Brothers: Male Dominance and Technological Change.* London: Pluto.

Collins, Patricia Hill. 1990. *Black Feminist Thought: Knowledge, Consciousness, and the Politics of Empowerment.* New York: Routledge, Chapman & Hall.

Connell, R. W. 1989. *Gender and Power.* Stanford, CA: Stanford University Press.

———. 1995. *Masculinities.* Berkeley: University of California Press.

Cowan, Ruth Schwartz. 1983. *More Work for Mother.* New York: Basic Books.

Crenshaw, Kimberlé. 1989. "Demarginalizing the Intersection of Race and Sex: A Black Feminist Critique of Antidiscrimination Doctrine, Feminist Theory, and Antiracist Politics." *University of Chicago Legal Forum* 139.

———. 1992. "Whose Story Is It Anyway? Feminist and Anti-racist Appropriations of Anita Hill." Pp. 402-40 in *Race-ing Justice, En-gendering Power: Essays on Anita Hill, Clarence Thomas, and the Construction of Social Reality*, edited by Toni Morrison. New York: Pantheon.

Davis, F. James. 1991. *Who Is Black?* College Park: Pennsylvania State University Press.

Degler, Carl. 1980. *At Odds: Woman and the American Family from the Revolution to the Present.* New York: Oxford University Press.

Deutsch, Sarah. 1987. *No Separate Refuge: Culture, Class and Gender on an Anglo-Hispanic Frontier in the American Southwest, 1880-1920.* New York: Oxford University Press.

Dill, Bonnie Thornton. 1980. "The Means to Put My Children Through: Childrearing Goals and Strategies among Black Female Domestic Servants." Pp. 107-24 in *The Black Woman*, edited by La Frances Rogers Rose. Beverly Hills, CA: Sage.

Dominguez, Virginia. 1986. *White by Definition: Social Classification in Creole Louisiana.* New Brunswick, NJ: Rutgers University Press.

Du Bois, W. E. B. 1935. *Black Reconstruction in America, 1860-1880.* New York: Harcourt Brace.

———. [1903] 1989. "The Souls of White Folks." In *Darkwater: Voices from within the Veil.* New York: Bantam.

Dyer, Richard. 1988. White. *Screen* 29, no. 4:44-65.

Echols, Alice. 1989. *Daring to Be Bad: Radical Feminism in America, 1967-1975.* Minneapolis: University of Minnesota Press.

Epstein, Barbara. 1981. *The Politics of Domesticity: Women, Evangelism and Temperance in Nineteenth Century America.* Middletown, CT: Wesleyan University Press.

Espiritu, Yen. 1992. *Asian American Panethnicity: Bridging Institutions and Identities.* Philadelphia: Temple University Press.

Fields, Barbara J. 1982. "Ideology and Race in American History." Pp. 143-78 in *Region, Race and Reconstruction*, edited by James MacPherson and M. Morgan Kousser. New York: Oxford University Press.

———. 1990. "Slavery, Race and Ideology in the United States of America." *New Left Review* 181:95-118.

Forbath, William. 1996. "Race, Class and Citizenship." Unpublished manuscript.

Foucault, Michel. 1977. *Discipline and Punish: The Birth of the Prison.* Translated by Alan Sheridan. New York: Pantheon.

———. 1978. *The History of Sexuality.* Vol. 1, *An Introduction.* Translated by Alan Sheridan. New York: Vintage.

Frankenberg, Ruth. 1993. *White Women, Race Matters: The Social Construction of Whiteness.* Minneapolis: University of Minnesota Press.

———. 1994. "Whiteness and Americanness: Examining Constructions of Race, Culture and Nation in White Women's Life Narratives." Pp. 62-77 in *Race,* edited by Steven Gregory and Roger Sanjek. New Brunswick, NJ: Rutgers University Press.

———, ed. 1997. *Locating Whiteness.* Durham, NC: Duke University Press.

Fraser, Nancy and Linda Gordon. 1994. "A Genealogy of *Dependency*: Tracing a Keyword of the U.S. Welfare State." *Signs* 19:309-36.

Freeman, Jo. 1995. "The Revolution for Women in Law and Public Policy." Pp. 365-404 in *Women: A Feminist Perspective,* edited by Jo Freeman. Mountain View, CA: Mayfield.

Fuchs, Lawrence H. 1983. *Hawaii Pono: An Ethnic and Political History.* Honolulu: Bess.

Garcia, Alma. 1989. "The Development of Chicana Feminist Discourse, 1970-1980." *Gender & Society* 3:217-38.

Garcia, Mario. 1981. *Desert Immigrants: The Mexicans of El Paso, 1880-1920.* New Haven, CT: Yale University Press.

Gilkes, Cheryl Townsend. 1985. " 'Together and in Harness': Women's Traditions in the Sanctified Church." *Signs* 10:678-99.

Glenn, Evelyn Nakano. 1986. *Issei, Nisei, Warbride: Three Generations of Japanese American Women in Domestic Service.* Philadelphia: Temple University Press.

———. 1992. "From Servitude to Service Work: Historical Continuities in the Racial Division of Paid Reproductive Labor." *Signs* 18:1-43.

Gordon, Linda. 1994. *Pitied but Not Entitled: Single Mothers and the History of Welfare 1890-1935.* New York: Free Press.

Gramsci, Antonio. 1971. *Selections from the Prison Notebooks.* Edited and translated by Quintin Hoare and Geoffrey Nowell Smith. New York: International.

Gunderson, Joan R. 1987. "Independence, Citizenship, and the American Revolution." *Signs* 13:59-77.

Gutierrez, David. 1995. *Walls and Mirrors: Mexican Americans, Mexican Immigrants, and the Politics of Ethnicity.* Berkeley: University of California Press.

Hall, Stuart and David Held. 1989. "Citizens and Citizenship." Pp. 173-88 in *New Times,* edited by Stuart Hall and Jacques Martin. London: Lawrence & Wishart.

Haney Lopez, Ian F. 1996. *White by Law: The Legal Construction of Race.* New York: New York University Press.

Harris, Angela. 1990. "Race and Essentialism in Feminist Legal Theory." *Stanford Law Review* 42:581-616.

Harris, Cheryl I. 1993. "Whiteness as Property." *Harvard Law Review* 106:1707-91.

Hartmann, Heidi I. 1976. "Capitalism, Patriarchy, and Job Segregation by Sex." *Signs* 1:137-69.

Higginbotham, Evelyn Brooks. 1992. "African-American Women's History and the Metalanguage of Race." *Signs* 17:251-74.

hooks, bell. 1992. "Representing Whiteness in the Black Imagination." Pp. 338-46 in *Cultural Studies,* edited by Lawrence Grossberg, Cary Nelson, and Paula A. Treichler. New York: Routledge.

Horsman, Reginald. 1981. *Race and Manifest Destiny.* Cambridge, MA: Harvard University Press.

Hull, Gloria T., Patricia Bell Scott, and Barbara Smith, eds. 1982. *All the Women Are White, All the Blacks Are Men, but Some of Us Are Brave: Black Women's Studies.* Old Westbury, NY: Feminist Press.

Ignatiev, Noel. 1995. *How the Irish became White.* New York: Routledge.

Jordan, Winthrop. 1968. *White over Black: American Attitudes toward the Negro, 1550-1812.* Chapel Hill: University of North Carolina Press.

Kaminsky, Amy. 1994. "Gender, Race, Raza." *Feminist Studies* 20:3-32.

Kaplan, Elaine Bell. 1987. " 'I Don't Do No Windows': Competition between the Domestic Worker and the Housewife." In *Competition: A Feminist Taboo?* edited by Valerie Minor and Helen E. Longino. New York: Feminist Press.

Katzman, David. 1978. *Seven Days a Week: Women and Domestic Service in Industrializing America.* New York: Oxford University Press.

———. 1982. *Plain Folk: The Life Stories of Undistinguished Americans.* Urbana: University of Illinois Press.

Kim, Elaine. 1993. "Home Is Where the Han Is: A Korean American Perspective on the Los Angeles Upheavals." Pp. 215-35 in *Reading Rodney King, Reading Urban Uprising,* edited by Robert Gooding-Williams. New York: Routledge.

Klein, Alan M. 1993. *Little Big Men: Bodybuilding Subculture and Gender Construction.* Albany: State University of New York Press.

Laslett, Barbara and Johanna Brenner. 1989. "Gender and Social Reproduction: Historical Perspectives." *Annual Review of Sociology* 15:381-404.

Levins Morales, Aurora. 1989. "Between Two Worlds." *Women's Review of Books* 7 (December):3-4.

Lind, Andrew W. 1951. "The Changing Position of Domestic Service in Hawaii." *Social Process in Hawaii* 15:71-87.

Litwak, Leon F. 1961. *North of Slavery: The Negro in the Free States, 1790-1860.* Chicago: University of Chicago Press.

Liu, Tessie. 1991. "Teaching Differences among Women from a Historical Perspective: Rethinking Race and Gender as Social Categories. *Women's Studies International Forum* 14, no. 4.

Lorber, Judith. 1994. *Paradoxes of Gender.* New Haven, CT: Yale University Press.

Lowe, Lisa. 1996. *Immigrant Acts.* Durham, NC: Duke University Press.

MacKinnon, Catharine A. 1989. *Toward a Feminist Theory of the State.* Cambridge, MA: Harvard University Press.

Marshall, T. H. 1950. *Citizenship and Social Class and Other Essays.* Cambridge: Cambridge University Press.

Messerschmidt, James W. 1993. *Masculinities and Crime: Critique and Reconceptualization.* Lanham, MD: Rowman & Littlefield.

Messner, Michael A. 1992. *Power at Play: Sports and the Problem of Masculinity.* Boston: Beacon.

Michel, Sonya. 1996. "A Tale of Two States." Presented at the Women's Studies Colloquium, University of California, Berkeley.

Mink, Gwendolyn. 1994. *The Wages of Motherhood.* Ithaca, NY: Cornell University Press.

Moraga, Cherríe. 1986. "From a Long Line of Vendidas: Chicanas and Feminism." Pp. 173-90 in *Feminist Studies/Critical Studies,* edited by Teresa de Lauretis. Bloomington: Indiana University Press.

Myrdal, Gunnar (with R. Sterner and A. Rose). 1944. *An American Dilemma: The Negro Problem and Modern Democracy.* New York: Harper & Row.

Nakashima, Cynthia L. 1992. "The Invisible Monster: The Creation and Denial of Mixed Race People in America." Pp. 162-78 in *Racially Mixed People in America,* edited by Maria P. P. Root. Newbury Park, CA: Sage.

Nelson, Barbara. 1990. "The Origins of the Two-Channel Welfare State: Workman's Compensation and Mothers' Aid." Pp. 123-51 in *Women, the State and Welfare,* edited by Linda Gordon. Madison: University of Wisconsin Press.

Okin, Susan. 1979. *Women in Western Political Thought.* Princeton, NJ: Princeton University Press.

Omi, Michael and Howard Winant. 1986. *Racial Formation in the United States from the 1960s to the 1980s.* New York: Routledge.

————. 1994. *Racial Formation in the United States: 1960-1990.* 2d ed. New York: Routledge.

Ong, Aiwa. 1996. "Cultural Citizenship as Subject Making: Immigrants Negotiate Racial and Cultural Boundaries in the United States." *Current Anthropology* 37:737-61.

Palmer, Phyllis Marynick. 1989. *Domesticity and Dirt.* Philadelphia: Temple University Press.

Palumbo-Liu, David. 1994. "Los Angeles, Asians and Perverse Ventriloquisms: On the Functions of Asian America in the Recent American Imaginary." *Public Culture* 6:365-81.

Parrenas, Rhacel. 1998. "The Global Servants: Filipina Servants in Rome and Los Angeles." Ph.D. dissertation in progress, University of California Berkeley.

Pascoe, Peggy. 1990. *Relations of Rescue.* New York: Oxford University Press.

————. 1991. "Race, Gender, and Intercultural Relations: The Case of Interracial Marriage." *Frontiers* 12, no. 1:5-18.

————. 1996. "Miscegenation Law, Court Cases, and Ideologies of 'Race' in Twentieth-Century America." *Journal of American History* 83 (June):44-69.

Pateman, Carole. 1988. *The Sexual Contract.* Cambridge: Polity.

————. 1989. *The Disorder of Women.* Stanford, CA: Stanford University Press.

Pocock, J. G. A. 1985. "The Ideal of Citizenship since Classical Times." Pp. 29-52 in *Theorizing Citizenship,* edited by Ronald Beiner. Albany: State University of New York Press.

Reich, Michael. 1981. *Racial Inequality.* Princeton, NJ: Princeton University Press.

Ringer, Benjamin B. 1983. *We the People and Others: Duality and America's Treatment of Its Racial Minorities.* New York: Tavistock.

Ringer, Benjamin B. and Elinor Lawless. 1989. *Race, Ethnicity and Society.* New York: Routledge.

Roediger, David. 1991. *The Wages of Whiteness: Race and the Making of the American Working Class.* London: Verso.

————. 1994. *Towards the Abolition of Whiteness.* London: Verso.

Rollins, Judith. 1985. *Between Women: Domestics and Their Employers.* Philadelphia: Temple University Press.

Romero, Mary. 1992. *Maid in the U.S.A.* New York: Routledge.

Root, Maria P. P., ed. 1992. *Racially Mixed People in America.* Newbury Park, CA: Sage.

————, ed. 1995. *The Multiracial Experience: Racial Borders as the New Frontier.* London: Sage.

Rose, Sonya O. 1986. "Gender at Work: Sex, Class and Industrial Capitalism." *History Workshop* 21:113-31.

———. 1995. "Class Formation and the Quintessential Worker." Unpublished manuscript.

Rubin, Gayle. 1975. "The Traffic in Women: Notes on the Political Economy of Sex." Pp. 157-210 in *Toward an Anthropology of Women,* edited by Rayna R. Reiter. New York: Monthly Review Press.

Rubin, Lillian Breslow. 1994. *Families on the Fault Line.* New York: HarperCollins.

Ruiz, Vicki. 1987. *Cannery Women, Cannery Lives: Mexican Women, Unionization and the California Food Processing Industry, 1939-1950.* Albuquerque: University of New Mexico Press.

Ryan, Mary P. 1981. *Cradle of the Middle Class: The Family in Oneida County, New York, 1790-1865.* Cambridge: Cambridge University Press.

Sacks, Karen Brodkin. 1989. "Toward a Unified Theory of Class, Race and Gender." *American Ethnologist* 16:534-50.

———. 1994. "How the Jews became White Folks." Pp. 78-102 in *Race,* edited by Steven Gregory and Roger Sanjek. New Brunswick, NJ: Rutgers University Press.

Sapiro, Virginia. 1986. "The Gender Basis of American Social Policy." *Political Science Quarterly* 101:221-38.

Scott, Joan W. 1986. "Gender: A Useful Category of Historical Analysis." *American Historical Review* 91:1053-75.

Seccombe, Wally. 1986. "Patriarchy Stabilized: The Construction of the Male Breadwinner Wage Norm in Nineteenth Century Britain." *Social History* 11:53-76.

Shinagawa, Larry and Gin Pang. 1996. "Asian American Panethnicity and Intermarriage." *Amerasia Journal* 22, no. 1:1-25.

Smith, Rogers M. 1988. " 'One United People': Second-Class Female Citizenship and the American Quest for Community." *Yale Journal of Law and the Humanities* 1:229-93.

Spickard, Paul. 1989. *Mixed Blood: Intermarriage and Ethnic Identity in Twentieth-Century America.* Madison: University of Wisconsin Press.

Staples, Robert. 1982. *Black Masculinity: The Black Man's Role in America.* San Francisco: Black Scholar.

Stigler, George J. 1946. "Domestic Servants in the United States, 1900-1940." Occasional Paper 24, National Bureau of Economic Research, New York.

Stoler, Ann. 1996. "Carnal Knowledge and Imperial Power: Gender, Race and Morality in Colonial Asia." Pp. 209-66 in *Feminism and History,* edited by Joan W. Scott. New York: Oxford University Press.

Strasser, Susan. 1982. *Never Done: A History of American Housework.* New York: Pantheon.

Thorne, Barrie. 1993. *Gender Play: Girls and Boys in School.* New Brunswick, NJ: Rutgers University Press.

U.S. Department of Labor, Bureau of Labor Statistics. 1993. *Occupational Outlook Quarterly* (Fall).

Ware, Vron. 1992. *Beyond the Pale: White Women, Racism and History.* London: Verso.

Watson, Amey. 1937. "Domestic Service." In *Encyclopedia of the Social Sciences.* New York: Macmillan.

West, Candace and Sarah Fenstermaker. 1995. "Doing Difference." *Gender & Society* 9:8-37.

West, Candace and Don Zimmerman. 1987. "Doing Gender." *Gender & Society* 1:125-51.

Wong, Sau-ling. 1995. "Denationalization Reconsidered." *Amerasia Journal* 21:1-27.

Wray, Matt and Annalee Newitz, eds. 1997. *White Trash: Race and Class in America.* New York: Routledge.

Wright, Lawrence. 1994. "One Drop of Blood." *New Yorker,* July, pp. 46-55.

Yamamoto, Eric. 1995. "Rethinking Alliances: Agency, Responsibility and Interracial Justice." *UCLA Asian Pacific American Law Journal* 3, no. 1:33-74.

Young, Iris Marion. 1989. "Polity and Group Difference: A Critique of the Ideal of Universal Citizenship." *Ethics* 99:250-74.

Zavella, Patricia. 1987. *Women's Work and Chicano Families: Cannery Workers of the Santa Clara Valley.* Ithaca, NY: Cornell University Press.

CHAPTER 2

Rewriting Class, Race, and Gender

Problems in Feminist Rethinking

JOAN ACKER

In the early days of the contemporary women's movement, feminist critics of male-centered social theory identified class as one of their first conceptual targets, arguing that the concept had not included women.[1] Although debates around women and class or capitalism and patriarchy were intense and often transforming, these debates declined as core problems, such as how to decide the class location of unpaid housewives, remained unresolved. Feminist social scientists shifted their focus from theorizing women and class to empirical studies of gender and work by the end of the 1970s. In the 1980s, responding to the criticisms of Third World feminists and women of color, much theoretical attention was directed to the intersections of gender, race, and class. Within this new focus, the old problems with class analysis were not addressed. In much of this work, class is taken for granted as unproblematic, whereas race and gender are extensively analyzed. With the development of postmodern/poststructuralist feminism, many leading feminist theorists on the left turned to issues of representation, culture, and identity, in effect abandoning class as a central theoretical concept (Barrett 1992). However, feminists still need class theory if they are to understand women's subordination, for that subordination, in *all* its

AUTHOR'S NOTE: This chapter is a revised and expanded version of an article published in *Sosiologisk tidsskrift*, 1997, vol. 5, no. 2:93-109.

variety, is still tied to the economic inequalities of industrial societies. In this chapter, I review this history and discuss a feminist conceptualization of class that emerges from the efforts to comprehend how gender, class, and race are linked in the ongoing development of capitalism.

Feminist Critiques of Class

At the end of the 1960s and into the 1970s, feminists argued that class theory, whether Marxist, Weberian, or occupational/functional, either ignored women altogether or assumed that women's class positions are determined by those of the men to whom they are attached, thus ignoring women's own paid work as determinants of their class locations (Acker 1973). Moreover, although class theories claimed to encompass major societal structures of inequality and exploitation, they failed to account for the relatively greater subordination and exploitation experienced by women compared with the men who share their class locations. Ideas of class, feminists argued, were built on implicit images of the male worker, ignoring the different conditions and contexts of women's paid and unpaid work; consequently, class concepts were not gender-neutral as they were claimed to be. Instead, they were premised upon gendered assumptions. Women were not absent in theories of class; they were invisible, defined as nonworkers.

The concept of class is understood in a variety of ways.[2] For example, the word *class* is often used to describe hierarchies of material wealth, authority, and status linked to the occupational structure. Such descriptive schemes are usually based on the occupations of men and thus suffer from the problems listed above. Adding women's occupations to job hierarchies does not erase the implicit modeling of the structure on men's jobs. Women's jobs do not fit properly in the male models: Because of sex-typing and sex segregation, the pay and status of women's jobs do not rise with increased experience and technical demands as do the pay and status of men's jobs (Acker 1980; Crompton 1993:96). Some researchers attempted to integrate women's unpaid work in the home into such occupational schemes by measuring the status of the occupation "housewife" (Bose 1973). However, this effort further revealed the implicit male model in these schemes. According to the model, a correlation should exist between status and income; however, the occupation housewife falls in the middle status range, but produces no income at all (Bose 1973). Although adequately revised descriptions of inequality are useful, many feminists were more interested in theories that dealt with the dynamics of class processes, such as the ongoing economic, political, and social activities that create sharp differences in power, wealth, and well-being. Marxist theory was the most prominent conceptualization of class dynamics and struggle. Although Marxist class theory presented all the difficulties discussed above, many feminists, including myself, attempted to use and adapt it. Marxism seemed a reasonable place for feminists to begin, because its central focus is on the social relations of economic oppression and exploitation and how systems of domination function and may be overcome. Many feminists were trying to both understand and change the world, and Marxist theory seemed to be the most useful conceptual and political tool.

The starting point for much of Marxist feminism was a structural analysis of class. Focusing on economic relations between capitalist and worker at the most abstract level, Marxist feminists derived class from these relations, as well as class positions and class boundaries. In this view, class structure consists of empty places; it is a structure of positions determined by the relations of production within a mode of production. The structure is indifferent about who fills the empty places (Wright 1985). Into some positions go women, into others go men, and patriarchy determines these placements (Hartmann 1981). Similarly, race or ethnicity may play a part in determining which actors turn up in which positions. However, gender and race have nothing to do with the way the structure itself is constituted. In the structural Marxist view, "Marxist categories, like capital itself, are sex-blind" (Hartmann 1981:10-11). Further, "if capitalists organize work in a particular way, nothing about capital itself determines who (that is, which individuals with which ascriptive characteristics) shall occupy the higher, and who the lower rungs of the wage labor force" (Hartmann 1981:23-24). Thus, class is conceptualized at an analytic level where gender is simply an ascriptive characteristic of individuals and groups of individuals.

Marxist feminists and socialist feminists attempted to rectify the defects in Marxist class theory in a number of different ways that can be roughly grouped under the designations of political economy of housework theories (e.g., Hamilton and Barrett 1986; Seccombe 1974) and capitalism/patriarchy theories (Barrett 1980; Eisenstein 1979; Hartmann 1976, 1981; Kuhn and Wolpe 1978). In the political economy of housework debate, theorists argued that unpaid housework creates value by reproducing the labor power of workers in both present and future generations, and that this value is appropriated by capitalists. Thus, women's work contributes to surplus value and profit. Because the value they produce becomes realized in the process of commodity production, women can be considered part of the working class in their own right.

Capitalism/patriarchy, also called dual systems, theorists argued that patriarchy, a system of male dominance and control over women, exists in close association with capitalism. Theorists differed in how they understood the bases of patriarchy and the relationships between patriarchy and capitalism. One view was that patriarchy is rooted in male control of human reproduction and sexuality; male control in this private arena structures women's fates in the more public world of class and capitalism. The other view was that patriarchy is rooted in men's economic interests, which cut across class lines (Hartmann 1976). "The argument is that capitalism develops out of a previously patriarchal society and preserves patriarchy as part of the system of control. In the process of development, male workers gain a privileged position in the wage-based economy" (Acker 1980:31). Male workers and employers cooperate to maintain that privileged position for both economic and ideological reasons. Thus, organized male privilege relegates women to subordinate places in the class structure.

Both the political economy of housework and capitalism/patriarchy theories were extensively criticized and defended (Molyneux 1979; Young 1981), but neither direction provided a satisfactory resolution to the theoretical problems (Beechey 1987). The political economy of housework focused too much on unpaid domestic labor, failing to address gender inequalities in paid work that were also part of women's class experiences. Those who argued for this approach disagreed about precisely how unpaid labor contributed to the capitalist's profits and whether capitalists paid for this labor through the "family wage" or paid workers less than the costs of the reproduction of their labor power because some costs were assumed by the housewife's unpaid work. Thus, this theoretical approach foundered on a narrow and economistic attempt to fit women's unpaid work into the abstract analysis of surplus value and the abstract concept of class linked to this analysis.

Capitalism/patriarchy and other dual systems theories, on the other hand, sidestepped the problems with class analysis by creating a separate system to explain the special subordination of women, leaving intact the original class concept that had been widely criticized as implicitly based on a model of the male worker. Another criticism of dual systems theories was that they posit analytically independent structures, such as gender and class, implying that some social relations are gender relations whereas others are something else. This conceptualization seems to ignore the actuality that many gender relations are simultaneously class relations and that class relations, as concrete practices rather than as theoretical abstractions, are often also gender relations (Acker 1989b; Pollert 1996). Finally, as a consequence of the assignment of women's subordination to a separate system, class came to be seen as less central for explaining women's subordination than for explaining men's subordination in capitalist societies.

In spite of the difficulties in feminist attempts to rethink Marxist class theory, these interventions established that women's unpaid domestic labor is valuable, and that the oppression of women is systemic and cannot be located solely within the family and reproduction. However, this theorizing left untouched the central conception of class, which still contained the assumptions that made women invisible: lack of or unsatisfactory analysis of domestic labor and abstract, apparently gender-neutral concepts that were grounded on male models of both worker and employer.[3]

The lively debates of the late 1960s and the 1970s about the structural causes of women's subordination, including women's class relations and their locations in class structures, failed to produce a new grand theory in which women and their work was as central as men and their work (Acker 1980; Sokoloff 1980). As Beechey (1987) observes:

> By the end of the seventies theoretical analyses of women's work had reached a kind of impasse. People debated the pros and cons of different ways of theorizing the relationship between production and reproduction, patriarchy and capitalism, without making much progress. However, both feminist politics and research into women's employment were beginning to point in new directions. (pp. 11-12)

One new direction was to focus on concrete studies of particular historical instances of women's inequality and subordination at work in capitalist societies, to understand the intersections of gender and class in changing occupations (Cockburn 1983), in industries and organizations (Game and Pringle 1983; Cockburn 1985), and in the labor process (Knights and Willmott 1986). Crompton and Jones (1984) analyzed the gender divisions in the "service class." Walby (1986) theorized marriage as a class system related to other class systems. A debate about whether or not women's class positions are "really" determined by those of their husbands appeared in British journals. Many of these arguments are represented in a collection of essays edited by Crompton and Mann (1986). All of these issues were discussed at a major international conference on gender and class in Antwerp in 1988, yet very little new thinking was presented.

This impasse led some feminists to try to transcend dual systems theory and produce accounts of class societies in which gender and class are united in one system of relations (Acker 1988, 1989a). For example, Weinbaum and Bridges (1976) suggested that the work of consumption of goods and services is a way that women's unpaid labor is necessary to capitalism and ties women into the system of production and class. This analysis is insightful, but, like other theories connecting domestic labor to the economy, it leaves out women's paid work and its relationship to women's unpaid labor. In "Class, Gender, and the Relations of Distribution" (Acker 1988), I argued that we need to expand our notions of class relations to include relations of distribution if we are to conceptualize class in a way that can include unpaid, mostly women, workers and others outside the paid labor force, such as the long-term unemployed. The wage relation, I suggested, is integral to production but is also a form of distribution. Other relations of distribution are located in the family and the welfare state. Both relations of production and relations of distribution are gendered and intrinsically interconnected. A major lack in this reconceptualization was that I did not deal with the social and economic contributions of domestic labor. Wright (1989) used a similar strategy, conceptualizing family relations and relations to the state as links between individuals and productive resources. These mediated class relations, along with direct class relations, constitute the class structure. Wright did not develop the concept of mediated class relations, and continued to employ his categorical scheme based on occupational position (see also Baxter 1994). These efforts all had a fundamental problem: They left intact the central conceptualization of class that had been criticized by feminists, only adding on notions of "relations" relevant to women's work. Glucksmann (1990), a British sociologist, attempted another solution, arguing that there is a "total social organization of labour" encompassing in one structure both commodity production and domestic production and, further, that class relations in the world of production can be understood only in terms of this overall organization of work. These ideas were promising, but

Glucksmann did not analyze those economic relations that I tried to capture with the idea of distribution and Wright referred to as "mediated" class relations. Thus, none of us accomplished what we were attempting: to overcome the problems of dual systems analysis by positing one multifaceted system of relations.

I had, at least partly, to agree with Cockburn (1986), who argued that we were not really successful in bringing class and gender together, that in practice we were still talking about two systems. Thus, some discussion of gender and class continued through the 1980s, but, on the whole, at least in the United States, there was remarkably little attention to theoretical problems in linking gender and class, and the issue slipped from the forefront of feminist concerns. This lack of interest in problems of structure contributed in the 1980s to a number of shifts in feminist thinking—the postmodernist/poststructuralist turn, a turn from class and gender consciousness to identity, and from theorizing class as a system of economic relations to theorizing how gender enters into the process of conceptualization and social construction of class locations and subjective processes (Barrett and Phillips 1992).

Many feminist scholars continued to use the term *class,* but without much attention to the earlier debates. On the whole, those doing empirical studies of women's paid and unpaid work tended to use ideas that were less contentious than class, such as sex segregation or occupational sex-typing (e.g., Reskin and Hartmann 1986), human capital theory, queuing theory (Reskin and Roos 1990), or even rational choice theory (England and Farkas 1986), bypassing class altogether. Case studies of workplaces and organizations might identify the subject as, for example, working-class women, but what *working-class* might mean was unexplored, or emerged in its particularity from the case study material.

The Emergence of Triple Oppression: Gender, Race, and Class

In the meantime, in the United States and Britain, challenges from women of color, articulated in their theoretical, empirical, and political work, began to make clear that a great deal of feminist theorizing assumed a White, middle-class woman similar to the women doing the theorizing. If they were to deal adequately with the issues they said they were trying to understand, feminists could not be concerned only with class and gender—they also had to take race/ethnicity seriously.[4] Thus, gender, class, and race became the triple oppressions that must be theorized. Many recognized that an additive model of gender, race, and class as distinct dimensions or systems would violate the experience that feminists were attempting to capture with their theorizing. For example, a woman who is Black (White), Spanish (English) speaking, and a doctor (waitress) does not experience herself in disjointed segments of gender, race, ethnicity, and class; rather, all these elements are produced and reproduced within the same everyday experiencing of her life. Theory would have to reflect that reality and the diverse patterning and interplay of processes of domination, collusion, and protest. Third World feminists (e.g., Mohanty 1991) and feminists of color (e.g., Collins 1990) began to talk about race, class, and gender as intrinsic to each other, as social constructions, realities, identities emerging in particular historical moments and local places, but shaped by processes such as colonialist capital expansion, nation building, and war.

This perspective is an answer to extensive feminist critiques of essentialist and/or universalizing theory that posits a universal (White) man or woman. It also has roots in the work of theorists who argue that dominant processes of knowledge production erase the human subject and create an objectified conceptual world in which no woman (or man with little power) has a voice. The solution to this problem of invisibility and lack of voice is to begin an active search for knowledge in the everyday experiences of concrete women. The meaning of *experience* has been much discussed. My usage follows that of Smith (1987): *Experience* refers to the ordinary, practical activities of daily life, as well as the problems, frustrations, and happinesses of life. Using everyday experience as the starting point of investigation does not mean that the sociologist attends only to what is visible in the local and everyday place. On the contrary, the idea is that the place for beginning investigation is in the problematics of everyday life, but this investigation inevitably must move beyond that into "extralocal" relations that shape the local. Similarly, interpretation or explanation is not to be found only in the meanings that activities and events hold for the participants or in their own intentions and views of causation. Class relations, for example, often originate in extralocal places and may not be completely visible in local sites. Insisting that feminist work must be concrete and rooted in the standpoints or experiences of a multiplicity of different women (and men) leads to a view of class, gender, and race (and ethnicity, nationality, and so on) as complexly interrelated at a multiplicity of sites within particular historical developments.

There is, as yet, no consensus on what such a formulation of complex interrelations means. Some authors take an ethnomethodological approach, in which these interconnections occur primarily in face-to-face encounters (West and Fenstermaker 1995). Others emphasize interlocking oppressions as macro-level structures (Collins 1995). Some write about interacting systems or dimensions, which could imply a development of dual systems theory into triple systems or even multiple systems theory. That would be unfortunate, I think, because the problems of dual systems theorizing would only be amplified. For example, as I have argued above, positing patriarchy and capitalism or gender and class as separate systems has usually left standing the old analyses of capitalism and class based on (White) male models of work and life, while the situation of women is analyzed separately and gender subordination is consigned to its own, usually peripheral, niche. Adding racial and ethnic systems has a similar effect. All women and men of color are still peripheral to the analysis.

Another question involves the meanings of the separate terms. Debates about the meanings of *gender* and *women* have been at the center of feminist discourse for some time (e.g., Nicholson 1994). Although there are different positions, these positions are fairly clear. Gender is variously defined as socially constructed roles, a social institution, cultural phenomena, personality characteristics, and identities (Acker 1992; Lorber 1994). Scholars agree that gender is socially constructed, diverse, and varies historically and cross-culturally. Similarly, the complexities of race and ethnicity have been discussed extensively in recent years (e.g., hooks 1981, 1984; Collins 1990). Scholars see race as socially and politically constructed in particular historical processes of war, colonization, slavery, immigration, and migration. Many different racial categories and identities emerge, with the category "White" almost always in dominant positions in the Northern industrial countries. However, in spite of, or perhaps because of, all these difficulties in adapting "class" to our emerging requirements of feminist thinking, in many efforts to include race, gender, and class in the same analysis, the concept of class is used uncritically, as though the idea were self-evident and unproblematic. Recent energetic debates on gender and race have transformed these concepts, but the old class debate still lurks in the background, unresolved and probably unremembered.

What is wrong with that? We all know what *working-class* and *middle-class* mean; these ideas are necessary for making sense of our daily worlds. Why not just make do with our commonsense notions of class? What is wrong, I think, is that this usage elides the earlier critique of class, and this elision, or failure of memory, leaves the idea of class unspecified, but still carrying the old assumptions that exclude White women, racial minorities, and Third World people. As a result, class may become less and less illuminating in this time of dramatic social change. In addition, class may disappear into our analysis of gender and race, which would be an ironic turn of events.

Another reason for not "making do" with our commonsense notions of class is that the rapid and frequently alarming changes under way on a global basis are, to a large extent, changes produced by capitalist processes of accumulation. Capitalism cannot be deconstructed away; the apparently accelerating changes that are feminizing the world labor force, destroying the old male working classes in the most industrialized countries, and fragmenting the means of survival for many, making millionaires while impoverishing masses of people (to name just a few of the processes) show how much we need an analysis of capitalism to comprehend what is happening. Class is a linking concept that can mediate between the generalized and global expressions of capitalist processes and the concrete experiences of ordinary people who are simultaneously coping with these processes and producing a changing reality. A central question is, then, What sort of analysis of capitalism and class, along with understandings of race, gender, and other processes of difference, might help us to comprehend and, possibly, think about how to deal with this changing world?

Rethinking Class

The preceding discussion suggests some of the elements that I believe should enter into a rethinking of class. I do not pretend to have created a new conceptualization of class; I want only to suggest ways of thinking and doing research that could inform such a project. These are, first, the recognition that class is formed in and through processes that also create and re-create racial and gender formations; second, the understanding of class not as abstract structures into which people are inserted but as something accomplished through active practices that constitute social relations and structures; third, the recognition that class, along with gender and race/ethnicity, should be understood from the standpoints or locations of many different people, women and men; and fourth, that a concept of class adequate for feminist purposes must be broadened and anchored within a larger notion of the economic than is now used.

Gender, Race, and Class Interrelated in Practice

To begin with, class must be seen as formed through gender and race, just as gender and race are formed through class processes, historically varying across time and space. A great deal of knowledge exists about these processes; they are visible through many different points of entry. For example, economists Amott and Matthaei (1996) bring together research that demonstrates the dynamic interrelationships among gender, race, and class in the history of the United States (see also Dill 1988). They show how women's experiences with work and class have been shaped by the particular ways in which their racial/ethnic groups have been incorporated into the nation. For Chicanas, the process began with the Spanish invasion and colonization of Mexico, followed by the Mexican-American war that resulted in the annexation by the United States of Mexico's northern territories and the expropriation of land owned by former Mexicans. African American women's history is rooted in slavery and the brutalities of subsequent racial exploitation and exclusion. In contrast, Asian American women were imported into the American economy as low-wage workers, often farmworkers, prostitutes, and domestic servants. The category "Asian American women" encompasses many different ethnic groups with different histories and cultures, and thus with different gender/race/class experiences. Similarly, other racial/ethnic groups have different histories, shaping different class/gender experiences.

In U.S. sociology, African American, Asian American, and Chicana scholars (among others) are also providing a great deal of new knowledge about gender/race/class relations (e.g., Baca Zinn and Dill 1994; Collins 1990; Glenn 1986). Among these, Romero (1992) describes Chicana domestic workers and how their lives are shaped by gender, class, and race. Chow's (1994) study of Asian American women in the workforce shows how work bureaucracy and mixes of race, class, and gender discrimination shape their experiences and how these women develop strategies to resist unfair treatment, maintain their dignity, and assure family survival.

A growing literature explicitly examines the interplay of race, gender, and class as organized interests in policy development and social movements (e.g., Barnett 1993; Blankenship 1993; Deitch 1993). For example, Deitch (1993) analyzes how in the U.S. Congress, White male southern opponents of the Civil Rights Act inserted into Title VII of the act the category "sex" as a prohibited basis for employment discrimination, and how complex politics of race and class allowed that category to remain and become law. Subsequently, Title VII became the basis for some of the greatest achievements of the women's movement.

Finally, we are beginning to see analyses of Whiteness, the racial formation that is so invisible to those who enjoy its privileges (Frankenberg 1993) yet so visible to those whom Whites construct as "other" and so central to class/race/gender processes. Third World women scholars examining colonial and postcolonial developments in this perspective have shown how identities and actions are formed and manipulated as part of changes brought about by White colonialism/capitalism (Mohanty 1991; Rowbotham and Mitter 1994). Mohanty (1991) argues, for example, that "some of the effects of colonial policies and regulations are the reempowering of landholding groups, the granting of property rights to men, the exclusion of women from ownership, and the 'freezing' of patriarchal practices of marriage, succession, and adoption into laws" (p. 19). The history of capitalism is a history of the enslavement, domination, and genocide of peoples of color carried out by White people as well as a history of production and exploitation of White workers.

We probably know more about how gender, class, and race are intertwined in the lives of members of relatively subordinated groups than we do about the lives of those in more influential positions. An example of intersections in the practices of the influential comes from my own work on gender and politics in Sweden (Acker 1992, 1994a, 1994b). There, the strength of the male-dominated labor movement grew partly out of the image of the Swedish family composed of a male breadwinner and female housewife. This image supported a durable labor-capital compromise that made it possible for labor to define women's issues in such a way that they would not threaten men's power in unions, work organizations, government, or political life. Men union leaders used the concept of class and claims to class solidarity to silence women, defining some issues as inadmissible and criticizing cross-class feminist organizing as bourgeois and antilabor. In the process, the meaning of working-class consciousness came to include denigration and proscription of any actions defined as feminist (Hermansson 1993). Moreover, predatory masculine behavior, including actions that would now be seen as sexual harassment, were part of men's working-class solidarity and discouraged women's participation in unions and leftist political parties (Hermansson 1993). Men's power and dominance were taboo subjects within the labor movement, perhaps because of its active support for many social policies that benefited women.

The prohibitions against such talk fell in the wake of Social Democratic defeat in 1991, and labor unions and Social Democrats began to take measures to include women and women's issues in new ways. For example, the LO (a blue-collar labor federation) emphasized raising the pay of low-wage workers, mostly women, with unprecedented vigor. The Social Democratic Party decided that half the candidates would be women in the fall 1994 elections, contributing to the party's success at the polls. The gender composition of the labor movement has changed, and women have been able to reconstitute its gender/class consciousness from one that protected men's interests to one that attempts to incorporate more thoroughly the interests of women.

However, White hegemony in the labor movement was not problematized, even as an increasingly dark-skinned immigrant population grew and that population was consigned to low-paid, relatively unskilled jobs. Race has now become a more open issue in the labor movement, as immigrants, especially immigrant women, have become those with the highest unemployment rates in the population.

Sweden is not an isolated case; White masculinity and male bonding serve to cement class solidarity and consciousness in many other places. Looking at gender, class, and race historically may illuminate how White masculinity, in particular, is implicated in the emergence of central capitalist relations. As Kessler-Harris (1993) asks, "How then do we understand the particular relations out of which some men rose to power?" (p. 198). What particular forms of masculinity emerged within, shaped, and were shaped by changing economic relations or changing opportunities in the colonies and at home, for example? What are the links between masculinity and the wage relation? In theory, the wage relation appears as an abstract form. Concretely, wages have always been structured around distinctions of both gender and race. Perhaps the emergence of the abstract form, as a generalized form of power, happened through the actions of men who found meaning, necessity, and action within a particular form of masculinity (Connell 1995).

In *The Sexual Contract,* Pateman (1988) suggests a sense in which the wage relation, viewed as a contract between the worker and the employer, may itself be fundamentally gendered. She argues that the idea that labor power can be separated from the self and sold as the individual's property is dependent upon the concept of the abstract individual of liberal theory. That abstract individual has no body—indeed, cannot have a body if that individual is to represent a generalized human being. Examination of the genesis of the idea reveals that "the individual" is indeed a man. When the individual has a female body, problems of separation of the self from the body's ability to labor become evident, particularly when we consider that one meaning of to labor is to give birth. If we can argue that labor power cannot really be separated from the embodied self, then what we sell in the wage contract is that body, that self. The embodied self is always gendered, thus the wage relation, too, is gendered.

Social Relations as Active Practices

Another element in my feminist rethinking of class is to understand class as social relations, not as criteria to define locations in a pregiven structure of hierarchies and exploitations, but as activities and practices in which people engage as they earn their livings, organize and coordinate their work, and struggle for survival. This view of class has a long history, of course (see Thompson 1963). These activities and the meanings integral to them are shaped by gender and race/ethnicity as these identifications are constructed, reconstructed, contested, and controlled. In this conceptualization, I have been influenced by Smith's (1987, 1990a) notion of relations of ruling as "extended" social relations that link local experiences into extralocal places where practices of coordinating, administrating, and managing set the requirements, the conditions for what people do in the local. Extralocal places are also local for the people who are actively creating "the relations of ruling." This way of looking at social relations is, of course, similar to the way social relations have been defined by others. In contemporary capitalism, Smith argues, the relations of ruling are increasingly abstract, intellectualized, generalizing, and textually mediated. For example, job evaluation systems produced by large international consulting firms provide textual guides for reproducing and legitimating work hierarchies in which class, gender, and often racial inequalities are perpetuated (Acker 1989a). Their use involves complex series of activities that link the wage of a particular employee into generalized management practices. Such textual tools of management help to reproduce similar inequalities in many different countries. They are complex and often mystifying to workers, even as they help to organize gender/class/race relations.

This understanding of social relations does not produce a simple picture of how the world works, but is a method that allows one to discover class relations rather than derive them from abstract, a priori formulations. In *The Crossroads of Class and Gender*, Benería and Roldán (1987) demonstrate this approach. Starting from the concrete working and living situations of women doing industrial homework, they examine the chains of relations between workers and businesses that tie most of these workers to multinational firms and the world economy. They show how class and gender relations are constantly formed and reformed as women and men negotiate their lives in the family and household and in the wider economy, within particular historical and cultural contexts. This is a dynamic and multifaceted picture of class, gender, and ethnic processes, dramatically different from a categorical approach that begins with assigning individuals and families to theoretical class positions and then investigates the correlations of class position with other variables such as political allegiances.

Beginning in the Standpoints of Women (and Men)

Another element in a feminist rethinking follows from the above and from the feminist insight that efforts to develop knowledge should start from the standpoints of women. Again, I have found Smith's particular development of the notion of standpoint to be very useful. Standpoints can be seen as points of entry into relations of ruling, or, in this case, into class/gender/race relations. Most contemporary class theories, whether Marxist or any other, take standpoints within the relations of ruling. This does not mean that Marxist class theorists favor the present structure, but that their discursive, conceptual organization is linked into the forms of knowledge of the relations of ruling. What class theories build in as relevant is what is relevant from a standpoint within the relations of ruling. How capital functions is the central question; certain things are relevant and visible from that standpoint, whereas others, such as child care and families, are not (Smith 1990b). The discourse of class arising from within this perspective has a gendered substructure in the divisions between the "economy" and the life-support activities assigned primarily to women that are invisible from inside that discourse.

From the standpoints of a multiplicity of women, many other and different things are relevant, most of them probably of little interest to capital, but posing critical class/gender/race issues for the women involved. From these many different standpoints, it is possible to look back at the relations of ruling to see how they are being constructed. For example, from the perspective of capital, poor mothers on welfare in the United States are of little interest, at best members of an economically draining "underclass" caught in a web of dependency. From the perspectives of those women, their class as well as gender and race situations look quite different. They put together a livelihood from a number of sources—public assistance, work, family, husbands, and friends (Edin and Lein 1997). Public assistance payments are never enough to cover the cost of living, but neither are wages from the jobs usually available to them. The costs of health care and day care are high and cannot be covered by minimum-wage work. The only feasible avenue is to combine income from various sources in different mixes over time (Spalter-Roth and Hartmann 1993). A lot of effort goes into maintaining this pattern of survival as these women negotiate within complex relations of ruling. All of this work constitutes their class situation. They are not marginal to capitalism, as the term *underclass* implies, because they are enmeshed within its relations. But they are marginal from the standpoint of capital, serving an ideological function as images of sin and failure.

Using the idea of standpoint may also be helpful in broadening the understanding of class/gender/race in contemporary capitalism to a global view. A Norwegian woman lawyer is linked into global class relations in ways that are different from those of a woman garment worker finishing blouses in her home in South Korea, for example. Starting from the lives of these different women allows the complexity, variety, and linkages of capitalist relations to come into view.

Broadening Class and "the Economic"

Another facet of a feminist rethinking of class has to do with what counts as "class relations." As the above discussion implies, basing our understanding of class on relations of paid production or market processes provides too narrow a view. Whether we want to understand women's class situations, societal structures of inequality, or bases of social movements outside male-dominated labor organizations, such conceptual boundaries impede analysis. But these conceptual boundaries are difficult to breach unless we take a standpoint outside the discursive terrain of dominant class theories. Thus, broadening "the economic" depends upon relocating the observer.

Taking a broader view of class relations involves expanding our notion of the economic. What has been taken as the economy is discursively and politically defined and redefined, usually within the boundaries of relevance established by capitalist practices. Activities are usually defined as economic only as they are commodified, involve a money exchange, or can be counted in monetary terms.[5] When the same activities are decommodified, as when customers bag their own groceries or pump their own gasoline, the activities are no longer seen as economic (Glazer 1993). Feminists have long argued that unpaid domestic or reproductive labor should be seen as part of the economic, should be "counted" (see, e.g., Folbre 1994; Waring 1988), and efforts to do this are under way in a number of countries. But I think that is still too narrow to capture the multiplicity of ways in which people today are affected by and drawn into capitalist accumulation processes, and pushed out again. I have given one example above in the discussion of the class position of the unemployed single mother receiving welfare benefits. More broadly, class relations include other processes through which people acquire economic support, such as the relations of distribution of the welfare state and distribution through family ties (Acker 1988).

These processes are influenced by how local communities and families function to sustain and organize reproduction and production. Kessler-Harris (1993) suggests that class should be "defined as an outgrowth of a broader system of production that includes family, home and community" (p. 199), in which wage work and markets are only a part. Masculinity and femininity, as well as racial identities, shape the way this broad system functions. "Both masculinity and femininity, but particularly aggressive masculinity, can be seen as instruments of economic organization—including the organization of conceptions about how wage work might be structured as well as the organization of the workplace in particular" (Kessler-Harris 1993:199). Recent research and theory on men as managers and managers as men supports such an argument (Collinson and Hearn 1994, 1996). Bureaucratic practices and hierarchies have historically been invented and controlled by men (Ferguson 1984). Burris (1996) describes different types of managerial, controlling masculinity that emerge along with changing organizational and technological forms. Reed (1996) compares the masculinity of nineteenth- and twentieth-century entrepreneurialism, dissecting

Rupert Murdoch as a prime example of a "mutually reinforcing entrepreneurialism and masculinity with elements of pre-modern adventure capitalist action" (p. 119). These are only samples of the considerable literature that now exists linking masculinities to economic organization and change. An implication of this literature for a redefinition of the economic and of class is that class processes cannot be understood without dissolving the boundaries between action and structure: Men as entrepreneurs and managers act within particular historical contexts, constructing those contexts as their masculine identities are also constructed in that process. Women and femininities can also be analyzed in this way, but the global actors who have led the large-scale transformations of which class relations are a part have almost always been men.

In the past, class analyses have been restricted primarily to the boundaries of particular nation-states. Quite obviously, this is also too narrow a view. Changes are now creating great complexity on a global basis as more and more people are incorporated into capitalist relations. These processes have been referred to in many different ways (see Mingione 1991): as informal economies, casualized work, contingent work, development, the decline of rural life, and, at the other end of affluence, the new global information economy. Millions of "unemployed"—meaning those who are not working in steady and regulated jobs or their own businesses—are managing their sustenance in some way, even if at minimal levels. A move to a global concept of class would help to push White middle-class feminists in wealthy countries toward a comprehension of how their existence is embedded in class relations that also include those "unemployed." Race and gender are also embedded in these relations. Bannerji's *Thinking Through* (1995) is a particularly useful book for White feminists. Bannerji describes going to Canada to study, finding that she "was part of that war of raced classes" (p. 9). Interpreting her own experiences, she analyzes the "commonsense racism" she encountered even among White leftist feminists, situating both her own experiences and those of other feminists within postcolonial worlds. Thus, she combines the immediate concreteness of daily experience with a sophisticated theoretical analysis of race, gender, and class in changing global relations.

Unless our concepts of class are to become more and more parochial and irrelevant, we must devise some way of incorporating this changing reality. I think that this is the most difficult part of the task. We can talk about class relations as relations of survival, as provisioning activities, seeing different forms of provisioning (Nelson 1993) as ways of coping with changing economic circumstances and ensuring survival. I use the term *survival* in a provisional sense, not intending to limit the meaning to activities performed to stave off hunger and poverty. The term may be too limited, because it should also apply to the affluent, for whom survival is not a central issue, although survival at a desired level of consumption could be central. The concept should also capture the structuring of relations through the multiplicity of power relations that organize, manage, and control much of production. Such a view of class relations would include, for example, the women in some African countries who have developed new forms of self-employment as former means of sustenance have been eroded by the replacement of women-controlled subsistence farming by men-controlled commercial agriculture. It would also point us toward the changes in the global economy that have created the necessity for such moves, connecting these women's fates within capitalist relations to, for example, the International Monetary Fund. With a slight shift in perspective, we could then talk about how both gender and race/ethnicity are reproduced within the ongoing restructuring of class.

Conclusion

The concept of class takes much of its significance from class struggle within capitalist states. The subordination of women, colonialism, slavery—all part of capitalist development—were incorporated into class organization as the "other," the outsiders against which White masculine class identity was formed. Class theorists, writing from a standpoint from which these outsiders were invisible, made the outsiders invisible in the theory. Women's movements and anticolonialism and antislavery struggles were thus divorced from class struggle, which was seen as paramount. To try to remake the idea of class is not to deny its importance, both intellectually and politically, but only to say that it is time to recognize the always present realities of gender, race, and ethnicity, and to recognize them with a view of class that does not continually re-create them as outside and unimportant. I have suggested some of the dimensions of this different view of class: that class relations are embedded in ongoing societal processes that also create and re-create gender and race relations; that class must be understood as active practices continually under way, rather than as abstract structures; that understanding of class relations, along with race and gender relations, must be developed from the standpoints of many differently located people; and that our notions of class relations and of the economic must be broadened to relations and processes that are not now considered to be properly economic.

I have sketched a fluid view of class as an ongoing production of gender and racially formed economic relations, rooted in family and communities as well as in the global organization of capital. How can we think about and describe the overall class relations of a particular society or of the global economy? The relatively simple images of a hierarchy of positions or a pattern of classes that includes, for example, the bourgeoisie, the middle classes, and the working class will not do. This notion of class structure suggests a relatively static model of relations and processes and implies a particular image of capitalism that may no longer be accurate, if it ever was.

I want to suggest a different image. Capitalism looks to me like a mutating monster, engulfing and extruding, changing forms, moving from one place to another, spawning abstract, disembodied technological marvels while re-creating nineteenth-century sweatshops, organizing itself through ever more abstract, textually mediated relations, but also through the most old-fashioned direct relations of exploitation, using up the water, the earth, and the trees and creating great wealth alongside global impoverishment—in other words, doing what it has always done, but more efficiently and using much more impressive technology. This monster is not disorganized, but is mutating in unexpected ways. For example, the new mafia in Russia is a form of private enterprise, as are the world drug cartels. Down in the street, local drug entrepreneurs show that they understand the logic of capitalism. The monster has a World Bank and international financial markets (where many mutations take place). Such organization should not be thought of as brains and circulatory system, for the monster I have in mind is not analogous to a living body. It has a certain, very general, logic—exploitation and accumulation—understood by millions of people who use the logic in often creative ways under a great variety of conditions. Some of these conditions are consciously constructed, as when governments both protect and control capitalist activities. But predictions about where the monster will engulf and extrude, where and when it will change form, are not possible, anymore than we can predict the exact forms of innovations in the arts. As the mutations continue, classes change, as do the forms of gender and racial oppression.

The monster image is only a suggestion; I offer it because I think that it is time for new images that might give us more creative ways of imagining points and processes of intervention and change.

Notes

1. This chapter is based primarily on work done in the United States and, to a lesser extent, in Britain and Sweden. Feminist debates cross many borders, and so much has been written that it is impossible for me to be sure that I have thoroughly covered the international literature.

2. See Crompton (1993) for a thorough discussion of the various meanings of class.

3. Eventually, some mainstream theorists, mostly men, responded to the feminist criticism by trying to bring women into their analyses (e.g., Wright 1989). By and large, their responses were to allow that women in the labor force could have a class position of their own and to try to theorize the particular class positions of women, but they did not bring unpaid work or gender into their fundamental notions of class structure and class formation.

4. Race and ethnicity are not the same phenomena, but the two are often conflated in the U.S. and British literature, as Allen and Macey (1994) point out. They argue that *race* refers to politically, socially, and economically formed categories based on skin color, whereas *ethnicity* refers to cultural and historical group ties and identities. Race and ethnicity may overlap, and different ethnicities often exist within racial categories. Allen and Macey also point out that nation is a basis for difference and conflict that is quite different from both race and ethnicity, although often in dynamic interaction with both.

5. Some economists, such as Becker (1981), have used economic models of rational choice to examine all sorts of noneconomic processes. This is not what I have in mind when I suggest that we need to extend the boundaries of what are defined as economic activities.

References

Acker, Joan. 1973. "Women and Social Stratification: A Case of Intellectual Sexism." *American Journal of Sociology* 78:936-45.

———. 1980. "Women and Stratification: A Review of Recent Literature." *Contemporary Sociology* 9:25-35.

———. 1988. "Class, Gender, and the Relations of Distribution." *Signs* 13:473-97.

———. 1989a. *Doing Comparable Worth: Gender, Class, and Pay Equity.* Philadelphia: Temple University Press.

———. 1989b. "The Problem with Patriarchy." *Sociology* 23:235-40.

———. 1992. Reformer och kvinnor I den framtida valfardsstaten. In *Kvinnors och mans liv och arbete (Women's and Men's Life and Work),* edited by Joan Acker et al. Stockholm: SNS Forlag.

———. 1994a. "Two Discourses of Reform: Women in the Future Swedish Welfare State." Unpublished manuscript.

———. 1994b. "Women, Families, and Public Policy in Sweden." In *Women, the Family, and Policy: A Global Perspective,* edited by Esther Ngan-Ling Chow and Catherine White Berheide. Albany: State University of New York Press.

Allen, Sheila and Marie Macey. 1994. "Some Issues of Race, Ethnicity and Nationalism in the 'New' Europe: Rethinking Sociological Paradigms." In *Economic Restructuring and Social Exclusion,* edited by Phillip Brown and Rosemary Crompton. London: UCL.

Amott, Teresa and Julie Matthaei. 1996. *Race, Gender, and Work.* Boston: South End.

Baca Zinn, Maxine and Bonnie Thornton Dill, eds. 1994. *Women of Color in U.S. Society.* Philadelphia: Temple University Press.

Bannerji, Himani. 1995. *Thinking Through: Essays on Feminism, Marxism, and Anti-racism.* Toronto: Women's Press.

Barnett, Bernice McNair. 1993. "Invisible Southern Black Women Leaders in the Civil Rights Movement: The Triple Constraints of Gender, Race, and Class." *Gender & Society* 7:162-82.

Barrett, Michèle. 1980. *Women's Oppression Today: Problems in Marxist Feminist Analysis.* London: Verso.

———. 1992. "Words and Things: Materialism and Method in Contemporary Feminist Analysis." In *Destabilizing Theory,* edited by Michèle Barrett and Anne Phillips. Stanford, CA: Stanford University Press.

Barrett, Michèle and Anne Phillips, eds. 1992. *Destabilizing Theory.* Stanford, CA: Stanford University Press.

Baxter, Janeen. 1994. "Is Husband's Class Enough? Class Location and Class Identity in the United States, Sweden, Norway, and Australia. *American Sociological Review* 59:220-35.

Becker, Gary. 1981. *A Treatise on the Family.* Cambridge, MA: Harvard University Press.

Beechey, Veronica. 1987. *Unequal Work.* London: Verso.

Benería, Lourdes and Martha Roldán. 1987. *The Crossroads of Class and Gender: Industrial Homework, Subcontracting, and Household Dynamics in Mexico City.* Chicago: University of Chicago Press.

Blankenship, Kim M. 1993. "Bringing Gender and Race In: U.S. Employment Discrimination Policy." *Gender & Society* 7: 204-26.

Bose, Christine E. 1973. *Jobs and Gender: Sex and Occupational Prestige.* Baltimore: Johns Hopkins University, Center for Metropolitan Planning and Research.

Burris, Beverly H. 1996. "Technocracy, Patriarchy and Management." In *Men as Managers, Managers as Men: Critical Perspectives on Men, Masculinities, and Managements,* edited by David L. Collinson and Jeff Hearn. London: Sage.

Chow, Esther Ngan-Ling. 1994. "Asian American Women at Work." In *Women of Color in U.S. Society,* edited by Maxine Baca Zinn and Bonnie Thornton Dill. Philadelphia: Temple University Press.

Cockburn, Cynthia. 1983. *Brothers.* London: Pluto.

———. 1985. *Machinery of Dominance.* London: Pluto.

———. 1986. "The Relations of Technology: What Implications for Theories of Sex and Class?" In *Gender and Stratification,* edited by Rosemary Crompton and Michael Mann. Cambridge, MA: Polity.

Collins, Patricia Hill. 1990. *Black Feminist Thought: Knowledge, Consciousness, and the Politics of Empowerment.* New York: Routledge, Chapman & Hall.

———. 1995. "Symposium on West and Fenstermaker's 'Doing Difference.' " *Gender & Society* 9:491-94.

Collinson, David L. and Jeff Hearn. 1994. "Naming Men as Men: Implications for Work, Organization and Management." *Gender, Work and Organization* 1:2-22.

———, eds. 1996. *Men as Managers, Managers as Men: Critical Perspectives on Men, Masculinities, and Managements.* London: Sage.

Connell, R. W. 1995. *Masculinities.* Berkeley: University of California Press.

Crompton, Rosemary. 1993. *Class and Stratification: An Introduction to Current Debates.* Cambridge, MA: Polity.

Crompton, Rosemary and Gareth Jones. 1984. *White-Collar Proletariat: Deskilling and Gender in Clerical Work.* Philadelphia: Temple University Press.

Crompton, Rosemary and Michael Mann, eds. 1986. *Gender and Stratification.* Cambridge, MA: Polity.

Deitch, Cynthia. 1993. "Gender, Race, and Class Politics and the Inclusion of Women in Title VII of the 1964 Civil Rights Act." *Gender & Society* 7:183-203.

Dill, Bonnie Thornton. 1988. "Our Mothers' Grief: Racial-Ethnic Women and the Maintenance of Families." *Journal of Family History* 13:415-31.

Edin, Kathryn and Laura Lein. 1997. *Making Ends Meet: How Single Mothers Survive Welfare and Low-Wage Work.* New York: Russell Sage Foundation.

Eisenstein, Zillah. 1979. *Capitalist Patriarchy and the Case for Socialist Feminism.* New York: Monthly Review Press.

England, Paula and George Farkas. 1986. *Households, Employment and Gender: A Social, Economic and Demographic View.* New York: Aldine.

Ferguson, Kathy E. 1984. *The Feminist Case against Bureaucracy.* Philadelphia: Temple University Press.

Folbre, Nancy. 1994. *Who Pays for the Kids? Gender and the Structures of Constraint.* London: Routledge.

Frankenberg, Ruth. 1993. *White Women, Race Matters: The Social Construction of Whiteness.* Minneapolis: University of Minnesota Press.

Game, Ann and Rosemary Pringle. 1983. *Gender at Work.* London: Pluto.

Glazer, Nona Y. 1993. *Women's Paid and Unpaid Labor.* Philadelphia: Temple University Press.

Glenn, Evelyn Nakano. 1986. *Issei, Nisei, Warbride: Three Generations of Japanese American Women in Domestic Service.* Philadelphia: Temple University Press.

Glucksmann, Miriam. 1990. *Women Assemble.* London: Routledge.

Hamilton, Roberta and Michèle Barrett. 1986. *The Politics of Diversity.* London: Verso.

Hartmann, Heidi I. 1976. "Capitalism, Patriarchy, and Job Segregation by Sex." *Signs* 1:137-69.

———. 1981. "The Unhappy Marriage of Marxism and Feminism: Towards a More Progressive Union." In *The Unhappy Marriage of Marxism and Feminism,* edited by Heidi I. Hartmann et al. London: Pluto.

Hermansson, Ann-Sofie. 1993. *Arbetarrörelsen och Feminismen (The Labor Movement and Feminism).* Stockholm: Utbildningsfolaget Brevskolan.

hooks, bell. 1981. *Ain't I a Woman: Black Women and Feminism.* Boston: South End.

———. 1984. *Feminist Theory: From Margin to Center.* Boston: South End.

Kessler-Harris, Alice. 1993. "Treating the Male as 'Other': Redefining the Parameters of Labor History." *Labor History* 34:190-204.

Knights, David and Hugh Willmott. 1986. *Gender and the Labour Process.* Aldershot, England: Gower.

Kuhn, Annette and AnnMarie Wolpe, eds. 1978. *Feminism and Materialism.* London: Routledge & Kegan Paul.

Lorber, Judith. 1994. *Paradoxes of Gender.* New Haven, CT: Yale University Press.

Mingione, Enzo. 1991. *Fragmented Societies: A Sociology of Economic Life beyond the Market Paradigm.* Oxford: Basil Blackwell.

Mohanty, Chandra Talpade. 1991. "Cartographies of Struggle: Third World Women and the Politics of Feminism." In *Third World Women and the Politics of Feminism,* edited by Chandra Talpade Mohanty, Ann Russo, and Lourdes Torres. Bloomington: Indiana University Press.

Molyneux, Maxine. 1979. "Beyond the Domestic Labour Debate." *New Left Review* 116:3-28.

Nelson, Julie A. 1993. "The Study of Choice or the Study of Provisioning? Gender and the Definition of Economics." In *Beyond Economic Man: Feminist Theory and Economics,* edited by Marianne A. Ferber and Julie A. Nelson. Chicago: University of Chicago Press.

Nicholson, Linda J. 1994. "Interpreting Gender." *Signs* 20:79-105.

Pateman, Carole. 1988. *The Sexual Contract.* Cambridge, MA: Polity.

Pollert, Anna. 1996. "Gender and Class Revisited: Or, the Poverty of 'Patriarchy.' " *Sociology* 30:639-59.

Reed, Rosslyn. 1996. "Entrepreneurialism and Paternalism in Australian Management: A Gender Critique of the 'Self-Made' Man." In *Men as Managers, Managers as Men: Critical Perspectives on Men, Masculinities, and Managements,* edited by David L. Collinson and Jeff Hearn. London: Sage.

Reskin, Barbara F. and Heidi I. Hartmann. 1986. *Women's Work, Men's Work: Sex Segregation on the Job.* Washington, DC: National Academy Press.

Reskin, Barbara F. and Patricia A. Roos. 1990. *Job Queues, Gender Queues.* Philadelphia: Temple University Press.

Romero, Mary. 1992. *Maid in the U.S.A.* New York: Routledge.

Rowbotham, Sheila and Swasti Mitter, eds. 1994. *Dignity and Daily Bread: New Forms of Economic Organising among Poor Women in the Third World and the First.* London: Routledge.

Seccombe, Wally. 1974. "The Housewife and Her Labour Under Capitalism." *New Left Review* 83:3-24.

Smith, Dorothy E. 1987. *The Everyday World as Problematic.* Boston: Northeastern University Press.

———. 1990a. *The Conceptual Practices of Power: A Feminist Sociology of Knowledge.* Toronto: University of Toronto Press.

———. 1990b. "Feminist Reflections on Political Economy." *Studies in Political Economy* 30 (Autumn):37-60.

Sokoloff, Natalie J. 1980. *Between Money and Love: The Dialectics of Women's Home and Market Work.* New York: Praeger.

Spalter-Roth, Roberta M. and Heidi I. Hartmann. 1993. *Dependence on Men, the Market, or the State: The Rhetoric and Reality of Welfare Reform.* Washington, DC: Institute for Women's Policy Research.

Thompson, E. P. 1963. *The Making of the English Working Class.* New York: Vintage.

Walby, Sylvia. 1986. *Patriarchy at Work*. Minneapolis: University of Minnesota Press.

Waring, Marilyn. 1988. *If Women Counted*. San Francisco: Harper & Row.

Weinbaum, Batya and Amy Bridges. 1976. "The Other Side of the Paycheck." *Monthly Review,* July-August.

West, Candace and Sarah Fenstermaker. 1995. "Doing Difference." *Gender & Society* 9:8-37.

Wright, Eric Olin. 1985. *Classes*. London: New Left.

———. 1989. "Women in the Class Structure." *Politics and Society* 17:1-34.

Young, Iris Marion. 1981. "Beyond the Unhappy Marriage: A Critique of the Dual Systems Theory." In *The Unhappy Marriage of Marxism and Feminism,* edited by Heidi I. Hartmann et al. London: Pluto.

CHAPTER 3

Some Reflections on Gender and Politics

JOAN WALLACH SCOTT

The scholarship on gender and politics has been so prolific and far-reaching in the past ten years that it is impossible to summarize or synthesize it all. I have chosen, instead, to explore a few of the underlying assumptions of some of this work, with an eye to provoking critical reassessment, if not revision and reconceptualization, of the terms that have been most used in our analyses.

The Sex/Gender Distinction:
"Useful in principle, but by no means widely observed"

The usage note at the entry for "gender" in the *American Heritage Dictionary of the English Language* (3d ed., 1992) reads as follows:

> Traditionally, *gender* has been used primarily to refer to the grammatical categories of "masculine," "feminine," and "neuter"; but in recent years the word has become well established in its use to refer to sex-based categories, as in phrases such as *gender gap* and *the politics of gender*. This usage is supported by the practice of many anthropologists, who reserve *sex* for reference to biological categories, while using *gender* to refer to social or cultural categories. According to this rule, one would say *The effectiveness of the medication appears to depend on the sex* (not *gender*) *of the patient*, but *In peasant societies, gender* (not *sex*) *roles are likely to be more clearly defined*. This distinction is useful in principle, but it is by no means widely observed, and considerable variation in usage occurs at all levels. (p. 754)

That last sentence is crucial, both as a reminder of the futility of insisting upon precise linguistic usages and of the difficulty feminists have had in separating social designations from their physical referents. No matter how insistently feminist theorists have refined the term *gender* (purging it of all "natural" connotations while promoting its status as a "social construction"), they have been unable to prevent its corruption. In popular conversation, the terms *sex* and *gender* are as often used synonymously as oppositionally; indeed, sometimes it seems that *gender* is simply a polite euphemism for *sex*. And judging from the number of scholarly books and articles that take *gender* and *women* to be synonymous, academics are not much better than the general public at maintaining the distinction between the physical and the social (nature and culture, body and mind) that the introduction of the use of *gender* was meant to achieve.

Although there have been ongoing efforts to address the definitional confusion—ranging from calls for more careful policing of the term *gender* to suggestions that it be abandoned altogether—I don't think that is the way to approach the matter (Bock 1989; Hawkesworth 1997; Nicholson 1986, 1994). Rather, I think we need to read the tendency to conflate sex and gender as symptomatic of certain abiding problems (Sedgwick 1990).[1] One of these has to do with the difficulty of representing bodies as entirely social contrivances within the terms of the opposition between nature and culture. As long as the two realms are conceived as antithetical, bodies (and sex) will seem inadequately accounted for by reference to social construction alone. *Gender* will not replace *sex* in discussions of sexual difference; instead, *gender* will always refer to sex as the ultimate ground of its meaning. When sex resides within gender in this way, nothing can prevent its being identified with (or as) gender itself. What seems then to be conceptual and terminological confusion is in fact an accurate representation of the lack of sharp distinction between the two terms.

The seeming clarity of the distinction between sex and gender obscures the fact that both are forms of knowledge. Employing the opposition "natural versus constructed" perpetuates the idea that there is a transparent "nature" that can somehow be known apart from the knowledge we produce about it (Haraway 1991). But, in fact, "nature" and "sex" are concepts with histories (Butler 1993). They are articulated by language, and their meanings have changed over time and across cultures. When the sex/gender opposition neglects the role of language in the construction of nature, it works to secure the natural (prelinguistic, ahistorical) status of sex—exactly what the introduction of the use of the term *gender* was meant to undermine (Adams [1979] 1990). Perhaps the conflation of *sex* and *gender* in ordinary usage can be considered a correction of the "mistake" that would place sex outside language. Instead, those who use the terms interchangeably seem to be saying, both sex and gender are ascriptions of meaning, variable ways of differentiating bodies in the (albeit different) domains of the physical and the social. If that is the case, of what use is it to insist on a distinction between sex and gender?

Yet another reason it has been difficult to maintain a clear distinction between sex and gender has to do with the universalizing impulses of both feminism (a political movement originating in the West at the moment of its eighteenth-century democratic revolutions) and social science (whose origins are roughly contemporaneous with feminism). The universalizing impulses of feminism and social science have operated to produce a view of women (across time and cultures) as fundamentally homogeneous by taking as self-evident the fundamental difference of "women" from "men" (Riley 1988). Even when national and/or cultural differences are acknowledged, these are treated as second-order phenomena, so many variations on a universal theme in which gender always means the same thing: an asymmetrical, if not antagonistic, relationship between women and men that organizes the different functions of each into separate activities and spaces. But if gender—the unvarying fact of sexual difference—is universal, what, other than biology, can finally explain its universality? If gender means the social forms imposed on existing differences between women and men, then nature (bodies, sex) is left in place as the determining factor of difference. If the study of women automatically leads to "gender analysis," then a form of essentialism is driving the investigation: The presence of physical females is taken to mean that a system of difference—already known to us—is in effect (Collier and Yanagisako 1987). When "gender" assumes the prior existence of sexual difference, indeed is based unproblematically upon it, then sharp conceptual distinctions between sex and gender are impossible to maintain.

But maybe it is not necessary to maintain those distinctions; maybe it is more useful to accept the lack of precision the editors of the *American Heritage Dictionary* have identified. If sex and gender are both taken to be concepts—forms of knowledge—then they are closely related, if not indistinguishable. If both are knowledges, then gender cannot be said to reflect sex or to be imposed on it; rather, sex becomes an effect of gender. Gender, the social rules that attempt to organize the relationships of men and women in societies, produces the knowledge we have of sex and sexual difference (in our culture by equating sex with nature). Both sex and gender are expressions of certain beliefs about sexual difference; they are organizations of perception rather than transparent descriptions or reflections of nature (Keates 1992). If sex, gender, and sexual difference are *effects*—discursively and historically produced— then we cannot take them as points of origin for our analysis. Instead, we must ask the following kinds of questions: How do laws, rules, and institutional arrangements refer to and implement differences between the sexes? In what terms? How have different societies organized gender relationships? In what terms has sexual difference been articulated? How have medical or legal discourses—the discourses of the patient and the citizen, for example—produced knowledges said to reflect the truth about the nature of women and men (Foucault 1980; Laqueur 1990)? What has been the connection between gender and politics? Has sexual difference been invoked differently in different kinds of political/social movements? How, and in what terms? What is the nature of the appeal? What kinds of psychic investments are appealed to and/or produced in the social organization of the differences between the sexes? What is the specific link made in articulations of sexual difference to other kinds of difference (race, class, ethnicity, and so on)?

These kinds of questions require specific readings of particular instances. They do not assume that gender is always the driving force of politics; indeed, they allow for the possibility that there may be little or no relationship between gender and politics. Nor do they assume an invariant meaning for gender itself. Rather, they take it to be a changing and complex social and psychic phenomenon. Still, readings need to be informed by theory or theories—that is, by attempts to detect some logic (or logics) underlying the varied manifestations of human behavior. Theory has never been absent from feminist scholarship; the debates among Marxists, structuralists, poststructuralists, and those relying on psychoanalysis have enlivened the field over the past several decades, creating productive tensions even in the midst of angry exchange. One result of this activity has been the pressure to complicate analyses in the terms suggested by Rubin in her 1975 article "The Traffic in Women": "Eventually, someone will have to write a new version of [Engels's] *The*

Origins of the Family, Private Property, and the State, recognizing the mutual interdependence of sexuality, economics, and politics without underestimating the full significance of each in human society" (p. 145).

The kind of synthesis Rubin calls for requires thinking about sexuality in the same terms as economics and politics—that is, as a complex human activity rather than as the reflection or implementation of physical fact. Theorizing human sexuality has been the province of psychoanalysis in this century. "It is essential," Freud wrote ([1905] 1953), "to understand clearly that the concepts of 'masculine' and 'feminine,' whose meaning seems so unambiguous to ordinary people, are among the most confused that occur in science." "In human beings," he continued, "pure masculinity or femininity is not to be found either in a psychological or a biological sense. Every individual on the contrary displays a mixture of the character-traits belonging to his own and to the opposite sex; and he shows a combination of activity and passivity whether or not these last character-traits tally with his biological ones" (pp. 219-20). For Freud, the self-identification of a person as either male or female is a complex process—cultural, physical, and psychological—revolving around the myth of castration. The French psychoanalyst Lacan (1977) goes further, insisting that "man" and "woman" were not biological descriptions, but signifiers of the symbolic positions assumed by human subjects. And for both Freud and Lacan, sexual identity is never stable, never finally settled; it is secured only through its repeated performance (necessarily in relation to others).

For Freud, it is the repressive function of civilization that, in the name of the reproduction of the species, directs diffuse sexual energies into a monogamous, heterosexual path. ("The requirement . . . that there shall be a single kind of sexual life for everyone, disregards the dissimilarities, whether innate or acquired, in the sexual constitution of human beings; it cuts off a fair number of them from sexual enjoyment, and so becomes the source of serious injustice" [Freud (1930) 1953:104].) The difference between the sexes, then, is a social achievement (the price of "civilization"), though not in the sense that the opposition between gender and sex (culture and nature) implies. The cultural is not a planned operation, rationally imposed on physical bodies and then "internalized" by subjects. From a psychoanalytic perspective, the psychological, the social, and the physical do not exist independent of one another; they are instead inextricably combined, constituted in and by psychic processes that are crucially informed by the unconscious.

Freud's great contribution to the study of the human psyche (and through it to the production of sexual difference) is the theorizing of the unconscious. According to Freud, the unconscious is the site of repressed instincts and the desires that follow from them. Although it is not directly accessible to consciousness, the unconscious nonetheless has a discernible influence on human actions. Unconscious desires are expressed in slips of the tongue, jokes, dreams, and fantasies; these expressions take symbolic form—they are condensations and displacements of meaning, not direct representations, and they must be interpreted as such. Fantasies express unconscious desires and enact their fulfillment (and the complicated consequences of such fulfillment); they inform memory, imaginatively reconstructing and reshaping the past.

To the extent that fantasy shapes representations, actions, and memories, it becomes a crucial component of human behavior. To the extent that it offers general explanations for the origin of human subjects and their defining characteristics of sexuality and sexual difference, fantasy is not just a component of the psychic life of individuals. It partakes of the mythic structure of Western culture. Laplanche and Pontalis (1986) define as primary or original fantasies those that "relate to problems of origin which present themselves to all human beings: the origin of the individual (primal scene), the origin of sexuality (seduction), the origin of the difference between the sexes (castration)" (p. 19).

These origin stories are not restricted to sexuality as if it were a separate department of human existence. Fantasy spills over into all aspects of life. In patriarchal cultures, masculinity is signified not only by possession of a penis and by paternity, but (depending on time and place) by the statuses of soldier, property holder, scientist, and citizen, statuses from which women are necessarily excluded, because to include them would be to acknowledge that biological sex, on the one hand, and subjective identification with symbolic masculine or feminine positions, on the other, are not the same. The human imagination (propelled at least in part by unconscious desire) plays fast and loose with the boundaries social scientists would establish: The realm of economics is never simply about the satisfaction of basic needs, that of politics is never only about struggles among rationally motivated, self-interested actors. These domains are also inflected by phantasmatic projections that mobilize individual desires into collective identifications. It is in this sense that Freud suggests that fantasy is crucially implicated in politics. In his essay, "Fetishism" ([1927] 1953), for example, he makes an explicit connection between castration anxiety and political fear. After suggesting that the sight of his mother's genitals terrifies the young boy, who then reacts by denying that his mother lacks a penis, Freud goes on: "For if a woman had been castrated, then his own possession of a penis was in danger; and against that there rose in rebellion the portion of his narcissism which Nature has, as a precaution, attached to that particular organ. In later life a grown man may perhaps experience a similar panic when the cry goes up that Throne and Altar are in danger, and similar illogical consequences will ensue" (p. 153).

Although the example used seems to relate to the development of an individual boy's sense of sexual difference, Freud extends it to the collective experience of politics. The implication is, as Hertz (1983) has suggested, that political threats can be experienced as sexual threats (and vice versa). Hertz points out that several generations of commentators figured the French revolutions of the eighteenth and nineteenth centuries as harpies and Medusas, "the furies of hell, in the abused shape of the vilest of women," in the words of the English conservative Edmund Burke (quoted in Hertz 1983:27). In Hertz's reading, social upheaval is understood as the loss of what men hold most dear: property, power, social standing, family prestige, bodily integrity. And masculinity is associated in this conservative political discourse with upholding the status quo; the protection of order means protecting Throne, Altar, and the boundaries of sexual difference. The meanings are inextricably linked: The phantasmatic (in this case fear of the loss of the phallus) informs the meanings of property and family; the realities of social and economic power become supports for the symbolic phallus. Fantasy then has tangible manifestations, material outcomes.

There is no resolving the ambiguity of the relationship between imagination and reality, no guarantee, Freud ([1909] 1953:206-8) argues elsewhere, that memory (a "complicated process of remodeling") literally recounts lived external objective reality, no getting away from the fact that fantasy is itself a form of reality (psychic reality) and that it is powerfully enmeshed in perception. The perception of sexual difference is at once bound by the rules of "civilization" and animated by unconscious fantasies that exceed all boundaries. It defies neat separation into the categories of "sex" and "gender," which—by establishing two sets of fixed oppositions: nature versus culture and men versus women—obliterate the ways in which the unconscious refuses oppositions of any kind. ("What we call our 'unconscious'—the deepest strata of our minds, made up of instinctual impulses—knows nothing that is negative, and no negation; in it contradictories coincide" [Freud (1915) 1953:296].) I would argue, then, that the sex/gender distinction, which feminists used to extend the field of observation of sex and sexuality from the physical to the social and cultural, in fact had a more limiting effect. It not only split the physical off from the social (granting it "natural" status in the process), but also removed all the ambiguity that fantasy lends to the subject identities "man" and "woman," and to the ways in which the body materializes the psyche (Shepherdson 1997). Studying the "politics of gender" became a matter of tracking the legislation and inculcation of "roles" (the definitive organization of male and female into man and woman) rather than documenting a project whose very impossibility (creating a fixed and enduring opposition man/woman) defined the terms of its operations. These kinds of analyses of gender roles and the politics of their production lent support to the enterprise of the human sciences as Foucault (1972) has critically described them: dedicated to denying the operations of the unconscious by producing man as a rational subject and installing the "sovereignty of [his] consciousness," those very qualities that had "unceasingly eluded him for over a hundred years" (p. 14). These analyses, in other words, were an aspect of the ideological production of "man" as an entirely rational being and of politics as the activity of fully rational agents.

To insist that the "construction" of sexual difference involves unconscious processes is not, however, the same as saying that psychoanalysis is the only theory we can use. Indeed, the kind of historicizing of gender I am suggesting is often rejected by psychoanalytic theorists who take sexual difference to be a fixed, immutable relationship—the point from which history emanates or at which subjects enter history. But it seems to me that fulfilling Rubin's call for a theorization of the interdependence of the economic, the political, and the sexual cannot ignore the operations of fantasy in domains once restricted entirely to questions of need, self-interest, reason, and power. What concretely would this mean for the study of gender, understood as the articulation and implementation of knowledge about the differences between the sexes?

First, it would mean discarding the idea (inherent in the notion of gender as a "category") that there is anything fixed or known in advance about the terms *men* and *women* and the relationship between them. ("Woman cannot be taken as a transparent name for an eternal object"

[Adams and Minson (1978) 1990:82].) The new questions to be asked are: How are these terms being used in the particular contexts in which they are invoked? What is at stake in attempts to enforce boundaries between the sexes? What kinds of differences are being implemented?

Second, "men" and "women" are ideals established to regulate and channel behavior, not empirical descriptions of actual people, who will always fall short of fulfilling the ideals. How do social and political institutions offer the possibility (the illusion, the fantasy) of fulfilling the ideals? How are sexual identities secured and/or enacted through identification with various social positions or occupations (Reynolds 1996; Roberts 1994)? Conversely, how are relationships of power consolidated by appeals to sexual difference? How do appeals to unconscious desire figure in the articulations of power? Is there an erotics of power?

Third, there is discrepancy, even contradiction, in the cultural norms and social roles offered to articulate the difference between the sexes (even if sexual difference itself is a recurring theme). That means one has to read for specific meanings rather than assume uniformity in all spheres and aspects of social life. And it means relinquishing simple assessments of "women's" position in terms of progress and regress, instead limiting these characterizations to specific arenas such as the job market or the law. In what spheres does the performance of normative sex roles matter? In what spheres is sexual difference an irrelevant consideration? What are the manifestations of contradiction? How are they expressed? regulated? redressed? repressed? How have changes in one sphere influenced changes in another? Has the vote, for example, meant increased job opportunity or a change in courtship practices?

These questions push toward different kinds of analyses from those that tried to assess the impact of particular regimes or policies on women (Did women's condition improve or deteriorate with the French Revolution?) or the emancipatory effect on women of the vote or of increased labor force participation. They do not assume the abiding existence of a homogeneous collectivity called "women" upon which measurable experiences are visited. Rather, they interrogate the production of the category "women" itself as a historical or political event, whose circumstances and effects are the object of analysis. Unless feminism is defined as a score-keeping enterprise, this approach seems to me to be well within the purview of feminist concerns. Instead of reinscribing the naturalized terms of difference (sex) upon which systems of differentiation and discrimination (gender) have been built, analysis begins at an earlier point in the process, asking how sexual difference is itself articulated as a principle and practice of social organization.

Gender and Politics: Formations of Fantasy

Often the relationship between politics and gender is conceived in terms of independent systems or processes interacting with one another. There is political mobilization (nationalism, class struggle, ethnic or religious solidarity) and political transformation (revolution, legal reform, democratization) and there is gender (the normative roles assigned to men and women, the social constructions of biological reality), and the question posed is, How does one affect the other? Recent scholarship suggests that this way of posing the problem obscures the interdependence of the two systems or processes. The characteristics that mark the differences between the sexes (what matters and does not matter in our physical and psychic constitutions) do not exist apart from, but rather are produced through, the theories and practices of politics—understood not only as the mobilization of force to achieve a certain interest, but as enabled by appeals to fantasy. ("Politics without fantasy," without the manipulation of unconscious modes of enjoyment, "is an illusion," writes the Slovenian philosopher Salecl [1990:52].)

One feminist approach to the study of the social and political revolutions of the eighteenth century to the twentieth century has been devoted to establishing that the exclusion of women from citizenship was discriminatory (Nelson and Chowdhury 1994). The denial of citizenship placed women at a disadvantage compared to men in the eyes of the law, depriving them of the kind of influential public role enjoyed by some elite women under prerevolutionary regimes (e.g., Landes 1988). The conclusion of many of these studies echoes the now-famous comment of historian Kelly-Gadol (1977) about the Renaissance. There may have been a Renaissance in the sixteenth century, she said, but by most measures of progress, there was no renaissance for women. Similarly, it has been pointed out, women did not enjoy the benefits of democracy as citizens in 1776 or 1789 (although that did not prevent them from engaging in political action). And although later socialist revolutions brought the recognition of formal rights for women, these did not end hierarchies based on sex, or translate into genuine equality.

The impact of major revolutionary upheavals on women, in other words, has not been progressive (Boxer and Quataert 1978).[2]

These challenges to simple narratives of progress have been useful as a way of contesting the universalist claims of some democratic and socialist movements (Taylor 1983). They have also insisted on the complexity of women's political action and documented the many forms it took (Kerber 1980, 1997; Norton 1980, 1996). At the same time, however, they have not usually problematized the terms of sexual difference itself; *gender* means a set of fixed oppositional categories, male and female, and "politics" alters or perpetuates relationships between women and men. The question of how sexual difference is constituted by politics (how, to put it another way, masculinity is secured by attributing its antithesis to femininity and in what terms) is not directly addressed.

Yet at crucial moments in the articulation of democratic politics there have been arguments about the terms being used to distinguish between the sexes, as well as about the relevance of using any male/female oppositions at all. Take the case of citizenship in the French Revolution. The revolutionaries, inspired they said by Rousseau, claimed that women could not be citizens because of their difference from men: They were dependent, lacking reason and autonomy, more suited for domesticity and child rearing, incapable of the creative actions that self-representation requires (Zerilli 1994). Some among them, such as the Marquis de Condorcet ([1790] 1976), disagreed, insisting that physical differences of any kind are irrelevant considerations for politics. "Why should those exposed to pregnancies and other passing indispositions, not be allowed to exercise rights that no one imagines denying to those who have gout all winter or who catch cold quickly?" (p. 98). And feminist Olympe de Gouges ([1791] 1980) called upon legislators to "look, search, and distinguish, if you can, the sexes in the administration of nature. Everywhere you will find them mingled (or mistaken for one another—*confondus*)" (p. 89). The political decision associating citizenship with maleness, both suggested, introduced sexual difference where it does not and ought not to exist. Women became visible in their difference in the sphere of politics only when they were barred on the ground of their sex. Sexual difference was, then, the effect, not the cause, of women's exclusion. To see it as the cause is to accept the "natural" explanation offered by the revolutionaries to justify their actions. ("Since when is it permitted to give up one's sex and meddle in the affairs of government?" asked the Jacobin politician Chaumette in response to a demand by women for political rights. "Since when is it decent to see women abandoning the pious cares of their households, the cribs of their children, to come to public places, to harangues in the galleries, at the bar of the Senate? Is it to men that nature confided domestic cares? Has she given us breasts to feed our children?" [(1793) 1980:220].)

How then might we account for the exclusion of women from the exercise of what were announced as universal human rights? There have been suggestions offered that address the theme of representation, pointing out that the revolutionaries contrasted "feminine" aristocratic styles of artifice and illusion with "masculine" bourgeois styles of objectivity and rationality. The attack on the aristocracy then was coupled with a repudiation of feminine influences in the public sphere. In the course of the revolution, this interpretation concludes, women and aristocrats were denied the rights of self-representation for similar reasons (Landes 1988). Others have invoked Freud's discussion of the Oedipus complex to characterize the French Revolution as the collective revolt of sons against the power of their father (the king). In this interpretation, the common ground that ensured democratic fraternity was established by the possession and exchange of women (Hunt 1992). Yet another interpretation identifies the ways in which notions of "the body" (really of marked bodies) were used to imaginatively reconfigure ideas of public space (Outram 1989). Another version maintains that the introduction of the idea of formal equality through the figure of the abstract individual posed a new problem for social organization and individual identity. When hierarchy was presumed to be the natural form of society, social roles and subjective identities coincided; one was born into one's place. The idea of equality among autonomous individuals raised the question of identity in a new way. "Only when people were perceived as formally equal did sexual difference as such become thinkable" (Salecl 1994:117; see also Sonenscher 1987:10). Individuals were said to be autonomous, yet their identity depended on recognition by an other. Without external confirmation, without a sense of separation from an other or others, individuality has no defining boundaries, hence no distinguishable existence (Warner 1992). But equality among individuals meant that each was independent of others. How to reconcile the apparent contradiction between dependence and independence? The revolutionaries developed many solutions: distinctions between active and passive citizens, between those who were economically and socially dependent and independent, and between women and men. Redefining existing patriarchal rules in terms of biologically based sexual difference maintained the fiction of an autonomous individuality that was at once universal and masculine. The "others" whose recognition confirmed men's individuality were not themselves considered to be individuals—they were women (Scott 1996). It is at this point that we enter the register of fantasy: Autonomy and independence, the power of self-representation and the possession of rights, were figured as phallic functions, attributed to those with a biological penis. And the birth of the nation (the bringing to life of the social contract) demonstrated the generative potential of the phallus: Politics was entirely men's labor (Cornell 1991).

Another example of the interconnections between politics and sexual difference comes from contemporary Poland. There, argues Watson (1993), a sociologist, the advent of democratization and the transition from communism to liberal capitalism has been marked by a "rise of masculinism" in the sphere of civil society. Appeals to "traditional" or "natural" differences between the sexes have been invoked to rescind rights women enjoyed as a matter of course under state socialism. Democracy is being hailed as a return to normalcy in gender relations; in this way social inequality and sexual difference become mutually reinforcing references. Under state socialism, Watson points out,

> the lack of civil society and private property had an ambivalent significance for gender relations. On the one hand, the constraints on the scope for autonomous public action . . . brought a substantial leveling of relations between women and men. This dimension of equality was further reinforced by the encoding of legal rights for women based on the assumption of full employment. On the other hand, the absence of civil society also fostered the neo-traditional organization of society, one aspect of which was the valorization and entrenchment of traditional definitions of gender. It is the combined effect of these two sets of influences that is responsible for the fact that in Eastern Europe, deep-seated notions of gender difference often go hand in hand with a lack of any real sense of gender inequality. (p. 71)

In the new arrangement, she continues, civil society has become the arena for men's action, whereas the private sphere of family and household—once the center for resistance to a public sphere synonymous with an authoritarian state—has become limited to the domestic concerns of women.

The political empowerment of men does not rest on claims to superior experience (women were prominent members of government under the old regimes), skills, or qualifications (educational opportunities, too, were granted to both sexes under communism), but rather on sexual difference. A Polish official put it this way: "It is impossible to speak of discrimination against women. Nature gave them a different role to that of men. The ideal must still be the woman-mother, for whom pregnancy is a blessing" (quoted in Watson 1993:73). The assault on abortion rights, in Poland associated with the political ascendancy of the Catholic Church, is an example of an explicit attempt to realize the ideal. "We will nationalize those bellies!" proclaimed a member of the Polish Senate (quoted in Watson 1993:73). The issue here is not simply population policy (freeing families from state direction) or economic retrenchment (the removal of women from the labor force so they will not compete with men) or the reassertion of deeply felt religious belief. It is, rather, the evocation of a phantasmatic association among the power of the state, the unequal access to and distribution of its resources, and the masculinity of its representatives. To recall an old feminist slogan in a new context: The personal (in the sense of deeply felt conscious and unconscious processes of identification) is the political (in the sense of structured relations of power), and the political, the personal.

Does the Presence of Women Always Call for Gender Analysis?

One of the important effects of feminist activism and scholarship has been to point to the ways in which seemingly neutral categories are in fact sexed. Thus the abstract individual, the foundation of liberal democracy, has been revealed to be male (Elshtain 1981; Fauré 1991; Pateman 1988); declarations of human rights have been shown to be limited in intent and practice to men (Okin 1979; Reynolds 1986); certain professions and activities (science preeminently among them) have been redescribed as masculine (Glazer and Slater 1987; Keller 1985; Rossiter 1982, 1995); and the designation *worker* has turned out to refer to the productive capacity and skills of men, even though it has rarely carried the explicit qualification that *woman worker* does (Phillips and Taylor [1980] 1996; Scott 1993). It has been precisely in rendering explicit implicit assumptions about sex and sexual difference that feminists have raised the consciousness of scholars and policy makers about the inequities suffered by many women. Whether it was a matter of denouncing the "lie" of a republican revolution that promised equality and denied citizenship to women, or of making visible the translucent barrier of the "glass ceiling" (Federal Glass Ceiling Commission 1995), feminists have enabled us to see how divisions between women and men have constituted, and been constituted by, the social and political arrangements of societies.

The exposure of the ways in which seemingly neutral classification has masked the exclusion of women has been important to the feminist project in several ways. It has identified the subtle and historically varied ways in which discrimination has operated, and it has consolidated the identity of women as a political constituency (of those who experience and perhaps also resist discrimination) in the present and the past. Feminists have, in this way, found exemplary models for their behavior; they have established "traditions" into which they have projected themselves. But the designation of "women" as an inherently political category has sometimes tended to conflate the appearance of women in, say, mixed political crowds with the existence of a collective feminine consciousness that can be analyzed in terms of "gender," that is, as a result or reflection of treatment experienced by them as "women" (Ortner 1996; Rosaldo 1980; Tsing 1990; Young 1994). It is one thing to argue that the appearance of women in the ranks of protesters contradicts the presumption that femaleness precludes public activism, and quite another to say that their presence exemplifies a peculiarly "women's" consciousness. The presence of women in the crowds that marched to Versailles to bring King Louis XVI back to Paris during the French Revolution was motivated by economic concerns about the impact of high prices on poor families and fears about the political direction of the revolution. Although "gender" was at play (in the composition of the crowd and in accounts of it),[3] feminist consciousness was not. In contrast, the demands of women to be accorded the status of active citizens with voting rights were the expression of an "interest" specific to women as a group. The point is that the presence of physical females is not always a sure sign that "women" are a separate political category, that they have been mobilized as women. Yet some of the work that tries to attribute peculiarly female or feminine motives to women in social movements assumes exactly that. The projection of a separate women's interest into a situation where it is not operating naturalizes "women," because their interest is taken to preexist the political context of the crowd's action and the terms of its mobilization.

An insistence that we be precise about what kind of gender analysis is appropriate is at the heart of the argument Czech sociologist Havelkova (1997) makes about developments in her country since 1989. As she seeks to explain misunderstandings between West and East European feminists, she cautions against the automatic assumption that problems faced by women are to be necessarily defined as addressing or repressing "women's interests." Her choice of prostitution to illustrate her argument is particularly provocative, given that it involves the sale of sex—the exploitation of women's bodies. Still, Havelkova insists that when we examine the situation in the Czech Republic, issues other than gender come to the fore:

> Prostitution . . . is concentrated mostly around the Czech-German border, [and] is regarded primarily as a problem posed by the abruptly opened border and the disproportion between the Czech and German currencies. The customers are German, the prostitutes Czech. Prostitutes report that they earn in one night more than their mothers earn in a whole month in the factory. So this problem is framed by the broader problem of the relative economic position of the country. (p. 57)

Havelkova suggests that, in this instance, gender is beside the point, or, if not beside the point, then a lesser consideration for economic and political analysis. Prostitution is one of many indicators of a relative economic impoverishment that has also affected men (at the level of their bodies, too, in the form of hunger, stress, and elevated mortality). Protest, if it emerges, and policy initiatives, when they are taken, will (rightly, Havelkova implies) address not sexual, but economic hierarchies in the geopolitical terms of national interest. It is as Czechs (in relation to German hegemony) and not separately as men or women that people are, in this instance, experiencing the vagaries of market capitalism.

Havelkova (1997) extends her argument by insisting that, although there are many ways in which women are treated differently from men, this has not produced the kind of consciousness Western feminists have been led to expect. Women have long participated in the Czech labor force, and they are used to confronting problems strategically. Moreover, "one effect of the totalitarian experience is that both women and men think politically rather than psychologically. On the one hand, this leads to a lesser degree of sensitivity on gender issues, but on the other, it also makes women feel politically equal." The results of this, she concludes, are not to be underestimated in the future. "When women . . . start to see the political relevance of the gender difference, they will most likely see it in the context of and in proportion to other political realities" (p. 59).

Havelkova's call for attention to the specificities of the Czech situation refuses to separate structural factors from subjective perception. If she refers to "women" as a social category throughout her essay, she does so in order to dispute Western feminist interpretations. But she denies there is any "women's interest" that inevitably attaches to "women." Instead, in her thinking, the articulation of "women's interest" marks the emergence of a separate women's political identity, the terms of which relate to the way in which sexual difference has been articulated in a specific historical context. Havelkova seems to have little doubt that some kind of feminist movement will emerge—given the heightened gender inequalities appearing in the arenas of politics and the labor force (a sign that lines of sexual difference are indeed being drawn) and given the international (United Nations-sponsored) framework that, since the Beijing Conference of 1995, has called for universal human rights for women. But her insistence that perceptions of inequality are discursively shaped in historical contexts means that we must not take the emergence of this feminism as a sign of women's coming into some predetermined consciousness—a state already experienced, already known by inhabitants of "advanced" countries of the West. Rather, "there is a history of feminism in the Czech Republic; it needs to be understood in its own terms and in its changing relation to Western feminism" (Havelkova 1997:61).

The Subject of Rights

From the Enlightenment to the Beijing Conference, the question of universal human rights has had important repercussions for feminists (Human Rights Watch 1995). The idea that all individuals are (in the words of the American Declaration of Independence) "endowed by their Creator with certain unalienable rights" enabled men and women to imagine societies of perfect equality and to mobilize collectively to achieve them.

Although appeals for "rights" have informed feminist protests—they were surely the basis for suffrage campaigns in the past and have recently provided something of a common ground for women's movements all over the world—there has not been unanimity about the wisdom of these appeals. Some have argued (echoing long-standing debates between socialists and liberals) that formal rights mask social antagonisms, that attention to rights precludes attention to inequities of class, gender, and race (Gibson-Graham 1996). "Equality between men and women or even between women in different circumstances may be iniquitous," writes South African educator and political activist Ramphele (1997). "We need to problematize equality and develop an equity framework that enables us and our various societies to address the needs of people—men and women—in an equitable way, bearing in mind the differential impact of race, class, age, and other constraints on power relations" (p. 36). Others have replied that without formal rights there can be no attention to substantive issues; in democratic societies, at least, representation of the needs and interests of social groups depends on individuals' access to political power. Arguing for the vote in 1881, French suffragist Auclert wrote, "Until woman has the power to intervene to defend her interests wherever they are at stake, any change in the economic or political condition of society will not ameliorate her condition." Still others have insisted that claims for rights by social groups (such as women) imply an inverse causality for the process by which laws create subjects and attribute agency to them (Butler 1992; Spivak 1992). "Legal recognition is a real and circular process. It recognizes the things that correspond to the definitions it constructs" (Adams and Minson [1978] 1990:99). To imply otherwise essentializes identities and removes them from the historical contexts that create them. Legal appeals that attach rights to persons imply that the rights of women, fathers, and fetuses are inherent, when, in fact, it is the law that creates rights by attributing them to classes or individuals. Legal recognition of subjects and their rights also permits state regulation (of women's bodies, say, in the name of paternal or fetal rights). So rights are not an unqualified good (Brown 1995). Countering this view is the one that insists that rights confer not only specific social identities, but a more general recognition of humanity. Thus Williams (1991) maintains that "for the historically disempowered, the conferring of rights is symbolic of all the denied aspects of their humanity: rights imply a respect that places one in the referential range of self and others, that elevates one's status from human body to social being" (p. 153).

By far the most intense discussions have addressed the issue of universalism itself: Is it a genuinely inclusive concept, violated only in practice, or is it inherently exclusionary, a way of (mis)representing a set of particularistic normative standards as if they were neutral

("Universalism" 1995)? Put more concretely, are notions of individual rights historically and culturally Western? "I should like to see the word *universal* banned altogether from discussion of African literature until such a time as people cease to use it as a synonym for the narrow, self-serving parochialism of Europe, until their horizon extends to include all the world," Nigerian writer Achebe (1989:9) has stated. Is the abstract individual, the bearer of those rights, merely a synonym for men? That is the suggestion of French feminists campaigning for parity—a law that will designate half the seats in the National Assembly for women. ("It is paradoxical, but interesting to argue that it was universalism that best maintained the sexualization of power, and that parity attempts, by contrast, to desexualize power by extending it to both sexes. Parity would thus be the real universalism" [Collin 1995:103; see also Scott 1997].) Do men and women reason in "different voices," as Gilligan (1982) has suggested? Is universalism, then, Western patriarchalism in disguise? Is it accurate to say, as MacKinnon (1983) does, that "abstract rights will authorize the male experience of the world" (p. 658)?

The positions taken in these debates often conflate two separate issues that are, in fact, not reducible to one another: the general and the particular, the abstract and the concrete, the enduring and the historical, principle and practice. They are (futile) attempts to resolve a paradox at the heart of universalist discourse that Brown (1995), a political theorist, has described this way:

> The question of the liberatory or egalitarian force of rights is always historically and culturally circumscribed; rights have no inherent political semiotic, no innate capacity either to advance or impede radical democratic ideals. Yet rights necessarily operate in and as an ahistorical, acultural, acontextual idiom: they claim distance from specific political contexts and historical vicissitudes, and they necessarily participate in a discourse of enduring universality rather than provisionality or partiality. Thus, while the measure of their political efficacy requires a high degree of historical and social specificity, rights operate as a political discourse of the general, the generic, and universal. (p. 97)

And that, Brown concludes, is as it should be. "It is . . . in their abstraction from the particulars of our lives—and in their figuration of an egalitarian political community—that they may be most valuable in the democratic transformation of these particulars" (p. 134). Put in other terms, it is because they allow us to imagine (and thus to strive to create) a different order of social and political life, and not because they are attached to a set of specific objects or because they are a universal human possession, that rights are effective.

Here the notion of fantasy may again be useful. "The discourse of universal rights . . . presents a fantasy scenario in which society and the individual are perceived as whole, as non-split. In the fantasy, society is understood as something that can be rationally organized, as a community that can be non-conflictual if only it respects human rights" (Salecl 1994:127). Rights then articulate a desire that can never be entirely satisfied, but whose articulation involves the assertion of that humanness upon which equality must rest. It is not possession but aspiration that provides common ground. "It is not the case that human beings as such have rights, but that none remain without rights" (Salecl 1994:133),[4] that is, without the ability to wish for or imagine autonomy, agency, transformation. This formulation can be interpreted to admit of no exclusions; the operations of desire are not in the first instance limited by social differences, although they may be directed at different objects. In that sense, this notion of rights could be read as universalistic. It is admittedly abstract, but unlike the abstract individual, this understanding of rights carries with it no necessary personification, no figure (historically, the White Western male) who embodies a standard that functions to exclude those who are different from it. Women's claims for rights, from this vantage point, would be analyzed as an insistence on their (symbolic and actual) position as desiring subjects, individuals whose desire rested not on their possession of some physical trait or the performance of a specified biological function, but on the very constitution of their being—a being conceptualized through an other's recognition, necessarily expressed in words that are always inadequate for the full representation of the self and that, therefore, leave one yearning for completeness. Such completeness, paradoxically, would mark the end of individuation, the death of the individual subject, because, according to Lacan, individual subjects come into being as divided or alienated selves because they are dependent on the recognition of others for confirmation of their individuality. Individuality—autonomous, independent, self-creating—relies for its existence on distinction from and recognition by an other. Moreover, individuality (one's sense of self) exists only in its representation and, by definition, representation is not the real or originary thing. But the self cannot do without representation and without others, though it is conceived as entirely self-sufficient. Achievement of the ideal of self-sufficiency would dissolve exactly those boundaries between self and other upon which realization of selfhood depends (Lacan 1959-60). From this it follows that community might be conceived not in terms of commonality, but as an association of individuals paradoxically united by their dependence on difference (Agamben 1993; Miami Theory Collective 1991; Nancy 1991).

Changing one term—*rights* as aspiration rather than possession—requires changing another—*individual* becomes more rather than less abstract. It also permits us to establish a critical distance on contemporary debates about rights and to ask some historical questions about them. How did *rights* come to be understood as something individuals possess? How did gender figure in the articulation of this possessive individualism? What, historically and cross-culturally, have been the relationships between notions of possession and representations of sexual difference? How did the fantasy of political egalitarianism (the democratic vision) interact with (supplement? challenge? contradict?) the fantasies of human origin that, at least in the West, make sexual difference fundamental to individual identities? How has this happened differently in different places at different times? And what are the implications of the answers to these questions for our understanding of the new "globalization" of feminism as a matter of securing women's "human rights" ("Conference Reports" 1996)?

These questions return us to some of those with which I began this essay. They are questions that make the articulation of sexual difference itself the problem to be investigated, that take psychic realities seriously in examinations not only of ideology and subjectivity, but also of political, economic, and social institutions and the power relations they attempt to implement (Connell 1987). They are questions that grant the vagaries and complexities of individual sexual (and other) identities, assuming that social regulation is about reducing multiplicity to manageable normative categories. These questions open the possibility of thinking about individual identity as that which is constrained by, but always exceeds, any categorization imposed on it. If political and social identities always operate reductively, the question becomes, How? What is left over or left out in the process of producing (and reproducing) categories of collective identity? What are the stakes in such reductions? Have they been contested? How? And by whom?

All of these are questions that can be answered only in terms of specific historical/cultural instances. They necessarily problematize and historicize the categories that are our objects of study, as well as those we deploy in our own analyses. By positing a distinction between our discursive constructions and those of other times and places, we establish a certain reflexivity on our own stakes and intentions (granting even the place of desire in serious scholarly endeavors). In this way, we open ourselves to history, to the idea and possibility that things have been, and will be, different from what they are now.

Notes

1. Sedgwick (1990) talks about sex/gender as delineating "a problematical *space* rather than a crisp distinction," and she uses the term *gender* to "denominate" that space (p. 29).

2. For additional citations, see the last section of this essay, headed "The Subject of Rights."

3. Historical accounts depend on descriptions that mingle fantasy and reality, as Hertz (1983) points out. What is the effect on the portrait of a crowd when authors use the trope of an unruly female to figure a revolution? How do historians distinguish in these descriptions between a certain exaggeration for effect and the actual events that they purport to recount? Can we make a distinction? What kind of reading practices are required to do this? These are questions that classic "crowd studies" do not usually ask (Rudé 1973; Tilly 1986) and that serious attention to unconscious processes demands.

4. I have taken liberties here with Salecl's (1994) discussion, which more centrally turns on Lacan's theory of sexual difference. For Lacan the subject comes into being through language that rests on sexual difference, so presumably there cannot be an individual who is not sexed. But the point of Salecl's argument is that when rights are reconceived as expressions of desire rather than things we possess, we do away with the abstract individual. Then desire—human aspiration, the direction of human imagination—can be the basis for a more egalitarian politics. The question is, I guess, whether, in this way of thinking about it, desire is inflected by sexual difference.

References

Achebe, C. 1989. "Impediments to Dialogue between North and South." Pp. 14-19 in *Hopes and Impediments: Selected Essays.* New York: Doubleday.

Adams, P. [1979] 1990. "A Note on the Distinction between Sexual Division and Sexual Differences." Pp. 102-9 in *The Woman in Question: m/f,* edited by P. Adams and E. Cowie. Cambridge: MIT Press.

Adams, P. and J. Minson, J. [1978] 1990. "The 'Subject' of Feminism."
Pp. 81-101 in *The Woman in Question: m/f*, edited by P. Adams and E. Cowie.
Cambridge: MIT Press.

Agamben, G. 1993. *The Coming Community.* Translated by M. Hardt.
Minneapolis: University of Minnesota Press.

Auclert, H. 1881. *La Citoyenne*, February 13.

Bock, G. 1989. "Women's History and Gender History: Aspects of an
International Debate." *Gender and History* 1:7-30.

Boxer, M. and J. Quataert. 1978. *Socialist Women: European Socialist Feminism
in the Nineteenth and Early Twentieth Centuries.* New York: Elsevier.

Brown, W. 1995. *States of Injury: Power and Freedom in Late Modernity.*
Princeton, NJ: Princeton University Press.

Butler, J. 1992. "Contingent Foundations: Feminism and the Question of
'Postmodernism.' " Pp. 3-21 in *Feminists Theorize the Political*, edited by J.
Butler and J. W. Scott. New York: Routledge.

———. 1993. *Bodies That Matter: On the Discursive Limits of "Sex."* New York:
Routledge.

Chaumette. [1793] 1980. "Women's Deputations Barred from Sessions of the
Paris Commune." Pp. 219-20 in *Women in Revolutionary Paris, 1789-1795*,
edited by D. G. Levy, H. B. Applewhite, and M. D. Johnson. Urbana:
University of Illinois Press.

Collier, J. F. and S. J. Yanagisako, eds. 1987. *Gender and Kinship: Essays toward
a Unified Analysis.* Stanford, CA: Stanford University Press.

Collin, F. 1995. "Actualité de la parté." *Projets Féministes* 4-5.

Condorcet. [1790] 1976. "On the Admission of Women to the Rights of
Citizenship." In *Condorcet: Selected Writings*, edited by K. M. Baker.
Indianapolis: Bobbs-Merrill.

"Conference Reports [from Beijing]." 1996. *Signs* 22:181-226.

Connell, R. W. 1987. *Gender and Power: Society, the Person and Sexual Politics.*
Stanford, CA: Stanford University Press.

Cornell, D. 1991. *Beyond Accommodation: Ethical Feminism, Deconstruction, and
the Law.* New York: Routledge.

de Gouges, O. [1791] 1980. "The Declaration of the Rights of Women."
Pp. 87-96 in *Women in Revolutionary Paris, 1789-1795*, edited by D. G. Levy,
H. B. Applewhite, and M. D. Johnson. Urbana: University of Illinois Press.

Elshtain, J. B. 1981. *Public Man, Private Woman: Women in Social and Political
Thought.* Princeton, NJ: Princeton University Press.

Fauré, C. 1991. *Democracy without Women: Feminism and the Rise of Liberal
Individualism in France.* Translated by C. Gorbman and J. Berks. Bloomington:
Indiana University Press.

Federal Glass Ceiling Commission. 1995. *A Solid Investment: Making Full Use of the Nation's Human Capital: Recommendations of the Federal Glass Ceiling Commission.* Washington, DC: Federal Glass Ceiling Commission.

Foucault, M. 1972. *The Archaeology of Knowledge.* Translated by A. M. Sheridan Smith. New York: Harper & Row.

———. 1980. *The History of Sexuality.* Vol. 1. Translated by Robert Hurley. New York: Vintage.

Freud, S. [1905] 1953. "Three Essays on Sexuality." Pp. 125-72 in *The Standard Edition of the Complete Psychological Works of Sigmund Freud,* vol. 7, edited and translated by J. Strachey. London: Hogarth.

———. [1909] 1953. "Notes upon a Case of Obsessional Neurosis." Pp. 153-320 in *The Standard Edition of the Complete Psychological Works of Sigmund Freud,* vol. 10, edited and translated by J. Strachey. London: Hogarth.

———. [1915] 1953. "Thoughts for the Times on War and Death." Pp. 273-301 in *The Standard Edition of the Complete Psychological Works of Sigmund Freud,* vol. 14, edited and translated by J. Strachey. London: Hogarth.

———. [1927] 1953. "Fetishism." Pp. 273-302 in *The Standard Edition of the Complete Psychological Works of Sigmund Freud,* vol. 21, edited and translated by J. Strachey. London: Hogarth.

———. [1930] 1953. "Civilization and Its Discontents." Pp. 59-145 in *The Standard Edition of the Complete Psychological Works of Sigmund Freud,* vol. 21, edited and translated by J. Strachey. London: Hogarth.

Gibson-Graham, J. K. 1996. *The End of Capitalism (as We Knew It): A Feminist Critique of Political Economy.* Oxford: Basil Blackwell.

Gilligan, C. 1982. *In a Different Voice: Psychological Theory and Women's Development.* Cambridge, MA: Harvard University Press.

Glazer, P. M. and Slater, M. 1987. *Unequal Colleagues: The Entrance of Women into the Professions, 1890-1940.* New Brunswick, NJ: Rutgers University Press.

Haraway, D. J. 1991. " 'Gender' for a Marxist Dictionary: The Sexual Politics of a Word." Pp. 127-48 in *Simians, Cyborgs, and Women: The Reinvention of Nature.* New York: Routledge.

Havelkova, H. 1997. "Transitory and Persistent Differences: Feminism East and West." Pp. 56-62 in *Transitions, Environments, Translations: Feminisms in International Politics,* edited by J. W. Scott, C. Kaplan, and D. Keates. New York: Routledge.

Hawkesworth, M. 1997. "Confounding Gender." *Signs* 22:649-85 (with comments and replies by McKenna and Kessler, Smith, Scott and Connell, pp. 687-713).

Hertz, N. 1983. "Medusa's Head: Male Hysteria under Political Pressure." *Representations* 4:27-54.

Human Rights Watch. 1995. *The Human Rights Watch Global Report on Women's Human Rights*. New York: Human Rights Watch.

Hunt, L. 1992. *The Family Romance of the French Revolution*. Berkeley: University of California Press.

Keates, D. 1992. "Sexual Difference." Pp. 402-5 in *Feminism and Psychoanalysis: A Critical Dictionary*, edited by E. Wright. Oxford: Basil Blackwell.

Keller, E. F. 1985. *Reflections on Gender and Science*. New Haven, CT: Yale University Press.

Kelly-Gadol, J. 1977. "Did Women Have a Renaissance?" Pp. 137-64 in *Becoming Visible: Women in European History*, edited by R. Bridenthal and C. Koonz. Boston: Houghton Mifflin.

Kerber, L. K. 1980. *Women of the Republic: Intellect and Ideology in Revolutionary America*. Chapel Hill: University of North Carolina Press.

———. 1997. *Toward an Intellectual History of Women*. Chapel Hill: University of North Carolina Press.

Lacan, J. 1959-60. *The Ethics of Psychoanalysis, 1959-60*. Edited by J.-A. Miller and translated by D. Porter. New York: W. W. Norton.

———. 1977. *Écrits: A Selection*. Translated by A. Sheridan. New York: W. W. Norton.

Landes, J. B. 1988. *Women and the Public Sphere in the Age of the French Revolution*. Ithaca, NY: Cornell University Press.

Laplanche, J. and J.-B. Pontalis. 1986. "Fantasy and the Origins of Sexuality." Pp. 5-34 in *Formations of Fantasy*, edited by V. Burgin, J. Donald, and C. Kaplan. London: Methuen.

Laqueur, T. 1990. *Making Sex: Body and Gender from the Greeks to Freud*. Cambridge, MA: Harvard University Press.

MacKinnon, C. A. 1983. "Feminism, Marxism, Method, and the State: Toward Feminist Jurisprudence." *Signs* 8:635-58.

Miami Theory Collective. 1991. *Community at Loose Ends*. Minneapolis: University of Minnesota Press.

Nancy, J.-L. 1991. *The Inoperative Community*. Minneapolis: University of Minnesota Press.

Nelson, B. J. and N. Chowdhury, eds. 1994. *Women and Politics Worldwide*. New Haven, CT: Yale University Press.

Nicholson, L. J. 1986. *Gender and History: The Limits of Social Theory in the Age of the Family*. New York: Columbia University Press.

———. 1994. "Interpreting 'Gender,' " *Signs* 20:79-105.

Norton, M. B. 1980. *Liberty's Daughters: The Revolutionary Experience of American Women, 1750-1800*. Boston: Little, Brown.

————. 1996. *Founding Mothers and Fathers: Gendered Power and the Forming of American Society.* New York: Alfred A. Knopf.

Okin, S. M. 1979. *Women in Western Political Thought.* Princeton, NJ: Princeton University Press.

Ortner, S. 1996. "The Problem of 'Women' as an Analytic Category." Pp. 116-38 in *Making Gender: The Politics and Erotics of Culture,* edited by S. Ortner. Boston: Beacon.

Outram, D. 1989. *The Body and the French Revolution: Sex, Class and Political Culture.* New Haven, CT: Yale University Press.

Pateman, C. 1988. *The Sexual Contract.* Stanford, CA: Stanford University Press.

Phillips, A. and B. Taylor. [1980] 1996. "Sex and Skill: Notes toward a Feminist Economics." Pp. 317-30 in *Feminism and History,* edited by J. W. Scott. Oxford: Oxford University Press.

Ramphele, M. 1997. "Whither Feminism?" Pp. 334-38 in *Transitions, Environments, Translations: Feminisms in International Politics,* edited by J. W. Scott, C. Kaplan, and D. Keates. New York: Routledge.

Reynolds, S., ed. 1986. *Women, State, and Revolution: Essays on Power and Gender in Europe since 1789.* Brighton: Harvester.

————. 1996. *France between the Wars: Gender and Politics.* London: Routledge.

Riley, D. 1988. *"Am I That Name?" Feminism and the Category of "Women" in History.* London: Macmillan.

Roberts, M. L. 1994. *Civilization without Sexes: Reconstructing Gender in Postwar France, 1917-1927.* Chicago: University of Chicago Press.

Rosaldo, M. Z. 1980. "The Use and Abuse of Anthropology: Reflections on Feminism and Cross-Cultural Understanding." *Signs* 5:389-417.

Rossiter, M. W. 1982. *Women Scientists in America: Struggles and Strategies to 1940.* Baltimore: Johns Hopkins University Press.

————. 1995. *Women Scientists in America: Before Affirmative Action, 1940-1972.* Baltimore: Johns Hopkins University Press.

Rubin, G. 1975. "The Traffic in Women: Notes on the 'Political Economy' of Sex." Pp. 157-210 in *Toward an Anthropology of Women,* edited by R. R. Reiter. London: Monthly Review Press.

Rudé, G. 1973. *The Crowd in the French Revolution.* London: Oxford University Press.

Salecl, R. 1990. "Society Doesn't Exist." *American Journal of Semiotics* 7:45-52.

————. 1994. *The Spoils of Freedom: Psychoanalysis and Feminism after the Fall of Socialism.* London: Routledge.

Scott, J. W. 1993. "The Woman Worker." Pp. 399-426 in *A History of Women,* vol. 4, edited by G. Duby and M. Perrot. Cambridge, MA: Harvard University Press.

————. 1996. *Only Paradoxes to Offer: French Feminists and the Rights of Man.* Cambridge, MA: Harvard University Press.

————. 1997. " 'La Querelle des Femmes' in Late Twentieth Century France." *New Left Review* (November-December).

Sedgwick, E. K. 1990. *Epistemology of the Closet.* Berkeley: University of California Press.

Shepherdson, C. 1997. "The Epoch of the Body: Need, Demand and the Drive in Kojève and Lacan." In *Perspectives on Embodiment: Essays from the NEH Institute at Santa Cruz,* edited by H. Haber and G. Weiss. New York: Routledge.

Sonenscher, M. 1987. *The Hatters of Eighteenth-Century France.* Berkeley: University of California Press.

Spivak, G. C. 1992. "French Feminism Revisited: Ethics and Politics." Pp. 54-85 in *Feminists Theorize the Political,* edited by J. Butler and J. W. Scott. New York: Routledge.

Taylor, B. 1983. *Eve and the New Jerusalem: Socialism and Feminism in the Nineteenth Century.* New York: Pantheon.

Tilly, C. 1986. *The Contentious French: Four Centuries of Popular Struggle.* Cambridge, MA: Harvard University Press.

Tsing, A. L. 1990. "Gender and Performance in Meratus Dispute Settlement." Pp. 95-125 in *Power and Difference: Gender in Island Southeast Asia,* edited by J. Atkinson and S. Errington. Stanford, CA: Stanford University Press.

"Universalism." 1995. Special issue. *Differences: A Journal of Feminist Cultural Studies* 7 (Spring).

Warner, M. 1992. "Thoreau's Bottom." *Raritan* 11:53-79.

Watson, P. 1993. "The Rise of Masculinism in Eastern Europe." *New Left Review* 198:71-82.

Williams, P. J. 1991. *The Alchemy of Race and Rights: Diary of a Law Professor.* Cambridge, MA: Harvard University Press.

Young, I. M. 1994. "Gender as Seriality: Thinking about Women as a Social Collective." *Signs* 19:713-38.

Zerilli, L. 1994. *Signifying Woman: Culture and Chaos in Rousseau, Burke, and Mill.* Ithaca, NY: Cornell University Press.

PART II

THE MACROSOCIAL
ORGANIZATION OF GENDER

CHAPTER 4

Feminist Thinking about the Welfare State

ANETTE BORCHORST

During the past 15 years, feminist scholarship addressing the welfare state has become a voluminous research field that has yielded valuable insights into the impact on gender relations of crucial aspects of state regulation. During the early phases of feminist scholarship, feminists did not take much interest in analyzing the state, but in the late 1970s and early 1980s some scholars, especially those related to the Marxist feminist tradition, engaged in what they saw as a first step toward building a feminist theory of the state. Since then, a growing number of comparative studies of welfare states has revealed fundamental variations in their gendering effects. Today, building a generic feminist theory of the state appears futile to most scholars, and it is widely acknowledged that there are far-reaching differences among welfare states. Throughout this process, the object has been narrowed, shifting from the state in general to aspects of welfare policies in particular. By the same token, researchers have become more explicit about what specific state formation they study and how far their conclusions can be stretched. Furthermore, analytic and methodological approaches have been widened, and a multifaceted view of the state has emerged. It is acknowledged that states are built around a number of institutions and that different actors struggle to influence the policy process.

Empirical analyses of how welfare states have been influenced by political actors have become numerous, including an increasing number of historical studies of the forming of welfare states. Studies of specific welfare policies and their effects have contributed to more differentiated conclusions about what policies affect gender relations and how. Another theme that has come more into focus is the role of women's agency. Initially, women were seen primarily as passive victims of state intervention or as recipients of state benefits, but as the welfare state debate has progressed, their role as policy makers, individually or collectively, has been investigated more thoroughly. A wealth of studies of the role of women, especially in the historical development of welfare states, have been published.

In this chapter my aim is to synthesize feminist scholarly thought on the welfare state. I do not offer a complete account of the research tradition, given its complexity. Rather, I identify key debates that appear to have been stimulating for other scholars and have triggered discussions of the gendering effects of welfare states across national borders. I begin with a summary of the first wave of studies set off by Anglo-American scholars in the late 1970s and early 1980s. I then turn to Scandinavian scholarship on this topic in the 1980s, which I consider to be a second wave of thought. The heart of the chapter then deals with different themes and approaches during the past 10-15 years of feminist scholarship, concentrating on debates related to the comparative welfare state paradigm and the citizenship tradition. The latter is intrinsically linked to the former, but to some extent these constitute separate research strands, and for analytic purposes I discuss them separately. Afterward, I discuss the predominantly American debate that has centered on women's agency in the forming of welfare states, and I address the different approaches and notions of the welfare state inherent in feminist welfare state research.

The First Wave: British/American State Theory

During the late 1970s, the project of building a feminist theory of the state was initiated by Marxist feminists. Characteristically, the British feminist Wilson (1977) concluded that the welfare state first and foremost controls "the way in which the woman does her job in the home of servicing the worker and bringing up their children" (p. 40). She saw the state as mainly repressive, and in her account, the role of ideology was highlighted. She argued that women were continuously defined as wives and mothers, even though they increasingly sought employment outside the home, and they were caught between their situation as low-paid workers and their official definition as primarily mothers.

In a similar vein, another British scholar, McIntosh (1978), concluded that the state sustains the subordination of women by initiating and guiding changes in the family household according to the capital's need, but exercises its control over women indirectly, by confirming men's dominant position in the family and leaving them control in this sphere (p. 257). Like Wilson, McIntosh tended to subsume gender inequality under class inequality. This implied that she regarded men as being dominant mainly as capitalists and less as men (p. 259).

American Marxist feminists, particularly Eisenstein and Hartmann, developed a dual systems theory of capitalism and patriarchy. The implication of this dual oppression was that men not only had privileges according to their class, but also as men, and that even working-class men participated historically in subordinating women. Hartmann and Eisenstein defined the role of the state as an intermediator between the two systems; however, they differed in their perceptions of the basis of patriarchal power. Hartmann (1981) claimed that men's control over women's labor power is decisive, and considered the family wage the cornerstone of sexual division of labor (pp. 15, 25). Eisenstein (1983) asserted that patriarchy's dynamic of power is centered in attempts to control women's options in relation to motherhood and mothering (p. 44). Eisenstein argued that the state institutionalizes a division between private and public as a female-male distinction, and she made a distinction between familial patriarchy and social patriarchy as two separate but interrelated structures. The first related to patriarchy as it appears in family life; this, Eisenstein found, had been undermined by the integration of women into the labor force. The latter she argued was actually strengthened through patriarchal control within the labor force (Eisenstein 1981:204).

This approach emphasized the repressive nature of the state vis-à-vis women, and its suspicion of the state reflected feelings toward the state found in the new feminist movement at the time, especially among its socialist and radical branches. The ideas were not uncontested, and the concepts of patriarchy and dual systems theory were subject to a lively debate among feminists (e.g., Sargent, 1981; Barrett, 1988).

This first wave of feminist scholarly studies adopted a very general approach to the state, and was not very explicit about whether the object of analysis was the state itself or its welfare policies in particular. These studies tended to ignore contradictions within the state, to overemphasize the oppressive nature of the state, and to ignore women's role in supporting or mitigating patriarchal power. The authors were, however, all aware of such problems. Wilson (1977:13) questioned the idea of the state as a conscious conspiracy or a rational monolith, and McIntosh (1978:281) criticized the perception of society as an integrated whole with equilibrium-seeking mechanisms. Eisenstein (1981) observed internal conflicts between different factions of the state and contradictory policies of American governments of the 1980s. Regardless, they all failed to allow these reservations to modify their theoretical conclusions, and tended to portray the state as a conspiratorial bloc that manipulates women's consciousness.

Another major shortcoming of these early contributions was that despite the authors' overt focus on state regulations of their own nations, they seemed to assume that their conclusions would apply equally well to other state structures, and only sporadically expressed awareness of possible differences among liberal, social democratic, and other state formations. Yet however severe the weaknesses of their approach, this first wave of studies did serve as a catalyst for a whole new research agenda during the coming years, and was inspiring and thought-provoking for feminists in other countries.

The Second Wave: Scandinavian Theories of the Welfare State

Many Scandinavian feminists were inspired by British and American literature, even though they argued that the situation in Scandinavia differed.[1] They described how social democratic governments in the postwar period had emphasized egalitarian ideals and class cooperation, and how equality had been articulated as a central political goal and had been pursued through the enactment of redistributive policies. Equality policies applied, above all, to reducing class differences, but gender equality had also received attention. Sweden and Denmark had experienced a large-scale entry of women into the labor force since the 1960s (Norway a decade later), and Scandinavian scholars noted that this development had been facilitated by the extension of the welfare state, particularly in the caregiving sector. The welfare state became an important provider of care, especially for small children during the daytime, but to some extent also for the elderly. Health care was considered a responsibility of the state. The result was far-reaching change in the boundaries between private and public, called by some "reproduction going public" (Hernes 1987). The collective mobilization of women begun in the 1970s by the new feminist movement and the increasing political representation of women, which had reached about 30 percent by the mid-1980s, were seen as cause and effect of the development of the welfare states.

Many Scandinavian scholars interpreted these changes as a reorganization of patriarchy (Holter 1984:19), as a shift from private to public dependence for women (Hernes 1984), or argued that family patriarchy had been weakened, whereas social patriarchy had been strengthened (Borchorst and Siim 1987). Such far-reaching changes notwithstanding, they shared the belief that male dominance was still a fundamental structuring principle of these societies. However, during the 1980s a considerable gap between more optimistic and pessimistic views of the developments in Scandinavia emerged.

The first innovation in this literature was to differentiate among the roles that characterized the relations between individuals and the state. Hernes (1984) named three—citizens, employees, and welfare clients— and found that in all three roles women's lives were more determined by state policies than were men's. But Hernes did not discuss whether this dependency was negative or positive for women. Danish political scientists Borchorst and Siim (1987:146) suggested a fourth category— consumers of public services such as child care—was useful for distinguishing between different forms and levels of dependence, and they restricted the client role to recipients of income maintenance. They argued that when women were rendered totally economically dependent on the state, which was the situation in some liberal countries, it furthered social control and stigmatization, whereas a role as consumers of child-care services, as in Scandinavia, facilitated women's participation in the labor force, and thus their economic independence of husbands as well as of the state (see also Siim 1988:174ff.; Borchorst 1994:58). Siim (1988) argued that there are important socioeconomic, cultural, and power differences among women in these different roles and contended that there are no alternatives in modern states to women's dependency on the state. The distinction among roles served as an analytic tool for understanding both gender differences and cross-national differences in the gendering effects, and so it marked a break with the view of a linear development from private to public patriarchy. It was, however, too vague to be adequate for more systematic empirical purposes.

The Swedish historian Hirdmann (1990) then prompted a broad debate in Sweden and among Scandinavian feminists on pessimistic versus optimistic appraisal of the gendering effects of the welfare state.

She argued that during the postwar period, two forces had been at play in the Swedish welfare state: a gender integrative one that pulled women into the labor force and a segregative force that differentiated between "the big world," which was male dominated, and "the small life" predominantly related to women. The gender system had been modernized through a change from a housewife contract to an equality contract, but gender segregation and gender hierarchy had been preserved. She claimed that the Swedish welfare state was characterized by an escalating gender conflict, in which women were considered the problem. It is noteworthy that Hirdmann's interpretation of the Swedish welfare state was conducted at the request of the Swedish government and published as a government report.

Several scholars, notably Hernes, added to the pessimistic interpretations by emphasizing that Scandinavian countries had ascribed the corporate channel a very central role in political decision making in the postwar period. This channel is based on formalized access of organizations and institutions, above all employers' organizations and unions, and is the least participative, most hierarchical, and most elitist form of political power (Hernes 1984:30). Because women had not gained access to the corporate channel, they had been objects more than subjects of policy—in other words, they had mainly been "policy takers," whereas men had been "policy makers" or participants in the political process. This led Hernes (1982:32; 1984:31) to characterize the Scandinavian state form as a "tutelary state" for women, yet she also later concluded that Scandinavian welfare states, and especially Sweden and Norway, had the potential to be woman-friendly. She defined a woman-friendly state as one that enables "women to have a natural relationship to their children, their work, and public life," and that "would not force harder choices on women than on men, or permit unjust treatment on the basis of sex" (1987:15). The difference between this conclusion and her notion of the tutelary state is explained by the different aspects of the state under consideration. The state's woman-friendly potential is related to the extension of care and a focus on women as recipients of state benefits, whereas the "tutelary" characterization was derived from a view of the welfare state from the perspective of political power. Both conclusions were descriptive and tentative, but served to nurture feminist debates about the effects of not only Scandinavian but also other welfare states.

The view of Scandinavian welfare states as woman-friendly did not remain uncontested. Considering motherhood and child care, Leira

(1989) pointed to distinct differences separating Sweden and Denmark from Norway, the latter being the least advantageous for women. She also criticized the notion of a woman-friendly welfare state for exaggerating the impact of the welfare state, and for "glossing over the fact that women have both similar and different interests and aims" (Leira 1993:50).

Despite the division between optimistic and pessimistic interpretations, the overall picture was that Scandinavian welfare states were more favorable to women than were Anglo-Saxon ones. Scandinavian women were far from equal with men in terms of political influence, yet women had gained a foothold at different levels of the state, as politicians, bureaucrats, and professional staff in care facilities. Hence analyses of the state could not be built merely on assumptions of patriarchal dominance and female oppression. The Scandinavian experience laid the groundwork for a more sophisticated understanding of how changing gender relations had structured welfare states and vice versa.

Because this second wave of scholarship put the Scandinavian welfare states into a social democratic context and some of the work was published in English, it had an impact on feminist scholarly thinking beyond Scandinavia. It inspired scholars to be explicit about the national and political backgrounds of the welfare states they studied. With the acknowledgment that there were distinct differences between liberal and social democratic state formations by the end of the 1980s, the project of building a general feminist theory of the state seemed to be abandoned (Pateman 1989; Allen 1990).

Variations in Welfare States

As differences and variations among welfare states came to the fore, many feminists adopted a comparative approach. A growing dialogue among scholars of different national backgrounds stimulated interest in cross-national differences in the mix of state, market, and family.

Mainstream considerations of welfare states constituted a starting point for many feminist scholars. In particular, the power resource theory of welfare states (Esping-Andersen and Korpi 1987; Esping-Andersen 1990) drew attention to the market-modifying forces of welfare states and their capacity to mitigate class inequality. It also paid attention to the degree to which state benefits are provided as citizens' rights (Esping-Andersen 1990:21). A focal point of the power resource school was the rejection of the hitherto dominant theory of the emergence of welfare states, which had seen them as a by-product of the industrialization process. The qualitative innovations of the power resource school were its shift of explanatory variables from the economy to politics and its focus on differences among welfare states instead of similarities. Empirically, the focus moved from the level of social expenditures to the effects for individuals of income transfers such as old-age pensions and unemployment benefits.

Central to this approach was the idea that different class alliances, as they had crystallized at the governmental level, had produced different welfare state models with varying levels of stratification. A leading theme was the impact of social policy on stratification, but also, conversely, whether the welfare state is a system of stratification in its own right. The comparative mainstream approach devised typologies for understanding patterns of variations among welfare states. One of the most cited examples was Esping-Andersen's (1990) clustering of 18 Western democracies into three welfare regimes: liberal, conservative, and social democratic. These regimes are characterized by different configurations of the three societal arenas—market, state, and the family—in the solution of social problems. Although all three regimes regard a market economy with some degree of state intervention as desirable and ascribe some importance to the family in the solution of social problems, each tends to highlight the role of one of these arenas. The liberal welfare regime above all seeks to keep market forces sovereign. Much more than the others, the conservative regime highlights the role of the family, and the social democratic regime has extended the role of the state far more than the two other models. The archetypical examples of the liberal regime are the United States, Canada, and Australia, where the welfare state is characterized by predominantly means-tested benefits, modest universal transfers, and modest social-insurance plans. The conservative regime type is found in Austria, France, Germany, and Italy, where rights are attached to class and status, and compulsory insurance schemes tied to the labor market prevail. Their strong belief that the state should interfere only when the family's capacity to solve social problems and take care of its members is exhausted is called the *principle of subsidiarity.* The social democratic welfare state, exemplified by the Scandinavian countries, has pursued equality among the classes through its policies, and it has enacted many universal benefits based on citizens' rights. Some benefits are graduated according to accustomed earnings, and family costs are socialized (Esping-Andersen 1990:26ff.).

The three regimes exhibit varying degrees of decommodification, which is a key concept for the power resource school. It measures the degree to which social rights "permit people to make their living standards independent of pure market forces" (Esping-Andersen 1990:3). The liberal regime minimizes decommodification, whereas the universalistic programs in Scandinavia are highly decommodifying. The conservative regime falls in between.

A striking number of feminists took up the ideas of the power resource school because this approach coincided with their dominant theoretical and empirical interests. First, it constituted a break with economic determinism and the simplistic approach to the state that had colored the first wave of feminist scholarship. Second, it provided conceptual tools for grasping the national differences among welfare states in relation to gender that had emerged as significant in the second wave. Third, decommodification as a key concept of the power resource school centered on one of the recurrent threads of feminist thinking, namely, the notion of dependence and independence. Yet gender received scant attention from the mainstream power resource school. In the 1990s, numerous feminist critiques emerged, showing how the conceptual framework was unsuited to examine how welfare states shape gender relations. They pointed to the fact that not only was the theory gender-blind, it had also been generated from a male standpoint, taking a male worker with a dependent family as the standard case.

Above all, feminists critiqued the overwhelming focus on the state-market nexus, and the concomitant neglect of the family as producer of welfare goods and services (Lewis 1992; Orloff 1993; Sainsbury 1994). The mainstream concept of decommodification focused solely on the state-market nexus and so did not adequately describe the interplay among state, market, and family, and the issue of independence for women. Mainstream analysis ignored the role of unpaid labor and the implications of women's responsibility for care of dependent persons for their position on the market (Sainsbury 1994). Lewis (1992) and Ostner (1994) put it well when they stated that women enter mainstream analysis only when they enter the labor market, and disappear again when they leave it.

On the empirical level, feminists argued that the centrality of income maintenance flawed Esping-Andersen's analysis, because the availability of public services, and especially care for small children, the sick, and the elderly, is crucial for the position of women. Welfare states vary considerably as to the level and content of these services, and the patterns of variation do not always correspond to the patterns of variation in income maintenance. The Dutch welfare state illustrates this point well. It has a high level of spending on income maintenance, and, in Esping-Andersen's analysis, it comes close to the social democratic cluster. However, its level of public services has been relatively low, and this has been especially true for child-care provision. The generous social security benefits in the Netherlands were designed to replace a family income, because these policies have been fundamentally structured by a breadwinner-caretaker family model (Bussemaker and Kersbergen 1994; Knijn 1994; Sainsbury 1996). When these kinds of benefits are examined, and when the situation of women is considered, the Netherlands looks more like a conservative state, and the basic assumptions of how welfare states cluster are challenged.

Broadly speaking, feminist critics responded in two different ways to the gender blindness of the power resource model. One strand sought to refashion the theory, whereas another proposed alternative typologies. Among those reframing the theory, Orloff (1993) suggested the incorporation of additional variables: the role of the family, gender stratification, access to paid work, and the ability to form autonomous households. By this she meant the possibility for women "to survive and support their children without having to marry to gain access to breadwinner's income" (p. 319). In a similar vein, O'Connor (1993) proposed that the concept of decommodification should be supplemented by the concept of personal autonomy, arguing that autonomy varies according to the range of services that insulate individuals both from personal dependence on family members and from public dependence on state agencies.

Among those proposing alternative typologies, Ostner and Lewis argued that the strength or weakness of the male breadwinner role, or the centrality of the family wage, serves as a predictor of the way in which women are treated in social systems. They categorized West European welfare states as strong, medium, or weak breadwinner states. A strong breadwinner model prescribes earning for men and homemaking for women, and tends to draw a firm dividing line between public and private responsibility for care work. Britain, Germany, and the Netherlands are the prime examples. A moderate breadwinner model was found in France, where women had been recognized as mothers as well as workers. Sweden and the other Nordic countries exemplified the weak breadwinner model, which has prevented a public-private dichotomy (Lewis, 1992; Lewis and Ostner 1994).

Lewis and Ostner's typology had a clear preliminary character, which they themselves admitted, but it did serve as a point of departure for many scholars. Sainsbury (1996) critiqued and expanded on their approach by distinguishing between a breadwinning model and an individual model. She stressed these different bases for entitlement as critical for women's dependence and autonomy and underlined variations in patterns of individualization and familism, expressed in the way social benefits are directed toward individuals or families. The first implies that women and men (and sometimes children) are entitled to benefits individually. The latter has often involved benefits directed to the man as head of household. In her comparison of the United Kingdom, the United States, the Netherlands, and Sweden, Sainsbury demonstrated that it is crucial for women whether their entitlements are derived from their status as wives, mothers, or workers. She found that individualization furthered women's independence, but also involved some pitfalls if state policies do not encourage women's labor market participation and if adequate day-care facilities are not provided.

Rethinking the typologies of welfare states has also directed attention to variations in the extent to which women are responsible for care of dependent persons such as small children, the sick, and the elderly (Ungerson 1990; Lewis and Ostner 1994; Sainsbury 1994). One interpretation of the extension of public responsibility for care, notably in the Scandinavian countries, was that this implied an emptying of functions in the family, or that reproduction had gone public. Yet, in a thought-provoking article, Balbo (1987) argued that tasks were not simply transferred from the family to the state. Applying the metaphor of patchwork, she argued that when some of these tasks are removed from the family, a lot of adapting is needed to satisfy human needs, and this servicing work is still done by women.

Feminist studies of countries belonging to the same clusters have revealed considerable variations (O'Connor 1999; Leira 1993). In this way, the feminist paradigm has contributed to the ongoing discussion of the relevance of the regime typology. Many scholars have reached the conclusion that it is not possible to capture all aspects of the effects of regimes on different groups of women and men using one-dimensional typologies.

The emphasis on typologies has also led feminists to ask whether welfare states are becoming more similar or more different. A factor that may affect trends toward convergence or divergence is the restructuring process that most welfare states in the West have been undergoing during the past decade. Many feminists argue that the trend toward privatization of public activities, in the direction of both the market and the family, hits women disproportionally, because more women than men are public employees, clients of welfare, and consumers of public services (Hernes 1987; Lewis and Ostner 1994; Borchorst 1994).

Single mothers have often been chosen as the focus of feminist analysis of welfare states. They constitute a strategic group to illustrate how welfare state policies affect gender relations, because they are not engaged in a gender-determined division of care and breadwinning, and often appear as a problematic group in public discourse (Gordon 1994; Knijn 1994; Hobson 1994; Hobson and Lewis 1997). Comparisons among welfare states and their policies toward single parents reveal great variation. In some countries, they are much more likely to be poor than in others, and in some countries stigmatization and control are much more evident than in others. Single mothers seem to fare best when their labor market participation is high and when benefits and services are universalized (Sainsbury 1996; Hobson and Lewis 1997).

In sum, by the 1990s, feminist research on welfare states had turned comparative, corresponding to the trend in mainstream research, even though there are still few systematic comparative studies from a gender point of view. Feminist scholarly studies of the welfare state constituted an important corrective to the power resource school. The bottom line of the feminist argument was that the neglect of gender, the family, and public services distorts understanding of their similarities and differences and so obscures important aspects of welfare states. The inclusion of gender provides a more sophisticated understanding of the effects of social benefits for the welfare of women, men, and children. A weakness of the feminist comparative paradigm, which also colors part of the mainstream literature, is the overwhelming focus on recipients—the role of women as policy takers, rather than as policy makers.

Gendered Citizenship and the Welfare State

During the late 1980s and the 1990s, citizenship emerged as a core concept in the discussions of welfare states. The key elements of the concept are rights and obligations tied to membership in a community. The concept is both descriptive and normative in essence, and it is embodied in a broader discussion of political thought and theories of democracy. In this context, I will concentrate on the social aspects of the conception.

The citizenship tradition revolves around the thinking of Marshall (1964), who defines citizenship as a "status bestowed on those who are full members of a community" (p. 92). He argues that three different types of citizenship developed in historical stages: Civil rights connected to individual freedom—for instance, freedom of speech and property rights—in the eighteenth century; political rights, notably the vote, in the nineteenth century; and social rights, including the right to a minimum of social and economic welfare, in the twentieth century.

Just as in the comparative welfare state literature, feminists rooted in the citizenship tradition have critiqued mainstream thought for overlooking women and omitting gender. Marshall sees social rights as a means to mitigate class inequality, and his approach does not encompass ethnicity, race, or gender. He only very superficially mentions the situation of women, and he does not explore whether citizenship implies the same rights and duties for all individuals. His de-emphasis of the situation of women is tied to the fact that the male worker serves as his ideal type of citizen, and his framework is constructed on a male norm. For example, Marshall ignores married women's lack of basic civil rights, such as rights over their persons, property, and children, in the mid-nineteenth century (Pateman 1996). A variety of feminist studies have shown that Marshall's sequence of citizenship rights does not hold in the case of women. Throughout the world, women obtained important social rights before they got political rights (Hernes 1987; Gordon 1990; Bock and Thane 1991; Koven and Michel 1993). Marshall excludes women's house and care work from his discussion of citizenship duties, and women are disproportionally excluded from social citizenship when his argument for social rights changes from asserting unconditioned rights to rights conditioned on employment (see Pateman 1996).

Different strands of political thought advocate very different interpretations of citizenship. Broadly speaking, three main traditions can be identified: a liberal, a republican, and a socialist. The three traditions differ in their perceptions of the balance between rights and duties, and they enshrine very different perceptions of the scope of citizenship, particularly with regard to the extent of social citizenship. The liberal tradition operates with a narrow concept of citizenship, stressing civil and political rights and the freedom of individuals. The republican tradition highlights obligation and active political citizenship. The socialist position has also been oriented toward rights, but treats substantive social rights as more salient than do the other two traditions. The social democratic notion of citizenship has been vested in a participatory, egalitarian ideal (Pateman 1989; Siim 1994; Lister 1998).

Feminists have been critical of all three traditions. They have demonstrated that the liberal tradition has been premised on a public-private split, a crucial aspect of which has been the gendered division of paid and unpaid work. Pateman (1989) notes that the key criterion of citizenship is independence, and liberal thought tends to perceive women as dependent and so second-class citizens. Republicanism is also problematic, because it is particularly demanding for women, who are disadvantaged by the gender division of time (Lister 1998). The socialist model operates with a dual model of citizenship, differentiating between citizenship for the carer and citizenship for the worker, who do not share equal rights (Leira 1989, 1993).

The approach to the state taken by feminists with a background in the liberal tradition and feminists rooted in the socialist tradition still differs perceptibly. Scholars with liberal backgrounds are more often negative toward state regulations, sometimes suggesting that public policies will simply replace women's dependence on individual husbands with control by a bureaucratic state. Scandinavian scholars are less skeptical of the state, and they more often talk about an interplay between women and the state, especially with regard to care. Despite these differences, feminists agree that women's dependence and independence constitute a key issue. Feminists have argued convincingly that the process of independence is different for men and women due to their different position on the market and in the family. Yet independence has many different connotations and may vary greatly in the way it is crystallized in public policies. What dependence *means* becomes a central problem for researchers.

Some argue that it is too simplistic to equate private and public dependence. Thus Hernes (1984:40) argues that dependence changes character when it becomes public and subject to regulation and support. This implies that different roles, such as client and caretaker, may produce different sorts of dependencies (Borchorst and Siim 1987). Although liberal feminists may think that the alternative to dependence on the state is personal autonomy, Siim (1988:175) argues it is more likely to be dependence on market forces.

Fraser and Gordon (1994) explore the stigmatizing and gendered meanings of dependency discourses in the American context. They identify four different registers of dependency: an economic, a political, a moral, and a psychological. They argue that the semantics of dependency have shifted in correspondence to different phases in the history of American welfare. In the contemporary policy discourse, they see two streams, one drawing on rhetoric of pauperism and the other relating to neoclassical economics. Similarly, Knijn (1994) argues that the concept of dependency contains both a structural and a personal aspect. She demonstrates that the Dutch welfare state supported autonomous motherhood for single mothers from the 1970s, but in the early 1990s the structural dependency of single mothers on the state came under attack. At that time a shift occurred from a care discourse to an individuation discourse, which claimed that single mothers should provide for themselves and their children. The discursive approach shows that the concept of dependency and its stigmatizing connotations change over time, and both Fraser and Gordon and Knijn argue for a redescription of the notion in order to allow new, emancipatory visions to emerge.

Women's independence also hinges on control over their bodies and their reproductive capacities. Women's abilities to participate in society as independent individuals are undermined by the control of their bodies in the family, the workplace, and public spaces (Orloff 1993:309). In the case of contraception, abortion, and child care, Pateman (1989) shows how rights have had a different meaning for women, and Shaver (1993) asserts that control over one's body has a taken-for-granted character for men, but not for women. In the case of policies toward woman battering, rape, and sexual harassment in Sweden and the United States, Elman (1996) reaches the interesting conclusion that the Swedish state rebuffs intervention on behalf of women in the case of sexual violence, whereas the United States has been more open to solutions to gender-specific oppression. She ascribes this to differences between the centralized Swedish state structure and the fragmented federalist American state.

Feminists have also engaged in the project of generating a gender-sensitive approach to citizenship. They argue that women's access to citizenship entitlements is not the same as men's, and that men and women make claims based on their different positions. Walby (1997) poses the question of whether the concept of citizenship is so imbued with gender-specific assumptions that it should be abandoned altogether, arguing that it has no significant meaning in the private sphere. Yet she also finds that it has the potential to explore varying degrees of social integration and participation as a national project. Some scholars also point to the problem that the citizenship conception is anchored in the context of nation-states. This excludes a global and transnational approach to differences in citizenship (Yuval-Davis, 1997). A crucial point of feminist thinking is to discuss how gender, race, and ethnicity intersect, thus bringing the issue of diversity among women to the fore. Some scholars have shown that welfare state policies often affect women differently, according to race, class, and ethnicity, and they have argued that much of feminist scholarship has tended to take a White, middle-class norm as its reference point (Mink 1990; O'Connor 1993, 1996; Lister 1998; Yuval-Davis, 1997). The issue of race and ethnicity has been particularly present in studies of the American and British welfare states, because it has been very visible in these countries.

Closely connected to this discussion is the issue of whether gender is a universal category or whether it should be deconstructed, as post-structural feminists argue. Whereas an essentialist approach to gender most certainly implies the fallacy of reducing women's identity to one single position and ignoring differences among women (Mouffe 1992), I agree with Lister (1998), who notes that a poststructuralist position may entail a danger "that 'woman' is simply deconstructed and left in fragments, there is no woman left to be a citizen" (p. 77).

Fraser (1989) adopts a discourse-oriented approach to how people make claims for social provision and points to the contested character of needs claims. Because the interpretation of people's needs is by no means unproblematic, or fixed by categories such as gender and race, it matters who defines needs and from what interests. Fraser shifts attention from distribution of needs satisfactions to "the politics of needs interpretation." She also challenges the idea that rights are inherently individualistic or bourgeois-liberal or that they should be separated from needs. She traces the role of women's agency in developing alternative interpretations of rights and advocates a translation of justified needs claims into social rights (p. 183).

In sum, a central issue for feminists has been how care fits into the configuration of citizenship rights and obligations. As Leira (1989) states, a concept of citizenship is lacking that "recognizes the importance of care to society and encompasses those citizens whose adult lives comprise both economic provision and caring commitments" (p. 208). Although some feminist scholars seek to replace an ethic of care with an ethic of rights, others have argued for a synthesis. The strength of the citizenship approach is that by tying together rights and duties, it provides an opportunity to look at state activities from above as well as from below. The concept of citizenship has proven to be fruitful in cross-national analyses of welfare states and is capable of encompassing variations in the relation between states and citizens, individually or collectively. Yet the concept is very fragmented and its meaning is contested, and it is telling that almost all dimensions of social life have been squeezed into this language. The concept thus tends to become slippery, especially if the underlying political theory is not made explicit.

Women's Agency, Materialism, and the Construction of Welfare States

In the 1990s, the role of women's agency has become a separate and important issue on the feminist research agenda. Most such studies have focused on the early history of welfare states, examining the parallel development of the women's movement and the welfare state in Western Europe and North America. This trend has stimulated interest in the welfare state among feminists in the United States, who had been less attracted to this topic than had feminist scholars in other countries (Gordon 1990:9).

Some feminists have been correcting the picture presented by mainstream historical scholarship, which had neglected social provisions targeted to women and mothers, and downplayed the fact that many women were struggling for social rights before they obtained the right to vote. As a response to these shortcomings, feminists have highlighted women's activities from the 1880s to the 1930s. They have concluded that women were a driving force in the enactment of maternity and family-centered policies as individual reformers in women's charity groups, religious groups, and women's rights organizations. Women reformers sought to obtain a recognition of women's role as mothers and to define the needs of mothers and children, and succeeded in transforming these needs into public policy. Feminist scholarship has also shown that women's groups and organizations by no means agreed on which policies to pursue. The reformers argued both for the right to be different from men without being discriminated against and, from an equality perspective, for the right to be treated the same (Gordon 1990; Bock and Thane 1991; Koven and Michel 1993).

Several scholars characterize women's politics during this period as "maternalism," but the conception has carried various meanings. Bock and Thane (1991) use the concept rather descriptively as a perspective on certain cultural, moral, and intellectual processes, whereas Koven and Michel (1993) focus their attention on discourse and ideology attached to care, nurturance, and morality. Koven and Michel identify two levels of operation of maternalism: the positive appraisal of private domesticity and the legitimation of women's "public relationship to politics and the state, to community, workplace, and marketplace" (p. 6). Gordon (1993) identifies three different components of maternalism: One is the conviction that women reformers should act in a motherly way toward the poor; the second is that their work, experience, and/or destiny as mothers qualifies them to lead reform campaigns; and the third is the idea that money should be given directly to women, and especially to single mothers (pp. 147f.). Hence maternalism has been used not only to characterize various aspects of women's agency, but also to differentiate ideas underlying the institution of policies and as a characteristic of the target group itself.

Several studies illustrate the ambiguous meanings and uses of the concept, historically as in the present. Throughout the early history of welfare states, different groups of women fought to define its content. In France, for example, a Catholic women's organization was successful in its efforts to get an unwaged mother's allowance, but the organization aligned its campaign with nationalist and pronatalist interests, and French feminists criticized how the issue was divorced from women's rights (Pedersen 1993).

Comparative studies particularly appear to stimulate explanations of the interplay between women's agency and the institution of benefits for mothers and children. Bock and Thane (1991) conclude on the basis of studies of European countries that authoritarian welfare states adopted polices that contrasted sharply with feminist maternalism, whereas women's needs were incorporated more readily in policy making in democratic welfare states, which were more receptive to women's movements. Koven and Michel (1993) hypothesize that strong states, defined as "those with well-developed domestic-welfare bureaucracies and long traditions of government intervention," such as Germany and France, allowed women's agency less space than weak states like the United States and, to a lesser extent, Great Britain. But they also find that countries where women's movements were weak also offered the least generous benefits for women and children before 1920 (pp. 24, 25). Skocpol (1992), however, finds the distinction between strong and weak states too crude to grasp the differences in women's agency and the variations in how responsive states were to women's organizations. She suggests that a more complex appraisal of state institutions, political systems, and patterns of political organization may be needed to explain differences in social policy making, for instance, between the United States and Britain (p. 37).

In the case of the United States, a particularly lively debate has taken place among scholars exploring the early history of social benefits. Scholars agree that a gender-differentiated system emerged in the United States relatively early compared with other countries, but never developed into a modern universal welfare state. Nelson (1990) emphasizes how a two-tier system of welfare provision developed from workman's compensation and mothers' aid during the Progressive Era, whereas Skocpol (1992) offers a more positive interpretation of the impact of maternalism, and argues that the United States came close to forging a maternalist welfare state largely administered by female professionals. She contends that maternalism, especially federations of local women's clubs, were more influential during the Progressive Era than paternalism, particularly in the form of unions, and points to three factors that contributed to the comparatively better opportunities afforded American maternalism: First, institutional religion did not constitute the same kind of restraint on women's voluntary associations as elsewhere; second, American women gained more and better education sooner than any other women in the world; and third, American women reacted more vigorously against their exclusion from politics (pp. 51f.).

Skocpol's analysis prompted debate around the question of how to evaluate the role of women's agency and how to interpret the impact of welfare provisions instituted during the Progressive Era. Wikander, Kessler-Harris, and Lewis (1995) emphasize that labor legislation for women in the United States offered the weakest set of protections of any industrial state, and they question whether the European welfare states were much more paternalistic than the American. Kessler-Harris (1995) notes that the female reformers stressed women's role as workers rather than as mothers, and she suggests that maternalism is not an adequate characterization of this period. She finds it suggestive that maternity leave was not introduced in the United States, as it had been in many European countries, and argues that the American legislation did less to protect motherhood than to remove women from the labor market. Gordon (1993) criticizes Skocpol for missing the gendered meaning of welfare strategies. In her view, Skocpol ascribes too much importance to formal politics and state actors, and too little to social-structural power relations such as race and class. Gordon sees the achievements of women during the Progressive Era as much more ambiguous in value than does Skocpol, and she underlines their stigmatizing legacy. These two scholars differ in the way they perceive gender relations, with Skocpol's (1993) theory of gender more implicit and based on a model that does "not bifurcate gender identities into 'male' and 'female'" (p. 169), whereas Gordon analyzes gender relations in a framework of structural inequality and emphasizes differences in power among women, particularly between reformers and recipients of benefits.

This debate over maternalism has accentuated the question of the impact women's agency has had on differences among women, particularly whether female reformers have fought for welfare provisions that turned out to foster discrimination against women. Gordon (1990:13f.) mentions protective labor legislation and AFDC as examples of this. Furthermore, many benefits that have been considered as reforms for women were accessible only for women of certain ethnic and racial backgrounds. Other benefits had different impacts on different social groups of women due to their different life situations. Mink (1990) demonstrates that benefits to mothers during the New Deal in the United States granted women some kind of social citizenship, but it was tied to women's dependency on men and implied a racially biased regulation of women's lives, notably in the South. Other scholars have shown that women administrators created innovative welfare approaches, like health visiting in Britain, but were also involved in controlling and regulating women from less privileged classes (Bock and Thane 1991; Koven and Michel, 1993).

Overall, the studies of maternalism suggest positive effects of women's agency during the early history of welfare states. Koven and Michel (1993) find that women's relationship not only to "civilization" but to each other, to men, to the state, and to society were dramatically changed, arguing that at least White, middle-class women thereby obtained an avenue into the state (p. 29). The studies also applaud maternalist policies that were enacted because they entailed political responsiveness toward women's and children's needs (Bock and Thane 1991; Koven and Michel 1993). Skocpol (1992:33) suggests that the achievements of maternalism during the Progressive Era in the United States implied a celebration of a universal civic value of mothering by mothers of all classes and races. Yet other scholars also point to the paradoxical legacy of maternalism, particularly with regard to the situation of poor women and women of other racial background than the White, middle-class reformers and bureaucrats. The celebration of motherhood also served to maintain the family wage system as a cornerstone of most societies, and thereby also confirmed women's dependency on men (Gordon 1990; Koven and Michel 1993).

Is the State Patriarchal?

In light of the research reviewed above, feminist scholars have asked whether patriarchy is a concept that can be usefully applied to states. Some feminists have pointed to the problem that patriarchy as a concept was originally designed to characterize rule by older men in a societal form quite different from today's, and urge that the concept be abandoned altogether (Barrett 1988; Dahlerup 1987; Gordon 1990; Watson 1990). Others, such as Pateman (1988) and Walby (1990), still see usefulness in the concept and are trying to expand its analytic capacity. Walby (1990, 1997) argues, for example, that the public and private types of patriarchy constitute a continuum rather than a dichotomy, and she has suggested an analytic separation of degree and forms of patriarchal power. Pateman (1988), who approaches the concept by means of classical political theory, contends that patriarchalism from the start has had two dimensions: the paternal, which relates to the father-son relation, and the masculine, which involves the husband-wife relation. She finds that the concept is "the only term with which to capture the specificities of the subjection and oppression of *women* and to distinguish this from other forms of domination" (p. 103). Both Pateman and Walby argue that the concept of patriarchy per se is not universalistic or ahistorical, nor does it discount the role of women's agency.

Any conception of male power, whether or not in terms of patriarchy, clearly needs to be historically contextualized as well as specific about what states are being discussed. Yet not all theorists provide the needed context or specificity. Some researchers highlight the controlling and bureaucratic aspects of the state. For example, Fraser (1989:154ff.) analyzes the American social welfare system as a juridical-administrative-therapeutic state apparatus that serves to disempower women, without specifying how broadly her model should be generalized. Pateman (1989) characterizes the British, American, and Australian welfare states as patriarchal welfare states that directly and indirectly have reinforced women's identity as men's dependents. Lewis and Ostner (1994) pick out certain European welfare states as strong breadwinner states, which have tended to draw a firm dividing line between public and private spheres. Marx Ferree (1995) suggests that the different identities and interests of the feminist movement in the two parts of the unified Germany relate to the existence of a public patriarchy in the former East Germany and a private in West Germany. Although the state can disempower women, the welfare state has also offered women political resources and potential for change (Piven 1990; Orloff 1993; Skocpol 1992). Australian scholars have pointed to positive experiences of women entering the political and bureaucratic arena of the Australian state in the 1970s and 1980s, particularly the role of the so-called femocrats and the machinery of women's policy (Watson 1990). In Scandinavian countries the edge of the hostility toward the state was taken off in the 1980s, when much of the scholarship stressed the empowerment of women and woman-friendly policies; however, Scandinavian scholars by no means offer merely a rosy picture of women's experiences with the welfare state. Indeed, many point to ambiguous experiences (Borchorst 1994; Siim 1988) or to the Janus-faced character of the welfare state (Leira 1989; Hirdmann 1990).

In sum, the differing evaluations of welfare states' effects on women's power to some extent reflect variations in the success of feminists in conquering different spaces in politics in different countries. This pattern also varies within specific countries over time. Contradictory forces may also be active simultaneously, and women's multi-statused relation to the state implies that they may benefit from some provisions, but not from others. Women of different generational, social, or racial backgrounds may also experience different effects of policies. The same types of policies may even produce different outcomes in different countries. The different views of feminist scholars may therefore derive not only from the fact that they study different countries, but also from the fact that they focus on different policies or different groups of women. Still, Dahlerup (1994) reaches the far-reaching conclusion that women in all industrialized and urbanized state formations with market economies need state intervention on their behalf, such as redistribution of money to single mothers, public services such as child-care facilities, and protection against physical violence. Her conclusion is based on the assumption that women have better possibilities of gaining power through the state than through the market.

Conclusions

Feminist thinking on gender and welfare states exhibits continuity as well as change. Continuity is evident in that the leading theme has been insistence on the salience of gender both as a dependent and an independent variable in the structuring of welfare states. Topics such as unpaid work, care, and dependency have been recurrent threads running through the feminist account. The research tradition has also undergone some fundamental changes since it emerged in the 1970s, and the theoretical and methodological approaches that have been adopted have become more differentiated and multifaceted. The objective of feminist scholarship on this topic has, on the one hand, been narrowed from generating a theory of the state in general to evaluating particular aspects of welfare state interventions. On the other hand, the empirical focus has been broadened, turning both comparative and historical. It has enriched the whole paradigm that welfare states are frequently analyzed in the light of their historical legacy and from a deeper knowledge of their specificity and resemblance to other welfare states. Thus feminist accounts have shifted from claims of generalized similarities to discussion and explanation of differences, with a simultaneous interest in recurrent patterns and tendencies toward convergence.

This research field has been greatly fertilized by the cross-national and cross-disciplinary dialogue among feminist scholars, particularly as studies are carried out to expand, test, and critique the conclusions of other scholars. Conceptions or findings by feminist as well as mainstream scholars have been put to the test and reformulated by others. Although many feminist scholars engage in dialogue with male colleagues within their disciplines, pessimists note that mainstream thinkers still avoid rendering gender an integral part of their analyses. Despite gender-neutral language, mainstream studies of the state still neglect the position of women and generalize from a male norm. Still, the cross-fertilization process continues, and optimists would anticipate that a more gender-sensitive analysis will emerge in the future.

In her impressive review of the feminist welfare state tradition, O'Connor (1996:104) claims that there has been a development from focusing on women to discussing gender. I find that this does not give an adequate picture of feminist research, because it is still mainly focused only on women. One reason is that when feminist scholars seek to incorporate gender, it often implies adding the missing female perspective or rethinking and reformulating conceptions that are generated from a male norm. Yet there does appear to be a trend toward analyzing gender, and this tendency will probably continue at the same time as feminist scholarship undoubtedly will insist on the need to undertake detailed examinations of particular aspects of women's experiences with the welfare state.

A major challenge for feminist thinking about the welfare state is to avoid essentialism, by not treating gender as a universal category, and at the same time to capture gender as a fundamental structuring principle in modern societies. Several scholars, notably those with American and British backgrounds, have engaged in the conceptualization of differences among women according to race, ethnicity, and class. They have demonstrated that race and class cannot simply be added to a gender-sensitive analysis. Instead, it is crucial to explore how gender, race, and class intersect in the welfare state. European scholars, especially Scandinavians, are latecomers in this area, presumably because the issue of race and ethnicity has not been considered salient in their countries. The increasing number of immigrants and refugees in Europe, as well as the urge to adopt more global perspectives on the distribution of welfare, contributes to the incorporation of this issue in all countries.

An intriguing final question is whether the academic and political branches of feminism can benefit from each other. This account has reflected disagreements about what constitutes reform and regress for women in terms of the impact of state intervention. In some cases, the same kinds of phenomena have been interpreted differently by feminist scholars in different countries and even within the same countries, among other things because we are dealing with complex changes that may have ambiguous effects or different impacts for different groups of women. This reflects the need for an ongoing cross-national (and, I would add, cross-disciplinary) dialogue among feminist scholars. In order to make sure that gender does not disappear from the welfare state agenda, and that potentials, paradoxes, and traps for feminist strategies for more gender-equalized welfare states are being thoroughly debated, it is, however, crucial that this discussion not be restricted to the academic level.

Note

1. There is a lot of confusion about which countries actually are part of Scandinavia. In this text, Scandinavia is considered to comprise Norway, Sweden, and Denmark. The Nordic countries include these three countries and Finland and Iceland.

References

Allen, Judith. 1990. "Does Feminism Need a Theory of the State?" Pp. 3-20 in *Playing the State: Australian Feminist Interventions,* edited by Sophie Watson. London: Verso.

Balbo, Laura. 1987. "Crazy Quilts: Rethinking the Welfare State Debate from a Woman's Point of View." Pp. 45-71 in *Women and the State: The Shifting Boundaries of Public and Private,* edited by Anne Showstack Sassoon. London: Hutchinson.

Barrett, Michèle. 1988. *Women's Oppression Today: The Marxist/Feminist Encounter.* London: Verso.

Bock, Gisela and Pat Thane. 1991. *Maternity and Gender Policies: Women and the Rise of the European Welfare States 1880s-1950s.* Cornwall: Routledge.

Borchorst, Anette. 1994. "The Scandinavian Welfare State: Patriarchal, Gender Neutral or Woman-Friendly?" *International Journal of Contemporary Sociology* 31:45-67.

Borchorst, Anette and Birte Siim. 1987. "Women and the Advanced Welfare State: A New Kind of Patriarchal Power?" Pp. 128-57 in *Women and the State: The Shifting Boundaries of Public and Private,* edited by Anne Showstack Sassoon. London: Hutchinson.

Bussemaker, Jet and Kees van Kersbergen. 1994. "Gender and Welfare States: Some Theoretical Reflections." Pp. 8-25 in *Gendering Welfare States,* edited by Diane Sainsbury. London: Sage.

Dahlerup, Drude. 1987. "Confusing Concepts—Confusing Reality: A Theoretical Discussion of the Patriarchal State." Pp. 167-81 in *Women and the State: The Shifting Boundaries of Public and Private,* edited by Anne Showstack Sassoon. London: Hutchinson.

———. 1994. "Learning to Live with the State. State, Market, and Civil Society: Women's Needs for State Intervention in East and West." *Women's Studies International Forum* 17, nos. 2-3:117-27.

Eisenstein, Zillah. 1981. *The Radical Future of Liberal Feminism,* New York: Longman.

———. 1983. "The State, the Patriarchal Family, and Working Mothers." Pp. 41-58 in *Families, Politics and Public Policy,* edited by Irene Diamond. New York: Longman.

Elman, R. Amy. 1996. *Sexual Subordination and State Intervention: Comparing Sweden and the U.S.* Providence, RI: Berghahn.

Esping-Andersen, Gøsta. 1990. *The Three Worlds of Welfare Capitalism.* Princeton, NJ: Princeton University Press.

Esping-Andersen, Gøsta and Walter Korpi. 1987. "From Poor Relief to Institutional Welfare States: The Development of Scandinavian Social

Policy." In *The Scandinavian Model: Welfare States and Welfare Research,* edited by Robert Erikson et al. Armonk, NY: M. E. Sharpe.

Ferree, Myra Marx. 1995. "Patriarchies and Feminisms: The Two Women's Movements of Post-unification Germany." *Social Politics* 2:10-24.

Fraser, Nancy. 1989. "Women, Welfare, and the Politics of Needs Interpretation." Pp. 144-60 in *Unruly Practices: Power, Discourse and Gender in Contemporary Social Theory,* edited by Nancy Fraser. Minneapolis: University of Minnesota Press.

Fraser, Nancy and Linda Gordon. 1994. " 'Dependency' Demystified: Inscriptions of Power in a Keyword of the Welfare State." *Social Politics* 1:4-31.

Gordon, Linda, ed. 1990. *Women, the State and Welfare.* Madison: University of Wisconsin Press.

———. 1993. "Gender, State and Society: A Debate with Theda Skocpol." *Contention* 2, no. 3:139-56.

———. 1994. *Pitied but Not Entitled: Single Mothers and the History of Welfare 1890-1935.* New York: Free Press.

Hartmann, Heidi I. 1981. "The Unhappy Marriage between Marxism and Feminism." Pp. 1-41 in *Women and Revolution,* edited by Lydia Sargent. Boston: South End.

Hernes, Helga. 1982. *Staten—kvinner ingen adgang?* Oslo: Universitetsforlaget.

———. 1984. "Women and the Welfare State: The Transition from Private to Public Dependence." Pp. 20-46 in *Patriarchy in a Welfare Society,* edited by Harriet Holter. Oslo: Universitetsforlaget.

———. 1987. *Welfare State and Woman Power.* Oslo: Norwegian University Press.

Hirdmann, Yvonne. 1990. *Demokrati och makt i Sverige.* Stockholm: Statens Offentliga Utredninger.

Hobson, Barbara. 1994. "Solo Mothers, Social Policy Regimes, and the Logics of Gender." Pp. 170-88 in *Gendering Welfare States,* edited by Diane Sainsbury. London: Sage.

Hobson, Barbara and Jane Lewis, eds. 1997. *Lone Mothers in European Welfare Regimes.* London: Jessica Kingsley.

Holter, Harriet. 1984. "Women's Research and Social Theory." Pp. 9-25 in *Patriarchy in a Welfare Society,* edited by Harriet Holter. Oslo: Universitetsforlaget.

Kessler-Harris, Alice. 1995. "The Paradox of Motherhood: Night Work Restrictions in the United States." Pp. 337-57 in *Protecting Women: Labor Legislation in Europe, the United States and Australia, 1880-1920,* edited by Ulla Wikander, Alice Kessler-Harris, and Jane Lewis. Urbana: University of Illinois Press.

Knijn, Trudie. 1994. "Fish without Bikes: Revision of the Dutch Welfare State and Its Consequences for the (In)Dependence of Single Mothers." *Social Politics* 1:83-105.

Koven, Seth and Sonya Michel, eds. 1993. *Mothers of a New World: Maternalist Politics and the Origins of Welfare States.* New York: Routledge.

Leira, Arnlaug. 1989. *Models of Motherhood: Welfare State Policies and Everyday Practices: The Scandinavian Experience.* Oslo: Institutt for Samfunnsforskning.

———. 1993. " 'The Woman-Friendly' Welfare State? The Case of Norway and Sweden." Pp. 49-71 in *Women and Social Policies in Europe: Work, Family and the State,* edited by Jane Lewis. Aldershot: Edward Elgar.

Lewis, Jane. 1992. "Gender and the Development of Welfare Regimes." *Journal of European Social Policy* 2, no. 3:159-73.

Lewis, Jane and Ilona Ostner. 1994. "Gender and the Evolution of European Social Policies." Zes-Arbeitspapier No. 4, Universität Bremen.

Lister, Ruth. 1998. *Citizenship: Feminist Perspectives.* New York: Macmillan.

Marshall, T. H. 1964. *Class, Citizenship and Social Development.* Chicago: University of Chicago Press.

McIntosh, Mary. 1978. "The State and the Oppression of Women." Pp. 254-89 in *Feminism and Materialism,* edited by Annette Kuhn and AnnMarie Wolpe. London: Routledge & Kegan Paul.

Mink, Gwendolyn. 1990. "The Lady and the Tramp: Gender, Race and the Origins of the American Welfare State." Pp. 92-122 in *Women, the State and Welfare,* edited by Linda Gordon. Madison: University of Wisconsin Press.

Mouffe, Chantal. 1992. "Feminism, Citizenship, and Radical Democratic Politics." Pp. 315-31 in *Dimensions of Radical Democracy,* edited by Chantal Mouffe. London: Verso.

Nelson, Barbara. 1990. "The Origins of the Two-Channel Welfare State: Workman's Compensation and Mothers' Aid." Pp. 123-51 in *Women, the State and Welfare,* edited by Linda Gordon. Madison: University of Wisconsin Press.

O'Connor, Julia S. 1993. "Gender, Class and Citizenship in the Comparative Analysis of Welfare State Regimes: Theoretical and Methodological Issues." *British Journal of Sociology* 44:501-18.

———. 1996. "From Women in the Welfare State to Gendering Welfare State Regimes." *Current Sociology* 44, no. 2:1-124.

O'Connor, Julia S., Ann Shola Orloff and Sheila Shaver (1999). States, Markets, Families: Gender, Liberalism and Social Policy in Australia, Canada, Great Britain and the United States. Cambridge, UK: Cambridge University Press.

Orloff, Ann Shola. 1993. "Gender and the Social Rights of Citizenship: The Comparative Analysis of Gender Relations and Welfare States." *American Sociological Review* 58: 303-28.

Ostner, Ilona. 1994. "Independence and Dependency: Options and Constraints for Women over the Life Course." *Women's Studies International Forum* 17, nos. 3/4:129-40.

Pateman, Carole. 1988. "The Patriarchal Welfare State." Pp. 231-78 in *Democracy and the State,* edited by A. Gutmann. Princeton, NJ: Princeton University Press.

———. 1989. *The Disorder of Women: Democracy, Feminism and Political Theory.* Cambridge, MA: Polity.

———. 1996. "Democratization and Citizenship in the 1990s: The Legacy of T. H. Marshal." Vilhelm Aubert Memorial Lecture, Institute for Social Research, Oslo.

Pedersen, Susan. 1993. "Catholicism, Feminism, and the Politics of the Family during the Late Third Republic." Pp. 246-76 in *Mothers of a New World: Maternalist Politics and the Origins of Welfare States,* edited by Seth Koven and Sonya Michel. New York: Routledge.

Piven, Frances Fox. 1990. "Ideology and the State: Women, Power, and the Welfare State." Pp. 250-264 in *Women, the State, and Welfare,* edited by Linda Gordon. Madison: University of Wisconsin Press.

Sainsbury, Diane, ed. 1994. *Gendering Welfare States.* London: Sage.

———. 1996. *Gender Equality and Welfare States.* Cambridge: Cambridge University Press.

Sargent, Lydia, ed. 1981. *Women and the Revolution: A Discussion of the Unhappy Marriage of Marxism and Feminism.* Boston: South End.

Shaver, Sheila. 1993. "Body Rights, Social Rights and the Liberal Welfare State. *Critical Social Policy* 13, no. 39:66-93.

Siim, Birte. 1988. "Towards a Feminist Rethinking of the Welfare State." Pp. 160-86 in *The Political Interests of Gender,* edited by Kathleen B. Jones and Ann G. Jónasdóttir. London: Sage.

———. 1994. *Det kønnede demokrati—Kvinders medborgeskab i de skandinaviske velfærdsstater.* Freia, tekst 12. Aalborg: Aalborg Universitycenter.

Skocpol, Theda. 1992. *Protecting Soldiers and Mothers.* Cambridge, MA: Harvard University Press.

———. 1993. "Soldiers, Workers, Mothers: Gendered Identities in Early U.S. Social Policy." *Contention* 2, no. 3:157-89.

Ungerson, Clare, ed. 1990. *Women and Community Care: Gender and Caring in Modern Welfare States.* Brighton: Wheatsheaf.

Walby, Sylvia. 1990. *Theorizing Patriarchy.* Cambridge: Basil Blackwell.

———. 1997. *Gender Transformations.* London: Routledge.

Watson, Sophie, ed. 1990. *Playing the State: Australian Feminist Interventions.* London: Verso.

Wikander, Ulla, Alice Kessler-Harris, and Jane Lewis. 1995. "Introduction." Pp. 1-27 in *Protecting Women: Labor Legislation in Europe, the United States and Australia, 1880-1920,* edited by Ulla Wikander, Alice Kessler-Harris, and Jane Lewis. Urbana: University of Illinois Press.

Wilson, Elizabeth. 1977. *Women and the Welfare State.* London: Tavistock.

Yuval-Davis, Nira. 1997. "Women, Citizenship and Difference." Presented at "The Causes of Women's Exclusion: Actors, Processes and Institutions," Seminar 2 of the EC Programme "Gender and Citizenship: Social Integration and Social Exclusion in European Welfare States," University of Turin, Italy, April 4-6, 1997.

CHAPTER 5

Gender and
the Global Economy

VALENTINE M. MOGHADAM

In what way does a gender perspective deepen our understanding of global economic processes? How has the recognition that women and men are differently situated in and affected by socioeconomic processes influenced economic thinking and policy making? As sociologists, how do we approach gender *theoretically* in relation to the global economy, and in terms of its intersection with class, race/ethnicity, and the state? In what sense are economic restructuring and globalization *gendered*?

The scholarship on gender and the global economy has advanced considerably since the early 1980s. It is produced mainly by researchers working in the interdisciplinary field originally known as women-in-development and now called gender and development. It builds on earlier research—carried out largely within national frameworks, utilizing ethnographic methods, and focused on underdeveloped or Third World societies—on the way the gender division of labor shapes women's roles in production and reproduction (e.g., Afshar 1985; Boserup 1987; Young, Walkowitz, and McCollough 1981). Advancement in the field has occurred partly because the dramatic economic changes of structural adjustment and globalization have forced researchers to examine the implications of those changes for women and

AUTHOR'S NOTE: For helpful comments on the first draft of this chapter, I am grateful to my colleague Maura Toro-Morn and to Myra Marx Ferree, Beth Hess, and Judith Lorber. My colleague Manfred Steger provided additional and cogent comments when I presented this material at our women's studies weekly seminar on globalization. The analysis and any deficiencies are mine.

gender relations, and partly because feminists are beginning to theorize the way that gender shapes some of these processes and is in turn affected by them.[1] The now prodigious body of knowledge produced by feminist social scientists on development, women, and gender has not only shaped the evolution of the field itself, but is having some influence on practitioners and policy makers in international development agencies such as the United Nations and, to a lesser degree, the World Bank. Moreover, gender issues are being considered by some development economists (e.g., Collier 1989; Drèze and Sen 1989; Haddad et al. 1995; Karshenas 1997; Taylor 1995) and macrosociologists (especially Sklair 1991; see also Chase-Dunn 1989).

Theoretical work on gender and the world economy is only in its early stages—and necessarily so, as empirical research documenting gender-specific effects has had to be carried out first in order to provide evidence for the generalizations and larger theoretical claims. Many more studies exist on the effects of economic processes on women (e.g., Afshar and Dennis 1992; Beneria and Feldman 1992; Joekes and Weston 1995) than on the way that gender is inscribed in the macroeconomy or in the social structure, hence shaping socioeconomic outcomes. Still, researchers have sought explanations for economic impacts in terms of gender relations, ideologies, or bias (e.g., Elson 1991; Fernandez-Kelly 1989; Moghadam 1993; Pearson 1992; Redclift and Stewart 1991). Feminist economists are beginning to engage their more conventional colleagues with theoretical models and empirical evidence about the gendered nature of macroeconomic policies and especially structural adjustment (see the contributions in "Gender and Structural Adjustment," 1995). Sociologists are also producing important works that explore the gender aspects of economic restructuring, the way that gender shapes the labor process, and the impact of women's employment on gender relations (Blumberg et al. 1995; Feldman 1992; Moghadam 1995; Tiano 1994; Ward 1990). Feminists are working individually and collectively on gender processes in a (capitalist) *world* economy, or they are explicitly situating their national studies in global developments.

The objective of this chapter is to show how a gender perspective deepens our understanding of the global economy and of how women and men are involved in and affected by the global economy. By *gender,* I mean an asymmetrical social relationship between women and men based on perceived sex differences, and an ideology regarding their roles, rights, and values as workers, owners, citizens, and parents. The differential positions of women and men in the spheres of production and reproduction reflect the social relations of gender and are perpetuated by gender ideologies, whereas economic differences among women result from the inequalities of class and ethnicity, structured by the mode of production. By *global economy*, I mean the increasingly integrated and interdependent system of capital-labor flows across regions, between states, and through transnational corporations and international financial institutions, in the form of capital investments, technology transfer, financial exchanges, and increased trade, as well as the various forms of the deployment of labor, by which global accumulation takes place. The regions across and within which capital accumulation takes place may be understood in terms of geographic units (e.g., Latin America, sub-Saharan Africa, Southeast Asia, North America), in terms of income levels (high-, middle-, and low-income countries) or stages of industrialization (developing/industrializing countries—the South; developed/postindustrial countries—the North), or in terms of the economic zones of the world-system (core, periphery, and semiperiphery). All of these imply uneven development and unequal power relations. In illuminating the gender dynamics of economic and employment processes at the global level, I will focus in this chapter on structural adjustment in developing countries, the transition to a market economy in the former socialist world, recession and unemployment in the developed countries, the increasing labor force participation of women, and the growing informalization of labor arrangements. This focus on structure will be complemented in the final section by attention to expressions of women's agency, including the emergence of women's organizations and transnational networks that are responding to global economic issues.

The Global Economy: Economic Restructuring and Globalization

It may be useful to begin this discussion by outlining the main features of the contemporary global economy, in order that the gender aspects, as well as the contributions of gender analysis, be understood in their context.[2] What follows is a descriptive account.

The term *global economy* has gained currency because of the increasingly integrated processes of production and trade and the rapidity with which financial transactions occur across borders and regions. These are made possible by advances in information technologies and in transportation, by expanded forms of investment, and by the end of protectionist trade regimes through new agreements such as the Uruguay Round and the formation of the World Trade Organization. There has been much discussion in recent years of two dimensions of the global economy: economic restructuring and globalization. *Economic restructuring* refers to changes in the organization of production, and may take place at the global, regional, national, or firm level. *Globalization* refers to the outward-oriented and transnational nature of economic activity, the importance of national competitiveness, and the increasing integration of markets, all of which have employment, price, and wage implications. These processes have taken place through a number of interrelated processes at the regional and national levels.

In developing countries there has been a shift from an exclusive concentration on the extraction and export of raw materials and on agricultural production to the production of manufactured goods and the growth of the services sector. The earlier strategy of import-substitution industrialization, which favored the production of intermediate-level capital goods and consumer products for the home market, has been replaced by a strategy that favors the production of goods for export to world markets. In particular, newly industrialized countries (NICs) have effected the transition from agrarian, peasant, and low-income countries to industrialized, proletarianized, and upper middle-income countries. The first generation of these countries—South Korea, Taiwan, Hong Kong, and Singapore—began as producers of cheap and sometimes low-quality goods but now export sophisticated products. They are also investing in other developing countries; for example, Vietnam is now a site for capital investments from South Korea, Hong Kong, and Taiwan, mainly in textiles, handicrafts, and tourism. Among developing countries, the industrializing countries are the most integrated in the global economy, but other Asian economies that are advancing rapidly include Malaysia, Thailand, the Philippines, and China. There, qualified but cheap labor and competitive goods attract considerable foreign investment from the North as well as from the NICs. The first- and second-generation NICs have formed their own regional economic institution, the Association of Southeast Asian Nations. In other regions, such as Latin America, foreign investments and domestic capital investments have contributed to the expansion of competitive industries, such as Brazil's shoe manufacturers, who exports to world markets.

A principal player in the global economy is the transnational corporation, now numbering some 40,000 parent firms and some 250,000 foreign affiliates. Most of the stock of foreign direct investment flows among the United States and the North American Free Trade Agreement (NAFTA) countries (Canada and Mexico), the countries of the European Union, and Japan, with significant flows also between Japan and Southeast Asia. China receives a substantial amount of foreign investment, accounting for 40 percent of all flows into developing countries in 1994, and worth $34 billion (United Nations Conference on Trade and Development [UNCTAD] 1995:103).

Elsewhere in the developing world, and especially in sub-Saharan Africa and the Middle East, countries are less integrated into the global economy or remain on the periphery because their trade regimes are still restricted and intraregional trade is limited, or because of political instability or the relative underdevelopment of human resources. In addition, these two regions have suffered the consequences of high interest rates on loans from international commercial banks, the fall of commodities prices (e.g., oil and cocoa), and huge military expenditures. Africa has experienced deindustrialization as well as a number of debilitating civil conflicts. The Middle East and North Africa have seen the rise of fundamentalist movements that claim to offer religiously derived solutions to socioeconomic difficulties and cultural changes, including the reinstitutionalization of patriarchal gender relations (Moghadam 1994). Africa and the Middle East receive far smaller shares of total world investment than do other regions. In 1994, the value of foreign investment in the Middle East and Africa (including North African as well as sub-Saharan countries) was $34.5 billion and $53.1 billion, respectively. This compares with $186.2 billion in Latin America and the Caribbean and $305.1 billion in East, South, and Southeast Asia (see UNCTAD 1995, table 5:112-13).

Integration into the global economy is being touted as the only solution to economic crisis and as the only path to economic growth open to developing countries, given the end of the communist bloc and its alternative socialist economic system. As a first step toward global economic integration, countries are encouraged to implement structural adjustment policies, which aim to balance budgets and increase competitiveness through trade and price liberalization. In order to reduce the public sector wage bill and encourage growth of the private sector, developing countries have denationalized state holdings, privatized social services, invited foreign investment, and promoted exports. The international financial institutions, especially the World Bank and the International Monetary Fund, are the chief instigators of this free market policy shift, known as neoliberal economics. These institutions have clout because of the very favorable terms they offer when extending loans to developing countries. Structural adjustment policies were first implemented in some African and Latin American countries as a result of the debt crisis of the early 1980s. They were extended to other countries, including Malaysia, in the mid-1980s, and they were adopted in a number of Middle Eastern countries, including Jordan and Egypt, in the 1990s.

Structural adjustment has been a very controversial topic in the development studies literature; some development economists find that it has worked in some places but not in others, whereas other economists have regarded the entire turn to be a disaster for national sovereignty and for people's well-being. The feminist literature on development has been especially critical, charging structural adjustment with carrying out its objectives on the backs of the poor and especially poor women. They have had to assume extra productive and reproductive activities in order to survive the austerities of adjustment and stabilization policies, including higher prices, and to compensate for the withdrawal or reduction of government subsidies of food and services.

Integration into the global economy has also extended to the former socialist world. The centrally planned economies of Eastern Europe and the Soviet Union once had their own system of production, trade, and assistance, along with their own economic institutions. These extended benefits not only to socialist developing countries such as Vietnam and Cuba, but also to a number of friendly developing countries. That system was dissolved between 1989 and 1991, and the former socialist countries began the process of transition to a market economy and integration in the capitalist global economy.

In the developed world, integration has meant increased foreign investments to developing countries through bilateral and multilateral agreements, the formation of regional blocs such as NAFTA and the European Union (EU), the relocation of production sites to developing countries, and the shift from assembly-line manufacturing to postindustrial, high-tech service economies. Inequalities have widened in many developed countries, most dramatically in the United States, and unemployment has increased in EU countries. These developments have led to calls for more protection of declining industries and regulation of immigration, and opposing calls for the free flow of capital and of immigrant labor.

The adverse effects of economic restructuring have been felt within all regions, and especially by their respective labor forces. With increased trade, the prices of imported goods often compete with the prices of domestic products, forcing domestic capitalists to attempt to cut labor costs. In the developed countries, as plants relocate to sites elsewhere in search of cheaper costs of labor and production, jobs disappear and wages erode in the declining industrial sectors. As the developed countries shift from manufacturing to high-tech services, blue-collar unemployment grows, along with the expansion of part-time and temporary jobs at the expense of the kind of stable employment that men came to expect during "the golden age of capitalism" (Marglin and Schor 1990). Developing countries have seen a shift from internally oriented to externally oriented growth strategies and the shrinkage of large public sectors and nationalized industries. The result has been an expansion of informal sectors and self-employment. In both developing and developed regions, the stable, organized, and mostly male labor force has become increasingly "flexible" and "feminized." In most of the former socialist world, restructuring has led to loss of output, the creation of unemployment, and increased poverty.

What role does gender play, and how does a gender perspective advance our understanding of these economic processes?

Restructuring, Women's Labor, and Gender Ideology

Through institutions such as the transnational corporation and the state, the global economy generates capital largely through the exploitation of labor, but it is not indifferent to the gender and ethnicity of that labor. Gender and racial ideologies have been deployed to favor White male workers and exclude others, but they have also been used to integrate and exploit the labor power of women and of members of disadvantaged racial and ethnic groups in the interest of profit making. In the current global environment of open economies, new trade regimes, and competitive export industries, global accumulation relies heavily on the work of women, both waged and unwaged, in formal sectors and in the home, in manufacturing, and in public and private services. This phenomenon has been termed the "feminization of labor." Standing (1989) has hypothesized that the increasing globalization of production and the pursuit of flexible forms of labor to retain or increase competitiveness, as well as changing job structures in industrial enterprises, favor the feminization of employment in the dual sense of an increase in the numbers of women in the labor force and a deterioration of work conditions (labor standards, income, and employment status). Women have been gaining an increasing share of many kinds of jobs, but in the context of a decline in the social power of labor and growing unemployment, their labor market participation has not been accompanied by a redistribution of domestic, household, and child-care responsibilities. Moreover, women are still disadvantaged in the new labor markets in terms of wages, training, and occupational segregation. They are also disproportionately involved in forms of employment increasingly used to maximize profits: temporary, part-time, casual, and home-based work. Generally speaking, the situation is better or worse for women depending on the type of state and the strength of the economy. Women workers in the welfare states of Northern Europe fare best, followed by women in other strong Western economies. In Eastern Europe and the former Soviet Union, the economic status of working women changed dramatically for the worse following the collapse of communism. In much of the developing world, a class of women professionals and workers employed in the public sector and in the private sector has certainly emerged due to rising educational attainment, changing aspirations, economic need, and the demand for relatively cheap labor. However, vast numbers of economically active women in the developing world lack formal training, work in the informal sector, have no access to social security, and live in poverty.

Proletarianization

As world markets have expanded, a process of female proletarianization has taken place. In developing countries—and especially in Southeast and East Asia, parts of Latin America and the Caribbean, and Tunisia and Morocco—more and more women have been drawn into the labor-intensive and low-wage textile and garment industries, as well as into electronics and pharmaceuticals, which produce both for the home market and for export. The surge in women's waged employment in developing countries began in the 1970s, following an earlier period of capitalist development and economic growth that was characterized by the displacement of labor and craft work, commercialization of agriculture, and rural-urban migration (see Boserup 1987). Some have called the earlier marginalization of women "housewife-ization" (Mies 1986); others have described it as the "U pattern" of female labor force participation in early modernization.

During the 1970s, it was observed that export processing zones along the U.S.-Mexico border and in Southeast Asia, established by transnational corporations to take advantage of low labor costs in developing countries, were hiring mainly women (Elson and Pearson 1981; Nash and Fernandez-Kelly 1983). By the early 1980s, it was clear that the new industrialization in what was then called the Third World was drawing heavily on women workers. Many studies by women-in-development specialists and socialist feminists centered on the role played by the available pool of relatively cheap female labor. Gender ideologies emphasizing the "nimble fingers" of young women workers and their capacity for hard work, especially in the Southeast Asian economies (Heyzer 1986; Lim 1985), facilitated the recruitment of women for unskilled and semiskilled work in labor-intensive industries at wages lower than men would accept, and in conditions that unions would not permit. In South Korea in 1985, women's earnings were only 47 percent of equivalent men's earnings; in Singapore, the figure was 63 percent (Pearson 1992:231). In Latin America, women entered the labor force at a time when average wages were falling dramatically. Around the world, women's share of total industrial labor rarely exceeds 30 to 40 percent, but "the percentage of women workers in export processing factories producing textiles, electronics components and garments is much higher, with figures as high as 90% in some cases" (Pearson 1992:231). A 1984 study of the export promotion zone in Bombay, India, showed that 98 percent of its workers were women (Shah et al. 1994:WS-42). Studies commissioned by INSTRAW, a U.N. agency, led Joekes to conclude that "exports of manufactures from developing countries have been made up in the main of the kinds of goods normally produced by female labor: industrialization in the post-war period has been as much *female* led as *export* led" (Joekes and INSTRAW 1987:81).

Professionalization

The process of the feminization of labor continued throughout the recessionary 1980s, not only in the manufacturing sector, but also in public services, where throughout the world women's share has grown to 30 to 50 percent—at a time when public sector wages, like industrial wages, have been declining. It is significant that in Iran, Egypt, and Turkey, women's share of public service employment (including jobs as teachers and university professors in public schools and state universities, nurses and doctors in state hospitals, and workers and administrators across the ministries) has increased at a time when salaries have eroded tremendously. At the same time, the more lucrative and expanding private sector is absorbing more men (Moghadam 1998).

The proletarianization and professionalization of women have cultural repercussions and sometimes entail gender conflicts. During the 1980s, the increasing participation of women in the labor force in Middle Eastern countries was accompanied by subtle and overt pressures on them to conform to religious dictates concerning dress. Hence in Egypt, many professional women came to don modest dress and to cover their heads. One may hypothesize that in the earlier stage of the Islamist movement, the influx of women in the workforce raised fears of competition with men, leading to calls for the redomestication of women, as occurred immediately after the Iranian revolution. In the current stage, with the labor force participation of women now a fait accompli, Islamists in Turkey, Iran, Egypt, Sudan, and Yemen are not calling on women to withdraw from the labor force—indeed, many of their female adherents are educated and employed—but they do insist on veiling and on spatial and functional segregation. Only the most determined and secular women resist these pressures as they seek employment in public and private services.

As world trade in services has increased and global firms engage in outsourcing, the involvement of women in various occupations and professions of the service sector has grown. Women around the world have made impressive inroads into professional services such as law, banking, accounting, computing, and architecture; into tourism-related occupations; and into information services, as offshore airline booking agents, mail order and credit card service operators, word processors for publishers, telephone operators, and so on. The world trade in services also favors women's labor migration, in contrast to the demand for men manufacturing workers during the earlier periods of industrialization in Europe and the United States. Mexican, Central American, and Caribbean women have migrated to the United States to work as nurses, nannies, and domestics; Filipinas and Sri Lankans have gone to neighboring countries as well as to the Middle East to work as waitresses, nurses, nannies, and domestics; Argentine women have traveled to Italy to work as nurses; and an increasing number of Moroccan, Tunisian, and Algerian women have migrated alone to work in various occupations in France, Italy, and Spain.

The surge in women's employment is not only characteristic of developing countries. In 16 European countries, the increase in the number of women in the labor force from 1983 to 1991 was quite dramatic, whereas it was relatively modest for men. In six countries, the number of employed men actually fell during this period, most significantly by 3.4 percent in Belgium (European System of Documentation on Employment 1994:11-14). Moreover, the feminization of labor denotes not only the influx of women into relatively low-paying jobs, but the growth of part-time and temporary work among *men*, especially in New Zealand, the United Kingdom, and the Netherlands, mainly in retail trade, hotels and catering, banking, and insurance (United Nations 1991:190). Indeed, in the Netherlands, men's part-time work in 1992 was as high as 13.4 percent of total male employment, up from 5.5 percent in 1979 (UNESCO 1995).

The Nordic countries, including Finland, now have the highest rate of employment among women, with North America following close behind. Scandinavian women moved into the labor market in the 1960s and 1970s mainly through part-time jobs. (In Finland, women work in full-time jobs.) Yet in this region such work, most of it in the public sector, is characterized by normal working conditions, regularized pay, permanent employment, and social security. Kvande and Rasmussen (1994) describe the changes in the labor market in Norway as "the women's revolution." They argue that restructuring has led to a growth in jobs for women rather than for men, and point out that unemployment rates are higher for men than for women. Indeed, in Norway's postindustrial society, "women have moved into the labor market, often with the aid of welfare facilities to help take care of dependents whether they are young, old or disabled" (p. 6). They conclude that these radical changes in the labor market could fundamentally alter gender relations in Norway; state policies have in turn encouraged fathers to engage in full-time child care by raising the financial compensation for parental leave.

The Informal Sector

At the same time that women have been entering the formal labor force in record numbers in the developed countries, much of the increase in female labor force participation in developing countries has occurred in the informal sectors of the economy. The informal sector is usually defined as that which is outside the purview of the state and social security. Unregistered and small-scale urban enterprises, homework, and self-employment may fall into this category, and they include an array of commercial and productive activities. The extent of the urban informal sector and its links to the formal sector are matters of dispute, and women's involvement in it have not always been captured in the official statistics. Official statistics have traditionally overlooked women in the agricultural sector, and only in recent years have developing countries corrected this. For example, Egypt's 1988 labor force sample survey included a new questionnaire that discovered many more women in agriculture and urban informal services (Moghadam 1998). Similarly, in India, the total work participation rate for women increased between 1981 and 1991, a function partly of better enumeration of women in the urban informal and rural sectors of the economy (Shah et al. 1994:WS-41).

In the urban areas of developing countries, many formal jobs have become "informalized" as employers seek to increase "flexibility" and lower labor and production costs through subcontracting, as Beneria and Roldán (1987) show in their study of Mexico City. The growth of informalization is observed also in developed countries (Fernandez-Kelly and Garcia 1989). Drawing on existing gender ideologies regarding women's roles, their attachment to family, and the perceived lower value of their work, subcontracting arrangements encourage the persistence of home-based work. Many women accept this kind of work— with its insecurity, low wages, and absence of benefits—as a convenient form of income generation that allows them to carry out domestic responsibilities and care for children; some deny that it is "work," preferring to call it a hobby or a form of amusement, in order not to counter cultural codes or gender ideologies that idealize housewifery (see Cinar 1994; Dangler 1994; MacLeod 1996). One study comparing the work patterns and self-definitions of dressmakers and tailors in Rio de Janeiro's garment industry concluded that gender ideologies act on subcontracting practices to render men's work independent craft work, "while for women conditions of subordination bring their position closer to that of a typical wage worker" (Abreu and Sorj 1994:14). Informalization in developed and developing countries requires a gender perspective to understand "the process whereby employers seeking competitive edges in domestic and international markets can tap into not only 'cheap labor,' which is both female and male, but also into a substratum of labor, predominantly female, that is outside of formal relationships" (Fernandez-Kelly 1989:13). Table 5.1 provides data on nonwage employment—including agricultural activities—in a sample of developing countries.

TABLE 5.1

Shares of Men and Women Workers in Nonwage Employment (percentages of total)

Country	Year	Men	Women
Bolivia	1991	42	70
El Salvador	1991	28	48
Egypt	1989	46	74
Ghana	1989	69	92
Indonesia	1989	70	79
Korea, Republic	1991	38	43
Pakistan	1992	66	77
Peru	1991	39	55
Thailand	1989	71	76
Tunisia	1989	36	51
Turkey	1991	55	80

Source: World Bank (1995, table 11.3:73).

The Income Gap

The social relations of gender account for the pervasive income gap between men and women workers, a gap that is detrimental to women but lucrative to employers. On average, women earn 75 percent of men's wages (United Nations Development Program [UNDP] 1995:36), with Sweden, Sri Lanka, and Vietnam at the upper and more egalitarian end (90 percent) and Bangladesh, Chile, China, Cyprus, South Korea, the Philippines, and Syria at the lower and more unequal end (42-61 percent). The gender-based income gap is found mainly in the private sector, whereas the public sector tends to reward women more equitably. In Egypt, women's wages in the private sector are about half those of comparable men workers, whereas in the government sector women are paid the same as men (World Bank 1995:73). Some of the difference in the income gap is certainly based on lower education and intermittent employment among women workers, yet gender bias accounts for much of the difference in earnings. In some countries, women earn less than men despite higher qualifications, a problem that is especially acute in the private sector. For example, in Ecuador, Jamaica, and the Philippines, "women actually have more education and experience, on average, than men, but get paid between 20 and 30 percent less" (World

Bank 1995:45). Labor market segmentation along gender lines perpetuates the income gap. For example, in the computing and information processing sectors, the majority of high-skilled jobs go to male workers, and women are concentrated in low-skilled jobs (Pearson and Mitter 1993:50).

Unemployment

Considering the social relations of gender and the function of gender ideologies, it should come as no surprise that despite women's key role in the global economy, unemployment rates of women are very high. Global unemployment is partly a function of the nature of global economic restructuring itself, which has entailed massive retrenchment of labor in many developing countries, in the former socialist countries now undergoing marketization, and in the developed countries. Unemployment rates are especially high in Algeria, Jamaica, Jordan, Egypt, Morocco, Nicaragua, Poland, the Slovak Republic, and Turkey (World Bank 1995:29). Yet although men's unemployment is high, it is often higher for women (Moghadam 1995). In many developing countries unemployed women are new entrants to the labor force, who are seeking but not finding jobs (as in Egypt, Iran, Turkey, and Chile, where women's unemployment can be as high as 30 percent, compared with 10 percent for men). In certain countries where restructuring has occurred in enterprises employing large numbers of women, or in export sectors that have lost markets, the unemployment rates of women may also reflect job losses by previously employed women—as in Malaysia in the mid-1980s; Vietnam in the late 1980s; Poland, Bulgaria, and Russia in the early 1990s; and Morocco, Tunisia, and Turkey more recently. The fact that in Russia and Poland women's unemployment is higher than men's despite women's higher educational attainment and their long work experience is suggestive of the existence of gender bias in labor markets, often influenced by the gender ideology that men are primary breadwinners and more deserving of the better jobs.

A gender perspective also allows us to understand changes in the skill-designation and downgrading of jobs resulting from technical improvements. As noted above, many enterprises producing textiles and electronics, especially those for export, rely heavily on women workers. And yet as more sophisticated technology is used to produce these goods, women workers tend to be replaced by men or recruited at a slower pace, as appears to have been occurring in the Mexican *maquiladoras* (Sklair 1993) and in the textiles industries of Spain and Italy.

In all regions, high unemployment represents the downside of globalization and economic restructuring, especially for women workers, who must contend with not only the class biases but also the gender biases of free market economics. The feminization of unemployment, therefore, is as much a characteristic of the global economy as is the feminization of labor.

Summary

The above discussion highlights the ways in which women have been incorporated into the global economy as a source of relatively cheap labor. The simultaneous emergence and expansion of formal and informal employment among women can be explained in terms of labor market segmentation, various management strategies to extract surplus value or increase profitability, and the depressed status of unions. I have argued that the global economy is maintained by *gendered* labor, with definitions of skill, allocation of resources, occupational distribution, and modes of remuneration shaped by asymmetrical gender relations and by gender ideologies defining the roles and rights of men and women and of the relative value of their labor. But the effects have not been uniformly negative, for there have been unintended consequences of women's economic participation. Tiano (1994) and Kim (1997) provide detailed accounts of how women workers in the Mexican *maquilas* and in a South Korean free export zone, respectively, accommodate and resist the dominating forces of global capitalism and patriarchy. Others have shown that the entry of women into the labor force in large numbers has important implications for changes in gender relations and ideologies within the household and the larger society, and for women's gender consciousness and activism (Kahne and Giele 1992; Moghadam 1996; Safa 1996). I shall return to this point at the conclusion of this chapter.

Structural Adjustment and the
Feminization of Poverty: Making Gender Visible

Much of the development and economics literature on globalization and restructuring is largely devoid of any consideration of gender. In the sociology of development, standard texts do not integrate a gender dimension into their analyses (see, e.g., Booth 1994; Evans and Stephens

1988; Kincaid and Portes 1994). It has been up to feminist researchers to make women visible, and to show how women have been marginalized, segregated, and exploited by the development process. Subsequently, they have demonstrated the adverse implications for development projects of ignoring women's productive and reproductive roles. Currently, they are theorizing the relationship between gender and macroeconomic processes and mapping out strategies for transformation. Their contributions to a gender analysis of structural adjustment, which have come to influence policy makers, represent an important case in point.

As mentioned above, structural adjustment policies have been controversial in the development community. The now-classic UNICEF study *Adjustment with a Human Face* (Cornia, Jolly, and Stewart 1987) highlighted the social costs of adjustment and provided empirical evidence of the deterioration of social conditions in 10 countries undergoing adjustment. Subsequent studies found that there have been differential impacts on the various categories of the poor, including the "chronic" poor, the "borderline" poor, and the "new" or "working" poor. In the early 1980s, critical voices argued that adjustment and stabilization programs in developing countries were having particularly adverse effects on women. In September 1982, the U.N. Division for the Advancement of Women organized a meeting on "women and the international development strategy." One of the participants, Margarida da Gama Santos, a senior economist with the Ministry of Industry in Portugal, presented a prescient paper outlining the likely impacts of adjustment policies on women's employment patterns and on their household responsibilities (da Gama Santos 1985). She recognized that the gender division of labor and the differential positions of women and men in the spheres of production and reproduction would mean that the new policy shifts would lead to very different outcomes for women and men, although these gender differences would differ further by social class and by economic sector. In sum, the burden of adjustment falls on the urban poor, the working class, and women (see Elson 1991).

Structural adjustment policies—with their attendant price increases, elimination of subsidies, social service decreases, and introduction or increase of "user fees" for "cost recovery" in the provision of schooling and health care—heighten the risk and vulnerability of women and children in households where the distribution of consumption and the provision of health care and education favor men or income-earning adults. Structural adjustment causes women to bear most of the responsibility of coping with increased prices and shrinking incomes, because in most instances they are responsible for household budgeting and maintenance. Rising unemployment and reduced wages for men in a given household lead to increased economic activity on the part of women and children. This occurs also in households headed by women—an increasing proportion of all households in most regions. Household survival strategies include increases in the unpaid as well as paid labor of women, as discussed in the previous section. In Guayaquil, Ecuador, the proportion of wives working outside the household jumped from 45 percent to 95 percent during structural adjustment (World Bank 1995:106). In Ghana, women working in the informal sector saw their wages decline as excess labor released from formal employment moved into informal activities (World Bank 1995:107). In the Philippines, mean household size increased as relatives pooled their resources. One study found that the combined effects of economic crisis and structural adjustment in Peru led to a significant increase in poverty, with worse outcomes for households headed by women. According to Tanski (1994), who cites an official study: "In 1985-86, 16.9% of all male-headed households were poor and 17.4% of all households headed by women were poor. In 1990, 43.5% of all households headed by males were poor and 47.5% of all female-headed households were poor. . . . At the same time, there was a 1.2% increase in the proportion of households headed by females" (p. 1633). This global economic context was the focus of Standing's (1989) seminal paper on the feminization of labor and subsequent studies on the "feminization of poverty" (see Moghadam 1997; United Nations 1995).

The literature dealing with structural adjustment and women consists of empirical studies focusing on the unequal distribution of the burden of adjustment between men and women within households and labor markets (e.g., Afshar and Dennis 1992; Bakker 1994b; Beneria and Feldman 1992; Elson 1991; Sparr 1994; UNICEF 1989) and theoretical studies that challenge the presumed gender neutrality of theoretical and policy models (see Bakker 1994a; "Gender and Structural Adjustment" 1995). Why do economic crises and structural adjustment hurt women more than they do men? The reasons have to do with both the social relations of gender and the nature of market reforms. Intrahousehold inequalities, unequal allocation of resources, and the traditional gender division of labor within the home all contribute to the outcome. In some parts of the world, and especially in large patriarchal households, women do not enjoy the same relationship to their own labor as do men. They cannot organize and distribute their labor time as they see fit, they engage in considerable unpaid domestic labor, they may receive unequal amounts of food, and the products of their labor (including handicrafts and rugs) are often appropriated and disposed of by their husbands or fathers (see, e.g., Morvaridi 1992, on women agricultural workers in Turkey). Elsewhere, the decline in men's wages and increases in household poverty force women to seek employment or informal-type work. Poor parents may remove daughters from school to help at home or to bring in income. Labor market segmentation, low wages, and the lack of help for child rearing add to women's plight. Market reforms by their very nature place the burden of adjustment and change on labor; most vulnerable are women workers, whether they work in the formal or informal economy or in the home. Empirical evidence from Latin America, South Asia, sub-Saharan Africa, the Middle East, China, Vietnam, Central and Eastern Europe, and Russia confirms feminist criticisms of the gender bias in structural adjustment and economic liberalization more broadly. The effects of gender on the economy, and the effects of globalization and restructuring on women, include the following:

- Customary biases and intrahousehold inequalities lead to lower consumption by and fewer benefits for women and girls among lower-income groups.

- The mobility of labor that is assumed by free market economics and encouraged by structural adjustment policies does not take into account that women's geographic and occupational mobility is constrained by family and child-rearing responsibilities.

- The legal and regulatory framework often does not treat women as autonomous citizens, but rather as dependents or minors—with the result that in many countries women cannot own or inherit property, seek jobs, or take out loans without the permission of their husbands or fathers.

- Structural adjustment policies overstretch women's labor time by increasing women's productive activities (higher labor force participation due to economic need and household survival strategy) and reproductive burdens (in that women have to compensate in caregiving for cutbacks in social services). Working-class women and urban poor women are particularly hard hit.

- Because of women's concentration in government jobs in many developing countries, and because the private sector discriminates against women or is otherwise "unfriendly" to women and unwilling to provide support structures for working mothers, middle-class women may suffer disproportionately from policies that aim to contract the public sector wage bill by slowing down public sector hiring.

- Industrial restructuring or privatization affects women adversely, because women tend to be laid off first due to gender bias, but also because women workers tend to be concentrated in the lower rungs of the occupational ladder, in unskilled production jobs, or in over-staffed administrative and clerical positions.

- The poverty-inducing aspect of structural adjustment hits women hard and is especially hard on female-headed households with children.

- Labor market discrimination and job segregation result in women's being concentrated in the low-wage employment sectors, in the informal sector, and in the contingent of "flexible labor."

Economists at the World Bank have begun to take heed of the research documenting the close connection between gender differences and structural adjustment outcomes, as well as the wide-ranging criticisms of the adverse social effects of free market policies on labor, the poor, and women. The World Bank's *World Development Report 1995*, which focuses on workers in an integrating global economy, includes observations on women workers and the gender-specific effects of structural adjustment, as some of the citations above suggest. A World Bank Gender Consultative Group was formed in early 1996, consisting of gender-and-development experts from different regions of the world economy, whose task it is to advise World Bank officials on the gender aspects of economic restructuring, poverty, and social policies. There has been more serious consideration of gender issues across the U.N. system, with policies, programs, and projects now expected to specify their gender aspects at the planning, implementation, monitoring, and evaluation stages. Many of the publications and annual reports produced by the specialized agencies, programs, and funds of the U.N. system now routinely provide gender-disaggregated data and information on women. The Fourth World Conference on Women (Beijing, September 1995) drew on gender expertise in the preparatory phases and continues to do so in the follow-up. The Human Development

Report Office of the United Nations Development Program, which has been publishing its influential *Human Development Report* since 1990, devoted the 1995 report to a systematic analysis of gender inequalities and changes in the "capabilities" of women; the office routinely commissions background papers from gender-and-development specialists for its annual reports. And, as mentioned above, development economists such as Paul Collier, Jean Drèze, Amartya Sen, Lance Taylor, Lawrence Haddad, and Massoud Karshenas are beginning to consider gender in their own economic analyses.

Gender Dynamics of the Global Economy: A Theoretical Framework

In this section I return to the questions raised at the outset by tying together the theoretical strands that have been woven into this essay. I use a world-system theoretical framework, which, despite its rigidity and inattention to gender, has several advantages. First, it is a pertinent point of departure for a development social scientist, as it consists of concepts and methods, including its historical, global, and comparative sweep, that are consonant with non-West-centered social theories. Second, its insistence on the existence of a *world* system, integrated unevenly across economic zones and incorporating commodity chains and different forms of labor, has stood the test of time, given today's consensus, described above, concerning the global economy, globalization, integration of markets, informalization of labor markets, and so on. Third, world-system theory may be more amenable to the integration of gender analysis because of its built-in premises regarding social inequalities and its studies of class, race, gender, and households in the world-system (see Berquist 1984; Chase-Dunn 1989; Smith, Wallerstein, and Evers 1984; Smith et al. 1988; Smith and Wallerstein 1992; Timberlake 1985; Ward 1984, 1990). Fourth, because the theory concerns not only a world *economy* but also a system of states and cultures (Wallerstein 1991), it is better equipped to explain such phenomena as the rise of "identity politics" (including fundamentalisms) and the social and economic bases of cultural revivalist movements. Fifth, world-system theory provides a useful framework for understanding the links among structural adjustment in developing countries, privatization in the former socialist countries, competition between states and economies, and the changing fortunes of labor. It also provides an adequate explanation for global inequalities, economic crises, the hegemonic role of certain ("core") states and international financial institutions, the peripheralization of other states, and the significance of middle-income industrializing ("semiperipheral") states.

It is beyond the scope of this chapter to outline the main features of the world-system perspective, which include "long waves" of economic expansion and contraction; a hierarchy of states and markets within the three economic zones of core, periphery, and semiperiphery involving various "commodity chains"; the idea of the "hegemonic transition"; and forms of global, national, and labor market stratification (that is, "core workers" and "peripheral workers").[3] Although class has been elaborated, the place of *gender* in the world-system perspective remains undertheorized. However, at a very general level of analysis, one may begin to explain gender hierarchies and positions of women across the globe and within societies in terms of core, periphery, and semiperiphery locations. For example, in an early study, Ward (1984) found that peripheral status negatively affects women's share of the labor force and increases pressures for fertility. Defining peripheral status as "economic dependency" and a concentration of foreign investments in commodities, and utilizing 1960s and 1970s data sets, Ward found that this status leads to greater inequalities—not only between countries and between classes within countries, but between women and men. Women have limited job opportunities in the formal sector (the jobs go to men), are relegated to unpaid work in the informal sector, and are encouraged to have more children. Ward's most significant contribution, in my view, is her demonstration that fertility increases in the periphery because women's socioeconomic position vis-à-vis men is low, because women have less control over their fertility, and because children are needed as labor inputs and for old-age security, especially in agrarian settings.

In contrast, greater diversity in the structure of production and trade positively affects women's share of the labor force and decreases fertility rates, the pattern in the core and the semiperiphery. Most countries within the semiperiphery have seen dramatic declines in fertility, as more and more women have assumed nonagricultural employment, as described in preceding sections. In core countries, too, mass education, salaried employment, and social security programs have led to low birthrates. Within a society, differences in fertility are explained by the different class positions of women, which is why fertility behavior differs among poor, peasant, proletarian, and professional women. Thus location within economic zone and location within class structure are strong predictors of fertility behavior and child-care needs of women, and of their patterns of employment.

More recently, Ward (1993) has been critical of world-system theory for its overemphasis on exchange, accumulation, and class, and for its inability or unwillingness to theorize the gendered nature of production and the links between the formal sector and women's informal and domestic labor. She also takes issue with the recent work on households by Smith and Wallerstein (1992), who argue that "the appropriate operational unit for analyzing the ways in which people fit into the 'labor force' is not the individual but the 'household', defined for these purposes as the social unit that effectively over long periods of time enables individuals, of varying ages of both sexes, to pool income coming from multiple sources in order to ensure their individual and collective reproduction and well-being" (p. 13). Wallerstein, Smith, and their collaborators feel that this approach will explain how people respond to economic stagnation, expansion, and other cycles and trends; it recognizes the contribution of unwaged labor to the reproduction of the labor force and the capitalist system, and it offers a "micro" perspective on antisystemic movements. Ward (1993), however, finds that the household perspective "ignores the divergent interests of men and women within households"; it "obscures how women's socioeconomic roles in waged and nonwaged labor and housework are intertwined"; it "ignores how women have been systematically denied access to formal waged labor under the global economy"; and it leads to "male biases in how work and households are defined in their theories" (pp. 52-55).

Ward's critique is not unlike that of feminist economists who have taken issue with the work of Gary Becker and the new household economics, who highlight intrahousehold inequalities or who feel that the bargaining model of intrahousehold "cooperative conflict" associated with Drèze and Sen is a more useful framework than is conventional household economics. If the concept of household is to be useful, it should incorporate the existence of gender differences, for, as shown earlier in this chapter, intrahousehold inequalities and the traditional gender division of labor are critical factors in explaining differential effects and responses to economic crises and new economic policies for women and men. At the same time, one may dispute Ward's contention that women have been "systematically denied access to formal waged labor under the global economy." As this chapter has shown, there has been a tremendous increase in women's employment, not only in core countries but in semiperipheral countries as well—at the same time that informalization and unemployment have been expanding. World-system theorists correctly recognize the *different modes of remuneration of labor*, which they explain in terms of interconnections among various production processes, or "commodity chains," some of which are core-like and some of which are peripheral (see Wallerstein and Smith 1992:16).

The capitalist world-economy functions by means of the deployment of labor that is both waged and nonwaged. In recent decades, the involvement of women in both kinds of labor arrangements has been striking, as I have emphasized here. Capitalist accumulation is achieved through the surplus extraction of labor, and this includes the paid and unpaid economic activities of women, whether in male-headed or female-headed households. Global accumulation as the driving force of the world-system not only hinges on class and regional differences across economic zones, it is a gendered process as well, predicated upon gender differences in the spheres of production and reproduction. The various forms of the deployment of women's labor reflect asymmetrical gender relations and patriarchal gender ideologies—but the involvement of women in the global economy and in national labor forces has also served to interrogate and modify gender relations and ideologies.

Conclusions: Women's Responses to Globalization

It should come as no surprise that the massive entry of women into the workforce around the world, whether as professionals or as proletarians, has coincided with the political mobilization of women and the expansion of women's organizations of all types. In a number of advanced industrialized countries (the United States, Australia, the Nordic countries), women are the largest growing union constituency. In Japan, the Asian Women Workers' Center studies and promotes the rights of women workers throughout East and Southeast Asia and publishes a newsletter called *Resource Materials on Women's Labor in Japan*. In Taiwan, the Grassroots Women Workers Centre engages in various activities, including defense of the rights of immigrant women workers, and publishes a newsletter called *Female Workers in Taiwan*. Similar activities are carried out in Hong Kong by the Committee for Asian Women. In Morocco, feminist groups have come to the assistance of factory women who went on strike over sexual harassment. In Guatemala, women workers at an export shirt-making factory won a union contract, the first in a Guatemalan *maquiladora*. In India, the Self-Employed Women's Association (SEWA) operates as a trade union and a consciousness-raising feminist organization. In Israel, Arab women workers ignored by the Histadrut formed the Arab Women Workers Project.[4]

In the Middle East and North Africa, the involvement of women in paid employment has resulted in the politicization of women and of gender issues. In Tunisia, the National Commission on Working Women was created in July 1991 within the Tunisian General Federation of Workers. The commission has 27 branches throughout Tunisia, and carries out surveys and studies pertaining to women and the workplace. In Turkey, 41 percent of manufacturing workers are unionized, although they are mainly men. Only 6 percent of public sector workers are unionized due to legal restrictions, but even so, the leader of at least one public sector union has been a woman who regularly criticized government policy. In Morocco, a Roundtable on the Rights of Workers was organized in 1995 by the Democratic League of Women's Rights, and a committee structure was subsequently formed, consisting of 12 participating organizations. The group seeks to revise the labor code to take into account women's conditions, to include domestic workers in the definition of wageworkers and the delineation of their rights and benefits, to set the minimum work age at 15, and to provide workers on maternity leave with full salary and a job-back guarantee. In November 1995, some 500 women textile workers employed by the Manufacture du Maroc factory outside Rabat went on strike for two weeks to protest "repeated violence" against several women employees. This included the arbitrary dismissal of the general secretary of the factory's union of women workers, her subsequent rape by a foreman, and the firing of 17 women workers who protested the union leader's dismissal and rape. Morocco's Association of Democratic Women then set out to "mobilize human rights organizations and all the women's organizations" in defense of the women workers. The incident not only shows the vulnerability of women at the workplace, but the capacity of women workers to fight in defense of their rights and the ability of the feminist organizations to mobilize support for women workers (Moghadam 1998, chap. 9).

In addition to these and other grassroots organizations of women workers, feminist networks in the North and in the South are increasingly involved in issues pertaining to women and the global economy. These include Network Women in Development Europe (WIDE), based in Brussels and consisting of 12 national branches; Development Alternatives with Women for a New Era (DAWN), based in Fiji and with active branches in Latin America and South Asia; Women Working Worldwide, a coordinating group based in London; the International Association for Feminist Economics and the International Women's Tribune Center, both based in the United States; the Asia-Pacific Research and Resource Organization for Women (ARROW), based in Kuala Lumpur; Women Living under Muslim Laws, based in Montpelier, France, and with an active branch, Shirkat Gah, in Lahore, Pakistan; and ISIS International Women's Information and Communication Service, with one center in Quezon City, Philippines, and another in Santiago, Chile. In addition, the International Confederation of Free Trade Unions and Public Services International have active women's departments.

These national women's organizations and transnational feminist networks are linked together in ways that suggest a global women's movement. The organizations are increasingly networking and coordinating their activities, engaging in dialogue and forms of cooperation and mutual support, sending representatives to meetings in other countries and regions, and utilizing a similar vocabulary to describe women's disadvantages and the desired alternatives. Many of the above-named organizations were involved in the myriad preparatory activities for the Fourth World Conference on Women held in Beijing in September 1995 and the parallel Forum of Non-governmental Organizations; some were also involved with preparations for the World Summit for Social Development (Copenhagen, March 1995), where trade union representation was considerable.[5]

Historically, the labor movement has been constituted largely by men, and the culture of the labor movement and of unions has been rather masculine. In many countries, particularly in northern Europe, Italy, Australia, and North America, union membership is taking on a female face (Eaton 1992; Hastings and Coleman 1992). During the past decade, women have made their way into positions of power in Australian trade unions at a time when overall union membership began to decline. The numbers of women on the national peak council, the Australian Council of Trade Unions, rose from zero to one-third; in the state of South Australia the three major white-collar unions (teachers, nurses, public servants) are all currently led by women. All these gains have been made since the mid-1980s (Franzway 1994).

In global terms, the highest union density is found in Northern Europe—Denmark, Finland, Norway, and Sweden—and it is there that women's participation as workers and as union officials is the greatest. In those countries, union density is very high in community, social, and personal services (68-87 percent); in trade, restaurants, and hotels (47-49 percent); and in manufacturing (80-100 percent) in both the public and private sectors. Women are making up an increasing share of union membership, especially in services, with the most impressive figures found in Denmark. Danish women represent 42 and 62 percent of the two main union federations; they are 30 and 39 percent of the delegates to the union congress and 13 and 41 percent of members of leading committees, as well as 10 and 30 percent of leaders of individual unions (see Hastings and Coleman 1992; Klausen 1997). On at least one occasion that I know of during the 1990s, the Danish labor movement sent an all-woman delegation to the annual Congress of the International Labour Organization in Geneva. In Finland, women constitute 45 percent of the membership of one of the two labor confederations (SAK); they also constitute about 37.5 percent of delegates to the SAK Congress and 40 percent of the union council. The proportions of women in union leadership positions are also increasing in Germany, Portugal, Italy, the Netherlands, France, and England.

What can we conclude from the massive entry of women into the global economy, from women's activism and feminist networks around the world, and from the increasing participation of women workers in unions? My tentative conclusions are as follows. First, many feminist organizations are middle-class and often elite, but class lines are increasingly blurred as women professionals and women proletarians find common cause around personal, economic, and social issues, including violence against women, poverty, job security, land rights, the redistribution and socialization of domestic work, reproductive health and rights, and women's citizenship. Second, the mobilization of women into feminist groups and women's nongovernmental organizations, as well as the increasing participation of women in unions, has occurred on the part of women with education and work experience, and represents their response to continuing problems for women in the areas of literacy, education, employment, health, poverty, violence, human rights, and political participation. And third, if there is a specter haunting the global economy, it may very well be that of its "Other," a global women's movement.

Notes

1. For discussions of the evolution of the WID/GAD framework, see Rathgeber (1990), Scott (1986), and Razavi and Miller (1995).

2. Useful descriptions of the global economy may be found in the following annual publications: the International Labor Organization's *World Labor Report*, the UNDP's *Human Development Report*, the World Bank's *World Development Report* and *Trends in Developing Economies*, and the United Nations's *World Economic Survey* and *World Social and Economic Situation*.

3. For a useful introduction to the world-system perspective, see Shannon (1989). For elaboration, see Thompson (1983), Chase-Dunn (1989), and various issues of *Review*, published by the Braudel Center at SUNY-Binghamton. For the full treatment, see Wallerstein (1974, 1979, 1989).

4. Information in this paragraph is based on newsletters I have received. On SEWA, see Rose (1992).

5. Information in these paragraphs is based on various publications I have received, and on my own observations in Copenhagen and Beijing.

References

Abreu, Alice R. de P. and Bila Sorj. 1994. "Subcontracting and Gender: Dressmakers and Tailors in the Garment Industry in Rio de Janeiro, Brazil." Paper presented at the 13th World Congress of Sociology, July 18-23, Bielefeld, Germany.

Afshar, Haleh, ed. 1985. *Women, Work and Ideology in the Third World*. London: Tavistock.

Afshar, Haleh and Carolyne Dennis, eds. 1992. *Women and Adjustment Policies in the Third World*. London: Macmillan.

Bakker, Isabella, ed. 1994a. "Introduction: Engendering Macro-economic Policy Reform in the Era of Global Restructuring and Adjustment." Pp. 1-29 in *The Strategic Silence: Gender and Economic Policy*, edited by Isabella Bakker. London: Zed.

———, ed. 1994b. *The Strategic Silence: Gender and Economic Policy*. London: Zed.

Beneria, Lourdes and Shelley Feldman, eds. 1992. *Unequal Burden: Economic Crises, Persistent Poverty, and Women's Work*. Boulder, CO: Westview.

Beneria, Lourdes and Martha Roldán. 1987. *The Crossroads of Class and Gender: Industrial Homework, Subcontracting, and Household Dynamics in Mexico City*. Chicago: University of Chicago Press.

Berquist, Charles, ed. 1984. *Labor in the Capitalist World-Economy*. Newbury Park, CA: Sage.

Blumberg, Rae Lesser, Cathy A. Rakowski, Irene Tinker, and Michael Monteon, eds. 1995. *Engendering Wealth and Well-Being.* Boulder, CO: Westview.

Booth, David, ed. 1994. *Rethinking Social Development: Theory, Research and Practice.* Harlow, UK: Longman Scientific and Technical.

Boserup, Ester. 1987. *Women and Economic Development.* 2d ed. New York: St. Martin's.

Chase-Dunn, Christopher. 1989. *Global Formation: Structures of the World-Economy.* New York: Basil Blackwell.

Cinar, Mine. 1994. "Unskilled Urban Migrant Women and Disguised Employment: Homeworking Women in Istanbul, Turkey." *World Development* 22:369-80.

Collier, Paul. 1989. *Women and Structural Adjustment.* Oxford: Oxford University, Unit for the Study of African Economies.

Cornia, Giovanni A., Richard Jolly, and Frances Stewart, eds. 1987. *Adjustment with a Human Face.* Oxford: Clarendon.

da Gama Santos, Margarida. 1985. "The Impact of Adjustment Programmes on Women in Developing Countries." *Public Enterprise* 5:287-97.

Dangler, Jaimie Faricella. 1994. *Hidden in the Home: The Role of the Waged Homework in the Modern World-Economy.* Albany: State University of New York Press.

Drèze, Jean and Amartya Sen. 1989. *Hunger and Public Action.* Oxford: Clarendon.

Eaton, Susan C. 1992. "Women Workers, Unions and Industrial Sectors in North America." IDP Working Paper 1, International Labor Organization, Geneva.

Elson, Diane, ed. 1991. *Male Bias in the Development Process.* London: Macmillan.

Elson, Diane and Ruth Pearson. 1981. "Nimble Fingers Make Cheap Workers: An Analysis of Women's Employment in Third World Export Manufacturing." *Feminist Review* (Spring):87-107.

European System of Documentation on Employment. 1994. *Employment Observatory: Trends.* Bulletin 19.

Evans, Peter and John Stephens. 1988. "Development in the World Economy." In *The Handbook of Sociology,* edited by Neil J. Smelser. Newbury Park, CA: Sage.

Feldman, Shelley. 1992. "Crisis, Islam, and Gender in Bangladesh: The Social Construction of a Female Labor Force." In *Unequal Burden: Economic Crises, Persistent Poverty, and Women's Work,* edited by Lourdes Beneria and Shelley Feldman. Boulder, CO: Westview.

Fernandez-Kelly, Patricia. 1989. "Broadening the Scope: Gender and the Study of International Economic Development." *Sociological Forum* 4, no. 4:11-35.

Fernandez-Kelly, Patricia and Anna M. Garcia. 1989. "Informalization at the Core: Hispanic Women, Homework, and the Advanced Capitalist State." In *The Informal Economy: Studies in Advanced and Less Developed Countries,* edited by Alejandro Portes, M. Castells, and L. Benton. Baltimore: Johns Hopkins University Press.

Franzway, Suzanne. 1994. "Women Working in Australian Unions." Prepared for the annual meeting of the International Sociological Association, July 18-23, Bielefeld, Germany.

"Gender and Structural Adjustment." 1995. Symposium. *World Development* 23, no. 11.

Haddad, Lawrence et al. 1995. "The Gender Dimensions of Economic Adjustment Policies: Potential Interactions and Evidence to Date." *World Development* 23:881-96.

Hastings, Sue and Martha Coleman. 1992. "Women Workers and Unions in Europe: An Analysis by Industrial Sector." IDP Working Paper 4, International Labor Organization, Geneva.

Heyzer, Noeleen. 1986. *Working Women in South East Asia.* London: Open University Press.

Joekes, Susan and INSTRAW. 1987. *Women in the Global Economy: An INSTRAW Study.* New York: Oxford University Press.

Joekes, Susan and Ann Weston. 1995. *Women and the New Trade Agenda.* New York: UNIFEM.

Kahne, Hilda and Janet Z. Giele, eds. 1992. *Women's Work and Women's Lives: The Continuing Struggle Worldwide.* Boulder, CO: Westview.

Karshenas, Massoud. 1997. "Female Employment, Economic Liberalization, and Competitiveness in the Middle East." Economic Research Forum Working Paper, Cairo.

Kim, Seung-Kyung. 1997. *Class Struggle or Family Struggle? The Lives of Women Factory Workers in South Korea.* Cambridge: Cambridge University Press.

Kincaid, Douglas and Alejandro Portes, eds. 1994. *Comparative National Development: Society and Economy in the New World Order.* Chapel Hill: University of North Carolina Press.

Klausen, Jytte. 1997. "The Declining Significance of Male Workers: Trade Unions' Responses to Changing Labor Markets." In *Crisis and Conflict in Contemporary Capitalism,* edited by Peter Lange, Gary Marks, Herbert Kitchelt, and John D. Stephens. Cambridge: Cambridge University Press.

Kvande, Elin and B. Rasmussen. 1994. "Changing Gender Relations in the Labor Market." Presented at the 13th World Congress of Sociology, July 18-23, Bielefeld, Germany.

Lim, Linda. 1985. *Women Workers in Multinational Enterprises in Developing Countries.* Geneva: International Labor Organization.

MacLeod, Arlene Elowe. 1996. "Transforming Women's Identity: The Intersection of Household and Workplace in Cairo." In *Development, Change and Gender in Cairo: A View from the Household,* edited by Diane Singerman and Homa Hoodfar. Bloomington: Indiana University Press.

Marglin, Stephen and Juliet Schor, eds. 1990. *The Golden Age of Capitalism.* Oxford: Clarendon.

Martin, William G., ed. 1990. *Semiperipheral States in the World-Economy.* New York: Greenwood.

Mies, Maria. 1986. *Patriarchy and Accumulation on a World Scale.* London: Zed.

Moghadam, Valentine M. 1993. "Bringing the Third World In: A Comparative Analysis of Gender and Restructuring in the Third World and in State Socialist Societies." In *Democratic Reform and the Position of Women in Transitional Economies,* edited by Valentine M. Moghadam. Oxford: Clarendon.

———. 1994. "Women and Identity Politics in Theoretical and Comparative Perspective." In *Identity Politics and Women: Cultural Reassertions and Feminisms in International Perspective,* edited by Valentine M. Moghadam. Boulder, CO: Westview.

———. 1995. "Gender Aspects of Employment and Unemployment in a Global Perspective." In *Global Employment: An Investigation into the Future of Work,* edited by Mihaly Simai. London: Zed.

———. 1996. "Introduction and Overview." In *Patriarchy and Development: Women's Positions at the End of the Twentieth Century,* edited by Valentine M. Moghadam. Oxford: Clarendon.

———. 1997. "The Feminization of Poverty? Notes on a Concept and Trends." Occasional Paper No. 2 (August), Illinois State University, Women's Studies Program.

———. 1998. *Women, Work, and Economic Reform in the Middle East and North Africa.* Boulder, CO: Lynne Rienner.

Morvaridi, Behrooz. 1992. "Gender Relations in Agriculture: Women in Turkey." *Economic Development and Cultural Change* 40:567-86.

Nash, June and Maria Fernandez-Kelly, eds. 1983. *Women, Men, and the International Division of Labor.* Albany: State University of New York Press.

Pearson, Ruth. 1992. "Gender Issues in Industrialization." In *Industrialization and Development*, edited by Tom Hewitt, Hazel Johnson, and David Wield. Oxford: Oxford University Press.

Pearson, Ruth and Swasti Mitter. 1993. "Employment and Working Conditions of Low-Skilled Information-Processing Workers in Less-Developed Countries." *International Labour Review* 132, no. 1:49-64.

Rathgeber, Eva. 1990. "WID, WAD, GAD: Trends in Research and Practice." *Journal of Developing Areas* 24:489-502.

Razavi, Shahrashoub and Carole Miller. 1995. "From WID to GAD: Conceptual Shifts in the Women and Development Discourse." Occasional Paper 1, United Nations Research Institute for Social Development, Geneva.

Redclift, Nanneke and M. Thea Stewart, eds. 1991. *Working Women: International Perspectives on Women and Gender Ideology.* London: Routledge.

Rose, Kalima. 1992. *Where Women Are Leaders: The SEWA Movement in India.* London: Zed.

Safa, Helen. 1996. "Gender Inequality and Women's Wage Labor: A Theoretical and Empirical Analysis." In *Patriarchy and Development: Women's Positions at the End of the Twentieth Century*, edited by Valentine M. Moghadam. Oxford: Clarendon.

Scott, Alison MacEwan. 1986. "Women and Industrialization: Examining the 'Female Marginalisation' Thesis." *Journal of Development Studies* 22:649-80.

Shah, Nandita et al. 1994. "Structural Adjustment, Feminisation of Labor Force and Organisational Strategies." *Economic and Political Weekly* 29, no. 18: WS-39–WS-48.

Shannon, Thomas Richard. 1989. *An Introduction to the World-System Perspective.* Boulder, CO: Westview.

Sklair, Leslie. 1991. *A Sociology of the Global System.* Baltimore: Johns Hopkins University Press.

———. 1993. *Assembling for Development: The Maquila Industry in Mexico and the United States.* San Diego: University of California, Center for U.S.-Mexican Studies.

Smith, Joan et al., eds. 1988. *Racism and Sexism in the World-System.* Westport, CT: Greenwood.

Smith, Joan and Immanuel Wallerstein, eds. 1992. *Creating and Transforming Households: The Constraints of the World-Economy.* Cambridge: Cambridge University Press and Maison des Sciences de l'Homme.

Smith, Joan, Immanuel Wallerstein, and Harry Evers, eds. 1984. *Households and the World-Economy.* Beverly Hills, CA: Sage.

Sparr, Pam, ed. 1994. *Mortgaging Women's Lives: Feminist Critiques of Structural Adjustment.* London: Zed.

Standing, Guy. 1989. "Global Feminization through Flexible Labor." *World Development* 17:1077-95.

Tanski, Janet. 1994. "The Impact of Crisis, Stabilization and Structural Adjustment on Women in Lima, Peru." *World Development* 22:1627-42.

Taylor, Lance. 1995. "Environmental and Gender Feedbacks in Macroeconomics." *World Development* 23, no. 11.

Thompson, William. 1983. *Contending Approaches in World-System Analysis.* Beverly Hills, CA: Sage.

Tiano, Susan. 1994. *Patriarchy on the Line: Labor, Gender, and Ideology in the Mexican Maquila Industry.* Philadelphia: Temple University Press.

Timberlake, Michael, ed. 1985. *Urbanization in the World-Economy.* New York: Academic Press.

UNESCO. 1995. *World Education Report 1995.* Paris: UNESCO.

UNICEF. 1989. *The Invisible Adjustment: Poor Women and the Economic Crisis.* Santiago: Americas and Caribbean Regional Office, UNICEF.

United Nations. 1991. *World Economic Survey 1991.* New York: United Nations/DIESA.

———. 1995. *The World's Women 1995: Trends and Statistics.* New York: United Nations.

United Nations Conference on Trade and Development (UNCTAD). 1995. "World Investment Report 1995: Transnational Corporations and Competitiveness." *Transnational Corporations* 4, no. 3:101-65.

United Nations Development Program (UNDP). 1995. *The Human Development Report 1995.* New York: Oxford University Press.

Wallerstein, Immanuel. 1974. *The Modern World-System.* New York: Academic Press.

———. 1979. *The Capitalist World-System.* Cambridge: Cambridge University Press.

———. 1989. *The Modern World-System III.* New York: Academic Press.

———. 1991. *Geopolitics and Geoculture: Essays on the Changing World System.* Cambridge: Cambridge University Press.

Wallerstein, Immanuel and Joan Smith. 1992. "Households as an Institution in the World-Economy." In *Creating and Transforming Households: The Constraints of the World-Economy,* edited by Joan Smith and Immanuel Wallerstein. Cambridge: Cambridge University Press.

Ward, Kathryn. 1984. *Women in the World-System: Its Impact on Status and Fertility.* New York: Praeger.

———, ed. 1990. *Women Workers and Global Restructuring.* Ithaca, NY: ILR.

————. 1993. "Reconceptualizing World System Theory to Include Women." In *Theory on Gender/Feminism on Theory,* edited by Paula England. New York: Aldine.

World Bank. 1995. *World Development Report 1995: Workers in an Integrating World.* New York: Oxford University Press.

Young, Kate, C. Walkowitz, and R. McCollough, eds. 1981. *Of Marriage and the Market: Women's Subordination in International Perspective.* London: CSE.

CHAPTER 6

Gender, Work, Who Cares?!

Production, Reproduction,
Deindustrialization, and Business as Usual

LISA D. BRUSH

At the heart of classical sociology, and of the industrial regime that is its object of study, is the division between enterprises and households. Industrialism establishes a world of work and markets detached from the realm of domesticity. Work and family occupy separate sites with distinct rules of interaction. Enterprise and household exemplify segregated spheres of human endeavor: production (making things) and reproduction (tending hearth and family).

Both production and reproduction are gendered. Making things, and making things happen, is masculine; caring for people, especially reproducing the next generation, is feminine. Moreover, the distinction between production and reproduction renders women and men not just separate, but unequal. Men's productive activity *counts* historically and financially. Women's reproductive activity yields, at best, private and nonpecuniary rewards; at worst, exploitation from business, intrusive

AUTHOR'S NOTE: I prepared and presented an early version of this chapter as a guest of the Social Science Faculty at the University of Augsburg. Thanks for financial and intellectual support from my hosts there, especially Dr. Andrea Maurer; from my Berlin comrade Dr. Edgar Göll; and from Professor Burkhart Holzner, director of the University of Pittsburgh's Center for International Studies. Kathy Blee, Ruth Colker, Tom Fararo, and Judy Taylor were astute, speedy readers who, along with the editors, provided helpful suggestions and encouragement. Flaws resulting from failure or inability to heed their advice remain my responsibility.

scrutiny from church and state, and abuse from individual men. In short, *industrial societies organize gender.* Men are workers, women are mothers.

But also: *Gender organizes industrial societies* (Lorber 1994). The compulsory distinction between masculine and feminine, the marginalization of women's experiences, and the justification of both difference and subordination through appeals to anatomy, hormones, genes, or evolution—all mark the division between production and reproduction in terms of gender (Bem 1993). Gender segregation and discrimination mean that running enterprises and reaping the rewards of production are still largely male preserves (Reskin and Padavic 1994). Conversely, caring for home and family is women's lot (Shelton 1992). The distinction between production and reproduction is gendered to its core. Workers are men, mothers are women.

Yet, as I will demonstrate in this chapter, when social scientists examine the gendered social organization of industrial societies, the distinction between production and reproduction looks suspiciously unstable and political. In study after study, the assumed asymmetry of women and men, and their enduring assignment to home and work, respectively, proves descriptively false and normatively sexist as well as rife with class and race bias.

I organize my review of the past decade of feminist research on gender, production, and reproduction around the crises and transitions associated with *deindustrialization.* Deindustrialization is a complex, global phenomenon with three discernible dimensions. First is the depreciation of old manufacturing capacity, which leaves behind "shuttered factories, displaced workers, and a newly emerging group of ghost towns" (Bluestone and Harrison 1982:6). Second is technologies that generate "high-tech," information-based, producer service occupations (accountants, lawyers, engineers, computer systems analysts) at the expense of jobs for craft workers and factory operatives. Third is the shift to "high-touch" occupations in consumer or "people services," such as retail, food, accommodation, entertainment, and personal and health care, which are increasingly part of the paid market (Boyd, Mulvilhill, and Myles 1995).

At the center of the technological, economic, and social changes associated with deindustrialization is the concept of *work.* Investigating the gendering of production and reproduction pushes social scientists toward new understandings of work, who does it, where it happens, and with what rewards. Using gendered analyses, feminist scholars have redefined work in the marketplace and work in the home, paid and unpaid. A gendered analysis of production and reproduction shows that enterprises and households are not separate sectors but mutually constitutive sites of gender (and race and class) struggles over the tasks, meaning, and value of work. Feminist social scientists have remedied the theoretical and empirical neglect of gender at work that perpetuated the gendered distinction between production and repro-duction in classic studies of industrial societies. But the conventional analysis of deindustrialization, which proclaims crises of jobs and families, remains based on a framework that either incorporates only the most traditional and rudimentary notions of gender—including the sharp distinction between production and reproduction—or ignores feminist insights altogether. This chapter uses the decade's accumu-lated insights to substantiate the simple feminist claim that analysts would not prophesy the end of work if women's contributions to production and reproduction really counted. I conclude by pointing to some of the implications—for both mainstream and feminist social science—of gendered research and theory about production, reproduc-tion, and the crises commonly associated with deindustrialization.

The Conventional Deindustrialization Story: A Tale of Three Crises

Events and trends of the past 20 years have transformed the indus-trialized societies of the North Atlantic. In what follows, I describe the changes in the economy that have undermined old ways of generating and distributing wealth. I chart the new expectations, pressures, and social arrangements for caring that have shifted old patterns of house-hold and family formation. Finally, I examine the new constraints on public spending that have eroded welfare state programs and enabled government officials to impose austerity regimes and turn over regula-tion, ownership, and provision of income security and services to entrepreneurs, philanthropists, and unpaid caregivers. The results of these transformations in business, family, and the welfare state are commonly understood as the triple crises of production, reproduction, and the institutions and policies that, in industrial democracies, histori-cally bridge the two.

The Crisis in "Production"

As manufacturing has shifted to the Pacific Rim, the smokestack industries of steel, coal, automobiles, glass, and arms that built regions such as the Ohio Valley in the United States, the West Midlands in England, the Lorraine and Nord-Pas-de-Calais in France, Upper Silesia in Poland, and the German Rhine-Ruhr area have declined (Hesse 1988). For example, plant closings in the United States eliminated more than 900,000 manufacturing jobs per year in the late 1970s and early 1980s, and at least 10 percent of the job loss was permanent (that is, unreplaced by other manufacturing jobs; Harris 1984).

At first glance, increased employment in high-technology manufacturing (e.g., computers, electronics, and pharmaceuticals), business services and financial industries (e.g., banking and insurance), food and medical services, entertainment (including gaming), and retail sales balances the declines associated with deindustrialization. In fact, the U.S. economy has produced more than 35 million jobs since 1973, and is in this regard the envy of Europe.

Upon closer inspection, however, high-tech and service sector employment appears a poor replacement for industrial manufacturing jobs. Firms are smaller, career ladders shorter, and part-time, contract, and temporary employment more common in the service sector than in industrial manufacturing (Boje 1991). The combination of international competition and the shift from milling steel or riveting cars to flipping burgers or emptying bedpans has depressed wages of "low-skilled" workers, thereby increasing inequality in many North Atlantic countries. In the United States, median earnings in trade and service industries are only 60 to 80 percent of median earnings in the goods-producing sector (Burtless 1990). The expanding service sector, filled with "McJobs," has not kept up, especially in terms of salary and benefits. This is the reality behind the gallows humor of the vendor outside my building, one of whose most popular T-shirts asks on the front, "What are the five most important words to a college graduate?" and answers on the back, "You want fries with that?"

The conventional account of deindustrialization notes that firms producing goods and services in the global economy are under pressure to lower costs. They do so either by reducing the workforce, including everyone from supervisory management to production line workers, or by moving to areas where labor, infrastructure, and tax costs are lower, including free trade and export processing zones internationally and historically depressed and relatively union-free national regions. As a consequence of these strategies, and successful attacks on organized labor and the welfare state, the institutions that once organized the "normal" male life course—assembly lines and mass production, reliable and generous accords between powerful trade unions and stable firms, and linear careers and job security—are obsolete. These changes are conventionally interpreted as a crisis in production.

Ultimately, some commentators speculate, the crisis of production associated with deindustrialization will reach the point where we face a "jobless future" (Aronowitz and DeFazio 1994), "the end of work" (Rifkin 1995). The argument is that shifts from manufacturing to service occupations and to part-time, subcontracted, and temporary employment destroy the notion of a "job" as a collection of tasks and rewards with continuity over time. In addition, computers and other technological innovations replace human labor and skill. The result is a global epidemic of un- and underemployment. This speculation largely ignores the fact that industrial manufacturing jobs are lopsidedly men's work, whereas women are closely associated with clerical, retail, personal service, and hospitality work—precisely the growth areas in deindustrializing economies. It also ignores the fact that industrial production in export processing zones and historically impoverished districts (such as the Mississippi delta in the United States) frequently employs women. Without being overly sanguine about its effects, I would argue that what is actually occurring is a *feminization* of work. The assumption that the typical worker is a man with an uninterrupted employment history in heavy industrial manufacturing has collided with the fact that more and more workers are being treated as women have been treated historically—that is, as unskilled, temporary, and unorganizable service or light manufacturing labor (e.g., in food processing or in garment, textile, and electronics manufacturing). Assessing deindustrialization requires a feminist analysis, if only because the crisis in production is so obviously gendered (Amott 1993). Along with this crisis of production comes a crisis of its conceptual twin, reproduction.

The Crisis in "Reproduction"

According to the conventional account, the long-term unemployment and neighborhood blight that accompany deindustrialization have put new pressures on families and communities—the places where individuals and societies reproduce themselves. As decisions by corporate managers reduce the employment opportunities, standard of living, and security that many male workers once enjoyed, families must cope with layoffs, income decline, underemployment, debt, and the physical and mental health effects of job loss and increased inequality (Bluestone and Harrison 1982).

Moreover, if men's jobs once provided the material basis for marriage, family, and community life, deindustrialization (combined with concentration of poor people in districts that have been most devastated by job loss) decimates neighborhoods, households, and couples as well as individuals. Poor, racially segregated areas where a majority of adults have jobs are different from poor, racially segregated areas where only a minority of adults do. A 33-year-old mother from a poor Chicago neighborhood where joblessness is rampant put it this way:

> If you live in an area in your neighborhood where you have people that don't work, don't have no means of support, you know, don't have no jobs, who're gonna break into your house to steal what you have, to sell to get them some money, then you can't live in a neighborhood and try to concentrate on gettin' ahead, then you get to work and you have to worry if somebody's breakin' into your house or not. So, you know, it's best to try to move in a decent area, to live in a community with people that works. (quoted in Wilson 1996:11)

According to this view, jobs are essential to social organization. Widespread joblessness threatens the ability of neighborhood residents to establish social networks, to supervise and take responsibility for neighborhood problems, and to participate in formal, informal, and volunteer organizations that constitute the common life of any neighborhood (Wilson 1996). Thus deindustrialization means that families, neighborhoods, cities, and entire regions may be unable to sustain a new generation. The crisis of production generates a crisis of reproduction.

Adjusted for inflation, the average hourly wage for a young male high school graduate in the United States fell 28.1 percent ($2.96/hour) between 1973 and 1995. The drop for similarly educated and experienced women was 19 percent in the same period (Garnett 1997). As wages stagnate and fall, one way to maintain household income is to send more family members into the labor market. As a result, more people are working longer hours for fewer rewards than in the past, with devastating effects on the time and attention required for community and family life (Schor 1991; Hochschild 1997). Householders around the world turn to moonlighting and long hours, informal self-employment, industrial homework (frequently at piecework rates below the minimum wage), criminal activity (e.g., working without proper visas as well as trafficking in contraband goods and services), self-provisioning (in vegetable gardens, for example), and barter (Mingione 1985; Pahl and Wallace 1985; Bullock 1994). All this activity results from people's efforts to keep a roof overhead and food on the table—in short, to reproduce their own labor power and raise the next generation of workers. In conventional accounts, however, much of it does not count as "work," especially when done by women.

Of special concern in the conventional account of the crisis of reproduction is the increasing prevalence and impoverished plight of single mothers. Women face a particular disadvantage when they try to support children on their own, as increasing numbers are attempting to do (Kamerman 1995). The connections between single motherhood and deindustrialization vary cross-nationally with the extent of supportive public policies and the conditions of women's employment. For example, the income of single-mother families ranges from less than half (in the United States) to almost nine-tenths (in Sweden) of income in two-parent families, and the poverty rates for the children of single mothers vary similarly (McLanahan and Garfinkel 1995). In addition, in the United States, household formation, marriage, births out of wedlock, and poverty rates all vary tremendously by race. But across the industrial world, children in female-headed households are more likely to be poor than their counterparts in two-parent households, and everywhere their numbers are growing.

The official debates over "welfare" and the vilification of poor single mothers frequently ignore the problem of creating enough high-wage jobs to support families on the earnings of a single employee. If they *do* focus on jobs, they think only of the men as workers, noting, for example, that the proportion of men who are employed in a typical week in ghetto neighborhoods has plummeted since the 1950s (Wilson 1996). But poor women, even women on public assistance, also work. In fact, local labor market conditions help explain intercity differences in poor single mothers' strategies to make up the gap between their families' needs and what government transfers and low-wage work provide. Tight labor markets, for example, provide more opportunities and also increase poor single mothers' income from friends and family, while the availability of informal and underground work shapes the range of single mothers' survival strategies; both of these labor market issues reflect trends characteristic of deindustrialization (Edin and Lein 1997).

Just as the conventional account of deindustrialization focuses attention on men's job losses, it places women at the center of the crisis in reproduction. The gendered association of reproduction with women means that single mothers can easily become scapegoats for changes that are structural features of deindustrialization. Single mothers become the targets of concern over both the work ethic and family values. When politicians and policy commentators admonish people not to have children they cannot afford, they make an increasingly elusive and precarious economic self-sufficiency the prerequisite of childbearing, thus denying reproductive freedom to poor people (as, e.g., Murray 1994 proposes). Scapegoating single mothers as the cause of the crisis of reproduction also has important racist overtones in the United States, and has reached a distinctly eugenic pitch among conservatives determined to dismantle government programs that might mitigate some of the worst economic and social effects of deindustrialization (Herrnstein and Murray 1996). The crisis of reproduction, ironically, is read as a consequence of individual failings rather than a predictable outcome of maintaining an archaic, gendered distinction between production and reproduction and systematically undervaluing women's contributions to both (Sidel 1996). I return to this point in the next section, but first I turn to the third dimension of the conventional account of deindustrialization, the crisis of the welfare state.

Privatization, Welfare Wars, and the "Crisis of the State"

The conventional wisdom notes that deindustrialization, with its twin crises of production and reproduction, creates a new environment for government institutions and social policies. The combination of global competition and new ways of organizing production shifts the balance of class forces on which the industrial democracies built their welfare states, and reduces the influence of organized labor on national politics. The result is more government dependence on the employment- and revenue-generating capacities of the business sector, strong fiscal and political pressure to cut public spending, and increasingly strident free market, antiunion, work ethic rhetoric. Social and economic policies used to maintain consumer demand through the redistributive mechanisms of *welfare* states and the military-industrial complex of *warfare* states. Now, social and economic policies are driven by post-Cold War efforts to improve international competitiveness (by decreasing the costs and increasing the flexibility of labor) through the establishment of austere *workfare* states (Jessop 1994).

One of the basic trends of this transition is *privatization*. Privatization has two distinct but related dimensions. The first is the transfer of state-owned enterprises—sometimes entire sectors considered the "commanding heights" of the economy—to the market. The second is the transfer of services and benefits previously provided, regulated, or subsidized by national and local government to markets, philanthropic organizations, or family members, thus sending former recipients "into the arms of (usually female) relatives, charity, or chance" (Brush 1987:276). The two types of privatization appear in different proportions depending on the level of nationalization of extractive, telecommunications, and manufacturing industries and the extent of publicly financed or administered income security, health care, education, and the like (Anderson and Hill 1996).

In the economies of the former state socialist and communist countries of Central and Eastern Europe, the effort to transfer assets from the state to the private sector combines the transition to market-driven economics and the dismantling of bureaucratic, one-party regimes. In capitalist countries such as the United Kingdom (the bellwether of privatization in the North Atlantic), politicians have portrayed government as too large and untrustworthy and the market as the best means of allocating resources. Caught between the rock of resistance to tax increases and the hard place of demand for public services in hard and unequal times, capitalist welfare state administrators have used contracting out, vouchers, and subsidies. Privatization both reduces public spending and responsibility for services and undermines the power of public sector trade unions.

The stated goal of privatization is to reduce costs and improve efficiency through the combination of increased competition, reduced public sector jobs and unions, and diminished bureaucracy. The stated goal of the war on welfare—cutting benefits and entitlements and pillorying recipients—is to shore up the work ethic and traditional family values while eliminating taxpayer support for reducing poverty and inequality. What frequently goes without saying in the conventional account is that privatization and welfare reform are efforts to keep production and reproduction going without redressing gender (and race and class) inequality. I show in the next section how feminist perspectives revise conventional notions of deindustrialization's triple crises, in large part by redefining "work."

His and Hers Crises: Redefining "Work"

Even without explicitly addressing gender or the distinct character of women's experiences, the conventional description of deindustrialization recognizes that *reproduction* means more than making babies (Laslett and Brenner 1989). And increasingly, even mainstream analysts of deindustrialization recognize that the shift is less one from goods to services than it is one from unpaid to paid service work, further blurring the line between production and reproduction.

But an explicitly feminist analysis goes much further, suggesting, for example, that there are in fact two gender-specific sides to deindustrialization: "his and hers" crises, so to speak. The *decline* in traditionally male manufacturing occupations associated with deindustrialization has coincided with a sharp *increase* in women's labor force participation. In the United States, the increase is especially remarkable for married women, mothers, and women of privileged racial/ethnic and class groups who could previously depend on the wages of fathers or husbands to support them at home (Amott and Matthaei 1996; Browne 1997). As feminists pointed out a decade ago, women's increased employment hardly constitutes a windfall if women workers continue to find themselves sequestered in jobs with low wages, little security, limited recognition of their skills, and few of the benefits that make it easier to combine earning and mothering (Sternlieb and Baker 1987). The decline in family-supporting jobs in manufacturing means that remedies designed to improve opportunities for individuals, such as affirmative action or human capital investment, will not necessarily help women achieve autonomy and equality. Such strategies fail to increase the availability of living-wage jobs; individualist remedies do not necessarily change the ladder of opportunities (Kuhn and Bluestone 1987).

At the same time, because the ladder of opportunities is so thoroughly gendered, even the individualist step of moving some women up a rung can change the balance of power in homes and firms. As married women in particular cease to be wholly dependent on their husbands' wages, the economic balance of power in families shifts. This shift brings changes at home as well as challenges to business, as women carry family-related concerns with them into the workplace (Kessler-Harris and Sacks 1987). In all these respects, deindustrialization means something quite different for women and men. Moreover, the fact that family survival frequently relies on women's skills, networks, and unpaid labor means privatization and economic restructuring have deeply gendered effects (Dalla Costa and Dalla Costa 1995).

Gender-blind analyses divide the world into public and private in ways that obscure how gender organizes production. Feminist reassessment of the conventional wisdom about deindustrialization expands the definition of "work," with interesting consequences both for assessments of these trends and for the distinction between production and reproduction. Feminists have made strides toward redefining "the economy" to include the gendered ways in which labor power is reproduced on both daily and intergenerational scales. It should come as no surprise, therefore, that the extent and character of the crises of deindustrialization depend on whether your perspective is that of a man or a woman losing a $28/hour manufacturing or high-salaried middle-management job, a man or a woman trying to schedule shift work and overtime without neglecting their children, a pieceworker for a multinational electronics or garment manufacturer in an export processing zone, or an immigrant doing live-in domestic work for cramped room, scanty and grudging board, and subminimum wage. But it is not only individual circumstances that are gendered. Specific tasks and their value—their definition as "work"—are also at stake (England 1992). In this section, I assess the changing picture of who workers are and where work happens, based on evidence provided by feminist scholars who continue to press the gendered question of what counts as work.

Who Is a Worker?

Women were among the first waged workers of the industrial age, laboring in factories around the world and joining and often launching struggles over wages, working conditions, and the collective power of labor (Kessler-Harris 1981). The message that proper White women were pure, pious, and above all *domestic* grew especially shrill just as young women in Jacksonian (1800-1840) New England left home and entered thread and textile mills (Lerner 1979). Interestingly enough, in light of this history, part of the perceived crises in production and reproduction is rooted in the fact that the workers employers think of as "productive" are increasingly female. Although this perception is based in ignorance of women's historic labor force participation, it is also true that in the United States in 1995, a record 61 million women were working or looking for work—almost half of all U.S. labor force participants (Women's Bureau 1996b). The proportion of the total labor force who are women varies from between 40 and 50 percent in East Asia, North America, and the countries of the former Soviet Union to less than 20 percent in North Africa and western Asia (Bullock 1994). The feminization of the labor force certainly appears to be a long-term, global trend.

In the countries of the European Union (EU), for example, where deindustrialization has caused rampant long-term unemployment for men, more than 80 percent of the new jobs created since 1961 have been filled by women (Rubery, Fagan, and Smith 1995). Deindustrialization has also challenged the standardization of employment, structuring weekly hours into either very long or involuntarily short spans. In Britain, for example, the 1989 Hours of Work Survey showed that more than 40 percent of men spent more than 45 hours a week at their workplaces, as did 10 percent of women (Fagan 1996). More than 20 percent of both men and women in all occupations in the EU say they "usually" work on Saturdays, and 8 percent on Sundays. One European in seven works more than 45 hours a week. Such "unsocial" hours make it particularly difficult to combine earning and caring work (Rubery et al. 1995).

None of this sounds as if people in deindustrializing countries are facing the "end of work." Redistributing the total volume of working hours in the EU so everyone aged 20 to 59 worked just 30 hours a week would employ 90 percent of Europeans in this age group (Rubery et al. 1995). Such a redistribution of waged work could also help men and women renegotiate the division of domestic labor, but only if caregiving outside the labor market were valued more highly than it is now (Plantenga 1996). There is far too much pressure on productivity in competitive economies to imagine that the world of leisure is at hand. To a feminist optimist, however, redefining "work" to value women's caring and to remedy economic inequality may well mean the end of the gendered distinction between production and reproduction.

Also to a feminist optimist, women's expanding labor force participation threatens the stereotypically masculine character of production. In the increasingly competitive global economy, firms are realizing that management cannot afford to discriminate just because talent wears a skirt. Women managers like Judith Rogala, who went from being a flight attendant at TWA to the position of executive vice president of the office supply giant Office Depot, leave "a trail of interactive, participatory management and higher profits" by eliminating costly status symbols like company cars and special parking spaces, making management more accessible through employee hot lines, and insisting on balance between work and family life (Rosener 1995:118-19). Rogala has counterparts in firms around the world (Adler and Izraeli 1994).

Women are also slowly changing the face of traditionally male occupations such as commodities and wholesale sales representatives, metal and plastic processing machine operators, and chemical technicians, all of which are between 20 and 25 percent female in the United States (Women's Bureau 1996a). Fed up with low pay and sometimes with the physical and skill limits of traditional women's work (clerical and secretarial jobs, nursing, waiting tables, elementary school teaching), some women enjoy the hard work, satisfaction, and financial benefits they experience in trades such as welding (Ferguson 1994). At the same time, men may turn to "women's work" when family circumstances mean they have to care for ailing elderly relatives (Applegate and Kaye 1993), when temperament or political commitment draws them to occupations such as elementary school teaching (Allan 1993), or when the need to earn a fast buck working limited hours makes working in strip joints an appealingly lucrative prospect (Tewksbury 1993).

It is not just the gendered face of production that is changing. The most optimistic accounts claim that the traditional assignment of women to home and men to the labor force is crumbling from both sides. Families with employed husbands and stay-at-home wives represent a shrinking minority of U.S. families. Women's increased labor force participation means the gendered distinction between production and reproduction is crumbling as well, as fewer households can afford to divide earning and caring between breadwinning men and housekeeping women (Barnett and Rivers 1996). In the same way (albeit not in nearly the same proportions) that women are taking advantage of increased autonomy, fulfillment of ambition, and opportunity to provide for themselves and their families, men are discovering the rewards of investing time in trustworthy relationships with their children and rearranging priorities so that fatherhood can include meaningful, intimate interaction (Coltrane 1996).

In fact, deindustrialization disrupts notions of masculinity as being centrally about providing for wife and family through tough or skilled labor (Connell 1995). Men formerly able to use employment in the U.S. auto industry, for example, to fulfill the manly role of provider ("a good Catholic man—a steady churchgoer with a steady factory income, a station wagon parked under the elms and a wife with an automatic door on her womb"; Hamper 1991:10) have learned how fragile this construction of proper manhood is. Some White working-class men and boys respond to the deindustrial corrosion of their work-defined race and gender privileges by scapegoating racial "Others" as drug-addicted, violent, filthy, and sexually unacceptable; mocking gay men to affirm their aggressively heterosexual masculinity; and holding on, "desperate and vigilant, to identities of white race and male gender as though these could gain them credit in increasingly class-segregated worlds" (Fine et al. 1997:66).

Although a feminist optimist can find evidence that the traditional notion that men work and women stay home is markedly unstable, other research (much of it reviewed elsewhere in this volume) suggests that change has gone not nearly far enough. Despite the slowly dawning consciousness that sometimes the best man for the job is a woman, the segregation of men and women on the job persists on a global scale (Jacobs and Lim 1995). Cashier, secretary, elementary school teacher, and registered nurse or nurse's aide are all among the 10 largest occupations for White, Black, Asian, and Hispanic women in the United States; not one of those occupations is among the top 10 for men of any race. Truck driver, construction laborer, and janitor are all among the 10 largest occupations for White, Black, and Hispanic men in the United States; neither truck driver nor construction laborer appears among the top 10 for women of any race, and janitor appears in the top 10 only for Black and Hispanic women (Reskin and Padavic 1994).

The shift from goods production to services characteristic of deindustrialization could have helped women gain access to job opportunities in relatively high-status, nonmanual jobs in rapidly expanding service industries. Industrial and occupational restructuring seems instead to generate ever more low-wage jobs in service occupations where women predominate (Tienda, Smith, and Ortiz 1987). Women remain subordinate tokens in many nontraditional occupations, in which they frequently receive insufficient training, discriminatory supervision, and a combination of blatant racist and sexist hostility that can make their working lives extremely difficult (Yoder and Aniakudo 1997).

To add insult to injury, besides persistently doing women's work, women still earn women's wages. In the United States, where the trend toward equal pay has been among the fastest, the wage gap decreased by about a dime during the two decades following passage of the Equal Pay Act in 1963 (Reskin and Padavic 1994). "At that rate," as performance artist Laurie Anderson puts it in her piece "Beautiful Red Dress" (1989), "it will be 2083 before we make a buck." And women still face exclusionary old-boys' networks, recalcitrant coworkers and union officials, and sexual and gender harassment.

For example, Nancy Pease (1992), a heavy equipment operator who testified before a U.S. House of Representatives investigation on sexual harassment in nontraditional occupations, tells of being the only woman in a department of 70, the head of which greeted her this way: "I can't wait to get you in my shop. I am going to make you cry every day. . . . I don't think you belong here, I don't want you here. My wife's not here, you shouldn't be here" (p. 33). Pease was "subjected to daily comments on the size and the shape of [her] breasts" and to descriptions of pornographic movies from her direct supervisor in one unit. She was sprayed down with a fire extinguisher in front of coworkers by another supervisor who objected to hearing her voice in conversation. She received so many physical threats that she carried an iron pipe in her gym bag (pp. 33-35).

Given the evidence of the persistent inequality between women and men in the labor market and on the job, the changes in labor force participation do not prove that gender no longer matters. Instead, feminist research demonstrates the enduring importance of gender in the organization of production. Gender and sexual harassment happen at work in part because of the persistent stereotypical association of men and masculinity with production and women and femininity with reproduction. Gender hierarchy persists despite major historical transformations in economic and social structures because taken-for-granted interactional processes reinscribe gender inequality onto new social arrangements and institutions (Ridgeway 1997). Even more important, feminist research suggests that relations between women and men are built in large part on the complex feedback loop between enterprises and households, two territories that look increasingly similar as work sites.

Where Work Also Happens, or, Why Do You Think They Call It House**work**?

The caring work of families is typically hidden in the privacy of people's homes. It is frequently performed out of duty, affection, or self-preservation rather than for pay. It is nonetheless work. This work is considered simultaneously to be demeaning drudgery and the fulfilling height of the feminine family roles of wife and mother (Romero 1992). Because caring, especially when it is domestic, is not considered work, it fails to earn for women the respect and consideration that men's employment earns for them (Ferree 1984; Hunt and Hunt 1987). Feminist researchers, building on empirical studies of housewifery such as Oakley's 1974 classic *Woman's Work,* continue to substantiate the fundamental claim that reproductive tasks, whether performed at home for kin, in other people's homes for wages, or through institutions such as hotels, nursing homes, elementary schools, or restaurants, add value and "produce goods and services for one's own use or in exchange for pay or support" and therefore fit the technical criteria for "work" (Reskin and Padavic 1994:1).

Reproductive labor has been transformed by new technologies (e.g., electricity, indoor plumbing, and the appliances they make possible) and by the mass marketing of consumer goods formerly made at home (clothing and foodstuffs). Many aspects of housework are less arduous and skilled in industrialized countries than they were for previous generations of women (and remain in poor or war-torn countries where maintaining shelter and finding fuel, food, and potable water are major tasks). Yet new technologies and consumerism, combined with changing notions of gender and family, have raised standards of cleanliness and other maternal and housewifely duties, thus adding to the housework load. This at least partly explains why the hours per week U.S. women spent doing housework varied less than 10 percent (51 to 56 hours) between 1924 and 1974 (Vanek 1974), before declining to 41 hours a week (compared with 20 hours a week for men) by 1987 (Shelton 1992). Cooking and serving meals, washing dishes, doing laundry, cleaning up indoors and out, taking care of pets and houseplants, doing household paperwork, maintaining house and car, shopping, and running errands all take time and energy and contribute significant value to individual and family life. And adding child care increases the workload of domestic laborers enormously.

Indeed, the work of housework goes beyond material tasks; cooking for and feeding family members, for example, "involves connecting household members with the larger society and the day-to-day production of the kind of group life we know as 'family' " (DeVault 1987:179). Critics of deindustrialization warn about crime, family breakdown, and other social ills that burgeon when the discipline of work disappears

(Wilson 1996). They appear to forget that reproduction—especially caring for people—is also a discipline, imposed disproportionately on women, that requires equally high levels of reliability, attentiveness, and commitment (Baines, Evans, and Neysmith 1991). Feminist research that sees housewifery and mothering as work sharply contradicts the notion that paid jobs are the only way to discipline individuals and structure community life (Naples 1991).

Some of the most taxing elements of housework, moreover, remain largely *women's* work, even in two-earner couples. Men spend fewer than half the weekly hours preparing meals, cleaning the house, and doing laundry that are put in by women who are also full-time workers (Shelton 1992). There is significant variation in couples' arrangements, however. "Drudge wives," women in dual-earner couples who take on virtually all the housework in the classic "second shift" described by Hochschild (1989), coexist with relatively egalitarian couples and modified traditional arrangements. Still, the gendered division of household tasks generally means that women spend more time than their husbands doing repetitive, everyday, "low-control" tasks (Barnett and Rivers 1996; Ferree 1991).

Interestingly, in a period of "globalization," similar patterns of housework hold across countries as different as China, the United States, Great Britain, and Japan. Cross-nationally, comparable data on the division of household tasks show considerable variation in the degrees to which women, men, or both partners equally perform specific tasks in dual-earner couples. In none of those countries, however, do men alone undertake cleaning the house, washing clothes, or cooking as much as 15 percent of the time. Even in China, where equal sharing is most common among these four countries, it is a minority household strategy; in Japan, 9 out of 10 wives employed full-time do all the cleaning, cooking, and laundry; and in Great Britain, wives working full-time are solely responsible for these domestic tasks in two-thirds to nine-tenths of households, depending on the chores (Stockman, Bonney, and Xuewen 1995).

Mothering, in particular, is work—by definition, women's work. Mothers provide for, nurture, protect, and train children, all tasks that require resources, time, and labor to add value to goods and services as well as to children's lives (Polakow 1993; Ruddick 1995). The mother-work of ensuring children's (and community) survival, identity, and empowerment—reproduction in the most literal sense—can be especially labor-intensive and life-consuming for women whose struggles to raise healthy children in racist neighborhoods and societies regularly interweave home and enterprise, private and political concerns (Collins 1994; Naples 1992). Making a home from substandard housing, protecting children in violent neighborhoods, and navigating the bureaucratic public health and welfare states are all part of mother-work for poor women, especially single mothers (Oliker 1995). Fathering, too, can be as time-consuming and rewarding as mothering, and receives as little recognition as "real work" (Coltrane 1996). Both mothering and fathering are forms of reproduction that are not counted as work when they are performed for love at home rather than for money on the market. Also, they involve skills—changing diapers and otherwise providing for physical comfort, interpreting needs, resolving conflict, building trustworthy relationships—that are typically devalued because supposedly anyone can do them and because they are typed as "feminine" (Daniels 1987).

Domestic labor is more clearly "work" when it is paid for. The service economy of deindustrialized societies signals, on the one hand, that reproductive tasks (cooking, child care) are increasingly performed outside the home, for money. On the other hand, it also marks the commodification of reproductive labor in private households, as women employed in the labor market seek to shift their work in the home to paid domestic workers (Rerrich 1994). After all, why nag your husband to pick up his dirty socks when you can hire a maid (Romero 1992)? Middle-class Chinese women in Hong Kong have hired approximately 150,000 mostly Filipina domestic workers to facilitate their extensive entry into the labor force (Constable 1997). More than 40 percent of U.S. parents with annual family incomes above $75,000 have hired domestic caregivers to work with their children; depending on the race and class differences between employer and employee, caregivers may also be expected to perform housework along with child care (Wrigley 1995). Paid domestic workers' race, class, and sometimes immigrant status means they do a double shift of housework—one unpaid for their own families, and one for pay in other people's homes.

"Home" is also a site of women's resistance to the devaluing of their time and labor, and thus a place where a form of gendered (and raced) class struggle happens. The Black women household workers interviewed by Dill (1988) used "confrontation, chicanery, or cajolery" to assert self-respect, demand decent conditions, and build careers in the face of "social inequities that unjustly consigned Black women and their daughters to this low-status, low-paid, and dirtiest of women's jobs" (pp. 37-47, 51). Class relations (and race, too) happen in spaces where women do reproductive work for other women (Glenn 1992).

Home—supposedly private, reproductive space—is in addition the site of paid labor for off-site employers. Industrial homework blurs the line between home and factory and figures centrally in debates over working conditions and protective labor legislation that have raged for a century (Boris 1994). Women also work in the "underground economy," labor that goes uncounted both because of where it happens and because it often includes illegal activities such as selling sex, drugs, or stolen goods (Mitter 1994). The gendered invisibility of women's illegal employment allows pundits and politicians to claim—quite wrongly— that these women show no commitment to self-sufficiency or the work ethic (Edin and Lein 1997). Women also work in formal and informal organizations, building social movements, administering welfare, and cleaning up after the patriarchy, although their caring often does not count as "work" (Boria et al. 1993).

What you think of as "work"—as production as opposed to reproduction—depends on where you look (Messias et al. 1997). Feminist researchers have made a powerful contribution to the redefinition of work by looking from the standpoint of women's experiences. The move of reproductive labor from home to market, one of the central characteristics of deindustrialization, has not eroded the conventional gender division of power, but instead "appears to be contributing to its consolidation and even its growth" (Boyd et al. 1995:193). Moreover, the profitability of much service sector work—considered "production" when performed for pay—is subsidized by caring labor—considered "reproduction" (or love or duty) when women do it for no pay (Glazer 1993). The realities of women's productive and reproductive labor raise questions about the future of work that tend to be invisible in conventional, gender-blind accounts of deindustrialization.

What Counts? Redefining Work, Social Science, and Gender

The question of what counts as work is related to who does it (men "labor," women "love") and where (in the formal labor market, in the underground economy, or in the "domestic" realm). Conventional economics privileges the public marketplace and marginalizes both paid and unpaid caring work (Beasley 1994). What counts as work also depends on the social construction of *skill* and *value*—qualities of "production" that feminist research reveals as deeply gendered. Feminist research shows the empirical impossibility of sustaining the ideological exclusion of caring—reproduction—from the realm of activities that not only sustain but also add value to individual and community life. After a brief assessment of the gendered project of redefining skill, care, and work in deindustrializing societies, I conclude by summarizing some implications—for both mainstream and feminist social science—of the research reviewed in this chapter.

Skill, Caring, and the Redefinition of Work

As they redesign production around new technologies, employers in both the manufacturing and service sectors re-create a sharp distinction between skilled and unskilled workers and, in fact, women and men on the job (Walby 1989). The load levels of machines, timing of shifts, and the gender reassignment of reengineered tasks are not purely technological but also managerial decisions, representing social (and sexist) constructions of "skill" as well as notions of who is a "worker." By design, assignment, and socially constructed preferences, women's relationships to the changing technologies characteristic of deindustrialization make the value of women's skills particularly problematic (Jenson 1989).

The realities of women's caring obliterate the conventional boundary between production and reproduction. As waged work, caring for people—especially the young, the old, and the overworked—is notoriously underpaid. The reasons, while complex, have everything to do with gendered notions of skill and value that permeate labor markets and workplaces. Indeed, low wages in the service sector are the common focus of struggles for comparable worth (that is, equal pay for work of equal value) for at least two entwined reasons. First, neither tending people nor comforting them is thought to require special skills or training. Second, the most common caregivers—especially at a level not recognized as "professional"—are women (Acker 1989; Phillips and Taylor 1980). Moreover, caring for people literally does not count at all when it happens at home, for free. Unpaid caring work is excluded from macroeconomic statistics such as the gross domestic product, which purport to measure the "productivity" of the economy (Anderson 1991). In Germany, Italy, Norway, and France, supplementary accounts for nonmarket work allow for recognizing the value of reproductive labor, but in the United States this innovation has languished in policy limbo (Folbre 1995:15).

There is only one way to proclaim the "end of work" when this much caring—both paid and unpaid—is going on: by perpetuating the notion that women's time, effort, and responsibilities do not count. The dominant solution, in a U.S. society where public school children need tutoring and elders need looking after, seems to be to call on people to volunteer still more of their precious time. Appeals to voluntarism, although they may discipline citizens to repair fragmented deindustrialized communities, merely mask the unremunerated subsidy women have provided to both employers and government and increase women's time poverty (Glazer 1984). Privatizing the crises of production and reproduction through calls for unpaid community service treats deindustrialization as a failure of moral will rather than a failure to realize that women have long helped reproduce the market economy, and it perpetuates the false division between production and reproduction. The past decade (and more) of feminist research shows this indisputably; the task remains of shaping how we think about and respond to deindustrialization around these insights.

Reinvigorating Social Science and Feminism

Characterizing production and reproduction as complementary but distinct elements in a functional whole "tends to exaggerate the differences and occlude the similarities" between the two realms (Fraser 1989:119). The functionalism of classical social science epitomizes and indeed institutionalizes the "men are workers, women are mothers" notion of gender. What is increasingly obvious is that work and home are not the distinct, gendered realms portrayed in classical sociology. On the one hand, not only does the labor force look increasingly "feminized," but also markets and enterprises are places where difference and dominance are constructed in gender and race as well as class terms. On the other hand, households are important sites of class and race as well as gender relations, where long-unrecognized and -undervalued work happens, and where people struggle daily over money, care, privilege, and identity. The crises of production and reproduction are *both* about changes that could transform gender relations (as well as class and race relations). In the medium term—the next 10 years of research and activism—one of the most important implications of feminist assessments of production and reproduction is that dichotomy-driven theories cannot capture the complexity of these realities, and are insufficient for feminist social science.

In fact, the accumulated knowledge of the past 10 years of feminist social science flies in the face of the tidy dichotomy between men producing goods and services for exchange in rational, bureaucratic factories and offices, and women reproducing family members in caring homes. Production and reproduction are not segregated into neat spatial or logical realms. People in factories, offices, and unemployment lines are all making class and gender as well as race and sexuality. People in kitchens, bedrooms, and bathrooms are adding value to goods and services for themselves and others. Discipline and skill are gendered features of caring, whether performed at home by a relative for love or in a hospital by a stranger for money—indeed, even when care providers are driven to comfort strangers for pay by the need to support loved ones at home. Investigating how deindustrializing societies organize gender and how gender organizes deindustrializing societies reinforces a basic social science insight: Human beings are always and everywhere making not just things, but people and social relations.

Some analysts seem to think class is irrelevant in postindustrial societies. Yet the organization of production, groupings based on control over skills and resources, and decisions about value all matter tremendously in the global transformation for which deindustrialization is shorthand. What is irrelevant (or perhaps obsolete) is the narrow and exclusionary claim that class only matters or happens for men in paid work. Feminist redefinitions of work—specifically, analyses that acknowledge rather than sever the links between enterprises and families, production and reproduction—can usefully complicate a more global definition of class with race and gender. Surely the crises of production and reproduction attendant on deindustrialization signal not the end of work but the beginning of new struggles over inequality and poverty, and over ecologically and democratically sustainable strategies for global as well as individual and familial survival.

Indeed, feminists can help people interpret the transitions and dislocations of deindustrialization. Deindustrialization generates plenty of "private troubles" and makes it hard to grasp the broader context of social change (Mills 1959). Feminist analyses that acknowledge people's sense of "crisis" around work, family, and government can defuse the scapegoating people do as their commonsense response to feeling beleaguered, impoverished, and disenfranchised by social change. Feminist studies of deindustrialization and the gendered organization of paid and unpaid work can contribute to people's interpreting their experiences in the context of economic and social forces they can organize to understand and shape. But feminism can strengthen people's sociological imaginations in this way only if we can explain that—and how—production and reproduction, paid and unpaid work, gender difference and male dominance are connected. By gendering our macro-level models of society—our theories of changing regimes of production, of labor markets and world trade, of the development and decline of welfare states—feminist social science can make such connections apparent not only at the level of individual interactions, households, and enterprises but also at the level of global and historical change.

Marshaled to feminist ends—for example, to pose the realities of women's low-paid and unpaid caring against the growing insistence that waged labor is the only acceptable way to contribute to society—research of the type I have reviewed here can bridge the gap between pocketbook issues and sexual politics, between feminist theory and women's movement practice (Brush 1997; Hartmann et al. 1996). Feminist organizing appears to be more effective than relying on government, party, or union (Elman 1996), and research that challenges business as usual—in social science, in policy, in offices and factories, and at home—can provide feminists with the empirical and conceptual tools to help mobilize women on their own behalf.

References

Acker, J. 1989. *Doing Comparable Worth: Gender, Class, and Pay Equity.* Philadelphia: Temple University Press.

Adler, N. J. and D. N. Izraeli. 1994. *Competitive Frontiers: Women Managers in a Global Economy.* Cambridge, MA: Blackwell Business.

Allan, J. 1993. "Male Elementary Teachers: Experiences and Perspectives." Pp. 113-27 in *Doing "Women's Work": Men in Nontraditional Occupations,* edited by C. L. Williams. Newbury Park, CA: Sage.

Amott, T. 1993. *Caught in the Crisis: Women and the U.S. Economy Today.* New York: Monthly Review Press.

Amott, T. and J. Matthaei. 1996. *Race, Gender, and Work: A Multicultural Economic History of Women in the United States.* Rev. ed. Boston: South End.

Anderson, L. 1989. "Beautiful Red Dress." On *Strange Angels* (Record album). New York: Warner Bros. Records.

Anderson, V. 1991. *Alternative Economic Indicators.* London: Routledge.

Anderson, T. L. and P. J. Hill, eds. 1996. *The Privatization Process: A Worldwide Perspective.* Lanham, MD: Rowman & Littlefield.

Applegate, J. S. and L. W. Kaye. 1993. "Male Elder Caregivers." Pp. 152-67 in *Doing "Women's Work": Men in Nontraditional Occupations,* edited by C. L. Williams. Newbury Park, CA: Sage.

Aronowitz, S. and W. DeFazio. 1994. *The Jobless Future: Sci-Tech and the Dogma of Work.* Minneapolis: University of Minnesota Press.

Baines, C. T., P. M. Evans, and S. M. Neysmith, eds. 1991. *Women's Caring: Feminist Perspectives on Social Welfare.* Toronto: McClelland & Stewart.

Barnett, R. C. and C. Rivers. 1996. *She Works, He Works: How Two-Income Families Are Happier, Healthier, and Better-Off.* San Francisco: Harper.

Beasley, C. 1994. *Sexual Economyths: Conceiving a Feminist Economics.* New York: St. Martin's.

Bem, S. L. 1993. *The Lenses of Gender: Transforming the Debate on Sexual Inequality.* New Haven, CT: Yale University Press.

Bluestone, B. and B. Harrison. 1982. *The Deindustrialization of America: Plant Closings, Community Abandonment, and the Dismantling of Basic Industry.* New York: Basic Books.

Boje, T. P. 1991. "Flexibility and Fragmentation in the Labour Market." Pp. 137-65 in *Towards a New Europe? Structural Change in the European Economy,* edited by A. Amin and M. Dietrich. Hants, UK: Edward Elgar.

Boria, M. S., C. Bevilaqua, H. Gualtieri, Y. Hernandez, J. A. Jimenez, E. Sorenson, and D. Weber. 1993. "July 18, 1988, at a Sexual Assault and Battered Women's Center." Pp. 193-200 in *Violence against Women: The Bloody Footprints,* edited by P. B. Bart and E. G. Moran. Newbury Park, CA: Sage.

Boris, E. 1994. *Home to Work: Motherhood and the Politics of Industrial Homework in the United States.* Cambridge: Cambridge University Press.

Boyd, M., M. A. Mulvilhill, and J. Myles. 1995. "Gender, Power, and Postindustrialism." Pp. 178-206 in *Gender Inequality at Work,* edited by J. A. Jacobs. Thousand Oaks, CA: Sage.

Browne, I. 1997. "Explaining the Black-White Gap in Labor Force Participation among Women Heading Households." *American Sociological Review* 62:236-52.

Brush, L. D. 1987. "Understanding the Welfare Wars: Privatization in Britain under Thatcher." *Berkeley Journal of Sociology* 32:261-79.

————. 1997. "Harm, Moralism, and the Struggle for the Soul of Feminism." *Violence Against Women* 3:237-56.

Bullock, S. 1994. *Women and Work.* London: Zed.

Burtless, G. 1990. *A Future of Lousy Jobs? The Changing Structure of U.S. Wages.* Washington, DC: Brookings Institution.

Collins, P. H. 1994. "Shifting the Center: Race, Class, and Feminist Theorizing about Motherhood." Pp. 56-74 in *Representations of Motherhood,* edited by

D. Bassin, M. Honey, and M. M. Kaplan. New Haven, CT: Yale University Press.

Coltrane, S. 1996. *Family Man: Fatherhood, Housework, and Gender Equity.* New York: Oxford University Press.

Connell, R. W. 1995. *Masculinities.* Berkeley: University of California Press.

Constable, N. 1997. *Maid to Order in Hong Kong: Stories of Filipina Workers.* Ithaca, NY: Cornell University Press.

Dalla Costa, M. and G. F. Dalla Costa, eds. 1995. *Paying the Price: Women and the Politics of International Economic Strategy.* London: Zed.

Daniels, A. K. 1987. "Invisible Work." *Social Problems* 34:403-15.

DeVault, M. L. 1987. "Doing Housework: Feeding and Family Life." Pp. 178-91 in *Families and Work,* edited by N. Gerstel and H. E. Gross. Philadelphia: Temple University Press.

Dill, B. T. 1988. " 'Making Your Job Good Yourself': Domestic Service and the Construction of Personal Dignity." Pp. 33-52 in *Women and the Politics of Empowerment,* edited by A. Bookman and S. Morgen. Philadelphia: Temple University Press.

Edin, K. and L. Lein. 1997. "Work, Welfare, and Single Mothers' Economic Survival Strategies." *American Sociological Review* 61:253-66.

Elman, R. A. 1996. *Sexual Subordination and State Intervention: Comparing Sweden and the U.S.* Providence, RI: Berghahn.

England, P. 1992. *Comparable Worth: Theories and Evidence.* New York: Aldine de Gruyter.

Fagan, C. 1996. "Gendered Time Schedules: Paid Work in Great Britain." *Social Politics* 3:72-106.

Ferguson, T. C. (with M. Sharples). 1994. *Blue Collar Women: Trailblazing Women Take on Men-Only Jobs.* Liberty Corner, NJ: New Horizon.

Ferree, M. M. 1984. "Sacrifice, Satisfaction, and Social Change: Employment and the Family." Pp. 61-79 in *My Troubles Are Going to Have Trouble with Me: Everyday Trials and Triumphs of Women Workers,* edited by K. B. Sacks and D. Remy. New Brunswick, NJ: Rutgers University Press.

———. 1991. "The Gender Division of Labor in Two-Earner Marriages: Dimensions of Variability and Change." *Journal of Family Issues* 12:158-80.

Fine, M., L. Weis, J. Addelston, and J. Marusza. 1997. "(In)Secure Times: Constructing White Working-Class Masculinities in the Late 20th Century." *Gender & Society* 11:52-68.

Folbre, N. 1995. "Domesticate the Gross Product." In *Real World Macro,* 12th ed., edited by R. Albelda, M. Breslow, J. Miller, B. Reed, B. Snyder, and the Dollars & Sense Collective. Somerville, MA: Dollars & Sense.

Fraser, N. 1989. *Unruly Practices: Power, Discourse and Gender in Contemporary Social Theory.* Minneapolis: University of Minnesota Press.

Garnett, S. 1997. "It's Tough to Be Young Today." *Dollars & Sense* 213 (September-October):50.

Glazer, N. Y. 1984. "Servants to Capital: Unpaid Domestic Labor and Paid Work." *Review of Radical Political Economics* 16:61-87.

———. 1993. *Women's Paid and Unpaid Labor: The Work Transfer in Health Care and Retailing.* Philadelphia: Temple University Press.

Glenn, E. N. 1992. "From Servitude to Service Work: Historical Continuities in the Racial Division of Paid Reproductive Labor." *Signs* 18:1-43.

Hamper, B. 1991. *Rivethead: Tales from the Assembly Line.* New York: Warner.

Harris, C. S. 1984. "The Magnitude of Job Loss from Plant Closings and the Generation of Replacement Jobs: Some Recent Evidence." *Annals of the American Academy of Political and Social Science* 475:15-27.

Hartmann, H. I., E. Bravo, C. Bunch, N. Hartsock, R. Spalter-Roth, L. Williams, and M. Blanco. 1996. "Bringing Together Feminist Theory and Practice: A Collective Interview." *Signs* 21:917-51.

Herrnstein, R. J. and C. Murray. 1996. *The Bell Curve: Intelligence and Class Structure in American Life.* New York: Free Press.

Hesse, J. J., ed. 1988. *Regional Structural Change and Industrial Policy in International Perspective: U.S., Great Britain, France, Federal Republic of Germany.* Baden-Baden, Germany: Nomos.

Hochschild, A. R. (with A. Machung). 1989. *The Second Shift.* New York: Penguin.

———. 1997. *The Time Bind: When Work Becomes Home and Home Becomes Work.* New York: Metropolitan.

Hunt, J. G. and L. L. Hunt. 1987. "Male Resistance to Role Symmetry in Dual-Earner Households: Three Alternative Explanations." Pp. 192-203 in *Families and Work,* edited by N. Gerstel and H. E. Gross. Philadelphia: Temple University Press.

Jacobs, J. A. & S. T. Lim. 1995. "Trends in Occupational and Industrial Sex Segregation in 56 Countries, 1960-1980." Pp. 259-93 in *Gender Inequality at Work,* edited by J. A. Jacobs. Thousand Oaks, CA: Sage.

Jenson, J. 1989. "The Talents of Women, the Skills of Men: Flexible Specialization and Women. Pp. 141-55 in *The Transformation of Work? Skill, Flexibility and the Labour Process,* edited by S. Wood. London: Unwin Hyman.

Jessop, B. 1994. "Post-Fordism and the State." Pp. 251-79 in *Post-Fordism: A Reader,* edited by A. Amin. Oxford: Basil Blackwell.

Kamerman, S. B. 1995. "Gender Role and Family Structure Changes in the Advanced Industrialized West: Implications for Social Policy." Pp. 231-56 in *Poverty, Inequality, and the Future of Social Policy: Western States in the New*

World Order, edited by K. McFate, R. Lawson, and W. J. Wilson. New York: Russell Sage Foundation.

Kessler-Harris, A. 1981. *Women Have Always Worked: An Historical Overview.* Old Westbury, NY: Feminist Press.

Kessler-Harris, A. and K. B. Sacks. 1987. "The Demise of Domesticity in America." Pp. 65-84 in *Women, Households, and the Economy,* edited by L. Beneria and C. R. Stimpson. New Brunswick, NJ: Rutgers University Press.

Kuhn, S. and B. Bluestone. 1987. "Economic Restructuring and the Female Labor Market: The Impact of Industrial Change on Women." Pp. 3-32 in *Women, Households, and the Economy,* edited by L. Beneria and C. R. Stimpson. New Brunswick, NJ: Rutgers University Press.

Laslett, B. and J. Brenner. 1989. "Gender and Social Reproduction: Historical Perspectives." *Annual Review of Sociology* 15:381-404.

Lerner, G. 1979. "The Lady and the Mill Girl: Changes in the Status of Women in the Age of Jackson." Pp. 15-30 in *The Majority Finds Its Past: Placing Women in History.* Oxford: Oxford University Press.

Lorber, J. 1994. *Paradoxes of Gender.* New Haven, CT: Yale University Press.

McLanahan, S. and I. Garfinkel. 1995. "Single-Mother Families and Social Policy: Lessons for the U.S. from Canada, France, and Sweden." Pp. 367-83 in *Poverty, Inequality, and the Future of Social Policy: Western States in the New World Order,* edited by K. McFate, R. Lawson, and W. J. Wilson. New York: Russell Sage Foundation.

Messias, D. K. H., E. Im, A. Page, H. Revev, J. Spiers, L. Yoder, and A. I. Meleis. 1997. "Defining and Redefining Work: Implications for Women's Health." *Gender & Society* 11:296-323.

Mills, C. W. 1959. *The Sociological Imagination.* New York: Oxford University Press.

Mingione, E. 1985. "Social Reproduction of the Surplus Labour Force: The Case of Southern Italy." Pp. 14-54 in *Beyond Employment: Household, Gender and Subsistence,* edited by N. Redclift and E. Mingione. Oxford: Basil Blackwell.

Mitter, S. 1994. "On Organising Women in Casualised Work: A Global Overview." Pp. 14-52 in *Dignity and Daily Bread: New Forms of Economic Organising among Poor Women in the Third World and the First,* edited by S. Rowbotham & S. Mitter. London: Routledge.

Murray, C. 1994. "What to Do about Welfare." *Commentary* 98:26-34.

Naples, N. 1991. " 'Just What Needed to Be Done': The Political Practice of Women Community Workers in Low-Income Neighborhoods." *Gender & Society* 5:478-94.

————. 1992. "Activist Mothering: Cross-Generational Continuity in the Community Work of Women from Low-Income Urban Neighborhoods." *Gender & Society* 6:441-63.

Oakley, A. 1974. *Woman's Work: The Housewife, Past and Present.* New York: Vintage.

Oliker, S. J. 1995. "Work Commitment and Constraint among Mothers on Workfare." *Journal of Contemporary Ethnography* 24:165-95.

Pahl, R. E. and C. Wallace. 1985. "Household Work Strategies in Economic Recession." Pp. 189-227 in *Beyond Employment: Household, Gender and Subsistence,* edited by N. Redclift and E. Mingione. Oxford: Basil Blackwell.

Pease, N. C. 1992. Statement of Nancy C. Pease, Smithville, NJ. Pp. 31-36 in U.S. House of Representatives Committee on Education and Labor, *Hearing on Sexual Harassment in Nontraditional Occupations.* Washington, DC: Government Printing Office.

Phillips, A. and B. Taylor. 1980. "Sex and Skill: Notes towards a Feminist Economics." *Feminist Review* 6:79-88.

Plantenga, J. 1996. "For Women Only? The Rise of Part-Time Work in the Netherlands." *Social Politics* 3:57-71.

Polakow, V. 1993. *Lives on the Edge: Single Mothers and Their Children in the Other America.* Chicago: University of Chicago Press.

Rerrich, M. S. 1994. "Modernizing the Patriarchal Family in West Germany: Some Findings on the Redistribution of Family Work between Women." *European Journal of Women's Studies* 3:27-37.

Reskin, B. F. and I. Padavic. 1994. *Women and Men at Work.* Thousand Oaks, CA: Pine Forge Press.

Ridgeway, C. L. 1997. "Interaction and the Conservation of Gender Inequality: Considering Employment." *American Sociological Review* 62:218-35.

Rifkin, J. 1995. *The End of Work: The Decline of the Global Labor Force and the Dawn of the Post-market Era.* New York: G. P. Putnam.

Romero, M. 1992. *Maid in the U.S.A.* New York: Routledge.

Rosener, J. B. 1995. *America's Competitive Secret: Utilizing Women as a Management Strategy.* New York: Oxford University Press.

Rubery, J., C. Fagan, and M. Smith. 1995. *Bulletin on Women and Employment in the EU.* No. 7. (Published by the Equal Opportunities Commission serving the European Union, Brussels.)

Ruddick, S. 1995. *Maternal Thinking: Toward a Politics of Peace.* Boston: Beacon.

Schor, J. B. 1991. *The Overworked American: The Unexpected Decline of Leisure.* New York: Basic Books.

Shelton, B. A. 1992. *Women, Men, and Time: Gender Differences in Paid Work, Housework, and Leisure.* Westport, CT: Greenwood.

Sidel, R. 1996. *Keeping Women and Children Last: America's War on the Poor.* New York: Penguin.

Sternlieb, G. and C. W. Baker. 1987. "Placing Deindustrialization in Perspective." Pp. 85-107 in *Women, Households, and the Economy,* edited by L. Beneria and C. R. Stimpson. New Brunswick, NJ: Rutgers University Press.

Stockman, N., N. Bonney, and S. Xuewen. 1995. *Women's Work in East and West: The Dual Burden of Employment and Family Life.* Armonk, NY: M. E. Sharpe.

Tewksbury, R. 1993. "Male Strippers: Men Objectifying Men." Pp. 168-81 in *Doing "Women's Work": Men in Nontraditional Occupations,* edited by C. L. Williams. Newbury Park, CA: Sage.

Tienda, M., S. A. Smith, and V. Ortiz. 1987. "Industrial Restructuring, Gender Segregation, and Sex Differences in Earnings." *American Sociological Review* 52:195-210.

Vanek, J. 1974. "Time Spent in Housework." *Scientific American* 231 (November):116-20.

Walby, S. 1989. "Flexibility and the Changing Sexual Division of Labour." Pp. 127-40 in *The Transformation of Work? Skill, Flexibility and the Labour Process,* edited by S. Wood. London: Unwin Hyman.

Wilson, W. J. 1996. *When Work Disappears: The World of the New Urban Poor.* New York: Knopf.

Women's Bureau. 1996a. "Nontraditional Occupations for Women" [On-line]. Available: www.dol.gov/dol/wb/public/ wb_pubs/nontra96.htm

Women's Bureau. 1996b. "20 Facts on Women Workers" [On-line]. Available: www.dol.gov/dol/wb/public/wb_pubs/20f96.htm

Wrigley, J. 1995. *Other People's Children.* New York: Basic Books.

Yoder, J. D. and P. Aniakudo. 1997. " 'Outsider within' the Firehouse: Subordination and Difference in the Social Interactions of African American Women Firefighters." *Gender & Society* 11:324-41.

PART III

GENDER, DISCOURSE, AND CULTURE

CHAPTER 7

"Woman" as Symbol and Women as Agents

*Gendered Religious
Discourses and Practices*

SUSAN STARR SERED

During the past half century, issues of gender and religion have been confronted and negotiated around the world in a variety of contexts with a variety of outcomes—many of which seem inconsistent (Callaway and Creevey 1994; Neitz 1987; Shiman 1986). For example, the autonomy of Catholic nuns and women pastors has expanded greatly, but the Church continues to refuse to ordain women as priests (Iadarola 1985; Wallace 1993). Muslim women's access to religious learning has increased enormously, at the same time that unveiled women are stoned on the streets of Iran (Darrow 1985). And in Africa, women have founded new religions (Jules-Rosette 1979), while Muslim and Christian clergy attempt to suppress women's traditional religious forms (Callaway and Creevey 1994).

The twentieth century has been a period of dramatic shifts in gendered religious patterns. The pace of these changes provides scholars with opportunities to examine the construction and deconstruction of gendered religious institutions and the negotiation of gendered religious roles. Scholars have examined which symbolic complexes endure over time, how religions adapt or fail to change when women's and men's social roles are realigned, and what sorts of discourses have been generated to promote or discourage such realignments. Gendered religious shifts have occurred in all world religions and in many tribal religions. Clearly, any attempt to summarize patterns of changes cannot be comprehensive; even within particular religious traditions, gender configurations have shifted in different ways for different groups. My aim in this essay is to draw attention to some of the more significant gendered realignments of religion, and to review the impacts of gender analyses on religious studies.

From the perspective of gender analysis, religion during the twentieth century has followed a path different from that of other social institutions. Although women throughout the world certainly still suffer from economic and political discrimination and disadvantages, there has been, internationally, a growing belief in gender equality. In the religious sphere, in contrast, the development of Jewish, Christian, Muslim, and Hindu feminist discourses has been paralleled by the development of fundamentalist discourses that give renewed—and often harshly unprecedented—emphasis to patriarchal values (Hawley 1994). A preliminary question we must ask is why religion has "behaved" differently than other social institutions in regard to gender and change.

When analyzing gender in religious systems it is crucial to understand that two ontologically different sets of issues are involved. The first centers on *women*—that is, actual people who have varying degrees of agency within specific social situations. Women as agents can demand rights, enter into negotiations, and protest unfair treatment. In religious contexts, agency is expressed in such activities as the ability to state one's religious needs freely, to image the divine and address the divine as one sees fit, to gather together openly with others of like mind in order to carry out rituals, and to choose freely which rituals and ceremonies to join or eschew. The second set of issues centers on *Woman*—a symbolic construct conflating gender, sex, and sexuality, and comprised of allegory, ideology, metaphor, fantasy, and (at least in male-dominated religions) men's psychological projections. Although Woman may have little grounding in the real experiences of women, in religious interactions these two ontologically distinct categories tend to be conflated. Woman as a symbol is often associated with some of the deepest, most compelling, and most tenacious theological and mythological structures in religious traditions, and these structures imprint the lives of women involved in those traditions.

What I have said about women and Woman seems, in many ways, also to be true of nonreligious matters. In political and economic arenas in the United States, for example, women are both agents (e.g., members of the workforce and voters) and symbols (e.g., of sexuality). Yet despite certain similarities, religious and secular gender conflicts do differ in important ways. Religious conflicts entail a dimension that is generally absent from other types of conflict—religious conflicts tend to be, by definition, conflicts over symbols (symbols are, after all, the currency of religion). In religious conflicts the issue of divine legitimation comes into play; religious symbols are eternal symbols—they are symbols of the very order of Heaven and Earth, and thus intrinsically difficult to change. Because symbols are what religion does best, the tension between women and Woman is particularly strong. Founding myths, creation myths, etiological myths all proclaim that the way that "we" do gender is natural and sacred.

It is often at the fuzzy meeting points of symbol and agency (Woman and women) that we find the most extensive control of women, as well as conflict regarding that control. From the point of view of patriarchal institutions, women are problematic symbols because they always "threaten" to turn into agents. For example, in many Middle Eastern societies, virginity is an important symbol of a family's honor, but one that can be ruined through the agency of the woman on whose body that symbol is imprinted. Because women know themselves to be agents, many cultures do things to women's bodies to encourage or force them to internalize an understanding of themselves as symbols. These "things" are often expressed through the language of religious ritual and ideology (Daly 1978), but can also directly and literally be cut into the body, through genital mutilation of young girls—infibulation and clitoridectomy (Lutkehaus and Roscoe 1995).[1] As Boddy (1989) has argued, genital mutilation is an expression of the overdetermination of women's gender—in my terms, of the process of converting an agent into a symbol. The infibulated woman has been taught or coerced into seeing herself and presenting herself to others as more of a symbol than an agent. Through practices such as genital mutilation, women are *transmuted* into cultural icons, and the medium of that transmutation is often religious.[2]

Because of the precariousness of the link between women and Woman (that is, the threat that women will shake off Woman), religious ideologies typically include a fallback position for when symbolism of the "good" Woman doesn't take—for situations in which women do not sufficiently internalize Woman. That fallback position is the "bad" Woman—the demonness, the source of original sin, Lilith, the witch. Women who do not comply with cultural symbols of "Good Woman" run the risk of having cultural symbols of "Bad Woman" forcibly imprinted onto their bodies: They may be stoned, raped, burned, or symbolically branded with "scarlet letters."

Thus, because religions deal in eternal, deeply rooted, psychically compelling, divinely mandated symbols, gender conflicts in religion tend to develop differently than conflicts in other institutional spheres. In addition, we may find that conflicts in other arenas are sometimes framed as religious conflicts in order that individuals may claim that "right" is on their side. For example, contemporary Middle Eastern frustration with or resistance to economic and cultural exploitation at the hands of the West is often framed in Islamic religious symbols— including that of the veiled Woman's body (Hawley 1994).

Scholars of religion in the humanities have accorded most of their attention to Woman (goddesses, demonesses, myths, and so on), whereas social scientists have focused on women (for example, patterns of church attendance). This dichotomy has hindered the study of gender and religion to a significant degree: The lives of women are shaped by cultural understandings of Woman, just as images of Woman are, at least to some extent, shaped by interactions with real women. Shaw (1994) expresses this notion nicely in her study of women in Tantric Buddhism:

> The religious lives of women unfold within a matrix of beliefs about women's capacities and the nature and value of femaleness. Beliefs and attitudes shaping women's self-perception—such as the symbolic content and interpretation of their religious practices—are just as important as material objects they wield and physical actions they perform. (p. 35)

Cultural symbols (such as Woman), because of their resonant mythic, ritualistic, and ideological power, have something of a life of their own, regardless of temporal social changes. The independence of cultural symbols, however, is neither absolute nor static. A variety of social forces (e.g., urbanization, transitions from village to state economies, the breakup of extended families, and new technologies) affect both women's agency through access to social and economic resources *and* cultural images of Woman as a symbol.

Symbols are generated and sustained in settings in which some people have more access to resources than do others, and so can impose their interpretations of situations and practices on the less privileged (Williams 1996). Thus, although there is no necessary association between women's experiences and any particular symbolization of Woman (such as goddess or demonness), the more agency women have, the more control they have over the creation and interpretation of symbols. Where any particular group of women falls along the agent-symbol continuum depends on the group's access to social resources. In some instances, the agency of women may grow strong enough to overpower the oppressive symbolic Woman, allowing the creation of gynocentric symbols, myths, and rituals that transform the image of Woman and that augment women's agency (Plaskow and Christ 1989). In other instances, the resources and thus agency of women may decrease, and the oppressive power of Woman as a symbol may correspondingly escalate.

Ratte's (1985) outstanding analysis of the early Hindu nationalist movement shows that at different stages in the development of the movement, men and women made conscious selections of particular Woman symbols from the vast mythical repertoire of Hindu tradition:

> Men, understandably, wanted to create an ideology which would not only inspire themselves and other men to act, but which would endow the male patriot with sufficient power and authority to succeed in what he undertook. Sharing power with women was acceptable if, as in the representations of both goddess and mother, powerful female figures played an inspirational role while remaining in the background, removed from the field of action. Women, however, looked for symbols that would include the desirable notion of complementarity while at the same time freeing women from domestic roles in order to make their active presence in the social and political realms both useful and necessary. In choosing the epic heroines women were fortunate in finding within their cultural and religious heritage a traditional symbol broad enough to encompass women's need for and experience of autonomy and involvement, and society's need to give clear meanings, traditionally justified, to the notions of duty and virtue. (p. 369)

In other situations, women seeking to expand their agency have rejected Woman images from their cultural repertoire and embellished Man images. For example, Esquivel (1987), like certain other Christian women of Central and South America, describes Jesus as a symbol of liberation for women and the poor, and the Virgin Mary as a symbol of passivity and suffering.

In the remainder of this essay, using a concept of gender that incorporates women as agents and Woman as symbols, I shall look at several of the more significant patterns of gendered religious realignment in the twentieth century.

The Old Ways under Attack

Throughout the world, traditional ways have been encroached upon and threatened by what can be labeled the *modern Western industrial-cultural complex*. This encroachment has had a twofold effect on understandings of gender and religion. On the one hand, in many societies, when the traditional ways come under attack, Woman becomes strengthened as a symbol of all that used to be thought good and noble. The elevation of Woman as a symbol of the good old ways tends to coincide with the oppression of women whose behavior is not in line with the reified ideal. These kinds of situations have been analyzed primarily by scholars studying religious fundamentalism. On the other hand, in those societies where men's traditional lifestyles become disrupted earlier or more thoroughly than women's, women may find that they are able to take over ritual resources that formerly belonged to men (who no longer want or can use them), or they may find that their own customary rituals have gained a new legitimacy by now representing both men and women.

Decreased Agency for Women

In many situations, Western hegemonic culture has led to a diminution of indigenous religious authority. Although the kinds of structural changes that lead to the decline of native religious authority often affect men and women in parallel ways, a closer look suggests that within specific cultural situations, the decline of one gender's religious opportunities is typically accompanied by the ascent of the other's.

Often, men's traditional religious forms—centralized and literate—have better fitted the culture of the modern world, and therefore have more easily survived than have women's traditional religious forms. Moreover, because the enforcers of Western hegemony are often men, we find cross-culturally that traditional male institutions become legitimated by colonial governments and international agencies, whereas women's institutions are ignored.[3]

Among the indigenous Bari of Colombia, for example, modernization (i.e., contact with Western capitalism) has meant a forced transition from egalitarianism to male dominance. In the ritual realm, the Bari traditionally exhibited full gender symmetry. Their primary ritual, Los Cantos, involved singing and exchange of gifts by pairs of men and women. In recent years, women no longer participate in Los Cantos. Buenaventura-Posso and Brown (1980) see this exclusion as part of a constellation of changes that includes the artificial creation of male chiefs where there had been no chiefs at all; forced breakup of the collective living unit and its replacement by the patriarchal nuclear family, with women dependent upon wage-earning men; elimination of women's traditional tasks and the shift of women's work from production to service; and the usurpation of women's role in healing by distribution of modern medicines through men chosen by the government.

In many societies, the decline of the midwife as a female ritual specialist with expertise in both health care and religion has had profound effects on women's religious power (Paul and Paul 1975; Cosminsky 1982).[4] As modern technology penetrates the traditional female reproductive sphere—a sphere that was both physical and spiritual—women lose important specialist functions. Not only midwives, but traditional fertility, infertility, and child health experts, most of whom were women, are replaced by modern medical personnel. Even when the new experts are themselves women, the traditional knowledge of women is denigrated. The medicalization and resultant despiritualization of childbirth and fertility—relating to birth as a biotechnical rather than a magical-spiritual event—has, in many cases, undermined one of the most important repositories of women's religious power. We can perhaps see a connection between the decline of women's agency in traditional midwifery and the alienated Woman at the mercy of "the hierarchical atmosphere of the hospital, the definition of childbirth as a medical emergency, the fragmentation of body from mind" (Rich [1976] 1986:176; see also Martin 1987).

Okinawa provides an illuminating case study of these issues. It is the only known society in the world in which women have dominated the official, mainstream religion for at least the past 500 years (the period for which we have documentation). Yet since the end of the nineteenth century, women's religious leadership has been eroded by the Japanese policy of compulsory land registration. In traditional Okinawan villages, high-ranked priestesses owned land that they passed on to their successors (usually their daughters). This land explicitly gave the priestesses the economic autonomy necessary for them to remain unmarried. With Japanese annexation, Okinawan land was registered in the names of male "heads of household," and all over Okinawa, priestesses lost their land to male relatives (Lebra 1966). In Henza Village, where I carried out fieldwork during 1994-95, the previous head priestess had lost her house to her brother, a situation that, according to the oldest living priestess in the village, had profound effects upon the spiritual potency and social status of the current head priestess.

Since World War II, young women in Okinawan cities have begun dancing in young men's *eisaa* groups (typically in a very subordinate role), and they have stopped dancing in traditional women's *usudeku* groups. This phenomenon illustrates a widespread pattern in which women's rituals fade away as men's rituals become normative for both men and women. In Okinawan cities, *eisaa* dancing has become both a municipally supported economic extravaganza and a public expression of Okinawan (versus Japanese or American) culture. No contemporary women's ritual is comparable in scope and visibility to contemporary men's *eisaa*.

Throughout the twentieth century, Okinawan men have become more integrated into Japanese political and economic structures than have Okinawan women. Recently, a men's fishing ritual known as *haari* (a boat race) has become part of the public, community-oriented folklore of Henza and other villages, and is blossoming under municipal auspices. The priestesses' traditional rituals, many of which are performed in the sacred groves deep inside the jungle, do not lend themselves to the kind of public display found at the newly expanded men's rituals. Lebra (1966) notes that in many villages, "the male political leaders are loath to allot funds for [priestesses'] ritual purposes. . . . This changed attitude undoubtedly derives from the influence of Japanese culture, which accords the male a higher status in all spheres of action, religious as well as secular" (p. 78). I would add that the Japanese are not alone in exerting a patriarchal influence upon Okinawan culture; their efforts have been complemented by the American military occupation and the Western cinema.

The Okinawan example is particularly instructive because the Okinawan priestess is both agent and symbol; the priestess is the embodiment of *kami-sama*—divinity. As a symbol, the Okinawan priestess is self-created, giving birth to herself through a series of dreams and rituals (Sered forthcoming). Okinawan priestesses are indeed symbols, but of divinity, not of Woman. In fact, Okinawan culture is characterized by an almost total absence of gender ideology, although all priestesses and most shamans are women, Okinawans do not offer any ideological reasons to explain why this is the case. Unlike in many male-dominated religions, religious leadership in Okinawa is not explained in terms of gender characteristics.

Okinawa is one of the few known societies in which women traditionally have generated the key cultural symbols, but with the decline in women's social resources, they are losing their power to create and manipulate symbols. The new symbols of Woman—Western cinema stars and high-heeled, saccharine-voiced Japanese welcome girls—function to spread an ideology of women as uninterested in agency.

Religious Fundamentalism

We turn now to an extreme variation on the theme of women's diminished agency in religion in the wake of decreased access to significant social resources. In the context of religious fundamentalism, women not only have little or no power to generate and manipulate symbols, but actually are themselves reduced to being symbols.

Lazarus-Yafe (1988:37) has noted that fundamentalist groups typically reject legal steps aimed at reducing inequality between women and men and exclude women from leadership positions within their own groups. In a superb analysis that introduces Hawley's edited volume *Fundamentalism and Gender,* Hawley and Proudfoot (1994) explain the centrality of gender ideology among fundamentalist groups: First, religious fundamentalism is often associated with a feeling of being beleaguered and wronged, which is then projected onto women as the origin or symbol of moral decline. "Fundamentalist groups typically see themselves as victims of someone else's violence, physically or otherwise. They feel battered by the onslaughts of the modern world—not technologically, perhaps, but from a moral and communitarian point of view" (p. 21). Men in fundamentalist groups feel that they cannot control the outside forces that increasingly determine their lives, so they turn their attention to controlling the "Other" in their midst—Woman. In many fundamentalist discourses,

> women's behavior is regarded not only as being symptomatic of cosmic dislocation but as being its cause. Embodying the other that is at once intimate and ubiquitous, women serve as a fine canvas on which to project feelings of general besetment. They are close enough to serve as targets, yet pervasive enough to symbolize the cosmic dimensions of the challenge. For every text that places well-domesticated womanhood on a religious pedestal, another one announces that, if uncontrolled, women are the root of all evil; and to the perception of many fundamentalists, the loosening of women is a prominent feature of modern Western secularism. (p. 27)

Women in many societies deem it advantageous to participate in the fundamentalist enterprise for many of the same reasons as men. Women, perhaps even more than men in certain situations, may feel beset upon or denigrated by the demands of industrial and postindustrial societies, demands that their own socialization or inclination make difficult to fulfill.

In Muslim fundamentalist discourse, turning to religion is typically presented as a way of turning away from the West, culturally and materially. Ayatollah Khomeini compared the modest Muslim woman to the Western "floozie":

> The coquettes who put on makeup and go into the street showing off their necks, their hair, their shapes, did not fight against the Shah. They never did anything good, not those. They do not know how to be useful, neither socially, nor politically, nor professionally. (quoted in Betteridge 1983:122; compare Karim 1992)

In this view, Muslim women neither bear the full blame for their own degeneracy nor are they given full authority to restore their own dignity; Western society is accused of manipulating women's behavior, which then justifies Islamic control of women. In Islamic fundamentalist rhetoric, Woman is presented as a symbol—onto Woman's body is mapped either Western degeneracy or Islamic purity.

> Colonialism was fully aware of the sensitive and vital role of woman in the formation of the individual and of human society. They considered her the best tool for subjugation of the nations. Therefore, under such pretexts as social activity, the arts, freedom, etc., they pushed her to degeneracy and degradation, and made of her a doll who not only forgot her human role, but became the best tool for emptying others of their humanity. . . . In Western societies where capitalism is dominant . . . women's liberation is nothing but the liberty to be naked, to prostitute oneself. (Najmabadi 1991:67)

The defense against this degradation is to encourage women—and Woman—to be "a queen crowned in her kingdom and her home" (Haddad 1985:287).

In many ways, the Islamic fundamentalist rhetoric resembles Christian fundamentalist and Jewish orthodox rhetoric, especially in the emphasis given to control of sexuality and procreation. These themes are most consistently associated with Woman because in these areas men look upon women as most immutably "Other." As Moghadam (1994) has argued: "Because of their reproductive capacity, women are seen as the transmitters of group values and traditions and as *agents* of socialization of the young. When group identity becomes intensified, women are elevated to the status of *symbol* of the community and are compelled to assume the burden of the reproduction of the group" (p. 18; emphasis added).

A second aspect of gendered fundamentalism analyzed by Hawley and Proudfoot (1994) concerns devotion to restoring the idealized past:

> Fundamentalist religion, more than most, capitalizes on the strength of the connection between religion and childhood. In its devotion to restoring a golden age—a time better structured and more innocent than the present—it pulls toward the center of religious experience the more broadly felt adult need to solidify ties with a nurturing childhood. Not surprisingly, the figure massively responsible for nurturance in childhood—mother—is often give a prominent *symbolic* position in religious groups for whom this act of reconnection is a very substantial concern. (p. 31; emphasis added)

Third, fundamentalist men express a brand of "religious machismo" in which they as men must defend women against threats (often sexual threats) from the outside world. In particular, fundamentalist men see themselves as defending Woman—who becomes a symbol of their community. Woman and women here are conflated, as Hawley and Proudfoot contend: "These two kinds of women, the symbolic and the real, reinforce one another. Symbols of endangered womanhood can be more easily sustained if they are nourished in an environment where real women must depend on men to defend them; and the converse is also true" (p. 33). Put differently, in situations in which women have limited agency and therefore are dependent upon men to support and protect them, the symbol Woman tends to take on greater salience, leading to efforts to impress upon women's bodies and souls the imprint of Woman. The elevation of Woman is achieved through the suppression of women's autonomy.

As a highly charged symbolic category, Woman (and women's bodies) easily becomes the battlefield upon which secular and religious institutions engage in combat. Significantly, in the abortion controversy in the United States, the right-to-choose faction uses language of agency and the right-to-life side uses language of symbols. According to Papanek (1994), the language of prochoice stresses the importance of women's own choices: "While there are many differences of opinion on the 'Pro-Choice' side, there is a consistent tendency to emphasize individual autonomy with respect to reproductive issues" (p. 51). In contrast, antiabortion rhetoric often draws upon an explicitly religious discourse in which women's agency is disregarded, the fetus takes center stage, and women are reduced to symbolic vessels housing unborn children.

Women as Guardians of the Good Old Ways

In the preceding discussion of religious fundamentalism, I have argued that nostalgia for the good old days can lead to suppression of women's agency and the elevation of Woman as a symbol of the hallowed past. I now turn to another set of examples that illustrates a related theme.

In the wake of contact with the modern Western industrial-cultural complex, some women may come to be seen as guardians of local old ways, as experts in the traditional religion. In my own research among elderly Jewish women of Kurdish and Yemenite origin who live in Jerusalem (Sered 1992), I found their children and grandchildren often made comments such as, "My mother is closer to God than I am," or "The way my mother does it [religion] is better, but I myself am not strong enough to do it like she does." Even modern children and grandchildren who consider much of the old women's Judaism to be "superstition" turn to their elderly women relatives for information concerning the old ways, most especially concerning death and mourning. Children and grandchildren usually do not know exactly how the old women perform the rituals—nor do they care to learn. Their grandmothers may pray in Arabic, Kurdish, or another language that the younger generation does not know, and the youngsters rarely accompany the old women on pilgrimages to holy tombs. The old women's sacred knowledge has come to be surrounded by an aura of mystery that was not connected to women's rituals in Kurdistan or Yemen. Even the old women's cooking has taken on a new mystique: they proudly describe their traditional foods as needing special knowledge to prepare—"Not just anyone can do it."

While it is true that the spiritual prowess of elderly Kurdish and Yemenite women has become exalted, it is critical to understand that these same women are situated on just about the lowest rung of the sociocultural ladder in Israeli society. They are old and weak in a society that glorifies youth and strength; they are Middle Eastern in a society in which European (Ashkenazi) is higher on the hierarchy; they are sick, illiterate, and poor. In other words, their exalted symbolic status does not translate into any form of agency. Women who in the old days were the repositories of critical cultural knowledge in the realms of health and ritual have now become icons: sometimes negative icons of "superstition" and sometimes cutely positive icons of "folklore."

Much of the time that I spent with the women was in the context of a local senior citizens' day center where three times each week the women are addressed by a rabbi or *rabbanit* (rabbi's wife). Often, the theme of the address is that they should follow Jewish law rather than traditional customs—that they should ask rabbis' opinions about matters of Jewish observance, something these women were not accustomed to doing in the "old country," where women consulted other, more experienced women regarding ritual matters. In short, despite (or because of) their authentic ritual knowledge, these women are treated to systematic lessons in male dominance.

To take another example that, although not a twentieth-century one, illustrates beautifully the themes I have been addressing, Silverblatt (1980) writes that Andean women in the colonial period "were increasingly viewed by indigenous society as the defenders of ancient traditions and thus were encouraged to assume leading roles in the carrying out of native ritual" (p. 177). These rituals, however, began to diminish in legitimacy as colonial authorities introduced their own rituals. As a result, one effect of colonialism has been an enhancement of men's social position vis-à-vis women, legitimated by the introduction of a religious framework dominated by men in which Woman in the guise of the Virgin Mary has all but conquered women (see Gutierrez 1992).

Increasingly, in the Muslim world, the religious establishment has become concerned with stamping out indigenous women's rituals. For example, in Nubia, women's traditional dancing on the sheikh's birthday has become the target of attack by educated Muslim men (Kennedy 1978:92). Among Muslims in Sri Lanka, public observance of female puberty rituals has disappeared in major coastal settlements at the same time that the spread of greater pan-Islamic consciousness has placed increased emphasis upon "respectability" and the seclusion of women (McGilvray 1982; see also Bowen 1992; Karim 1992). In Iran, women's *sofreh* gatherings, at which they share votive meals, have been criticized for being pseudoreligious, nonorthodox, and unsponsored by official (male) religious leaders (Jamzadeh and Mills 1986). This erasing of women's agency (as expressed in certain traditional women's rituals) has been accompanied by fundamentalist discourse stressing Woman— purity and seclusion.

New Opportunities for Women's Agency

We sometimes find that the modern Western industrial-cultural complex can have a more negative effect upon men's institutions than upon women's institutions. For example, in some societies men's hunting activities have declined, or male-dominated corporate groups such as patrilineages have disintegrated, affecting men's agency adversely. Because these institutions tend to be associated with symbol systems (including Woman symbols), the decline of these institutions may stimulate the decline of Woman and the ascent of women. In certain circumstances, an outside source has bolstered women's agency, as in parts of the world where Christian missions have made a particular appeal to women through schools and clinics and the abolition of polygyny.

A key theme emerges when we look at societies in which women's religious agency has expanded: Agency, remember, is dependent upon access to social resources. Women's religious agency often increases in situations characterized by the absence of indigenous men who have the resources to propagate Woman as a symbol. For example, in rural Sudan, men's emigration from the villages has led to a strengthening of matrilineal ties and the expansion of women's autonomous religion. Conversely, in urban areas of the Middle East and Islamic Africa, where men's social and economic resources far exceed women's, urban fundamentalism has enhanced Woman rather than women.

Throughout parts of Africa and the Middle East a phenomenon loosely labeled zar (spirit-possession) religion has been spreading rapidly. The primary ritual complex of zar religion centers on contact with and expression of spirits; in group rituals, some or many women become possessed by their "zars." Zar groups are composed predominantly of women, and the vast majority of zar leaders are women (see Sered 1994). Traditional anthropological analysis of zar religion has explained it as an expression of women's social and sexual frustration amplified by the migration of men from the villages to the cities (Lewis 1975). More recently, however, feminist anthropologist Boddy (1989) has offered an entirely different analysis based on women's opportunities to bond with other women.

Boddy describes a typical contemporary family history in a Sudanese village: After the wedding, the groom goes back to the city to work while the bride "remains in her natal household until after the births of several children. . . . The ratio of adult women to adult men in [the village] is understandably high: 2.2:1. *Yet it is a situation which many women say they prefer"* (pp. 40-41; emphasis added). Boddy found that among village women there "is an explicit preference for women who are near relatives to live together" (p. 41). Even women who live with their husbands' kin generally return to their own mothers' homes during pregnancy, remaining there for a prolonged period after the birth, often extending such visits to quasi-permanent residence. Boddy notes the growing "tendency toward matrilocal residence and matrifocal groupings" (p. 83) in the village she studied.

Village women manage their households and maintain informal networks of exchange of food, child care, support, and information with other women. Women have a great deal of say regarding whom their children marry, because in this highly gender-segregated society only women can provide information about potential brides. Women prefer their sons to marry within the women's own families and not their husbands' families. And indeed, marriage of a son to the mother's brother's daughter is more frequent than marriage to the father's sister's daughter, thus strengthening the bonds among matrilineally related women.

The women spend a great deal of their time socializing and visiting, especially with sick neighbors and relatives, new mothers, girls and boys after infibulation and circumcision, and mourners. The women nowadays are freer to go out visiting because so many men have left the village, so that women's movements are less controlled by concerns of modesty. It is in this social world, relatively free of the presence of men, that zar religion has grown in popularity. Zar has spread among Sudanese women at the same time as women have become more autonomous—more in control of what is (for them) significant social and economic resources, and less constricted by men's presence. As women's agency has grown, so have their religious involvement and opportunities for religious leadership.[5]

In a variety of cultural situations in the twentieth century, women have become prominent in ritual activities and roles that were once exclusively men's. A theme in many of the studies looking at these situations is that the expansion of women's religious role is linked to women's expanded access to significant resources. For example, Powers (1986:194) has found Oglala women on the Pine Ridge Reservation in South Dakota participating in rituals that had once been restricted to men: the sun dance, the vision quest, and the sweat lodge have opened to women. Women's higher level of participation in rituals that were

formerly done by men can be explained as a function of the disintegration of men's social institutions in the wake of European conquest: In
many Native American communities today there simply are not enough
men able to fill the traditional roles. Among the Iroquois, "rituals once
associated with the exclusively male spheres of hunting and war activities are now said to further agricultural aims. As symbolic associations
with the crops are developed, women and feminine symbols acquire
new roles within men's rites" (Shimony 1980:253). Thus, where European conquest has more thoroughly destroyed men's activities (hunting
and war) than women's agricultural and domestic work, ritual attention
has shifted to arenas in which women have resources and high levels
of agency.

Among the Mapuche of southern Chile, the advent of the reservation system has prevented men from engaging in the traditional role of
mobile warriors and cattle herders, yet has allowed women to maintain
their own traditional subsistence modes. As a result, men more than
women have moved into wage labor and assimilated into modern
Chilean society. In the wake of these economic and social changes,
women have replaced men as shamans (*machis*). "Male *machis* are
disappearing because they are criticized for being unmasculine by the
Chilean/Catholic society. . . . Women who become *machis* are empowered because they have moral authority over the Mapuche community"
(Bacigalupo 1996:118).[6] However, women's power is confined to the
local scene, whereas men become integrated into the natural economy.

Christian influence has mixed effects. Throughout much of Africa
and Oceania, Christian missionaries have augmented women's agency
via schools and clinics, and have even offered shelter to women who
wish to leave their tribes or villages. As a result, in Zululand, for
instance, more women than men attend Christian churches, and women
serve as local church leaders; in some churches women may act as media
for a risen Bantu Christ. Sundkler (1961) suggests several reasons for
these phenomena: Men feel that clothes and Christianity are "unmanly,"
men prefer polygynous marriages, boys are busy looking after cattle
and have no time to go to church schools, and church women's organizations that help with loans attract many women. Thus, whereas in
traditional Zulu magic and ritual women had only minor roles, in the
mission churches the influence of women is enhanced.[7]

Christian missionaries often subvert men's agency in more direct
ways. For example, in Melanesia, missionaries have tried to obliterate
the men's "homosexual" rituals that had played a crucial role in the

establishment of the men's community (Lindenbaum 1987). In some villages in highland Papua New Guinea, missionaries have required male Christian converts to display their sacred flutes to women, from whom these ritual objects had traditionally been hidden (Sexton 1984). As a result, a traditional source of male supremacy has become demystified.

Because Christianity imposes its own Woman symbols, it is not clear whether in the long run the presence of Christian missions augments women's agency. However, in parts of Christianized Africa indigenous women have broken off from the mission churches, founded their own churches, and developed their own religious symbols, which possibly will have enhanced power to sustain women's agency (Jules-Rosette 1979). Although only a minority of African independent churches are led by women, Hackett (1994) argues that "within this milieu women may achieve full independence in religious activities and transcend traditional taboos and attitudes, while in contrast many of the historic churches perpetrate and reinforce sex stereotypes" (p. 62).

Woman or Women?

When women acquire greater agency, they often are tempted to demand a larger piece of the religious pie. These demands, not surprisingly, may lead to conflict. Cross-culturally, in situations of religious conflict, perceptions of the conflict as involving women or Woman can have enormous effects upon the outcome. A good example is ordination in Christian churches. In most Protestant churches, the role of minister or pastor is understood to be one of agency—the minister or pastor leads and teaches. And in most Protestant churches, after varying amounts of debate and dispute, women have been ordained as ministers. In the Catholic Church, on the other hand, where the role of priest is inherently symbolic, disputes over the ordination of women remain unresolved, precisely because Christ's (and the priest's) sex and celibate sexuality are seen as having symbolic value. Catholic priests, in other words, can be considered "Man" rather than merely "men." As the Vatican Congregation for the Doctrine of the Faith explained in 1977, there is a "sacramental bond between Christ, maleness and priesthood" (Iadarola 1985:469).

Hampson's (1987) analysis of the discourse surrounding the ordination of women in the Anglican Church emphasizes the issue of symbols:

> In the Anglican church, a "symbolic" church in which the priest in the eucharist is held to be by many in some sense a "representative" of Christ, the argument [against ordaining women] has in the first place centered around Christ's maleness. . . . Those opposed to women's ordination may say that symbols are profound. It is not insignificant that God became incarnate as a man, or that "he" has revealed that we should call him "Father." (p. 142)[8]

Those in favor of women's ordination, in contrast, have consistently used a language of agency. Ruether (1994:277) demonstrates that efforts to ordain women in Protestant churches in the United States have paralleled moves toward women's equality in the secular sphere. Brereton and Klein (1980:186-87) show that calls for women's ordination have consistently pointed to the fact that women *already* are carrying out leadership roles within the churches.

During the past 10 years in Israel, a series of cases have unfolded that have challenged in different ways the traditional orthodox Jewish religious gender roles that had been institutionalized by the modern Israeli state.[9] Three recent cases, presented below, all received a great deal of publicity in the newspapers, and all eventually reached the Israeli Supreme Court. In two of the cases—a struggle over the right of women to serve on municipal religious councils and a battle by women to serve on the electoral bodies that elect chief rabbis—women successfully challenged the male-dominated religious establishment (represented by the Ministry of Religion and certain prominent rabbis) and their demands for change were met. The third case, known popularly as the "Women of the Wall," concerns the right of women to pray as a group at the Western Wall in Jerusalem (in traditional Jewish contexts only men pray as a group) and to carry and read from the Torah (sacred scroll).

The first two cases were resolved through a process of redefinition: Both sides to each dispute agreed that the case really did not involve religious matters, but rather was concerned with the secular—budgets and politics. In the third case, the dispute continues, and the rhetoric used by those who oppose the women's right to pray as they wish at the Western Wall has been filled with invective hurled at women who have breached the traditional Jewish norms of conduct through the appropriation of key religious symbols (Sered 1997).

In the cases concerning women serving on municipal religious councils and electoral bodies, women were seen by both sides to the dispute as agents. The contested question was to what extent women's agency is equal to men's. In the case of the Women of the Wall, in contrast, the issue is understood to be one of Woman. The Women of the Wall are themselves seen as a symbol, symbolically desecrating Judaism's holiest symbolic site. In the first two cases, the gravity of gender was neutralized through the presentation of the changes as secular, and thus as fundamentally irrelevant to Judaism—as involving mere women rather than Woman. Significantly, in both of these cases, the redefinition of the issues as secular was made possible because the religious establishment eventually understood that women would be allowed to serve on these bodies whether or not the rabbis agreed. The side that had greater resources (in these cases, the backing of the Supreme Court and the support of the Israeli secular press) was able to force a redefinition of the issue from one of Woman to one of women.

The Women of the Wall could not downplay religion (after all, their struggle had to do with prayer), and so they chose to downplay gender. (They rarely speak of women's rights, but rather base their claims on Jewish law and on the value of religious pluralism.) This strategy has not carried any weight with the religious establishment, for whom women's gender, sex, and sexuality are never tangential categories, but rather divinely created ones integrally bound into religious duties and taboos. The Women of the Wall, portrayed by the Israeli media as foreign, American Reform Jews, lack the social resources to force the employment of their own notions of their group as women rather than Woman.[10]

If we look at modern Israeli society, we see that significant advances in the status of women have already taken place: education for girls, votes for women, women working outside the home, and women serving in the Parliament and the military. Accordingly, in the cases interpreted as involving secular power, women negotiated minivictories quite in keeping with Israeli secular norms. In the case understood as involving sacred power, on the other hand, the Women of the Wall have challenged the mythic charter of the Jewish people, and Woman as a symbol is an intrinsic part of that charter. They are, therefore, not likely to win their fight.

Feminist Discourse

Within the larger religious traditions (Judaism, Christianity, Islam, Buddhism, Hinduism), there has been an enormous flowering of feminist writing over the past few decades. The bulk of this literature is organized around three themes (these themes or schools of thought are not mutually exclusive):

1. The original message of the religion's founder was liberating for women, and thus the contemporary feminist agenda should be to strip away the historically later layers of gender discrimination.
2. The "problem of women" is deeply rooted in the symbols of the religious tradition, and thus the contemporary feminist agenda should be the creation of new women-oriented rituals and symbolic interpretations.
3. The religious tradition is not only irredeemably patriarchal but it is actually responsible for the sustenance of secular patriarchy, and thus the contemporary feminist agenda should be the creation of new religions that reflect women's spirituality.

Feminists who want to restore a religion's putatively egalitarian tradition claim that the religion under discussion is inherently good for women—that the fundamental message of Jesus, the Buddha, Muhammad, or the Torah was one that significantly improved the status of women in the given historical context in which the religion emerged. These feminists argue that those who came after the founder misinterpreted or ignored the egalitarian core of the religion. The solution, then, is to find within the religion alternative sources and texts that will enable contemporary men and women to return to the essentially nonsexist baseline of the religion. For example, Saadawi (1982) situates the source of patriarchy in economic forces (rather than divine creation) and presents Muhammad as liberator of women (although those who came after him lost that part of his message).

Reformist religious feminists are convinced that manifestations of sexism within the religion do not indicate that the core of the religion is sexist; these manifestations are distortions of the religion's true essence. They feel that a synthesis of religion and feminism is not only possible but probably inevitable, and therefore there is sufficient room within the traditional religion for feminists to maneuver. This discourse gives particular attention to issues of agency (to the ordination of women, to discrimination against women in religious courts, and to women's right to participate in communal rituals), but generally avoids discussion of symbols—and especially of symbols of the divine. Thus Ozick (1983) argues that the problem with the status of women in Judaism is not God or Torah—both of which are eternal—but rather specific social factors that are open to change. Women can increase their agency by studying Jewish texts and history, and then convince rabbis to grant women more agency in matters such as divorce.

The second group of feminist religious writers understands the problem of women in religion to be systemic, not a dispensable by-product of unfortunate social or historical circumstances or random oversights that can be corrected through the changing of a few laws or customs. These writers focus on the problem of imaging divinity as male; the male divinity serves both to reinforce a patriarchal social order and to teach women to internalize their inferiority. This critique empha-sizes symbols and argues that patriarchal symbols undercut women's agency.

Arguing from this perspective, Plaskow (1983) responded to the paper by Ozick cited above by making it clear that to her mind, the problem for women is theological—not merely sociological. For Plaskow, Jewish law (or specific laws) is not the cause of women's oppression; rather, it is the legal manifestation of a patriarchal system. She notes with dismay:

> The Jewish women's movement of the past decade has been and re-mains a civil-rights movement rather than a movement for "women's liberation." It has been a movement concerned with the images and status of women in Jewish religious and communal life, and with *halakhic* [legal] and institutional changes. It has been less concerned with analysis of the origins and bases of women's oppression that render change necessary. It has focused on getting women a piece of the Jewish pie; it has not wanted to bake a new one! (p. 223)

Despite their broad-based critique, the writers in this second group remain committed to the traditional religious *community*, if not to all of the traditional religious texts, laws, and symbols. The womanist move-ment, for instance, has been developed by African American women dedicated to combining women's spirituality and feminism without aban-doning their commitment to the African American community (Alice Walker is the most famous example of a womanist author). Womanists pay particular attention to traditional African American values of shar-ing and mutual help in the struggle for survival, liberation, mother-daughter relationships, and rituals that strengthen women's spirit (Williams 1989). Similarly, certain Jewish feminists have devoted espe-cially creative attention to the devising of new women's communal rituals that transform traditional Jewish symbols. Examples include the spread of Jewish women's Rosh Hodesh groups, which celebrate the new moon, women-oriented Passover seders and *hagadot*, and new *midrashim* (biblical exegesis) and blessings (see, e.g., Falk 1989). Catholic and Protestant feminist theologians have developed an ethic that puts women's experiences at the center of moral choices. They work through an umbrella organization, called Woman-Church, that is made up of feminist groups engaged in reconstructing ethics and sexual morality.

Whereas the reformist critique is framed solely in issues of agency and rights, and the feminist stream described in the preceding paragraphs deconstructs Woman as a key religious symbol, a third and more radical group of spiritual feminist writers have developed a multi-layered discourse that entirely repudiates religions that oppress women through the reification of male-imaged Woman. In the by-now classic opening paragraph of *Beyond God the Father*, Mary Daly (1973) sets out the spiritual feminist argument:[11]

> The biblical and popular image of God as a great patriarch in heaven, rewarding and punishing according to his mysterious and seemingly arbitrary will, has dominated the imagination of millions over thousands of years. The symbol of the Father God, spawned in the human imagination and sustained as plausible by patriarchy, has in turn rendered service to this type of society by making its mechanisms for the oppression of women appear right and fitting. (p. 13)

In the context of a discussion of the pointlessness of putting a skirt on God and calling that nonpatriarchy, she remarks that "the stereotypically male symbols of Christianity do not lend themselves to . . . easy adaptation by feminism" (p. 25). In other words, the core symbols themselves are patriarchal; if one tries to "extract" the patriarchy, one is left with nothing.

Denouncing traditional religions as irredeemably patriarchal, some spiritual feminists have developed their own forms of spiritual expression. These forms elevate a goddess or goddesses as positive symbols of Woman and enlist spirituality in the interests of enhancing women's agency. Perhaps the best-known representative of this school is Starhawk (1987), whose writings demonstrate the interrelationships among goddess symbols, human liberation, personal transformation, antimilitarism, community building, ecofeminism, and magic.

Starhawk, like dozens of other spiritual feminists, is engaged in self-consciously generating a body of religious writing that gives expression to women's agency. Although spiritual feminists devote a great deal of attention to discovering, inventing, and reinventing goddess symbols, their approach is characterized by an explicit effort to avoid reification of Woman. For example, it is common to find in spiritual feminist writings multiple representations of goddesses, denials that "the Goddess" has particular or unchanging traits that everybody must acknowledge, and commitment to the notion that goddesses and women are involved in a reciprocal and joint enterprise to discover their own agencies.

The enormous role of books and articles in both the discourses of religious feminists of various schools and the discourses of religious fundamentalists merits comment. When real women read religious texts in which Woman is denigrated, elaborated, mystified, put on a pedestal, mythologized, or legislated, subject meets object. When the subject has access to significant social resources, and thus comes to the text from a position of agency, the text is likely to be critiqued, deconstructed, reconstructed, and perhaps ultimately rejected and replaced. When the subject lacks significant social resources, the objectified Woman in the text functions to suppress the readers' agency further (El-Or 1994).

Directions for the Future

Gender-based analyses have had an enormous impact on the study of women and religion in the humanities. Feminist theory has become mainstream in many divinity schools, theology schools, and departments of religion. In addition to the scientific study of texts (e.g., Fiorenza 1989), feminists have critiqued their own religious traditions, fomented change, and taken on leadership roles within established religious institutions. Feminist approaches have changed the way that men and women think about religion both inside and outside of the academy. An exciting corpus of feminist and womanist theology and ritual has developed over the past 25 years. Women within major institutional religions have won the battle for ordination in many sects and have changed the face of divinity studies. Women theologians are formulating alternative nonoppressive, women-centered ethics, ritual, and liturgy. And women are creating goddess-based religion where they can find their own spiritual paths entirely outside of traditional, male-dominated religions.

Hopefully, the next round of feminist writing about religion will make a greater effort toward the cross-fertilization between the humanities and the social sciences. Social scientists have a great deal to learn from the careful textual analysis that allows a historical view of religious development, detailed understandings of myths and symbols, insight into the power of religion to engage and motivate believers, and engaged depictions of human religious beliefs. At the same time, historians of religion have a great deal to learn from the study of social structure that gives meaning to texts and rituals, and that facilitates examination of human agency in context. The next round could fruitfully take a more subtle look at the interplay of myths, symbols, rituals, life experiences, resources, social contexts, and social structure. The overview of literature presented in this chapter shows issues of both agency and symbolism to be relevant to the exploration of gender and religion. Integration of the study of women and the study of Woman will offer insight into the interaction between cultural symbols and real people, and will foster better understanding of religion's power to engender other social institutions.

Notes

1. Circumcision cuts religion into male bodies as well.

2. Although the textual basis of the tradition is far from clear, throughout the Muslim world women *believe* that "female circumcision" is required by Islamic law.

3. See Bell (1993) on Australia, Silverblatt (1980) on the Andes, Forman (1984) on Oceania, and Davis (1984) on Thailand.

4. In some societies, the midwife is also the practitioner of genital mutilation, a role constellation that gives her a great deal of power over other women.

5. The growth of matrifocal households and women-led zar religious groups has not, however, resulted in the abolishment of genital mutilation of young girls. The overarching cultural ideology in the Sudan remains patriarchal (Boddy 1989).

6. See also Watkins (1996) on the Nyeshangte of northern Nepal and Young (1987) on urban Hinduism.

7. See also Bond (1987) on Presbyterian Church membership among the Yombe and Forman (1984:155) on Oceania.

8. In 1992 the Church of England voted for ordination of women to the priesthood (see Ruether 1994:279).

9. These cases are not the first time that issues of gender and religion have made the front pages of Israeli newspapers. The rights of women to vote and to be elected split religious Jews into two camps before the establishment of the state of Israel, and arguments concerning military exemptions for religious girls have reemerged periodically over the past 50 years.

10. The secular newspapers have been antagonistic to the Women of the Wall, thus depriving them of a major social resource. Although this may still change, as of this writing the Women of the Wall have also been deprived of the court backing that could be seen as a key social resource. Although the Supreme Court has not been overtly antagonistic, it has allowed the case to drag on for years.

11. *Spiritual feminism* is the term used by post-Christian, wicca, pagan, or goddess-oriented feminists. See Plaskow and Christ (1989) and Eller (1995).

References

Bacigalupo, Ana Mariella. 1996. "Mapuche Women's Empowerment as Shamans-Healers (*Machis*) in Chile." Pp. 57-129 in *Annual Review of Women in World Religions*, vol. 4, edited by Arvind Sharma and Katherine K. Young. Albany: State University of New York Press.

Bell, Diane. 1983. *Daughters of the Dreaming*. Melbourne: McPhee Gribble/George Allen & Unwin.

Betteridge, Anne H. 1983. "To Veil or Not to Veil: A Matter of Protest or Policy." In *Women and Revolution in Iran*, edited by Guity Nashat. Boulder, CO: Westview.

Boddy, Janice. 1989. *Wombs and Alien Spirits: Women, Men, and the Zar Cult in Northern Sudan*. Madison: University of Wisconsin Press.

Bond, George C. 1987. "Ancestors and Protestants: Religious Coexistence in the Social Field of a Zambian Community." *American Ethnologist* 14:55-72.

Bowen, John R. 1992. "On Scriptural Essentialism and Ritual Variation: Muslim Sacrifice in Sumatra and Morocco." *American Ethnologist* 19:656-71.

Brereton, Virginia Lieson and Christa Ressmeyer Klein. 1980. "American Women in Ministry: A History of Protestant Beginning Points." Pp. 171-90 in *Women in American Religion*, edited by Janet Wilson James. Philadelphia: University of Pennsylvania Press.

Buenaventura-Posso, Elisa and Susan E. Brown. 1980. "Forced Transition from Egalitarianism to Male Dominance: The Bari of Columbia." Pp. 109-33 in *Women and Colonialization: Anthropological Perspectives*, edited by Mona Etienne and Eleanor Leacock. New York: J. F. Bergin.

Callaway, Barbara and Lucy Creevey. 1994. *Women, Religion, and Politics in West Africa: The Heritage of Islam.* Boulder, CO: Lynne Rienner.

Cosminsky, S. 1982. "Childbirth and Change: A Guatemalan Study." Pp. 205-29 in *Ethnography of Fertility and Birth,* edited by Carol MacCormack. London: Academic Press.

Daly, Mary. 1973. *Beyond God the Father.* Boston: Beacon.

———. 1978. *Gyn/Ecology: The Metaethics of Radical Feminism.* Boston: Beacon.

Darrow, William. 1985. "Women's Place and the Place of Women in the Iranian Revolution." Pp. 307-20 in *Women, Religion and Social Change,* edited by Yvonne Yazbeck Haddad and Ellison Banks Findly. Albany: State University of New York Press.

Davis, Richard. 1984. "Muang Matrifocality." *Mankind* 14:263-71.

Eller, Cynthia. 1995. *Living in the Lap of the Goddess: The Feminist Spirituality Movement in America.* Boston: Beacon.

El-Or, Tamar. 1994. *Educated and Ignorant: Ultraorthodox Jewish Women and Their World.* Boulder, CO: Lynne Rienner.

el Saadawi, Nawal. 1982. "Woman and Islam." *Women's Studies International Forum* 5:193-206.

Esquivel, Julia. 1987. "Christian Women and the Struggle for Justice in Central America." Pp. 22-32 in *Speaking of Faith: Global Perspectives on Women, Religion, and Social Change,* edited by Diana Eck and Devaki Jain. Philadelphia: New Society.

Falk, Marcia. 1989. "Notes on Composing New Blessings." Pp. 128-38 in *Weaving the Visions: New Patterns in Feminist Spirituality,* edited by Judith Plaskow and Carol Christ. San Francisco: Harper & Row.

Fiorenza, Elisabeth Schussler. 1989. "In Search of Women's Heritage." Pp. 29-38 in *Weaving the Visions: New Patterns in Feminist Spirituality,* edited by Judith Plaskow and Carol Christ. San Francisco: Harper & Row.

Forman, Charles. 1984. " 'Sing to the Lord a New Song': Women in the Churches of Oceania." Pp. 153-72 in *Rethinking Women's Roles: Perspectives from the Pacific,* edited by Denise O'Brien and Sharon Tiffany. Berkeley: University of California Press.

Gutierrez, Ramon A. 1992. *When Jesus Came, the Corn Mothers Went Away: Marriage, Sexuality, and Power in New Mexico, 1500-1846.* Stanford, CA: Stanford University Press.

Hackett, Rosalind I. J. 1994. "Women in African Religions." Pp. 61-92 in *Religion and Women,* edited by Arvind Sharma and Katherine K. Young. Albany: State University of New York Press.

Haddad, Yvonne Yazbeck. 1985. "Islam, Women and Revolution in Twentieth-Century Arab Thought." Pp. 275-306 in *Women, Religion, and Social*

Change, edited by Yvonne Yazbeck Haddad and Ellison Banks Findly. Albany: State University of New York Press.

Hampson, Daphne. 1987. "Women, Ordination and the Christian Church." Pp. 138-47 in *Speaking of Faith: Global Perspectives on Women, Religion, and Social Change,* edited by Diana Eck and Devaki Jain. Philadelphia: New Society.

Hawley, John Stratton, ed. 1994. *Fundamentalism and Gender.* New York: Oxford University Press.

Hawley, John Stratton and Wayne Proudfoot. 1994. "Introduction." Pp. 3-46 in *Fundamentalism and Gender,* edited by John Stratton Hawley. New York: Oxford University Press.

Iadarola, Antoinette. 1985. "The American Catholic Bishops and Woman: From the Nineteenth Amendment to ERA." Pp. 457-76 in *Women, Religion, and Social Change,* edited by Yvonne Yazbeck Haddad and Ellison Banks Findly. Albany: State University of New York Press.

Jamzadeh, Laal and Margaret Mills. 1986. "Iranian Sofreh: From Collective to Female Ritual." Pp. 23-65 in *Gender and Religion: On the Complexity of Symbols,* edited by Caroline Walker Bynum, Stevan Harrell, and Paula Richman. Boston: Beacon.

Jules-Rosette, Bennetta. 1979. *New Religions of Africa.* Norwood, NJ: Ablex.

Karim, Wazir Jahan. 1992. *Women and Culture: Between Malay Adat and Islam.* Boulder, CO: Westview.

Kennedy, John G. 1978. *Nubian Ceremonial Life.* Berkeley: University of California Press.

Lazarus-Yafe, Hava. 1988. "Contemporary Fundamentalism: Judaism, Christianity, Islam." *Jerusalem Quarterly* 47:27-39.

Lebra, William P. 1966. *Okinawan Religion.* Honolulu: University of Hawaii Press.

Lewis, I. M. 1975. *Ecstatic Religion.* 1971. Harmondsworth: Penguin.

Lindenbaum, Shirley. 1987. "The Mystification of Female Labors." In *Gender and Kinship: Essays Toward a Unified Analysis,* edited by Jane Fishburne Collier and Sylvia Junko Yanagisako. Stanford, CA: Stanford University Press.

Lutkehaus, Nancy and Paul Roscoe, eds. 1995. *Gender Rituals: Female Initiation in Melanesia.* New York: Routledge.

Martin, Emily. 1987. *The Woman in the Body.* Boston: Beacon.

McGilvray, D. B. 1982. "Sexual Power and Fertility in Sri Lanka: Batticaloa Tamils and Moors." Pp. 25-73 in *Ethnography of Fertility and Birth,* edited by Carol MacCormack. London: Academic Press.

Moghadam, Valentine M. 1994. "Women and Identity Politics in Theoretical and Comparative Perspective." Pp. 3-26 in *Identity Politics and Women:*

Cultural Reassertions and Feminisms in International Perspective, edited by Valentine M. Moghadam. Boulder, CO: Westview.

Najmabadi, Afsaneh. 1991. "Hazards of Modernity and Morality: Women, State and Ideology in Contemporary Iran." Pp. 48-76 in *Women, Islam and the State,* edited by Deniz Kandiyoti. Philadelphia: Temple University Press.

Neitz, Mary. 1987. *Charisma and Community: A Study of Religious Commitment within the Charismatic Renewal.* New Brunswick, NJ: Transaction.

Ozick, Cynthia. 1983. "Notes toward Finding the Right Question." Pp. 120-51 in *On Being a Jewish Feminist,* edited by Susannah Heschel. New York: Schocken.

Papanek, Hanna. 1994. "The Ideal Woman and the Ideal Society: Control and Autonomy in the Construction of Identity." Pp. 42-75 in *Identity Politics and Women: Cultural Reassertions and Feminisms in International Perspective,* edited by Valentine M. Moghadam. Boulder, CO: Westview.

Paul, Lois and Benjamin Paul. 1975. "The Maya Midwife as Sacred Specialist: A Guatemalan Case." *American Ethnologist* 2:707-20.

Plaskow, Judith. 1983. "The Right Question Is Theological." Pp. 223-33 in *On Being a Jewish Feminist,* edited by Susannah Heschel. New York: Schocken.

Plaskow, Judith and Carol Christ, eds. 1989. *Weaving the Visions: New Patterns in Feminist Spirituality.* San Francisco: Harper & Row.

Powers, Marla. 1986. *Oglala Women.* Chicago: University of Chicago Press.

Ratte, Lou. 1985. "Goddesses, Mothers, and Heroines: Hindu Women and the Feminine in the Early Nationalist Movement." Pp. 351-76 in *Women, Religion, and Social Change,* edited by Yvonne Yazbeck Haddad and Ellison Banks Findly. Albany: State University of New York Press.

Rich, Adrienne. [1976] 1986. *Of Woman Born: Motherhood as Experience and Institution.* New York: W. W. Norton.

Ruether, Rosemary. 1994. "Christianity and Women in the Modern World." Pp. 267-302 in *Today's Woman in World Religions,* edited by Arvind Sharma and Katherine K. Young. Albany: State University of New York Press.

Sered, Susan Starr. 1992. *Women as Ritual Experts: The Religious Lives of Elderly Jewish Women in Jerusalem.* New York: Oxford University Press.

———. 1994. *Priestess, Mother, Sacred Sister: Religions Dominated by Women.* New York: Oxford University Press.

———. 1997. "Women and Religious Change in Israel: Rebellion or Revolution." *Sociology of Religion* 58(1):1-24.

———. 1999. *Women of the Sacred Groves: Divine Priestesses of Okinawa.* New York: Oxford University Press.

Sexton, Lorraine Dusak. 1984. "Pigs, Pearlshells, and 'Women's Work': Collective Response to Change in Highland Papua New Guinea." Pp. 120-52 in *Rethinking Women's Roles: Perspectives from the Pacific,* edited by Sharon Tiffany. Berkeley: University of California Press.

Shaw, Miranda. 1994. *Passionate Enlightenment: Women in Tantric Buddhism.* Princeton, NJ: Princeton University Press.

Shiman, Lillian Lewis. 1986. " 'Changes Are Dangerous': Women and Temperance in Victorian England." Pp. 193-215 in *Religion in the Lives of English Women 1760-1930,* edited by Gail Malmgreen. Bloomington: Indiana University Press.

Shimony, Annemarie. 1980. "Women of Influence and Prestige among the Native American Iroquois." Pp. 243-59 in *Unspoken Worlds: Women's Religious Lives in Non-Western Cultures,* edited by Nancy Falk and Rita Gross. San Francisco: Harper & Row.

Silverblatt, Irene. 1980. "Andean Women under Spanish Rule." Pp. 149-85 in *Women and Colonization: Anthropological Perspectives,* edited by Mona Etienne and Eleanor Leacock. New York: J. F. Bergin.

Starhawk. 1987. *Truth or Dare.* New York: Harper & Row.

Sundkler, Bengt. 1961. *Bantu Prophets in South Africa.* London: Oxford University Press.

Wallace, Ruth. 1993. "The Social Construction of a New Leadership Role: Catholic Women Pastors." *Sociology of Religion* 54(1):31-42.

Watkins, Joanne. 1996. *Spirited Women: Gender, Religion, and Cultural Identity in the Nepal Himalaya.* New York: Columbia University Press.

Williams, Delores S. 1989. "Womanist Theology." Pp. 179-86 in *Weaving the Visions: New Patterns in Feminist Spirituality,* edited by Judith Plaskow and Carol Christ. San Francisco: Harper & Row.

Williams, Rhys H. 1996. "Introduction: Sociology of Culture and Sociology of Religion." *Sociology of Religion* 57(1):1-6.

Young, Katherine K. 1987. "Hinduism." Pp. 59-104 in *Women in World Religions,* edited by Arvind Sharma and Katherine K. Young. Albany: State University of New York Press.

CHAPTER 8

Sex, Text, and Context

(In) Between
Feminism and Cultural Studies

SUZANNA DANUTA WALTERS

Surely in these days of image-driven presidents and sound-bite social policy, of Murphy Browns and Madonnas, O.J. mania and televisual Sapphic smooching, no responsible social theorist would dare to question the centrality of *culture* (however one defines it) and the absolute necessity for critical media analysis. And just as surely—as Hillary is pilloried and family values subvert feminist values—no equally responsible social theorist can question the centrality of *gender* as a determinant of identity, a configuration of power, an institutional rubric, and an embodied social location.

Cultural studies from its inception positioned itself against, or at least in argument with, traditional ways of knowing and the territorial divisions of academic endeavor. Definitions of cultural studies are hard to come by, but suffice it to say that the field is marked precisely by its eclecticism, its wide-ranging negotiation with a daunting variety of analytic subjects, and its explicitly political concern with questions of

AUTHOR'S NOTE: Portions of this chapter were previously published, in somewhat altered form, in the following places: *Material Girls: Making Sense of Feminist Cultural Theory* (University of California Press, 1995); "Material Girls: Feminism and Cultural Studies," in *Current Perspectives in Social Theory*, vol. 12, edited by Ben Agger (JAI Press, 1992); and "From Here to Queer: Radical Feminism, Postmodernism, and the Lesbian Menace (or, Why Can't a Woman Be More Like a Fag?)," in *Signs*, vol. 21, no. 4 (Summer 1996):830-69.

ideology, power, hegemony, and struggle. Unlike more traditional models of cultural analysis (literary criticism, art history, mass media studies), cultural studies sets its sights both wide and deep: "Culture" becomes not so much an "object" to be analyzed as an interrogation of a "way of life" and set of practices that produce identity, subjectivity, and, always, gender.

Significantly, cultural studies does not limit itself to any particular form of culture: Its practitioners study "high literature" and fanzines, art films and cereal boxes, museum attendance and the politics of bowling, PBS and MTV. In so doing, cultural studies explicitly deconstructs the high/low culture divide and, in fact, reveals that divide to be the result of political and academic power struggles, struggles that often revolve around issues of canonization, cultural "capital" and access, and the production of identities in and through cultural representations.

Born of the political and intellectual ferment of the post-World War II years, and thus reared on structuralism, poststructuralism, semiotics, linguistic theory, and associated tropes of social theory, and weaned on the challenges of the new social movements, cultural studies did not resist the introduction of gendered analysis that more established disciplines did. Feminism—and the centrality of gender as a formative conceptual tool—was already a part of the intellectual and political landscape when cultural studies began to force its way into the established field of vision.

Because of these always politicized concerns with "culture" as *practice* rather than discrete object, gender analysis found a fairly welcoming environment. More to the point, *feminism* found a welcome home. For the introduction of gender need not—as we have seen time and time again—be necessarily feminist. Gender can be understood simply as a neutral conceptual variable, a mode of demarcation, rather than a broad-based theoretical framework with an implicit, if not always explicit, politics. My language here will be one of *feminism* more than gender, a language I feel a bit more comfortable with because it explicitly indicates a political and politicized analysis: a theoretical stance that is informed by a desire to make the world different for all kinds of gendered beings, particularly those most victimized by the gender system.

Although there was some initial resistance from New Left scholars of working-class (male) cultures, the field as a whole is striking in its early and rapid engagement with feminism. Cultural studies firmly situates itself within and between the interstices of radical identity theorization—of gender, of race, of sexuality, of class, of ethnicity—which may be why it is on the firing line in the so-called culture wars. Its political agenda and overt concern with the structures and practices of domination have made it a target, alongside women's studies, in the right-wing battle against a transformed curriculum.

Thus the questions posed by this book appear a bit different when applied to cultural studies. Struggles were there, of course (where there is feminism, there is struggle!), but the drama of gender was enacted along somewhat different lines, with less acrimony and less of the sense of absolute challenge and disruption that followed the introduction of gender into the traditional disciplines. Nevertheless, feminist cultural studies is not without its *internal* divisions and struggles, fault lines that often mirror debates within cultural studies writ large and feminist theory as well.

The early work in feminist cultural criticism—like much of early feminist theory generally—was preeminently concerned with exposing the depth and range of sexist images and stereotypes that pervaded mass culture. In these early accounts, gender itself was not really problematized or even called into question (in the ways we do now, for example, by stressing the construction of gender as itself the construction of gendered inequality). Rather, the concern was with inequity, misrepresentation, and stereotype. Although these were laudatory concerns (and remain so), they were severely limited in their understanding of the complex process of the production and consumption of cultural representation.

Researchers in this tradition—what I have called the "images of women" approach[1]—produced both quantitative and qualitative work that was largely *descriptive* of the offending representations and then, prescriptively, argued for more inclusion and more diversity. The assumption was that there was a direct one-to-one relationship between images and social relations and identities: Sexist images produce (or, alternately, reflect) sexist identities and practices. Thus the transformation of those images will initiate or signal transformations in the larger social body. Strip away the sexist imagery, so the argument goes, and you will be able to reveal women as they "really are."

The flip side of this reflection model is a view of the media derived from theories of sex roles and socialization. If the reflection model posits the media as a mirror to social "reality," the socialization model argues that the media teach us sex-stereotyped roles and behaviors, and in both models, meaning is viewed as "read off" the images themselves in a direct, coherent, and uncontradictory way. The socialization hypothesis (in its starkest form, often called the hypodermic model) assumes a one-way flow between image and viewer, with the image acting on the viewer by prescribing roles and behaviors to a largely unspecified and undifferentiated "receiver" of the cultural message. In other words, there is no sense of the role of the spectator in constructing meaning; an image simply "means" something (determined by its characterization and content) that then is unproblematically "picked up" by the viewer. Along with reflection and socialization, the third fundamental ingredient of the "images" perspective has to do with *stereotypes* that limit women's options and possibilities in the "real world." Thus early feminist cultural criticism maintained fairly simplistic notions of both "gender" and "culture," and worked within methodological frameworks that rarely challenged the academic status quo.

Both the What and the How: Theoretical
Reframings and Methodological Transformations

Inevitably, these approaches came under substantive attack. Simply put, feminist cultural studies underwent a shift from an "images of woman" perspective to "woman as image," and in that shift was a transformation into a truly gendered analysis of representation. A concern with the position of women in narratives and within particular genres, attention to the ways in which patriarchy not only structures content but informs our very "way of seeing," and an emphasis on the "constructedness" and "productiveness" of images have provided the bases for revealing and deconstructive analyses of media texts.

For example, seeing Madonna as a stereotype of the sexually objectified woman gives us little insight into the complex reactions of the young girls who idolize her as a signifier of their own nascent sexuality. This focus on stereotypes in the early work, although important, failed to address their social origin and thus ignored the most interesting aspect of the analysis of stereotypes: How is it that they have meaning for us? Stereotypes work only because they must, in some way, speak to perceptions of "real" attributes or qualities. In other words, stereotypes often enlarge upon or even parody aspects of personality or group identity that—within a culture—share a certain "commonsense" veracity. Although there are certainly some stereotypes that are simply "made up" out of whole cloth (e.g., blondes have more fun and/or are "ditsy"), the majority of stereotypes emerge from naturalizing selective traits of certain groups. For instance, the stereotype that women are more relational and emotionally sensitive than men is based on no small amount of experiential reality. But most stereotypes are not neutral; they are deeply embedded in structures of oppression and domination and become prescriptions for behavior and modes of social control. So the stereotype of women as more emotional has vast social and political implications and reverberations, such as justification for certain forms of job discrimination.

Although stereotypes certainly "exist" in the mass media, it is important to ask more complex questions about how, exactly, we come to recognize certain images and representations *as stereotypes.* Who gets to say what is a stereotype and what is a more "realistic" portrayal? Does the identification of a stereotype by a critic help us to understand how that image is "read" by spectators? For some, the character Roseanne on the hit sitcom of the same name is anything but a stereotype. Rather, her fans see in her a working-class heroine, a tough, witty woman who refuses to conform to male standards of beauty and who remains proudly sexual as well. For others, she is more like Ralph Kramden in drag, reinforcing the stereotype that working-class women are fat, lazy, dirty, and careless in their child-rearing practices. It is thus very difficult to identify stereotypes, particularly if one sees meaning as being produced in some sort of a relational context.

Stereotypes change and mutate and evolve over different time periods and within different cultural contexts. So, for example, Madonna successfully used the stereotype of the conniving blonde bombshell (itself already parodied by Marilyn Monroe in the film *Gentlemen Prefer Blondes*) in her music video "Material Girl," in which she both employed the stereotype and deconstructed it at the same time, by showing it to be just another "performance." In other words, stereotypes are not fixed false beliefs, but rather shifting and contested meanings, the result of interactive processes of production and "reading." Assuming the transparency of images ignores the social context of image production, the role of the viewer in creating meaning, and the specificity of the mass media form itself.

Central to this new "signification" paradigm in cultural studies, then, is an invigorated concern with the *productiveness* of images. If images of women are no longer to be seen as simple reflections (or misreflections) of "real" women, then feminists have to develop an analysis that stresses how representations actually *construct* gender. As

Byars (1991) argues, "Representation is not reflection but rather an active process of selecting and presenting, of structuring and shaping, of making things *mean*" (p. 69). In other words, the new critical analyses examine how our cultural images produce this very category "woman" and thus (re)produce gender distinctions and gender dominance. For example, what is it about the history of film as a public visual medium that so often dichotomizes women into the virginal heroine or the sexualized "whore"? How does the living-room location of TV help to determine the kinds of images of women produced there? These questions are not just about *what* (sexist) images are produced, but *how* they are produced and come to have meaning for us. One might ask not just "what" the icon of Madonna means, but "how" she is produced as an icon. How do young girls come to know her as an icon? How do her gay male fans know her differently? How, therefore, does Madonna's cultural meaning differ by the gender and sexuality of her viewers? The new claim is that the entire cultural notion of "woman" is itself constructed in and through images rather than somehow "residing" in the images themselves.

Most important, the introduction of gender changed what *mattered* in cultural studies. If it were not for the introduction of gendered analysis into cultural studies, we might never, for example, have enjoyed the rich and detailed studies of soap operas or melodrama or pornography. Feminist cultural theorists transformed the very object of study by foregrounding gendered discourse in popular culture. As Lury (1995) points out, feminists altered cultural studies by insisting that cultural objects and cultural processes are not gender neutral: "The dominant presumption that culture itself is gender-neutral, that it is only specific uses of culture which are problematic from a feminist point of view, obscures the ways in which culture itself is constituted in relation to gender and other social and political categories" (p. 33). Examples of this approach can be found in Radway's (1984) and Modleski's (1982) marvelous work on romance novels and soap operas, work that was directly informed by feminist questions concerning the gendered nature of cultural reception, or the fascinating analyses of the strange world of fan culture (e.g., Penley 1992), or the studies of the female audiences of talk shows (see particularly Shattuc 1997). My own work on the representations of mothers and daughters has been informed by the "gender and genre" issues developed by feminist film theorists.

By focusing on what women actually do with popular representations, and how they might do things differently than male cultural consumers, feminist critics transformed not only the questions that were asked but the object of study itself.[2] The most demeaned forms of popular culture rose in intellectual stature as a direct result of feminist interventions into cultural studies. Popular forms with primarily female audiences have been—no surprise—typically ignored or put to the margins. These forms have now emerged as central, not only for what they reveal about the gendered nature of the production and consumption of images, but for what they reveal about the relationship between cultural canons and gendered identities. Soap operas and romance novels, understood as the province of women and thus devalued, now became revalued as sources for substantive and revealing cultural critique.

As the "what" was transformed, with forms of popular culture previously ignored or marginalized receiving explicit and detailed attention, the "how" was also transformed. New methodologies of cultural analysis have emerged as particularly relevant for the understanding of gendered representation. Specifically, reception theory, spectatorship studies, and ethnographic work emerged as specifically feminist methods of cultural criticism.

Soaps Я Us: Gender and Cultural Production

Although a nongendered analysis tended to see the act of producing a mass cultural object as somewhat neutral (or, in the left-wing versions, the aesthetic expression of capitalist domination), feminists working in cultural studies began to argue that culture is "always already" gendered. This claim manifests itself on many levels. First, there is the rather literal question of the gendered and sexed identity of the cultural producers. If gender is implicated everywhere, not simply tacked on, then perhaps it matters whose gendered identity produces culture. Certainly, most of our mass cultural output is produced by men, within the context of male-dominant media institutions. Do women cultural workers produce different kinds of cultural objects? Is there a "woman's film" that bears the distinct and recognizable marks of its women producers? And how might that film be different from the "woman's film" of the 1940s produced by "sympathetic" male directors? Or is the process itself so male dominated from the start that the gender of the producer washes out?[3] In other words, is representation itself so predicated on the objectification of women, on a male gaze and an implied male spectator, that even the most valiant attempts to subvert this trajectory are hopelessly doomed to failure? And what do we make of gender-targeted productions such as the Lifetime cable television network, which cannily advertises itself as "television for women"?[4]

If cultural production itself is gendered, then it stands to reason that the genres that make up our organization of cultural life are gendered as well. Genre analysis has a long history in cultural studies, but, not so accidentally, the genres that got introduced into the critical canon first were those in which the dramas of masculine identity are played out: film noir, westerns, cops shows on TV, detective novels. More and more, feminist cultural critics have been interested in the relationship between gender and genre, between the construction of sexual difference and the specific signifying practices of a particular type of representation. Do some genres that have typically been presented for a female audience (melodramas, soap operas, romances) offer themselves up more to a feminist reading? Are there "feminine forms" of representation, and, if so, do they construct women differently than "masculine" forms? Is there a "female address" implied in many genres that focus on women's lives and women characters (e.g., nighttime soaps such as *Melrose Place* that occupy themselves with the soap-opera world of revolving-door relationships, thought to be the emotional province of women)?

Much of this discussion over "female forms" has centered on film and television melodrama. Melodramas, "woman's films," or "the weepies," as they were often called (and perhaps called "chick flicks" now!), have historically been seen as the "lowest" form of mass culture, not worthy of the critical attention paid to genres such as the western or film noir, in which male subjectivity figures so heavily. It is not surprising that genres associated with both a female audience and "feminine" subject matters (the family, personal relationships, love) should be found unworthy of critical attention by male cultural critics. Feminist critics have reclaimed these films, television shows, and novels as worthwhile subjects for analysis, and some of the most interesting work in recent years (Modleski's on romance gothics, TV soaps, and Hitchcock; Radway's study of female romance readers; Brunsdon's work on British soap operas; the excellent British Film Institute collection on melodrama) has come out of this attempt to deal with the question of "gender and genre."

The study of soap operas has been central to the new feminist work on genre, especially that of Modleski (1982), Hobson (1990), and Nochimson (1992). These theorists argue that soaps, which appear so ridden with stereotypical and sexualized images of women, actually construct a space for the female viewer and for female subjectivity through their nonlinear, fragmented narrative form as well as through the structure of domestic spectatorship. Nochimson (1992) argues that "by opening up narrative linearity, soap opera does not merely give a potential female subject the chance to cut a wide swath or gain spectator identification; it actually insists that she be set free" (p. 30). Moores (1990) is convinced that "soap opera's multi-levelled, open-ended narrative structures demand a viewer who is able to identify with a range of characters. Such a cultural competence is brought to the text by many women viewers as a consequence of their social placing as housewives and mothers" (pp. 20-21). In *Loving with a Vengeance*, Modleski (1982) sees a feminist potential in television soap operas precisely because of their generic conventions and narrative structure, as does Kuhn (1984) in her work on women's genres: "Their characteristic narrative patterns, their foregrounding of 'female' skills in dealing with personal and domestic crises, and the capacity of their programme formats and scheduling to key into the rhythms of women's work in the home all address a female spectator" (p. 20).

Modleski (1982) sees a possibility in these genres for the creation of female "ways of seeing" that are not constrained by the male gaze and its associated dominance over female subjectivity. In fact, she even argues for the *radical* potential of forms such as the soap opera, noting that "the disorder of the form conveys a structure of feeling appropriate to the experience of the woman in the home whose activities and concerns are dispersed and lacking a center. But precisely because of its decentered nature this most discredited genre can be aligned with advanced feminist aesthetics and advanced critical theory as a whole" (p. 111). For Modleski, then, the soap opera offers possibilities in both form and content. Its open-ended and overlapping and repetitive structure allows its women fans who are working at home to enter into the text without necessarily "neglecting" their home duties. Unlike most ongoing serials, soaps are characterized by a phenomenally slow pace; soap fans *always* joke that they haven't watched *General Hospital* in five years and then come back to find Luke and Laura *still* trying to work out their relationship! Because many women's lives are so often interrupted by the exigencies of managing domesticity, this slow-paced structure may allow for a kind of engagement that is specifically gendered.

Not only are soaps structured like the rhythms of many women's lives, but the narrative content of most soaps is the stuff of relationships, intimacies, sexuality, family—concerns often central to women that contrast with the current dominance of "action/blockbuster" films, where people are more likely to relate to cyborgs and dinosaurs than to each other. It is no coincidence, then, that the content and narrative structure of soaps has changed in recent years, as more and more women work outside the home and are thus not readily available as the predicted audience. Indeed, in an attempt to increase viewership among teens and college kids (while still maintaining the female stay-at-home audience) soaps have moved beyond the living room and bedroom and into the world of work, spy-ring intrigue, and action-adventure spectacularism.

Clearly, much of the work on soap operas is in opposition to the hierarchies of critical analysis, in which "women's genres" are inevitably placed at the bottom, and where "women are . . . seen as the passive victims of the deceptive message of soap operas, just as the ideology of mass culture sees the audience as unwitting and pathetic victims of the commercial culture industry" (Moores 1990:20-21). Countering this view, Nochimson (1992), drawing heavily on the work of Modleski and others, argues:

> Soap opera assumes an essential femininity and masculinity, but there the similarity ends, for soap opera looks with a critical eye at Hollywood's rigid interpretation of gender roles: women tucked securely under the influence of men. Hollywood fantasy is the fantasy of patriarchy. In soap opera, by contrast, another kind of yearning emerges, one rarely permitted expression in our culture. Soap opera includes a female subject. (p. 2)

Film melodrama has also come under close scrutiny because of the possibilities in a genre that both "speaks" to a female audience *and* foregrounds women, rendering it open to a feminist reading and available to a female audience. Like soap operas, the woman's film, or melodrama, is seen as a particular site of female agency and exploration and "is distinguished by its female protagonist, female point of view and its narrative which most often revolves around the traditional realms of women's experience: the familial, the domestic, the romantic—those arenas where love, emotion and relationships take precedence over action and events" (LaPlace 1987:139). Not only can the melodrama "invite" a female audience, it can perhaps provoke her to resist the "resolution" that so often inscribes women in positions of subordination. Gledhill (1987) argues that melodrama must draw on the discourses of women's social reality in order for a female audience to be "won over," and there is possibility for contestation here: "Thus in twentieth-century melodrama the dual role of woman as symbol for the whole culture and as representative of a historical, gendered point of view produces a struggle between male and female voices: the symbol cannot be owned, but is contested" (p. 37).

Byars (1988) echoes these concerns, arguing that melodramas may have a compensatory function and, at the same time, may also provide a space for female self-definition, precisely because of the centrality of women's lives to the "woman's film":

> The narrative structure of the female-oriented family melodrama indicates the attempt to fill such a compensatory emotional function, the attempt to fulfill needs unmet in daily life. While this would seem to support the view that these are "politically conservative" texts, it should be noted, following Radway, that they also function to transmit a "female voice"—a vision of the world based in continuity rather than separation. (p. 121)

Melodrama, then, is often seen in terms of its excess, its inability to fully enclose and recuperate (for patriarchy) the woman. This excess can be understood in a number of senses: first, a visual excess (e.g., the lush film style of Douglas Sirk, which seems dizzyingly unreal in its Technicolor garishness), and, second, an excess of emotional weight (e.g., nighttime TV melodramas such as *Melrose Place* that contain endless emotional crescendos, unlike the more typical dramatic singular moment). It is in this "excess" and in the contradictions inherent in the subject of the genre (relationships, family, love, sex) that contestation can be located and analyzed. Indeed, the structural excess of much of our cultural output has recently been understood as at least potentially feminist. If women's gender identity has been represented so often as that which is constrained, reined in, curtailed, circumscribed by rigid boundaries of home and marriage, then representations that overflow these boundaries can also open up possibilities for gender challenge and deconstruction.

The hit sitcom *Roseanne* (not, of course, a melodrama, yet representative of a different kind of excess) provides one such example of a cultural image of a woman that, arguably, radically disrupts established gender protocol: She is unabashedly fat and unabashedly sexual, a mother and a worker, a wife and an autonomous person, ribald and controlling in a world that defines these as nonfeminine and the exclusive province of men, and knowingly funny, but not in a self-abnegating manner. Her rebellious excess signals, to many critics, her adamant refusal to follow the gendered rules of the game; she thus opens up space for women in the traditional heartland of the prime-time domesticom.

Melodramas, TV soaps, and other "women's genres" are therefore of interest to feminist critics for a number of reasons. Not only is there a possibility that they speak to and thus help to construct a female viewer, but they also deal thematically and narratively with issues that are central to many women's lives. They often present a domestic world fraught with contradictions and struggles, so that the "resolution" of these contradictions appears tenuous at best. Whether the contradictions opened up by these women's genres actually serve as "progressive" forces in women's lives or whether they are merely "escape valves" for women's frustrations and anxieties has been hotly contested by feminist critics. On the one hand, Ang (1985), who conducted a substantive study of the TV series *Dallas,* argues that it is important not to assume that the acceptance of oppression in soap operas equals the acceptance of oppression in "real life": "This acceptance (just like protest) takes place within the world of fantasy, not outside it. It says nothing about the positions and standpoints that the same women occupy in 'real life.' After all, watching soap operas is never the only thing they do. In other activities, other positions will be (or have to be) assumed" (pp. 134-35). On the other hand, the domesticity of the melodrama might serve to mire women further in that realm as the only one available to them.

Classically "female" forms have not been the only ones subject to feminist reexamination. Indeed, there is a growing body of work that is interested in those genres that appear most *unavailable* to a female audience, such as film noir:

> In the classical Hollywood cinema, there are two types of films within which the contradictions involved in the patriarchal representation of woman becomes most acute—melodrama and film noir. . . . What is particularly interesting about film noir for a feminist analysis is the way in which the issue of knowledge and its possibility or impossibility is articulated with questions concerning femininity and visibility. The woman confounds the relation between the visible and the knowable at the same time that she is made into an object for the gaze. (Doane 1991:103)

Other feminists have examined gangster films and cop shows in an attempt to locate questions of female identity in a broader generic context and to explore the contradictions in representations that explicitly deny women centrality and voice. If woman is almost obsessively visible and narratively central in melodrama and soap opera, she is marked precisely by her invisibility and her narrative unknowability in genres more typically understood as "masculine," such as film noir. But the almost anonymous femmes fatales offer interesting possibilities for feminist readings, in that a space for female action in the public world is curiously opened up (even if to be "shut down" by narrative resolutions that solve the enigma of woman by eliminating her). In addition, typically "male" genres such as science fiction have increasingly been examined for their curious construction of femininity. The hugely popular films *Alien* and *The Terminator* (and their many later iterations) are compelling examples of the ways in which science fiction and action genres use "hardbodied women" to sexualize women differently (around power and strength) while at the same time firmly locating female action heroines in their social sites as mothers and caretakers. Thus lean, tough Sigourney Weaver renders the final battle scene a great struggle between good and bad (alien) mothers, and buff Linda Hamilton fights for her right to be the mother of the (unborn) male freedom fighter.

The Male Gaze and Beyond: Gender and Cultural Consumption

If the introduction of a rigorously gendered analysis of culture transformed how we think about its production, it also deeply altered how we think about the consumption or reception of a cultural object. If it matters who produces representations and if those generic forms are seen to be themselves thoroughly embedded within a gendered order, then it also matters who is sitting in the movie theater, who is watching the TV, who is listening to the music. Nowhere is the impact of gendered, feminist analysis more palpable than in work on spectatorship and the audience. It is surely no accident that a more respectful focus on the cultural "consumer" should be so attractive to feminist scholars. Because the notion of passivity that traditional reception studies invoked carried such problematic assumptions for women (the association of women with passivity and the stereotypical image of the glassy-eyed housewife starring blankly at the TV screen), it is no surprise that these were soon replaced within feminist cultural studies by the image of the overworked wife and mother cleverly negotiating with the flow of televisual production.[5]

Because "looking" or "sight" is obviously such an important part of the reception of an image, it made sense to examine the ways in which looking at images is constructed by gender and the social relations of patriarchal power. If it is true that women are so often represented as sexual spectacle, as "on display" for men, what are the processes that produce woman as sexual spectacle?

Mulvey's ([1975] 1981) early work on the male gaze offers a recognition that viewing is itself a gendered phenomenon and carries with it relations of power and access that are made manifest within the image by the generally male director/cameraperson and by the presumed male spectator. Her work has been *critical* for feminist cultural theorists, even as it has been challenged and pushed beyond its original moorings. Introducing the issue of male power into the most intimate aspect of the representational process, sight, Mulvey argues that the objectification of women is not an "added-on" attraction, but rather endemic to the very structure of image-making. Silverman (1984) states the significance of the concept of the gaze:

> It is by now axiomatic that the female subject is the object rather than the subject of the gaze in mainstream narrative cinema. She is excluded from authoritative vision not only at the level of the enunciation, but at that of the fiction. At the same time she functions as an organizing spectacle, as the lack which structures the symbolic order and sustains the relay of male glances. (p. 131)

Mulvey and others have argued that there are two main pleasures of looking in Hollywood film: voyeurism and fetishism. The voyeuristic look gets pleasure in seeing without being seen, and is associated with power and control. The eye of the camera is like the eye looking through the peephole: "Voyeurism is a way of taking sexual pleasure by looking at rather than being close to a particular object of desire, like a Peeping Tom. And Peeping Toms can always stay in control. Whatever may be going on, the Peeping Tom can always determine his own meanings for what he sees" (Coward 1985:76-77).

The fetishistic look has to do with endowment of sexual meaning. Mulvey here relies strongly on Freud's essay on fetishism, suggesting "that the erotic spectacle of woman unconsciously reactivates the moment in which the male child discovers his mother's lack of a penis" (Studlar 1990:230), thus producing a sense of horror. The fetishism then derives from the disavowal and denial of that "castration," the boy/man turns an object into a "symbolic replacement of the mother's missing penis" (Studlar 1990:230). In film, fetishism often takes the form of a sexualization of women's bodies or parts of their bodies, ascribing a phallic connotation to a female body part (legs, breasts) in order to reclaim the woman and rid oneself of the threat of otherness generally and the threat of castration specifically: "Woman as representation signifies castration, inducing voyeuristic or fetishistic mechanisms to circumvent her threat" (Mulvey 1989:25). This fetishistic look is also clearly part of the representation of women in advertising, to the point where women are represented only as body parts: "In ads women are frequently represented in a 'fragmented' way. . . . Women are signified by their lips, legs, hair, eyes or hands, which stand, metonymically—the part for the whole—for, in this case, the 'sexual' woman. Men, on the other hand, are less often 'dismembered' " (Winship 1987:25). In ads, women are urged to think of their bodies as "things" that need to be molded, shaped, remade into a male conception of female perfection. The fragmentation of the female body into body parts that women should then "improve" or "work on" often results in women's having self-hating relationships with their bodies (see particularly Bordo 1993).

More by implication than by explicit analysis, Mulvey addresses the problem of the female spectator in a visual world constructed for male pleasure. The male viewer may revel in his fetishistic scopophilia, getting pleasure (and control) from what he sees from a distance, but the female viewer is condemned to a narcissistic pleasure, a "pleasure in closeness, in reflection and in identification with an image" (Betterton 1987:220). In other words, the female gaze (for Mulvey not so much a gaze as a passive spectating position) seems to be characterized either by narcissism or by a kind of masochistic identification with one's own objectification. There is no space for an authentic female gaze, because the spectator is inevitably addressed as male, and female viewers are forced to look with the male protagonist. Doane (1988) argues that identity itself is unavailable to the female spectator, bound up as it is with the processes of voyeurism and fetishism. For Doane, "the female spectator . . . in buying her ticket, must deny her sex. There are no images either *for* her or *of* her" (p. 26). In this view, women spectators are caught between a rock and a hard place: Either see yourself as men see you (as a sexual object) or cross-identify and see yourself as the man objectifying the woman (you). Either way, there is not much room here for theorizing female spectatorship as anything but troubled, to say the least.

In reviewing this work, it is important to make a distinction between the terms *audience* and *spectator*, because each is tied to a specific intellectual tradition and the terms are used quite differently in the analysis of representation and reception. *Audience* refers, typically, to the actual people who sit and watch—who consume—a media production. *Spectator*, particularly as the term has been used by feminist film critics, refers to the *subject position* constructed by the representation. The spectator is not a "real woman," but is instead a viewing position constructed by the signifying practice itself. The text constructs us *as spectators*, that is, as sites or locations for the enactment of specific psychic processes such as voyeurism. These two modes of understanding the viewer and the viewing process have provoked much discussion and debate. Are we to focus on actual audiences, and thus necessarily engage in some sort of nontextual, empirical research? Or would we do better to read the cultural texts for what they *imply* about the people who are consuming/viewing them? Kuhn (1984) makes a distinction between the "social audience" as a "group of people who buy tickets at the box office, or who switch on the TV sets; people who can be surveyed, counted and categorized according to age, sex and socioeconomic status" and the "spectator," who is constructed in relation to the text (p. 23). This distinction entails profoundly different methodologies. Psychoanalytic critics impute or imply "spectator positions" from analysis of the text because they believe that the text itself situates women and men in universal and repeatable ways. The text, therefore, remains central. Less psychoanalytically inclined theorists might engage in ethnographic audience research to ascertain how individuals or groups interpret and experience certain media events.

Feminists working with the theory of the male gaze strongly indicted classic Hollywood cinema as being the primary culprit in producing images of woman as spectacle for male desire:

> Women are passive; men are active. Men carry the narrative action forward; women are the stuff of ocular spectacle, there to serve as the locus of the male's desire to savor them visually. Indeed, Mulvey maintains, on screen, women in Hollywood film tend to slow down the narrative or arrest the action, since action must often be frozen, for example, in order to pose female characters so as to afford the opportunity for their erotic contemplation. (Carroll 1990:351)

The issue of "point of view" becomes crucial here, as Mulvey and others have argued that the narrative structure and "mise-en-scène" of classic Hollywood film literally acted out the male gaze by "stylistically . . . confining the spectator to the point of view of the narrative hero" (Devereaux 1990:341). For Mulvey, many aspects of dominant filmmaking contribute to the construction of the woman as sexualized spectacle: the kinds of camera shots (e.g., close-ups), costuming, lighting, makeup, and so on.

The implications of Mulvey's version of the "male gaze" were dramatic: a disavowal of narrative cinema and the construction of a feminist avant-garde that destroyed narrative pleasure, a pleasure that, in her reading, was both masochistic and reproductive of male dominance. Indeed, Mulvey herself attempted to produce just such an avant-garde film, *Riddles of the Sphinx*, made with Peter Wollen. Mulvey (1989) has argued strongly that Hollywood films are bankrupt for feminists, because "the mass of mainstream film, and the conventions within which it has consciously evolved, portray a hermetically sealed world which unwinds magically, indifferent to the presence of the audience, producing for them a sense of separation and playing on their voyeuristic phantasy" (p. 17). If the pleasure of film is, for women, always tainted by a male gaze that controls and objectifies, then we must reject that very pleasure. This point, too, has evoked great debate, both for its absolute rejection of those films from which many of us derive so much pleasure as well as for its insistence on an avant-garde film practice that only earnest film students really seem to enjoy.

Most problematic, perhaps, was Mulvey's assertion of a monolithic male gaze. Not only did it present a picture of a seamless web of patriarchal narrative, but it consigned women spectators to the (unhappy) positions of utter absence or self-negating masochism. Disheartened by the rigidity and hopelessness of this paradigm, feminist critics began to reevaluate the concept of the gaze: "To say that women *can* and *do* look actively and erotically at images of men and other women disrupts the stifling categories of a theory which assumes that such a look is somehow always bound to be male" (Moore 1988:49). This reevaluation has taken many forms. First, there was the direct challenge to the concept of the gaze: Is it overly generalized? Is film really so monolithic? What about other visual media? Is it appropriate to use such deliberately psychoanalytic concepts to discuss the *social* process of filmgoing? And, most important, is the gaze inevitably male? Are women forever condemned to consume images of our own objectification? Are we really structured as the "lack" that must be fetishized to reduce the threat that lack poses? And what about women's gaze? Certainly, women *do* go to the movies, watch TV, listen to pop music—so how, as Pribram (1988) asks, "have we come to perceive all forms of filmic gaze as male when women have always taken up their proportionate share of seats in the cinema? How have we come to understand cinematic pleasure (narrative, erotic, and so on) as pleasurable to the male viewer, but not the female? Why have we failed to see our own presence in the audience when women have always watched—and loved—film?" (p. 1). Feminist work on audiences and spectatorship addresses central questions around power and resistance. How do representations construct viewing positions for the audience member and, in doing so, construct subjectivities and identities as well? How is pleasure produced in the processes of both production and reception? How does the particular social and cultural location of a viewer influence the way she or he "reads" a media text? And, in a broader sense, what impact does the larger social context have on the interpretive possibilities available to any socially situated reader, and on what is produced at all?

Against the Grain: Spectators, Audiences, Resistance

The notion of the implied spectator derived from textual analysis avoids the empiricism of earlier notions of the audience member as number to be counted, but it has its own set of problems. Gray (1987) argues that "such analyses have tended to assume an ideal (female) reader, inscribed within the feminine subject position offered by the text and further emphasized by the assumed cultural competencies of the reader. The risk inherent in this enterprise is the conflation of the 'implied' and the 'real' reader" (p. 33). In other words, it is vital to maintain a distinction between how an actual woman experiences a cultural event and the assumption, through a textual analysis, of how she will experience that event. Gray and many others have expressed concern over the possible conflation of these two "readers," a conflation that can result in a new kind of invisibility for the embodied female reader.

Feminists interested in the "social audience" often engage in ethnographic research in which they interview women to ascertain exactly (or as exactly as possible, given the problems inherent in interview situations and in conducting participant observation) how they consume/interpret a representation and what they do in the process of making meaning out of it. This work often owes a greater debt to anthropology and sociology than to textual literary criticism. In other work, there is an attempt to theorize an audience not simply from the textual operations but from a social and historical analysis that goes beyond the individual, idiosyncratic consumer. For example, one could draw on historical data, popular journalism, fan letters, production information, and other sources along with an analysis of the text (and perhaps interviews as well) to then presume certain kinds of viewing possibilities.

One substantive feminist strategy for challenging the ideological dominance of popular representations has been the practice of "reading against the grain," in which films or television shows are "read" for their absences and ruptures in an attempt to reveal the internal contradictions and produce an interpretation that challenges the dominant reading of the film as well as its coherence and closure. In so doing, feminists have challenged the view of classic narrative that sees it as impenetrable and completely unified. Critics have questioned the ability of the narrative to bring women "back into line," thus continuing to challenge the "images of women" approach. There is often a disjuncture between the ideological desire to put the woman in "her place" at the end of the film and the actual structure of the narrative, which sometimes contradicts that "resolution." It is in these contradictions, these excesses, that feminist film critics have often located the possibility of rereading the film so that these moments become highlighted and revealed.

Such recent feminist work around spectatorship is designed to "reclaim" or "recapture" popular texts for a feminist reader, rereading films or other representations that have previously been understood to be exemplars of patriarchal representations. In an article on *Gentleman Prefer Blondes,* which has typically been understood as the epitome of voyeuristic male cinema, Arbuthnot and Seneca (1990) set out to "chronicle our search to understand our pleasure in this film" (p. 112). These authors argue for the empowering vision of the friendship between the two female characters played by Jane Russell and Marilyn Monroe that "invites the female viewer to join them, through identification, in valuing other women and ourselves" (p. 113). They convincingly argue their case that the women in the film resist male objectification and in fact "return the look" both to the men in the film and, with love and respect, to each other so that "we read, then, beneath the superficial story of heterosexual romance in *Gentlemen Prefer Blondes*, a feminist text which both denies men pleasure to some degree, and more importantly, celebrates women's pleasure in each other" (p. 113). Indeed, the final shot of Marilyn Monroe and Jane Russell in a double wedding displaces the expected foregrounding of heterosexual romance by explicitly centering the last image on a close-up of the two women gazing happily at each other (with their soon-to-be spouses visually disappeared).

One of my favorite examples of Hollywood's failure, narratively, to produce coherent and believable closure is the classic film *Blonde Venus*, starring Marlene Dietrich. In this film, Marlene (herself an enigmatic star figure, thus extratextually resistant as well) plays Helen Faraday, a woman who is married to a scientist stricken ill by one of his experiments. A former singer, Helen goes back to the stage to raise the money needed to send her husband to Switzerland for the cure he must have to survive. Remade now as "the Blonde Venus," she is befriended by a rich playboy (played by Cary Grant) who gives her the necessary money and, of course, falls in love with her as well. Helen sends her husband off for the cure and, eventually, moves in with her rich new friend. When her husband returns early, he discovers her "secret" and threatens to take their young son away from her. Thus begins Helen's downward spiral, as she runs from town to town, keeping just one step ahead of the police. Eventually, thinking it best for the child, she gives up her son to his father and sinks into alcoholic degeneracy. But, again, she is reincarnated and turns up in Europe, a cold and "masculine" star once again.[6] The film ends with her return to New York and her reunion with husband and son, who "take her back." She is put in her proper place, once again, as wife and mother.

Now, although this ostensibly reads like the classic narrative of wayward woman punished for her errant ways and finally, repentant, brought back to the domestic fold, the story is, upon closer examination, fraught with inconsistencies and confusions that make that neat closure seem artificial and silly. By looking closely at the narrative structure, we can see, for example, that Helen's initial punishment (what turns her into a bad, sexual woman that then justifies the loss of her child and then motivates the reunion) seems itself unjustified. For Helen has become "bad" only to save her husband's life; his brutal rejection of her upon his return thus appears unjustified and spiteful. Thus the main narrative motivation for Helen's punishment and "resurrection" is highly tendentious, to say the least.

In addition, in most representations when a mother loses her child, she must first be shown to be a truly horrible mother—the ideology of motherhood is so strong in our culture that she must be depicted as deeply neglectful in order to merit the punishment of loss. But in *Blonde Venus* we have no doubt that she is, even in the worst of circumstances, a wonderful and loving mother. In addition, extratextual factors play into our disbelief. Dietrich was a powerful and sexual Hollywood star. The depiction of her as a chastened wife, begging to go back to her tradition-bound husband, must have struck a false note with many viewers, particularly women viewers who idolized Marlene's independence and power. And the rumors of her lesbianism, which abounded in Hollywood at the time, must have seemed at odds with her depiction as a domesticated heterosexual housewife. Thus by the film's end we experience little narrative justification for this reunion, for this reining in of a woman. Many feminists argue that it is precisely this narrative inconsistency that we should seek out—to elaborate and make visible the cracks in the supposedly airtight case that is male-dominant imagery.

Feminist work on spectatorship has also focused on the phenomena of stars and the fans who identify with, imitate, adore, and revile them, suggesting that a female gaze is activated or encouraged by the presence of certain kinds of female icons, such as Bette Davis, Katharine Hepburn, Marlene Dietrich, and Madonna (see particularly Ang 1985, 1991; Brunt 1992; Doane 1991; Gledhill 1988; Mayne 1993; Radway 1984). The most interesting work on female stars and their fans has been around the possibility of a "lesbian gaze," a theme explored by Weiss (1991) in her study of the space for lesbian desire in watching such stars as Marlene Dietrich (especially when she kisses a woman in the cabaret scene from *Morocco*), Katharine Hepburn, and Greta Garbo. Weiss argues that it is the combination of the stars' extrafilmic personas (the supposed lesbianism of both Dietrich and Garbo) and the actual textual representations (the kiss in the cabaret, the masculinized or androgynous attire) that "provided an alternative model upon which lesbian spectators could draw" (p. 293).

Weiss here explicitly challenges the psychoanalytic model of spectatorship as one that "can only see lesbian desire as a function of assuming a masculine heterosexual position" (p. 290) and instead offers up an analysis of lesbian spectatorship that locates the lesbian filmgoer in a social and historical context, a context of homophobia both within and outside the film industry. Ellsworth (1990) writes about how feminist reviewers "appropriated *Personal Best* into oppositional spaces constructed by feminist political practice" (p. 183) in order to both challenge dominant meanings and help construct a shared, collective space for a feminist subjectivity. Ellsworth found that lesbian-feminist reviewers (themselves also, of course, spectators) deliberately and boldly rewrote and redefined this film to such an extent that they "named and eroticized" moments in the film. Identification and empowerment was achieved not through a simple "reading against the grain," but through a complex process that utilized the already existing cultural codes of lesbian culture to "bring out" and validate the lesbianism that appeared to be defeated in the film's overt narrative. Focusing on lesbian spectatorship disrupts the coherence of the theory of the male gaze by revealing the heterosexism implicit in Mulvey's framework (e.g., the assumption that the object of desire is always cross-gendered). It also reveals the activeness of viewing, as marginalized groups repeatedly construct subtexts and "different endings" in an attempt to locate desire and identity in a representational world produced by heterosexual dominance.

Feminist Decodings: Gender and Cultural Methodology

This concern for discovering a female gaze or female spectator position has close links with a newly invigorated tendency toward ethnographic research:

> The problem, of course, was how to find out what these reading strategies were and where the subcultural resistance was located. Because the analyst's desire was somehow to construct a knowledge of the "other"—or more precisely, the other's knowledge—a resort to anthropological or sociological methodologies seemed inevitable. This approach, which has come to be termed "ethnographic," makes use of such techniques as participant observation and audience interviews. (Bergstrom and Doane 1989:11)

This new ethnography—drawing as it does from radical anthropologists and oral historians—rigorously interrogates its own practice and is careful to avoid the undertheorized empiricism of the old mass-comm audience research as well as the subjectivism and relativism of much literary criticism. Reception issues in cultural studies, too, have particular resonance for feminist researchers of popular culture. If women are so often the objects and not the subjects of research, so often the spectacle of popular culture and rarely the articulated voice, then to give women access to that voice seems a crucial step. Feminist analysis has always stressed, both epistemologically and methodologically, the contextual and interactive nature of meaning-making. An emphasis on process is a feminist maxim, often laughed at but too rarely paid attention to substantively. Thus the insight that cultural meaning is not simply immanent in the text but produced at least in part by actual audiences in particular social contexts, bringing with them specific cultural "capital," is familiar to feminist researchers. Indeed, much of the best of recent cultural ethnography is deeply feminist in both epistemological orientation and subject of study.

The turn to anthropological and sociological methodologies (interviews, participant observation, focus groups, historical contextualization) emerged out of an attempt to uncover and interpret the nature of alternative reading strategies. It also emerged out of a critique of the overreliance on the "text" of culture, an overreliance that often resulted in the designation of the consumers of popular culture as blank slates, and duped blank slates at that. Again, it seems obvious to me that feminist cultural critics would have a particular problem with a cultural analysis that assigns women that status of the unvoiced: Been there, done that.

Radway's (1984) work on women romance readers is a unique attempt to develop a specifically feminist methodology of cultural analysis. It has been replicated, commented on, and criticized by numerous feminist cultural theorists. Radway's subjects (much like the male working-class subjects of earlier British work on subcultures) are neither duped consumers of cultural commodities nor simply enjoying themselves "innocently." Radway's romance readers see themselves as involved in a process with other women, one allowing them respite from the demands of husband and children. In that sense, these readers are doing more than simply escaping from the drudgery of housework; although their reading is, to some extent, compensatory, it also allows them to glimpse ways of life unlike their own and to question some of their own assumptions and options. For example, the male characters in romance novels, although often initially harsh and distant, are usually brought around to a position of warmth and accessibility, a male identity not necessarily found in the "real lives" of the readers themselves. The women readers of Radway's study use romance novels in ways that are, contradictorily, helpful in negotiating their everyday existence and, ultimately, reproductive of that very existence. Radway's insistence on blending the ethnographic and the textual, the anthropological and the psychoanalytic, broke down methodological barriers that had been firmly in place for years. Her attempt to integrate critical and ethnographic impulses with a thorough feminist politics creates a quite interesting set of research possibilities for feminist cultural critics.

Much contemporary television research follows this model, exemplified by the work of Hobson (1990), who argues from her interviews that

> women use television programs as part of their general discourse on their own lives, the lives of their families and friends and to add interest to their working lives. It adds to the critique of audiences as passive viewers by putting forward the hypothesis that it is the discussion after television programs have been viewed which completes the process of communication and locates television programs as part of popular culture. (p. 62)

Thus reading romances or watching TV soaps is not merely, or only, a compensatory activity that further mires women in the muck of patriarchal domination; rather, "the use of events within fiction to explore experiences which were perhaps too personal or painful to talk about to a complete work group is a beneficial and creative way of extending the value of the program into their own lives" (p. 65).

Many other feminists have used ethnographic methods to determine these different reading positions. Bobo (1988) conducted group interviews to analyze the reception/interpretation of the film *The Color Purple* "to examine the way in which a specific audience creates meaning from a mainstream text and uses the reconstructed meaning to empower themselves and their social group" (p. 93). Drawing on Hall's theory of encoding/decoding, as well as historical analysis that locates this particular film in a larger context of films about Blacks made by White male directors, Bobo paints a picture of a complex process whereby a Black female audience brings to the film a knowledge of the stereotypes that will be employed and then (consciously or unconsciously) negotiates with those images to glean something for themselves: "Given the similarities of *The Color Purple* to past films that have portrayed Black people negatively, Black women's positive reaction to the film seems inconceivable. However, their stated comments and published reports prove that Black women not only like the film but have formed a strong attachment to it. The film is significant in their lives" (p. 101). Bobo places this reception in the context of "cultural competencies" surrounding the emergence of a "canon" of Black women writers: "Black women's response to the film *The Color Purple* is not coincidental, nor is it insignificant. It is in keeping with the recent emergence of a body of critical works about the heritage of Black women writers, the recent appearance of other novels by Black women written in the same vein as *The Color Purple* and, very importantly, the fact that there is a knowledgeable core of Black women readers of both literary and filmic texts" (p. 107).

I am now in the midst of my own work on lesbian and gay culture, a section of which examines the cultural phenomenon of the televisual and "real-life" coming out of the lead character in the sitcom *Ellen* and actor Ellen DeGeneres. My feminist methodology is similar to that of Bobo's, engaging with the larger context of reception—a context of newly established lesbian visibility, of organized parties to view the episode, of increased antigay activism, of "lesbian chic." In other words, attention to the fullness of reception contexts seems a particularly feminist approach to cultural analysis. So the meaning of the cultural phenomenon of *Ellen* is not to be found solely in a reference to the relevant television text, but in and around the circulating discourses that "took up" the television event (before and after it actually occurred) and layered it with a vast network of meanings.

Such work broadens out what we mean by reception, for it enlarges the context of reception beyond the actual moment of viewing and "reading" to a larger circuit of engagements that include discussing the shows with friends and family: "By not asking merely, What do people do with the text? (stop) but, What do they do with the text *in the real world?*, a way is offered for 'audience' to mean more than merely receiver or reader of others' encodings" (Brunt 1992:76).

Away with All Posts: Predicaments for
Twenty-First-Century Feminist Cultural Studies

So, what now for feminist cultural studies? It seems to me that the most interesting new work and most promising research agendas center on questions of reception, pleasure, and agency. The question is: Who/what has the power to determine meaning? Is it the actual viewer, who makes of the image what she will, or is it the image itself that determines certain readings from the viewers? Although this new attention to the "female gaze" is to be lauded, it has the danger of overlooking the often violent reality of male domination and male objectification of women in images. The motivation for much of this spectatorship (or "female gaze") theory is to move us away from situating women as victims, completely determined by the totalistic male gaze and therefore unable to do anything but consume our own objectification—an uninspiring place, to be sure. Female gaze theory locates resistance in women's ways of seeing images and constructing meaning. In addition, it gives substantive weight to the theoretical position that argues that meaning is not just apparent in the text but is actively made in an interaction between viewer and image.

Nevertheless, we must remain aware of the institutional and representational strictures placed on our experience of popular culture. Women certainly are not the passive viewers cultural theory often has made us out to be; however, we are also not wholly free to make resistant reading out of whole cloth. Images are so often filled with dominant cultural messages that, although a few women may read radically against the grain, the vast majority of us will feel the weight of the dominant and interpret the codes without much semiotic play. Gray (1987) alerts us to the dangers of a too-celebratory approach: "What seems to be happening here, and it is a worrying trend, is that by celebrating on the one hand an active audience for popular forms and on the other those popular forms which the audience 'enjoy,' we appear to be throwing the whole enterprise of a cultural critique out of the window" (p. 28). Even feminist "reading against the grain" is not the whole answer to "reclaiming" mainstream representations. Refusing the explicit narrative that seems to insist on the subordination of women and reading instead secret subversions and protofeminist counternarratives can be empowering, but it can also miss out on the (unequal) power of mass-produced imagery. A feminist critic may "read" *Dynasty* as an over-the-top camp tale of active, sexual women, but this does not necessarily mean that the majority of women viewers will do that, or that the dominant meaning is not still resolutely patriarchal. We must be careful not to "find" resistance and ideological slippage under every apparently hegemonic rock of popular culture, simply because we want them to be there. Feminist attention to narrative needs to traverse both these grounds—exposing the male-centered plots of popular culture and constructing alternative readings that tell a more empowering story. And these alternative readings need not be produced wholly in the minds of the academic feminist critic, but can themselves be unpacked and analyzed from the narratives of audiences.

Gledhill (1988) argues for the term *negotiation* to replace both the reflectionist models of "images of women" and the determinism and ahistoricism of "cine-psychoanalysis":

> For the term "negotiation" implies the holding together of opposite sides in an ongoing process of give-and-take. As a model of meaning production, negotiation conceives cultural exchange as the intersection of processes of production and reception, in which overlapping but non-matching determinations operate. Meaning is neither imposed, nor passively imbibed, but arises out of a struggle or negotiation between competing frames of reference, motivation and experience. (pp. 67-68)

Gledhill goes on to argue that we negotiate at every level: Organized feminists put pressure on various media institutions to produce more complex images; critics debate the meaning of texts; audiences actively "read" what they are offered. But she also argues that "concern with the pleasures or identifications of actual audiences seems to ignore the long-term task of overthrowing dominant structures, within which resistant or emergent voices struggle on unequal terms" (p. 71).

In other words, we need to ask what women do with all this resistance, how they use it and work with it in their everyday lives, because, as Press (1991) argues, "if women's tendency to resist hegemony through creative interpretations of television truly stops in the kitchen, then this evidence of resistance must be counted as something else. Theorists of resistance must develop some means for assessing the political effectiveness of the resistance they chronicle" (p. 177). "Resistance," if it is to have any meaning at all, must be concerned with actually changing the social conditions of women's lives.

For all these cautionary provisos, the recent work in female spectatorship bodes well for feminist cultural studies. In its multilayered and intertextual approach, it begins to break down the stubborn barriers between the ethnographic and the ideological, the contextual and the textual, production and reception. Trends in cultural studies themselves coincide with recent developments within feminist theory. As feminism has grown beyond the initial stages and fully taken its place within both the academy specifically and intellectual life more broadly conceived, it has shifted away from documenting patriarchal oppression and toward a more nuanced and perhaps inward examination of the production of gender as a viable category. So too has feminist cultural studies moved away from the documentation of "negative" and stereotyped portrayals of women to an examination of the multiplicities of meaning and interpretive possibilities. No longer are we as interested (only) in revealing the nefarious ways in which Woman has been figured in popular images; now we are more concerned with exploring the very construction of Woman as a stable category and thus with destabilizing gender itself.[7]

But I fear that this trend may have gone too far. To put it simply: How do we account for the multiplicity of interpretive locations and reading strategies that women make in various situations without falling into the traps of individualism and particularism? Or, as Pearce (1995) asks trenchantly:

> If it was no longer tenable to represent women as a group, where did that leave the woman reader, or, indeed, the feminist reader? Could there be any such thing as a reading position that was gendered, simplistically, male or female? How could a text direct itself to a male or female audience when those terms, in themselves, are inclusive of so many differences and contradictions as to render them meaningless? (p. 87)

If "woman" is a gendered fiction—a fiction of gender—then how can we speak of a female gaze, resistant or not?

How do we analyze cultural material so as to explore the contradictions contained within mainstream representations without necessarily interpreting contradiction as coequal to collective transgression of patriarchal norms? And, for me the crucial question, how can we still work actively with concepts of power, domination, and ideology without defining most women as "cultural dupes" or consigning them to the nether regions of false consciousness? How do we do justice to the very real pleasures experienced in the consumption of popular culture (even that which appears by most accounts to do us at least ideological harm) without mistaking this pleasure for resistance, much less revolution?

The future of feminist cultural studies must wrestle with these tough questions and find ways to speak of power *and* agency, domination *and* resistance, subjection *and* subversion. A more thoroughly contextual and intertextual approach that is rooted in materialism seems to me a significant direction to move toward. If it is no longer possible to think of patriarchal representations (and patriarchal power generally) as a monolithic force that reproduces itself almost automatically and is consumed generically, it is equally impossible to analyze representations of women without reckoning with the stubborn persistence of very real, very structured forms of male domination, and very specifically situated real audiences. Gender, as Butler (1990) has correctly pointed out, is a performative sign that re-creates itself precisely in the repetition of its performance. But it is a sign that has embodied, material effects.

The concept of "performance" has dominated recent feminist theory as well as gay/lesbian/queer theory. Butler is obviously key here, as her work has come to signify a radical move in both theoretical arenas. The notions of gender play and performance that she elaborates have been the starting points for any number of new works in feminist and queer theory. Butler (1990) is explicit that the performance of gender is never a simple voluntary act (like choosing the clothes one puts on in the morning) and is always already constituted by the rules and histories of gender. She also reiterates the ambiguity of drag, arguing carefully that "drag is not unproblematically subversive . . . [and] there is no guarantee that ex sing the naturalized status of heterosexuality will lead to its subversion" (p. 231). Yet the analysis of performance still remains removed from social and cultural contexts that enable or disenable their radical enactment.

The performance motif may be the perfect trope for our funky times, producing a sense of enticing activity amid the depressing ruins of late capitalism. It obviously speaks to the pastiche-like world of images and signs that have come to signify what it means to live in the postmodern (see Madonna or Michael Jackson or Princess Diana if you doubt this), yet this hand can be, and has been, overplayed. In particular, this performance trope becomes vacuous when it is decontextualized, and overblown when it is bandied about as the new hope for a confused world. Theories of gender as play and performance need to be intimately and systematically connected with the power of gender (really, the power of male power) to constrain, control, violate, and configure. Too often, mere lip service is given to the specific historical, social, and political configurations that make certain conditions possible and others constrained.

Hennessy (1994) notes in her critique of Butler (and others) the lack of attention to the material context of "gender performance": "What does it mean to say that what can be seen as parodic and what gender parody makes visible depends on a context in which subversive confusions can be fostered? What exactly is meant by 'context' here?" (p. 40). Without substantive engagement with complex sociopolitical realities, those performance tropes appear as entertaining but ultimately depoliticized academic exercises.

There is great insight and merit in understanding gender and sexual identity as processes, acquisitions, enactments, creations (and Butler [1990] is right to credit Simone de Beauvoir with this profound insight), and Butler and others have done us a great service by elaborating the dissimulating possibilities of simulation. But this insight gets lost if it is not theorized with a deep understanding of the limitations and constraints within which we "perform" gender. Without some elaborated social and cultural context, the theory of performance is deeply ahistorical and therefore ironically (because postmodernism fashions itself as particularism par excellence) universalistic, avoiding a discussion of the contexts (race, class, ethnicity, and the like) that make particular "performances" more or less likely to be possible in the first place. It is not enough to assert that all performance of gender takes place within complex and specific regimes of power and domination; those regimes must be explicitly part of the analytic structure of the performance trope, rather than asides to be tossed around and then ignored.[8]

In the rush to avoid consigning women to the status of helpless victims of the male gaze and phallocentric culture, too many cultural critics have begun to go on a postmodern Easter egg hunt, searching for resistance and subversive pleasure within every page of *Playboy* and in every trip to the mall. It may be fun to go to the mall, and one may even find forms of female solidarity amid the cacophony of consumerism, but the feminist cultural critic needs to begin to suggest connections between mall pleasures and everyday life, between the consumption of commodities and resistances to commodification.

It is, of course, central for feminist cultural critics to reckon with the pleasures of popular culture, for no matter how we might cringe at its often blatant sexism and homophobia and racism, we do dearly love it. Although more assuredly feminist forms of visual culture are being developed and need to be actively pursued, we certainly cannot consign the pleasures of popular culture to an intellectual no-fly zone. But neither can we glibly equate pleasures with resistance, or even with subversion. Readings against the patriarchal grain, acts of cultural cannibalism, appropriations of masculinized forms for female fun are not necessarily socially progressive moves. They can be, but that is, as they say, an empirical question.

We must not forget that it is vitally important to continue to articulate the links between popular pleasures and collective struggles. What is the relationship between feminist appropriations of popular culture (say, the willful misreading of *Cagney & Lacey* as lesbian text) and extratextual feminist politics? Struggles at the site of the sign do have their own political salience, but there is a difference between reading a TV text radically and fighting for safe and legal abortion. I don't mean to be flip here; rather, I want to re-ask the question of why we study culture at all. I cannot be satisfied with feminist cultural analyses that do not at least attempt to plot relationships between certain cultural phenomena and other social movements, social processes, social struggles. There is no more vivid example of the need for this linkage than in the current explosion of representations of lesbians and gay men. This cultural visibility must be understood in the larger context of antigay activism and referenda, the commodification of gay life, the growth of a "legitimate" gay rights movement, and niche marketing to gay consumers. How else to analyze the simultaneous proliferation of gay weddings on TV and anti-gay marriage legislation? The narrow particularism of much of contemporary cultural criticism avoids these connections as the leperlike markings of grand narrative and metatheory, but we forgo the big picture at our peril. In some ways, I think the difference between what I would call ideology critique and the newer, French-accented analyses of culture is not a question of text versus context, or sociology versus lit crit. Rather, the debate is really one between the context as implicated in the text, as in fact the analytic site, and a theory of culture in which context provides only background or decorative wallpaper. For example, in examining the new visibility of lesbians in the media, one would attempt to *integrate* an analysis of the social conjuncture (e.g., antigay referenda, rise in hate crimes, a gay-positive president, the search for a "gay gene") with the more formal or textual analyses of the representations themselves. Thus "lesbian chic" would be understood in a fully social sense, and the examination of particular images would be informed by—and implicated in—a larger sociohistorical frame. This method is in contrast to a kind of cultural analysis that often begins with a brief survey of the "social scene" only to move on to a textual analysis seemingly uninformed by that initial move.

Ethnographic research—and emphasis on varying interpretive possibilities—does address context, but it can lead to a kind of wishywashy pluralism in which "people in modern mediatized societies are complex and contradictory, mass cultural texts are complex and contradictory, therefore people using them produce complex and contradictory culture" (Morris 1990:24-25). It is vital to remember that an ethnographic approach involves a great deal of interpretation on the part of the critic; it cannot give the "guarantee" of truth anymore than a purely textual analysis can.

Other studies stand as examples of the possibility of reuniting text and context within a critical feminist perspective. In this regard, an emphasis on some sort of (nonempiricist, e.g., not holding up quantitative data as scientific truth) empirical research should be part of the project, particularly if one attempts to turn the feminist phrase "The personal is political" into a methodological principle. Methodologically, this would entail a move away from the focus on either the isolated text or the aggregate viewer, and a move toward an engagement with the lived experience of actual women. I want to stress that this engagement need not be seen literally—as interviews or ethnographies. Rather, the methods increasingly being used by feminist cultural critics are refreshingly eclectic, merging sophisticated textual analyses with social history, genre criticism with object relations, interviews with fan mail. Indeed, these intertextual, contextual critics are redefining what we mean by *audience* and what we mean by the phrase *empirical research.* These are not, I would suggest, self-evident terms, but themselves need critical development and elaboration. Feminist cultural criticism should continue to push at these boundaries, while always maintaining a firm commitment to asking fundamentally *feminist* questions of cultural processes.

Notes

1. For a thorough examination of the history of feminist cultural theory, see my *Material Girls* (Walters 1995). Here, I present a quite truncated version of that rather more complicated story.

2. Of course, male cultural critics were and are examining the particular ways in which men and boys engage with various cultural practices. Yet in a world structured around the power of gender (not just gender as a benign category), these studies are feminist only insofar as they reveal the construction of gendered identities as itself the construction of relations of power. Feminist cultural work encourages the study of forms of culture that are typically engaged in by men and boys, to the extent that it problematizes gender and gendered power.

3. There is an obvious parallel here to work in feminist theory—particularly French feminism—around what has been called *ecriture feminine,* or women's writing, or what feminist psychologists and moral theorists have called women's "different voice" and "ways of knowing."

4. See particularly the special issue of *Camera Obscura* (nos. 33-34, 1994) devoted to analysis of the Lifetime network. Many of the authors address the complex relations of gender, genre, and spectatorship implied in an explicit television address to women, and focus specifically on how "woman" (upscale, White, working women with a touch of scaled-down feminist angst) is constructed through the actual programming and the marketing strategies as well.

5. Lynn Spigel (1992) and others have written of the early days of television production, in which advertisers evinced great concern and ambivalence toward women as cultural consumers, both anxious to get women in front of the tube and purchasing their products and, at the same time, worried that the presence of TV in the family home would disrupt traditional relations of power.

6. Much has been made of Dietrich's costuming in the film; indeed, her masculine attire is always present at her most self-defining (and therefore "unfeminine") moments.

7. For example, the whole madness surrounding the "family values" debate and Dan Quayle's attack on sitcom single mom Murphy Brown was not awful only because of the antifeminist ethos it revealed. Rather, the constructed entity "single mother" became contested and was matched against her equally constructed "opposite"—the heterosexual wife and mother who stays at home. One could not understand the *Murphy Brown* debacle simply by reference to theories of stereotypes or "negative images"; rather, one needed recourse to theories of intertextuality (the relation between print media and TV sitcoms and talk shows and public policy; the eerie slippage between "real" single moms and "fictional" single moms).

8. Again, I would note here that Butler's most recent work seems to address, rather successfully, many of my concerns. Nevertheless, I still am concerned that much of the discussion around drag, performance,

crossing, and so on remains deeply decontextualized, or that the context seems to be solely a textual and representational one.

References

Ang, Ien. 1985. *Watching Dallas: Soap Operas and the Melodramatic Imagination.* London: Methuen.

———. 1991. *Desperately Seeking the Audience.* New York: Routledge.

Arbuthnot, Lucie and Gail Seneca. 1990. "Pre-text and Text in *Gentlemen Prefer Blondes.*" Pp. 112-25 in *Issues in Feminist Film Criticism,* edited by Patricia Erens. Bloomington: Indiana University Press.

Bergstrom, Janet and Mary Ann Doane. 1989. "The Female Spectator: Contexts and Directions." *Camera Obscura* 20-21:5-27.

Betterton, Rosemary. 1987. "How Do Women Look? The Female Nude in the Work of Suzanne Valadon." Pp. 217-34 in *Looking On: Images of Femininity in the Visual Arts and Media,* edited by Rosemary Betterton. London: Pandora.

Bobo, Jacqueline. 1988. "*The Color Purple*: Black Women as Cultural Readers." Pp. 90-109 in *Female Spectators: Looking at Film and Television,* edited by E. Deidre Pribram. London: Verso.

Bordo, Susan. 1993. *Unbearable Weight: Feminism, Western Culture, and the Body.* Berkeley: University of California Press.

Brunt, Rosalind. 1992. "Engaging with the Popular: Audiences for Mass Culture and What to Say about Them." Pp. 69-80 in *Cultural Studies,* edited by Lawrence Grossberg, Cary Nelson, and Paula A. Treichler. New York: Routledge.

Butler, Judith. 1990. *Gender Trouble: Feminism and the Subversion of Identity.* New York: Routledge.

Byars, Jackie. 1988. "Gazes/Voices/Power: Expanding Psychoanalysis for Feminist Film and Television Theory." Pp. 110-31 in *Female Spectators: Looking at Film and Television,* edited by E. Deidre Pribram. London: Verso.

———. 1991. *All That Hollywood Allows: Re-reading Gender in 1950s Melodrama.* Chapel Hill: University of North Carolina Press.

Carroll, Noel. 1990. "The Image of Women in Film: A Defense of a Paradigm." *Journal of Aesthetics and Art Criticism* 48:349-60.

Coward, Rosalind. 1985. *Female Desires: How They Are Sought, Bought and Packaged.* New York: Grove.

Devereaux, Mary. 1990. "Oppressive Texts, Resisting Readers, and the Gendered Spectator." *Journal of Aesthetics and Art Criticism* 48:337-48.

Doane, Mary Ann. 1988. "Woman's Stake: Filming the Female Body." Pp. 22-36 in *Feminism and Film Theory,* edited by Constance Penley. New York: Routledge.

———. 1991. *Femmes Fatales: Feminism, Film Theory, Psychoanalysis.* New York: Routledge.

Ellsworth, Elizabeth. 1990. "Illicit Pleasures: Feminist Spectators and *Personal Best.*" Pp. 183-96 in *Issues in Feminist Film Criticism,* edited by Patricia Erens. Bloomington: Indiana University Press.

Gledhill, Christine. 1987. "The Melodramatic Field: An Investigation." Pp. 5-42 in *Home Is Where the Heart Is: Studies in Melodrama and the Women's Film,* edited by Christine Gledhill. London: British Film Institute.

———. 1988. "Pleasurable Negotiations." Pp. 64-89 in *Female Spectators: Looking at Film and Television,* edited by E. Deidre Pribram. London: Verso.

Gray, Ann. 1987. "Reading the Audience." *Screen* 283:24-35.

Hennessy, Rosemary. 1994. "Queer Visibility in Commodity Culture." *Cultural Critique,* pp. 31-76.

Hobson, Dorothy. 1990. "Women Audiences and the Workplace." Pp. 61-74 in *Television and Women's Culture,* edited by Mary Ellen Brown. London: Sage.

Kuhn, Annette. 1984. "Women's Genres." *Screen* 251:18-28.

LaPlace, Maria. 1987. "Producing and Consuming the Woman's Film." Pp. 138-66 in *Home Is Where the Heart Is: Studies in Melodrama and the Women's Film,* edited by Christine Gledhill. London: British Film Institute.

Lury, Celia. 1995. "The Rights and Wrongs of Culture: Issues of Theory and Methodology." Pp. 33-45 in *Feminist Cultural Theory: Process and Production,* edited by Beverley Skeggs. Manchester: Manchester University Press.

Mayne, Judith. 1993. *Cinema and Spectatorship.* New York: Routledge.

Modleski, Tania. 1982. *Loving with a Vengeance: Mass-Produced Fantasies for Women.* London: Methuen.

Moore, Suzanne. 1988. "Here's Looking at You Kid." Pp. 44-59 in *The Female Gaze: Women as Viewers of Popular Culture,* edited by Lorraine Gamman and Margaret Marshment. London: Women's Press.

Moores, Shaun. 1990. "Texts, Readers and Contexts of Meaning: Developments in the Study of Media Audiences." *Media, Culture & Society* 12:9-29.

Morris, Meaghan. 1990. "Banality in Cultural Studies." Pp. 14-43 in *Logics of Television: Essays in Cultural Criticism,* edited by Patricia Mellencamp. Bloomington: Indiana University Press.

Mulvey, Laura. [1975] 1981. "Visual Pleasure and Narrative Cinema." Pp. 12-15 in *Popular Television and Film,* edited by Tony Bennett et al. London: British Film Institute/Open University Press.

———. 1989. *Visual and Other Pleasures.* Bloomington: Indiana University Press.

Nochimson, Martha. 1992. *No End to Her: Soap Opera and the Female Subject.* Berkeley: University of California Press.

Pearce, Lynne. 1995. "Finding a Place from Which to Write: The Methodology of Feminist Textual Practice." Pp. 81-96 in *Feminist Cultural Theory: Process and Production*, edited by Beverley Skeggs. Manchester: Manchester University Press.

Penley, Constance. 1992. "Feminism, Psychoanalysis, and the Study of Popular Culture." Pp. 479-500 in *Cultural Studies*, edited by Lawrence Grossberg, Cary Nelson, and Paula A. Treichler. New York: Routledge.

Press, Andrea. 1991. *Women Watching Television: Gender, Class and Generation in the American Television Experience*. Philadelphia: University of Pennsylvania Press.

Pribram, E. Deidre. 1988. "Introduction." Pp. 1-11 in *Female Spectators: Looking at Film and Television*, edited by E. Deidre Pribram. London: Verso.

Radway, Janice. 1984. *Reading the Romance: Women, Patriarchy, and Popular Literature*. Chapel Hill: University of North Carolina Press.

Shattuc, Jane. 1997. *The Talking Cure: TV, Talk Shows, and Women*. New York: Routledge.

Silverman, Kaja. 1984. "Dis-embodying the Female Voice." Pp. 131-49 in *Re-vision: Essays in Feminist Film Criticism*, edited by Mary Ann Doane, Patricia Mellencamp, and Linda Williams. Los Angeles: American Film Institute.

Spigel, Lynn. 1992. *Make Room for TV: Television and the Family Ideal in Postwar America*. Chicago: University of Chicago Press.

Studlar, Gaylyn. 1990. "Masochism, Masquerade, and the Erotic Metamorphoses of Marlene Dietrich." Pp. 229-49 in *Fabrications: Costume and the Female Body*, edited by Jane Gaines and Charlotte Herzog. New York: Routledge.

Walters, Suzanna Danuta. 1992. "Material Girls: Feminism and Cultural Studies." *Current Perspectives in Social Theory 12*, edited by Ben Agger. Greenwich, CT: JAI.

———. 1995. *Material Girls: Making Sense of Feminist Cultural Theory*. Berkeley: University of California Press.

———. Summer 1996. "From Here to Queer: Radical Feminism, Postmodernism, and the Lesbian Menace (or, Why Can't a Woman Be More Like a Fag?)." *Signs*, 21(4):830-69.

Weiss, Andrea. 1991. " 'A Queer Feeling When I Look at You': Hollywood Stars and Lesbian Spectatorship in the 1930s." Pp. 293-99 in *Stardom: Industry of Desire*, edited by Christine Gledhill. London: Routledge.

Winship, Janet. 1987. "Handling Sex." Pp. 25-39 in *Looking On: Images of Femininity in the Visual Arts and Media*, edited by Rosemary Betterton. London: Pandora.

PART IV

GENDER IN
SOCIAL INSTITUTIONS

CHAPTER 9

Moving Beyond Gender

Intersectionality and
Scientific Knowledge

PATRICIA HILL COLLINS

In the United States, feminist analyses of science have moved in important new directions since the mid-1980s. Where earlier feminist scholarship focused on barriers confronting aspiring women scientists, more recent work has emphasized science as a deeply gendered enterprise. As Fox Keller and Longino (1996b) put it, "Gender opened an entirely new window on the nature of scientific inquiry" (p. 2). Spurred on by insights culled from the history (Keller 1985; Harding 1986), philosophy (Harding 1991), and sociology of science (Smith 1990), feminist scholarship raised a number of new and important questions about the content, practice, and traditional goals of science. As a result, the choice and definition of scientific problems, the design and interpretation of experiments, and even the very definitions of modern science have all been criticized as reflecting male biases and priorities (see, e.g., Keller and Longino 1996a, pt. IV).

By distinguishing among scientific epistemologies, methodologies, and research methods, Harding (1987) provides a useful schema for clarifying some definitional issues that shape feminist critiques of science. Within Harding's schema, "epistemology" constitutes an overarching theory of knowledge (e.g., positivism). In contrast, "methodology" encompasses the broad principles of how to conduct research and

AUTHOR'S NOTE: I wish to thank the editors of this volume for their invaluable editorial assistance, as well as Nicole Trombley for her suggestions and ideas on this topic.

how theory is to be applied (e.g., qualitative and quantitative). "Methods" are the particular techniques used in the course of scientific research (e.g., interviewing and survey analysis). As Jayaratne and Stewart (1991) suggest, "It follows from these definitions that first, quantitative and qualitative 'methods' are simply specific research procedures; second, 'feminist methodology' or a 'feminist perspective on methodology' must be taken to refer to a much broader theory of how to do feminist research. There may, then, be a 'feminist methodology' without any particular 'feminist methods' " (p. 92).

Feminist critiques of scientific epistemology have led to detailed analyses of positivism, especially the pervasive gender biases associated with positivist science. Claiming the existence of absolute truths and an objective reality structured by invariant rules, positivist science argues that the underlying structure of social as well as physical phenomena can be uncovered. This approach to science has guided the intellectual orientations and practices of a range of academic disciplines in the United States and Europe (Ross 1991). Feminist scholars have unpacked these and other assumptions of positivism in order to demonstrate how positivism's epistemological assumptions shape specific conceptions of sex and gender.

Within these epistemological debates, the dual constructs of objectivity and rationality have garnered special attention. Positivist science typically advances two fundamental beliefs to legitimate its claims. The first is that empiricism or hypothesis-testing against objectively collected data is the basis of natural and social sciences. Belief in objectivity lies at the core of empirical research. Particularistic concerns are to be erased by a commitment to a universality that science allegedly provides. Second, rationalism or abstract reasoning about systems of thought and the logical coherence of ideas, more characteristic of philosophy and literary studies, also remains central to the construction of scientific knowledge. To varying degrees, feminist scholarship has taken on different dimensions of this philosophy. Whereas earlier work questioned science as masculinist, more recent work presents more nuanced critiques and alternative feminist research methods (Reinharz 1992).

Jayaratne and Stewart (1991) provide a useful summary of the substance of feminist critiques of scientific methodology. Although the initial dialogue on feminist methodology originated in criticism of traditional quantitative research, the critique now addresses a broad range of issues. Feminists have criticized scientific methodologies for selecting sexist and elitist research topics; using biased research designs, including the selection of only male subjects; maintaining an exploitative relationship between scientific researchers and the subjects of scientific research; fostering an illusion of objectivity; using quantitative data in simplistic and superficial ways; improperly interpreting and overgeneralizing scientific findings; and inadequately disseminating scientific data (Jayaratne and Stewart 1991:86). Collectively, feminist analyses of scientific epistemology, research methodology, and research methods have generated interest in alternatives to mainstream, positivist science.

Despite these important contributions, certain conceptualizations of gender that permeate this literature limit the feminist perspective. By the mid-1980s, a healthy debate emerged within feminist circles that focused on the diversity among women as well as the implications of this diversity for conceptualizations of gender (Spelman 1988). The irony of a recurrent pattern in feminist theory that reflected the viewpoints of White middle-class women of North America and Western Europe is not lost on philosopher Nicholson (1990), who notes that "the underlying problem was . . . the failure, common to many forms of academic scholarship, to recognize the embeddedness of its own assumptions within a specific historical context" (pp. 1-2). With the exceptions described below, feminist scholarship on scientific knowledge remains largely untouched by this insight. Because it generally ignores how gender mutually constructs and is constructed by race, class, ethnicity, and other major systems of domination, feminist analysis of science may be similarly unable to "recognize the embeddedness of its own assumptions."

In this essay, I explore how feminist analyses of gender and scientific knowledge might benefit from closer association with emerging scholarship on intersectionality. The construct of intersectionality references two types of relationships: the interconnectedness of ideas and the social structures in which they occur, and the intersecting hierarchies of gender, race, economic class, sexuality, and ethnicity. Viewing gender within a logic of intersectionality redefines it as a constellation of ideas and social practices that are historically situated within and that mutually construct multiple systems of oppression.

I limit my discussion here to how the intersection of race and gender operates within scientific discourse and practice. In developing my argument, I pursue three major lines of investigation. First, I discuss the persistent disjuncture between scientific knowledge and scientific practice that, when linked to a nonintersectional gender analysis, shapes much of the feminist scholarship on science. Second, I examine two main areas of feminist scholarship: questions of gendered epistemologies and methodologies and the relationship of science to modernity. Finally, using African American women's experiences, I suggest how working from within assumptions of intersectionality might generate new directions for feminist analyses of science.

Science as Discourse and Practice: Parallel and Intersectional Analyses

The theme of intersectionality that attracted substantial attention in the 1980s and 1990s can usefully be applied to rethinking questions of gender, race, and scientific knowledge.[1] The initial emphasis on race, social class, and gender has expanded to include intersections involving sexuality, ethnicity, and nationalism (Anthias and Yuval-Davis 1992; Parker et al. 1992).[2] Work on the interplay of race, class, and gender in Weimar and Nazi Germany (Bridenthal, Grossmann, and Kaplan 1984); the centrality of primatology in framing gendered and raced views of nature in modern science (Haraway 1989); race, gender, and sexuality in the colonial conquest (McClintock 1995); and the workings of race, class, and gender in African American women's lives (Mullings 1997)— all illustrate intersectional analyses.

One emphasis emerging from intersectional frameworks concerns the connections between scientific knowledge and scientific practices (Fausto-Sterling 1992a). As Mies (1991) argues, "If we understand feminist research and science as part of the historical movement out of which it has emerged, then it is . . . impossible to cling to the dichotomy between thought and action, science and politics. We are then left with no alternative but to question contemplative science, which veils power and exploitation, as something which divides historical reality into separate areas" (pp. 64-65). Those feminist scholars of science who reject this "dichotomy between thought and action, science and politics" develop intersectional analyses of gender and race that investigate the relationship between knowledge and power. For example, in *Primate Visions*, Haraway (1989) examines how racialized colonial discourse and gender ideologies shaped the scientific contours of the field of primatology. In her important essay, "Race and Gender: The Role of Analogy in Science," Stepan (1990) provides a provocative framework for examining intersections of gender and race in the construction of nineteenth-century science. In her edited volume, *The "Racial" Economy of Science,* Harding (1993b) aims to build a bridge between feminist scholarship of science and that of race. In *Myths of Gender,* Fausto-Sterling (1992b) provides an intersectional analysis of biology, and in her work on "Hottentot" women in Europe, she explores intersections of gender, race, and nation (Fausto-Sterling 1995).

The work of these scholars suggests that gender and race operate within science less as *parallel* dimensions in constructing scientific knowledge than as *intersecting* dimensions of social organization where knowledge and power are intimately linked. Conceptualizing race and gender as parallel dimensions allows researchers to focus on one dimension and then the other, so that one can imagine a "pure" gender or "pure" race unaffected by the other. Prioritizing gender and race in this fashion fosters assumptions that race and gender constitute similar yet essentially distinct constructs. Feminist analyses of science that examine gender while making little mention of race work within assumptions of parallelism. For example, Rosser's (1993) useful seven-stage model for changing science identifies a pool of scientists, a curriculum, the curriculum's theoretical underpinnings, and pedagogical techniques as four factors present at each stage of change. Stage one consists of a community of scientists who are White middle- to upper-class men from relatively homogeneous backgrounds. Stages two through five are characterized by "more women entering science." At stage six, "more people of color and individuals of different classes, ethnicities, and sexual orientations, as well as more women become scientists" (Rosser 1993:73). From this statement, one must assume that White women constitute the "women entering science," paving the way for everyone else. Rosser's assumptions of parallelism preclude an analysis that sees women as already including the differences she adds in later in her model. Examining Western science's relationship to gender and race as intersectional constructs alters this type of thinking.

In preparing this chapter, I revisited selected "classic" works in the feminist analyses of science (see, e.g., Harding and Hintikka 1983; Harding 1986; Keller 1985) in order to establish a baseline for examining the degree to which intersectional analyses are currently affecting this field. Because my own work is in the sociology of knowledge, I was interested in science as a particular type of knowledge and in feminist analyses of scientific discourse as a critique of accepted views of science as objective and universalistic. Given the range of edited volumes, journal articles, and book-length monographs published in this area, as well as a growing research community dedicated to feminist analyses of science, I decided to focus my investigation on three important anthologies published in 1996: *The Equity Equation: Fostering the Advancement of Women in the Sciences, Mathematics, and Engineering* (Davis et al. 1996), *Feminism and Science* (Keller and Longino 1996a), and *Gender and Scientific Authority* (Laslett et al. 1996). These anthologies contain some of the most significant work available in feminist analyses of science and provide a minimap of some key questions and concerns in this area of inquiry.

Two things stood out for me in all three volumes. First, none of the three anthologies takes Fausto-Sterling's (1992a) advice that the intersections of scientific knowledge with scientific practice merit a major focus of investigation. Instead, each specializes in one area or the other. For example, the ten chapters in *The Equity Equation* make little mention of scientific knowledge—their concern lies in addressing the barriers that women confront in the life, physical, behavioral, and social sciences, whether as practicing professionals or as students. In contrast, both *Feminism and Science* and *Gender and Scientific Authority* take up questions of scientific knowledge, but examine scientific practices only through historical analysis. Despite Harding's (1993a) suggestion that science studies need a critical component similar to the relationship of literary criticism to novels, poetry, and traditional forms of literature, or cultural studies to film, media, and other productions of popular culture, analyses that examine scientific knowledge in relation to contemporary scientific practices remain rare.

The emphasis on either scientific practice or scientific knowledge reflects a comparable problem within Western feminist analyses overall, namely, the investigation of *either* questions of theory (knowledge) *or* activism (power). Given the richness of work following the discovery, in the United States, of French theorist Foucault's (1979) analyses of knowledge *and* power, this trend seems especially ironic.[3] Discounting the linkages between knowledge and power encourages the reintroduction of the kinds of hierarchies that feminist analyses have repeatedly questioned, in this case, valuing the scholarship of those doing "philosophy of science" or "theory" over that of those doing the "applied" or "activist" work of increasing the numbers of women in scientific professions. More important, when some feminists focus on increasing the numbers of women in science while others examine scientific discourse, texts, and ideas, questions of how praxis and scientific knowledges structure one another are obscured.

The second theme is both an outcome and a cause of the first. Separating questions of scientific knowledge from questions of scientific practice fosters a homogeneous conception of gender. If the absence of women is critical in the production of scientific knowledge, then the absence of racial, ethnic, and social class diversity among women who critique science certainly must have an impact on the knowledge produced. Whether intentional or not, feminist scholarship on scientific knowledge seems wedded to the experiences of White, Western, and economically privileged women. If the experiences of a relatively narrow group of women become normative for gender theory, then critiques of science are also compromised.

Of the three anthologies, *The Equity Equation* seems most sensitive to questions of diversity among women and how such diversity might intersect with comparably complex theories of gender. For example, examining women's progress in the sciences from the perspective of diversity, Chu Clewell and Ginorio (1996) searched for work on women in science attentive to issues of race, class, sexuality, and disability. To their chagrin, they found little. Referring to the extensive bibliography accompanying their article, they note, "had we cited only studies that address any two issues together (for example, ethnicity and gender or disability and gender) we would have had a very short list" (p. 164).

The lack of attention to diversity in the literature on women's participation in science is mirrored by an accompanying lack of attention to issues of diversity in theoretical work on science. As evidenced in their comprehensive introduction, the editors of *Gender and Scientific Authority* recognize the complexity of concepts of gender. Accepted feminist views on gender generally cluster around varying positions concerning the degree to which sex and/or gender are socially constructed. In contrast to traditional science, which assumes a biological base, some feminists see gender as a social construct. This perspective assumes either that there are two fairly similar sexes distorted by social practices into two genders with purposefully different characteristics or that two sexes exist whose essential differences are rendered unequal by social practices. Another perspective claims that *both* sex and gender are socially constructed. In this view, bodies differ in many ways physiologically, but it is social practices that transform them to fit into the salient categories of a society, the most pervasive of which are "female" and "male" and "women" and "men" (Lorber 1993). Social constructionist gender theory has paid much less attention to how bodies are transformed into racial, ethnic, and other categories. In the

United States, for example, women's bodies are socially shaped as age-specific, as of particular race or ethnic origin, as expressing a specific sexuality, as able-bodied or disabled, as fertile or infertile. Those who have power (which means those who produce knowledge) determine which categories are deemed normal and which are deviant. Analyses that confine themselves to global gender categories are a vast improvement over the presentation of scientific knowledge as ungendered, but work that does not take into consideration the diversity among women and men is limited.

In sum, the question of diversity in science must apply not only to scientists and their categories of knowledge, but also to critics of science. For instance, Fox Keller and Longino (1996b) note that all of the contributors to *Feminism and Science* are White and Western. They then express the wish that "the construction of a multinational and multicultural feminist academic community will, we hope, soon encompass science studies as well, bring new questions, new perspectives, new transformations to this provocative and challenging subject" (p. 13). Despite their wish for a more inclusive feminist scientific community, these authors situate social change *outside* of science. They look to an activist feminist community of nonscientists to work on bringing more African American, working-class, and other historically excluded women into science. The task of critiquing scientific knowledge becomes the province of those already *inside* science. The absence from feminist critiques of science of those who might raise different questions about science, including questions concerning the emphases in feminist critiques of science, limits the critique itself.

Because feminist analyses of science routinely overlook how science is central to manufacturing not just gender, but race and other systems of domination, they typically miss opportunities to develop more complex understandings of science as knowledge and practice. Consider, for example, sociologist Essed's (1991) study of forms of everyday racism that Black women professionals encounter in racially desegregated settings. Essed's work points to the connections between scientific and racist thinking, and does so by examining the experiences of women typically excluded from science and from feminist critiques of science. Essed found that Black women became reduced to their perceived "essence" for purposes of manipulation, discrimination, and exclusion. Scientific methodologies grounded in reducing complex phenomena to units that can be statistically manipulated participate in a similar logic. Thus, Essed's lengthy treatment of the logic and practices of everyday racism bears a remarkable resemblance to scientific norms valued within positivist epistemologies and methodologies and the scientific practices they support. Both processes—the treatment of actual Black women in physical space and the manipulation of scientific material in symbolic space—rely on similar cognitive frameworks.

Gendered Epistemologies and Methodologies

Situating feminist critiques of scientific epistemologies and methodologies within complexities of gender and race potentially generates new avenues of investigation. Consider, for example, how scientific and theoretical commitment to abstraction changes if gender is conceptualized as a more complex category of analysis. As Bannerji (1995) notes, "An abstraction is created when the different social moments which constitute the 'concrete' being of any social organization and existence are pulled apart, and each part assumed to have a substantive, self-regulating structure. This becomes apparent when we see gender, race and class each considered as a separate issue—as ground for separate oppressions" (p. 49). Western science analyzes social phenomena by violating the concrete—"pulling apart" the concrete and assigning essential qualities to each part.

Understanding African American women's experiences in the context of a eugenicist discourse illustrates the limitations of abstractions and shows the potential contributions of an intersectional analysis. At minimum, gender and race are both necessary for understanding the meaning of eugenics for African American women. As Davis (1981) noted some time ago, the discourse on eugenics remains vitally important to African American women. Unlike contemporary dialogues that obscure women's participation in maintaining and/or challenging racial hierarchies, the eugenics movements of the early twentieth century were quite outspoken in linking gender, race, and women's biology to proposed social policies. Common to eugenics movements throughout the world was the view that *biology* is central to solving *social* problems. Societies that embraced eugenic philosophies typically transformed social issues such as crime and poverty into medical or biological issues. Eugenic approaches thus combined a "philosophy of biological determinism with a belief that science might provide a technical fix for social problems" (Proctor 1988:286).

Despite wishful thinking that eugenicist thinking has waned, its sedimented meanings persist (Duster 1990). In a provocative essay titled "Out of Eugenics: The Historical Politics of the Human Genome," Kevles (1992) traces the history of contemporary genetics scholarship from its origins in nineteenth-century eugenicist thinking and contextualizes the contemporary Human Genome Project in this history. Fausto-Sterling (1992a) also argues that these links between eugenics and the Human Genome Project constitute an important site of convergence for feminism and science. Thus, the discourse of eugenics in the United States represents a historically specific, concrete social location where race, gender, social class, and nation mutually construct one another.

The logic of eugenics represents a point of convergence within intersecting hierarchies of gender and race. The eugenics discourse demonstrates how race and gender intersect in shaping social practices as well as how they cognitively intersect. Gender and race apparently share a common epistemological foundation that relies on constructions of a "mythical norm" and "othering" associated with dichotomous thinking (Lorde 1984). Within a dichotomous logic, social and natural phenomena are classified and compartmentalized into oppositional categories—White/Black, smart/dumb, rich/poor, man/woman, rational/emotional, healthy/sick, virgins/whores, real men/faggots, real women/dykes, saved/sinner, master/slave, heterosexual/homosexual, adult/child, and science/nonscience. The normal/deviant construct overlays this entire enterprise. Moreover, these oppositional categories intersect so that the qualities on the favorable side of these dichotomies coalesce to form the "normal." "Real" men, for example, are constructed as White, smart, rich, rational, masters, and potential scientists. In contrast, those groups deemed farthest away from the norm—that is, those that purportedly possess a higher incidence of negatives— become derogated. Representations of and practices targeted toward African American women, African American men, White women, and other groups depend on varying patterns of convergence of dichotomies. Particular constellations of qualities represent the "essences" peculiar to these groups, distinguishing them from elite White men as the essentially normal and normative group. These dichotomies are not just horizontal differences of complementarity—they reflect hierarchical differences that elevate the normal over the deviant. Normality and deviance require one another to be comprehensible, yet, because they are defined in opposition to one another, and as essential categories, reconciliation or compromise is not possible. Normality and deviance remain dichotomous and hierarchical.

This same dichotomous thinking that shapes race and gender also seems essential to Western science (Harding 1986). This quest to measure, classify, and understand normality and deviance through attention to differences of all sorts has long constituted a linchpin of science as practiced in the United States and European colonial powers. Moreover, within this common logic that houses science, gender, and race, understandings of gender will be comparably fragmented. This fragmentation results from the placement of women in historically constructed, socially defined niches that will limit what they see, hear, and experience. Any group that aims to generalize from its own location, including feminist theorists of science, will express only a partial perspective (Haraway 1988). Ironically, although feminist critics take on questions of objectivity, rationality, and abstraction expressed by male colleagues, they duplicate these same failings when it comes to their own work. By emphasizing the dichotomy of greatest concern—in this case, male/female—feminists inadvertently forward a critique of science that ignores the connectedness of other dichotomies. Expanding the circle of feminists engaged in critique would not extract feminist critiques of science from the limits of Western dichotomous thinking. However, it would mean that a greater array of issues would emerge.

Feminist critiques of science show how science is gendered. However, science is not only gendered—it remains profoundly raced (Tucker 1994).[4] Gender analyses that rely too heavily upon the experiences of middle-class White women in the West inadvertently replicate structures of racial privilege while claiming to dismantle gender privilege. African American women's difficulties in entering scientific professions signal much more than gender discrimination. Rather, African American women serve as a dual reminder of long-standing exclusionary practices in Western science grounded in *both* gender *and* race.

Yet, although African American women are certainly harmed by being excluded from science, much more is at stake here. Given Western science's fascination with quantitative methodology, empiricism, and rationality as superior ways of understanding the world, African American women scientists encounter a difficult intellectual space. By their physical presence, Black women transgress and change the very boundaries of what constitutes the discipline. Their presence creates issues where absence has long been the norm. Moreover, African American women's entrance into scientific professions also has an important symbolic impact. The often heated debates about quantitative versus qualitative methodology (see, e.g., Sprague and Zimmerman 1989;

Jayaratne and Stewart 1991) tap much deeper issues of what science should be. The quantitative, abstract, objective, physical, or "hard" sciences—the male, the White, the Subject, the Universal—define themselves in opposition to the qualitative, contextualized, interpretive, natural, social, or "soft" sciences—the female, the Black, the Other, the Different. Paralleling this cognitive structure is a bureaucratic structure that has long made similar assessments of the membership of the profession. Thus, this perspective long equated the *absence* of Black women in science with scientific excellence.

Black women's absence becomes configured as absence of difference (embodied in both Blacks and women and thus accentuated in Black women) and the absence of what that difference represents—that is, feminine, soft, nonrigorous, qualitative. Within this logic, the presence of Black women as scientific practitioners and as subjects of study commensurate with White men may signal to White men and White women the seeming deterioration of scientific professions. Increased attention to quantitative rigor allegedly addresses both of these concerns by reinstituting a cognitive structure that aligns itself symbolically with Whiteness, maleness, and elitism, while simultaneously reproducing in the real world an accompanying hierarchy of social relations within scientific disciplines. Thus, what appear to be merely methodological questions may mask deep-seated questions of the contested terrain of science and its position in intersecting race and gender hierarchies. Feminist analyses of science that confine themselves to gender only, at best, simply miss this complexity; at worst, they participate in reconfiguring long-standing racial hierarchies associated with Western science.

Science and Modernity

Refocusing attention to intersections of gender and race challenges the dichotomous thinking that juxtaposes modernity to postmodernity as well as analyses of the significance of science in this enterprise.[5] Scientific knowledge constitutes the signature discourse of modernity, one founded on a rational, empiricist, objective, and seemingly enlightened approach to social phenomena. It also underpins bureaucratic organizations, where merit is supposed to be determined through the use of objective, fair standards. Scientific discourse claims to allow fair hierarchies to emerge, protecting society against the injustice of favoring special interests or particular groups of people. Within dominant scholarship, modernity is a "condition in which society must legitimate itself by its own self-generated principles, without appeal to external verities, deities, authorities, or traditions" (McGowan 1991:3). Within this logic, science becomes a tool for discovering general principles of society that transcend prejudices, superstition, and what are seen as limiting human concerns. By revealing truths about human nature, society, and history, science potentially advances social progress by abolishing long-standing prejudices and ignorance (Seidman and Wagner 1992). As Rabinow and Sullivan (1987) suggest, "The dream of modern Western man to be freed from his passions, his unconscious, his history and his traditions through the liberating use of reason has been the deepest theme of contemporary social-scientific thought" (p. 2). From the perspective of early modernist thinkers, this twofold project was an improvement over the passionate, historically grounded, and superstitious world that preceded the so-called Enlightenment.

Feminist analyses have shown how this construction of modernity was inherently gendered. They note that women were associated with the premodern—the passionate, the concrete, the embodied presence, the experiential, intuitive knowledge. In this sense, science as a modern enterprise and scientific knowledge as modern knowledge required that an emotional, female Other be banished from knowledge construction in order to foreground the centrality of practicing scientists who were rational men. Scientific knowledge was constructed in opposition to women's intuitive, irrational knowledge. Feminists also show that belief in objective science manufactures consent for the continuation of gender subordination under conditions of modernity. Scientific knowledge is commonly portrayed as inherently oppositional to knowledges that preceded it, a conceptualization that feminist historical studies of science and medicine have challenged.

Introducing race problematizes Western definitions of "modernity," the participation of scientific knowledge in the construction of modernity, and, by implication, postmodernity. Recontextualizing modernity and Western science in political and economic contexts of domination, conquest, and oppression permits alternative interpretations to emerge. The gender-only feminist critiques of science may be less oppositional than meets the eye. For people of color, Western perspectives on modernity have long been problematic (Gilroy 1993). Discussions of modernity that assess it only within its own assumptions, that contrast it with what came before in Europe, or that discuss its gendered formations in isolation from other social contexts fail to see the interconnections that concepts of modernity have with people not typically thought of as "modern" (see, e.g., McClintock 1995; Young 1995). Modernity lacks meaning without a corresponding "primitive." "Modern" societies viewed themselves as different from more "primitive" societies rooted in superstition and religious tradition by defining their own characteristic form of social organization and social values as rational and therefore "scientific." Western perspectives routinely assume that modernity as reflected in science is the highest form of civilization. Modernity cannot be assessed exclusively through a gender lens focused on women within European nation-states, nor solely in relation to the so-called Dark Ages of Europe.

Alternative analyses of modernity and Western science stress their links to European expansion into and subsequent colonization of Africa, Asia, and North and South America (Gilroy 1993; Said 1993; McClintock 1995). *Modernity* as a term promulgated in Western arguments signals development and progress, the move from the so-called Dark Ages of medieval Europe into the so-called Enlightenment of modernity. This transition was thought to represent progress and freedom from backwardness, superstition, primitiveness, underdevelopment, and witchcraft. This version of the history and meaning of modernity fits a male-controlled, Western interpretation of the introduction of industrial capitalism on a global scale, as well as political arrangements such as slavery in the United States, the Caribbean, and Brazil; genocide against Native peoples in North and South America; the colonization of Africa and parts of Asia; and the introduction of imperial relations across the globe.

Such constructions of modernity rely not just upon notions of gender applied to European and American White women within national boundaries; they also require a cognitive structure of racial reasoning that seems remarkably similar to scientific reasoning (see Goldberg 1993). The first premise lies in constructing people of color as culturally backward, immature, or "primitive" in relation to putatively developed, adult, "modern" White American and European men and women. Seen as childlike, people of color and their premodern cultures are constructed as essentially intuitive, spontaneous, and irrational. The next step is to claim that people of color need guidance of some sort in order to handle modernity, the cultural equivalent of adulthood. However, perceived variations among "primitive" peoples meant that docile and "noble" groups might benefit from benevolent guidance, whereas others who were "naturally" sexually volatile and violent required strict control. A final feature of this logic argues that Whites are destined and obliged to control and dominate "primitive" peoples and their territories (Torgovnick 1990).

Combining feminist and antiracist analyses of science and modernity suggests that science defined itself not solely in opposition to unraced women, or to ungendered Africans, but to groups that seemingly were raced and gendered (Stepan 1990). Thus, notions of science, race, gender, and modernity are integrally linked. The terms *modernity* and, by association, *science* become suspect in such a recontextualization, as does the uncritical valorizing use of terms such as *postmodernity* and *feminist science*. Investigation of the connections between scientific knowledge and intersecting systems of power or hierarchical power relations would be strengthened by feminist analyses that, at minimum, consider gender as operating in tandem with race. Rather than viewing modernity as a passive backdrop for the development of the natural, physical, behavioral, and social sciences, scientific professions helped manufacture and legitimate notions of modernity through a racialized and gendered production of scientific knowledge. These cognitive structures of scientific discourse in turn remain central in shaping public policy directed against people of color and women that has occurred in conjunction with capitalist development in the past and in the present.

Both gender and race remain ignored within analyses of how important scientific knowledge has been in shaping modernity. Moreover, this neglect obscures how science hegemonically shapes contemporary power relations. The enchantment with postmodernist contributions to knowledge, particularly its increasing emphasis on discourse analysis and the constructed nature of things, without sufficiently interrogating why these options emerge now, obscures the power of science to co-opt and incorporate even the most sincere critiques. Mainstream science operates as such a powerful discourse and set of social practices that, to many, it appears to be invincible. Rather than admitting this fact, theories that reject science altogether can claim an oppositional identity for themselves while actually presenting an ineffective challenge to science itself. Such decontextualized, social constructionist arguments may be especially attractive within the field of feminist analyses of gender and science at this historical moment, because they minimize the persistence of power relations in shaping their own critical knowledge (Collins 1997b).

Simple attention to patterns of exclusion leads directly to the much larger question of the participation of scientific professions and scientific knowledge in manufacturing structures of power. Even though it is often confined to analyzing gender, some feminist scholarship has investigated scientific culpability in reproducing and/or challenging women's oppression. Within this tradition, science as practiced in the United States and in former colonial powers such as Great Britain can be best understood as the theoretical orientation of White men actively engaged in conquering not only the world of the mind, but the actual physical world. This framework consists of "a way of looking at the world characteristic of the dominant white, male, Eurocentric ruling class, a way of dividing up the world that puts an omnipotent subject at the center and constructs marginal Others as sets of negative qualities" (Hartsock 1990:161), or in the words of Smith (1990), a sociologist, "conceptual imperialism." In other words, the locations of scientific disciplines within hierarchical power relations shape scientific knowledge, and this knowledge in turn legitimates the power relations. As Smith describes these relations of ruling: "To begin with the theoretical formulations of the discipline and to construe the actualities of people's activities as expressions of the already given is to generate ideology, not knowledge" (p. 48).

Feminists working in applied areas of medicine and nursing may be more cognizant of the connections of knowledge and structures of power than are those in more theoretical areas. Those feminist scientists who are fortunate enough to see the connections between women's lives as they are situated in hierarchical power relations may be better able to resist the tendency to universalize "women" as raceless, classless, albeit gendered human beings. It is no accident that some of the best work that synthesizes social structural analysis with discourse analysis and that remains focused on issues of intersections of gender and race is done by scientists who refuse to relinquish questions of how their science affects social practices. The work of biologist Fausto-Sterling, who teaches in a medical school, remains exemplary in this regard. Her essay, "Gender, Race and Nation: The Comparative Anatomy of 'Hottentot' Women in Europe, 1815-1817" (1995), illustrates the strengths of work that synthesizes intersections of knowledge and power with those of gender and race. In contrast to other uses of the text and graphics about this much-written-about African woman, Fausto-Sterling chooses to use the "Hottentot Venus" as a lens for examining early science and its implications in structures of race, gender, class, and nation.

African American Women, Intersectionality, and
New Directions for Feminist Critiques of Science

In my own work, I use African American women's experiences as objects and agents of knowledge to rethink a variety of topics. In the case of scientific knowledge, I emphasize African American women's experiences, not because they are more important or "privileged," but to invoke one particular social history as a way of interrogating patterns in feminist discourse. Thinking through the question of gender and scientific knowledge, not from the seemingly objective "view from above" or the postmodern "view from nowhere," but from a particular "view from here"—that is, centered in Black women's particular concerns—represents an epistemological and political choice that reflects my views concerning the current state of scholarship on gender and scientific knowledge.[6]

Although all women are affected by scientific discourses on gender that frame core constructs, interpretive paradigms, and epistemologies of scientific knowledge in Western science, African American women occupy a specific social location. Assumptions about Black women's presumed sexual promiscuity, lower morals, inferior intelligence, and heightened fertility have long permeated research in a variety of scientific disciplines. Whether given researchers set out to prove, disprove, or ignore these assumptions, they operate as received wisdom that must be addressed. During the period when biology, sociology, anthropology, chemistry, and other scientific disciplines were being formed, Black women were denied positions as scientists. This treatment of African American women as objects rather than creators of scientific knowledge occurred during an important period for Western science characterized by the emergence of scientific authority in explaining social realities (Ross 1991). Ironically, the continued treatment of African American women as invisible within feminist analyses, as well as silences concerning the exclusion of African American women from science as a profession, replicates earlier patterns of mainstream science. African American women's experiences with exclusion were far from unique. Rather, they offer a vantage point for viewing the more general process; many groups were excluded from what counted as scientific knowledge. However, I use African American women's experiences neither to illustrate a more general principle applicable to all women nor to stand as proxy for the experiences of other groups of women—that is, as emblematic of women of color or the "subaltern." Rather, I examine African American women from one specific, historical social location that can be used to stimulate dialogues among groups that have engaged in comparable analyses of the embeddedness of their own knowledge and experience (Collins 1998).

As the preceding discussions of scientific methodology and science and modernity illustrate, an intersectional approach might address some of the limitations of exclusively gendered analyses of science. Working from a situated standpoint as I do in this essay may also shed light on the process of intersectionality itself. One approach to developing intersectional analyses consists of selecting a specific social location, social practice, group history, or topic, and subjecting it to an intersectional analysis. This approach means choosing a concrete topic that is already the subject of investigation and trying to find the combined effects of race, class, gender, sexuality, and nation, where before only one or two interpretive categories were used. This process of stressing the particular as a site of intersectionality—in this case, the concreteness of African American women's experiences and, for example, the eugenics discourse—reverses the process of abstraction so central to Western science. An intersectional approach *grounded* in the particular starts with specific locations as points of origin, and aims to build abstractions not by pulling apart various pieces of social reality, but by investigating connections among what are deemed separate dimensions. From this perspective, one would not just add race to feminist analyses of science. Rather, as was the case with the discourse of eugenics, one must assume that gender and race mutually construct both one another and scientific knowledge. This approach views concrete histories of natural, physical, behavioral, and social sciences as specific locations where intersectionality operates.

Working with the assumptions of intersectionality can foster a rethinking of the relationship between conceptions of gender in Western science and the hierarchical power relations grounded in intersections of race, gender, social class, age, and nationality. In contrast to views of science that see both its practice and discourse as divorced from history and power relations, such analysis explores science's long-standing contested social location within such power relations. Neither modernity nor its characteristic scientific discourses were uniformly neutral, value-free, controlling, or emancipatory. Instead, science developed within, helped construct, and also resisted the power relations of capitalism, nationalism, colonialism, and imperialism. Scientific disciplines played a central part in constructing gender- and race-specific under-standings of modernity. Modernity was not a passive backdrop for the development of Western science. Scientific discourses helped manufacture and legitimate notions of modernity through dichotomous ideas about the primitive, which were associated with race, and women's biology and psychology, associated with gender. These cognitive structures of scientific discourse in turn shaped public policy directed against people of color, who were thought to have only race, and against women, who were defined only by gender.

Science was central in manufacturing consent for and in challenging the social policies associated with colonialism, imperialism, slavery, and other social hierarchies. Does Western science continue in this role? Do feminist critiques and constructions of gender and scientific knowledge similarly replicate and challenge extant hierarchical power relations? With its commitment to objectivity, rationality, and the search for reliable truths that transcend belief, opinion, or "stories," scientific knowledge continues to offer a powerful weapon for confronting bureaucratic structures of domination. Science speaks the language of power because it *is* the language of power. However, science is about much more than language or discourse. Given its significance in Western thought, scientific knowledge and the practices it constructs and defends are intersecting dimensions of the struggle to shape reality. Whether feminist analyses of science maintain this struggle remains to be seen.

Notes

1. This notion of intersectionality is closely aligned with developments in Black women's studies. The scholarship and activism of Black women in the United States provides a useful direction in addressing these questions. In the early 1980s, several African American women scholar-activists called for a new approach to analyzing Black women's experiences. Claiming that African American women's experiences were shaped not just by race, but by gender, social class, and sexuality, works such as *Women, Race, and Class* by Davis (1981), "A Black Feminist Statement" drafted by the Combahee River Collective (1982), and Lorde's (1984) classic volume *Sister Outsider* stand as groundbreaking works that explored interconnections among systems of oppression. Subsequent work aimed to name this interconnected relationship with terms such as "matrix of domination" (Collins 1990), and "intersectionality" (Crenshaw

1991) and were increasingly applied to the connections among systems of oppression.

2. Sexuality was one of the emphases in early work by African American women. Black lesbians were at the forefront of raising the issue of intersectionality. However, homophobia in African American communities, as evidenced by the reactions to the works of early modern Black feminists such as Alice Walker, Ntozake Shange, and Michele Wallace, effectively muted an intersectional analysis that emphasized race, social class, gender, and sexuality. The absence of a developed tradition of queer theory in the academy also worked against more comprehensive intersectional analyses. For early intersectional analyses that included sexuality, see the essays in Smith's (1983) edited volume *Home Girls: A Black Feminist Anthology.*

3. This trend may result, in part, from a particular reading of Foucault. Foucault's (1979) text *Discipline and Punish* is a historical study of how the organization of prisons generated new ways of organizing knowledge, referred to by Foucault as "disciplinary knowledge." Because his analysis of the links between disciplinary knowledge and prison structures includes examination of actual historical cases, Foucault's leadership in analyzing the links between knowledge and institutional power is especially useful. However, subsequent uses of Foucault's ideas that decontextualize this historical narrative with the intent of summarizing the essential elements of Foucault's analysis of knowledge-power relationships may erase the most important contributions of his theory. Hartsock's (1990) critique of Foucault's analysis of power takes issue with the use of ideas attributed to Foucault.

4. I can only speculate about why the absence has been minimized in feminist analyses of scientific practice and knowledge. Possibly the question of diversity among women as participants in science is perceived as merely a technical question far removed from analysis of scientific knowledge. In the current backlash against theories that link knowledge to group standpoints, presuppositions that diversity of scientific membership may produce diverse scientific knowledges might appear to open a Pandora's box. The growing political clout of postmodernism within the academy and the increasing disenchantment of progressive intellectuals with prior forms of political activity may also be contributing factors (Collins 1997a, 1997b).

5. Chow (1993) distinguishes between modernism as the sum total of artistic innovations from Europe and North America and modernity as a force of cultural expansionism whose foundations are not only emancipatory but also Eurocentric and patriarchal. For a related discussion of the centrality of Blackness to definitions of modernity, see Gilroy (1993).

6. Despite the increasing reluctance of feminists to ground analyses of knowledge in actual social conditions, I remain convinced that, for African American women and others in similar social locations, ignoring social conditions of race and gender is not simply politically naive but foolish. The recent flurry of attention within feminist scholarship to the supposed limits of standpoint epistemology, a "view from here" approach, illustrates this tendency. In my article for a symposium in *Signs* devoted to standpoint theory, I explore how an increasing willingness to recast standpoint theory solely as a theory of truth erases questions of power (Collins 1997a). I develop these ideas more fully in *Fighting Words* (1998).

References

Anthias, Floya and Nira Yuval-Davis. 1992. *Racialized Boundaries: Race, Nation, Gender, Colour and Class in Anti-Racist Struggle.* New York: Routledge.

Bannerji, Himani. 1995. *Thinking Through: Essays on Feminism, Marxism, and Anti-Racism.* Toronto: Women's Press.

Bridenthal, Renate, Atina Grossmann, and Marion Kaplan, eds. 1984. *When Biology Became Destiny: Women in Weimar and Nazi Germany.* New York: Monthly Review Press.

Chow, Rey. 1993. *Writing Diaspora: Tactics of Intervention in Contemporary Cultural Studies.* Bloomington: Indiana University Press.

Clewell, Beatriz Chu and Angela B. Ginorio. 1996. "Examining Women's Progress in the Sciences from the Perspective of Diversity." Pp. 163-231 in *The Equity Equation: Fostering the Advancement of Women in the Sciences, Mathematics, and Engineering,* edited by Cinda-Sue Davis, Angela B. Ginorio, Carol S. Hollenshead, Barbara B. Lazarus, Paula Rayman, and Associates. San Francisco: Jossey-Bass.

Collins, Patricia Hill. 1990. *Black Feminist Thought: Knowledge, Consciousness, and the Politics of Empowerment.* New York: Routledge, Chapman & Hall.

————.1997a. "Comment on Hekman's 'Truth and Method: Feminist Standpoint Theory Revisited': Where's the Power?" *Signs* 22:375-81.

————.1997b. "How Much Difference Is Too Much? Black Feminist Thought and the Politics of Postmodern Social Theory." *Current Perspectives in Social Theory* 17:3-37.

————. 1998. *Fighting Words: Black Women and the Search for Justice.* Minneapolis: University of Minnesota Press.

Combahee River Collective. 1982. "A Black Feminist Statement." Pp. 13-22 in *All the Women Are White, All the Blacks Are Men, but Some of Us Are Brave:*

Black Women's Studies, edited by Gloria T. Hull, Patricia Bell Scott, and Barbara Smith. Old Westbury, NY: Feminist Press.

Crenshaw, Kimberle Williams. 1991. "Mapping the Margins: Intersectionality, Identity Politics, and Violence against Women of Color." *Stanford Law Review* 43:1241-99.

Davis, Angela Y. 1981. *Women, Race, and Class.* New York: Random House.

Davis, Cinda-Sue, Angela B. Ginorio, Carol S. Hollenshead, Barbara B. Lazarus, Paula Rayman, and Associates, eds. 1996. *The Equity Equation: Fostering the Advancement of Women in the Sciences, Mathematics, and Engineering.* San Francisco: Jossey-Bass.

Duster, Troy. 1990. *Backdoor to Eugenics.* New York: Routledge.

Essed, Philomena. 1991. *Understanding Everyday Racism: An Interdisciplinary Theory.* Newbury Park, CA: Sage.

Fausto-Sterling, Anne. 1992a. "Building Two-Way Streets: The Case of Feminism and Science." *NWSA Journal* 4:336-49.

———. 1992b. *Myths of Gender: Biological Theories about Women and Men.* 2d ed. New York: Basic Books.

———. 1995. "Gender, Race and Nation: The Comparative Anatomy of 'Hottentot' Women in Europe, 1815-1817." Pp. 19-48 in *Deviant Bodies: Critical Perspectives on Difference in Science and Popular Culture,* edited by Jennifer Terry and Jacqueline Urla. Bloomington: Indiana University Press.

Foucault, Michel. 1979. *Discipline and Punish: The Birth of the Prison.* New York: Schocken.

Gilroy, Paul. 1993. *The Black Atlantic: Modernity and Double Consciousness.* Cambridge, MA: Harvard University Press.

Goldberg, David Theo. 1993. *Racist Culture: Philosophy and the Politics of Meaning.* Cambridge, MA: Basil Blackwell.

Haraway, Donna J. 1988. "Situated Knowledges: The Science Question in Feminism and the Privilege of Partial Perspective." *Feminist Studies* 14:575-99.

———. 1989. *Primate Visions: Gender, Race, and Nature in the World of Modern Science.* New York: Routledge.

Harding, Sandra. 1986. *The Science Question in Feminism.* Ithaca, NY: Cornell University Press.

———. 1987. "Introduction: Is There a Feminist Method?" Pp. 1-14 in *Feminism and Methodology,* edited by Sandra Harding. Bloomington: Indiana University Press.

———. 1991. *Whose Science? Whose Knowledge? Thinking from Women's Lives.* Ithaca, NY: Cornell University Press.

———. 1993a. "Forum: Feminism and Science." *NWSA Journal* 5:49-55.

————. 1993b. *The "Racial" Economy of Science.* Bloomington: Indiana University Press.

Harding, Sandra and Merrill B. Hintikka, eds. 1983. *Discovering Reality: Feminist Perspectives on Epistemology, Metaphysics, Methodology and Philosophy of Science.* Dordrecht, Netherlands: Reidel.

Hartsock, Nancy. 1990. "Foucault on Power: A Theory for Women?" Pp. 157-75 in *Feminism/Postmodernism,* edited by Linda J. Nicholson. New York: Routledge.

Jayaratne, Toby Epstein and Abigail J. Stewart. 1991. "Quantitative and Qualitative Methods in the Social Sciences: Current Feminist Issues and Practical Strategies." Pp. 85-106 in *Beyond Methodology: Feminist Scholarship as Lived Research,* edited by Mary Margaret Fonow and Judith A. Cook. Bloomington: Indiana University Press.

Keller, Evelyn Fox. 1985. *Reflections on Gender and Science.* New Haven, CT: Yale University Press.

Keller, Evelyn Fox and Helen E. Longino, eds. 1996a. *Feminism and Science.* New York: Oxford University Press.

————. 1996b. "Introduction." Pp. 1-14 in *Feminism and Science,* edited by Evelyn Fox Keller and Helen E. Longino. New York: Oxford University Press.

Kevles, Daniel J. 1992. "Out of Eugenics: The Historical Politics of the Human Genome." Pp. 3-36 in *The Code of Codes: Scientific and Social Issues in the Human Genome Project,* edited by Daniel Kevles and Leroy Hood. Cambridge, MA: Harvard University Press.

Laslett, Barbara, Sally Gregory Kohlstedt, Helen Longino, and Evelynn Hammonds, eds. 1996. *Gender and Scientific Authority.* Chicago: University of Chicago Press.

Lorber, Judith. 1993. "Believing Is Seeing: Biology as Ideology." *Gender & Society* 7:568-81.

Lorde, Audre. 1984. *Sister Outsider.* Trumansburg, NY: Crossing Press.

McClintock, Anne. 1995. *Imperial Leather: Race, Gender, and Sexuality in the Colonial Contest.* New York: Routledge.

McGowan, John. 1991. *Postmodernism and Its Critics.* Ithaca, NY: Cornell University Press.

Mies, Maria. 1991. "Women's Research or Feminist Research? The Debate Surrounding Feminist Science and Methodology." Pp. 60-84 in *Beyond Methodology: Feminist Scholarship as Lived Research,* edited by Mary Margaret Fonow and Judith A. Cook. Bloomington: Indiana University Press.

Mullings, Leith. 1997. *On Our Own Terms: Race, Class, and Gender in the Lives of African American Women.* New York: Routledge.

Nicholson, Linda J. 1990. "Introduction." In *Feminism/Postmodernism,* edited by Linda J. Nicholson. New York: Routledge.

Parker, Andrew, Mary Russo, Doris Sommer, and Patricia Yaeger, eds. 1992. *Nationalisms and Sexualities*. New York: Routledge.

Proctor, Robert N. 1988. *Racial Hygiene: Medicine under the Nazis*. Cambridge, MA: Harvard University Press.

Rabinow, Paul and William M. Sullivan. 1987. "The Interpretive Turn: A Second Look." Pp. 1-30 in *Interpretive Social Science, A Second Look*, edited by Paul Rabinow and William M. Sullivan. Berkeley: University of California Press.

Reinharz, Shulamit. 1992. *Feminist Methods in Social Research*. New York: Oxford University Press.

Ross, Dorothy. 1991. *The Origins of American Social Science*. New York: Cambridge University Press.

Rosser, Sue. 1993. "Forum: Feminism and Science." *NWSA Journal* 5:65-76.

Said, Edward. 1993. *Culture and Imperialism*. New York: Alfred A. Knopf.

Seidman, Steven and David G. Wagner. 1992. "Introduction." Pp. 1-14 in *Postmodernism and Social Theory*, edited by Steven Seidman and David G. Wagner. Cambridge, MA: Basil Blackwell.

Smith, Barbara. 1983. *Home Girls: A Black Feminist Anthology*. New York: Kitchen Table Press.

Smith, Dorothy E. 1990. *The Conceptual Practices of Power: A Feminist Sociology of Knowledge*. Toronto: University of Toronto Press.

Spelman, Elizabeth V. 1988. *Inessential Woman: Problems of Exclusion in Feminist Thought*. Boston: Beacon.

Sprague, Joey and Mary K. Zimmerman. 1989. "Quality and Quantity: Reconstructing Feminist Methodology." *American Sociologist* 20:71-86

Stepan, Nancy. 1990. "Race and Gender: The Role of Analogy in Science." Pp. 38-57 in *Anatomy of Racism*, edited by David Goldberg. Minneapolis: University of Minnesota Press.

Torgovnick, Marianna. 1990. *Gone Primitive: Savage Intellects, Modern Lives*. Chicago: University of Chicago Press.

Tucker, William H. 1994. *The Science and Politics of Racial Research*. Urbana: University of Illinois Press.

Young, Robert J. C. 1995. *Colonial Desire: Hybridity in Theory, Culture and Race*. New York: Routledge.

CHAPTER 10

Gender and Sexuality
in Organizations

PATRICIA YANCEY MARTIN
DAVID L. COLLINSON

Throughout the twentieth century, theories of organization, management, and industrial relations have taken for granted that men are the
shop-floor workers, trade union members and officials, supervisors,
middle managers, CEOs, and company directors. Even when women
have constituted the majority, gender has been ignored or all workers
have been treated analytically as if they had no gender (see Acker and
Van Houten 1974). Today, many influential theoretical paradigms and
organizational perspectives continue to represent management and
organizations as gender-free (Calas and Smircich 1996). According to
these theories, workers are recruited and hired on the basis of "true"
qualifications, placed in jobs that best fit their skills and knowledge, and
rewarded according to their "objective" performance (Acker 1990).
Gender and sexuality are irrelevant at work, these theories argue, thus
they do not affect organizational structures, cultures, or dynamics.

A feminist critical reading of this literature reveals that such theories
contradict the experiences of many men and, more starkly, most
women. New conceptualizations and analyses bring in more accurate
analyses of real workplaces and workers. They include nondualistic and nonessentialist concepts of gender, and they address power,
make cultural resources and worker identity visible, and consider how

AUTHORS' NOTE: We are grateful to Mary Rogers, Judith Lorber, Myra Marx
Ferree, Nicole Raeburn, and Beth Hess for suggestions that enhanced our
chapter's organization, content, and clarity.

organizational practices construct and maintain gender at work. Intersecting these concerns is the issue of agency, including the ability of individuals and collectivities to resist gender stereotyping and discrimination and to protest sexual harassment.

In this chapter, we focus on recent concerns to show how their use in research and analyses has changed organizational theory. At the end, we suggest some applications of this new thinking. First, we review six themes in earlier research and theory as a foundation for more recent work.

Concepts of Gender in Organization Theory

Previous Work

Sex segregation. Since Moss Kanter's (1977) pathbreaking study *Men and Women of the Corporation*, a great deal of attention has been paid to gender in organizations, and some to sexuality. One group of studies has explored the segregation of men and women in organizations in an attempt to understand its persistence, causes, and effects (Bielby and Baron 1986; Reskin and Roos 1990). These findings indicate that women and men rarely hold the same jobs in the same firm in the same work site. Sex segregation is pervasive horizontally in the types of work people are assigned and vertically in the status and power of the positions they hold (Cockburn 1988). The writers conclude that separating women and men allows employers to pay men more without the awareness of women workers, who might become dissatisfied (Loscocco and Spitze 1991). Cotter et al. (1997) suggest that occupational segregation alone can account for all of the difference at the macro level in women's and men's wages, by depressing women's wages in "men's" occupations and by devaluing "women's" jobs.

Devaluation of women's work. A second group of studies has analyzed the devaluation of women's work as evidenced in the lower earnings of *all* workers who hold "women's jobs" (England 1992; Steinberg 1990). We know that women's jobs (those populated mostly by women or normatively associated with women, e.g., schoolteacher, nurse, librarian, secretary) are devalued compared with men's jobs, but we know less about the dynamics of this result. One limitation of research on devaluation is its occupational focus. Some research has taken an *orga-*

nizational focus, however. For example, Cockburn's (1988) study of 11 organizations in the United Kingdom found that men managers adopted new technologies in ways that preserved men's greater access to the more interesting, mobile, autonomous, and better-paid jobs. Cohn (1985) found that in the nineteenth century, the British postal system began hiring women 80 years before the railway system did. He concludes that women's "cheap" labor appealed to a labor-intensive industry such as the postal service, whereas the capital-intensive railway industry had fewer workers and preserved even clerical jobs for men.

Gender composition. A third group of studies has focused on gender composition in various kinds of work contexts (Bird 1996; Martin and Harkreader 1993). Taking off from Moss Kanter (1977), these studies have examined how the gender composition of jobs, work units, and hierarchies affects relations between women and men and the material and psychological rewards they derive from work. This research has inconsistently supported Moss Kanter's finding that the situation of women improves as their numbers increase. In some instances, the influx of women has created a backlash and a rise in harassment.

Organizational culture as masculine. The "masculine ethic" among managers (Kanter 1977) in large-scale hierarchical organizations is also manifest on the shop floor, where working-class men socially construct gender and sexuality so as to resist management and bond with each other (Collinson 1988; see also Willis 1977). Cockburn's (1983) study of printers shows how the "hot-metal" skills of Linotype compositors have historically been protected as the exclusive province of men by claims that women are physically unable to handle the heavy type. Collinson (1992) shows how male engineering workers constructed a shared sense of masculine identity through discourses that valorized being practical and productive, being family breadwinners, having common sense, and being "able to swear when you like and give and take a joke like a man." New workers were tested to see whether they were "man enough" to take teasing and insults, and those who were able to "give it and take it" were accepted into the masculine subculture, whereas those who "snapped" were excluded. Such processes of collective identification differentiated the working-class men from office workers, supervisors, and managers, thus creating alternative masculinities in the organization (Connell 1995).

Using gender as an organizing principle. Another group of studies has explored how employers use gender to organize work and assign jobs (Leidner 1993). These studies show that perceptions of women's or men's suitedness for particular jobs are socially constructed (Hall 1993b). Elite men are generally shown to preserve the better jobs—those that are higher paying, more mobile, less repetitive, less boring, more secure—for other men who are, except for gender, often different from themselves (Cockburn 1988).

Gender as discourse, practice, and identity in organizations. Some studies have focused on the *practices* of gender and sexuality as something people "do" at work (Barrett 1996; Calvert and Ramsey 1996; Chase 1995; Hall 1993a; Holstein 1987; Lane 1996; Pierce 1995; Ranson and Reeves 1996). For example, some men managers enact authoritarian masculinity by precluding dissent, rejecting dialogue, and preferring coercive power based on dictatorial control and unquestioning obedience (Collinson and Hearn 1994). Such actions produce a brutal, aggressive masculinity for judging themselves and others. Others behave paternalistically, emphasizing the moral superiority of cooperation, the importance of trust in personal relations, and employees' need to invest in work tasks. In practicing entrepreneurial masculinity, some men managers prioritize profits, production, and costs and elevate economic efficiency and control over other criteria.

Women similarly construct femininity in the workplace. Kondo (1990) describes how Japanese women factory workers assert their gendered identities as surrogate mothers to young men workers. Their actions partly challenge male workers' highly masculine celebration of prowess on the job, yet their feminine identity, by drawing on conventional discourses about women, reinforces their own marginality as workers (see also Fletcher 1998).

Current Conceptualizations

Nondualistic and nonessentialist conceptions of gender. Prior conceptions of gender framed women and men as dualistic opposites. In the heyday of this conceptualization, women were equated with and consigned to the "private" sphere of home and family, whereas men were equated with and legitimated in the "public sphere" of paid work (Feldberg and Glenn 1979). Women were framed as weak, delicate, and needing protection; men were framed as strong and hardy protectors of women and children, even though many women were always in the public sphere as shopkeepers, innkeepers, and factory workers, and many men failed to "protect" women and children. The nineteenth-century separate spheres doctrine and cultural stereotypes that framed women as frail and dependent encouraged middle-class professional men, such as those who wrote management and organization theories, to depict bureaucratic organizations as men's domain. Relative to gender, they framed all members as men; relative to sexuality, they framed all members as heterosexuals.

Dualistic and essentialist conceptions assure that stereotyping will occur and that intragroup diversity based on social class, race/ethnicity, and age relative to gender and sexuality will be overlooked (Dunne 1997; Lorber 1994; Rogers forthcoming). Explorations of fluidity, multiplicity, contradictions, and the political aspects of gender and sexuality make visible the agency of organization members.

Power. Classical organization and management theories represent power at work as following the lines of official organizational positions and hierarchies. In this view, differences between women and men reflect *official positions* that have varying amounts of status, resources, and control; men and women are "equals" at work except for positional differences. Two decades of research challenge this claim, showing that men and women have different amounts and types of power due to gender and sexuality distinctions, not only official position. Furthermore, unofficial structures of asymmetrical power associated with gender and sexuality (and race/ethnicity) are overlaid onto official structures of power (Acker 1990; Grauerholz 1989; Rospenda, Richman, and Nawyn 1998; Wharton 1992). Those with official power thus are able to "do gender" and "do sexuality" in the course of "doing organization" without having to acknowledge what they are doing.

Cultural resources and member identity. Formerly, gender was portrayed as a trait of individuals that they enacted in ways consistent with their natural/biological tendencies or "sex role socialization." Rather than an inert legacy of early childhood learning, gender and sexuality are now being studied as *cultural resources* that members of organizations use for varied purposes in diverse and often inconsistent ways (Martin 1997). Members actively assert gender's relevance, for example, when they say women or men are better at certain jobs or use gender distinctions to control children at school—for example, by lining up boys and girls separately or pitting them against each other in contests (Thorne 1993). People in organizations also deny sexuality's relevance even as they work within social relations and structures and engage in practices that are pervasively organized by heterosexuality as well as gender (Dunne 1997; Gutek 1989; Stewart 1997).

In enacting gender, individuals frequently invest in discourses associated with their definitions of self and other. Recent poststructuralist research highlights the importance of identity and subjectivity for understanding the reproduction of gendered power relations in organizations (Kerfoot and Knights 1998). These studies focus on connections between discourse and gender identity and on the complex, ambiguous dynamics of subjectivity. For example, Kondo (1990) argues that gender identity is open, negotiable, shifting, and ambiguous. She views selves not as coherent, seamless, bounded, and whole but as multiple and fluid. Selves are constructed at work in the context of relations that are ambiguous, paradoxical, and characterized by power differences. This approach sees actors as "shot through with contradictions and creative tensions" (p. 224). It also reveals the paradoxical outcomes of ambiguous gender processes and the fragmented, contradictory nature of subjectivity (Henriques et al. 1984), while avoiding the reduction of men and women to passive carriers of early gender socialization.

Social construction and practice. Earlier conceptualizations of gender as made up of individual attributes meant that men and women would "naturally" have different interests and capacities and would therefore "naturally" behave differently at work, as elsewhere. A more current view is that gender is *socially constructed* by organization members *through gendered practices* situated within a specific, local system of gender relations (Acker 1990, 1995; Collinson and Hearn 1994; Roper 1996). Organizations are *sites* where men and women routinely "do masculinities" and "do femininities" (Messerschmidt 1996; Woodward 1996; see also Kerfoot and Knights 1998; Kleinman 1996).

Gender and sexuality are not just imported from the outside world; they shape the development, structure, culture, and dynamics of organizations (Britton 1997). To understand how gender and sexuality are produced, challenged, and transformed in organizations, one must study members' agency as *producers, reproducers, and modifiers* of organizational structure and practice (Burrell 1992; Ranson and Reeves 1996; Williams 1995). Members are not passive objects of organization culture, dynamics, and ideology; rather, they are active agents who construct gender and sexuality in both official and unofficial arenas.

From the points of critique noted above, feminist theories of gender, sexuality, and organizations have emerged.

Feminist Theories Applied to Gender and Organizations

Contending that gendered workplaces presuppose and reflect gender relations in the wider society, Marxist feminists analyze underlying conflicts and contradictions of economic interests in capitalist organizations. Attempts to interrelate patriarchy and capitalism are known as *dual systems theory,* an approach that frames gender dynamics as interwoven in complex ways with other features of organizations and the family, such as hierarchy, managerial control, culture, subordination, and resistance. Dual systems theory emphasizes social structures, however, and neglects the *social practices* that are their medium and outcome. In response to these criticisms, some writers have focused on how job segregation and other gender divisions are reproduced and challenged in ongoing organizational structures, cultures, and practices (Collinson, Knights, and Collinson 1990).

For example, historical research on the early Industrial Revolution shows that capitalists organized the first factories along gender lines (Marglin 1976). Women (and children) were recruited for drudge work under the scrutiny of men owners. Refusing to be "bossed," husbands and fathers shunned factory jobs but "allowed" their wives and daughters to accept them. Capitalists eventually lured husbands and fathers into factories by offering them supervisory jobs, with authority over women (and children). The patriarchal family made it easy for employers to collude with fathers and husbands in relegating women to unsanitary, backbreaking, tedious factory work. Women's lesser power at home, plus their desire to earn money or escape domestic work, explains their willingness to accept such jobs. Thus the societal *gender order* made it possible for early factory owners to exploit women (see also Wolf 1992). Casting gender as unintentionally imported into the factory misrepresents the conditions whereby factories, and other work sites at later dates, were gendered from the outset (Glucksmann 1990).

The founding conditions of organizations persist, so that an organization that begins with women in the lowliest jobs is likely to retain this pattern over time. Also, organizations of similar types imitate one another, in search of legitimacy (DiMaggio and Powell 1983). Early organizations were established along gender lines, with women excluded or assigned to lesser-valued jobs, so gendered workplaces are a legacy of social organization and culture. Almost no work organization situates women and men so as to make gender irrelevant.

Recently, postmodernist and poststructuralist feminist analyses have offered accounts of gendered power relations that focus not only on structure but also on agency, identity, and difference (Ely 1995; Hollway 1996; J. Martin 1990). These studies recognize men's and women's diverse, fragmented, and contradictory lives in and around organizations. Pringle (1988) found, for example, that women secretaries flirted with their men bosses to have fun and gain concessions. They did this knowingly, despite norms that proscribed such behavior. Men secretaries did not enact sexuality in relations with their bosses, but they used their superior gender status to resist their women bosses' power. They were more outspoken and less deferential with women bosses than with men bosses.

Social contexts that sexualize and delegitimate women but valorize and legitimate men for valued positions or opportunities mean that all official positions are "conditioned" by the gender and sexuality of position holders. Pierce's (1995) study of paralegals and litigators supports this conclusion. Men litigators accepted criticism from men paralegals, but not from women paralegals; they became angry with women subordinates who gave them less than complete approval and support. Assertive men litigators were admired by other men, but women who behaved similarly were denigrated. Yet women who displayed normative femininity—for example, compliance and supportiveness—were also discounted by men. Pierce concludes that men reward each other for displaying a range of masculinities, including the most competitive and adversarial kinds, yet they punish women who violate norms of femininity. Men also denigrate women litigators who are "too soft" or cooperative, however. The norms for women paralegals are clear, but women litigators receive contradictory messages from colleagues and the heads of their firms. These results show how gender and sexuality amplify and undercut the impact of "official position" and "objective performance" at work. We need to know more about such dynamics. These efforts should not conflate issues of gender and sexuality with *women*, however, because men are equally implicated in their relations with women and with other men (see Messerschmidt 1996; Ranson and Reeves 1996).

Men in Organizations

Men's power and influence are taken for granted in most organizational research and theory. For the social construction of men and masculinities at work to be visible as a social dynamic, this power and influence must be problematized (Morgan 1992). Paying attention to dominant or *hegemonic* masculinity (Connell 1995) focuses attention on practices that empower men, especially in bureaucratic organizations, such as acting competitive, defensive, and emotionally detached (Collinson and Hearn 1996). Despite these practices, men at work do build alliances with each other around shared interests and values, such as sexist and racist humor, sports, cars, sexual exploits, and alcohol consumption (Collinson and Hearn 1994). Their informal relations often transcend organizational boundaries, extending to professional meetings, work groups, sports activities, and postwork drinks (Morgan 1981). These symbolic and interactional bonds exclude women from informal work-related domains and maintain men's monopoly over organization resources, relations, and activities.

The office is the predominant work site in advanced capitalist economies. Until the late nineteenth century, men dominated office jobs in Britain and the United States as both lower-level clerks and upper-level bosses. With the introduction of typewriters and the standardization of clerical work, women's employment in clerical and secretarial office jobs increased rapidly. Women's clerical work today is undervalued and stereotyped as entailing "homemaker-like" tasks, such as arranging for food at meetings, decorating offices for special occasions, buying gifts, placating the boss, and making coffee. In contrast, men clerical workers and secretaries are often considered administrative assistants with narrowly focused duties.

In other occupations that women enter in substantial numbers, men try to preserve an imagery of "heroic" masculine traits (Dorsey 1994; Collinson et al. 1990; Leidner 1993). Thus salesmen contend they need to "take the knocks" in the aggressive marketplace. They use terms words as "intrepid," "valiant," and "forceful" to characterize their forays into the "dangerous" world of competitors and clients, where they work "against the odds." Formerly male-dominated professions and technical occupations such as physician, computer specialist, lawyer, and academic still revolve around masculinist values and practices and gender divisions that support men's monopoly of the better positions (Lorber 1984; Spencer and Podmore 1987; Witz and Savage 1992).

One way of maintaining men's symbolic monopoly at work is to segregate women and men in the organizational hierarchy. Senior management remains dramatically masculine (Collinson and Hearn 1996). Despite women's inroads into lower management grades, men predominate in senior posts in most industries and countries. Women make up less than 5 percent of senior management in Britain and the United States, and in Australia and many other countries the proportion is closer to 2 percent (Sinclair 1995). Because they are a small minority, women managers often reproduce masculine values and practices (Marshall 1995). They downplay their femaleness, especially with regard to pregnancy and childbirth, and accommodate their personal lives to their work schedules (J. Martin 1990). Yet women's strategies for gaining acceptance are more or less ineffective, because men managers constantly *mobilize masculinity* in work settings (Martin 1996, 1998; see also Sheppard 1989; Scase and Goffee 1989).

Martin (1998) identifies two clusters of masculinity dynamics that men mobilize at work. *Contest masculinities* consist of men's self-promotion, intragroup competition, and expropriation of others' labor and contributions, including women's and some men's. This behavior, reflective of organized sports (competing, winning, being number one, being "on top"), is used by men in bureaucratic hierarchies to stress the value of rising above others in rank and pay. These practices also reflect the values of capitalism that valorize market domination, "rational" choice and action, and aggressive competition (see also Connell 1995, chaps. 7, 9; Messerschmidt 1996).

When men use *in-group affirmative masculinities*, they affirm and support each other as men. Women are excluded because their opinions or behaviors are irrelevant; men seek approval of, or inclusion by, other men. For example, a woman bank vice president who works mostly around men may have to listen to men talk about a football game or golf outing during management meetings because powerful men start such talk or tolerate it in other men. Given her assumption that the men are bonding or enjoying their camaraderie, she sees no reason to join in—yet she is not free to leave the room either.

Women managers who feel isolated, excluded, or continuously tested on masculinist standards such as toughness, political maneuvering, and total commitment often leave the organization to become self-employed (Marshall 1995; McIlwee and Robinson 1992). Women who remain are likely to be in junior managerial positions that are increasingly feminized, downgraded, and deskilled. The most powerful, prestigious, and strategic globalized functions of transnational corporations thus stay in the hands of men (Calas and Smircich 1993; Harding 1996; see also Woodward 1996).

Sexuality in Organizations

Theories about organizations generally assert that sexuality has no legitimate place at work. Yet many people find life partners and partners for other sexual relationships at work. Additionally, sexual attraction, flirtation, manipulation, and coercion are pervasive in organizations (e.g., Hall 1993a) and are not easily legislated out of existence. One sexuality norm in organizations is the requirement for everyone to present him- or herself as heterosexual. Frequently, especially among men, homophobia is used to "keep each other in line" (Reskin and Padavic 1994). If sexuality were irrelevant in organizations, then "out" lesbians and gays would occasion little notice or comment; however, the opposite usually occurs. The identifiable homosexual (or bisexual) faces indignities and discrimination from presumptive heterosexuals (Dunne 1997; Raeburn 1998; Schneider 1993).

At a minimum, men use sexuality to establish a hierarchy that separates them from women and keeps women "in their place" (Pyke 1996). Numerous studies reveal how men at multiple hierarchical levels sexualize women at work (Hearn and Parkin 1987; Collinson and Collinson 1989). Hollway (1984) suggests that men invest in a "male sexual drive discourse" in which they frame men's sexuality as "incontinent," "out of control," and biologically driven. They thereby construct predatory sexual discourses and workplace cultures that derogate and undermine women (Cockburn 1983; Collinson 1992).

The greatest attention to sexuality in workplaces centers on sexual harassment. Since the late 1970s, numerous studies have documented sexual harassment as structural and commonplace rather than individual and rare (Rospenda et al. 1998; Wise and Stanley 1988). Sexual harassment involves violence, power, authority, and economic discrimination (MacKinnon 1979). Women's vulnerability to sexual harassment reflects their segregated, subordinated labor market position (Hadjifotiou 1983), and service sector employment may render them especially vulnerable because of pressures to "please customers" (Folgero and Fjeldstad 1995; Hochschild 1983; Adkins 1995). Walby (1988) views sexual harassment as a patriarchal strategy that men proactively use to keep women "in their place." Men's greater power gives them more *sexual authority* at work and conveys to women the message, "You're only a woman. And at that level you're vulnerable to me and any man" (Cockburn 1991:142). DiTomaso (1989) suggests that some work contexts license men to behave offensively so that their attempts to take sexual advantage become the norm. One respondent told her, "The men are different here than on the street. It's like they have been locked up for years" (p. 80).

Collinson and Collinson's (1996; see also 1992) study of sexual harassment in the British insurance sales industry delineates men's sexuality discourses and practices at work. Men sales agents subjected women colleagues to extensive sexual harassment; in one incident, a man displayed his penis to a woman. The men managers "normalized" other men's offensive practices with statements such as "It's a fact of life" and "It's just a bit of fun." They viewed men's harassment of women as "rites de passage," a gendered test of women's ability to deal with the "pressures" of working in a male-dominated occupation. They agreed that the women were responsible for "handling" sexual harassment and when one failed to "handle it well," they cast her as cause rather than victim of the dynamic.

Generally, men sexually harass women for the benefit of other men or to impress men colleagues (Kimmel 1996). Pinups of nude women and pornographic photos in workplaces signify in-group heterosexuality, conveying messages of exclusion to gay and bisexual men and of objectification to women. Work organizations are thus sites where men proclaim their heterosexuality by using women to establish relations with each other even while they *practice homosociality* by aggressively seeking out and preferring the company of other men (Lipman-Blumen 1976). Raeburn (1998) notes that the signification of heterosexuality at work is so pervasive as to be mandatory—for instance, displaying photographs of a spouse and children, wearing a wedding band, talking about wife, husband, or family-related concerns. These practices convey to gay and lesbian members their difference, requiring them to display discordant symbols—such as photos of a same-sex partner—or to remain silent and serve as audience for the heterosexual discourse and practice that are hegemonic in such contexts, thereby (re)constructing their own marginalization.

When harassment is extensive and women are discouraged from reporting, nearly any reaction by women is ineffective (Cockburn

1991:157). Separated from one another, women find that their strategies of resisting, integrating, showing indifference, distancing, and denial fail to produce beneficial results. Collinson and Collinson (1996) found that one woman who complained was labeled by the men as a "moaning feminist troublemaker"; another who tried to integrate into the male sexist culture was derided by the men as "unfeminine and aggressive." A third who tried to ignore the men's sexual innuendos was eventually ostracized. All responses by the women were framed by (men) line managers as evidence that the women were incompetent or "unable to fit in."

Far from diminishing, evidence suggests that sexual harassment is alive and well. A recent survey of 4,501 U.S. women medical doctors, ages 30 to 70, confirms this conclusion (Frank, Brogan, and Schiffman 1998). Fully 47.7 percent of the physicians reported having been targets of gender-based harassment, and 36.9 percent reported having been sexually harassed. The authors of the survey conclude that although "some may believe that problems of harassment will disappear in time, that they are simply a function of older, sexist physicians still being in practice," the picture is less sanguine. Even though women are 42 percent of all medical students, they conclude, "We may be continuing to train physicians in an environment where harassment is common."

Advancing a few women into male-dominated workplaces may reinforce rather than challenge harassment culture and practices (Collinson and Collinson 1996). If so, equal opportunity schemes that advance women into male-dominant arenas may subject them to increased harassment and distress (Martin 1994; Marshall 1995). Collinson and Collinson (1996) conclude that creating organizations that legitimate and value women equally with men will require a fundamental reconceptualization of their purposes, goals, and methods, not merely ameliorative policies to raise awareness or to reform "insensitive men."

In sum, men's power in organizations cannot be understood apart from sexuality. Organizations are social contexts with extensive resources that men use to enact sexuality, and the conflation of sexuality with women means that gender issues can be rendered invisible by powerful men, even as they engage in sexualized behavior. For example, in an interview with the first author, a 55-year-old White male vice president of a telecommunications company described a "personal policy" he had followed for 30 years. He described himself as a "Christian, happily married man, and father of four" who wanted to avoid any suspicion of sexual impropriety. His policy was to invite men but not women subordinates to accompany him on trips. When his out-of-town host was a man, they went out to dinner to prepare for the upcoming day's work. He did not go to dinner with a woman host. These practices prevented the vice president from getting to know women as well as he did men, from establishing working relations with women that were as close as his relationships with men, and from gaining firsthand knowledge of women's talents, skills, and potential. He realized only recently that his behavior had "hurt the careers of women for many years." He regretted that his policy prevented women from having the same opportunities as men and was more sympathetic toward women now, but his policy remained the same. "I still do not want anyone to accuse me of sexual misconduct. . . . I'm sorry but that's just the way it is." He was not concerned that his willingness to have dinner alone with a man could be interpreted as a sign of homosexual interest, furthermore (Hearn 1993). Yet women who openly prefer women's company and advancement at work have been accused of being lesbians (Katzenstein 1998).

Organizing for Change

With this rethinking of gender and sexuality, exciting developments are occurring in organizations. In this section we note two developments with promise for application in diverse kinds of organizations. The first concerns the founding of feminist organizations (Bordt 1997; Ferree and Martin 1995; P. Y. Martin 1990). The second is the increase in organizing for change inside mainstream institutions, such as for-profit corporations (Raeburn 1998), the U.S. military and the Catholic Church (Katzenstein 1998), and not-for-profit, charitable organizations (Ostrander 1995).

Feminist organizations. Since the start of second-wave feminism in the late 1960s, feminist organizations have eschewed masculinist practices and values, such as hierarchy, domination, exploitation, competition, manipulation, and control (see Pyke 1996). Feminist organizations try to promote equality, consensus, cooperation, democracy, and empowerment (P. Y. Martin 1990). During the nearly 30 years since they began, many remain committed to less hierarchical and more democratic practices and structures (Bordt 1997), in addition to the achievement of external movement goals. Although some feminist organizations are national in scope and policy oriented in nature, many are local, operating in community contexts, "doing the work of the movement" in largely invisible, unacknowledged ways (Ferree and Martin 1995).

Whereas Perrow (1986) characterizes small, local organizations, such as feminist organizations usually are, as "trivial" compared with multinational corporations and state government, we view them as consequential. Feminist organizations are permanent sites for activists to use in raising funds, educating the public, seeking legitimation within the mainstream, and retreating from antifeminist hostilities (Simonds 1996). Their members learn how to act in cooperative, nonexploitative ways as they organize, pursue political agendas, and obtain and use mainstream resources for women's movement ends. Whereas some early feminist organizations prohibited men's participation, many in the 1980s and 1990s let men participate, as long as they abided by feminist practices. They thus became a means of educating men as well as women in democratic methods and goals. Such organizations show that masculinist practices, structures, and values are not required for success, as depictions of bureaucracy and capitalism often insist.

Collective organization and action inside mainstream institutions. In the late 1980s and early 1990s, many employers became concerned about racial, ethnic, and gender diversity in the U.S. workforce. To help people of color and women "feel more accepted," they instituted diversity training and encouraged employees to form groups, caucuses, or networks based on varied identity groups. Employees formed such groups in many companies, consisting usually of African Americans, women in various professional categories, young professionals, Asian Americans, gays and lesbians, and similar groups. Some groups formed with corporate endorsement, others without. The latter normally refused funds, direction, or oversight from employers, for fear of being co-opted. Some groups had agendas to provide support and information only; others sought to change the organization. For example, gays, lesbians, and bisexuals created networks in corporations to raise awareness and provide support to nonheterosexual employees, gain benefits for same-gender partners, and fight discrimination (Raeburn 1998).

When employees band together in common purpose, gender and sexuality are revealed as far from immutable conditions and practices. Research on internal mobilizations around sex and gender shows that those who organize take risks, however (Taylor and Raeburn 1995). We need case studies, comparative work, and analysis of collective action in organizations so that we can understand mobilizations that have greater and lesser odds of success. We would benefit from knowing why people mobilize around gender and sexuality and the rewards and costs of doing so.

Katzenstein's (1998) research on the U.S. military and the Catholic Church shows that collective action by women in two of the most hierarchical, bureaucratic, and masculinist institutions in contemporary society has produced an array of changes. Military women have successfully used the courts to challenge women's exclusion from particular duties or positions. For example, U.S. Navy carriers can no longer exclude women, nor can women be denied certain combat jobs. Catholic women, unable to use the legal system to change church policy or practice, have shaped the church's political discourse and debates and brought about changes that more fully include women (see also Wallace 1992). Catholic women who keep organizing, writing letters, making speeches, and creating documents that call into question the legitimacy of church policies that exclude women constitute a form of "discursive politics" inside the mainstream church (Katzenstein 1998; Farrell 1991).

Ostrander's (1995) study of the Haymarket Fund, a not-for-profit organization in New England, describes how board members took extraordinary steps to challenge gender, race, class, and sexual elitism in their meetings and relations with the organizations they fund. At one point during Ostrander's fieldwork, the board included only two White men, one of whom requested that others challenge him even as he continued to dominate meetings by talking excessively, giving suggestions, and referring to others as representatives of their racial/ethnic, gender, or sexuality groups. Yet her results show how resolve and creativity ultimately challenged the masculinism, heterosexism, and racism that influenced members both within and outside the group.

Thoughts for the Future

In many practical respects, gender and sexuality at work are inseparable. "Doing femininity" involves "doing heterosexuality"—looking "sexy" in heterosexist ways, deferring to men in vaguely sexual ways, being partnered with a man, and so forth (Rogers forthcoming). "Doing masculinity" is, in contrast, largely "doing dominance" (see West and Zimmerman 1987). Sexual domination epitomizes gender dominance, in many ways, given that men's greater power *as* men and *as* occupants of powerful organizational positions allows them to treat women as sexual objects. Gender disadvantage combines with organizational disadvantage to make women's resistance to sexual harassment difficult. Whereas gender and sexuality intertwine in profound ways, gender and class as well as gender and race are less consequentially bound up with one another in organizations (Tomaskovic-Devey 1993). The gender/sexuality nexus is particularly consequential in organizations because sexuality is not supposed to find expression and gender is supposed to play a minimalist role. Yet sexuality and gender are extensively conflated in everyday practice in organizations, especially, but not solely, by men.

Given these conditions, a radical revisioning of organizational practices and theories will require attention to the issues we have reviewed and others as well. Along this line, the first author has identified some "feminist practices" that people in organizations can use to improve women's status and to increase democracy overall (Martin 1993). For example, she suggests that one ask the "woman question" when a new policy or practice is proposed, so members will consider whether it will have its intended effects for everyone or only for men (see also Eisenstein 1995). She recommends the use of "feminist practical reasoning," which starts with experience and reasons outward rather than starts with abstract principles that often fail to produce intended effects "on the ground." Other practices she recommends include promoting community and cooperation, empowering subordinates, and nurturing and caring for associates. She concludes: "Armed with feminist vision, tactics, and a sense of purpose, feminist managers can teach a corporation the way it should go and create a more responsive and responsible workplace—for women, minority men, and majority men alike" (Martin 1993:292).

To advance this fundamental revisioning, we need studies of *masculinities* relative to other elements of power, culture, subjectivity, and relations in organizations. We need especially to understand masculinity dynamics among men. Connell (1995) claims that masculinities that are compatible with capitalism and rational-technical bureaucracy make it possible to promote masculine values and practices without acknowledging them. We need more attention to men's *affiliative* relations at work to see whether they undercut competitiveness among men or merely restrict competition to men by, for example, excluding women. In what ways and with what consequences are masculinity practices and ideology interwoven with workplace dynamics, such as bureaucratic claims that "rationality" and efficiency inform decisions or that capitalist market imperatives require competition and domination to assure success? How do masculinities that are dominant in organizations produce racism and the marginalization of people of color, including highly educated and skilled African American women and men (Collins 1997)?

We also need research on *femininities* to explore women's agency and compliance. Pyke (1996) discusses "noncompliant femininity," which conveys a false impression of women's independence, and calls for research on how the "construction of femininities reflects and (re)constructs (or resists) the gender order and inter-male hierarchies" (p. 546). Organizations are peopled by women and men who construct both femininities and masculinities, and individual women can practice "masculinities" just as individual men can practice "femininities" (Connell 1995; Kerfoot and Knights 1998). However, only men can collectively mobilize masculinities and, in doing so, exclude both women and femininities (Martin 1998). Organizations are suffused with emotionality, and affect is the basis for much action, official and unofficial (Martin and Knopoff 1997). Socializing and affiliation on and off the job are denied by hegemonic theories of organization and management. Equated with women and femininities, they are ignored in men. Organization theory has not only neglected gender, sexuality, and women but also has rendered men's emotional ties at work invisible (Hearn 1993). Men's emotions may include fear and dismay more than liking and affirmation, but theories depicting men as guided primarily by rational, logical, unemotional sentiments are, we suggest, stereotypical and incorrect.

It would be most interesting to document the results where employers have taken steps to dismantle gender and sexuality inequalities in their own ranks. Some for-profit corporations (e.g., Microsoft, Walt Disney World) and state and local governments (e.g., the state of Washington; the cities of San Jose and San Francisco, California) have established employee benefits packages that include the same-sex partners of homosexuals or that redress pay inequities for women's jobs relative to men's. Which internal policies are helpful? How do organizational cultures, practices, and structures have to be changed so that organizations can effectively implement the policies they adopt? What ingredients of organization and action make a workplace supportive of equality?

Alliances between members of organizations and members of social movements beyond organizational borders can foster change in gender and sexuality at work (Eisenstein 1995). Such alliances will not readily occur, however, and the effort required to build and sustain them is great. Yet changes have occurred and some will continue. Our hope is that gender and sexuality, as well as race, will become less and less relevant to the social organization of work and that the myth of social neutrality in traditional organization theory will become the reality of the future.

References

Acker, Joan. 1990. "Hierarchies, Bodies, and Jobs: A Theory of Gendered Organizations." *Gender & Society* 4:139-58.

―――. 1995. "Feminist Goals and Organizing Processes." Pp. 137-44 in *Feminist Organizations: Harvest of the New Women's Movement,* edited by Myra Marx Ferree and Patricia Yancey Martin. Philadelphia: Temple University Press.

Acker, Joan and Donald Van Houten. 1974. "Differential Recruitment and Control: The Sex Structuring of Organizations." *Administrative Science Quarterly* 19:152-63.

Adkins, L. 1995. *Gendered Work: Sexuality, Family, and the Labour Market.* Buckingham: Open University Press.

Barrett, Frank J. 1996. "The Organizational Construction of Hegemonic Masculinity: The Case of the U.S. Navy." *Gender, Work, and Organization* 3:129-42.

Bielby, William T. and James N. Baron. 1986. "Men and Women at Work: Sex Segregation and Statistical Discrimination." *American Journal of Sociology* 91:759-99.

Bird, Sharon. 1996. "Welcome to the Men's Club: Homosociality and the Maintenance of Hegemonic Masculinity." *Gender & Society* 10:120-32.

Bordt, Rebecca L. 1997. *The Structure of Women's Nonprofit Organizations.* Bloomington: Indiana University Press.

Britton, Dana. 1997. "Gendered Organizational Logic: Policy and Practice in Men's and Women's Prisons." *Gender & Society* 11:796-818.

Burrell, Gibson. 1992. "Sex and Organizational Analysis." Pp. 71-92 in *Gendering Organizational Analysis,* edited by Albert J. Mills and Peta Tancred. Newbury Park, CA: Sage.

Calas, Marta B. and Linda Smircich. 1993. "Dangerous Liaisons: The 'Feminine-in-Management' Meets 'Globalization.' " *Business Horizons* (March-April):73-83.

―――. 1996. "From the Woman's 'Point of View': Feminist Approaches to Organization Studies." Pp. 218-57 in *Handbook of Organization Studies,* edited by Stewart R. Clegg, Cynthia Hardy, and Walter R. Nord. Thousand Oaks, CA: Sage.

Calvert, Linda McGee and V. Jean Ramsey. 1996. "Speaking as Female and White: A Non-dominant/Dominant Group Standpoint." *Organizations* 3:468-85.

Chase, Susan. 1995. *Ambiguous Empowerment: The Work Narratives of Women School Superintendents.* Amherst: University of Massachusetts Press.

Cockburn, Cynthia. 1983. *Brothers.* London: Pluto.

———. 1988. *Machinery of Dominance: Women, Men, and Technical Know-How.* Boston: South End.

———. 1991. *In the Way of Women: Men's Resistance to Sex Equality in Organizations.* London: Macmillan.

Cohn, Samuel. 1985. *The Process of Occupational Sex-Typing: The Feminization of Clerical Labor in Great Britain.* Philadelphia: Temple University Press.

Collins, Sharon. 1997. "Black Mobility in White Corporations: Up the Corporate Ladder but Out on a Limb." *Social Problems* 44:55-67.

Collinson, David L. 1988. "Engineering Humour: Masculinity, Joking and Conflict in Shopfloor Relations." *Organization Studies* 12:181-99.

———. 1992. *Managing the Shopfloor: Subjectivity, Masculinity and Workplace Culture.* Berlin: Walter de Gruyter.

Collinson, David L. and Margaret Collinson. 1989. "Sexuality in the Workplace: The Domination of Men's Sexuality." Pp. 91-109 in *The Sexuality of Organization,* edited by Jeff Hearn, Debra L. Sheppard, Peta Tancred-Sheriff, and Gibson Burrell. London: Sage.

———. 1992. "Mismanaging Sexual Harassment: Protecting the Perpetrator and Blaming the Victim." *Women in Management Review* 7:11-17.

Collinson, David L. and Jeff Hearn. 1994. "Naming Men as Men: Implications for Work, Organization and Management." *Gender, Work and Organization* 1:2-22.

———. 1996. "Breaking the Silence: On Men, Masculinities, and Managements." Pp. 1-24 in *Men as Managers, Managers as Men: Critical Perspectives on Men, Masculinities, and Managements,* edited by David L. Collinson and Jeff Hearn. London: Sage.

Collinson, David L., David Knights, and Margaret Collinson. 1990. *Managing to Discriminate.* London: Routledge.

Collinson, Margaret and David L. Collinson. 1996. "It's Only 'Dick': The Sexual Harassment of Women Managers in Insurance." *Work, Employment and Society* 10(1):29-56.

Connell, R. W. 1995. *Masculinities.* Berkeley: University of California Press.

Cotter, David A., JoAnn DeFiore, Joan M. Hermsen, Brenda Marsteller Kowalewski, and Reeve Vanneman. 1997. "All Women Benefit: The Macro-Level Effect of Occupational Integration on Gender Earnings Equality." *American Sociological Review* 62:714-34.

DiMaggio, Paul J. and Walter W. Powell. 1983. "The Iron Cage Revisited: Institutional Isomorphism and Collective Rationality in Organizational Fields." *American Sociological Review* 48:147-60.

DiTomaso, Nancy. 1989. "Sexuality in the Workplace: Discrimination and Harassment." Pp. 71-90 in *The Sexuality of Organization*, edited by Jeff Hearn, Debra L. Sheppard, Peta Tancred-Sheriff, and Gibson Burrell. London: Sage.

Dorsey, David. 1994. *The Force*. New York: Ballantine.

Dunne, Gillian A. 1997. *Lesbian Lifestyles: Women's Work and the Politics of Sexuality*. Toronto: University of Toronto Press.

Eisenstein, Hester. 1995. *Inside Agitators: The Femocrats in Australia*. Philadelphia: Temple University Press.

Ely, Robin. 1995. "The Role of Dominant Identity and Experience in Organizational Work on Diversity." Pp. 161-86 in *Diversity in Work Teams: Research Paradigms for a Changing Workplace*, edited by Susan E. Jackson and Marian N. Ruderman. Washington, DC: American Psychological Association.

England, Paula. 1992. *Comparable Worth: Theories and Evidence*. New York: Aldine de Gruyter.

Farrell, Susan A. 1991. " 'It's Our Church Too!': Women's Position in the Catholic Church Today." In *The Social Construction of Gender*, edited by Judith Lorber and Susan A. Farrell. Newbury Park, CA: Sage.

Feldberg, Roslyn and Evelyn Nakano Glenn. 1979. "Job versus Gender Models in the Sociology of Work." *Social Problems* 26:524-38.

Ferree, Myra Marx and Patricia Yancey Martin. 1995. "Feminist Organizations: Doing the Work of the Movement." Pp. 3-23 in *Feminist Organizations: Harvest of the New Women's Movement*, edited by Myra Marx Ferree and Patricia Yancey Martin. Philadelphia: Temple University Press.

Fletcher, Joyce. 1998. "Relational Practice: A Feminist Reconstruction of Work." *Journal of Management Inquiry* 7:163-86.

Folgero, I. S. and I. H. Fjeldstad. 1995. "On Duty—Off Guard: Cultural Norms and Sexual Harassment in Service Organizations." *Organization Studies* 16:299-314.

Frank, Erica, Donna J. Brogan, and Melissa Schiffman. 1998. "Prevalence and Correlates of Sexual Harassment among U.S. Women Physicians." *Archives of Internal Medicine* 158:352-58.

Glucksmann, Miriam. 1990. *Women Assemble: Women Workers and the New Industries in Interwar Britain*. New York: Routledge.

Grauerholz, Elizabeth. 1989. "Sexual Harassment of Women Professors by Students: Exploring the Dynamics of Power, Authority, and Gender in a University Setting." *Sex Roles* 21:798-801.

Gutek, Barbara A. 1989. "Sexuality in the Workplace: Key Issues in Social Research and Organizational Practice." Pp. 56-70 in *The Sexuality of Organization*, edited by Jeff Hearn, Debra L. Sheppard, Peta Tancred-Sheriff, and Gibson Burrell. London: Sage.

Hadjifotiou, N. 1983. *Women and Harassment at Work*. London: Pluto.

Hall, Elaine. 1993a. "Smiling, Deferring, and Flirting: Doing Gender by Giving 'Good Service.' " *Work and Occupations* 20:452-71.

————. 1993b. "Waitering/Waitressing: Engendering the Work of Table Service." *Gender & Society* 7:329-46.

Harding, Sandra. 1996. "European Expansion and the Organization of Modern Science: Isolated or Linked Historical Processes?" *Organization* 3:497-509.

Hearn, Jeff. 1993. "Emotive Subjects: Organizational Men, Organizational Masculinities and the (De)Construction of 'Emotions.' " Pp. 142-66 in *Emotions in Organizations*, edited by Stephen Fineman. London: Sage.

Hearn, Jeff and Wendy Parkin. 1987. *"Sex" at "Work": The Power and Paradox of Organisation Sexuality*. Brighton: Wheatsheaf.

Henriques, J., W. Hollway, C. Urwin, C. Venn, and V. Walkerdine, eds. 1984. *Changing the Subject*. London: Methuen.

Hochschild, Arlie R. 1983. *The Managed Heart: Commercialization of Human Feeling*. Berkeley: University of California Press.

Hollway, Wendy. 1984. "Gender Difference and the Production of Subjectivity." Pp. 227-63 in *Changing the Subject*, edited by J. Henriques, W. Hollway, C. Urwin, C. Venn, and V. Walkerdine. London: Methuen.

————. 1996. "Masculinities and Managements in the Transition: From Factory Hands to Sentimental Workers." In *Men as Managers, Managers as Men: Critical Perspectives on Men, Masculinities, and Managements*, edited by David L. Collinson and Jeff Hearn. London: Sage.

Holstein, James A. 1987. "Producing Gender Effects on Involuntary Mental Hospitalization." *Social Problems* 34:141-55.

Kanter, Rosabeth Moss. 1977. *Men and Women of the Corporation*. New York: Basic Books.

Katzenstein, Mary. 1998. *Faithful and Fearless: Moving Feminist Protest inside the Church and Military*. Princeton, NJ: Princeton University Press.

Kerfoot, Debra and David Knights. 1998. "Managing Masculinity in Contemporary Organizational Life: A 'Man'agerial Project." *Organizations* 5:7-26.

Kimmel, Michael. 1996. *Manhood in America: A Cultural History.* New York: Free Press.

Kleinman, Sheryl. 1996. *Opposing Ambitions: Gender and Identity in an Alternative Organization.* Chicago: University of Chicago Press.

Kondo, Dorrine. 1990. *Crafting Selves: Power, Gender, and Discourses of Identity in a Japanese Workplace.* Chicago: University of Chicago Press.

Lane, Phyllis M. Pace. 1996. "You Can't Walk a Straight Line with a Crooked Shoe." *Organization* 3:462-67.

Leidner, Robin. 1993. *Fast Food, Fast Talk: Interactive Service Work and the Routinization of Everyday Life.* Berkeley: University of California Press.

Lipman-Blumen, Jean. 1976. "Toward a Homosocial Theory of Sex Roles: An Explanation of Sex Segregation in Social Institutions." *Signs* 1:15-31.

Lorber, Judith. 1984. *Women Physicians: Careers, Status, and Power.* London: Tavistock.

———. 1994. *Paradoxes of Gender.* New Haven, CT: Yale University Press.

Loscocco, Karyn and Glenna Spitze. 1991. "The Organizational Context of Women's and Men's Pay Satisfaction." *Social Science Quarterly* 17:3-19.

MacKinnon, Catharine A. 1979. *The Sexual Harassment of Working Women.* New Haven, CT: Yale University Press.

Marglin, Stephen. 1976. "What Do Bosses Do? The Origins and Function of Hierarchy in Capitalist Production." Pp. 13-54 in *The Division of Labour: The Labour Process and Class Struggle in Capitalism,* edited by Andre Gorz. Sussex: Harvester.

Marshall, Judi. 1995. *Women Managers Moving On: Exploring Career and Life Choices.* London: Routledge.

Martin, Joanne. 1990. "Deconstructing Organizational Taboos: The Suppression of Gender Conflict in Organizations." *Organizational Science* 1:1-21.

———. 1994. "The Organization of Exclusion: Institutionalization of Sex Inequality, Gendered Faculty Jobs, and Gender Knowledge in Organizational Theory and Research." *Organization* 1:401-31.

Martin, Joanne and Kathleen Knopoff. 1997. "The Gendered Implications of Apparently Gender-Neutral Theory: Re-reading Weber." In *Ruffin Lecture Series,* vol. 3, *Business Ethics and Women's Studies,* edited by E. Freeman and A. Larson. Oxford: Oxford University Press.

Martin, Patricia Yancey. 1990. "Rethinking Feminist Organizations." *Gender & Society* 4:182-206.

———. 1993. "Feminist Practice in Organizations: Implications for Management." Pp. 274-96 in *Women in Management 4: Trends, Issues, and Challenges in Managerial Diversity,* edited by E. Fagenson. Newbury Park, CA: Sage.

————. 1996. "Gendering and Evaluating Dynamics: Men, Masculinities, and Managements." Pp. 186-209 in *Men as Managers, Managers as Men: Critical Perspectives on Men, Masculinities, and Managements,* edited by David L. Collinson and Jeff Hearn. London: Sage.

————. 1997. "Gender, Accounts, and Rape Processing Work." *Social Problems* 44:464-82.

————. 1998. "Theorizing Men as Men in Organizations: Men's Masculinity Mobilizations from (Some) Women's Standpoint(s)." Department of Sociology, Florida State University, Tallahassee. Unpublished manuscript.

Martin, Patricia Yancey and Steve Harkreader. 1993. "Multiple Gender Contexts and Employee Rewards." *Work and Occupations* 20:296-336.

McIlwee, Judith S. and J. Greg Robinson. 1992. *Women in Engineering: Gender, Power, and Workplace Culture.* Albany: State University of New York Press.

Messerschmidt, James W. 1996. "Managing to Kill: Masculinities and the Space Shuttle *Challenger* Explosion." Pp. 29-53 in *Masculinities in Organizations,* edited by Cliff Cheng. Thousand Oaks, CA: Sage.

Morgan, D. H. J. 1981. "Men, Masculinity, and the Process of Sociological Enquiry." Pp. 83-113 in *Doing Feminist Research,* edited by H. Roberts. London: Routledge.

————. 1992. *Discovering Men.* London: Routledge & Kegan Paul.

Ostrander, Susan. 1995. *Money for Change: Social Movement Philanthropy at Haymarket People's Fund.* Philadelphia: Temple University Press.

Perrow, Charles. 1986. *Complex Organizations: A Critical Essay.* New York: McGraw-Hill.

Pierce, Jennifer. 1995. *Gender Trials.* Berkeley: University of California Press.

Pringle, Rosemary. 1988. *Secretaries Talk: Sexuality, Power, and Work.* Sydney: Routledge, Chapman & Hall.

Pyke, Karen D. 1996. "Class-Based Masculinities: The Interdependence of Gender, Class, and Interpersonal Power." *Gender & Society* 10:527-49.

Raeburn, Nicole C. 1998. "The Rise of Lesbian, Gay, and Bisexual Rights in the Workplace." Ph.D. dissertation, Department of Sociology, Ohio State University, Columbus.

Ranson, Gillian and William Joseph Reeves. 1996. "Gender, Earnings, and Proportion of Women: Lessons from a High-Tech Occupation." *Gender & Society* 10:168-84.

Reskin, Barbara F. and Irene Padavic. 1994. *Women and Men at Work.* Thousand Oaks, CA: Pine Forge.

Reskin, Barbara F. and Patricia Roos. 1990. *Job Queues, Gender Queues: Explaining Women's Inroads into Male Occupations.* Philadelphia: Temple University Press.

Rogers, Mary. Forthcoming. *Our Barbies, Our Selves.* Thousand Oaks, CA: Sage.

Roper, Michael. 1996. " 'Seduction and Succession': Circuits of Homosexual Desire in Management." Pp. 210-226 in *Men as Managers, Managers as Men: Critical Perspectives on Men, Masculinities, and Managements,* edited by David L. Collinson and Jeff Hearn. London: Sage.

Rospenda, Kathleen M., Judith A. Richman, and Stephanie J. Nawyn. 1998. "Doing Power: The Confluence of Gender, Race, and Class in Contrapower Sexual Harassment." *Gender & Society* 12:40-60.

Scase, R. and R. Goffee. 1989. *Reluctant Managers.* London: Unwin Hyman.

Schneider, Beth. 1993. "Put Up and Shut Up: Workplace Sexual Assaults." Pp. 57-72 in *Violence against Women: The Bloody Footprints,* edited by Pauline B. Bart and Eileen G. Moran. Newbury Park CA: Sage.

Sheppard, D. L. 1989. "Organizations, Power, and Sexuality: The Image and Self-Image of Woman Managers." Pp. 139-57 in *The Sexuality of Organization,* edited by Jeff Hearn, Debra L. Sheppard, Peta Tancred-Sheriff, and Gibson Burrell. London: Sage.

Simonds, Wendy. 1996. *Abortion at Work: Ideology and Practice in a Feminist Clinic.* New Brunswick, NJ: Rutgers University Press.

Sinclair, A. 1995. "Sex and the MBA." *Organization* 2:295-317.

Spencer, A. and D. Podmore. 1987. *In a Man's World.* London: Tavistock.

Steinberg, Ronnie. 1990. "The Social Construction of Skill: Gender, Power, and Comparable Worth." *Work and Occupations* 17:449-82.

Stewart, James B. 1997. "Coming Out at Chrysler." *New Yorker,* July 21, pp. 38-49.

Taylor, Verta and Nicole C. Raeburn. 1995. "Identity Politics as High-Risk Activism: Career Consequences for Lesbian, Gay, and Bisexual Sociologists." *Social Problems* 42:252-73.

Thorne, Barrie. 1993. *Gender Play: Boys and Girls in School.* New Brunswick, NJ: Rutgers University Press.

Tomaskovic-Devey, Donald. 1993. *Gender and Racial Inequality at Work: The Sources and Consequences of Job Segregation.* Ithaca, NY: ILR.

Walby, Sylvia. 1988. *Gender Segregation at Work.* Philadelphia: Open University Press.

Wallace, Ruth A. 1992. *They Call Her Pastor: A New Role for Catholic Women.* Albany: State University of New York Press.

West, Candace and Don Zimmerman. 1987. "Doing Gender." *Gender & Society* 1:125-51.

Wharton, Amy S. 1992. "The Social Construction of Gender and Race in Organizations: A Social Identity and Group Mobilization Perspective."

Pp. 55-84 in *Research in the Sociology of Organizations 10*, edited by Pamela Tolbert and Samuel Bacharach. Greenwich, CT: JAI.

Williams, Christine. 1995. *Still a Man's World: Men Who Do Women's Work.* Berkeley: University of California Press.

Willis, Paul E. 1977. *Learning to Labor: How Working-Class Kids Get Working-Class Jobs.* New York: Columbia University Press.

Wise, Sue and Liz Stanley. 1988. *Georgie Porgie: Sexual Harassment in Everyday Life.* London: Pandora.

Witz, Anne and Mike Savage. 1992. "The Gender of Organizations." Pp. 3-62 in *Gender and Bureaucracy,* edited by Mike Savage and Anne Witz. Oxford: Basil Blackwell.

Wolf, Diane. 1992. *Factory Daughters: Gender, Household Dynamics, and Rural Industrialization in Java.* Berkeley: University of California Press.

Woodward, Alison. 1996. "Multinational Masculinities and European Bureaucracies." Pp. 167-85 in *Men as Managers, Managers as Men: Critical Perspectives on Men, Masculinities, and Managements,* edited by David L. Collinson and Jeff Hearn. London: Sage.

CHAPTER 11

Gender, Family Structure, and Social Structure

Racial Ethnic Families in the United States

ANNE R. ROSCHELLE

Of the many topics that could be covered in this chapter, I have chosen to focus on family poverty and the organization of racial ethnic families. Both have been profoundly shaped by gendered political and economic forces. In fact, the rise in family poverty and concomitant changes in family structure can be linked directly to macrostructural economic transformations occurring over the past three decades. Clearly, families must be understood within the broader societal context (Baca Zinn 1989; Toro-Morn 1995) rather than treated simply as reflections of micro-level household interactions. Because race, gender, and class are fundamental categories of social organization, they must become the locus of family research. I begin with a review of theoretical perspectives on racial ethnic families, particularly African Americans, Chicanos, and Puerto Ricans, who share a legacy of economic disenfranchisement and racialized oppression.[1] Using a gender perspective, I analyze the culture of poverty thesis, the cultural relativity or strength/resilience approach, and the structural perspective. I then propose an integrative theoretical framework in which race, class, and gender are treated as interlocking systems of oppression and resistance and apply it to a discussion of contemporary racial ethnic families in the United States.

The Culture of Poverty Thesis

The dominant theoretical position in American social sciences throughout the 1960s was that pathological elements inherent in minority cultures were responsible for deviant family structures. As a result, poverty was produced and reproduced by the intergenerational transmission of aberrant cultural norms and behaviors. Although this perspective was applied differently to African Americans, Chicanos, and Puerto Ricans, it reflected dominant cultural norms about "appropriate" gender relations and uniformly defined racial ethnic families as pathogenic.

With respect to African Americans, what little theorizing existed on the Black family up to the 1930s was based on the generally accepted assumption of biological inferiority. This essentialist perspective was used to define African American families that deviated from the White middle-class nuclear norm as unstable. In an attempt to refute biological explanations for Black family structure, Frazier (1932, 1939) identified two very different patterns of Black family life. The more prevalent type, according to Frazier, was a maritally unstable and sexually permissive matriarchal family, which he attributed to the disruptive forces of slavery, emancipation, and migration, which eroded long-standing bonds of kinship. The second, less common, type of family was the two-parent male-headed family, characterized by a small but growing middle-class and property-owning segment of the African American population. Although emphasizing that it was slavery rather than race that led to family breakdown, Frazier assumed that the majority of households were female centered, that out-of-wedlock births represented family "disorganization," and that such patterns were transmitted normatively from one generation to the next.

In fact, however, careful historical studies have shown that, following the Civil War, most Blacks, even former slaves in both North and South, in both rural and urban areas, lived in two-parent households (Gutman 1976; Tolnay 1997). Given that most of these families were headed by nonskilled workers, it was clear that Frazier's conflation of race, social class, and family type was fallacious. Despite the profoundly inhumane conditions of plantation life in the South, slavery did not destroy the Black family.

Despite Frazier's erroneous historical assumptions, the image of a dysfunctional "matriarchal" Black family gained widespread acceptance in 1965 with the publication of a report written by Daniel Patrick

Moynihan for the U.S. Department of Labor. *The Negro Family: The Case for National Action* (1965) detailed a "tangle of pathology" affecting Black communities that Moynihan attributed to the predominance of "matriarchal" families in which boys were dominated by women and subsequently grew up without adequate role models for healthy adult masculinity. Moynihan argued that low educational attainment, persistent unemployment, family disintegration, and poverty within the Black community were direct results of deviant cultural norms characterizing matriarchal families. Furthermore, he argued that poor Blacks have distinctive values, aspirations, psychological characteristics, and behavioral deficiencies that keep them impoverished. Through socialization, these deficiencies are transmitted intergenerationally, which results in a perpetual cycle of poverty. Finally, Moynihan rejected racism as a pivotal force in the perpetuation of poverty by asserting that the tangle of pathology was "capable of perpetuating itself without assistance from the white world" (Baca Zinn 1989). At the heart of Moynihan's analysis were race, class, and gender assumptions about the primacy of the patriarchal middle-class nuclear family in which men and women are compartmentalized into different domains with distinctive roles. Not surprisingly, Moynihan's major policy recommendation was for Black women to relinquish their putative control of the Black community and to restructure their families according to the middle-class patriarchal model.

In its valorization of the patriarchal nuclear family, this thesis overlooked the strengths of the African traditions of extended and fictive kinship networks, perceiving only "disorganization" in these alternative family patterns (Stack 1974). Black women have never been "matriarchs," given that they have historically been denied economic and political power. During the nineteenth century, unskilled Black male laborers consistently earned more than their female counterparts (Gutman 1976), and Black women continue to earn less than men in all race and education categories (U.S. Bureau of the Census 1997c:160). And although Black male unemployment rates are persistently high, this does not confer greater power to African American women. In fact, as I detail later in this chapter, families deprived of a "male" wage are at high risk of falling below the poverty threshold. Nevertheless, the pernicious image of the dominant Black matriarch persists, demonizing African American women among Whites as well as among many Black men.

The culture of poverty thesis also deflects attention from the social structural conditions that reduce the pool of potential marriage partners who could be adequate providers, conditions that increasingly apply to non-Blacks as well (see Brush, Chapter 6, this volume). With increasing numbers of Black men unemployed or underemployed, incarcerated, victims of homicide, or lost to the drug world, there are few prospects, however much Black women may desire stable and happy marriages. For example, in the early 1990s, for every three unmarried African American women in their 20s there was only one unmarried Black man with earnings above the poverty line (Lichter et al. 1992). Nonetheless, the current debate over changes in welfare policy has been dominated by the idea that poverty can be avoided and American taxpayers saved the cost of supporting single mothers if only "these women" would marry and stay attached to their husbands, regardless of the quality of those relationships. The idea that marriage is the solution to poverty has also generated internal antagonisms within the Black community, between those who consider male unemployment to be the major problem facing families and those who are most concerned with enhancing the well-being of single mothers and their children (Dill 1997).

Furthermore, this debate reflects the still unquestioned and invisible role of marriage as a major form of income redistribution in society. Without the mechanism of marriage to facilitate income transfers from men to women, the underlying gender inequalities in income and wealth become more obvious. Because of low male earnings and a tradition of female education and independence, marriage is a less effective redistributive mechanism for African American families today than it is for White families. Finally, the patriarchal assumption that marriage should be the primary means of reducing gender inequality in income conveniently ignores socially structured inequities found throughout the U.S. labor market.

With regard to the Chicano family, culture of poverty theorists applying the yardstick of a White middle-class nuclear ("Anglo") household should at least have derived some satisfaction in finding male dominance intact. Ironically, the patriarchal pattern that critics wish to see restored to Black families is transformed into a negative feature of Mexican American families. In this view, poverty among Chicanos can be traced to the debilitating effects of machismo and female passivity, in contrast to a presumably more egalitarian Anglo model (Mirande 1985). Chicano men are depicted, even by some Latino scholars, as neurotic, cruel and insensitive toward women, socially irresponsible, and locked into traditional notions of honor (Diaz-Guerrero 1975; Williams 1990). Conversely, Chicanas are portrayed as weak and submissive, kept in line by the threat and actuality of interpersonal violence (Andrade 1982; Ybarra 1983). Marriage is seen as placing few limits on men, but as completely constraining for women. This rigidly patriarchal structure is then assumed to have a negative effect on the achievement orientation and individualism of Chicano children, reducing their chances of success in American society (Mirande 1985; Roschelle 1997).

This depiction of Chicano families is both ahistorical and empirically dubious. No attempt is made to trace the effects of immigration policies or even of the long history of migration between Mexico and the southwestern states. There are no studies with large, representative samples, and little attention is paid to variations within the Chicano population, by regions, residential patterns, or occupational niches. Rather, an obsession with machismo seems to have overwhelmed researchers, so that even when studies find that the Chicano family is less authoritarian than hypothesized, the data are explained away as the effect of acculturation (e.g., Hawkes and Taylor 1975). Paradoxically, culture of poverty theorists assert that African Americans must achieve a patriarchal family composition as a means of transcending their pathological conditions, while simultaneously arguing that this same patriarchal structure is responsible for the impoverished conditions of Chicano families. This internal contradiction reflects conventional gender ideology, in which women are blamed for their children's economic disenfranchisement. In order to present both African American and Chicano families as pathological, one must idealize Anglo gender relationships, implicitly denying that male dominance, family violence, and unequal distribution of power are prevalent in many families of all races (Barrett 1988).

Because families of Latino origin are often studied as if they all share the same traditions and sociohistorical experiences, many of the traits attributed to Mexican American families have been used to characterize Puerto Rican families as well, particularly the rigid codes of masculinity and femininity. The most influential study of Puerto Rican family life to date was conducted by Harvard anthropologist Oscar Lewis in the early 1960s following a similar study he conducted in Mexico. Lewis (1966), who coined the expression "culture of poverty," portrayed Puerto Rican families as preoccupied with sexuality: male sexual violence, female sexual jealousy, and children's sexual precocity. In contrast to the image of the passive, powerless Chicana, Lewis's *Puertorriqueñas* were sexually aggressive and contemptuous of men. Subsequently,

Lewis argued that *Puertorriqueñas* were responsible for fatalism, dependency, and inferiority among their children and that they were to blame for the intergenerational transmission of poverty.

Arguing that Mexican families are pathological because of their patriarchal structure, whereas Puerto Rican families are deviant because of the strength of their women, signifies an inherent contradiction in Lewis's work. Once again, the underlying message is that "appropriate" gender relationships in the family are necessary to achieve individualized economic success. Mothers who are too independent (of a husband), too dependent (on public funds), too sexually dominated (by machismo), or too sexually aggressive (with unbridled desires) are "bad" for their children, who thereby become ill equipped to achieve labor market success or obtain a stable family life. These stereotypic assumptions tap into the same public sentiment as the Moynihan report, and so receive widespread publicity. One major problem with this approach, however, is that taking marital disruption and female-headed households as evidence of pathological functioning obscures and denigrates the ameliorative effects of extended kinship and friendship networks. In addition, any analysis that locates the cause of poverty primarily in family culture rather than in a long and well-documented history of political and economic marginalization becomes an intellectually sterile exercise in blaming the victim (Ryan 1972). The concept of a culture of poverty reinforces the Protestant ethic of work as a calling, of success as a sign of grace, and of individual responsibility as a sign of godliness. This hegemonic conceptualization allows contemporary White middle-class gender relations to appear as a "natural" timeless standard, and continues to have a profound impact on the lives of all racial ethnic women.

The Cultural Relativity Approach

The cultural relativity perspective arose as a response to the negative stereotypes perpetuated by culture of poverty theorists. This approach emphasizes the strength and resilience of racial ethnic families who endured despite grinding poverty and racial injustice. Researchers in this tradition focus on such positive factors as the strength of parent-child ties, informal support networks, extended family systems, and shared community responsibility for child care (Billingsley 1992). For example, this historical approach traces current African American familial patterns to traditional African practices, such as diverse forms of descent, extended family households, and the exclusive mother-infant bonds common in the West African societies from which slaves were taken, but that are labeled deviant by contemporary White American middle-class norms (Billingsley 1968, 1992). From this perspective, what deserves attention is not the apparent disorganization of African American families, but their amazing resilience in the face of forced migration, slavery, sexual violence, and postbellum discrimination. That African American families have survived at all is due primarily to Black women, who have relied on an extensive network of real and fictive female kin (Jarrett 1994).

Although this approach avoids the racism of culture of poverty theorists, it has several shortcomings. The links between varied family patterns in dozens of West African cultures 150 years ago and the situation of American Black families today are empirically tenuous. Attempting to disentangle cultural variables (traditional family patterns) from historical forces (wars and migrations) and social structural conditions (employment opportunities) requires a more painstaking analysis than many scholars have applied. The glorification of Black motherhood is also problematic. By glorifying Black mothers, scholars refuse to acknowledge many of the obstacles facing these women. In addition, by claiming that Black women are endowed with the capacity for devotion, self-sacrifice, and unconditional love to an inhuman degree, proponents of this perspective inadvertently foster the image of the superstrong Black mother (Collins 1990). This perspective also ignores African American mothers' own interpretations of their experience, as when the mothers of pregnant teenagers express anger and rejection of their daughters (Kaplan 1997). As Hill Collins (1990) notes, we require an Afrocentric feminist analysis of motherhood that debunks the image of both the matriarch and the superstrong Black mother and that accurately depicts the difficulties of raising children in poverty. Similarly, a more balanced approach that examines the broader social forces that produce pockets of poverty, joblessness, and despair as well as cultural responses to these macroeconomic forces is essential (Wilson 1991).

Similarly, as refutation to the implicit racism of the pathological models, the strength resilience perspective on Chicano families focuses on positive cultural traits, including close ties of affection and assistance between the generations, love for children, and extended social support networks. This norm of "familism" has been traced by some scholars to the Aztec culture of pre-Columbian Mexico (Mirande and Enriquez

1979; Del Castillo 1984). Historical documentation, based primarily on the customs of the upper strata, depicts an Aztec emphasis on arranged marriage, expectations of marital fidelity, limited access to divorce for both men and women, and joint family ownership of land. In addition, godparenthood or *compadrazgo*, then as now, served to enlarge a family's ties to others in the community. From this perspective, despite variations within the Chicano population, familism is a resource rather than a barrier to worldly success. Although it may be modified by urbanization and acculturation, *la familia* remains the central institution in the life of its members, the source of emotional support and material resources.

From this perspective, women are strong because they are responsible for maintaining the extended kin network, caring for young and old, and sacrificing their personhood in service to *la familia*. From a feminist perspective, however, it can be argued that such cultural ideals, now placed in a positive light, are every bit as constraining for women as were the negatively valued norms of passivity and subordination. The difference is that a glow of romantic nostalgia now envelops *la sufrida*, the self-effacing Chicana counterpart to the self-sacrificing African American mother (Segura and de la Torre 1997). In the hands of cultural relativists, the concept of machismo denotes family pride and respect rather than male dominance. A man must use his authority fairly or risk losing the respect of family members. What others have described as a rigid authoritarian structure is redefined as a stable family that is held together by mutual dependencies and patterns of assistance, in which each person's place is clearly established (Murillo 1971).

Yet this depiction is only a shift in normative interpretation. Negative stereotypes are replaced with positive stereotypes of the same characteristics, producing a romanticized caricature of the Chicano family, a picture that obscures both internal diversity and external sources of stress. In this view no less than in the culture of poverty thesis, formal normative prescriptions are presented as accurate descriptions of reality, leading to a simplistic view of an all-powerful Chicano husband/father and the self-effacing wife/mother. In reality, family dynamics are both more variable and more complex, with men wielding less and women more authority than commonly assumed. In addition, the longer the family has been in the United States and the more acculturated its members, the greater the challenge to traditional gender expectations (Segura 1994). The force of familism may erode with acculturation, as Chicana/os follow the pattern of other ethnic groups in adopting an Anglo middle-class pattern of independent and autonomous nuclear households (Williams 1990). However, in a more racially diverse and deindustrialized future, entirely different normative family patterns may emerge.

When the strength resilience model is applied to the Puerto Rican family, observers tend to note the lack of a thriving indigenous culture. Because of the mass bloodshed that occurred during the Spanish invasion, the Taino were virtually wiped out. As a result of this genocide, very little is known about the impact of their culture on subsequent family life (Fitzpatrick 1981). However, given the patriarchal structure of the traditional Puerto Rican family, it seems unlikely that the matrilineal Taino had an overwhelming influence on succeeding family patterns. As a result of insufficient historical data on Taino culture, and the fact that most Puerto Ricans identify with their Spanish ancestry, strength resilience theorists focus primarily on the effects that Spanish colonial rule had on development of the Puerto Rican family. After four centuries of Spanish colonial rule, it is not surprising to find norms that value patriarchy, machismo, and female passivity in family interaction. The centrality of family, strict supervision of young people, segregation of the sexes, arranged marriages, and separate spheres for husbands and wives often associated with traditional Puerto Rican families are given a positive twist by scholars in the cultural relativism tradition. From this vantage point, the family is seen as facilitating rather than impeding upward mobility and as nurturing and supportive rather than as smothering (Padilla 1987).

The depiction of Puerto Rican families differs in one crucial respect from its Chicano counterpart—in its portrayal of women. In contrast to the often idealized Chicana mother, rarely does one find a positive evaluation of Puerto Rican women as assertive members of the family and active agents of change, or of *hembrismo,* a concept of womanhood that connotes strength and the ability to survive (Comas-Diaz 1987). A more contemporary and nuanced reality, however, is portrayed by Toro-Morn (1994) and Alicea (1997) in their studies of how Puerto Rican migrant women juggle the traditional and modern aspects of their transnational community: "Puerto Rican women find themselves having to coordinate and negotiate between family needs, competing expectations, racism and poverty, and their own sense of agency and desire to do meaningful work, as well as to achieve personal satisfaction . . . [and] improve their positions of power vis-á-vis men" (Alicea 1997:622).

The transnational character of many Puerto Rican families, involving back-and-forth migration between the mainland and the island, is a hallmark of Puerto Rican culture, with the effect of making their migration less "permanent" or fixed than that of nineteenth-century European or twentieth-century Asian families.

But whether one sees family characteristics as obstacles or as resources, both the culture of poverty and cultural relativity perspectives place primary emphasis on traditional norms and patterns of behavior, transmitted through socialization. Both therefore elevate conventional or "deviant" gender relations within the family to the dubious honor of being the primary source of stratification outcomes. Families are seen as separate and autonomous from the rest of society. a sort of moated castle in which culture is created and preserved, and from which children venture forth only as (un)employable adolescents. As Baca Zinn (1990) has noted, any theory that extols the adaptive potential of previously denigrated traits runs the risk of overemphasizing strengths at the level of family culture while minimizing the persistent long-term external threats to the well-being of racial ethnic families. Cultural ideals are one thing; social structure is quite another.

The Structural Perspective

The structural perspective views the family as a social institution that is inextricably bound and influenced by the larger social structure. Racial and ethnic variations in family configuration are often regarded merely as reflections of class divisions, with special emphasis on how locations in stratification systems affect network participation. Hence the underlying assumption of this approach is that economic rather than cultural factors are responsible for family organization (Bean and Tienda 1987).

Although, in general, the three populations of concern in this chapter share common locations in various stratification hierarchies—education, occupation, and income—they have followed different historical trajectories, with different effects on women and men. Yet, despite all the economic and racial oppression they faced during the first half of this century, throughout the Great Depression and World War II, a majority of racial ethnic households in the United States consisted of stable married couples. Today, however, although a growing number of African Americans and Latinos have "made it" to the middle class in terms of education, white-collar occupations, and suburban residence, and many others maintain stable working-class households, about one-fourth of African Americans and one-third of Latinos live in households with incomes below the poverty level, and a stubborn minority of racial and ethnic poor remain locked in decaying urban centers.

Structural models focus on how macroeconomic forces have produced high rates of family poverty among particular subgroups, resulting in the reliance on extended family networks and the proliferation of female-headed households. For example, since 1945, employment discrimination, residential segregation, the decline of manufacturing, and the flight of skilled service jobs to the suburbs have taken their toll on a man's ability to earn a "family wage" (Massey and Denton 1993). In addition, although women of color and poor European American women have always worked in the paid labor market, they have consistently earned less than their male counterparts. Therefore, whereas many working- and middle-class couples were able to stay afloat financially through the wife's increased labor force participation, women trapped in America's inner cities found only low-waged work, if any, often in illegally operated sweatshops. Without adequate and affordable child care, even these jobs were beyond the reach of many single mothers.

Macro-level economic shifts also greatly reduced the tax base and led to the decay of the urban infrastructure, with disastrous effects on schools and community institutions that minister to families (Wilson 1997). In addition, White flight from the cities shifted the balance of power in state legislatures, further reducing resources available to urban residents. The result is that, in cities across the nation, there are ghettos of poverty-stricken Blacks and Latinos, an "underclass" composed largely of women and their children.

In addition, the situation of Chicanos has been exacerbated by the recent passage of restrictive immigration legislation, reflecting widespread xenophobia inflamed by politicians, that makes it increasingly difficult for family members to move across borders and maximize shared resources (Roschelle 1995). Each of these structural trends in the economy and the polity has weakened *la familia,* attenuating its ability to care for its own, eroding the base of male power, and thrusting women into the dual roles of breadwinner and caregiver, often making them dependent upon public assistance in order to handle both responsibilities.

As the job situation for low-skilled urban labor deteriorates in a society increasingly geared to a management/information-based position in the global economy, relatively untrained young men, Anglo as well as Black and Latino, will be attracted to the immediate payoff of illegal activities, resulting in high rates of incarceration and homicide. Other men join the military or migrate in search of jobs, further straining marriages and reducing the pool of eligible partners for inner-city women. The result, for many women, will be the now-familiar pattern of out-of-wedlock births and mother-headed families, with limited prospects for escaping poverty. Although marriage and/or a job may lift a household over the income threshold, an illness, job loss, or desertion by a husband or boyfriend will plunge it below the poverty line, and today there is no federal guarantee of a last-resort safety net. Under such circumstances, more than ever before, sheer survival depends on pooling the resources of the kinship network and on forging a support system of friends and neighbors, based on norms of reciprocity. Unfortunately, recent research indicates that the extended kinship networks traditionally associated with low-income racial ethnic families are largely unavailable (see, e.g., Cochran et al. 1990; Williams 1990; Menjivar 1997; Roschelle 1997).

Although the structural perspective recognizes the influence of socioeconomic constraints on families, it tends to discount the influence of culture on family organization. Although family organization is certainly affected by economic forces, it is crucial to examine how culture affects the way different groups respond to their economic circumstances. In addition, this perspective overlooks gender, as if it had no relationship to the social structure. Even as they acknowledge the power of structural factors, such models tend to assume that male-dominated nuclear families are appropriate, and so merely deplore the inability of racial ethnic men to earn a wage sufficient to support a family. In this view, marriage becomes the primary mechanism for lifting women and children out of poverty, and middle-class Anglo individualism is again seen as the standard for socialization into the values of work and personal responsibility. The structural perspective is devoid of any analysis of pay inequity, gender segregation, sexual harassment, or other forms of gender discrimination in the labor market. The tendency among structural theorists to romanticize the nuclear family is extremely problematic, because gender relations in American families have rarely conformed to the White middle-class male-breadwinner nuclear family idealized in the 1950s and still enshrined under the rubric of "traditional family values" (Coontz 1992; Stacey 1996). In fact, contrary to this idealized image of the family, poor women have always worked for pay, in or outside the home, in a variety of labor markets, and typically for very low wages (Bose 1996).

Finally, the propensity of structural theorists to attribute racial and ethnic variations in family organization solely to socioeconomic factors is extremely problematic. Puerto Ricans and Chicanos have the added resource (or burden) of maintaining transnational ties, in part because of the importance of transmitting the Spanish language and other cultural values to their children. In these cases, culture becomes a form of resistance to hegemonic standards of family and gender that permit dominant groups to interpret "difference" as pathology. Most important, phrasing the debate in terms of "culture versus social structure" has impeded the development of a more sophisticated theoretical framework focusing on the intersection of race, gender, and class (Collins 1990; Baca Zinn 1990).

Integrative Model

According to the integrative model, any analysis of family organization must include an examination of the impact of gender as well as cultural and structural elements on family organization, because each affects the other. This is especially, but not exclusively, true of minority families, which have had to adapt to the impact of racial and ethnic stratification so deeply embedded in American institutions. Race and ethnicity account for cultural variation, but distinctive histories of immigration and discrimination in the United States are part of the social structural impact on families. For the three populations examined here, economic and educational opportunities have been, for the most part, severely limited, so that families are disproportionately working-class or marginal to the labor force, with fluctuations depending on the state of the economy. It is also important to note that although many White families have been negatively affected by the same structural trends, leading to stagnant wages, departing fathers, pregnant teenagers, and disintegrating kinship networks, the public discourse tends to be racialized, with dependency on welfare incorrectly perceived as largely a "vice" of women of color (Massey 1997). Historically, however, African American mothers have been excluded from a variety of welfare programs on the grounds that they were "employable" when their labor was needed as agricultural workers or domestic servants, especially in the South (Piven and Cloward 1993; Quadagno 1994), a role increasingly occupied today by undocumented Latinas (Chang 1994). The

1960s War on Poverty extended to Blacks many of the benefits originally designed to support White families, ultimately unleashing a backlash against the welfare system itself, as I will discuss later in this chapter.

Gender intersects both culture and social structure. Within each racial ethnic population, cultural forces have generated particular norms and expectations for women, especially with regard to sexuality and dominance/deference behaviors within the family. Structurally, immigration contingencies and job opportunities have been gendered, which in turn affects family structure and functioning. For example, as Chicanas become more educated and enter the wage labor force, their power within the family is enhanced (Segura 1994). Ironically, perhaps, economic exploitation in sweatshops and *maquiladoras* offers women a limited degree of independence from repressive familism, although many will still turn their earnings over to fathers or husbands. It is also logical to expect that employment and acculturation will lead to lowered fertility, thus reducing the responsibilities of child rearing. Conversely, it is the relative lack of employment opportunities for men that has had the greatest effect on family structure of African Americans and Puerto Ricans.

In addition, where much previous work on families has accorded the male breadwinner pride of place and assumed a basic harmony of interests of family members, it is increasingly obvious that we must take into account the dynamics of gender, of family as contested terrain, and of women's relationship to family and work in the broader context of class and race inequality. Hence the need to conceptualize race, class, and gender as intersecting hierarchies of resources and rewards. In its analysis of multiple axes of race, gender, and class oppression, the integrative model tends to produce a "tapestry composed of threads of many different hues [rather] than one woven in a single color" (Fraser and Nicholson 1990), or, I might add, one made up of several separate layers.

A number of Black feminist scholars have been at the forefront of this theoretical development (e.g., Dill 1983; Collins 1990; Baca Zinn 1990). The crux of their argument is the simultaneity of oppression in an interactive rather than an additive model: How are these systems linked in the lives of racial ethnic women? And how do these processes vary among different racial ethnic populations? With respect to African American families, for example, the interplay between culture and social structure is illustrated by the pattern of informal adoption of children by nonbiological "other mothers," a reflection of the value placed on cooperative child rearing in many African societies—a traditional cultural remedy for a very modern structural situation, and yet one that exclusively involves women as caregivers (Collins 1990). Afrocentric alternatives to middle-class American norms can be very helpful to those in adverse circumstances. Similarly, for Chicano families caught between cultural ideals and structural realities, the extended support network represents a traditional solution to a modern problem. In both cases, women are at the center of these survival strategies.

Yet mothering has always been contested terrain. Although mothering seems to flow naturally from the biological division into male and female for reproduction, and thus to be universal and invariant, what is defined as "good mothering" is a highly ideological, culturally specific, and historically constituted ideal (Glenn 1994; Hays 1996). By shifting attention to the experience of women of color as mothers, the dominant model of intensive, child-centered, emotional labor is "decentered" in a way that allows us to appreciate how mother-work varies by race and class. Both in the past and today, women of greater economic privilege have been able to pass along the more physically arduous tasks of child care to working-class women and women of color, who have often had to raise both their own and their employers' children in two physically separated and profoundly unequal circumstances (Wong 1994). Women who employ others to help care for their children become "mother managers," and their experiences of child rearing and family life differ greatly from those of women for whom putting bread on the table is a priority (MacDonald 1998; Nelson 1990). The work of mothering for many women of color has had to focus on securing the physical safety and economic survival of their children, yet this struggle, not always successful, is a central aspect of mother-work that is virtually ignored or considered inferior to the "sensitive mothering" idealized in the White middle class and extolled in the professional and popular literature (O'Reilly 1996).

Avoiding the idealization of poor mothers' struggles as superhuman heroism and recognizing that they often fail to keep their families afloat is an important corrective to overly optimistic cultural relativism, but it is equally important to recognize the strengths of "other mothering" (Collins 1990), extended family supports (Stack and Burton 1994), and community activism as a maternal responsibility (MacDonald 1998; Naples 1998). The myth of separate spheres not only divided the appropriate "places" of women and men, but assigned families a fantasy location as "havens" from the stresses of macroeconomic forces and the possibilities of public policy (Ferree 1990). Reconnecting families to social structures and societal institutions begins to move us beyond the false opposition between "structural" and "cultural" models, to a view of family variation as simultaneously historical, cultural, and structural.

Although this model has produced a more nuanced view of past adaptive patterns among racial ethnic families, can it help us understand the consequences of more recent changes in the objective condition of the very poor—namely, the continued deterioration of the urban core and increased immiseration of former welfare recipients and of the lowest quintile of wage earners? Several recent studies have documented a gradual erosion of the kin and nonkin networks that once served to buffer low-income families from stressful environmental events (Menjivar 1997; Roschelle 1997). In addition, other sources of support—local, state, and national assistance programs—have been either terminated or curtailed, leaving an extremely vulnerable population of poor women and their children, a situation that disproportionately affects racial ethnic families. Here, then, is another location where the intersection of race, gender, and class and the simultaneity of oppression on family organization can fruitfully be examined.

The Feminization of Poverty

Although it is generally believed that the American "War on Poverty" was a failure because roughly the same number today as in 1960—40 million people—live in households with incomes below the poverty threshold, quite the opposite is the case. Indeed, in its first decade, the War on Poverty succeeded in reducing the proportion of poor Americans by half, from 20 percent to 10 percent by 1975. These reductions were dramatic for the major targets for relief—the elderly (whose poverty rate today is lowest of any age group) and White working-class married couples. Since 1980, however, the proportion of poor has gradually risen and currently fluctuates around 14 percent. When the "near poor" (within 25 percent of the income threshold) are included, the "truly disadvantaged" population rises to close to 15 percent. But where the poor of 1960 were the kinds of people with whom White Americans could sympathize—indeed, some might even have been family members—the poor of today are very different and hence much less likely to evoke a sympathetic response from Euro-American policy makers: They are darker, more foreign culturally, nonmarried, and, above all, women.

Women have always been more likely to be poor than have men, but the degree to which they dominate the poverty population today is unprecedented (Pearce 1978). In addition, what distinguishes today's poor women from previous cohorts is that they are most likely to be nonmarried. Teenage mothers, single mothers and their daughters, divorced women of any age, and elderly widows swell the ranks of the poor. And although Whites make up the great majority of poor women, racial ethnic women are disproportionately found among the teenage mothers and single parents. Of special concern is the proportion of American children being raised in households below or just above the poverty line. Currently one-fifth of all children under age 6, and two-thirds of all Black children live in single-parent households—a "generation at risk" (Carnegie Corporation 1994). Overall, about 40 percent of Black and Latino children in the United States live in households with incomes below the poverty line (U.S. Bureau of the Census 1997b).

Clearly, living in a single-parent family increases the likelihood of impoverishment, particularly when that parent is the mother. Currently 51 percent of families headed by an African American woman and 60 percent of Latino families headed by a single mother are poor. Not only are woman-headed single-parent families most prone to poverty, but the proportion of such families has doubled, from about 4 percent in 1970 to 9 percent of all U.S. households (U.S. Bureau of the Census 1997a). However, there are vast racial and ethnic differences in the incidence of single-parent households. Among Asian Americans and non-Hispanic Whites, 6 percent of households have a single parent, compared with 34 percent for Blacks and 17 percent for Hispanics.

There are several social structural reasons for the increase in women-headed families. Impoverished communities have fewer potential stable wage-earning fathers than in the past. In addition, the relatively high rates of incarceration, homicide, mental and physical illness, and unemployment among minority men decrease the pool of potentially marriageable men (Lichter et al. 1992; Raley 1996). Military service and migration in search of jobs further drains this pool of eligibles in urban centers. Finally, some women choose not to marry the fathers of their children because, rather than providing financial stability, they are often a drain on already scarce resources.

In addition, for those who do marry, the likelihood of divorce and desertion is inversely related to income level. Because money is what couples are most likely to fight about, it follows that the fewer the

resources, the greater the conflict, and hence the less stable the relationship (Kurz 1995). In addition, poverty and location in an urban center
increase the risk of drug addiction and involvement in the drug trade,
with devastating effects on families. Men who share the culture's general expectation of dominance within the family may lash out in violence at wives who fail to display what the men consider to be appropriate deference. Both drugs and domestic assault are primary causes
of divorce, disproportionately affecting less affluent couples (Kurz
1995).

Similarly, because teenage sexual activity and risks of pregnancy are
linked to family income, girls from poor families are more likely to
become pregnant than are their middle-class counterparts. However,
birthrates have declined for all American women since 1970, especially
for African Americans, and teenagers of any race are less likely to
become mothers today than they were in the past. What currently
makes teenage mothers a "social problem" is their marital status. Given
that one-half of all American women in 1950 were married by age 20,
the typical teenage mother at that time was a married woman, an
honorable status. The issue today, therefore, is not teenage motherhood
but unmarried motherhood, and when the unmarried mother is Black
or Latina, the level of societal opprobrium rises. As Nathanson (1997)
notes: "Teenage pregnancy has become the most powerful and threatening symbol of welfare failure in the United States because for many
it represents out-of-control female sexuality and procreation and a
population explosion of undesirables. That is, teenage pregnancy has
become a capacious sink for misogyny and racism" (p. 5).

"Illegitimacy" has always been an issue of patriarchal rights, evoked
to control women's sexuality, yet the treatment of unmarried mothers
and the value of their offspring has also been racially variable. In the
1950s, for example, pregnant White teenagers were treated as emotionally disturbed and were pressured to give up their babies for adoption.
Conversely, Black pregnant teens were perceived as immoral, and there
was no market for their children (Solinger 1994). Responses to unmarried teen pregnancy remain racialized today. The modal response for
White pregnant teenagers is abortion; for Blacks, single motherhood;
and for Hispanics, a "shotgun" marriage (Plotnick 1992).

Paradoxically, the same politicians who excoriate the "immoral"
conduct of pregnant teenagers regularly vote to deny them access to
family planning services. Thus have young Black and Latina single
mothers become our newest living symbols of racial ethnic inferiority,

signified by their uncontrollable sexuality. Once again, the Protestant ethic is invoked, this time to demonize sexually active young women. "Good" people keep their impulses in check, whereas the morally flawed cannot. Hegemonic constructions of sexuality are made evident in that magnificent paean to the nation's values "America the Beautiful," in which we proclaim, "Confirm thy soul in self-control, thy liberty in law." To succumb to the temptations of the flesh, and then to expect law-abiding taxpayers to pay for such transgressive behavior, is simply unacceptable. However, even the discourse around sin is racialized. White pregnant teens are conceptualized as having fallen only temporarily, whereas Black teenage mothers are defined as incurably immoral (Solinger 1994). Redemption, however, can be sought through the discipline of work. In the curiously gendered, racialized, and class-biased canon of American moralism, then, both nonwork and sexual license evoke condemnation. Nonworking mothers are honored, provided they can remain attached to a man with an adequate income; and sexually active older men are admired, provided that they are White. Universally denigrated, however, is the nonmarried racial ethnic mother, whether she works outside the home (and leaves her children unsupervised in a dangerous neighborhood) or not (inculcating welfare dependency). To whom can she turn for help?

The likelihood of receiving support payments from noncustodial fathers is minimal, particularly given that many of these men are themselves impoverished. Women below the poverty level are less likely to be awarded support and to receive it than are women above the poverty level. White women receive more support than women of color, although few families receive adequate sums. Going to court to pursue a claim requires resources that are not available to many poor women, and those who succeed typically receive only a few thousand dollars a year (U.S. Bureau of the Census 1997c:389-90). Failure to establish paternity is a major problem in obtaining child support for these unmarried mothers (Garfinkel and McLanahan 1994), especially for Black women, who have higher rates of out-of-wedlock births, so that paternity is established in less than one-third of these cases (Ellwood 1988; Nichols-Casebolt and Garfinkel 1991).

Poor mothers of all races do, however, have sources of income other than child support. In fact, one in four was officially recorded as having some labor force experience in 1996, although only a small percentage were full-time, year-round workers (U.S. Bureau of the Census 1997b). In addition, a large but unrecorded number of women are active in the "underground economy," which includes both legal and illegal work, usually off-the-books, and often involves labor in semilegal sweat-shops. However earned, poor women's incomes are rarely sufficient to lift them or their families above the poverty threshold. Single mothers are further disadvantaged by the demands of child care, which limit the number of hours they can work. Even when a single mother with two children works 40 hours a week, 52 weeks a year, for the minimum wage, her income is well below the $12,600 a year deemed sufficient for a family of three in 1996. Making ends meet is a perpetual preoccupation for all low-income women, involving continually shifting combinations of work, welfare, and gifts from family and friends, all of which are rarely enough to pay all the bills (Edin and Lein 1997).

Furthermore, because racial ethnic women are typically employed in lower-paying jobs or earn less than similarly located White women, the family income gap remains even under conditions of full employment. In fact, it has been estimated that even if Black single mothers worked full-time year-round in the same proportions as their White counterparts, the childhood poverty rate for Black children would still be one-third higher than it is for White children (Lichter and Eggebeen 1994).

Given the problematic vicissitudes of dependency on a male bread-winner, many single mothers have come to depend on various welfare programs devised by federal and state governments to ameliorate the immediate effects of poverty. Between 1945 and 1996, a minimal support system was cobbled together, representing a societal obligation to its less fortunate members. Welfare was available to women whose incomes fell below the poverty level and who met other specified criteria. Eligibility for state and federal aid was considered an "entitlement." The great majority of recipients of all social welfare programs in the United States are women, but, in the spirit of the work ethic, they are categorized as either "deserving" or "undeserving." The elderly and infirm ("worthy widows") are deemed to have earned societal support and sympathy, whereas younger, nonworking, sexually active poor women ("welfare queens") are seen as having forfeited all claims to compassion (Hess 1983; Brush 1997). Only the latter are considered to be dependent on welfare.

Thus "welfare dependency" became a lightning rod for politicians and a public seeking to purify the body politic. Programs that benefited unemployed men or the elderly remained intact, while those for child-bearing nonmarried women, double violators of the Puritan norms that inform the American sense of good and evil, were all but eliminated. The concept of "dependency"—with its negative connotations of femaleness, weakness, and subordination—has shifted from a description of relationships to a stigmatized and gendered personal identity (Fraser and Gordon 1994). For women, being dependent on a husband is honorable, but being dependent on public assistance is a sign of moral imperfection. For men, dependence on an employer is responsible behavior, whereas dependence on women is insufferable.

The debate over welfare reform emphasized the character-building potential of work and the destructive nature of being dependent on welfare. The public perception of welfare recipients was shaped by the political discourse and concomitant media representations which focused almost exclusively on Black women. Subsequently, the image that emerged in the public mind was of a lazy Black woman who refused to work, had numerous children to obtain additional benefits, refused to marry to protect her welfare entitlements, and remained dependent on welfare for a lifetime. In the spirit of the culture of poverty perspective, these women were also demonized for passing their welfare dependency and their pathogenic morality on to their children. Of course the worst sin associated with this cycle of poverty was the perceived enormity of the cost to the American taxpayer.

That public perceptions about the nature of welfare recipients were only minimally supported by empirical evidence mattered little. The image of the "welfare queen" resonated to the racism, xenophobia, and sexual dread engraved in the American psyche. Glaringly absent from the discourse on welfare reform were the facts that most poor women do work, but for very low wages; that they have an average of one to two children; that only about 12 percent remain on welfare for five or more consecutive years; and that marital rates are unrelated to welfare recipiency (O'Hare 1996). Similarly, it was rarely reported that most teenage mothers live with relatives and that family structure has only a weak effect on the school performance of Black youngsters (Heiss 1996). Finally, completely missing from the discussion was any mention that the cost of Aid to Families with Dependent Children (AFDC) in 1996 was around 2 percent of the federal budget and 5 percent of state budgets—roughly the same as a handful of B-2 bombers (U.S. Bureau of the Census 1997c:336-37, 375). Yet Congress overwhelmingly passed and President Clinton signed, to the applause of a grateful public, legislation that effectively ended welfare entitlements. As we approach the twenty-first century, the words *entitlement* and *dependency* signify the unfair demands made upon the public to support "undeserving" and immoral single mothers.

The new system ends the role of the federal government in providing direct cash assistance to the poor in favor of giving block grants to state governments to design and operate their own programs. To ensure that the states will not be more generous than the federal government had been, Congress enacted additional constraints—for example, that no family can receive assistance for more than five years. States can enact even more restrictive term limits, and are further allowed to deny cash benefits to children born to poor teenagers, as well as to any woman who has additional children while receiving assistance (a "family cap"). Some states, such as California, have opted to include the most draconian elements of welfare reform, such as denying benefits *forever* to anyone who has one felony drug conviction after January 1998. In addition, legal immigrants who have not become citizens are deemed ineligible for many benefits, and future newcomers will be denied any form of assistance for a period of five years. These provisions are clearly designed to discourage further Latino and Asian immigration. In return for control over these monies, the states must make an attempt to place former recipients in paid employment, even if their earnings do not reach the levels formerly provided by AFDC. Because the savings from this sweeping legislation are quite small, about $10 billion a year out of a $1.5 trillion federal budget, we must conclude that the purpose was less to balance the budget than to reform the unworthy. All in all, the new welfare system is a pointedly punitive set of regulations, in which fears about class, race, ethnicity, and gender have been crystallized into public policy. Although many non-Hispanic White women will be affected, the burden of the new provisions will fall most heavily on racial ethnic single mothers and their children. Very little in the new system will have much impact on men of any income level, except some added effort by the states to collect child support payments.

Will work purify the "fallen"? Will the "family cap" bring a drop in fertility? Will the threat of the withdrawal of benefits lead poor women into marriage and reduce the incidence of divorce? At this writing, one year into the new world of workfare, most states report a striking decline in the number of welfare recipients, primarily through restrictive eligibility requirements rather than steady employment, although there has been some movement toward increased labor force participation, helped by a tight labor market. Fears about what might happen if there is an economic downturn have been overwhelmed by the euphoria of continued job growth, albeit at the lower skill levels.

As for the "family cap," it appears to have had negligible effect on fertility, at least in New Jersey, where the cap was enacted in 1992 with the explicit intention of discouraging further childbearing by poor women (Romberg 1997). The belief that poor women will stop having children if they lose $60-$100 a month in benefits is a logical extension of the assumption that they have children in order to increase welfare payments, although there is no evidence to support either expectation.

Moving mothers from welfare to workfare is not a simple process. Many welfare recipients lack the educational qualifications or specialized training necessary for well-paying jobs. Other women need child care and after-school care for their preschool and school-age children. Many women will be forced to work in the secondary labor market in low-paying jobs with no health insurance. The loss of medical coverage could have drastic consequences for poor women and their children. Fortunately, some states, primarily those with relatively low racial ethnic populations, such as Oregon and Wisconsin, have made a serious effort to meet these needs. Other states have simply assigned welfare recipients to public service jobs. In general, as a function of employer preference and educational attainment, it will be easier to place White women in jobs than Latinas and African American women.

But once the easy-to-place women have been dropped from the welfare rolls, what about those women who are left? What will become of racial ethnic women trapped in the inner-city ghettos? What about the women who are undereducated, or drug addicted, or victims of family violence and sexual abuse, or the mentally ill? Where will these women and their children go for help once their five-year grace period expires? It will be several years before these questions can be answered, but extrapolating from existing patterns, we can assume that the kin and nonkin support network will become more crucial than ever to the survival of single-parent families. We also know that these support systems have been eroding under the impact of deteriorating conditions in the inner cities and many rural areas: the breakdown of educational facilities, the flight of jobs, the collapse of community associations, the destructive effects of drug use and trafficking, and the daily unending insults of poverty (Roschelle 1997). One consequence of the loss of federal and community safety nets may be a dramatic increase in the number of homeless families.

The ultimate effects of social structure on the family structures of impoverished racial ethnic groups may be to destroy what little is left of a kin-based safety net. The consequences for millions of children are beyond imagination, but it is their mothers who are the focus of attention of the moral entrepreneurs of the conservative right. Ironically, the massive attempt to change adult behavior embedded in the new welfare system is just the sort of "social engineering" the same critics derided when it was advocated by liberal politicians to ameliorate the effects of poverty. When the pioneers of the second wave of feminism adopted the slogan "The personal is political," they were not primarily thinking of poor women, yet it is precisely the least powerful among us who are most vulnerable to politically motivated interventions in their personal lives. At the intersection of race, class, and gender in the lives of racial ethnic poor women, we find the age-old fear of women's sexuality, the need to control and punish those who violate social mores, and the triumphalism of White male norms for family structure.

What can we learn about family functioning in general from the experiences of those who have been most affected by the simultaneity of race, class, and gender oppression? In terms of race and class, outcomes are not so very different for the millions of White working-class families struggling with stagnant wages, divorce and desertion, physical abuse, and single motherhood. The emergent study of Whites as a race suggests that there is a growing White underclass on the urban fringes characterized by many of the same traits so vociferously condemned when displayed by African American and Latina women and men, but who have been thus far shielded from public outrage by their Whiteness (Roediger 1994; Frankenberg 1997). Class as well as race counts. Family breakdown among the employed and nonpoor tends to be perceived as a personal problem, a bit of bad luck, rather than as a sign of moral turpitude.

In terms of gender politics, debates about the future of the family in the United States are increasingly being framed in terms of restoring men to their rightful place as heads of household and of returning mothers to their home-based caregiving duties. Even in the unlikely event that large numbers of women are willing to leave the labor force for childbearing and homemaking, could American businesses afford to provide a family wage for most of their male employees? As for staying married, several states are now revising their statutes to make divorce more difficult, although it is not clear that commitment and faithfulness can be legislated.

In the absence of evidence to the contrary, it seems logical to assume that current trends will continue. The economic situations of most households will not improve greatly, and the gap between rich and poor will continue to increase. Divorce, separation, and nonmarital motherhood will continue to produce single-parent households in which women will struggle to survive. Public supports for family stability and maintenance will continue to erode, until, perhaps, we recognize that the village needed to raise a child is the very community to which we belong.

Note

1. For reasons of space and commensurability, I limit discussion in this chapter to African American, Chicano, and Puerto Rican subpopulations, although many of my conclusions also apply to Asian American families. In large part because Asian immigrants were perceived as a "model minority" in terms of commitment to dominant American values regarding family and work, at least in the postwar years, they have been spared much of the recent virulence directed toward Blacks and Latinos.

References

Alicea, Marixsa. 1997. " 'A Chambered Nautilus': The Contradictory Nature of Puerto Rican Women's Role in the Social Construction of a Transnational Community." *Gender & Society* 11:597-626.

Andrade, Sally J. 1982. "Family Roles of Hispanic Women: Stereotypes, Empirical Findings, and Implications For Research." Pp. 95-106 in *Work, Family and Health: Latina Women in Transition*, edited by Ruth E. Zambrana. New York: Hispanic Research Center, Fordham University.

Baca Zinn, Maxine. 1989. "Family, Race, and Poverty in the Eighties." *Signs* 14:856-74.

———. 1990. "Family, Feminism, and Race in America." *Gender & Society* 4:68-82.

Barrett, Michele. 1988. *Women's Oppression Today: The Marxist/Feminist Encounter*. Rev. ed. London: Verso.

Bean, Frank D. and Marta Tienda. 1987. *The Hispanic Population in the United States*. New York: Russell Sage Foundation.

Billingsley, Andrew. 1968. *Black Families in White America*. Englewood Cliffs, NJ: Prentice Hall.

———. 1992. *Climbing Jacob's Ladder: The Enduring Legacy of African American Families*. New York: Simon & Schuster.

Bose, Christine. 1996. "Race, Ethnicity, Class, and Gender: Women's Work in Turn of the Century U.S." Presented at the annual meeting of the American Sociological Association, August, New York.

Brush, Lisa D. 1997. "Worthy Widows, Welfare Cheats: Proper Womanhood in Expert Needs Talk about Single Mothers in the United States: 1900-1988." *Gender & Society* 11:720-46.

Carnegie Corporation. 1994. *Starting Points: Meeting the Needs of Our Youngest Children.* New York: Carnegie Corporation.

Chang, Grace. 1994. "Undocumented Latinas: The New 'Employable Mothers.' " Pp. 259-86 in *Mothering: Ideology, Experience, and Agency,* edited by Evelyn Nakano Glenn, Grace Chang, and Linda Rennie Forcey. New York: Routledge.

Cochran, Moncrieff, Mary Larner, David Riley, Lars Gunnarson, and Charles R. Henerson. 1990. *Extending Families: The Social Networks of Parents and Their Children.* Cambridge: Cambridge University Press.

Collins, Patricia Hill. 1990. *Black Feminist Thought: Knowledge, Consciousness, and the Politics of Empowerment.* New York: Routledge.

Comas-Diaz, Lillian. 1987. "Feminist Therapy with Mainland Puerto Rican Women." *Psychology of Women Quarterly* 11:461-74.

Coontz, Stephanie. 1992. *The Way We Never Were: American Families and the Nostalgia Trap.* New York: Basic Books.

Del Castillo, Richard Griswold. 1984. *La Familia: Chicano Families in the Urban Southwest, 1848-the Present.* Notre Dame, IN: University of Notre Dame Press.

Diaz-Guerrero, Rogelio. 1975. *Psychology of the Mexican: Culture and Personality.* Austin: University of Texas Press.

Dill, Bonnie Thornton. 1983. "Race, Class and Gender: Prospects for an All Inclusive Sisterhood." *Feminist Studies* 9:131-50.

———. 1997. "Review Essay." *Contemporary Sociology* 26:418-21.

Edin, Kathryn and Laura Lein. 1997. *Making Ends Meet: How Single Mothers Survive Welfare and Low Wage Work.* New York: Russell Sage Foundation.

Ellwood, Daniel T. 1988. *Poor Support: Poverty in the American Family.* New York: Basic Books.

Ferree, Myra Marx. 1990. "Beyond Separate Spheres: Feminism and Family Research." *Journal of Marriage and the Family* 52: 866-84.

Fitzpatrick, Joseph P. 1981. "The Puerto Rican Family." Pp. 189-214 in *Ethnic Families in America: Patterns and Variations,* edited by Charles H. Mindel and Robert W. Haberstein. New York: Elsevier.

Frankenberg, Ruth, ed. 1997. *Displacing Whiteness: Essays in Social and Cultural Criticism.* Durham, NC: Duke University Press.

Fraser, Nancy and Linda Gordon. 1994. "A Genealogy of *Dependency*: Tracing a Keyword of the U.S. Welfare State." *Signs* 19:309-36.

Fraser, Nancy and Linda J. Nicholson. 1990. "Social Criticism without Philosophy: An Encounter between Feminism and Postmodernism." Pp. 19-38 in *Feminism/Postmodernism*, edited by Linda J. Nicholson. New York: Routledge.

Frazier, E. Franklin. 1932. *The Negro Family in Chicago*. Chicago: University of Chicago Press.

———. 1939. *The Negro Family in the United States*. Chicago: University of Chicago Press.

Garfinkel, Irwin and Sara S. McLanahan. 1994. "Single-Mother Families and Government Policy." Pp. 205-25 in *Confronting Poverty: Prescriptions for Change*, edited by Sheldon Danziger, Gary D. Sandefur, and Daniel H. Weinberg. Cambridge, MA: Harvard University Press.

Glenn, Evelyn Nakano. 1994. "Social Constructions of Mothering: A Thematic Overview." Pp. 1-32 in *Mothering: Ideology, Experience, and Agency*, edited by Evelyn Nakano Glenn, Grace Chang, and Linda Rennie Forcey. New York: Routledge.

Gutman, Herbert G. 1976. *The Black Family in Slavery and Freedom: 1750-1925*. New York: Vintage.

Hawkes, Glen R. and Mina Taylor. 1975. "Power Structure in Mexican and Mexican-American Farm Labor Families." *Journal of Marriage and the Family* 37:807-11.

Hays, Sharon. 1996. *The Cultural Contradictions of Motherhood*. New Haven, CT: Yale University Press.

Heiss, Jerold. 1996. "Effects of African American Family Structure on School Attitudes and Performance." *Social Problems* 43:246-67.

Hess, Beth B. 1983. "The New Faces of Poverty." *American Demographics* (May):26-31.

Jarrett, Robin L. 1994. "Living Poor: Family Life among Single Parent, African American Women." *Social Problems* 41:30-43.

Kaplan, Elaine Bell. 1997. *Not Our Kind of Girl: Unraveling the Myths of Teenage Black Motherhood*. Berkeley: University of California Press.

Kurz, Demie. 1995. *For Richer, for Poorer: Mothers Confront Divorce*. New York: Routledge.

Lewis, Oscar. 1966. *La Vida: A Puerto Rican Family in the Culture of Poverty-San Juan, New York*. New York: Random House.

Lichter, Daniel T. and David J. Eggebeen. 1994. "The Effect of Parental Employment on Child Poverty." *Journal of Marriage and the Family* 56:633-45.

Lichter, Daniel T., Diane K. McLaughlin, George Kephart, and David T. Landry. 1992. "Race and Retreat from Marriage." *American Sociological Review* 57:781-99.

MacDonald, Cameron. 1998. "Manufacturing Motherhood: The Shadow Work of Nannies and Au Pairs." *Qualitative Sociology* 2:25-54.

Massey, Douglas S. 1997. "Review Essay." *Contemporary Sociology* 26:416-18.

Massey, Douglas S. and Nancy A. Denton. 1993. *American Apartheid: Segregation and the Making of the Underclass.* Cambridge, MA: Harvard University Press.

Menjivar, Cecilia. 1997. "Immigrant Kinship Networks and the Impact of the Receiving Context: Salvadorans in San Francisco in the Early 1990's." *Social Problems* 44: 104-23.

Mirande, Alfredo. 1985. *The Chicano Experience: An Alternative Perspective.* Notre Dame, IN: University of Notre Dame Press.

Mirande, Alfredo and Evangelina Enriquez. 1979. *La Chicana: The Mexican American Woman.* Chicago: University of Chicago Press.

Moynihan, Daniel Patrick. 1965. *The Negro Family: The Case for National Action.* Washington, DC: U.S. Department of Labor, Office of Policy Planning and Research.

Murillo, N. 1971. "The Mexican American Family." Pp. 97-108 in *Chicanos: Social and Psychological Perspectives,* edited by N. N. Wagner and M. J. Haug. St. Louis, MO: C. V. Mosby.

Naples, Nancy. 1998. *Grassroots Warriors: Women, Community Workers, and the War on Poverty.* New York: Routledge.

Nathanson, Constance. 1997. "Review of *Dubious Conceptions: The Politics of Teenage Motherhood* by Kristen Luker." *Contemporary Sociology* 26:1-5.

Nelson, Margaret K. 1990. *Negotiated Care: The Experience of Family Day Care Providers.* Philadelphia: Temple University Press.

Nichols-Casebolt, Ann and Irwin Garfinkel. 1991. "Trends in Paternity Adjudications and Child Support Awards." *Social Science Quarterly* 73:83-97.

O'Hare, William. 1996. "U.S. Poverty Myths Explored." *Population Today* 24:1-2.

O'Reilly, Andrea. 1996. " 'Ain't That Love?': Antiracism and Racial Constructions of Motherhood." In *Everyday Acts against Racism,* edited by Maureen T. Reddy. Seattle, WA: Seal.

Padilla, Felix. 1987. *Puerto Rican Chicago.* Notre Dame, IN: University of Notre Dame Press.

Pearce, Diana M. 1978. "On the Edge: Marginal Women Workers and Employment Policy." Pp. 197-210 in *Ingredients for Women's Employment Policy,* edited by Christine Bose and Glenna Spitze. Albany: State University of New York Press.

Piven, Frances Fox and Richard A. Cloward. 1993. *Regulating the Poor: The Functions of Public Welfare*. New York: Vintage.

Plotnick, Robert D. 1992. "The Effects of Attitudes on Teenage Premarital Pregnancy and Its Resolution." *American Sociological Review* 57:800-811.

Quadagno, Jill. 1994. *The Color of Welfare: How Racism Undermined the War on Poverty*. Oxford: Oxford University Press.

Raley, R. Kelly. 1996. "Cohabitation, Marriageable Men, and Racial Differences in Marriage." *American Sociological Review* 61: 973-83.

Roediger, David R. 1994. *Toward the Abolition of Whiteness: Essays on Race, Politics, and the Working Class*. New York: Verso.

Romberg, Jon. 1997. "The Family Cap and Other Myths." *New York Times*, September 28, sec. 13NJ, p. 15.

Roschelle, Anne R. 1995. "The Political Mileage of Racism." *Peace Review* 7:443-47.

———. 1997. *No More Kin: Exploring Race, Class, and Gender in Family Networks*. Thousand Oaks, CA: Sage.

Ryan, William. 1972. *Blaming the Victim*. New York: Vintage.

Segura, Denise A. 1994. "Working at Motherhood: Chicana and Mexican Immigrant Mothers and Employment." Pp. 211-33 in *Mothering: Ideology, Experience, and Agency*, edited by Evelyn Nakano Glenn, Grace Chang, and Linda Rennie Forcey. New York: Routledge.

Segura, Denise A. and Adela de la Torre. 1997. "*La Sufrida*: Contradictions of Acculturation and Gender in Latina Health." In *Revisioning Women, Health, and Healing: Feminist, Cultural, and Technoscience Perspectives*, edited by Adele Clarke and Virginia Oleson. New York: Routledge.

Solinger, Rickie. 1994. "Race and Value: Black and White Illegitimate Babies, 1945-1965." Pp. 287-310 in *Mothering: Ideology, Experience, and Agency*, edited by Evelyn Nakano Glenn, Grace Chang, and Linda Rennie Forcey. New York, Routledge.

Stacey, Judith. 1996. *In the Name of the Family: Rethinking Family Values in the Postmodern Age*. Boston: Beacon.

Stack, Carol B. 1974. *All Our Kin: Strategies for Survival in a Black Community*. New York: Harper Colophon.

Stack, Carol B. and Linda M. Burton. 1994. "Kinscripts: Reflections on Family, Generation, and Culture." Pp. 33-44 in *Mothering: Ideology, Experience, and Agency*, edited by Evelyn Nakano Glenn, Grace Chang, and Linda Rennie Forcey. New York: Routledge.

Tolnay, Stewart E. 1997. "The Great Migration and Changes in the Northern Black Family, 1940-1990." *Social Forces* 75: 213-38.

Toro-Morn, Maura I. 1994. "The Family and Work Experiences of Puerto Rican Women Migrants in Chicago." Pp. 277-94 in *Resiliency in Ethnic*

Minority Families: Native and Immigrant American Families, edited by Hamilton I. McCubbin, Elizabeth A. Thompson, Anne I. Thompson, and Julie E. Fromer. Madison: University of Wisconsin Press.

———. 1995. "Gender, Class, Family, and Migration." *Gender & Society* 9:712-26.

U.S. Bureau of the Census. 1997a. *The Black Population of the United States: March 1996.* Current Population Reports P20-498, June. Washington, DC: Government Printing Office.

U.S. Bureau of the Census. 1997b. *Poverty in the United States: 1996.* Current Population Reports P60-198, September. Washington, DC: Government Printing Office.

U.S. Bureau of the Census. 1997c. *Statistical Abstract of the United States: 1997.* Washington, DC: Government Printing Office.

Williams, Norma. 1990. *The Mexican American Family: Tradition and Change.* New York: General Hall.

Wilson, William Julius. 1991. "Studying Inner-City Social Dislocations: The Challenge of Public Agenda Research" (1990 Presidential Address). *American Sociological Review* 56:1-14.

———. 1997. *When Work Disappears: The World of the New Urban Poor.* New York: Alfred A. Knopf.

Wong, Sau-ling C. 1994. "Diverted Mothering: Representations of Caregivers of Color in the Age of 'Multiculturalism.' " Pp. 67-95 in *Mothering: Ideology, Experience, and Agency,* edited by Evelyn Nakano Glenn, Grace Chang, and Linda Rennie Forcey. New York: Routledge.

Ybarra, Lea. 1983. "Empirical and Theoretical Developments in the Study of Chicano Families." Pp. 91-110 in *The State of Chicano Research on Family, Labor, and Migration: Proceedings of the First Stanford Symposium on Chicano Research and Public Policy,* edited by Armando Valdez and Albert Camarillo. Stanford, CA: Stanford Center for Chicano Research.

CHAPTER 12

Just Do . . . What?

Sport, Bodies, Gender

SHARI L. DWORKIN
MICHAEL A. MESSNER

Sport has proven to be one of the key institutional sites for the study of the social construction of gender. Organized sport, as we now know it, was created in the late nineteenth and early twentieth centuries by and for White middle-class men to bolster a sagging ideology of "natural superiority" over women and over race- and class-subordinated groups of men (Crosset 1990; Kimmel 1990; McKay 1991; Messner 1988; Whitson 1990). Thus, although sport was seemingly based in natural physical endowments, it was socially constructed out of the gender, race, and class-based stratification systems of Europe and the United States. Although some women have actively participated in organized sport, until very recently most girls and women have been largely excluded from participation. Those few who did participate were stereotyped as sexual and gender deviants, and were ghettoized in ways that did not challenge the doctrine of male superiority (Cahn 1994; Cayleff 1995; Lenskyj 1986). Although the segregation of men of color was challenged by concepts of fairness and civil rights for all men, combating the segregation of White women and women of color to feminized sport niches has been complicated by deeply ingrained beliefs in the muscular superiority of all men compared to all women.

It took a gender analysis of sports ideologies and commercialization to unravel the ways sport is organized to sell masculinity to men. Today, that same gender analysis is being applied to the deconstruction of the selling of a shifting imagery of physical femininity in women athletes.

Note, however, the persistence of the gender segregation so evident in organized sport from the beginning—in nearly all cases, men's and women's sports are carefully segregated, and men's sports are still assumed to be mostly for male spectators. Women's sports, however, to be successful, have to be attractive to men as well as women viewers. As a result, notions of conventional masculinity and femininity persist. Sport, as a cultural and commercial production, constructs and markets gender; besides making money, making gender may be sport's chief function.

It may appear ironic that an institution that has continued to contribute to the reconstitution of hegemonic masculinity throughout the twentieth century has become a key site for the development of a critical feminist scholarship on gender (e.g., Birrell 1988; Birrell and Cole 1994; Bryson 1987; Hall 1988, 1996; Hargreaves 1994; Messner and Sabo 1990; Theberge 1981). In fact, it is the very centrality of the body in sport practice and ideology that provides an opportunity to examine critically and illuminate the social construction of gender (Connell 1987; Lorber 1994). Feminist insights into the social construction of gendered and sexualized bodies have illuminated the lives of female and male body-builders (Bolin 1992a; Klein 1993), professional women golfers (Crosset 1995), an Australian "Iron Man" (Connell 1990), a professional trans-sexual tennis player (Birrell and Cole 1990), the "doing of gender" by men and women cheerleaders (Davis 1990), the "ironic" masculinity of gay male athletes (Pronger 1990), the construction of Black masculinities in sport (Majors 1990), the sports media's "denial of power" to women athletes (Duncan and Hasbrook 1988), the exploitation of older women's labor to support men's sport activities (Boyle and McKay 1995), the sexualization of women in the *Sports Illustrated* "swimsuit issue" (Davis 1997), and the possibilities of empowerment for women through sport participation (Theberge 1987).

Because of the centrality of gender in such studies, sport has become a fascinating subfield in which to revisit perennial feminist questions of structure and agency, as well as to explore more recent debates over embodiment, identity, and power. We begin this chapter with an examination of recent research on men and sport to reflect on the limitations of employing an analytic gender lens that ignores or marginalizes the centrality of race and class. Then we discuss the extent to which bodily agency by athletic women represents resistance to oppression by exploring three contexts: the Title IX struggle for sex equity in high school and college sports, the recent championing of women's athletic participation by corporate liberals such as Nike, and the contradictory meanings surrounding muscular female bodies.

Athletic Men: Paying the Price

When we disentangle the historical and contemporary relationship between sport and men's power, we must recognize the distinction between sport as a cultural practice that constructs dominant belief systems and the individual experience of sport as an athletic career. Clearly, for at least the past 100 years, the dominant cultural meanings surrounding athletic masculinity have served mostly to stabilize hegemonic masculinity in the face of challenges by women, working-class men, men of color, and immigrants (Crosset 1990; Kimmel 1990). However, the experience of male athletes is often fraught with contradiction and paradox. Although many male athletes may dream of being the next Michael Jordan, very few ever actually make a living playing sports (Messner 1992). Even for extremely successful male athletes, the rigor of attaining and maintaining athletic stardom often comes at the cost of emotional and interpersonal development (Connell 1990). And although athletic masculinity symbolizes an image of physical health and sexual virility, athletes commonly develop alienated relationships with their bodies, learning to relate to them like machines, tools, or even weapons to be "used up" to get a job done. As a result, many athletes and former athletes suffer from permanent injuries, poor health, and low life expectancy (Sabo 1994; White, Young, and McTeer 1995). In particular, it is disproportionately young men from poor socioeconomic and racial/ethnic backgrounds who pay these costs.

To put it simply, young men from race- or class-subordinated backgrounds disproportionately seek status, respect, empowerment, and upward mobility through athletic careers. Most of them do not make it to the mythical "top," but this majority is mostly invisible to the general public. Instead, those very few who do make it into the limelight—especially those in sports like football or boxing, that reward the most extreme possibilities of large, powerful, and violent male bodies—serve as public symbols of exemplary masculinity, with whom all men can identify *as men*, as separate and superior to women (Messner 1988, 1992). While serving to differentiate "men" from "women" symbolically, top male athletes—especially African American men in violent sports—are simultaneously available to be used by men as cultural symbols of differences among them. African American male athletes—

for instance, boxer Mike Tyson—have become icons of an atavistic masculinity, in comparison to whom White middle-class men can construct themselves as kinder, gentler "new men" (Messner 1993a). This imagery of Black men includes a package of sexual potency and muscular power wrapped in danger. Just as African American males have been used in the past to symbolize fears of a "primitive" sexuality unleashed (Hoch 1979; Davis 1981), Americans are increasingly obsessed with documenting the sexual misbehaviors of Black male athletes (Messner 1993b).

Men's sport, then, constructs masculinities in complex and contradictory ways. At a time in history when physical strength is of less and less practical significance in workplaces, especially in the professional and managerial jobs of most White, college-educated men, African American, poor, and working-class men have increasingly "taken over" the sports to which they have access. But having played sports is of little or no practical use to most of these young men once their athletic careers have ended. Athletic skills rarely transfer over into nonsports careers. The significance of successful African American male athletes in the current gender order is *not* that they challenge dominant social meanings or power relations. To the contrary, they serve to stabilize ideas of natural difference and hierarchy between women and men *and* among men of different social classes and races.

We can draw two conclusions from this brief discussion of men's sports. First, although we can see African American men's struggles to achieve success and respect through sport as a collective response to class and racial constraints, this agency operates largely to *reproduce*—rather than to *resist* or challenge—current race, class, and gender relations of power. Put another way, Black men's agency in sport is a key element in the current hegemony of the race, class, and gender order. As in the past, men at the bottom of the stratification system achieve limited upward mobility by providing entertainment and vicarious thrills for those more advantaged. Second, we can see by looking at men's sports that *simply* employing a "gender lens" to analyze sport critically is limiting, even dangerous. The current literature supports the claim that men's sport does continue to empower "men," but for the most part, it is not the men who are doing the playing who are being empowered. Clearly, when we speak of "sport and empowerment" for men, we need to ask, Which men? These two points—that "agency" is not necessarily synonymous with "resistance," and that we need to be very cautious about employing a simplistic gender lens to speak categorically about "men and sport"—will inform our examination of women's current movement into sports.

Sex Equity for "Women in Sport"

Since the passage of Title IX of the Education Act Amendments, adopted by Congress in 1972, girls' and women's sports in the United States have changed in dramatic, but paradoxical, ways. On the one hand, there is no denying the rapid movement toward equity in the number of female participants and programs for women and girls (Cahn 1994; Carpenter 1993). For example, in 1971, only 294,015 U.S. girls, compared with 3,666,917 boys, participated in interscholastic high school sports. By 1996, the number of girls participating had risen to 2,240,000, compared with 3,554,429 boys (Acosta and Carpenter 1996). Opportunities for women to play intercollegiate sports have also continued to rise. In 1978, right before the date for mandatory compliance with Title IX, colleges and universities offered an average of 5.61 women's sports per school. By 1988, the average had risen to 7.31 sports per school, and it continued to rise to an all-time high of 7.53 in 1996 (Acosta and Carpenter 1996). These numerical increases in opportunities to participate in such a masculine-structured institution as school sports prove the effectiveness of organizing politically and legally around the concept "woman." Indeed, the relative success of this post-Title IX liberal strategy of gender equity in sport was premised on the deployment of separate "male" and "female" sports.

On the one hand, at least within the confines of liberalism, a "strategic essentialism" that successfully deploys the category "woman" can result in moves toward greater distributive justice. And in this case, we can see that there are benefits that result when girls' and women's participation in sports increases. Research suggests that girls who play interscholastic sports tend to have higher self-esteem and greater self-confidence, more positive feelings about body image, lower school dropout rates, and lower levels of unwanted pregnancies than girls who do not play sports (Sabo and Women's Sports Foundation 1988; President's Council on Physical Fitness and Sports 1997). And it is likely that boys who play with, or watch, competent and powerful female athletes will develop a broader and more respectful view of women's physical capabilities than did earlier generations of boys and men (Messner and Sabo 1994).

Yet, Title IX has not yet yielded anything close to equity for girls and women within sports—more boys and men still play sports; they still have far more opportunities, from the peewee level through professional sports; and girls and women often have to struggle for access to uniforms, travel money, practice facilities, and scholarships that boys and men routinely take for granted (Lopiano 1993; Women's Sports Foundation 1997). But the dramatic movement of girls and women into sport—and the continued legal basis for challenges to inequities that are provided by Title IX precedents—makes sport an impressive example of a previously almost entirely masculine terrain that is now gender contested. The very existence of skilled and strong women athletes demanding recognition and equal access to resources is a destabilizing tendency in the current gender order.

On the other hand, there are obvious limits in the liberal quest for gender equity in sport. First, as the popularity, opportunities, and funding for women's sports have risen, the leadership positions have markedly shifted away from women to men. For example, in 1972 more than 90 percent of women's college teams had women coaches. By 1996, the proportion had dropped to 47.7 percent. Similarly, in 1972 more than 90 percent of women's college programs were headed by women athletic directors. By 1996, the figure had dropped to 18.5 percent (Acosta and Carpenter 1996). Radical critics of sport have argued that this shift toward men's control of girl and women athletes is but one indicator of the limits and dangers of a gender-blind model of equity that uncritically adopts the men's "military model" of sport (Nelson 1991). To be sure, this shift to men coaches was heroically resisted throughout the 1970s by many women coaches and athletic administrators behind the banner of the Association for Intercollegiate Athletics for Women (AIAW). The AIAW attempted to defend the idea that women's sport should be controlled by women, and should reflect the values of health, cooperation, and participation, rather than the values of cutthroat competition and star systems that dominated men's sports. But as the economic power of the National Collegiate Athletic Association (NCAA) (and its linkages with television) rapidly brought women's college sports under its aegis, "the AIAW faded quickly from the scene, closing down operations in 1982 and conceding final defeat in 1984 when it lost an antitrust suit against the NCAA" (Cahn 1994:257). Locally, most women's athletic departments were folded into male athletic departments, and the hiring of coaches for women's sports was placed in the hands of male athletic directors.

As women's sports has become controlled by men, it increasingly reflects the most valued characteristics of men's sports: "hierarchy, competitiveness and aggression" (Hall 1996:91). In the most "feminine" sports, men coaches are simultaneously demanding the aggressiveness of adult men athletes and the submissiveness of little girls—a most complex gender message! A poignant example of these dangers can be seen in women's gymnastics and ice-skating, where very young girls, typically coached mostly by men coaches who are often abusive, learn to practice with painful injuries and often develop severe eating disorders in order to keep their bodies "small, thin and prepubescent" (Ryan 1995:103).

Most people who followed media coverage of the 1996 Olympics still hold the image in their minds of a grinning coach Bela Karolyi cradling gymnast Kerri Strug in his arms, her leg in a brace, after she had courageously vaulted with a painful injury, and thus appeared to secure a gold medal for the U.S. team. Strug's deed resulted in a great deal of flag-waving and in numerous endorsement contracts for her, and it was lauded by the media as an act of bravery that symbolized the "arrival" of women's sports. But it can also be seen as an example of the limits and contradictions of the uncritical adoption of the dominant values of men's sports. The image of Karolyi's cradling the much smaller body of the young, injured Strug, so often replayed on television and prominently positioned in print coverage of the Olympics, illustrates two important points. First, the sports media today continue to frame women athletes ambivalently, symbolically denying them their power (Duncan and Hasbrook 1988). After all, it was not Strug's moment of triumphant power as she exploded off the vault, or even her difficult and painful landing on her injured leg that the media etched in all of our memories; instead, it was the aftermath of the actual athletic moment that the media seized upon. Here, an infantilized and vulnerable Strug appeared anything but powerful. It is unlikely that the sports media would frame a male athlete in a similar situation the same way. The second point that this popular image illustrates is that today, young girl and women athletes' bodies are in the literal and symbolic hands of men coaches. As Ryan's powerful book *Little Girls in Pretty Boxes* (1995) illustrates, Karolyi is seen by many as the most egregious in a system of men coaches who systematically submit aspiring young girl athletes to verbal, psychological, and physical abuse. The physical and psychological carnage that results from this professionalized system, whose main aim is to produce gold medalists for the United States every four years, is staggering. Recent discussions of exploitation, sexual harassment, and sexual abuse of young female athletes—especially those competing in the more "feminine" sports, such as swimming and gymnastics—by male coaches adds another frightening dimension to this picture (Nelson 1994; Tomlinson and Yorganci 1997).

In short, as girls and women push for equity in sport, they are moving—often uncritically—into a hierarchical system that has as its main goal to produce winners, champions, and profits. Although increased participation for girls and women apparently has its benefits at the lower levels, as the incentives mount for girl and women athletes to professionalize, they increasingly face many of the same limitations and dangers (in addition to some others, such as sexual harassment and rape) as those experienced by highly competitive men.

"If You Let Me Play . . ."

In recent years, corporate America has begun to awaken to the vast and lucrative potential markets that might be developed within and subsidiary to women's sports. The 1996 Olympics and its aftermath saw unprecedented amounts of money spent on television and magazine ads featuring women athletes. Two new professional women's basketball leagues were begun in 1996 and 1997, and one of them, the Women's National Basketball Association (WNBA), began with a substantial television contract—a factor that today is the best predictor of financial success in pro sports. Although many see these developments as merely the next step in the successful accomplishment of gender equity for women in sport, we argue that the increasingly corporate context of this trend calls for special critical scrutiny.

In recent years, athletic footwear advertisements by Reebok and Nike have exemplified the ways that corporations have made themselves champions of women's athletic participation. In the early 1990s, Reebok was first to seize the lion's share of the female athletic shoe market. But by the mid-1990s, Nike had made great gains with a highly successful advertising campaign that positioned the corporation as the champion of girls' and women's rights inside and outside of sports. One influential TV spot included images of athletically active girls and women, with the voice-over saying things like, "If you let me play, I'll be less likely to drop out of school," and "If you let me play, I'll be better able to say no to unwanted sexual activity." These ads made use of the research findings from such organizations as the Women's Sports Foundation, documenting the positive, healthy, and empowering aspects of athletic participation for girls. Couching this information in the language of individual empowerment, Nike sold it to girls and women in the form of athletic shoes.

To be sure, the power of these commercials lies partly in the fact that they almost never mentioned shoes or even the Nike name. The message is that individual girls will be happier, healthier, and more in charge of their lives if we "let them play." The Nike "swoosh" logo is subtly displayed in the corner of the ads so that the viewer knows who is the source of these liberating ideas. It is through this kind of campaign that Nike has positioned itself as what Cole and Hribar (1995) call a "celebrity feminist," a corporate liberal entity that has successfully appropriated and co-opted the language of individual empowerment underlying the dominant discourse of opportunity for girls and women in sports. Aspiring athletes are then encouraged by slick advertising campaigns to identify their own individual empowerment—in essence, *their relationship to feminism*—with that of the corporate entity that acts as a celebrity feminist. If "feminist identity" can be displayed most readily through the wearing of the Nike logo on shoes and other athletic apparel, then displaying the Nike "swoosh" on one's body becomes a statement to the world that one is an independent, empowered individual—a successful young woman of the nineties.

There are fundamental limitations to this kind of "empowerment." If radical feminists are correct in claiming that patriarchy reproduces itself largely through men's ability to dominate and exploit women's bodies, we might suggest a corollary: Corporations have found peace and profit with liberal feminism by co-opting a genuine quest by women for bodily agency and empowerment and channeling it toward a goal of physical achievement severely limited by its consumerist context. The kind of collective women's agency that emphasizes the building of institutions such as rape crisis centers, domestic violence shelters, and community women's athletic leagues is a *resistant agency* through which women have empowered themselves to fight against and change the institutions that oppress them. In contrast, individual women's agency expressed as identification with corporate consumerism is a *reproductive agency* that firmly situates women's actions and bodies within the structural gender order that oppresses them.

In addition, Nike's commitment to women's liberation is contradicted by its own corporate practices. In 1996, when it posted its largest profits, and its CEO Phillip Knight's stock was estimated to be worth $5 billion, the mostly women Indonesian workers who manufactured the shoes were paid about $2.25 a day. Workers who attempted to organize for higher pay and better working conditions were fired (Take Action for Girls 1996). Meanwhile, U.S. women's eager consumption of corporate celebrity feminism makes it almost impossible for them to see, much less to act upon, the exploitation of women workers halfway around the globe. In fact, it is likely that the kinds of individual "empowerment" that can be purchased through consumerism seriously reduce women's abilities even to identify their collective interests in changing institutions here within the United States.

Liberal feminism in sport has come full circle: a universalized concept of "women" was strategically deployed to push—with some impressive but limited success—for equal opportunities for women in sport. As these successes mounted, a key ideological support for hegemonic masculinity—the naturalized equation of male bodies with athletic ability and physical strength—was destabilized. But corporations have recently seized upon the individualist impulse of female empowerment that underlies liberal feminism, and have sold it back to women as an ideology and bodily practice that largely precludes any actual mobilizing around the collective concept of "women." Individual women are now implored by Nike to "Just do it"—just like the men "do it." Undoubtedly, many women strongly approve of, and feel good about, the Nike ads. But Nike's individualized and depoliticized "feminism" ignores how individuals who "do it" with Nike are implicated in an international system of racial, gender, and class exploitation of women workers in less developed nations.

Just as we argued in our discussion of the limits of sports for raising the status of working-class and African American men, here, too, gender analysis alone is not enough. It is not just muscular, or athletic, or "fit" bodies that must be considered in women's liberation—it is also laboring bodies as well. In fact, as we will argue next, a danger in contemporary reductionist understandings of empowerment as being synonymous with the development of one's body is that concentrating on toning muscles can easily transfer energies—especially those of women privileged by class and race—away from collective organizing to change institutions that disadvantage all women, but especially those who are poor, working-class, and racially disadvantaged.

Women and Muscles

In addition to the ever-increasing numbers of women who compete in high school and college sport, more and more women today engage in fitness activities, lift weights, and enjoy the power of carrying musculature. Much of the new emphasis and popularity of fitness and muscular development among women has emerged outside of organized sport. New bodily ideals can be said to have broadened from thin and slim to tight and toned, with an "allowance" for "substantial weight and bulk" (Bordo 1993:191). By some standards, today's more muscular woman can be viewed as embodying agency, power, and independence in a way that exemplifies resistance to patriarchal ideals. However, just as within sport, women's bodily agency in fitness activities can be contradictory. Is this bodily agency resistant and/or empowering, or is the fit, muscled ideal simply the latest bodily requirement for women, a form of "self-surveillance and obedience" in service to patriarchal capitalism (Bartky 1988)?

Some feminists argue that when women exercise their agency to develop bodily mobility and muscular power, these activities are self-affirming for women and antithetical to patriarchal definitions of women as passive, docile, and weak (MacKinnon 1987; Nelson 1991; Young 1990). By fighting for access to participation in sport and fitness, women have created an empowering arena where the meaning of gender is being contested and renegotiated, and where active rejections of dominant notions of femininity may be forged (e.g., Bolin 1992b; Gilroy 1989; Guthrie and Castelnuovo 1992; Kane and Lenskyj 1998; Lenskyj 1987; McDermott 1996; Theberge 1987). Other feminists, however, offer compelling counterarguments. First, there is the question as to whether bodily "empowerment" is merely a modern version of the "docile body," the intensely limiting and oppressive bodily management and scrutiny with which women learn to be complicit (Bordo 1993). For some women (especially those who are White, middle-class, and married heterosexuals) this complicit agency might result in more work on top of their already stifling "second shift" (Hochschild 1989)—a "third shift" that consists of long doses of effort invested in conforming to the latest touted bodily "requirement." It is these women, whose daily lives in families and careers might leave them feeling less than empowered, who would then respond to advertisements that encourage them to participate in sport and fitness in order to feel a sense of empowerment through their bodies. Couched in the logic of individualism and the Protestant work ethic, it seems that a woman needs only enact her free will and "just do it" in order to "have it all." But "doing it" the corporate individualist way involves a radical turning inward of agency toward the goal of transformation of one's own body, in contrast to a turning outward to mobilize for collective political purposes, with the goal of transforming social institutions. Clearly, despite its uplifting tone and seemingly patriotic commitment to American women, corporate slogans such as Nike's beg several questions, such as: Just do *what*? And *for whom*?

Just as the cult of true womanhood excluded numerous women from its "ideal" in the early nineteenth century, a similar conceptual vacuum arises here. After all, the dominant fitness industry message very likely "has no relevance to the majority of working-class women, or to Black women, or those from other ethnic minorities" (Hargreaves 1994:161). Bordo (1993) might disagree as she argues for the power of such messages to "normalize" across different races, classes, and sexualities. However, rather than being prematurely celebratory of bodily agency across categories of women, it may be argued that these newest images are fully compatible with the current "needs" of patriarchal capitalism for (especially and increasingly middle-class) women to be both active laborers and consumers (Bartky 1988).

Just as images of physically powerful and financially successful African American men ultimately did not challenge, but instead continued to construct a stratified race, class, and gender order, current images of athletic women appear to represent a broadening of the definitional boundaries of what Connell (1987) calls "emphasized femininity" to include more muscular development. But the resistant possibilities in images of athletic women are largely contained by the continued strong assertion of (and commercial rewards for) retaining a link between heterosexual attractiveness and body image. For instance, many lauded Olympic track star Florence Griffith-Joyner's muscularity as a challenge to the dominant image of femininity and to images of men as physically superior. However, Griffith-Joyner's muscularity existed alongside "rapier-like" nails, flowing hair, and spectacular outfits, which ultimately situated her body and its markings firmly within a commercialized modernization of heterosexual femininity (Messner forthcoming). Now more than ever, the commodification of women's bodies may mean that when women "just do it," they are "just doing" 1990s "heterosexy" femininity. In the media, these bodies are not unambiguously resistant images of powerful women, but rather an ambivalent framing or subtle trivialization or sexualization of women's bodies that under-mines their muscles and their athletic accomplishments (Duncan and Hasbrook 1988; Messner, Duncan, and Wachs 1996; Kane 1995; Kane and Lenskyj 1998). Female bodybuilders in particular illustrate these gender ambiguities. Research demonstrates that women can and do press and contest the limits of emphasized femininity. However, their agency is contained by the structure, rules, and ideologies of women's bodybuilding. For instance, Bolin (1992a, 1992b) found that the increas-ing size of the woman bodybuilder "beast" is acceptable only if "tamed" by "beauty." Female bodybuilders have faced penalties from judges for being too muscular, and they are rewarded for appearing with painted fingernails, dyed and highlighted hair, and breast implants. In short, their muscle size and body comportment is expected to be made con-sistent with emphasized femininity.

Researchers who study women's participation in fitness activities find the same tendency to adhere to emphasized femininity as is shown by women athletes and bodybuilders. They tend to avoid lifting weights "too much" for fear of being "too big." Instead, they engage in long doses of cardiovascular work, which is thought to emphasize tone and leanness (Dworkin forthcoming; Markula 1996). Just as women in male-dominated occupations often hit a glass ceiling that halts their professional advancement, there appears to be a glass ceiling on women's musculature that constrains the development of women's muscular strength. Defined according to the latest commodified eroti-cization of heterosexual femininity, most women (with differences by race, class, sexuality, age) remain acutely aware of how much muscle is "allowed," how much is "still" attractive.

Conclusion

Through an examination of gender, bodies, and sport, we have made three main points in this chapter that may illuminate more general attempts to understand and change the current gender order. First, although sport has been an arena for contesting the status quo by men of color and by White women and women of color, the positive results have been individual rather than collective. A few star athletes have become celebrities, but their popularity has not raised the overall status of disadvantaged men and women (although it may have upgraded the physical potentiality of middle-class White women). Second, whatever sport has accomplished in terms of equity, women's and men's sports are still segregated, and men's sports are still dominant in commercial value and in the media. Third, rather than breaking down conventional concepts of masculinity and femininity, organized sport has overblown the cultural hegemony of heterosexualized, aggressive, violent, heavily muscled male athletes and heterosexualized, flirtatious, moderately muscled female athletes who are accomplished and competitive but expected to be submissive to the control of men coaches and managers.

The link in all these outcomes is that organized sport is a commercial activity first and foremost. Organized sport is financially underwritten by corporations that sell shoes and clothing to a public looking for vicarious thrills and personal "fitness." The corporations capitalize on the celebrity of star athletes, who use individual achievements to make more money, rather than to help upgrade the communities from which they have come. Their endorsements sell individual achievement and conventional beauty and sexuality as well as Nikes and Reeboks. A further negative consequence to the upbeat message of "Just do it" is that many of the appurtenances of sport and fitness are produced by the labor of poorly paid, malnourished, and probably physically unfit women workers.

Does this mean that women's agency in sports and other physical activities is a dead end that should be abandoned by feminist activists? Absolutely not. We think that sport is like any other institution: We cannot abandon it, nor can we escape from it. Instead, we must struggle within it. When liberal reforms such as Title IX are fought for and won, the results—though not revolutionary—are often positive changes in individual lives. And these changes shift the context for current and future struggles over control of resources and over ideologies and symbols that support inequalities. But we think feminists need to fight on two fronts in the battle for equity in sports. On the one hand, we must continue to push for equal opportunities for girls and women in sports. On the other hand, although the research points to benefits for girls and women who play sports at the lower levels, many of the girls and women who are professionalized into corporate sports can expect—just as most of their men counterparts in corporate sports can—to pay emotional and physical costs.

But in challenging women's uncritical adoption of the dominant values of corporate sport, we must be cautious not to fall into the same trap as have past activists for girls' and women's sports. In the 1920s and 1930s, in the wake of two decades of burgeoning athleticism by girls and women, medical leaders and physical educators responded with what now appear to be hysterical fears that vigorous physical activity for girls and women carried enormous physical and psychological dangers (Cahn 1994). The result of these fears was the institutionalization of an "adapted model" (i.e., "tamed down" sports for women) that served to ghettoize women's sports, leaving the hegemonic masculinity of men's sport virtually unchallenged for the next 40 years. Given this history, today's advocates of women's sports walk a perilous tightrope: They must assert the positive value of vigorous physical activity and muscular strength for girls and women while simultaneously criticizing the unhealthy aspects of men's sports. A key to the accomplishment of this task must involve the development of a critical analysis of the dominant assumptions, beliefs, and practices of *men's* sports (Thompson 1988; Messner and Sabo 1994). In addition, we need to continue to explore feminist alternatives, for women and for men, to the "military model," with its emphasis on heroism, "playing through pain," and winning at all costs (Birrell and Richter 1987; Nelson 1991; Theberge 1985).

The activist fight for women and girls as a group will not be helped by simplistic scholarship that acts as a cheering section for numerical increases in women's athletic participation, or for the increasing visibility of women's athletics in televised ads. Nor will a simple "gender lens" that views sport uncritically in terms of undifferentiated and falsely universalized categories of "men" and "women" take us very far in framing questions and analyzing data. Different groups of men and of women disproportionately benefit from and pay the costs of the current social organization of sports. We need an analytic framework that appreciates the importance of class, racial, and sexual differences among both men and women while retaining the feminist impulse that places the need to empower the disadvantaged in the foreground.

Data from empirical observation of sport demonstrate the absence of absolute categorical differences between "men" and "women"—instead, there is a "continuum of performance" that, when acknowledged, can radically deconstruct dichotomous sex categories (Kane 1995). Obscuring this continuum are the social processes through which sport constructs and naturalizes differences and inequality between "men" and "women." Does this observation lead us down the path of radical deconstruction? We think the discussion in this chapter demonstrates just the opposite. The current poststructuralist preoccupation with deconstructing binary categories like "men and women" (e.g., Butler 1990; Sedgewick 1990) has produced new discourses and practices that disrupt and fracture these binaries (Lorber 1996). Yet simply deconstructing our *discourse* about binary categories does not necessarily challenge the material basis of master categories to which subordinate categories of people stand in binary opposition: the capitalist class, men, heterosexuals, Whites. In fact, quite the contrary may be true (Stein and Plummer 1994). As many feminists have pointed out, although it is certainly true that every woman is somewhat uniquely situated, a radical deconstruction of the concept "woman" could lead to an individualism that denies similarity of experience, thus leading to depoliticized subjects. We would argue that it is currently corporations such as Nike that are in the forefront of the widespread development of this sort of depoliticized individualist "empowerment" among women. Radical deconstruction, therefore, is very much in the interests of the most powerful institutions in our world, as it leaves us feeling (at best) individually "empowered," so long as we are able to continue to consume the right products, while making it unlikely we will identify common interests with others in challenging institutions.

Rather than a shift toward radical deconstruction, the research on gender, bodies, and sport suggests that it is essential to retain and build upon the concept of social structure, with its attendant emphasis on the importance of people's shared positions within social institutions (Duncan 1993; Messner 1992). Such a materialist analysis reveals how differential access to resources and opportunities and the varieties of structured constraints shape the contexts in which people think, interact, and construct political practices and discourse. A critical analysis of gender within a materialist, structural analysis of institutions entails a reassertion of the crucial importance (though not necessarily the primacy) of social class. Interestingly, as recent intellectual trends have taken many scholars away from the study of institutions toward a preoccupation with individuals, bodies, and difference, the literature has highlighted race, gender, and sexual identities in new and important ways, but social class has too often dropped out of the analysis. As we have demonstrated, discussions of the possibilities and limits of women's agency in gender equity struggles in sport, the co-optation of feminism by Nike's "celebrity feminism," and the current encouragement of physical fitness for middle-class women all need to be examined within the context of distributive justice. We also need a clear analysis of the position of women and men as workers in organized sport; as marketable celebrities; as workers in sweatshops making sport shoes, clothing, and equipment; and as consumers of these products and symbols. This analysis must be informed by feminist theories of the intersections of race, class, and gender (e.g., Baca Zinn and Dill 1996). Politically, this work can inform an alliance politics that is grounded simultaneously in a structural analysis of power and a recognition of differences and inequalities between and among women and men.

References

Acosta, R. Vivian and Linda Jean Carpenter. 1996. "Women in Intercollegiate Sport: A Longitudinal Study—Nineteen Year Update, 1977-1996." Brooklyn, NY: Department of Physical Education, Brooklyn College.

Baca Zinn, Maxine and Bonnie Thornton Dill. 1996. "Theorizing Difference from Multiracial Feminism." *Feminist Studies* 22:321-31.

Bartky, Sandra L. 1988. "Foucault, Femininity, and the Modernization of Patriarchal Power." In *Feminism and Foucault: Reflections on Resistance,* edited by I. Diamond and L. Quinby. Boston: Northeastern University Press.

Birrell, Susan. 1988. "Discourses on the Gender/Sport Relationship: From Women in Sport to Gender Relations." *Exercise and Sport Sciences Review* 16:159-200.

Birrell, Susan and Cheryl L. Cole. 1990. "Double Fault: Renee Richards and the Construction and Naturalization of Difference." *Sociology of Sport Journal* 7:1-21.

———, eds. 1994. *Women, Sport, and Culture.* Champaign, IL: Human Kinetics.

Birrell, Susan and Diana M. Richter. 1987. "Is a Diamond Forever? Feminist Transformations of Sport." *Women's Studies International Forum* 10:395-409.

Bolin, Anne. 1992a. "Flex Appeal, Food, and Fat: Competitive Bodybuilding, Gender, and Diet." *Play and Culture* 5:378-400.

———. 1992b. "Vandalized Vanity: Feminine Physique Betrayed and Portrayed." Pp. 79-90 in *Tattoo, Torture, Mutilation, and Adornment: The Denaturalization of the Body in Culture and Text,* edited by Frances E. Mascia-Lees and Patricia Sharpe. Albany: State University of New York Press.

Bordo, Susan. 1993. *Unbearable Weight: Feminism, Western Culture, and the Body.* Berkeley: University of California Press.

Boyle, Maree and Jim McKay. 1995. " 'You Leave Your Troubles at the Gate': A Case Study of the Exploitation of Older Women's Labor and 'Leisure' in Sport." *Gender & Society* 9:556-76.

Bryson, Lois. 1987. "Sport and the Maintenance of Masculine Hegemony." *Women's Studies International Forum* 10:349-60.

Butler, Judith. 1990. *Gender Trouble: Feminism and the Subversion of Identity.* New York: Routledge.

Cahn, Susan K. 1994. *Coming On Strong: Gender and Sexuality in Twentieth Century Women's Sport.* New York: Free Press.

Carpenter, Linda Jean. 1993. "Letters Home: My Life with Title IX." Pp. 79-94 in *Women in Sport: Issues and Controversies,* edited by Greta L. Cohen. Newbury Park, CA: Sage.

Cayleff, Susan. 1995. *Babe: The Life and Legend of Babe Didrikson Zaharias.* Urbana: University of Illinois Press.

Cole, Cheryl L. and Amy Hribar. 1995. "Celebrity Feminism: Nike Style Post-Fordism, Transcendence, and Consumer Power." *Sociology of Sport Journal* 12:347-69.

Connell, R. W. 1987. *Gender and Power.* Stanford, CA: Stanford University Press.

———. 1990. "An Iron Man: The Body and Some Contradictions of Hegemonic Masculinity." Pp. 83-95 in *Sport, Men and the Gender Order: Critical Feminist Perspectives,* edited by Michael A. Messner and Donald F. Sabo. Champaign, IL: Human Kinetics.

Crosset, Todd W. (1990). "Masculinity, Sexuality and the Development of Early Modern Sport." Pp. 45-54 in *Sport, Men and the Gender Order: Critical Feminist Perspectives,* edited by Michael A. Messner and Donald F. Sabo. Champaign, IL: Human Kinetics.

———. 1995. *Outsiders in the Clubhouse: The World of Women's Professional Golf.* Albany: State University of New York Press.

Davis, Angela Y. 1981. *Women, Race, and Class.* New York: Random House.

Davis, Laurel R. 1990. "Male Cheerleaders and the Naturalization of Gender." Pp. 153-62 in *Sport, Men and the Gender Order: Critical Feminist Perspectives,* edited by Michael A. Messner and Donald F. Sabo. Champaign, IL: Human Kinetics.

———. 1997. *The Swimsuit Issue and Sport: Hegemonic Masculinity in Sports Illustrated.* Albany: State University of New York Press.

Duncan, Margaret Carlisle. 1993. "Beyond Analyses of Sport Media Texts: An Argument for Formal Analyses of Institutional Structures." *Sociology of Sport Journal* 10:353-72.

Duncan, Margaret Carlisle and Cynthia A. Hasbrook. 1988. "Denial of Power in Televised Women's Sports." *Sociology of Sport Journal* 5:1-21.

Dworkin, Shari L. Forthcoming. "A Woman's Place Is in the . . . Cardiovascular Room? Gender Relations, the Body, and the Gym." In *Athletic Intruders,* edited by Anne Bolin and Jane Granskog. Albany: State University of New York Press.

Gilroy, S. 1989. "The Embody-ment of Power: Gender and Physical Activity." *Leisure Studies* 8:163-71.

Guthrie, Sharon R. and Shirley Castelnuovo. 1992. "Elite Women Bodybuilders: Model of Resistance or Compliance?" *Play and Culture* 5:378-400.

Hall, M. Ann. 1988. "The Discourse of Gender and Sport: From Femininity to Feminism." *Sociology of Sport Journal* 5:330-40.

———. 1996. *Feminism and Sporting Bodies: Essays on Theory and Practice.* Champaign, IL: Human Kinetics.

Hargreaves, Jennifer. 1994. *Sporting Females: Critical Issues in the History and Sociology of Women's Sport.* New York: Routledge.

Hoch, Paul. 1979. *White Hero Black Beast: Racism, Sexism and the Mask of Masculinity.* London: Pluto.

Hochschild, Arlie R. 1989. *The Second Shift.* New York: Avon.

Kane, Mary Jo. 1995. "Resistance/Transformation of the Oppositional Binary: Exposing Sport as a Continuum." *Journal of Sport and Social Issues* 19:191-218.

Kane, Mary Jo and Helen Lenskyj. 1998. "Media Treatment of Female Athletes: Issues of Gender and Sexualities." In *MediaSport: Cultural Sensibilities and Sport in the Media Age,* edited by Lawrence A. Wenner. London: Routledge.

Kimmel, Michael S. 1990. "Baseball and the Reconstitution of American Masculinity, 1880-1920." Pp. 55-66 in *Sport, Men and the Gender Order: Critical Feminist Perspectives,* edited by Michael A. Messner and Donald F. Sabo. Champaign, IL: Human Kinetics.

Klein, Alan. 1993. *Little Big Men.* Albany: State University of New York Press.

Lenskyj, Helen. 1986. *Out of Bounds: Women, Sport, and Sexuality.* Toronto: Women's Press.

———. 1987. "Female Sexuality and Women's Sport." *Women's Studies International Forum* 4:381-86.

Lopiano, Donna A. 1993. "Political Analysis: Gender Equity Strategies for the Future." Pp. 104-16 in *Women in Sport: Issues and Controversies,* edited by Greta L. Cohen. Newbury Park, CA: Sage.

Lorber, Judith. 1994. *Paradoxes of Gender.* New Haven, CT: Yale University Press.

———. 1996. "Beyond the Binaries: Depolarizing the Categories of Sex, Sexuality, and Gender." *Sociological Inquiry* 66:143-59.

MacKinnon, Catharine A. 1987. *Feminism Unmodified: Discourses on Life and Law.* Cambridge, MA: Harvard University Press.

Majors, Richard. 1990. "Cool Pose: Black Masculinity in Sports." Pp. 109-15 in *Sport, Men and the Gender Order: Critical Feminist Perspectives,* edited by Michael A. Messner and Donald F. Sabo. Champaign, IL: Human Kinetics.

Markula, Pirkko. 1996. "Firm but Shapely, Fit but Sexy, Strong but Thin: The Postmodern Aerobicizing Female Bodies." *Sociology of Sport Journal* 12:424-53.

McDermott, Lisa. 1996. "Towards a Feminist Understanding of Physicality within the Context of Women's Physically Active and Sporting Lives." *Sociology of Sport Journal* 13:12-30.

McKay, Jim. 1991. *No Pain, No Gain? Sport and Australian Culture.* Englewood Cliffs, NJ: Prentice Hall.

Messner, Michael A. 1988. "Sports and Male Domination: The Female Athlete as Contested Ideological Terrain." *Sociology of Sport Journal* 5:197-211.

———. 1992. *Power at Play: Sports and the Problem of Masculinity.* Boston: Beacon.

———. 1993a. " 'Changing Men' and Feminist Politics in the United States." *Theory and Society* 22:723-37.

———. 1993b. "White Men Misbehaving: Feminism, Afrocentrism, and the Promise of a Critical Standpoint." *Journal of Sport and Social Issues* 16:136-44.

———. Forthcoming. "Theorizing Gendered Bodies: Beyond the Subject/Object Dichotomy." In *Exercising Power: The Making and Remaking of the Body,* edited by Cheryl L. Cole, John Loy, and Michael A. Messner. Albany: State University of New York Press.

Messner, Michael A., Margaret Carlisle Duncan, and Faye Linda Wachs. 1996. "The Gender of Audience-Building: Televised Coverage of Men's and Women's NCAA Basketball." *Sociological Inquiry* 66:422-39.

Messner, Michael A. and Donald F. Sabo. 1990. "Towards a Critical Feminist Reappraisal of Sport, Men and the Gender Order." In *Sport, Men and the Gender Order: Critical Feminist Perspectives,* edited by Michael A. Messner and Donald F. Sabo. Champaign, IL: Human Kinetics.

———. 1994. *Sex, Violence and Power in Sports: Rethinking Masculinity.* Freedom, CA: Crossing Press.

Nelson, Mariah Burton. 1991. *Are We Winning Yet? How Women Are Changing Sports and Sports Are Changing Women.* New York: Random House.

———. 1994. *The Stronger Women Get, the More Men Love Football: Sexism and the American Culture of Sports.* New York: Avon.

President's Council on Physical Fitness and Sports. 1997. "Physical Activity and Sport in the Lives of Girls." Washington, DC: President's Council on Physical Fitness and Sports.

Pronger, Brian. 1990. *The Arena of Masculinity: Sports, Homosexuality, and the Meaning of Sex.* New York: St. Martin's.

Ryan, Joan. 1995. *Little Girls in Pretty Boxes: The Making and Breaking of Elite Gymnasts and Figure Skaters.* New York: Warner.

Sabo, Donald F. 1994. "Pigskin, Patriarchy, and Pain." Pp. 82-88 in *Sex, Violence and Power in Sports: Rethinking Masculinity*, by Michael A. Messner and Donald F. Sabo. Freedom, CA: Crossing Press.

Sabo, Donald F. and Women's Sports Foundation. 1988. *The Wilson Report: Moms, Dads, Daughters and Sports*. East Meadow, NY: Women's Sports Foundation.

Sedgewick, Eve K. (1990). *Epistemology of the Closet*. Berkeley: University of California Press.

Stein, Arlene and Ken Plummer. 1994. " 'I Can't Even Think Straight': Queer Theory and the Missing Sexual Revolution in Sociology." *Sociological Theory* 12:178-87.

Take Action for Girls. 1996. "The Two Faces of Nike." *Take Action for Girls Newsletter* 1 (November):2.

Theberge, Nancy. 1981. "A Critique of Critiques: Radical and Feminist Writings on Sport." *Social Forces* 60:341-53.

————. 1985. "Toward a Feminist Alternative to Sport as a Male Preserve." *Quest* 37:193-202.

————. 1987. "Sport and Women's Empowerment." *Women's Studies International Forum* 10:387-93.

Thompson, Shona M. 1988. "Challenging the Hegemony: New Zealand Women's Opposition to Rugby and the Reproduction of Capitalist Patriarchy." *International Review of the Sociology of Sport* 23:205-12.

Tomlinson, Alan and Ilkay Yorganci. 1997. "Male Coach/Female Athlete Relations: Gender and Power Relations in Competitive Sport." *Journal of Sport and Social Issues* 21:134-55.

White, Philip G., Kevin Young, and William G. McTeer. 1995. "Sport, Masculinity, and the Injured Body." Pp. 158-82 in *Men's Health and Illness: Gender, Power, and the Body*, edited by Donald F. Sabo and Frederick Gordon. Thousand Oaks, CA: Sage.

Whitson, David. 1990. "Sport in the Social Construction of Masculinity." Pp. 19-30 in *Sport, Men and the Gender Order: Critical Feminist Perspectives*, edited by Michael A. Messner and Donald F. Sabo. Champaign, IL: Human Kinetics.

Women's Sports Foundation. 1997. *The Women's Sports Foundation Gender Equity Report Card: A Survey of Athletic Opportunity in American Higher Education*. East Meadow, NY: Women's Sports Foundation.

Young, Iris M. 1990. *Throwing Like a Girl and Other Essays in Feminist Philosophy and Social Theory*. Bloomington: Indiana University Press.

PART V

GENDERING THE PERSON

CHAPTER 13

Gender, Power Dynamics, and Social Interaction

PETER GLICK
SUSAN T. FISKE

The scene is a birthing room, with the mother in the late stages of delivery, the excited father recording it all with his video camera, the doctor ready to receive the newborn infant. "You have a beautiful baby . . ." The doctor's voice trails off. "A beautiful baby what?" demands the father. "I don't know," the doctor responds. "I can't tell." So begins an episode of the television hospital drama *ER*. Subsequent tests reveal that the baby is chromosomally male; however, it would be easier medically to perform surgery to give him female genitalia (more extensive surgery would be needed for male genitalia, which would not be "fully functional" in adulthood). With simple surgery and hormones, he could be a "normal" she (though unable to reproduce). The discussion of how to proceed is dominated by the father, who had counted on having a son to carry on the family name. Because he does not want a son who will be impotent or a daughter whose gender appearance must be maintained through hormones, he decides that he and his wife should give the infant up for adoption.

This piece of dramatic fiction raises the questions explored in this chapter: Why are people intolerant of ambiguity concerning a person's sex category? Why is gender considered to be such an important part of an individual's identity? How can our most intimate cross-sex relationships involve both love and dominance? In this chapter we review the social psychology of sex and gender categorization and the effects that it has on how we perceive, feel about, and act toward others.[1]

Our intention, however, is not merely to summarize the research in encyclopedic fashion, but to propose a framework that places the psychology of gender relations into a social structural perspective. In the past, social psychologists, intent on understanding proximal causes of gender stereotyping and discrimination, have tended to ignore the wider social context in which gendered relations take place (though in recent years the tide has been changing rapidly). For instance, social psychologists often study people removed from their daily roles, diminishing the influence that gender has on behavior (Eagly 1987). Similarly, the dominant interpersonal perception approach to stereotyping and discrimination emphasizes psychological process often to the exclusion of social context in the attempt to adduce general principles of perception that underlie prejudice. Although we believe that such general principles exist, we argue that they can be fully articulated only through an examination of the *interrelationship between psychological process and social structural realities*. Indeed, through consideration of how past social psychological research fits with the work of sociologists and anthropologists, some of these principles become evident, as do some challenges to old assumptions about the nature of sexism.

Thus we focus on recent social psychological research findings that become particularly important when considered in relationship to gendered social structures. The first social psychological finding is that sex is *the* primary category by which people automatically classify others, and that this automatic process leads to the nonconscious activation of gender stereotypes even among perceivers who embrace nonsexist ideologies. We consider this finding in the context of male-dominated social institutions and a sex-segregated division of labor that make gender a socially useful construct that informs perceivers about others' alleged traits and how to treat them appropriately.

Second, social psychologists have increasingly questioned the notion that stereotypes are irrational and more highly resistant to change than other forms of generalizations (Allport 1954), as their research has revealed the subtle and sophisticated ways in which people handle information that challenges their stereotypes. For example, social psychologists have turned to the investigation of subtypes, stereotypes about smaller social groups, such as "career women" and "welfare mothers," that are defined by simultaneous membership in more than one group, such as the intersection of gender and role or gender and class in the examples above. Rather than being fixated on simple stereotypes of wide social groups, people readily form more specific and differentiated subcategories (Fiske and Neuberg 1990). A social structural perspective reveals *why* people are sensitive to such subgroupings as they reflect gender, race, ethnic, and class divisions embedded in the social structure. These structural realities lend stereotypes their social utility and also determine the *content* of stereotypes. Women are perceived as nurturant because of the roles they play and because of their lower status relative to men. Because stereotypes are not born of ignorance, but reflect social realities, changing them is not merely a matter of "education." Telling a young child that "women can be firefighters too" carries little weight when every firefighter the child sees is a man (Bigler forthcoming).

Third, recent research on sexism has challenged social psychologists' standard assumptions about the nature of prejudice.[2] Although prejudice has typically been viewed as Allport (1954) defines it, an antipathy toward a social group, it has become clear that women are viewed more favorably in certain ways than men and that sexism may be "benevolent" as well as hostile (Glick and Fiske 1996). We interpret these findings here in light of the dyadic dependencies created by complementary gender-based roles and heterosexual intimacy that lend women some power to fulfill or thwart men's goals. Because men's dominance coexists with a dependence on women, their conventional attitudes toward women are deeply ambivalent, encompassing love as well as dominance. Indeed, love itself can be a form of coercion if the offer of a man's love is contingent upon a woman's subordination (Jackman 1994). Thus we show how subjectively benevolent, as well as hostile, attitudes toward women serve to maintain a social structure that restricts women to lower-status roles.

Sex Categorization and Gender
Stereotyping as Primary and Automatic

As the "teaser" portion of the *ER* episode illustrates, a child (or any person) whose sex is indeterminable presents a dilemma that most Americans are ill equipped to handle. In real cases of hermaphroditism, as in this fictional account, a third option is never considered: leaving the child alone (Fausto-Sterling 1993). Does the infant really need surgery? Does it need to be treated either as a boy or as a girl? Medically, the answer might be no. Socially, most people do not hesitate to answer yes, for otherwise life becomes quite difficult: How would the parents respond to questions about the whether the baby is a boy or girl? What clothes would they buy? Would the child carry a Barbie lunch box or a Batman lunch box to school? Which public bathroom would the child use? How would such a child be treated by peers? One envisions a life of ambiguities, difficult questions, social predicaments, and ostracism.

Admittedly, purposeful "gender-bending" may be more popular among contemporary teens and adults than it was 30 years ago, but although a woman may wear "men's" clothes, the perceiver usually recognizes that the other is a woman (i.e., is able to place the target into one of the two standard sex categories). Failure to form a confident impression of another person's sex is rare. We typically categorize people by sex effortlessly, even nonconsciously, with diverse and profound effects on social interactions.

Since Allport's (1954) germinal book on prejudice, social psychologists have emphasized the normality of grouping people into social categories. Categorization is a basic and inescapable part of how we think about objects, sparing us the effort of dealing with each new object as a unique entity. Similarly, we categorize people into larger social groups along any number of dimensions—age, race, religious affiliation, and so on—that we find useful in determining how to interact with others (Fiske 1998; Fiske and Taylor 1991). There are as many potential systems of classification, however, as there are individuals who use them. In principle, each person could have his or her own idiosyncratic system (e.g., I might be sensitive to hair color and you to age). Although some variations occur due to differences in what each culture or each person deems important (Bem 1981; Higgins and Bargh 1987; Markus and Smith 1981), recent research indicates that one category transcends these differences, consistently emerging as the most automatic, pervasive, and earliest learned: sex (Fiske 1998; see also Harris 1991; Bem 1989).

When we encounter another person, we usually perform sex classification in the blink of an eye, typically faster than other socially important forms of categorization, such as identifying race (Zárate and Smith 1990). The speed and ubiquity with which we use sex to classify others is matched by the *primacy* of sex over other categories. Investigations of which features capture perceivers' attention suggest that sex is encoded more strongly than other socially important categories, such as race. In one research paradigm developed by Taylor and her colleagues (Taylor 1981; Taylor et al. 1978), participants view a series of people, identified only by name and photograph, making several statements. Later, participants are asked to match the statements to the people who made them. The errors a participant makes reveal which people that perceiver "lumps together." Taylor et al. (1978) found that within-sex confusions (e.g., mistaking a statement made by Karen as having been made by Nancy) were much more frequent than between-sex errors (e.g., recalling Karen's statement as one made by Tom). When targets vary by race (Black and White) as well as by sex, within-sex errors are more frequent than within-race errors, showing that people spontaneously make greater use of sex than of race when categorizing others (Stangor et al. 1992). Similar results have been obtained outside the laboratory. Using both recall and diary methodologies, Fiske, Haslam, and Fiske (1991) found that, in daily life, people of the same sex are more likely to be mistaken for each other than are people of similar age, race, height, build, or occupational role.

The speed of sex categorization suggests that it is an *automatic* process, part of the act of perceiving another person, done without conscious effort, and happening despite our volition. For instance, try to *look at,* but not to *read* the word at the end of this sentence, that is, perceive its shape without processing its meaning as a word: FEMALE. Perceiving this stimulus without understanding its meaning is impossible for literate individuals, for whom reading has become an automatic cognitive process. In a similar vein, our overlearned tendency to categorize people by sex occurs whether we want it to or not, and some of its effects occur without our conscious awareness. In other words, no matter how egalitarian an individual may be, he or she cannot be "sex-blind."

Categorizing others may begin with a simple male/female dichotomy, but it does not end there. Sex categorization automatically and nonconsciously activates gender stereotypes through a process known as "implicit stereotyping" (Banaji and Greenwald 1995; Banaji and Hardin 1996; Banaji, Hardin, and Rothman 1993; Blair and Banaji 1996). Banaji and her colleagues use a paradigm in which participants are exposed to "primes," words that activate a particular concept (Higgins, Rholes, and Jones 1977). Banaji et al. (1993) exposed participants to priming sentences by asking them to reorder sets of words to form sentences. Each sentence referred to a person by an initial, so that the person's sex was indeterminate (e.g., "J answered the phone"). For some participants, most sentences indicated stereotypically masculine-aggressive behavior (e.g., "R threatens other people"), whereas others received sentences that expressed stereotypically feminine-dependent behavior (e.g., "M can't make decisions"), and a third group unscrambled gender-neutral statements (e.g., "T crossed the street"). In a seemingly unrelated "reading comprehension task," the same participants read about either "Donald" or "Donna." When the stereotype evoked by the primes (e.g., assertive men, dependent women) matched the sex category of the target individual (Donald or Donna), stereotypic inferences were made even though the target person's behavior was ambiguous. No stereotyping effects were found in the gender-neutral prime condition; Donna was seen as no different from Donald *unless* participants were surreptitiously primed. The wide variety of gender-related primes that can lead to implicit stereotyping suggests that it may be a common, everyday occurrence. Banaji and Hardin (1996) obtained effects using gendered nouns (*mother, father, woman, man*), job titles (*secretary, mechanic*), role titles (*chairman, chairwoman*), and even ostensibly generic masculine terms (*mankind, layman*) as primes.

However, the lack of effect in the gender-neutral prime condition is consistent with research that demonstrates that when we deliberate in a conscious, rational manner we can short-circuit some effects of categorizing others (Devine 1989). Aware of the ubiquity of stereotypes, egalitarian individuals, such as well-intentioned college students, may try to compensate for the effects of stereotypes, a process that requires conscious deliberation (see Gilbert, Pelham, and Krull 1988). But because implicit stereotyping influences people's thoughts without their awareness, it occurs regardless of the consciously held attitudes of the individual, just as strongly for women as for men, and is unrelated to direct measures of overt sexism (Banaji and Hardin 1996).

In addition to the familiar observation that the media explicitly promote gender stereotyping, popular culture may play a particularly insidious role in such nonconscious priming. Rudman and Borgida (1996) had men view a series of actual television commercials as part of a "market research" study. The participants were either primed with commercials featuring women as sex objects (e.g., the "Swedish bikini team") or placed in a control condition in which they viewed nonsexist commercials for similar products. Later, the men who were primed were quicker to recognize sexist words (e.g., bimbo) and sexual double entendres (e.g., cherry), and to engage in sexually harassing behaviors when asked to interview a woman applying for a research assistant job. Similar to other implicit stereotyping effects, these outcomes occurred *independent* of the men's propensity to endorse sexist beliefs, indicating that the priming manipulation (compared with no priming) affected nonsexist men equally as strongly as it affected sexist men, although, overall, sexist men were more likely to engage in sexually harassing behavior.

In summary, recent research demonstrates that sex categorization (a) is *the* primary and most ubiquitous form of person categorization, (b) occurs without conscious awareness or control, and (c) evokes gender-based stereotypes and expectations. Sex categorization thus does more than place people into distinct groups, it is embedded within a wider system of gender constructs. This research reveals that sex and gender are of overwhelming importance, but does not tell us why.

The Importance of Sex and Gender

Categorization is a cognitive labor-saving device; by grouping people in categories and treating category members alike, people avoid the effort involved in perceiving each person as a wholly new stimulus about whom they know nothing. For example, research participants attempting to do two things at once, forming an impression of another person while simultaneously monitoring a tape about Indonesia, who were provided category labels (e.g., doctor, skinhead, artist) for the impression-formation task performed better on the competing task (Macrae, Milne, and Bodenhausen 1994). Having a category within which to place the targets allowed perceivers to form impressions more rapidly, thereby freeing more cognitive resources for the secondary task. But categorization simplifies perception only if category membership can be quickly and easily perceived, which is why social categories are usually based on physical characteristics.

That a person's sex category is associated with physical appearance is, however, insufficient to explain its overwhelming importance. After all, other physical traits, such as hair color, are rarely used as a basis of categorization, and some common social categories, such as homosexuality, are not associated with physical cues. Sex is an important category not only because of its physical salience, but because it is a socially useful category. As Stangor et al. (1992) note, "Features are attended to to the extent that they provide useful information" (p. 207), and sex categorization is socially useful because it is viewed as diagnostic of a wide range of others' personality dispositions.

But why is sex considered diagnostic of personality traits? We argue that it is crucial to consider gender in a wider, *social structural* sense. The social psychology of sex categorization rests fundamentally on the perceivers and targets both being located in gendered societies. Societies are structured such that social institutions, roles, and status are imbued with and depend on gender, which we define here as a set of social constructs associated with sex as a category. Logically, sex categorization preceded the development of gender constructs; the origins of gender constructs lie in a sex-segregated division of labor and status differences between men and women. Nevertheless, these emergent gender constructs, not sex categorization alone, explain why sex category is viewed as being informative about individuals' dispositions.

Divisions of labor, role differentiation, and status differences accompany other group distinctions (e.g., race and ethnicity), but conventional gender roles are unique in their relationship to human reproduction. Across cultures, women's work always includes the responsibility of bearing and rearing children (Eagly 1987). Women's greater reproductive investment in children is partially responsible for this cross-cultural consistency. Male dominance, or patriarchy, is also ubiquitous after the introduction of plow agriculture (Boserup 1986). Furthermore, heterosexuality creates powerful and intimate interpersonal dependencies between men and women, unlike the tendency of other groups to segregate themselves. Together, the sex-based division of labor, patriarchy, and heterosexuality strongly affect the structure of virtually all human societies.

Division of Labor

All known societies display a sex-based division of labor to some extent, although societies on the most egalitarian end of the scale show almost total overlap between men's and women's work (D'Andrade 1966; Harris 1991). The cross-cultural consistency of some of these patterns suggests that biological sex differences may be related to the origins of social practice. Nevertheless, categorical sex segregation persists even when new technologies render the original basis for this division of labor obsolete.

Thus one reason for the primacy of sex as a category is its relationship to social roles. Knowing what roles another person plays is socially useful information, because roles govern interactions with others. For instance, people expect that mothers are more experienced, and therefore more capable than fathers at comforting a sick child. And even when men and women nominally have similar roles, role "spillover" can occur (Gutek 1985). A woman secretary, for example, might be expected to do more "mothering" on the job than would a man secretary; because of the predominance of women in the job, taking care of people has become a part of the role. Furthermore, as Eagly (1987) notes, these role differences spawn gender stereotypes, notions about how different personality traits are associated with men and women. These stereotypes, which we review in more detail later, reinforce the perceived social utility of sex categorization.

Status and Power

It is theoretically possible to divide labor according to sex while considering men's and women's work to be of equal worth, but this kind of "separate but equal" system is not the human norm. Societies that have a sex-based division of labor invest men's work with greater social status (Chafetz 1990). With the important exception of the hunter-gatherer societies that dominated much of human history, patriarchy is the pancultural norm (O'Kelly and Carney 1986).

Patriarchy can be defined as the social arrangement in which men possess *structural power* by virtue of monopolizing high-status positions in important social, economic, legal, and religious institutions, as is the case in most modern industrial societies. Status powerfully affects how people interact with others. Compared with status inferiors, high-status people tend to initiate interactions, determine the course of conversations, and decide whether greater intimacy is allowed in the relationship (Goffman 1956; Henley and Kramarae 1994; Thorne and Henley 1975). High-power people can confirm their stereotypes of status inferiors by ignoring disconfirming information and focusing on information that fits their stereotypes. In contrast, status inferiors attend closely to the powerful, concentrating on the most informative, nonstereotypic information (Fiske 1993; Fiske and Dépret 1996). In short, people defer to those of higher status, who then exploit this deference to exert greater control over social interaction.

That men are used to having higher status than women is evident in situations where status is ostensibly equal. For instance, even when juries have equal numbers of men and women on them, men are elected "foreman" 90 percent of the time (Kerr, Harmon, and Graves 1982), and studies of who emerges as leader in leaderless groups have found that men are much more likely to get the role (Davis and Gilbert 1989; Eagly and Karau 1991).

Heterosexuality

In other intergroup relations, social role and status differences are also common. But gender role and status differences uniquely occur within the context of frequent and intimate contact between the groups (Fiske and Stevens 1993). Typically, when one social group holds structural power, its members not only exploit lower-status groups by forcing them into menial positions, but also enforce group distinctions through laws and social norms that segregate the groups as much as possible. Relations between men and women, however, are fundamentally different in this respect. Even in the most sexist societies, sexual relations between men and women have been necessary for group survival.

Certainly sexual intercourse can take place without psychological intimacy, and women and men can largely inhabit "separate worlds," as they do in many societies. But heterosexual reproduction generates interpersonal complexities beyond the sex act itself; men and women are also connected by kinship. In most societies, the first psychologically intimate relationship in a boy's life is with a woman, as babies are usually most firmly attached to their mothers (a fact of great concern to Freud, who devoted much of his thought to how boys manage to adopt a male gender identity when their initial identification is with a woman). This initial attachment is extremely powerful and has long-lasting effects on subsequent relationships with peers (Elicker, Englund, and Sroufe 1992) and romantic partners (Shaver and Hazan 1993).

Human infants, as any parent can attest, require an enormous amount of care over an extended period of time. Even in nonhuman species with such strong demands, pair-bonding between males and females is common, as two parents are more likely to ensure that the offspring survive to reproduce (Travis and Yeager 1991). It is not surprising, then, that sexual attraction and attachment tend to overlap in human adults (Shaver and Hazan 1993). Furthermore, humans are fundamentally social animals for whom survival has always been dependent on membership in cooperative groups, typically defined by extended kinship relations (Leakey 1978). Group harmony requires smooth relationships with members of both sexes; in our primate relatives, there is evidence that becoming the "alpha" male depends in no small part on having cooperative relations with the female members of the troop (Travis and Yeager 1991). These observations suggest a biological predisposition to form bonds of psychological intimacy that span a network of relationships among others of both sexes, kin or not (Caporael and Brewer 1991; Stevens and Fiske 1995). Heterosexual reproduction ensures that total gender segregation is impossible and that interpersonal intimacy between men and women is common.

Structural and Dyadic Power

Because intimate relationships between men and women create dyadic (two-person) dependencies that cross gender lines, even in clearly patriarchal societies in which men possess *structural power*, women often gain some measure of social control through *dyadic power*, power that accrues from men's interpersonal dependency on women (Guttentag and Secord 1983). Mothers may retain some measure of influence over their grown sons, and wives are often able to exercise influence over their husbands (Lips 1991; Rosaldo 1974). Men also can (and often do) possess dyadic power due to women's economic dependency, but women's dyadic power is not trivial for two reasons.

First, most people prefer to like and be liked by others (Newcomb 1961) and to have smooth and pleasant social interactions (Baumeister and Leary 1995), especially among intimates. Being accommodative and trying to inhibit destructive impulses is associated with greater satisfaction and commitment in intimate relationships (Rusbult et al. 1991). Thus, even if the man is "head of the household," it is generally more satisfying for him to rule with benevolence rather than hostility.

Second, women's influence over domestic tasks, such as child rearing, allows ample opportunities for resistance, even in very traditional cultures, that men would rather not elicit (Abu-Lughod 1990). Although many men rule the home by fear and violence, this often reflects a lack of social skills or a lack of economic resources to get the deference they expect (Pyke 1996; Straus and Smith 1992). In short, men's dyadic dependence on women significantly alters the balance of power in the "war between the sexes."

Ideological Consequences of Male Structural and Female Dyadic Power

Social structures do not perpetuate themselves independent of belief systems; they can be maintained only through shared ideologies that, for example, specify which roles *ought* to be fulfilled by women and which by men. Such ideologies do not merely specify "how things are," but serve as *legitimating myths* by providing "moral and intellectual justification for the differential distribution of power, privilege, and status among social groups within the social system" (Sidanius, Pratto, and Bobo 1994:999). Sexist ideologies are one example of legitimating myths that link social structure and the psychology of the individual, for adopting these beliefs affects responses to others on the basis of gender.

Social psychologists have given a great deal of attention to measuring individuals' adherence to patriarchal versus egalitarian beliefs about women's rights and roles. Most measures have focused on the hostile aspect of these ideologies, which typically characterize low-status groups as deserving their situation due to imputed traits such as stupidity, laziness, and immorality. A number of theorists, however, have noted that men's dependency on women tends to produce beliefs about women that are not solely negative (Eagly and Mladinic 1993; Guttentag and Secord 1983; Jackman 1994; Lipman-Blumen 1984). In earlier work, we have argued that the unique balance of male structural and female dyadic power is reflected in two related sets of gender ideologies: *hostile* and *benevolent* sexism (Glick and Fiske 1996). Hostile sexism is consistent with most definitions of sexism: patriarchal dominance, derogatory stereotypes of women, and an aggressive form of heterosexuality in which women are viewed as sexual objects. This hostile ideology is a gendered version of the forms of justification high-status groups typically use to rationalize their exploitation of low-status groups. Hostile sexism arises out of and serves to justify men's structural power through the belief that men are better than women, more qualified to wield power, and deserve to be in charge.

Benevolent sexism is also a sexist ideology that supports and justifies conventional gender roles and status differences, but characterizes these arrangements as being in women's best interests and imputes favorable traits to women. Benevolent sexism encompasses what is often referred to as male chivalry: protective forms of paternalism, idealized stereotypes of women (such as purity), and an intimate form of heterosexuality in which women are seen as necessary complements to men (their "better half") and even as powers in their own sphere (the "domestic goddess"). Although benevolent sexism is kinder and gentler in its overt attitudes toward women, it nevertheless also serves to legitimate women's subordination and often goes hand in hand with hostile sexist beliefs.

Despite the subjectively positive feelings it engenders, benevolent sexism remains patronizing toward women and provides a powerful ideological justification for traditional gender roles and patriarchy. The term *benevolent* is used to indicate the subjectively positive nature of these beliefs in the view of the person who endorses them. The man who sincerely subscribes to benevolent sexism no doubt believes that he has women's best interests at heart and may be genuinely puzzled when individual women disagree. Part of this puzzlement may come from inconsistent responses by women to benevolent sexism, with some women sharing his views and accepting, or even demanding, "chivalrous" treatment and others rejecting it as patronizing.

There are analogues to benevolent sexism in myths that have legitimated other group relations, such as the colonial belief in the "White man's burden" and similar justifications of slavery. Jackman (1994) argues that whenever groups in daily contact have a stable system of "expropriative" relations, in which the higher-status group exploits the labor of the lower-status group, such paternalistic ideologies develop for two reasons. First, they serve as a flattering self-justification for high-status group members ("We aren't exploiting them; they couldn't take care of themselves unless we told them what to do"), thus preventing cognitive dissonance between their codes of morality and their unfair treatment of the other group. Second, communicating this ideology to members of the lower-status group, along with rewards, such as easier jobs to those who seem to adopt these justifications, reduces resistance among the exploited group.

Although "benevolent" legitimating myths are not unique to relations between men and women, the intimate dyadic dependencies between them make benevolent sexism a uniquely powerful legitimating myth that can be traced from antiquity to the present day. The gender relations described in Homer's *Odyssey*, composed almost three millennia ago, are not at all foreign to the modern reader. Whereas the "White man's burden" has an archaic ring to it, belief in the "man's burden" as protector of women is alive and well today, despite its much more ancient roots. Hostile sexism, of course, has an equally ancient history; Eve and Pandora are blamed for letting evil and misery loose upon the world.

In summary, the persistence of both hostile and benevolent sexism can be attributed to the persistence of the social conditions that these ideologies justify: a sex-segregated division of labor, patriarchal power, and heterosexuality. The shared components and purposes of hostile and benevolent sexism make them intertwined aspects of traditional gender ideology, despite the opposite valences they represent in feelings expressed toward women. As a result, sexist men may be deeply ambivalent about women, as evinced in the cultural images they produce. "If woman had no existence save in the fiction written by men," Virginia Woolf ([1929] 1957) notes, "one would imagine her a person . . .

very various; heroic and mean; splendid and sordid; infinitely beautiful and hideous in the extreme" (p. 43). These ambivalent images persist in present-day popular culture (Faludi 1991).

Sexism and Everyday Social Interaction

The underlying social structural conditions of a sex-segregated division of labor and roles, patriarchal power, and heterosexuality manifest themselves at the level of individual social interactions, determining the manner in which people think about, feel about, and act toward women and men. These three domains (cognition, emotion, behavior) are the major outcome variables studied by social psychologists. In the area of intergroup relationships, *cognition* is represented by stereotypes (beliefs about the characteristics of groups and their members), *emotion* by prejudice (typically defined as antipathy toward members of other groups, but here considered as ambivalence), and *behavior* by discrimination (differential treatment of groups or individuals because of their group membership).

In reviewing each of these three outcome variables, we argue that the underlying ambivalence created by men's structural power and women's dyadic power polarizes reactions to women as a group: Stereotypes of women combine both highly valued traits (such as warmth) with disparaging ones (such as incompetence); prejudiced feelings toward women range from reverence to revulsion; and discriminatory behavior toward women includes benevolent, though patronizing, actions (helping the "damsel in distress") as well as overt hostility, coercion, and violence against women. Of particular interest is understanding how gender roles, power differences, and heterosexuality determine individual men's goals in interactions with women, for understanding these goals reveals the circumstances under which either the benevolent or the hostile aspects of sexism are activated.

Gender Stereotypes

There is an impressive degree of cross-cultural consistency in the content of gender stereotypes. In a study of 25 different countries with considerable geographic, economic, and cultural diversity, several consistent differences in perceptions of women and men emerged (Best and Williams 1993). Men are consistently characterized as more active and strong, whereas women are viewed as more passive and weak. Men are seen as high on dominance, autonomy, aggressiveness, exhibition, achievement, and endurance. In contrast, women are viewed as more deferent, abasing, nurturant, and affiliative.

In large measure, these pancultural consistencies in the content of gender stereotypes can be traced to the social structural consistencies in the division of labor and power. Roles have behavioral demands attached to them, and power (or the lack of it) strongly affects how people behave. As Eagly (1987) notes, gendered roles affect behavior through several mechanisms. First, a division of labor has direct effects as it requires the development of specific skills and behavior, as when taking care of young children requires one to develop sensitivity to others' needs. Second, differing roles generate social expectations about the behavior of men and women, which may be internalized through socialization and become part of the self-concept, so that, for example, many young girls come to prefer playing with dolls, whereas boys prefer rough-and-tumble play. Third, people tend to conform to prescribed roles out of compliance with social norms even when expectations are not internalized. This latter mechanism is not a trivial one, as it constrains the behavior of those individuals who would like to reject conventional gender roles.

Eagly (1987) argues that, like gender differences in behavior, gender stereotypes have their origins in the gender-based division of labor and the differential status assigned to male and female roles. Child rearing, in particular, requires the communal traits that have therefore become stereotypically associated with women: nurturant, able to soothe others' feelings, helpful, kind, gentle. In contrast, modern forms of competition typically require the agentic qualities associated with men: ambitious, aggressive, dominant, independent, self-confident. These role-based expectations are reflected in, and often enforced by, gender stereotypes that depict women as nurturers and men as competitors.

Power differences are a second source of the content of gender stereotypes (Conway, Pizzamiglio, and Mount 1996). People who are high in social status or power behave differently than those low in power. High-power individuals are more likely to dominate conversations, initiate interactions, assume leadership roles, feel self-confident, and disparage the contributions of those with lower power; all of these traits have become incorporated into social conceptions of what it means to be a man. Men are socialized to act in ways that are consistent with having social power, at least when they are interacting with women of a similar or lower social class to their own, preparing them to assume higher-status social roles. Men are expected—by themselves and others—to be more dominant, aggressive, decisive, strong, and confident.

How sexism interacts with other forms of discrimination, based on race, ethnicity, and class, has not been well studied by psychologists. Under some conditions the stereotypes of low-status groups parallel stereotypes of women. For example, almost 50 years ago, Hacker (1951) pointed out striking similarities between then-current stereotypes of African American men and of women in general; both were viewed as deferential, childlike, and content to serve their "betters." The ascription of "feminine" communal traits to low-status groups occurs when there are long-standing relations of stable status inequality between groups (see Jackman 1994). This, however, is likely to change when low-status groups begin to protest their oppression, at which point they are more likely to be stereotyped as aggressive, rather than communal, as can be seen both in current stereotypes of African Americans and of feminists.

Race, ethnicity, and class interact with gender in that people fit simultaneously into combinations of these categories (e.g., a Black female professional). Researchers are paying increasing attention to the importance of subtyping, using more specific categories, such as "housewives" and "welfare mothers," that represent combinations of race or ethnicity, class, and gender (Niemann et al. 1994). As yet, however, social psychologists have not adduced general principles about how such combinations are formed or how their content is determined.

Nor do we have an understanding of how the race, ethnicity, and class of *perceivers* affect sexism and gender prescriptions. For example, we still need to study whether men who are victims of racism or who have lower class status are more or less likely to be sexist (or to express sexism in different ways) than more privileged men. What is clear, however, is that people without power pay close attention to what the more powerful have to say, avoid challenging others directly, make tentative suggestions rather than express strong opinions, try to soothe others' feelings rather than assert themselves, and are more deferential and approval seeking—all of which are behaviors that women are encouraged to adopt (Lips 1991). These characteristics are evident in stereotypes of women as passive, weak, deferent, socially sensitive, and vulnerable.

Role and power differences alone are sufficient to create stereotypes. Research participants provided with information about fictitious cultures in which social subgroups are differentially assigned to domestic and work roles or differ in social status (Conway et al. 1996; Eagly and Steffen 1984) develop genderlike stereotypes about the groups. Behaviors required by domestic work and required of the relatively powerless come to be associated with women. In contrast, the traits required for work that is accorded higher social status and the characteristics of people with power become associated with men. These qualities are then seen as natural and immutable traits in men and women because people fail to perceive that many differences in behavior between men and women are created by the situational demands of the work they perform and by power differences (see Lorber 1994).

One of the fundamental findings of social psychology has been that people tend to infer dispositions that correspond to behavior without considering alternative situational attributions (Jones and Davis 1965; Ross, Amabile, and Steinmetz 1977). In other words, rather than considering that a person may be acting with deference due to a lack of power in the situation, and that the same person might act quite differently in situations where he or she has power, the perceiver tends to infer that the individual has a submissive personality. Thus gender stereotypes may be based in kernels of truth about differences in the behavior of men and women that occur *as a result of* differences in roles and power. Although biologically based sex differences may exist—for example, in physical aggression (Kenrick and Trost 1993)—that would also bolster gender stereotypes, social structural variables are not only sufficient to account for gender stereotypes, but also parsimoniously explain their similarity to certain race, ethnic, and class stereotypes.

Gender stereotypes are not simply the product of role and power differences; they also serve as part of the cement that keeps these social structures from collapsing. Through socialization and social norms, gender stereotypes maintain a sex-segregated division of labor and patriarchal power (Cejka and Eagly 1997). For instance, research on occupational choices shows that at a very early age, gender circumscribes children's aspirations—most children rule out careers that are stereotyped as being filled by members of the other sex (Gottfredson 1981). Because men are more likely than women actively to seek high-status, hierarchy-enhancing occupations (Pratto et al. 1997), sex segregation in the job market is more easily maintained. Men's dyadic dependency on women, however, causes positively evaluated traits to be included in stereotypes about women, alongside the less flattering justifications of women's lower status. For example, the traits associated with child rearing, such as nurturance and warmth, are viewed quite positively. In fact, there is evidence that (overall) people view the traits stereotypically associated with women more favorably than those associated with men (Eagly and Mladinic 1993). Women may not be seen as competent outside the home, but they are generally perceived as being *nice*.

The influence of gender stereotypes is particularly strong because, unlike many other stereotypes that are merely *descriptive,* gender stereotypes are also *prescriptive*—they represent norms of behavior from which deviations are punished (Fiske and Stevens 1993). For example, although the stereotype suggests that Jews are greedy, this is not viewed as a trait that Jews *should* have. In contrast, gender stereotypes suggest that women *ought* to be nurturant and men *ought* to be aggressive. The prescriptive nature of gender stereotypes illustrates how important gender distinctions are to social structure and how gender stereotypes serve to justify gender roles. In part, this demonstrates the higher-status group's dependency on the lower-status group; men are dependent on women to fill roles as wives and mothers so that men can devote their attention to achievement at work. As a result, men are motivated to have women accept these roles, to reward those who do and punish those who do not (Glick and Fiske forthcoming). Women of higher social class can avoid some of these constraints by hiring other women to take care of their children, whereas women of lower social class may be more constrained by gender-based prescriptions. Other prescriptions may be stronger for women of higher social class, such as appearance norms (Wolf 1991).

◆ If stereotypes reflect the social structure, then, surely, as social roles change so ought the stereotypes. Yet research shows that rather than altering the general stereotypes of men and women, exceptions and social changes are accommodated through a proliferation of subtypes. It has long been recognized that admitting that some people are exceptions to the overall stereotype is a mechanism by which the general stereotype can be kept intact (Allport 1954). When a group becomes sufficiently familiar (and men and women have an unusually high degree of contact), exceptions proliferate and perceivers come to rely on *subtypes*, characterizing specific subgroups, such as homemakers, grandmothers, career women, and debutantes (Taylor 1981). Recent research confirms that the overall stereotypes of men and women remain intact *because* exceptional cases can be subsumed into various subtypes (Hewstone et al. 1994). Men spontaneously use subtypes as the "basic" level of categorization (Deaux et al. 1985). These subtypes move beyond simple labeling of individuals as being male or female to incorporating various *gendered* categories. In particular, those who embrace conventional roles ("homemakers") are distinguished from women who have taken on nonconventional roles ("career women"), once again confirming the importance of the division of labor as a source of stereotypes. In some cases, the tendency to subtype can work in favor of women who pursue jobs typically held by men, as when a "career woman" is perceived as possessing the masculine traits required for the job (Glick, Zion, and Nelson 1988). However, because gender stereotypes are prescriptive, sexist men dislike women who are perceived as having masculine personalities (Fiske and Stevens 1993). We consider these emotional and evaluative responses below.

Gender Prejudice

Prejudice can be defined as the emotional or evaluative aspect of intergroup attitudes. Although sexism is usually defined as involving hostility toward women, we have argued that sexist men's feelings toward women are often ambivalent, that the peculiar combination of men's structural power and their dependency on women produces both hostile and benevolent sexism. The social structural variables relevant to gender—a sex-segregated division of labor, patriarchal power, and the dependencies created by heterosexual intimacy institutionalized in marriage and kinship relations—influence men's emotions toward women through their effects on *group-level goals*. For example, patriarchy creates an interest among men, as a group, to maintain the current power structure, because men's higher status as a group translates into greater self-esteem (Turner 1987). In general, at both the group and individual levels, the tenor of emotions toward specific groups depends on appraisals of whether the other group facilitates or challenges major goals, motives, or values (Fiske and Ruscher 1993; Smith 1993).

These social structural variables suggest a specific set of goals for men who desire to maintain conventional social relations with women that, in turn, enable prediction of how men who subscribe to conventional gender ideologies feel about specific subtypes of women. Patriarchy and a sex-segregated division of labor can be maintained only if women cooperate by adopting roles that complement and enable male roles. For instance, the role of "protector" does not exist unless there is someone who requires protection, and men's structural power is facilitated if they remain free to pursue high economic status without having to devote time to domestic chores or child rearing. Thus men who hold conventional careers are likely to evaluate women who fulfill support roles favorably, for such women enable men to maintain a sense of power and status while fulfilling their needs for sex and intimacy. Women who "buy into" the system help to support and validate it.

Women who challenge the system, however, are dangerous for men with a high stake in system maintenance. Women who seek careers in male-gendered areas—blue-collar jobs and elite professions—challenge conventional gender norms that are an important source of men's identity. Feminists also threaten patriarchal power by questioning gender role prescriptions and promoting the idea that women can, and have the right to, engage in male-gendered roles. Furthermore, successful, powerful women and feminists are seen as a threat to conventional arrangements in marriage, for they challenge men's greater control over marital decisions and ability to avoid domestic and child-rearing responsibilities. Right-wing authoritarians express particular dislike for feminists (Haddock and Zanna 1994). Thus sexist men have highly polarized views toward different groups of women, loving those who support conventional gender distinctions and hating those they perceive as challenging these social structures (Glick et al. 1997; Rhodebeck 1996).

In interactions between specific individuals, men's interaction goals are also affected by gender ideologies. A sexist man may react negatively when a woman, as opposed to a man, assumes a leadership role in a work group, for the former threatens aspects of self-esteem grounded in men's assumed superiority (Eagly, Makhijani, and Klonsky 1992). Psychological theory and research suggest that individuals gain self-esteem when they view themselves as outperforming other persons in areas that are relevant or important to them (Tesser 1988; Turner 1987). Such comparisons are more likely to be made among people who have close relations. Thus the success of a friend, sibling, or romantic partner in an area important to oneself can threaten one's self-esteem, whereas the other's failure can enhance it. This implies that a man can feel better about himself by thinking that individual women are less capable at those activities *he* deems important. Other men who perform well are also threats to self-esteem, but the presumption of men's superiority at male-gendered tasks makes a woman's successful performance in such areas particularly threatening, for it raises the specter of failure in comparison to an "inferior" class of people.

Belief in a gendered division of labor means, however, that a woman's superior performance on a task assigned to women poses no threat. In fact, in close relationships, a woman's superior performance at female-gendered tasks can create a great deal of pride, allowing the man to bask in reflected glory. Thus individual women who stick to female-gendered tasks and do not challenge men's control are likely to be rewarded with affection from sexist men; women who cross the line and succeed in besting men in areas important to them will be treated with hostility. Knowing this, either through her own or other women's experiences, can create significant pressure on a woman to avoid succeeding in such competitions.

But what about women's feelings toward men? The same social structural factors that create ambivalence on the part of men toward women may be responsible for women feeling ambivalence toward men. The fact that men have structural power is likely to create resentment among women, who, whether they consider themselves feminists or not, may chafe at the restrictions men impose and the power men are able to wield (Abu-Lughod 1990). At the same time, women are often dependent on men, but dyadic power accrues to them only within their intimate heterosexual relationships. Men's benevolent sexism offers women who conform the reward of protection, a means to gain social status, and perhaps some degree of influence by serving in a supporting role, the "woman behind every great man." Conversely, hostile reactions that nonconforming women must endure create an incentive for women to accept and justify conventional arrangements. Thus conforming women may view men as deserving their higher status, because men protect and provide for women, a view that would produce benevolent feelings toward men, who are the source of protection, status, and affection. A heterosexual orientation is likely to enhance these feelings among women for whom men also fulfill sexual needs that, at their best, promote affection and intimacy. Such benevolent feelings, just like men's benevolent sexism, may also be infantilizing. Women's benevolent sexism characterizes men as "naturally" irresponsible, insensitive, and unable to take care of themselves properly without a woman's help. In other words, it presumes that every man *needs* the support of a woman because of stereotypically masculine shortcomings.

Women's ambivalence toward men remains an unexplored area for empirical research. We are currently developing an instrument, the Ambivalence toward Men Inventory, to promote research in this area. Preliminary results suggest that women do have both hostile and benevolent feelings toward men and that the former predict more negative stereotypes of men, whereas the latter predict more positive stereotypes.

In short, the gender-based distinctions embedded in social structures create, at both the group and individual levels, ambivalent feelings toward persons in the other sex category, encouraging volatile and polarized reactions. These emotional reactions occur in a wide variety of daily social interactions, ranging from those involving peers at work to people's most intimate heterosexual relationships, and are at least partly responsible for discriminatory and coercive behavior.

Gender Discrimination and Coercion

Discrimination is the behavioral component of sexism: the differences in how people act toward men and women in daily social interaction as well as the institutional forms of gendered coercion and differential treatment that are embedded in many cultures' social structures. We have already reviewed evidence of institutional discrimination in the restriction of women to specific roles and their exclusion from positions of power. Here we concentrate on interpersonal forms of discrimination and coercive action.

As with stereotypes and prejudiced feelings, social psychologists have typically concentrated on hostile forms of discrimination against women, such as not hiring women for conventionally male-gendered jobs. The ambivalence inherent in gender ideologies, however, suggests that women are likely also to receive "preferential" treatment over men in contexts that convey heterosexual attraction or presume female "incapacity." In many interpersonal contexts, it is likely that women will receive more favorable treatment from men, compared with how men often treat one another. If, as we have hypothesized, benevolent sexism arises out of men's dependency on women in close interpersonal relationships, then discrimination that is perceived to be "in women's interest" is particularly likely to occur in informal social situations within family and other close relationships, and toward women who are perceived as embracing gendered roles that complement and enable men's roles.

Evidence from research on the differential treatment of women and men supports the existence of this "benevolent discrimination." Social norms encourage men to help the "damsel in distress," a behavioral enactment of a central benevolent sexism theme that a man's role is to be protector of women. For example, men are more likely to intervene in an emergency to help a woman than to help a man (Eagly and

Crowley 1986). Men are also more likely to behave in intimacy-seeking ways with women than with men, to stand closer to women (Riess and Salzer 1981), to touch women (Major, Schmidlin, and Williams 1990), and to self-disclose to women (Morton 1978). Thus, on a number of interpersonal measures, men are more likely to behave toward women in ways that are usually considered to be "prosocial" or that indicate attraction. It is just such behaviors, however, that can be intrusive or even harassing. Although sexual harassment is often a deliberately hostile act designed to "put a woman in her place," in many cases harassment may, from the perspective of the harasser, be subjectively benevolent (see Fiske and Glick 1995 for a taxonomy of subjectively hostile and benevolent forms of harassment). What this type of harasser is not aware of is that his attraction to a female subordinate is enhanced by his feeling of power over her (Bargh and Raymond 1995). This, in turn, may encourage him to be persistent, confident that the woman could not possibly turn him down.

In light of the social structural differences that determine gender ideologies and affect cross-sex relationships, the tendency of men to use closer interpersonal distances with, to self-disclose more to, and to be more likely to touch women may reflect differences in status, as higher-power individuals are more likely to control the progression of intimacy in interpersonal interactions (Thorne and Henley 1975). Thus the norm that men are to be the initiators of interaction helps to perpetuate their interpersonal power. Furthermore, all these behaviors can be preludes to developing a sexual relationship, suggesting ulterior motives for these actions. This combination of differences in power and roles, coupled with motivations for intimacy, precisely captures the concept of benevolent sexism and also sets the stage for possibly unwanted sexual approaches.

As a result, discrimination "in favor" of women is part of a system that reinforces a conventional division of labor and unequal power. Women must be protected and provided for because they are believed to be the "weaker sex." Individual women may be well aware of the fact that men who offer help often do so with the presumption that the woman is incapable of helping herself. Furthermore, men's sexual attraction toward women may lead them to discriminate in favor of a woman for reasons that she might consider demeaning. For example, in one experiment in which men were primed to view women as sexual objects by viewing sexist television commercials and later interviewed a woman for a job, "primed" men asked more sexist questions and rated the woman as less competent, but nevertheless gave more favorable salary and hiring recommendations (Rudman and Borgida 1996). These sexually aroused men were anxious to do a favor for the female applicant by helping her get hired, but not because they viewed her as competent. At best, the "favor" is a mixed one and perpetuates the idea that women are not competent, but just nice to look at. At worst, some participants' behavior was sexually harassing, as rated by the confederate who was interviewed and by observers.

Discrimination motivated by benevolent sexism poses a particularly insidious problem because it often does not seem coercive. It may appear to provide a benefit to, rather than to impose a cost on, members of the lower-status group, and the men who engage in such discrimination may be partially or completely unaware of the implicit messages they are sending. Yet it anchors and legitimates women's structural subordination. Benevolent discrimination often arises in close, affectionate relationships, making it difficult or even impossible to separate the role of sexist assumptions from communal helping norms (Clark and Mills 1979). But even benevolent discrimination can be coercive, with parents keeping daughters home "for their own good" and husbands withholding financial information from wives "so they won't have to worry."

These motivational ambiguities may lead both the actor and the recipient of benevolent forms of discrimination to view such acts as wholly positive behaviors stemming from laudable motives. And even when the recipient feels or suspects that an act is patronizing, she may nevertheless acquiesce without complaint for several reasons: the immediate benefits such discrimination offers, the difficulty of explaining to the man why his help is being rejected, his anticipated hostile or hurt reaction, and norms that call for gracious acceptance of another's helpful behavior. Furthermore, if the man has higher status in the situation, refusal becomes more difficult and dangerous. All of these factors conspire to make it easier to "go along to get along" than to create a scene or awkward social predicament by doing otherwise.

We have devoted considerable space to the "benevolent" form of discrimination because it has too often been overlooked, not to deny or minimize the other side of the equation. Hostile discrimination against women has been well documented, including the exclusion of women, hostile or violent behavior, derogatory epithets, and sexual harassment (Fiske and Glick 1995). Hostile discrimination is likely to occur when women violate gender prescriptions in domains, typically outside the home, in which men have successfully segregated themselves from women. Not surprisingly, much of the research on discrimination against women has examined hiring and promotion decisions in male-dominated jobs. Even though women in the United States are now in the paid workforce, they have been more likely to find employment in jobs resembling conventional female roles, such as taking care of children, doing domestic chores, and serving in roles subordinate to and in support of men. The preference for women in these roles is strong enough that men are likely to be discriminated against in hiring decisions for these occupations (Arvey et al. 1987). In contrast, there is ample evidence that equally qualified women are less likely to be hired or promoted in conventionally male-dominated jobs (Reskin and Padavic 1994).

In interpersonal interaction, hostile discrimination is most likely to occur when sexist men view a woman as violating prescriptive gender norms or as challenging men's social control. A meta-analysis of studies of reactions to men and women in leadership positions revealed that men react most negatively to women who assume a leadership role in a conventionally male-gendered domain and employ a high-power leadership style (Eagly et al. 1992). When women adopt the "masculine" style suited to successful performance in a male-gendered job, sexist men retaliate. For example, Ann Hopkins was denied partnership at Price-Waterhouse not due to poor performance, but because of her "masculine" personality (American Psychological Association 1991). Sexual harassment may also occur when women enter a domain from which they have previously been excluded, as in the military or on the Mitsubishi assembly line in Illinois, where it has been alleged that harassing behavior was widespread.

Nor is domestic life immune to the hostile side of sexist ambivalence. Intimate relationships provide ample opportunity for the experience of both positive and negative emotions and, in turn, hostile or benevolent behaviors. Men's violence in the home may be used to enforce wives' deference and to secure specific services (Kurz 1995). Some men refuse to accept any criticism or contradiction from their wives (Gottman 1994; Straus and Smith 1992). The fact that men's hostile acts often alternate with benevolent behavior, as in the "honeymoon" period that often follows an episode of physical abuse, reinforces the observation that sexist men are highly ambivalent about women. Sadly, this ambivalence is often at its most extreme and volatile in men's and women's closest relationships.

In conclusion, although women who accept conventional gender asymmetries may appear to reap the benefits of discrimination that favors them, this benevolent treatment is both patronizing and reinforces the assumption that women are less competent and are indeed the weaker sex. In contrast, women who reject such chivalry and seek equal treatment are likely to elicit hostile forms of discrimination from sexist men. Benevolent sexism is the carrot and hostile sexism the stick by which sexist men attempt to keep women in their place and preserve the social structure of male dominance.

Future Directions for Research

In this chapter we have emphasized the social psychological consequences of the gender-based social structures that pervade virtually all human societies. Our aim has been to provide a link between social structures (the sex-segregated division of labor, patriarchy, and heterosexuality), social ideologies (hostile and benevolent sexism), and the psychology of everyday social interactions between individual men and women (e.g., the application of gender stereotypes to individual women). With some notable exceptions—such as Tajfel's (1981) social identity theory and Eagly's (1987) social role theory—social psychologists have all too often considered the *psychology* of such processes as stereotyping without taking account of the wider social context in which these processes take place. We have tried to show the importance of linking the wider social context to psychological processes, for it is only by doing so that we can truly understand why and how gender has such profound effects on social interaction.

Explicit consideration of social structures—the legitimating myths that maintain them and the norms that enforce and encourage discrimination in daily life—suggest specific areas for further research. For example, social psychologists have paid too little attention to how stereotypes, prejudice, and discrimination interrelate. Influenced by an established interpersonal perception tradition, investigators of the social psychology of gender relations, and intergroup relations more generally, have long proceeded under the assumption that stereotypes cause prejudiced feelings and discriminatory behavior. Taking account of social structure suggests that this assumption is misleading, for discrimination is clearly embedded in social structures that can be seen as the roots of *both* stereotyping and discrimination. If so, then attacking people's stereotypes may not eliminate discrimination, as social psychologists often assume; education attempts can have only limited effects as long as material conditions (e.g., sex segregation in the labor market) remain the same. Similarly, the assumption that stereotypes cause prejudiced feelings has been questioned recently by researchers who have considered the impact of the wider social context on inter-group relations (Dovidio et al. 1996; Smith 1993).

More detailed investigation of the interplay between wider social forces and the psychology of the individual is of particular contemporary importance as gender relations continue to experience rapid change. Changes in the division of labor, for example, have undoubtedly promoted more progressive attitudes on the part of many individuals, but they have also promoted the creation of ideologies that appear to be progressive yet serve to resist these changes (Swim et al. 1995). Conventional stereotypes and other gender-related ideologies are flexible, able to accommodate changed social conditions (e.g., that most families now rely on women to work outside the home), but still to serve as rationalizations of male dominance.

Thus we urge more investigators (whether they are sociologists, anthropologists, or psychologists) to consider theoretical frameworks that link various levels of analysis—from social structure to shared ideologies to individual beliefs, feelings, and behavior—as a basis for generating research questions that address gender relations. Such frameworks have the power to reveal why gender is the most basic and influential form of intergroup distinction. It is through analysis of gender relations that researchers can most clearly illuminate how social roles, power and status, and interpersonal intimacy in the face of group distinctions affect each of us on a daily basis, both at work and in our closest relationships, in ways both subtle and profound.

Notes

1. We distinguish here between simple sex categorization, the dichotomous classification of people into the categories "men" and "women," and gender classification, which begins with, but goes beyond, mere sex categorization to include a variety of gendered subtypes into which men and women are placed (e.g., career women, homemakers). In general, we attempt to use the term *sex* when referring to the categorical dichotomy as such and the term *gender* when we mean to include constructs that are related to the categories, but go beyond them to elaborate on differences, constructing maleness and masculinity in relation to femaleness and femininity. Thus we refer to *gender stereotypes* rather than *sex stereotypes*,

because stereotypes about men and women generally occur at the subtype level and show considerable variation *within* sex categories (e.g., career women and homemakers are viewed as having quite different, even opposing, traits). Even as we provide this heuristic, we acknowledge that the line between sex and gender is often difficult to draw.

2. We define sexism here as the belief, either implicit or explicit, that women ought to be subordinate to men. By this definition, subjectively benevolent feelings and behavior toward women are considered to be sexist if they presume or support women's subordination.

References

Abu-Lughod, L. 1990. "The Romance of Resistance: Tracing Transformations of Power through Bedouin Women." Pp. 311-37 in *Beyond the Second Sex: New Directions in the Anthropology of Gender,* edited by P. R. Sanday and R. G. Goodenough. Philadelphia: University of Pennsylvania Press.

Allport, G. W. 1954. *The Nature of Prejudice.* Reading, MA: Addison-Wesley.

American Psychological Association. 1991. "In the Supreme Court of the United States: Price-Waterhouse v. Ann B. Hopkins; Amicus curiae brief for the American Psychological Association." *American Psychologist* 46:1061-70.

Arvey, R. D., H. E. Miller, R. Gould, and P. Burch. 1987. "Interview Validity for Selecting Sales Clerks." *Personnel Psychology 40:1-12.*

Banaji, M. R. and A. G. Greenwald. 1995. "Implicit Gender Stereotypes in Judgments of Fame." *Journal of Personality and Social Psychology 68:181-98.*

Banaji, M. R. and C. Hardin. 1996. "Automatic Stereotyping." *Psychological Science* 7:136-41.

Banaji, M. R., C. Hardin, and A. J. Rothman. 1993. "Implicit Stereotyping in Person Judgment." *Journal of Personality and Social Psychology* 65:272-81.

Bargh, J. A. and P. Raymond. 1995. "The Naive Misuse of Power: Nonconscious Sources of Sexual Harassment." *Journal of Social Issues* 51:85-96.

Baumeister, R. F. and M. R. Leary. 1995. "The Need to Belong: Desire for Interpersonal Attachments as a Fundamental Human Motivation." *Psychological Bulletin* 117:497-529.

Bem, S. L. 1981. "Gender Schema Theory: A Cognitive Account of Sex-Typing." *Psychological Review* 88:354-64.

———. 1989. "Genital Knowledge and Gender Constancy in Preschool Children." *Child Development* 60:649-62.

Best, D. L. and J. E. Williams. 1993. "A Cross-Cultural Viewpoint." Pp. 215-50 in *The Psychology of Gender,* edited by A. E. Beall and R. J. Sternberg. New York: Guilford.

Bigler, R. Forthcoming. "Countering Sexism." In *The Many Faces of Gender: The Multidimensional Model of Janet Taylor Spence,* edited by W. B. Swann, Jr., L. A. Gilbert, and J. Langlois. Washington, DC: American Psychological Association.

Blair, I. V. and M. R. Banaji. 1996. "Automatic and Controlled Processes in Stereotype Priming." *Journal of Personality and Social Psychology* 70:1142-63.

Boserup, E. 1986. *Women's Role in Economic Development.* Brookfield, VT: Gower.

Caporael, L. R. and M. B. Brewer. 1991. "The Quest for Human Nature: Social and Scientific Issues in Evolutionary Psychology." *Journal of Social Issues* 47:1-10.

Cejka, M. A. and A. H. Eagly. 1997. "Gender-Stereotyped Images of Occupations Correspond to the Sex Segregation of Employment." Center for Mission Research and Study at Maryknoll. Unpublished manuscript.

Chafetz, J. 1990. *Gender Equity: An Integrated Theory of Stability and Change.* Newbury Park, CA: Sage.

Clark, M. S. and J. Mills. 1979. "Interpersonal Attraction in Exchange and Communal Relationships." *Journal of Personality and Social Psychology* 37:12-24.

Conway, M., M. T. Pizzamiglio, and L. Mount. 1996. "Status, Communality, and Agency: Implications for Stereotypes of Gender and Other Groups." *Journal of Personality and Social Psychology* 71:25-38.

D'Andrade, R. G. 1966. "Sex Differences and Cultural Institutions." In *The Development of Sex Differences,* edited by E. E. Maccoby. Stanford, CA: Stanford University Press.

Davis, B. M. and L. A. Gilbert. 1989. "Effect of Dispositional and Situational Influences on Women's Dominance Expression in Mixed-Sex Dyads." *Journal of Personality and Social Psychology* 57:294-300.

Deaux, K., W. Winton, M. Crowley, and L. L. Lewis. 1985. "Level of Categorization and Content of Gender Stereotypes." *Social Cognition* 3:145-67.

Devine, P. G. 1989. "Stereotypes and Prejudice: Their Automatic and Controlled Components." *Journal of Personality and Social Psychology* 56:5-18.

Dovidio, J. F., J. C. Brigham, B. T. Johnson, and S. L. Gaertner. 1996. "Stereotyping, Prejudice, and Discrimination: Another Look." Pp. 276-319 in *Stereotypes and Stereotyping,* edited by C. N. Macrae, C. Stangor, and M. Hewstone. New York: Guilford.

Eagly, A. H. 1987. *Sex Differences in Social Behavior: A Social Role Interpretation.* Hillsdale, NJ: Lawrence Erlbaum.

Eagly, A. H. and M. Crowley. 1986. "Gender and Helping Behavior: A Meta-analytic Review of the Social Psychological Literature." *Psychological Bulletin* 100:283-308.

Eagly, A. H. and S. J. Karau. 1991. "Gender and the Emergence of Leaders: A Meta-analysis." *Journal of Personality and Social Psychology* 60:685-710.

Eagly, A. H., M. G. Makhijani, and B. G. Klonsky. 1992. "Gender and Evaluations of Leaders: A Meta-analysis." *Psychological Bulletin* 111:3-22.

Eagly, A. H. and A. Mladinic. 1993. "Are People Prejudiced against Women? Some Answers from Research on Attitudes, Gender Stereotypes, and Judgments of Competence." Pp. 1-35 in *European Review of Social Psychology*, vol. 5, edited by W. Stroebe and M. Hewstone. New York: John Wiley.

Eagly, A. H. and V. J. Steffen. 1984. "Gender Stereotypes Stem from the Distribution of Men and Women into Social Roles." *Journal of Personality and Social Psychology* 46:735-54.

Elicker, J., M. Englund, and L. A. Sroufe. 1992. "Predicting Peer Competence and Peer Relationships from Early Parent-Child Relationships." In *Family-Peer Relationships: Modes of Linkage*, edited by R. D. Parke and G. W. Ladd. Hillsdale, NJ: Lawrence Erlbaum.

Faludi, S. 1991. *Backlash: The Undeclared War against American Women*. Garden City, NY: Doubleday.

Fausto-Sterling, A. 1993. "The Five Sexes: Why Male and Female Are Not Enough." *Sciences* (March-April):20-25.

Fiske, A. P., N. Haslam, and S. T. Fiske. 1991. "Confusing One Person with Another: What Errors Reveal about the Elementary Forms of Social Relations." *Journal of Personality and Social Psychology* 60:656-74.

Fiske, S. T. 1993. "Controlling Other People: The Impact of Power on Stereotyping." *American Psychologist* 48:621-28.

Fiske, S. T. 1998. "Stereotyping, Prejudice, and Discrimination." Pp. 357-411 in *The Handbook of Social Psychology*, 4th ed., edited by D. Gilbert, S. T. Fiske, and G. Lindzey. Boston: McGraw-Hill. Distributed by Oxford University Press, New York.

Fiske, S. T. and E. Dépret. 1996. "Control, Interdependence, and Power: Understanding Social Cognition in Social Context." Pp. 31-61 in *European Review of Social Psychology*, vol. 7, edited by W. Stroebe and M. Hewstone. New York: John Wiley.

Fiske, S. T. and P. Glick. 1995. "Ambivalence and Stereotypes Cause Sexual Harassment: A Theory with Implications for Organizational Change." *Journal of Social Issues* 51:97-115.

Fiske, S. T. and S. L. Neuberg. 1990. "A Continuum of Impression Formation, from Category-Based to Individuating Processes: Influences of Information and Motivation on Attention and Interpretation." Pp. 1-74 in *Advances in Experimental Social Psychology*, vol. 23, edited by M. P. Zanna. New York: Academic Press.

Fiske, S. T. and J. B. Ruscher. 1993. "Negative Interdependence and Prejudice: Whence the Affect?" Pp. 239-68 in *Affect, Cognition, and Stereotyping: Interactive Processes in Group Perception*, edited by D. M. Mackie and D. L. Hamilton. New York: Academic Press.

Fiske, S. T. and L. E. Stevens. 1993. "What's So Special about Sex?" Pp. 173-96 in *Gender Issues in Contemporary Society*, edited by S. Oskamp and M. Costanzo. Newbury Park, CA: Sage.

Fiske, S. T. and S. E. Taylor. 1991. *Social Cognition*. 2d ed. New York: McGraw-Hill.

Gilbert, D. T., B. W. Pelham, and D. S. Krull. 1988. "On Cognitive Busyness: When Person Perceivers Meet Persons Perceived." *Journal of Personality and Social Psychology* 54:733-39.

Glick, P., J. Diebold, B. Bailey, and L. Zhu. 1997. "The Two Faces of Adam: Ambivalent Sexism and Polarized Attitudes toward Women." *Personality and Social Psychology Bulletin* 23:1334-44.

Glick, P. and S. T. Fiske. 1996. "The Ambivalent Sexism Inventory: Differentiating Hostile and Benevolent Sexism." *Journal of Personality and Social Psychology* 70:491-512.

———. Forthcoming. "Sexism and Other 'Isms': Interdependence, Status, and the Ambivalent Content of Stereotypes." In *The Many Faces of Gender: The Multidimensional Model of Janet Taylor Spence*, edited by W. B. Swann, Jr., L. A. Gilbert, and J. Langlois. Washington, DC: American Psychological Association.

Glick, P., C. Zion, and C. Nelson. 1988. "What Mediates Sex Discrimination in Hiring Decisions?" *Journal of Personality and Social Psychology* 55:178-86.

Goffman, E. 1956. "The Nature of Deference and Demeanor." *American Anthropologist* 58:473-502.

Gottfredson, L. S. 1981. "Circumscription and Compromise: A Developmental Theory of Occupational Aspirations." *Journal of Counseling Psychology Monograph* 28:545-79.

Gottman, J. M. 1994. *What Predicts Divorce?* Hillsdale, NJ: Lawrence Erlbaum.

Gutek, B. A. 1985. *Sex and the Workplace*. San Francisco: Jossey-Bass.

Guttentag, M. and P. F. Secord. 1983. *Too Many Women? The Sex Ratio Question*. Beverly Hills, CA: Sage.

Hacker, H. M. 1951. "Women as a Minority Group." *Social Forces* 30:60-69.

Haddock, G. and M. P. Zanna. 1994. "Preferring 'Housewives' to 'Feminists': Categorization and Favorability of Attitudes toward Women." *Psychology of Women Quarterly* 18:25-52.

Harris, M. 1991. *Cultural Anthropology*. 3d ed. New York: HarperCollins.

Henley, N. M. and C. Kramarae. 1994. "Gender, Power, and Miscommunication." In *The Women in Language Debate: A Sourcebook*, edited by C. Roman, S. Juhasz, and C. Miller. New Brunswick, NJ: Rutgers University Press.

Hewstone, M., C. N. Macrae, R. Griffiths, A. B. Milne, and R. Brown. 1994. "Cognitive Models of Stereotype Change: Measurement, Development, and Consequences of Subtyping." *Journal of Experimental Social Psychology* 30:505-26.

Higgins, E. T. and J. A. Bargh. 1987. "Social Cognition and Social Perception." *Annual Review of Psychology* 38:379-426.

Higgins, E. T., W. S. Rholes, and C. R. Jones. 1977. "Category Accessibility and Impression Formation." *Journal of Experimental Social Psychology* 13:141-54.

Jackman, M. R. 1994. *The Velvet Glove: Paternalism and Conflict in Gender, Class, and Race Relations.* Berkeley: University of California Press.

Jones, E. E. and K. E. Davis. 1965. "A Theory of Correspondent Inferences: From Acts to Dispositions." Pp. 219-66 in *Advances in Experimental Social Psychology,* vol. 2, edited by L. Berkowitz. New York: Academic Press.

Kenrick, D. T. and M. R. Trost. 1993. "The Evolutionary Perspective." Pp. 148-72 in *The Psychology of Gender,* edited by A. E. Beall and R. J. Sternberg. New York: Guilford.

Kerr, N. L., D. L. Harmon, and J. K. Graves. 1982. "Independence of Multiple Verdicts by Jurors and Juries." *Journal of Applied Social Psychology* 12:12-29.

Kurz, D. 1995. *For Richer, for Poorer: Mothers Confront Divorce.* New York: Routledge.

Leakey, R. E. 1978. *People of the Lake: Mankind and Its Beginnings.* New York: Avon.

Lipman-Blumen, J. 1984. *Gender Roles and Power.* Englewood Cliffs, NJ: Prentice Hall.

Lips, H. M. 1991. *Women, Men, and Power.* Mountain View, CA: Mayfield.

Lorber, J. 1994. *Paradoxes of Gender.* New Haven, CT: Yale University Press.

Macrae, C. N., A. B. Milne, and G. V. Bodenhausen. 1994. "Stereotypes as Energy-Saving Devices: A Peek inside the Cognitive Toolbox." *Journal of Personality and Social Psychology* 66:37-47.

Major, B., A. M. Schmidlin, and L. Williams. 1990. "Gender Patterns in Social Touch: The Impact of Setting and Age." *Journal of Personality and Social Psychology* 58:634-43.

Markus, H. R. and J. Smith. 1981. "The Influence of Self-Schemas on the Perception of Others." Pp. 233-62 in *Personality, Cognition, and Social Interaction,* edited by N. Cantor and J. F. Kihlstrom. Hillsdale, NJ: Lawrence Erlbaum.

Morton, T. U. 1978. "Intimacy and Reciprocity of Exchange: A Comparison of Spouses and Strangers. *Journal of Personality and Social Psychology* 36:72-81.

Niemann, Y. F., L. Jennings, R. M. Rozelle, J. C. Baxter, and E. Sullivan. 1994. "Use of Free Response and Cluster Analysis to Determine Stereotypes of Eight Groups." *Personality and Social Psychology Bulletin* 20:379-90.

Newcomb, T. M. 1961. *The Acquaintance Process.* New York: Holt, Rinehart & Winston.

O'Kelly, C. G. and L. S. Carney. 1986. *Women and Men in Society.* 2d ed. Belmont, CA: Wadsworth.

Pratto, F., L. M. Stallworth, J. Sidanius, and B. Siers. 1997. "The Gender Gap in Occupational Role Attainment: A Social Dominance Approach." *Journal of Personality and Social Psychology* 72:353-73.

Pyke, K. D. 1996. "Class-Based Masculinities: The Interdependence of Gender, Class, and Interpersonal Power." *Gender & Society* 10:527-49.

Reskin, B. F. and I. Padavic. 1994. *Women and Men at Work.* Thousand Oaks, CA: Pine Forge.

Rhodebeck, L. A. 1996. "The Structure of Men's and Women's Feminist Orientations: Feminist Identity and Feminist Opinion." *Gender & Society* 10:386-403.

Riess, M. and S. Salzer. 1981. "Individuals Avoid Invading the Space of Males but Not Females." Presented at the 89th Annual Meeting of the American Psychological Association, August, Los Angeles.

Rosaldo, M. Z. 1974. "Women, Culture, and Society: A Theoretical Overview." Pp. 1-16 in *Women, Culture, and Society,* edited by M. Z. Rosaldo and L. Lamphere. Stanford, CA: Stanford University Press.

Ross, L., T. M. Amabile, and J. L. Steinmetz. 1977. "Social Roles, Social Control, and Biases in Social-Perception Processes." *Journal of Personality and Social Psychology* 35:485-94.

Rudman, L. A. and E. Borgida. 1996. "The Afterglow of Construct Accessibility: The Behavioral Consequences of Priming Men to View Women as Sexual Objects." *Journal of Experimental Social Psychology* 31:493-517.

Rusbult, C. E., J. Verette, G. A. Whitney, L. F. Slovik, and I. Lipkus. 1991. "Accommodation Processes in Close Relationships: Theory and Preliminary Empirical Evidence." *Journal of Personality and Social Psychology* 60:53-78.

Shaver, P. R. and C. Hazan. 1993. "Adult Romantic Attachment: Theory and Evidence." Pp. 29-70 in *Advances in Personal Relationships,* vol. 4, edited by D. Perlman and W. H. Jones. London: Kingsley.

Sidanius, J., F. Pratto, and L. Bobo. 1994. "Social Dominance Orientation and the Political Psychology of Gender: A Case of Invariance?" *Journal of Personality and Social Psychology* 67:998-1011.

Smith, E. R. 1993. "Social Identity and Social Emotions: Toward a New Conceptualization of Prejudice." Pp. 297-316 in *Affect, Cognition, and*

Stereotyping: Interactive Processes in Group Perceptions, edited by D. M. Mackie and D. L. Hamilton. San Diego, CA: Academic Press.

Stangor, C., L. Lynch, C. Duan, and B. Glass. 1992. "Categorization of Individuals on the Basis of Multiple Social Features." *Journal of Personality and Social Psychology* 62:207-18.

Stevens, L. E. and S. T. Fiske. 1995. "Motivation and Cognition in Social Life: A Social Survival Perspective." *Social Cognition* 13:189-214.

Straus, M. A. and C. Smith. 1992. "Family Patterns and Primary Prevention of Family Violence." In *Physical Violence in American Families: Risk Factors and Adaptations to Violence in 8,145 Families,* edited by M. A. Straus and R. J. Gelles. New Brunswick, NJ: Transaction.

Swim, J. K., K. J. Aikin, W. S. Hall, and B. A. Hunter. 1995. "Sexism and Racism: Old-Fashioned and Modern Prejudices." *Journal of Personality and Social Psychology* 68:199-214.

Tajfel, H., ed. 1981. *Social Identity and Intergroup Relations.* London: Cambridge University Press.

Taylor, S. E. 1981. "A Categorization Approach to Stereotyping." Pp. 88-114 in *Cognitive Processes in Stereotyping and Intergroup Behavior,* edited by D. L. Hamilton. Hillsdale, NJ: Lawrence Erlbaum.

Taylor, S. E., S. T. Fiske, N. L. Etcoff, and A. Ruderman. 1978. "Categorical Bases of Person Memory and Stereotyping." *Journal of Personality and Social Psychology* 36:778-93.

Tesser, A. 1988. "Toward a Self-Evaluation Maintenance Model of Social Behavior." Pp. 181-227 in *Advances in Experimental Social Psychology,* vol. 21, edited by L. Berkowitz. New York: Academic Press.

Thorne, B. and N. M. Henley. 1975. "Difference and Dominance: An Overview of Language, Gender, and Society." Pp. 5-42 in *Language and Sex: Difference and Dominance,* edited by B. Thorne and N. M. Henley. Rowley, MA: Newbury House.

Travis, C. B. and C. P. Yeager. 1991. "Sexual Selection, Parental Investment, and Sexism." *Journal of Social Issues* 47:117-29.

Turner, J. C. 1987. *Rediscovering the Social Group: A Self-Categorization Theory.* Oxford: Basil Blackwell.

Wolf, N. 1991. *The Beauty Myth: How Images of Beauty Are Used against Women.* New York: William Morrow.

Woolf, V. [1929] 1957. *A Room of One's Own.* New York: Harcourt Brace Jovanovich.

Zárate, M. A. and E. R. Smith. 1990. "Person Categorization and Stereotyping." *Social Cognition* 8:161-85.

CHAPTER 14

Now You Can Choose!

Issues in Parenting and Procreation

BARBARA KATZ ROTHMAN

My oldest child is 23. I can date, with great precision, my concern with issues of procreation.

In 1973, when I was early-on pregnant, teaching the still-new "Sex Roles" course at Brooklyn College (a two-credit filler renamed from "Courtship and Marriage"), my friend and colleague Roslyn Weinman was teaching medical sociology. Roz's child was a toddler. We alone seemed to have missed the delayed childbearing message. Actually, at 26, I was the oldest pregnant woman I knew, lots older than Roz, and I thought I had delayed childbearing.

Roz and I were graduate students, lecturers in those glory days when full-time lecturer jobs were still available. I lost my job that year, bumped to part-time adjunct: Visibly pregnant, I was told I was obviously not serious about my career. It was a very particular moment in feminist history. Women, WOMEN were all anyone could think about those days. Women, not as mothers, with a very small *m* indeed, but as SISTERS, fully equal to our brothers. We didn't really have a vocabulary of "gender studies" worked out yet: I remember long discussions in which the uses of *sex* and *gender* were negotiated. Feminism was everywhere, reborn radiant, if maybe a bit limited.

AUTHOR'S NOTE: Portions of this chapter appear in Barbara Katz Rothman, *Genetic Maps and Human Imaginations: The Limits of Science in Understanding Who We Are.* Copyright 1998 Norton & Co.

Roz and I talked endlessly. The boundaries, if there ever were any, between the personal—the physically intimate, bodily bound personal—and the political and between the intellectual and the political all vanished into the thin air from which they probably sprang in the first place. What was happening in my pregnancy and birth, what was happening in the politics of women's health and "reproductive rights," and what was happening in the scholarly explosion of women's studies—all that happened at once, again and again, as Roz and I talked and talked and talked.

And I decided I wanted a home birth. It was not particularly about feminism, that decision. But feminism gave me a vocabulary to talk about it, a set of motives to legitimate it, the power to accomplish it, and an audience with which to share it. My first published piece was in *Ms.* magazine: "In Which a Sensible Woman Persuades Her Doctor, Her Family and Her Friends to Help Her Give Birth at Home" (1976). The editors at *Ms.* titled it, and it tells a lot, that title: They had rejected other articles submitted on home birth as too far out. Probably too New Age before New Age was a category: both too spiritual on the one hand and too mother-earthy on the other; too much that mix of the body and the soul that birth really is. My article was *sensible.*

I had not yet discovered midwives. I chose a feminist obstetrician—a phrase that now sounds suspiciously like "military intelligence" in its inherent contradiction. Not that the doctor was not both a feminist and an obstetrician, but I am not sure that the one identity really informed the other, that the two could ever be fully integrated. But at the time, both of us thought that they could. It was just a matter of being sensible. The simplest, most straightforward way to ground the home birth decision in a sensible, yet feminist way was to latch on to the concept of "choice." Choice covered a lot of territory. It had not yet been entirely folded into a code word for abortion, though one ought to have seen that coming.

So the issue of home birth distilled into choice—informed, sensible choice. Given the facts—the abysmal record of obstetrics, the untested and unproven nature of much of what they were doing in hospitals, the far more pleasant and emotionally supportive environment that home provides—home birth came to be a sensible choice. A home birth was a choice I made as an informed consumer, someone who weighed all the options, the safety records, the concerns of one sort or another that mattered to me. Having chosen, I then needed support for my choice, and where better to find it than with a feminist gynecologist-obstetrician, someone who supported "choice."

Choice radiated everywhere in those days, a one-size-fits all philosophy of feminism. Home birth, abortion, Little League teams, the two-step biopsy procedure for breast cancer, shaving armpits and legs, engineering degrees, bras—you name it, we wanted *choice*. It took me years to realize that while that made for excellent politics at the time, it was poor sociology.

"Choice" is an excellent, expandable concept, offering an opportunity to challenge the status quo (someone's lack of choice) while entirely accepting the dominant way of thinking in Western culture, It took a quarter of a century for the profound limits of choice to become clear. As Roberts (1997) spells it out in *Killing the Black Body*:

> The dominant view of liberty reserves most of its protection only for the most privileged members of society. This approach superimposes liberty on an already unjust social structure, which it seeks to reserve against unwarranted government interference. Liberty protects all citizens' choices from the most direct and egregious abuses of government power, but it does nothing to dismantle social arrangements that make it impossible for some people to make a choice in the first place. Liberty guards against government intrusion; it does not guarantee social justice. (p. 294)

In 1973 I was a feminist with a job—for a bit longer anyway—and a checkbook. If I wanted to hire an obstetrician to come to my home, that was my choice and my right. For women without jobs and checkbooks, let alone women without comfortable homes with heat, running water, husband, and family who could take time off from work and lend a hand, for women who were not, as I was, among the most privileged, the right might have been there, but the choice most assuredly was not.

The democratic ideal with which we were working is that each person is free to make her own choices—the capitalist system puts the limiting clause on that sentence: given what she can afford. Anybody with money can buy anything that is for sale, and given the capitalist ideal it is extremely difficult to argue why any given thing should not be for sale. If there is a market for it, so be it. And there was—and even more so today is—a market for home birth.

This is a very American understanding of choice, an extremely useful starting place for political action, but ultimately limited. To take a completely different arena of life, think about the civil rights movement's lunch counter sit-ins. The right to be served, the right to buy, was instantly understandable to White America outside of the South. The larger economic picture was lost in the close-ups of Black would-be customers denied service. The fact is that many of the people of African descent living in the South at that time could no more afford a Woolworth's lunch than they could afford a trip up to New York for an integrated lunch. Americans tend to see social justice as utopian, unattainable, wishful thinking, while viewing liberty as our birthright, guaranteed to us as citizens. And so anything that interferes with one's ability to purchase an available good or service, other than a lack of money, is seen as a terrific affront.

America, I have heard it said, does not have a culture; it has an economy. In such a context, choice is a useful, even essential, political tool and concept. But it has a way of flattening everything out, reducing everything to the same level, all individual choice. This consumerist model of choice is probably best represented by something like ice cream flavors: chocolate, vanilla, or raspberry swirl? Ordinary or exotic, the choices are in a sense equally weighted. Walk into an American ice cream store, and you will have a lot of choice, with all of the flavors costing the same. It is an entirely free choice.

But even consumer choices usually get a lot more complicated pretty quickly. I would, for example, like to choose the safest possible car. But I cannot afford a new car, and among used cars, I am limited to what is available, and what is in my price range. Am I sacrificing some safety quality of the brake system to get the lower-mileage car? I choose, and given the limited number of used cars available to me within my price range, I balance the factors that seem to matter most to me. Safety, mileage, size, cost—all get thrown into one pile, and somehow a decision has to emerge, and that decision will be counted as "my choice."

In procreation, the choices became *if, when* and *how*. Women had choices about whether or not to become mothers; to conceive at all or, having conceived accidentally, to continue the pregnancy or not. The decision about entering motherhood was quickly subsumed into the language of choice, and "choice" ultimately has come to represent primarily that one choice, the one we are "pro" as good feminists. Decisions about the timing of motherhood were similarly framed as choices, but mostly in one direction, namely, to postpone motherhood, to wait until we had finished school, established ourselves in careers, until we were ready. The choices about how to enter motherhood start with the relatively simple issue of where and with whom in attendance we would give birth, but over time have burgeoned into choices about a vast array of technological assists, substitutes, and impediments. The (liberal) feminist response to everything, from home birth to breast-feeding in public to egg harvesting to frozen embryos to prenatal diagnosis to surrogacy contracts to donor insemination for lesbian couples to IVF and the whole alphabet soup of infertility treatments, to *everything,* has been "choice."

My first indications of the ways the concept of choice was not working came when I was interviewing women about their decisions to use, or not to use, prenatal diagnosis (Rothman [1986] 1993). Testing was available to them, testing that would tell them if their fetuses had Down's syndrome, neural tube defects, or any of an increasingly large number of identifiable conditions. The women, deeply agonizing over this decision, used a phrase that continues to haunt me: "My only choice." Whatever they chose, to use the testing or not, to continue the pregnancy or to abort, the decision was often framed as an "only choice." What could that mean, that deep contradiction? It was a no-choice choice, a forced choice, a choice a woman makes when she is told she has a choice but sees only one way out.

A woman who lives in a fourth-floor walk-up in a city without curb cuts or services for people with disabilities and who terminates a pregnancy for neural tube defects is not exactly engaging in an exercise in free will, making a "choice." A woman who knows what state services will be like for her Down's syndrome child in the years after she has died, and who aborts rather than subject anyone to that treatment, is not experiencing a "choice."

Even access to the testing itself is not a matter of "choice." I did research in the Netherlands about how the midwives there were using, and not using, prenatal diagnosis in their practices. When I spoke to them about which women chose to use the testing, the differences between our two understandings of "choice" were all but laughable. In the United States, any woman who can afford the testing and who wants it feels she has a right to it. In the Netherlands, the midwives earnestly informed me that they always offer women over the age of 36 the choice of amniocentesis. It is absolutely the woman's choice, and her right to have that choice. No woman who is over 36 who wants the test is denied it; it is available for every eligible woman. But women under 36, I asked, what of their choice? "Oh, they're not eligible." End of discussion. The Netherlands had made a decision, as a society, as a community, and as a state, about what is reasonable in light of risks, of costs, of potential benefits all around. The point of demarcation was established as 36; the test was freely available to every woman over 36 who wanted it, and unavailable to every woman under 36.

The American in me bristled: You mean a 35½-year-old woman who wants the test can be refused it and then give birth to a baby with Down's syndrome, and that's the way it goes? Yup. Or more accurately, "Ja." That's the way it goes.

Yet as an American, I recognize the sad inevitability that within this country a 38-year-old woman who wants the test may not be able to afford it, even though she just as surely cannot afford a disabled child, and that's the way it goes. Just as a young woman who wants an abortion, who wants very much not to have a baby now but to finish school, who wants to grow up first, may not be able to afford the abortion she has a legal right to purchase. And that's the way it goes. Life, even our more morally responsive presidents have informed us, is not fair.

"Choice" was, all things considered, a good place to *start*. Choice offered feminists concerned with procreation a point of entry, a wedge into the discussion. But in this, as in the civil rights movement, it was only a start: Seating in the front of a bus matters only if you have the bus fare. Questions of social justice provide the context in which issues of choice can unfold.

In the area of procreation this is most clear—and most deeply ironic—as choice expands from decisions about the ways we want to enter motherhood to those affecting the kinds of babies we want to mother, including choices about the sex of our children. It started with Down's syndrome and neural tube defects, but it is most assuredly not stopping there. Any study of the introduction of new technology has to confront the problem of the technological imperative. Once people know how to do something, it is very hard for them not to do it. And once people know how to do something they do it more and more, often with wider and wider applications. If here, why not there? If then, why not now?

In philosophical terms, this problem is often discussed as "the slippery slope," a long slide down from the acceptable to the (morally) unacceptable uses of technology. In the case of prenatal diagnosis, the slope is usually graphed as moving from diagnosis and abortion for conditions incompatible with life, passing through the firm but contested territory of Down's syndrome and neural tube defects, floundering on the rocky terrain of socially undesirable conditions like deafness on down to obesity, bouncing along the questionable areas of "gay genes" and "alcoholism genes," and finally crashing into the great moral abyss of sex selection.

Now *that*, the bioethicists generally agree, is wrong. Using prenatal diagnosis and selective abortion "just because" you want one sex and not the other is generally considered wrong—not only by bioethicists but by lots of ordinary folk, too. It has become, I think, a fairly standard place to draw the line. For people who are doing something that risks making them uncomfortable, morally edgy, having a line somewhere is reassuring: This here may be a bit tricky, but that there is *wrong*.

I have heard countless physicians, geneticists, and genetic counselors use sex selection as the line, the unacceptable choice, which by its very existence makes what they *are* doing more acceptable. I am very uncomfortable with that line. It bothers me because it seems to make two demarcations, neither of which feels right. One is the line between "medical" and "nonmedical" conditions. The argument is that prenatal diagnosis and selective abortion for a "medical condition" is morally acceptable. The original language, which one still hears, is that those are "therapeutic" abortions. The implication is that a medical decision is a scientific, rational decision, and one that is morally sound because it is in the interests of health.

But what exactly makes a given disability a "medical condition" and sex *not*? Sex is a diagnosable genetic condition, associated with variations in phenotype, health, longevity, life chances. Is it that sex, while it does make a difference physically, should not matter that much socially? Is it that both sexes should have what they need to have a good life? Is it that sex ought not to be a basis for valuing people?

Then what is the difference between sex and any other "genetic condition"? This is precisely what disability activists are saying: Deaf people, people in wheelchairs, people who are blind, people with retarded mental development, all ought to be given what they need to have a good life, and all ought to be valued for what and for who they are. The problem, the disability activists are saying, lies with the society. And so it should be, one can easily argue, with sex. We ought to value our girls and our boys, welcome both equally. There is something wrong with a society in which people feel the need to do sex selection.

And that leads to the second demarcation that makes me so uncomfortable: "us" and "them." Over and over again, I have heard American and European physicians and geneticists point out that sex selection is a "Third World" problem, something done "over there" and requested by "immigrants." *We,* the doctors tell conference audiences, use prenatal diagnosis and selective abortion for sound medical reasons. *They* misuse the technology.

Each and every woman who uses this extraordinarily difficult technology of selective abortion is making a decision based on what she knows about the baby-to-be and what she knows about the world into which she might bring that baby. An Indian woman who knows what faces her third daughter is not making a morally different decision, it seems to me, than an American woman who knows what faces her child with Down's syndrome. I have spoken with women in both of these situations, who spoke with great love and longing for the baby-that-might-have-been, and much regret about the world that is. Each has said to me, "It wouldn't be fair to the baby, or to my other children."

I am not trying to show you how selective abortion for sex and selective abortion for disability are similar in order to show you that either is right or is wrong. Rather, I remain the sociologist: We need to look not at the individual decision, but at the social context, the world in which that decision is made. We must move beyond liberty and choice to the question of social justice. I can understand and respect a woman who chooses to terminate a pregnancy based on what she knows about the fetus and the world. I cannot understand or respect a society that places her in that position when it is not inevitable.

Let us move beyond sex to consider race. Race, too, is a "genetic" condition expressing itself in phenotype, health, longevity, and life chances. Whatever characteristics of skin, hair, and bone that a particular society defines as "racial," those characteristics will write themselves upon the body of the child. Several years ago, as a guest lecturer feeling somewhat defensive on the issues of disability, I tried to explain that it was not that the women who terminated pregnancies for Down's syndrome or other diagnoses were themselves "antidisability," or "ablist," not that they necessarily felt any repugnance toward people with disabilities. But they knew all too well what happens to these children in America when they grow up, when their parents die. Groping for a comparison, I said, let us consider a South African White women still living under apartheid, pregnant by her Black lover, who might choose an abortion rather than bring a mixed-race child into that situation. Does that make her a racist? I thought not; I thought she was doing what she felt she had to do as an individual living under impossible circumstances. If we were going to have discussions about regulating morality, it was not *her* morality with which we should start.

A young Black man came up to me afterward. But what about *Black South African women*? he asked. What were they supposed to do? They too are bearing their babies into that world. And indeed, what of those women? Haven't they sometimes made that same decision? It is not always about the otherness of the baby. Black women, Jewish women, women under a variety of racist regimes have contracepted, have aborted, and have committed infanticide to spare their babies the consequences of racist madness. When a woman kills her baby rather than have it sold downriver to speculators, or starved, tortured, or experimented upon, isn't that a mercy killing?

And what of women with disabilities? They have not been spared these decisions. Some years back, in one of the excesses of "talk radio," a show focused on the situation of a television news anchor's pregnancy. The woman had a genetic condition that resulted in missing fingers and toes, and knew the possibility of passing this condition on to her child. Some callers felt she had no right to continue the pregnancy without testing. The woman herself was obviously not all that severely disabled—she was, after all, a television news anchor, and so, by whatever American standards one brings to bear, doing just fine. But other women have been yet more disabled, have found the world too hostile a place for people with their condition, or their condition too difficult in itself, and have indeed chosen not to bring children like themselves into the world.

When the genetic technology for making these decisions was the technology of prenatal diagnosis and selective abortion, there was inevitably a strong leaning toward continuing the pregnancy. You have to have a good reason to abort a wanted pregnancy, and to some extent, the later the testing, the better the reason had to be. Thus the moral questions that arose focused on what might warrant an abortion: which conditions were serious enough, which too frivolous. Thus it turns out not to be so straightforward after all to draw a line that neatly divides "medical" and "other" grounds, that divides us with our good decisions from them with their bad ones. All decisions are made in a context, and there is no objective place to stand and judge.

But the technology is not stable. It shifts, and with the shifts come different questions. When you are not selecting *against*, but selecting *for*, the issue changes. Selective abortion has been a "slippery slope" problem. But when we think about selective implantation, selective *creation*, then I prefer a different image—that of the "camel's nose." That argument goes that once you let the camel's nose into the tent, it is very hard to keep the rest of the camel out. I prefer that image because I do not see a terrain along which we societal explorers move at our own risk, but rather a very aggressive camel: the biotech industries, highly motivated to get the nose and the rest of that profitable camel entrenched in our tents.

Sex selection is a perfect example of this process. Sex selection clinics have opened up around the world, offering methods of selection, of choosing the sex of a baby, that do not involve abortion. One is sperm sorting, using the technology of "artificial insemination" after separating out X- and Y-bearing sperm. This is of limited value, only increasing odds from roughly 50/50 to roughly 70/30, but thousands of people have paid for it, finding it worth trying. There are other, more elaborate procedures, with higher success rates combining variations on in vitro fertilization. Embryos outside of the body can be sexed and only those of the "right sex" implanted.

These are all technologies that are being marketed, that are available for a price. It is also possible to choose the *race* of your baby. Great Britain had a notorious case of a Black woman who requested an egg from a White woman for in vitro fertilization so she could spare her child the burdens of racism.

Sometimes people do sex selection to avoid the consequences of deep and profound sexism, and then it is, I think, comparable in every way to decisions women make about terminating pregnancies for disabilities. But, especially when abortion is not involved, sex selection is also marketed as a "consumer choice." Depending on how invasive a procedure she is willing to endure, and how much money she wants to spend, a woman can choose a method that at minimum increases her odds and at maximum virtually guarantees her having a child of chosen sex.

We are introducing choice into yet another arena of our lives. Choice always seems like a good thing to have, and from the point of view of the consumer, the purchaser, it probably is. But what about choice from the point of view of the—what? the consumed? purchased? Or let us be kind: the *chosen* child?

People in the adoption world have struggled with the idea of the chosen child. At first, it seemed such a satisfying bedtime tale: We chose you. It seemed, in adoption, a nice counterbalance to the implicit, understood but unstated fact of having been placed, made available in the first place. But it wasn't such a sweet tale after all. If a child is chosen, it is chosen *for* something. Why me? the child asks—What about me made you choose me? And suddenly parenthood becomes contingent. Chosen for being pretty, sweet, cute, for any given characteristic, implies that should you lose that characteristic, your chosen status is at risk. The child has to wonder, What if I get ugly, surly, stop being cute?

But if you choose a boy and get a boy, or choose a girl and get a girl, then what is the problem? The technology can be improved so that failure, the wrong sex, is not going to happen. So then, won't the child have been chosen for what it truly, indelibly is?

Who does such a thing? Who uses sex selection? A woman who has two sons and has always wanted a daughter? A family that has all girls and wants to "pass on the family name"? People do sex selection because they want a particular kind of child—or maybe, more accurately, because they want a particular kind of parenting experience, and they think sex selection will buy them that.

Sex is a diagnosable chromosomal condition. Choose for Y and you get a male; choose for X and you get a female. What exactly is it that you are choosing and getting?

Sometimes people call it "gender selection." I used to correct that, but I've stopped. *Sex* is the word social scientists use for the biological phenomenon of male/female. *Gender* we save for the social role, for being a boy, a girl, a man, a woman. A sperm cell or a zygote cannot possibly have "gender," but gender is what people are choosing when they select by sex. People who say they want a girl have something in mind—girlness, femininity, some set of characteristics that they expect will come in that girl-package that they think would not come with a boy. I have heard women say that they want the kind of relationship they had with their mothers; they think they cannot have that kind of relationship with a son. I have heard women talking about wanting to have the frills, the clothes, the manicures together, the pretty mother-daughter outfits, the fun of a prom gown and a wedding gown, that come with girls.

Can't you just see the disaster looming? That woman is not ready for a six-foot-tall, 300-pound daughter who wears nothing but denim and boots. People who want a son are probably none too pleased when he announces he wants ballet lessons. When people want a son or want a daughter, they want a host of characteristics that they believe are, and often believe *should be*, sex linked. Someone who wants a cuddly, warm, loving child who will remain close in adulthood chooses a girl. Someone who wants a child who will go out and accomplish great things in the world, bring glory to the family name, goes for a boy. The person is choosing sex, the chromosomes and the genitals, but he or she is also making a statement about personality, lifestyle, what he or she wants the child to be and to become. The person is opting for gender.

Sex is a very crude determinant of these personality and lifestyle traits. How much of gender is biological, "genetic," "nature," is a long-standing debate. But wherever you stand on that question, it is apparent that not every child is a living and breathing gender stereotype. Getting a girl or a boy does not guarantee a parent the characteristics he or she is seeking.

Well, lots of us are not what our parents had in mind, and so be it. What has changed with this technology is the implicit guarantee, offering the idea that parents can now choose, can hope to control the kind of child they will be parenting.

What are the characteristics that we think we can control when we plan our children? When we move past the list of diseases to be avoided, where are we? Sex is a crude genetic characteristic: It is writ large as a chromosome, but is only a loose indicator of what we might expect in a child. As the map of the human genome is unfolded and read, we expect finer and finer resolution. But we are looking at a map, not a crystal ball, and we are not dealing with three wishes from the blessing fairy. Our planning is limited to selecting among embryos, or selecting specific stretches of DNA to include in an embryo, and so our choices are limited to those things we believe are genetically determined.

But what exactly is that supposed to mean? The logic of genetic thinking, as Fox Keller (1995:3) sums it up, is that genes are the primary agents of life: They are the fundamental units of biological traits. In that logic, to read genes is to predict traits; and it follows then that to choose traits you have to choose the genes. Want a blue-eyed child? Select for the genes that cause blue eyes.

But are genes causes? Hubbard would never allow us to use the word *cause* for the action of a gene (see Hubbard and Wald 1993). Genes do not "do" anything; they are certainly not "for" anything. Genes are associated with, involved in, active in the production of proteins. And although I know Hubbard is correct, somehow I think that the language of a gene that causes something, like blue eyes or sickle-cell anemia, is a reasonable way to speak. What, after all, ever causes anything in this world?

I fell down the stairs and broke my ankle. But it is perhaps a bit more complicated. How did I come to be on the stairs? My Aunt Joan lent us the down payment for this house with its big staircase. I was carrying the Hanukkah presents at the time and couldn't see where I was going. Judah Maccabee fought some battle that Hanukkah commemorates. American Jews only make such a fuss over Hanukkah to compete with Christmas—actually, to compete with the commercialization of Christmas. And besides, some little child who shall remain nameless, lest godforbid she get a complex, left a plastic bag on the third-from-bottom step. And how can you break both bones in your ankle by falling three steps? Look at a skeleton sometime—the whole weight of the body tapers down to this absurdly thin point right above where the foot twists.

So what was the cause of my broken ankle? Aunt Joan, Judah Maccabee, Jesus Christ, American capitalism, a nameless child, or an orthopedic design flaw?

I do not know what ever causes anything. "Causality" in science is basically only a hypothesis you cannot disprove (yet). But with all of the hedging of my bets, I am still ready to sometimes use the word *cause* in connection with a gene. I know that genes only code for the production of proteins. They do not *do* anything, not even produce the protein, but still, in the more or less approximate way I am used to talking about causation, I feel comfortable saying that a gene causes, say, blue eyes. Sickle-cell anemia. What else?

We make this question hard to answer because we have painted ourselves into a corner with this nature/nurture thing; we have set up a dichotomy that exists nowhere but in our own heads, and then keep confronting it as if it were a fundamental truth of the universe. We make a list of characteristics, qualities, traits, states of being, and then see if we can assign them to the "nature" side by finding a "gene for" the characteristic. Is intelligence, sexual orientation, schizophrenia, the tendency to divorce, depression, or inability to spell genetic or not? The discussion too often seems to degenerate into "Is too!" "Is not!"

Two of the most public, vociferous, and politically important of these discussions have been the long-standing one focusing on the genetic component in intelligence and the more recent one focused on the "gay gene." Because the intelligence discussion has been hopelessly mired in the racism that surrounds it, let us take a look at the gay gene discussion: Is there a "gene for" being gay? For gay men, there does seem to be a genetic component, one of the pieces. Like every other gene, it speaks in probabilities, in odds. If an identical twin is gay, the chances of his twin being gay are 50 percent. That is considerably higher than chance, given that gay men make up less than 10 percent of all men, but very much lower than the odds on eye color matching in identical twins.

Burr (1996) has helpfully compared male sexual orientation with handedness. For both, we have a dominant and a minority orientation. About 92 percent of the population is right-handed. Left-handedness has at various times in history been treated as evil, sick, sinful, or an ordinary variation. Handedness is experienced as a very powerful given: It is not changeable by an act of will, though one can hide or pass if necessary. And so it seems to be with male homosexuality.

But is handedness "genetic"? If an identical twin is left-handed, the chances of his twin being left-handed are 12 percent. That is, the identical twin of a left-handed person is only one and a half times more likely to be left-handed than is the person sitting next to him on the bus. It is not a powerful argument for genetic causality. But neither does it make handedness a "lifestyle choice."

It seems as if what we are really talking about when we invoke genes is predestination versus free will. In our conversation, we talk as if the opposite of "genetic" were "a choice." Genes seem to function in our language and our thinking as inevitability, determination, predestination, *fate*. What the geneticists tell us is that genes work as probability factors that play a part in a causal equation. How can we think about human will, choice, agency, intentionality, if we are thinking about genes as causes? Go back to the stairs with me.

If you keep leaving things on the steps (and if I've said this once I've said it a thousand times), someone is going to get hurt. And if people march up and down the stairs day after day, year after year, it should be no surprise that eventually someone falls. And if you carry packages and cannot see where you are going, well, what do you expect? To each of these things, and probably a dozen more, maybe even one or two that are "genetic," having to do with bone structure, clumsiness, and distractibility, we can assign a probability rating. What are the odds of falling under each set of circumstances?

Now we are approaching some basic philosophical questions about determinism and inevitability. Was it inevitable that I break my leg? Given everything that happened in the world to that exact second—including the history of architecture, my relationship with Aunt Joan, the set of circumstances that brought that nameless child who shouldn't have a complex about this into my life, the invention of plastic, the evolution of the ankle—given all of it—was it inevitable? Did I have to put my foot there? Was it fate?

That is a fascinating philosophical question, but it is not terribly useful practically. For practical purposes, we focus on one or two of the factors that we think we can control. Do not leave things on the stairs. Watch where you are going. We act as if, and we have to act as if, we have control.

When genes become more and more important in our thinking, we start assigning them greater and greater causal power, moving them to more central positions. Sometimes that has meant giving up, that metaphorical throwing your hands up in the air and saying, "It's genetic," meaning "And that's that." Fate. Which is acceptable if the situation is one that we might want people to take their hands off of and leave be. So the "gay gene" might be useful as a political tool if invoking that gene becomes another way of saying, Give it up, you have to accept that some people are inevitably, determinedly, gay. But if the question we are looking at is not "Why are some men gay?" but "Why are more Black men in prisons than in colleges?" then saying "It's genetic" is quite dangerous. That of course is the underlying premise of racism: that there are genetic differences between categories of people. In the United States, such racist arguments resurface periodically, with books like *The Bell Curve* (Herrnstein and Murray 1994) making the best-seller lists as they invoke genetic determinist explanations for social problems.

In the context of procreation, from the perspective of would-be parents, what the developing technology of genetics might mean is that "It's genetic" is less a throwing-up-your-hands situation than a rolling-up-your-sleeves kind of problem. "It's genetic" might come to mean "Let's fix it," engineer it, construct it to order. Let *us* make the determination, let us predetermine: Let us *choose.*

Take that highly publicized "gay gene," XQ, now officially recorded as GAY1. Individual prospective parents of privilege should soon be able to include that—or any other given gene—in their list of things to select for or select against. Many people would be considerably more distressed to learn that their child is gay than to learn that he has some disability. The idea that there is a genetic component to being gay leads quickly to either selecting against that gene or engineering to change it. I picture that aggressive camel at the side of our tent, wearing its sign advertising sex selection; won't sexual orientation, for a slight additional fee, be available in the next package?

Does that kind of selection assure parents that their child will not be gay? Certainly not: A person without the "gay gene" can grow up to be gay just as a person with it can grow up to be straight. But with the selection, one shifts the odds, the probabilities. People have demonstrated their willingness to pay, in time, money, and physical risks and pain, to shift those odds even for sex selection. Knowing that the technology cannot guarantee a child of chosen sex, or if it is a child of chosen sex, cannot guarantee the "kind of girl" or "kind of boy" the parents seek, still they enter the sex selection clinics. People using prenatal diagnostic technologies know that whatever diseases are screened for and against, there are still no guarantees of a healthy, bright, happy child, but they find it worthwhile to do what they can to shift the odds in their favor. They rule out what they can, exercise control where they can. Offer more technology promising yet more control, and people will use it.

Gay is a highly politicized trait. But every day seems to bring some other "gene for" some other quality, characteristic, trait. Can we control all of it? Can we test and select and read and decode and splice our way to what we really want in our children, for our children?

And have we any right to do that? I am not talking about our legal rights, our rights as citizens. American liberal legal scholars can show that whatever our discomforts with treating children like consumer products, it is not in our civil libertarian tradition, and probably not in our interests, to try to stop each other from doing so. So I will not argue against "choice," not even the very limited kind of choices that are available to some people and not to others in so profoundly unjust a society. Rather, I am thinking about our moral rights as parents in our relationship with our children. Do we even want to have them custom-made? Would we have wanted our parents to have chosen our traits, predetermined whatever they could and wanted to about us? Whether a trait is what you like best or least about yourself, you probably would not like thinking about it as something your parents put on an order form.

As if they could. As if the traits and characteristics and parts of our being that we cared about were all separately and distinctively coded in "genes for," which in our determination we could choose for our children.

Parenthood does not come with guarantees. Motherhood, I have often said, is one more chance for a speeding truck to ruin your life. The world has plans for our children, and our children have plans for themselves; we will not be able to control this.

The demands of the information age drive us toward getting all the information, toward taking all the control we can. Perhaps wisdom lies in not always doing so, in making wise judgments about what information we want and what information we do not want; which choices we want to make and which choices are not ours to make.

Choices about if, when, and how to mother are ours to make. In a just and decent world, those choices would be available to all women and to all men who want to actively nurture in the way we call mothering. A good and just world, I believe, would provide people with opportunities to mother if that is what they want to do. A just world would provide women with genuine choices about pregnancy, and would support them in their choices about who will attend them and where as they labor to bring their children forth into the world. A good and just world would provide us with choices about *our* mothering. But it may go beyond what a good world, beyond what a just world should offer to give us choices about whom we will mother.

Our children are no more our property, subject to our consumerist choices, than we are the property of our parents. The geneticists like to talk about having unlocked the secrets of life, found the bible, the blueprint. The human genome, they tell us, is our book of life. We must not permit it to become a catalog.

References

Burr, Chandler. 1996. *A Separate Creation: The Search for the Biological Origins of Sexual Orientation.* New York: Hyperion.

Herrnstein, Richard J. and Charles Murray. 1994. *The Bell Curve: Intelligence and Class Structure in American Life.* New York: Free Press.

Hubbard, Ruth and Elijah Wald. 1993. *Exploding the Gene Myth.* Boston: Beacon.

Keller, Elizabeth Fox. 1995. *Refiguring Life: Metaphors of Twentieth-Century Biology.* New York: Columbia University Press.

Roberts, Dorothy. 1997. *Killing the Black Body: Race, Reproduction and the Meaning of Liberty.* New York: Pantheon.

Rothman, Barbara Katz. 1976. "In Which a Sensible Woman Persuades Her Doctor, Her Family and Her Friends to Help Her Give Birth at Home." *Ms.*, December.

———. [1986] 1993. *The Tentative Pregnancy: Prenatal Diagnosis and the Future of Motherhood.* New York: W. W. Norton.

CHAPTER 15

Embattled Terrain

Gender and Sexuality

JUDITH LORBER

In much recent feminist scholarship, the inclusion of gender as an organizing principle has enlarged the arena of shared concepts, research questions, and policy stances. With sexuality, however, many issues have two (or more) often embattled sides. Some of the debates involved are whether heterosexuality in Western societies is still dominated by men's objectification and exploitation of women's bodies or whether women are initiators and equal partners in consensual heterosexual encounters, whether prostitution is sex work or sexual slavery, and whether pornography is universally harmful or can be a legitimate part of varied sexual repertoires. These are divisive political splits, with some feminists fighting for women's freedom from sexual oppression and others for women's freedom to be sexual (Chancer 1998:1-58). The theoretical divisions center on concepts of sexuality, heterosexual relationships, and men's personal and structural dominance. Although feminists don't all line up on one side or the other, the debates have been intense. Chancer targets the "internal conundrum" of contemporary feminism as the source of the intensity—the intertwining of the personal and the political. In the case of sexuality, she says, "the feminist critique . . . raised the possibility that the very *fulfillments* and *pleasures*

AUTHOR'S NOTE: Parts of this chapter are adapted from *Paradoxes of Gender* (Yale University Press, 1994). I thank Myra and Beth for their editing, and Carolle Charles, Maren Lockwood Carden, Susan Farrell, Eileen Moran, and Barbara Katz Rothman for their astute comments on this chapter.

of the personal could also be the *undoing* and *bane* of the political" (p. 43).

Another set of issues concerns the origins and stability of heterosexual and homosexual sexuality and the significance of bisexuality. The area of transgendering (from cross-dressing to medicalized sex change) has raised questions of transgression and conformity. Here the debates, equally impassioned, are over the politics of identity. Transgendering and bisexuality implicitly deny the essentiality of binary, clearly distinguishable gender and sexual categories and their usefulness in theory, research, and politics (Lorber 1996; McIntosh 1993; Namaste 1994; Parlee 1996). The reaction by some lesbian and gay activists to transgressions that blur the boundaries illustrates the paradox that without clear categories, you have neither a politics of identity nor a politics of transgression (Gamson 1995). As Gamson (1998) says, "Both the category-strippers and the category-defenders are right: fixed identity categories are both the basis for oppression and the basis for political power" (p. 35).

At the heart of all of these debates are conceptualizations of gender and sexuality. Gender is not a homogeneous category, but involves status, identity, and display. *Gender status*—being taken as a man or a woman—in Western society implies dominance and assertiveness. *Gender identity*—the sense of self as a man or a woman, which can have various sexual identifications—presents interaction and legal issues. *Gender display*—being feminine versus being masculine according to late-twentieth-century postindustrial norms and expectations—involves sexualized behavior and appearance. *Sexuality* involves desired and actual sexual attraction, emotions, and fantasies, not just behavior. A *sexual identity* involves self-identification and a lifestyle; a *sexual status* involves social recognition of the identity (Klein, Sepekoff, and Wolf 1985; Person 1980). In the past decade, bisexuals and transgenders have become recognized social categories along with gays and lesbians, but the boundaries and definitions of each group, as well as their relationships to gender and sexual identity, transgression, and politics, present fascinating theoretical and conceptual issues (Bornstein 1994; Bristow and Wilson 1993; Garber 1992, 1995; Tucker 1995).

In the following analysis of the feminist discourse on gender and sexuality, I will argue that one side of these debates construes gender statuses, identities, and displays as both binary and stable, almost "essential," whereas the other sees them as derived from socialization

and social context and thus potentially both multiple and fluid. Although these contrasting views are often implicit, they have political
implications for feminist stances on sexuality. Liberal feminism's emphasis on sexual freedom assumes malleability and individual agency,
whereas radical feminism's more pessimistic view of the pervasive
sexual oppression of women by men reflects a belief in men's deep-
seated proclivities for domination and control, often through violence.
Psychoanalytic feminism sees men's sexual domination in heterosexual
relationships as rooted in their unconscious and unlikely to change
unless there are radical changes in gendered parenting. Lesbian feminists, like gay theorists and activists, recognize the political perils of
claims of biology or early childhood imprinting as the origins of sexual
orientation, but in organizing around identity, have tended to emphasize permanence in commitment to a gay or lesbian sexual status. Social
constructionists analyze the historical and cultural context in which
sexuality is "scripted," focusing politically on what sexual behaviors
are approved, tolerated, and tabooed for women and men of different
social groups. Sexuality, in this perspective, is a product of learning,
social pressures, and cultural values. Legal penalties, job loss, and
violence uphold the heterosexual social order, often defeating individual attempts at resistance and rebellion, but because everything is
socially produced, as social values change, so do the strictures on sexual
behavior. Postmodern feminism and queer theory take the most extreme view on the fluidity of gender and sexuality, arguing that they are
performances complete with costume changes and episodic dramatic
narratives; individuals can deliberately produce conformity or varying
degrees of social subversion.

The following discussion of heterosexuality, prostitution, pornography, and transgendering examines the theoretical assumptions on gender and sexuality in the different feminist perspectives and the conse-
quent political outcomes. I end this chapter with the possibilities of a
theoretical convergence, although I am pessimistic about the political
conflicts ending soon.

Heterosexuality: Rape or Cross-Purposes?

In the 1980s, radical feminists such as MacKinnon (1989) expanded
the concept of patriarchy by defining it as a worldwide system of
subordination of women by men through violence and sexual exploitation. At the core of the radical feminist view is the belief that all men are

capable of, if not prone to, rape, and all women are potential victims (Russell 1998). Thus, the threat of sexual violence is one of the most powerful means of men's control of women (Brownmiller 1975). Even if the violence is not direct, high culture and mass media sexualize and objectify women's bodies, encouraging attitudes that women are sexually available for any man's use (Kaplan 1983; Millett 1970). Sexual harassment is one of the most common manifestations of the covert sexual violence in Western societies: Unwanted sexual invitations, sexually loaded remarks and jokes, and inappropriate comments on dress or appearance—on the job, in school, and on the street—are routine experiences for women and girls. Overt sexual violence is manifest in all-too-frequent stranger, date, and gang rape and in sexual murders (Bart and Moran 1993; Caputi 1987; Crosette 1997).

The radical feminist concept of sexual violence was extended to romantic heterosexual relationships. The contention is that if all men derive power from their dominant social status, then any sexual relationship between women and men is intrinsically unequal: "Sexuality is conceived as . . . nothing less than the dynamic of sex as social hierarchy, its pleasure the experience of power in its gendered form" (MacKinnon 1989:xiii). Consent by women to heterosexual intercourse is, by this definition, not true consent, because it is often forced by emotional appeals and threats to end the relationship. If a woman fears that a date or friend or lover or husband will use physical violence if she does not give in, and she "consents," it is tantamount to rape. In this analysis, the line between consensual sex and rape is often hard to discern. According to MacKinnon (1987), men may clearly distinguish between "normal sex" and acts of sexual violence, but women do not:

> We have a deeper critique of what has been done to women's sexuality and who controls it. What we are saying is that sexuality in exactly these normal forms often *does* violate us. So long as we say that those things are abuses of violence, not sex, we fail to criticize what has been made of *sex*, what has been done to us *through* sex, because we leave the line between rape and intercourse, sexual harassment and sex roles . . . right where it is. (pp. 86-87)

In sum, in the radical feminist view, men's sexuality is imbued with barely concealed aggression. The finding that 25 percent of women in a U.S. national survey had experienced unwanted sex supports this view (Laumann et al. 1994). Radical feminists contrast men's sexuality with women's mutuality and tenderness: "Feminine sexuality, unlike the mediation of the visible which sustains phallic desire, is of the register of touching, nearness, presence, immediacy, contact" (Gallop 1982:30). Lesbian sexuality would then be the antithesis of male sexuality, especially anonymous "bath-house" encounters. Valverde (1985) says that because lesbian relationships reflect mother-daughter love, they are more emotionally encompassing and more powerfully erotic than heterosexual relationships are for women: "Because of this 'emotionalism' that women are conditioned to have, and the inevitable associations of the lover's body with the nurturing, all-powerful body of the mother, love between women can create some of the strongest bonds in human experience" (pp. 90-91).

The social constructionist view of sexuality agrees that in Western societies, men's sexual behavior is more instrumental and aggressive than women's, but places more emphasis on socialization and context than on innate differences in female and male sexuality. Some heterosexual and lesbian women enjoy sadomasochistic sex (English, Hollibaugh, and Rubin 1981). For many men, heterosexual as well as homosexual, objectified sexuality is not "good sex" (Stoltenberg 1990:101-14). However, inequality in sexual relationships is almost expected in contemporary society. A study of college-age women and men in dating relationships found that both felt the man appropriately had more power in the relationship; male-dominant relationships were also more long-lasting than female-dominant relationships, which were seen as nonnormative (Felmlee 1994).

In another study, women's and men's attitudes toward sexuality were not that different. Narratives on their sex lives written by White, middle-class, mostly heterosexual college students in the 1980s showed that women as well as men felt that they had a right to experiment sexually, that men as well as women were romantic, and that everyone believed that sex with affection was the best kind (Moffatt 1989:181-270). To be sexually eclectic, a man had to be able to respect his sex partner, whether their relationship was casual or long-term. Similarly, "to be an authentic sexual liberal, a woman, correspondingly, had to stop believing that if she fooled around she was a slut. Also, like a male romantic, she had to modify the neotraditional woman's stance so that she herself could enjoy casual sex without commitment" (p. 223).

Although there are both gender differences and significant overlap in current attitudes toward sexual behavior, women and men seem to be at cross-purposes in heterosexual relationships. For heterosexual men, norms of masculinity forbid open displays of affection for their men friends, to whom they are intensely loyal, even though they rely on women for emotional sustenance (Herek 1986). Women who become heterosexual relegate their emotional bonds with other women to "backup," while they search for one man to invest in emotionally for a long-term relationship (Cancian 1987). In their peer groups, the closeness of men's bonding is masked by sex talk, especially boasts of sexual conquests. The heterosexual boy's goal is supposed to be conquest: "To the young man, the woman becomes, in the most profound sense, a sexual object. Her body and mind are the object of a sexual game, to be won for his personal aggrandizement. Status goes to the winner, and sex is prized not as testament of love but as testimony to control of another human being" (Anderson 1990:114).

These sexual attitudes are deeply embedded in Western culture. The contradictions of men's continuing attachment to their friends and sexual objectification of women, and women's needing their friends for emotional solace while they pursue unrewarding romances, have been depicted in the songs, folklore, and fortune-telling rituals of the precommunist Russian working class (Bobroff 1983), the bawdy songs and stories of today's working-class Mexican men (Peña 1991), the street lore of late-twentieth-century African Americans (Anderson 1990:112-19), the sexual fantasies of White middle-class college students of the 1980s (Moffatt 1989:181-270), and the sexualization of adolescent girls in Germany in the 1970s (Haug et al. 1987).

According to psychoanalytic feminism, this asymmetry in heterosexual relationships is the outcome of the Oedipus complex—the psychological separation from the mother as a child develops a sense of individual identity but at the same time continues to want emotional closeness with her (Chodorow 1976). In Freudian theory, boys have to separate from their mothers and identify with their fathers in order to establish their masculinity. They develop strong ego boundaries and a capacity for the independent action, objectivity, and rational thinking so valued in Western culture, but also learn to repress their emotional attachment to their mothers.

Women are a threat to men's independence and masculine sexuality because they remind men of their dependence on their mothers. However, men need women for the emotional sustenance and intimacy they rarely give each other. Their ambivalence toward women is reflected in their proclivities to control women emotionally and objectify them sexually. In contrast, girls continue to identify with their mothers, and so they grow up with fluid ego boundaries that make them sensitive, empathic, and emotional. It is these qualities that make them potentially good mothers and responsive to men's emotional needs. But because the men in their lives have developed personalities that make them emotionally guarded, women turn to other women for intimacy. Thus, Rich (1980) contends that heterosexuality arises through the repression of a continuum of lesbian emotionality and desire by an intense process of socialization.

Whether the source is patriarchal oppression, social scripting, or the Oedipus complex, feminists have shown that men's sexuality holds many dangers for women, especially young women. Must they then constantly be protected from men's sexual predatoriness? The prevalence of rape, especially gang rape in supposedly friendly territory like fraternity houses, would so indicate (Sanday 1981). But some young women argue that such protection puts them back into the days of the taboo against premarital sex and the glorification of virginity (Roiphe 1993). Sexual protection laws for women have a long history of racial and ethnic contamination in the United States. Black women's and White women's legal standing as accusers of Black men and White men in rape cases are hardly equal. As Crenshaw (1991) notes:

> Rape statutes generally do not reflect *male* control over *female* sexuality, but *white* male regulation of *white* female sexuality. . . . When Black women were raped by white males, they were being raped not as women generally, but as Black women specifically. Their femaleness made them sexually vulnerable to racist domination, while their Blackness effectively denied them any protection. This white male power was reinforced by a judicial system in which the successful conviction of a white man for raping a Black woman was virtually unthinkable. (pp. 68-69)

A social construction analysis of rape shows that it is embedded in cultures and social attitudes, not in men's intrinsically violent sexuality. Reeves Sanday's (1981) cross-cultural analysis of 95 nonindustrial societies found that in 18 percent there was a high incidence of rape and concomitant cultural approval, whereas rape was rare or absent and culturally condemned in 47 percent (table 2:9). In the rape-free societies, women were respected for their procreative and productive roles, power was balanced between women and men, and interpersonal violence in general was condemned. In the rape-prone societies, men were dominant and regarded women as property, hostility was fostered between women and men, and sexual assault was part of the generalized use of violence in social conflict.

Even in a rape-prone society, not all men rape. To find out under what circumstances men in the United States commit rape, Scully and Marolla interviewed convicted rapists and compared them to other felons in the same prisons (Scully 1990). The rapists they interviewed were poorly educated and had held low-status jobs; many were serving sentences for more than one crime. The majority were under 35 years old; 54 percent were Black and 66 percent of their victims were White; 46 percent were White, and two of their victims were Black.[1] More than half had not lived with their biological parents when growing up, and about half had grown up in violent families. Their adolescent and adult sex lives had been active and unremarkable; almost half were either married or cohabiting at the time of the rape. The felons who were committed for crimes other than rape had similar social backgrounds, so there was nothing in upbringing or social characteristics that distinguished the rapists. What did distinguish the men convicted of violent sexual behavior was their hostility toward women and rigid beliefs that women should be sexually faithful and men should be tough, fearless, and able to conquer women sexually and defy authority. They also believed, more strongly than other felons, that women's own behavior causes men to rape, that women could avoid rape if they tried, that women secretly want to be raped and enjoy it, and that women use the charge of rape vindictively against innocent men. Some took pleasure in sexual violence, others in subduing a proud women; for still others, it was a bonus in a burglary or mugging. Given the culture's approval of sexual violence, Scully calls rape a low-risk, high-reward crime (pp. 137-69).

The social context of gang rapes shows that they are also rooted in gender norms of masculinity and a sexual double standard that blames the woman for complicity (Chancer 1987; Martin and Hummer 1989; Sanday 1990). In addition, gang rapes, or date rapes that turn into gang rapes, are part of men's bonding rituals in Western cultures. In an analysis of gang rapes in the United States, Reeves Sanday (1990) found a common pattern: "A vulnerable young woman, one who is seeking acceptance or who is high on drugs or alcohol, is taken to a room. She may or may not agree to have sex with one man. She then passes out, or is too weak or scared to protest, and a train of men have sex with her" (p. 1). This pattern "appears to be widespread not only among fraternities but in many other exclusively male contexts at colleges and universities in the United States, such as organized sports. It or its equivalent is also found outside universities where men band together in clubs, work groups, athletic teams, military units, and business conventions—in all the settings associated with the term 'stag party' " (p. 4). She argues that this behavior is a manifestation of both homo-sociality and homophobia: "In group sex, homoerotic desire is simulta-neously indulged, degraded, and extruded from the group. The fact that the woman involved is often unconscious highlights her status as a surrogate victim in a drama where the main agents are males interacting with one another" (pp. 12-13). The sexual show of masculinity is for each other, to show they are "real men." Men close ranks around one another when accused of gang rapes, and their families and communi-ties also support their behavior by decrying the promiscuity or irre-sponsibility of the victims, even when they are from the same commu-nity (Chancer 1987; Lefkowitz 1997; Martin and Hummer 1989).

From a social constructionist view, women need protection from the discourse of heterosexuality and its continued double standard, not men's sexuality. However, the double standard that condones and often glorifies men's sexual aggressiveness and condemns the same behavior in women reflects the dominance and subordination in the gendered social order. In the radical feminist view, that is the heart of sexual politics. By controlling women's bodies, men control a great part of women's lives. Sexual violence is one end of a continuum, not a pathol-ogy separate from what is normal. The viewpoints in the debate over heterosexuality and the politics of rape are not so far apart, but the continued virulence of the argument over whether women are constant victims of men's tacit and open sexual violence or are, for the most part, equal agents, speaks to a resonance with experiences that women cannot deny, even when they do not want to blame men in general. There is an ambivalence here that muddies feminist responses to men's egregious public sexual acting out and makes it difficult to maintain clear guidelines in cases of sexual harassment. As Chancer (1998) says, "Even today, the pleasures of sexuality and the pain inflicted by sexism remain stubbornly enmeshed in male-dominated societies like our own; it is difficult to extricate erotic joy from oppressive vulnerability" (p. 1).

So is the choice, as Segal (1994:318) puts it, feminism or fucking? Hardly, in her view: "Sexual pleasure is far too significant in our lives and culture for women not to be seeking to express our agency through it" (pp. 313-14). Sexual oppression is our lives, too, but for many of us lucky enough to have escaped physical violence, not our whole lives. A view of sexual behavior as socially constructed and contextualized, with a variety of behaviors and relationships, offers a perspective for an analysis of heterosexuality that does not preclude political activism against rape and violence, but also allows for heterosexual women's desires and sexual initiatives (Richardson 1996; Wilkinson and Kitzinger 1993).

Prostitution: Sex Work or Sexual Slavery?

A similar ambivalence imbues feminist positions on prostitution and other forms of sex work, some taking the point of view that it is women's right to use their bodies to make money (Chapkis 1997; Jenness 1990) and others claiming that prostitutes are virtual slaves in a worldwide sex industry (Barry [1979] 1983, 1995).

In the eighteenth and nineteenth centuries in Europe and the United States, women's selling or bartering sex for gifts, money, or favors was brought into public discourse and became subject to control and regulation by medicine and law, which had supplanted religion as the prime agencies of social control (Foucault 1978). Prostitution (known as "vice") became immoral work. Working-class women who had been able to augment their poor salaries or survive in hard times by selling sex were publicly stigmatized by vice campaigns (Corbin 1990; Hobson 1987; Rosen 1982; Walkowitz 1980). Condemned as sources of disease and moral pollution, they were subjected to medical examinations and treatment under contagious disease statutes or sent to prison as lawbreakers. Their customers, of course, were rarely included in these cleanup campaigns, although the ostensible intent was to protect customers' wives and unborn children from the scourge of syphilis. It was as difficult for middle-class feminists as for men reformers to see the working-class woman who sold sex as someone making a rational decision: "Middle class reformers could not grasp the motivations, moral codes, and survival strategies of poor women—that prostitution could appear as a viable alternative to low wages and lack of employment options. . . . Consequently, they advocated protection rather than punishment, which translated into policies that imposed strong controls over young women's lives, work, leisure, and relationships" (Hobson 1987:5). The result, as with so many other attempts to regulate sexual behavior, was to transform formerly private acts into a public problem and to stigmatize the women involved.

Today, prostitution is likely to be part of other illegal activities, especially selling drugs and organized crime, but even where it is not, it is usually an illegal way of making money (Miller 1986). Barry (1995) considers the global sex industry a form of sexual slavery because vulnerable young women from poor countries are lured by false promises into emigrating to rich countries, where they are frequently confined to brothels, deprived of their passports, and financially exploited. In many newly developing economies, especially in Southeast Asia and Eastern Europe, prostitution has become an export and tourist industry.

Just as the nineteenth-century campaign against prostitution implicated women in the spread of syphilis and gonorrhea, so, in the fight to halt the spread of AIDS, women sex workers were accused of being one of the main sources of HIV infections in heterosexual men (Campbell 1991; King 1990). In actuality, a woman is much more vulnerable to HIV infection from intercourse with an HIV-positive man than a man is from an HIV-positive woman—an ejaculation is an excellent conveyer of the virus, and semen stays in the vagina for days (Padian, Shiboski, and Jewell 1991). Ironically, it is harder for women to insist on condom use or safer sex practices in love relationships than in casual encounters or when partners are paying for sex. In one study of women of varied race and class, 74 percent of those with a main partner said they used condoms fewer than half of the times they had vaginal or anal intercourse, and 70 percent of those with client partners reported condom use more than half the time (Osmond et al. 1993). This study also found that when condoms were used, it was overwhelmingly because the woman made the decision and her partner agreed to it, and that women were more assertive and men more compliant when sex was for sale. However, the African American women were much more successful in getting their main partners to use condoms than the White women or Latinas, largely because they were in less stable relationships and thus less dependent economically on their main partners.

Attempting to reconcile the feminist positions about prostitution, Overall (1992) comes to the conclusion that it "makes sense to defend prostitutes' entitlement to do their work but not to defend prostitution itself as a practice under patriarchy" (p. 723). In this view, because women have fewer resources than men, and poor women, especially those from disadvantaged racial groups, have both limited economic choices and a degraded status, prostitution as work is intrinsically exploitative. However, sympathy and protection for the prostitute and condemnation of the worldwide sex industry does not point to clear policies. If feminists call for state intervention in the sex trade, some women will inevitably be criminalized for work that may be their only source of income or a considerably better source of income than a sweatshop factory job or round-the-clock domestic service. If adult sex work were decriminalized and workers better paid, unionized, entitled to benefits like health care and vacation pay, and there were no racial ethnic preference or children working in prostitution or pornography, would sex work still be an anathema? Or would there still be a revulsion against the sale of what should be an act of desire, if not affection?

A feminist analysis of prostitution has to look at the economic, gender, sexual, and psychological aspects (Chancer 1998:188-97; Hoigard and Finstad 1992). As work, the way it is organized and the extent of the worker's bargaining power are crucial elements. Child laborers of any kind are likely to be exploited. It does make a difference in sex work, as in any other kind of employment, whether the worker is a casual, off-the-books seller of services for money, food, clothes, jewelry, or drugs, or a "professional." Any permanent worker benefits from unionization or some sort of collective representation, as well as a clean, safe place to work, health services, sick leave, and vacations with pay (Alexander 1998). Equating organized sex work where the worker has bargaining power with slavery obscures the depths of degradation of authentic sexual slaves, such as the quarter of a million Korean and other "comfort women" used as sexual chattel for the "morale" of Japanese troops during World War II (Kazuko 1994), and the illegal aliens imported under false pretenses to work for a pittance in locked brothels in countries around the world (Specter 1998).

Gender is not the only crucial issue in the global sex industry, because women as well as men have profited as sex workers and as owners and managers. However, gender does enter into prostitution not only in regard to the overall balance of power between men and women but also in regard to the stigmatization of what are defined as illegitimate sexual relations (men with men, as well as women with men), that is, those not legitimated by an emotional or legal bond.[2] Western norms regarding the body are that it should not be sold for sexual or procreative purposes, even though there is a thriving market for sperm, eggs, and surrogate wombs (McKinley 1998). In the case of sex work, physical force and enslavement rarely exonerate the victim from stigmatization; as "fallen women," they hide their shameful histories lest their families be tainted. Once sullied, they lose value in the marriage market.

Both economic exploitation and sexual stigmatization victimize prostitutes—men and boys, women and girls. Patriarchy can certainly be blamed—it interpenetrates with capitalism, militarism, and imperialism in the sex industry in wartime and peacetime, encouraging and feeding on the belief that men must have constant and varied sexual services (Bailey and Farber 1992; Kazuko 1994). But women are implicated here, too, as upholders and beneficiaries of the economic, social, sexual, and gender arrangements that use other women and men as prostitutes and kept lovers, and at the same time excommunicate them from "polite society." A feminist analysis that sweeps everything together under one rubric, patriarchal sexual exploitation or free-agent sex work, loses the knowledge of sex workers' lives and customers' motivations, which are differentially shaped by gender statuses within social structures, as well as by cultural values and economic opportunities and constraints.

Pornography: Violence against Women or Erotic Enhancement?

Pornography is an even more embattled area in feminism than prostitution, with some feminists calling for its complete suppression and others arguing against censorship. Still others tout its erotic worth.[3]

The radical feminist view on pornography is that the symbolic sexual plunder of women in high culture and the mass media is often no different from the explicit sexual violence in hard-core productions (Dworkin 1987; Griffin 1982; MacKinnon 1987:125-213; Nead 1990). Both demean and exploit women. In many nineteenth-century paintings by men of artists' models, ballerinas, and barmaids, Nochlin (1988:34, 37-56) points out, the women selling services are also selling themselves sexually.

However, the radical feminist view goes much further, arguing that pornography is harmful to all women because of its conflation of sexuality and violence. MacKinnon (1987) says: "In pornography the violence *is* the sex. The inequality is the sex. Pornography does not work sexually without hierarchy. If there is no inequality, no violation, no dominance, no force, there is no sexual arousal" (p. 160). Russell (1998) argues that pornography feeds into western culture's misgyny and is an explicit encouragement to rape.

The pornographer's view of sexuality is no less essentialist than the radical feminist view, but there is much more overlap in the depiction of women's and men's sexual behavior. Pornography portrays women as sexual objects of men's lust and at the same time as sexually demanding and virtually insatiable; it portrays men as objectified by their enlarged penises, always sexually arousable and performance-perfect. The sex act is genitally specific and ends in explosive orgasms for the man and the woman—the "money shot" (Brod 1995; Faludi 1995; Williams 1989).

But there are sexual and symbolic gender differences between men and women actors. In her discussion of the pornographic portrayal of orgasm, Williams (1989) notes that it is male-focused not only for ideological reasons, but because there is a problem with the representation of female orgasms: "The irony . . . is that, while it is possible, in a certain limited and reductive way, to 'represent' the physical pleasure of the male by showing erection and ejaculation, this maximum visibility proves elusive in the parallel confession of female sexual pleasure. Anatomically, female orgasm takes place . . . in an 'invisible place' that cannot be easily seen" (p. 49). Women depict sexual desire in visual pornography (and in prostitution) without necessarily being aroused; as sexual actors in pornography (and in prostitution), men have to be aroused: "The male actor cannot merely depict arousal, because the audience looks for his erection as the sign of arousal. The only men who could depict arousal without enacting it are those who could sustain an erection in the absence of arousal" (Soble 1986:129; see also Faludi 1995).

Men's evident sexual prowess in visual pornography glorifies them as superstuds, so acting in pornographic films or live sex acts, posing for pornographic photographs, or selling sexual services does not debase them as much as it does women (Soble 1986:129-30). As audience, men spectators can identify with the studs and feel powerful; in gay pornography, a homosexual viewer can identify with the aggressive partner (Kimmel 1990:247-87). However, some men using pornography identify with the women as well, and women viewing pornography with men partners often find it sexually arousing (Putnam forthcoming).

Taking a Marxist perspective, Soble (1986) contends that under capitalism, "the use of pornography is an attempt to recoup in the domain of sexual fantasy what is denied to men in production and politics" (p. 81). Soble sees men who use pornography as powerless, although there is no evidence that it is used more by working-class men. In contrast, radical feminists see men who use pornography as potentially if not actually dangerous to women by virtue of their participation in a culture that encourages men's violence as a means of subordinating women. As for women's consensual participation in pornography, as actors or spectators, they would argue that it is a co-optation of women's sexual freedom to ends that are ultimately harmful to them.

The contrasting position—that pornography is erotica—puts it into the realm of fantasy and sexual enhancement. What pornography offers men, says Segal (1998) in an article critical of antipornography feminism, is fantasies of "infantile grandiosity" that they are sexually inexhaustible and irresistible and that there is always a ready and willing woman available: "Whether we respond with derision, sympathy, horror or indifference to what this suggests about men's ruling sexual trepidations will influence the stand we take on pornography" (p. 46). She argues that there is little proof that these fantasies inevitably translate into violence against real women. In her view, pornography is the least effective of the "phallocentric and misogynistic discourses fashioning our images of gender and sexuality" (p. 51), so its suppression would not do much to change the ways of our world (see also Chancer 1998:61-81). However, studies of the effects of pornography on men's attitudes toward women do demonstrate an increasing callousness and trivialization of the effects of rape (Donnerstein and Linz 1990; Zillmann and Bryant 1990).

In the psychoanalytic feminist view, women are objectified because they represent the female sexual identification and emotionality men had to repress in order to become like their fathers. If not only pornography but all of the mass media (and much of high culture as well) produce images of women that legitimate men's sexual objectification of them—what Kaplan (1983) calls "the male gaze"—why target pornography? Women as performers cannot escape men's voyeuristic gaze: In film, men directors look at them, men actors look at them, and men spectators look at them. Thus, no matter what role women play, they are sexualized because men look at them as desired or despised objects, and "men do not simply look; their gaze carries with it the power of action and of possession that is lacking in the female gaze" (p. 311).

As a result of this cultural phallocentricity, most of the sexual imagery in Western culture does not depict women's sexuality as experienced by women. Gilbert and Gubar (1988) argue that men publishers and critics are uncomfortable with women writers' images of women and sexuality. Some of these sexual metaphors appear in women novelists' and poets' descriptions of animals, birds, insects, flowers, jewels, water, and landscapes: "the Black Valley, the Divide, the Red Deeps," and "the little hard nut, the living stone, something precious in miniature to be fondled with the hand or cast away in wrath" (Moers 1977, 370, 387, 369-401). Such imagery is rarely used when men write about women. Do women need a pornography of their own?[4]

Suppose we lived in a scrupulously equal world where women and men had equal power, and all forms of sexuality were recognized as equally valid. Would there be equal numbers of pornographic magazines, movies, strip shows, erotic dancers, and any other sexual productions for heterosexual, homosexual, bisexual, transvestite, and sadomasochistic women as for the same groups of men? Would movies, television, books, and popular songs show women as sexual pursuers equally with men? Would pornography still be violence?[5]

Lesbigays, Transgenders, and Queers: Who's Who?

The feminist sex wars of the 1980s (Ferguson et al. 1984; Vance 1984) have not disappeared, but they have been superseded somewhat by the current arguments over bisexuality and transgendering. Framed by similar theories of gender and sexuality as essential or socially constructed, the issues here are the stability of sexual choice, the boundaries of sexual identities, and the politics of transgression (Gamson 1995, 1998; McIntosh 1993; Wilson 1993).

Fifty years ago, Kinsey used a seven-point scale to place people on a heterosexual-homosexual continuum of sexuality, from all male-female sexual acts to all male-male or all female-female (Kinsey, Pomeroy, and Martin 1948; Kinsey et al. 1953). What was revolutionary at the time were Kinsey's statistics showing that a significant proportion of Americans fell into the middle ranges of the scale: They had engaged in both heterosexual and homosexual sex. Yet no one seemed to pay much attention to what we now call bisexuality. All the rhetoric was in terms of binary sexual identities—heterosexual or homosexual.[6]

With the advent of the women's and the homosexual rights movements of the 1970s, it became clear that sexuality is gendered and that there are at least four sexual identities: heterosexual women and men, and lesbians and gays. The new nomenclature for homosexuals reflected the political and lifestyle split between lesbians and gays (McIntosh 1993; Taylor and Whittier 1992). Lesbian idealization of emotionally intimate sexuality and coupling was congruent with the feminist valorization of women's nurturant and expressive qualities. In contrast, the gay movement's pre-AIDS political stance called for liberation through anonymous and promiscuous sexual acts, almost a caricature of conventional masculine sexuality. Each type of sexual behavior could be attributed to female-male differences (sexuality as biology) or to choice and commitment (sexuality as socially constructed). Given that there are many gay men in long-term coupled relationships, often raising children (Weston 1991), and that there are lesbians who enjoy sadomasochistic sex and multiple partners (Hollibaugh and Moraga 1983), the evidence would seem to be on the side of a socially constructed sexual orientation rather than intrinsic male-female characteristics.

However, the debate over the origins and stability of homosexuality continues among sexologists and psychiatrists (Docter 1988; Green and Money 1969; Stoller 1985, Walters and Ross 1986) and among gays and lesbians writing about themselves (Abelove, Barale, and Halperin 1993; Bristow and Wilson 1993; Greenberg 1988; Kitzinger 1987; Stein 1992; Whisman 1996). Studies of *bisexuality* (serial or simultaneous same- and cross-sex sexual relationships) have shown how difficult it is to document the conventional sexual categories empirically (Klein and Wolf 1985; Rust 1995; Tucker 1995). Are we talking about desire, preference, identity, or social status? Sexual identities—heterosexual, homosexual, bisexual—are responses not just to psychic input but also to social and cultural strictures and pressures from family and friends. Because Western culture now constructs sexuality dichotomously (Laqueur 1990), many people whose sexual inclinations and experiences are bisexual are forced to choose between a heterosexual and homosexual identity as their "real" self.

Rust's (1992, 1993) research on bisexual and lesbian sexual identity found that 90 percent of the self-identified lesbians who answered her questionnaire had heterosexual relationships, 43 percent after coming out as lesbians, but these were discounted; what counted for these lesbians were their current relationships. The women who identified themselves as bisexual, in contrast, put more emphasis on their sexual attraction to both women and men. Assuming that all self-identified gay men and lesbians have exclusively same-sex partners not only renders invisible the complexities of sexuality but can also have disastrous health outcomes, as has been found in the spread of HIV infection and AIDS among lesbians (Goldstein 1995).

Gender shapes bisexual relationships as much as it does those that are heterosexual and homosexual. One early study found great variations in feelings and behavior within a small sample of bisexuals, but

although gender was irrelevant to their choice of partner, sexual scripting was not only gendered, but quite conventional, with both women
and men saying that women partners were more emotionally attuned
and men partners more physically sexual (Weinberg, Williams, and
Pryor 1994). The authors say that this gender-typing is paradoxical:

> In a group that often sets itself against societal norms, we were surprised
> to discover that bisexual respondents organized their sexual prefer-
> ences along the lines of traditional gender stereotypes. As with hetero-
> sexuals and homosexuals, gender is the building material from which
> they put together their sexuality. Unlike these groups, however, the
> edifice built is not restricted to one gender. (p. 57)

Rust (1995) found that her bisexual respondents spoke of being attracted to another person because of particular personality characteristics, ways of behaving, interests, intellect, looks, style. The physical
sex, sexual orientation, masculinity, femininity, and gender markers are
just the beginning set of parameters, and they might differ for a quick
sexual encounter, a romantic liaison, a long-term relationship. Rather
than comparing categories of gender or sexuality, researchers might
want to compare types of relationships.

As for group identification, gender and sexuality can play out in
many ways (Connell 1992). Sedgwick (1990) notes that some homosexuals (e.g., gay drag queens and butch lesbians) want to cross into the
other gender's social space, whereas for others (e.g., macho gay men
and lesbian separatists), "it is instead the most natural thing in the
world that people of the same gender, people grouped under the single
most determinative diacritical mark of social organization, people
whose economic, institutional, emotional, physical needs and knowledges may have so much in common, should bond together also on the
axis of sexual desire" (p. 87).

The issues of gender identification and display that Sedgwick raises
are even more problematized by transgenders—transsexuals, transvestites, and hermaphrodites. Transsexuals are individuals with cross-gender identification; some pass as members of the desired gender more or
less permanently through cross-dressing and renaming, while others
undergo medicalized sex change (hormones and surgery) and change
their legal and marital status as well (Bolin 1988; Morris 1975). Although
the initial medical research on transsexuals (Green and Money 1969)
accepted their insistence that they had believed they belonged in the
opposite gender from early childhood (indeed, that was a condition for

the surgery), stories began to emerge of the deliberate use of their mothers' hormones by boys and other manipulations of the medical teams (Garfinkel 1967:285-88). And it was also startling to those believing in clear-cut sex and sexual categorization to find that there are transsexuals who are homosexual in desire and behavior, both before and after surgery (Bolin 1988; Feinbloom et al. 1976).

Hermaphrodites and pseudohermaphrodites are people born with ambiguous genitalia or hormonal input (Fausto-Sterling 1993). In the Dominican Republic, there has been a genetic phenomenon in which children who looked female at birth and were brought up as girls produced male hormones at puberty. Their genitalia masculinized, their voices deepened, and they developed a male physical appearance (Imperato-McGinley et al. 1979). Most gradually changed to men's social roles—working outside the home, marrying, and becoming heads of households. Not all those who lived as men had fully functioning genitalia, and all were sterile. Some researchers who studied these pseudohermaphrodites claim that those who decided they would adopt men's identities and social roles despite having been raised as girls "appear to challenge both the theory of the immutability of gender identity after three or four years of age and the sex of rearing as the major factor in determining male-gender identity" (Imperato-McGinley et al. 1979:1236). They stress the effects of the hormonal input and secondary male sex characteristics at puberty. Others question whether the pseudohermaphrodites were reared unambiguously as girls, given their somewhat abnormal genitalia at birth, arguing that the community recognized and had names for a third sex category (Herdt 1990). At puberty, although virilization was not total, it provided the opportunity for the choice of the more attractive social role. In Papua New Guinea, many of these children were identified by experienced midwives at birth and reared anticipatorily as boys (Herdt 1990; Herdt and Davidson 1988). They went through boys' rituals as they grew up, but their identity as adult men was stigmatized; because of their small penises, they did not allow themselves to be fellated by adolescent boys, which made them fully men in that culture.

In Westernized countries, "clarifying" surgery has usually been done right after birth on children born with ambiguous genitalia to support an unambiguous gender categorization (Kessler 1990, 1998). In the past few years, there has been an intersex movement in protest against what is felt to be genital mutilation and the ruin of future sexual pleasure (Angier 1997; Cowley 1997). The sexual potentialities of true hermaphrodites with male and female genitalia who are not surgically altered can be gleaned from Fausto-Sterling's (1993) account of Emma, who was born in 1937 with a penis-like clitoris as well as a vagina. Raised as a girl, Emma used her penis in sexual relationships with women, and her vagina in sexual relations with her husband. She refused to have vaginal closure and to live as a man because it would have meant a divorce and her having to get a job. Emma's gender identity was that of a woman; she was physiologically bisexed, and thus able to be heterosexual in her sexual relations with her husband as well as with her women lovers.

Transvestism, or cross-dressing, is a familiar phenomenon in many societies throughout history, with many combinations and permutations of gender and sexual display, identity, and social status (Epstein and Straus 1991; Kates 1995; Nanda 1990; Williams 1986). In Western societies, women have dressed as men to work in nontraditional jobs, join the military, or enter other places where women are not allowed (Wheelwright 1989; Woodhouse 1989). Others cross-dress for performances (drag queens and kings), for parties and parades, for sexual pleasure, and just for kicks (Ekins 1997; Garber 1992). The two types of gender display—passing and transgressive—have totally different implications for gender identity and gender politics.

Passing both normalizes and disrupts conventional gender categories. Those who construct their gender against their sex assignment, whether through cross-dressing or surgical alteration of genitalia, reaffirm the conventional categories of man and woman, typically dressing conservatively and making their genitalia congruent with their outward gender display. Against this almost essentialist perspective, their own behavior sabotages the essentiality of the categories; in Garber's (1992) words, anyone who passes successfully (by crossing any boundaries) possesses "extraordinary power . . . to disrupt, expose, and challenge, putting in question the very notion of the 'original' and of stable identity" (p. 16). But only if they "unmask." Transgenders who pass as normal women or men achieve a successful transformation, but their achievement (and the gender resistance it entails) must remain a secret. As Gagné and Tewksbury (1998) say of their transgendered respondents:

> The need to come to terms with and publicly proclaim an alternative gender identity outweighed the fear of rejection and desire for self-preservation. But the need to avoid social erasure compelled a complete

(even if temporary) transformation. For most, identity achievement entailed the public expression of gender in ways that reflected an internalized sense of self, not one externally imposed upon them. Often this required enacting the gender of the "opposite" sex/gender category, the only known possibility available. (p. 86; see also Gagné, Tewksbury, and McGaughey 1997; Shapiro 1991)

Queers openly subvert binary gender and sexual categories through their deliberate mixtures of clothing, makeup, jewelry, hairstyles, and behavior. Transgression—queering—is their goal. By not constructing gender and sexuality in expected ways, they make visible, in Butler's (1990) term, the performativity on which the whole gender order depends. In their self-presentation, mixtures of partners in relationships, nonconventional combinations of housemates, and in-your-face political acts and cultural performances, they are saying to heterosexuals, "Get over it" and "Get used to it" (Warner 1993). Yet the more outrageous the behavior, the more the boundaries get drawn between "them" and "us" (Gamson 1998).

Despite the attempts of queer theorists to include lesbians, gays, bisexuals, transgenders, and hermaphrodites under one transgressive category, they themselves have broken up into multiple groups with different political goals. Lesbians, gays, and bisexuals are grouping under the rubric "lesbigay" in academic centers, and there is a *Journal of Gay, Lesbian, and Bisexual Identity,* which was started in 1996. Their agenda is the decentering of heterosexuality and the expansion of sexual possibilities. Nonetheless, there is still uneasiness between lesbians and bisexuals over the politics of identity, because the political stance of those lesbians and gays who argue that homosexuality is not a matter of choice is undermined by bisexual behavior and politics (McIntosh 1993; Rust 1995).

Transsexuals and transvestites now often call themselves transgenders. Although cross-dressing is a standard phase on the road to sex-change surgery, many transvestites do not even want to change their gender, let alone their genitalia. Ekins (1997) distinguishes three patterns among men—those related to sex ("body femaling"), sexuality ("erotic femaling"), and role behavior ("gender femaling"). Hermaphrodites are in an even more anomalous position. They can choose to live as men or women, but if they do not have "clarifying" surgery, their genitalia will not match their gender status. Even if they do have surgery, they are usually infertile. Although there has been some shared activism with groups opposing female genital mutilation (but not around infertility), for the most part hermaphrodites feel they don't fit in with any other gender, sex, or sexual group. It is not surprising that they have developed their own identity politics with a separate organization, Intersex Society of North America, which publishes a journal on the Internet, *Hermaphrodites with Attitude* (see also Angier 1996).

The double identity of belonging and not belonging to a category of stigmatized people has created hostility toward transsexuals and transgenders among some feminists and toward bisexual women among some lesbians. As Raymond (1979) says in arguing that male-to-female transsexuals are not women:

> We know that we are women who are born with female chromosomes and anatomy, and that whether or not we were socialized to be so-called normal women, patriarchy has treated and will treat us like women. Transsexuals have not had this same history. No man can have the history of being born and located in this culture as a woman. He can have the history of *wishing* to be a woman and of *acting* like a woman, but this gender experience is that of a transsexual, not of a woman. Surgery may confer the artifacts of outward and inward female organs but it cannot confer the history of being born a woman in this society. (p. 114; for a response, see Stone 1991)

On lesbian politics and bisexuality, Rust (1995) says: "Lesbians have become invested in a gender-based definition of lesbianism. Bisexuals, by challenging both dichotomous gender and dichotomous sexuality, challenge the very existence of lesbianism" (p. 59).

In sum, the content of the transgressions (gender status, sexual behavior, sexual identity, appearance, genitalia) and the divisions between those who want to pass as normal women and men and those who are open gender rebels make it theoretically and politically impossible to speak of "transgenders" as a unified category. This fragmentation of identity groups and their conflicting agendas undermine the possibilities for unified political action. As Gamson (1995) says, "In the contemporary American political environment, clear identity categories are both necessary and dangerous distortions, and moves to both fix and unfix them are reasonable" (p. 401). Without a political agenda for change, transgressiveness soon loses its sting:

> We transgress in order to insist that we are there, that we exist, and to place a distance between ourselves and the dominant culture. But we have to go further—we have to have an idea of how things could be different, otherwise transgression ends in mere posturing. In other

words, transgression on its own leads eventually to entropy, unless we carry within us some idea of transformation. It is therefore not transgression that should be our watchword, but transformation. (Wilson 1993, 116)

(In)conclusion

In this chapter, I have shown that the feminist differences over heterosexuality, prostitution, pornography, and multiple sexualities are to a great extent based on contrasting theories of gender. One gender perspective relies on clear and dichotomous categories of women and men with different sexual needs and behavior. In the contrasting perspective, gender is one of the social statuses that intersect with all the socially significant statuses, especially race and ethnicity, social class, sexual orientation, and age.

At the beginning of the second wave, radical feminists conceptualized women as an oppressed class whose bodies were under siege by dominant men. Today, there is much more emphasis on how the multiplicities and intersections of race, ethnicity, social class, and gender construct a hierarchy of domination in which the same people can be both oppressed and oppressors. There is also a recognition that a group identity is forged by socialization, education, economic and political opportunities, cultural values, history, place of residence, and sexual orientation, and that being a woman or a man intertwines with and shapes these experiences. To the extent that gender continues to structure social orders and power imbalances, it will be a prime organizing force in individual and group identity and in the social patterning of sexual behavior. But as postmodern theorists have shown, gender itself is a problematic category (Butler 1990; Flax 1987). Does a dual viewpoint that recognizes gender as structure and gender as performance offer policies for social change? If we want to redress the inequalities evident in the power of men over women's sexuality and in heterosexuality as the default sexuality, there has to be both behavioral change and a restructuring of laws and family relationships. Getting people to understand the constrictions of gender and sexual norms and expectations and encouraging resistance to them in daily life will not necessarily change social structures. Individuals and groups of people may resist or rebel, but the social order is very slow to change.

Queer theory emphasizes the impact of presentation of the self in the guise and costume most likely to produce or parody conformity.

Postmodern feminism is mainly concerned with deconstructing cultural productions, but its techniques have also been used on the more iron-bound and controlling discourses embedded in legal, religious, and political texts. Social construction feminism's analyses of the institutional and organizational practices that maintain the sexual/gender order could be combined with postmodern feminism and queer theory's deconstruction of how individuals do and undo gender and sexuality. Social construction feminism argues that the social order is constantly restabilized by individual action, but postmodern feminism and queer theory have shown how individuals can consciously and purposefully create disorder and instability, opening the way to social change. Postmodern feminism and queer theory's playfulness has the serious intent of making us think about what we take for granted—that men and women, homosexuals and heterosexuals, males and females, are totally different creatures, and that we cannot make and remake ourselves. Social construction feminism can show where the structural fault lines are, which would offer places for individuals, organizations, and social movements to pressure for long-lasting restructuring and a more equal social order for all kinds of people. Of course, rebels and transgressors will always find new contradictions, because, as queer theory teaches us, social orders can always use a little disorder.

Notes

1. These statistics reflect the prison population. In the majority of rapes in the United States, the victim and perpetrator are of the same race (Scully 1990:145-49).

2. Chancer (1998:173-99) notes that even women academics who study prostitutes, especially if they do it firsthand, are stigmatized.

3. For 20 years of feminist debates over pornography, see Chancer (1998), Dworkin (1981), Dworkin and MacKinnon (1988), Ellis (1984), English et al. (1981), Ferguson et al. (1984), Griffin (1982), Gubar and Hoff (1989), Itzen (1992), Kimmel (1990), Lederer (1980), Russell (1998), Steinem (1978), and Strossen (1995).

4. Snitow (1983) suggests that romance novels are women's pornography.

5. Chancer (1998:192) similarly asks whether prostitution would be the same social institution if there were equal numbers of women and men sex workers and customers, heterosexual and homosexual.

6. For a recent assessment of Kinsey's work, see Nardi and Schneider (1998).

References

Abelove, Henry, Michèle Aina Barale, and David M. Halperin, eds. 1993. *The Lesbian and Gay Studies Reader*. New York: Routledge.

Alexander, Priscilla. 1998. "Sex Work and Health: A Question of Safety in the Workplace." *Journal of the American Medical Women's Association* 53 (Spring):77-82.

Anderson, Elijah. 1990. *Streetwise: Race, Class, and Change in an Urban Community*. Chicago: University of Chicago Press.

Angier, Natalie. 1996. "Intersexual Healing: An Anomaly Finds a Group." *New York Times*, February 4, Week in Review, p. 14.

———. 1997. "New Debate over Surgery on Genitals." *New York Times*, May 13, pp. C1, C6.

Bailey, Beth and David Farber. 1992. *The First Strange Place: Race and Sex in World War II Hawaii*. Baltimore: Johns Hopkins University Press.

Barry, Kathleen. [1979] 1983. *Female Sexual Slavery*. New York: New York University Press.

———. 1995. *Prostitution of Sexuality: Global Exploitation of Women*. New York: New York University Press.

Bart, Pauline B. and Eileen G. Moran, eds. 1993. *Violence against Women: The Bloody Footprints*. Newbury Park, CA: Sage.

Bobroff, Anne. 1983. "Russian Working Women: Sexuality and Bonding Patterns in the Politics of Daily Life." Pp. 206-27 in *Powers of Desire: The Politics of Sexuality*, edited by Ann Snitow, Christine Stansell, and Sharon Thompson. New York: Monthly Review Press.

Bolin, Anne. 1988. *In Search of Eve: Transsexual Rites of Passage*. South Hadley, MA: Bergin & Garvey.

Bornstein, Kate. 1994. *Gender Outlaw: On Men, Women, and the Rest of Us*. New York: Vintage.

Bristow, Joseph and Angelia R. Wilson, eds. 1993. *Activating Theory: Lesbian, Gay, and Bisexual Politics*. London: Lawrence & Wishart.

Brod, Harry. 1995. "Pornography and the Alienation of Male Sexuality." Pp. 393-404 in *Men's Lives*, 3d ed., edited by Michael S. Kimmel and Michael A. Messner. Boston: Allyn & Bacon.

Brownmiller, Susan. 1975. *Against Our Will: Men, Women and Rape*. New York: Simon & Schuster.

Butler, Judith. 1990. *Gender Trouble: Feminism and the Subversion of Identity*. New York: Routledge.

Campbell, Carole A. 1991. "Prostitution, AIDS and Preventive Health Behavior." *Social Science and Medicine* 32:1367-78.

Cancian, Francesca M. 1987. *Love in America: Gender and Self-Development.* New York: Cambridge University Press.

Caputi, Jane. 1987. *The Age of Sex Crime.* Bowling Green, OH: Bowling Green University Popular Press.

Chancer, Lynn. 1987. "New Bedford, Massachusetts, March 6, 1983–March 22, 1984: The 'Before and After' of a Group Rape." *Gender & Society* 1:239-60.

———. 1998. *Reconcilable Differences: Confronting Beauty, Pornography, and the Future of Feminism.* Berkeley: University of California Press.

Chapkis, Wendy. 1997. *Live Sex Acts: Women Performing Exotic Labor.* New York: Routledge.

Chodorow, Nancy. 1976. "Oedipal Asymmetries and Heterosexual Knots." *Social Problems* 23:454-68.

Connell, R. W. 1992. "A Very Straight Gay: Masculinity, Homosexual Experience, and Gender." *American Sociological Review* 57:735-51.

Corbin, Alain. 1990. *Women for Hire: Prostitution and Sexuality in France after 1850.* Translated by Alan Sheridan. Cambridge, MA: Harvard University Press.

Cowley, Geoffrey. 1997. "Gender Limbo." *Newsweek,* May 19, pp. 64-66.

Crenshaw, Kimberlé. 1991. "Demarginalizing the Intersection of Race and Sex: A Black Feminist Critique of Antidiscrimination Doctrine, Feminist Theory, and Antiracist Politics." Pp. 57-80 in *Feminist Legal Theory: Readings in Law and Gender,* edited by Katharine T. Bartlett and Rosanne Kennedy. Boulder, CO: Westview.

Crosette, Barbara. 1997. "Violation: An Old Scourge of War Becomes Its Latest Crime." *New York Times,* June 14, Week in Review, pp. 1, 6.

Docter, Richard F. 1988. *Transvestites and Transsexuals: Toward a Theory of Cross-Gender Behavior.* New York: Plenum.

Donnerstein, Edward and Daniel Linz. 1990. "Mass Media, Sexual Violence, and Male Viewers: Current Theory and Research." Pp. 219-32 in *Men Confront Pornography,* edited by Michael S. Kimmel. New York: Meridian.

Dworkin, Andrea. 1981. *Pornography: Men Possessing Women.* New York: Perigee.

———. 1987. *Intercourse.* New York: Free Press.

Dworkin, Andrea and Catharine A. MacKinnon. 1988. *Pornography and Civil Rights.* Minneapolis: Organizing Against Pornography.

Ekins, Richard. 1997. *Male Femaling: A Grounded Theory Approach to Cross-Dressing and Sex-Changing.* New York: Routledge.

Ellis, Kate. 1984. "I'm Black and Blue from the Rolling Stones and I'm Not Sure How I Feel about It: Pornography and the Feminist Imagination." *Socialist Review* 14, nos. 3-4:103-25.

English, Deirdre, Amber Hollibaugh, and Gayle Rubin. 1981. "Talking Sex: A Conversation on Sexuality and Feminism." *Socialist Review* 11, no. 4:43-62.

Epstein, Julia and Kristina Straus, eds. 1991. *Body Guards: The Cultural Politics of Gender Ambiguity.* New York: Routledge.

Faludi, Susan. 1995. "The Money Shot." *New Yorker,* October 30, pp. 64-87.

Fausto-Sterling, Anne. 1993. "The Five Sexes: Why Male and Female Are Not Enough." *Sciences* (March-April):20-25.

Feinbloom, Deborah Heller, Michael Fleming, Valerie Kijewski, and Margo P. Schulter. 1976. "Lesbian/Feminist Orientation among Male-to-Female Transsexuals." *Journal of Homosexuality* 2, no. 1:59-71.

Felmlee, Diane H. 1994. "Who's on Top? Power in Romantic Relationships." *Sex Roles* 31:275-95.

Ferguson, Ann, Ilene Philipson, Irene Diamond, and Lee Quinby, and Carole S. Vance and Ann Barr Snitow. 1984. "Forum: The Feminist Sexuality Debates." *Signs* 10:106-35.

Flax, Jane. 1987. "Postmodernism and Gender Relations in Feminist Theory." *Signs* 12:621-43.

Foucault, Michel. 1978. *The History of Sexuality.* Vol. 1, *An Introduction.* Translated by Robert Hurley. New York: Random House.

Gagné, Patricia and Richard Tewksbury. 1998. "Conformity Pressures and Gender Resistance among Transgendered Individuals." *Social Problems* 45:81-101.

Gagné, Patricia, Richard Tewksbury, and Deanna McGaughey. 1997. "Coming Out and Crossing Over: Identity Formation and Proclamation in a Transgender Community." *Gender & Society* 11:478-508.

Gallop, Jane. 1982. *The Daughter's Seduction: Feminism and Psychoanalysis.* Ithaca, NY: Cornell University Press.

Gamson, Joshua G. 1995. "Must Identity Movements Self-Destruct? A Queer Dilemma." *Social Problems* 42:390-407.

———. 1998. "Publicity Traps: Television Talk Shows and Lesbian, Gay, Bisexual, and Transgender Visibility." *Sexualities* 1:11-41.

Garber, Marjorie. 1992. *Vested Interests: Cross-Dressing and Cultural Anxiety.* New York: Routledge.

———. 1995. *Vice Versa: Bisexuality and the Eroticism of Everyday Life.* New York: Simon & Schuster.

Garfinkel, Harold. 1967. *Studies in Ethnomethodology.* Englewood Cliffs, NJ: Prentice Hall.

Gilbert, Sandra M. and Susan Gubar. 1988. *No Man's Land: The Place of the Woman Writer in the Twentieth Century.* 2 vols. New Haven, CT: Yale University Press.

Goldstein, Nancy. 1995. "Lesbians and the Medical Profession: HIV / AIDS and the Pursuit of Visibility." *Women's Studies* 24:531-52.

Green, Richard and John Money, eds. 1969. *Transsexualism and Sex Reassignment*. Baltimore: Johns Hopkins University Press.

Greenberg, David F. 1988. *The Construction of Homosexuality*. Chicago: University of Chicago Press.

Griffin, Susan. 1982. *Pornography and Silence: Culture's Revenge against Nature*. San Francisco: Harper & Row.

Gubar, Susan and Joan Hoff. 1989. *For Adult Users Only: The Dilemma of Violent Pornography*. Bloomington: Indiana University Press.

Haug, Frigga et al. 1987. *Female Sexualization: A Collective Work of Memory*. London: Verso.

Herdt, Gilbert. 1990. "Mistaken Gender: 5α-Reductase Hermaphroditism and Biological Reductionism in Sexual Identity Reconsidered." *American Anthropologist* 92:433-46.

Herdt, Gilbert and Julian Davidson. 1988. "The Sambia 'Turnim-man': Sociocultural and Clinical Aspects of Gender Formation in Male Pseudohermaphrodites with 5α-Reductase Deficiency in Papua, New Guinea." *Archives of Sexual Behavior* 17:33-56.

Herek, Gregory M. 1986. "On Heterosexual Masculinity: Some Psychical Consequences of the Social Construction of Gender and Sexuality." *American Behavioral Scientist* 29:563-77.

Hobson, Barbara Meil. 1987. *Uneasy Virtue: The Politics of Prostitution and the American Reform Tradition*. New York: Basic Books.

Hoigard, Cecilie and Liv Finstad. 1992. *Backstreets: Prostitution, Money, and Love*. Translated by Katherine Hanson, Nancy Sipe, and Barbara Wilson. University Park: Pennsylvania University Press.

Hollibaugh, Amber and Cherrié Moraga. 1983. "What We're Rollin' Around in Bed With: Sexual Silences in Feminism." Pp. 394-405 in *Powers of Desire: The Politics of Sexuality*, edited by Ann Snitow, Christine Stansell, and Sharon Thompson. New York: Monthly Review Press.

Imperato-McGinley, Julianne, Ralph E. Peterson, Teofilo Gautier, and Erasmo Sturla. 1979. "Androgens and the Evolution of Male-Gender Identity among Male Pseudohermaphrodites with 5α-Reductase Deficiency." *New England Journal of Medicine* 300:1233-37.

Itzen, Catherine, ed. 1992. *Pornography: Women, Violence and Civil Liberties*. New York: Oxford University Press.

Jenness, Valerie. 1990. "From Sex as Sin to Sex as Work: COYOTE and the Reorganization of Prostitution as a Social Problem." *Social Problems* 37:403-20.

Kaplan, E. Anne. 1983. "Is the Gaze Male?" Pp. 309-27 in *Powers of Desire: The Politics of Sexuality,* edited by Ann Snitow, Christine Stansell, and Sharon Thompson. New York: Monthly Review Press.

Kates, Gary. 1995. *Monsieur d'Eon Is a Woman: A Tale of Political Intrigue and Sexual Masquerade.* New York: Basic Books.

Kazuko, Watanabe. 1994. "Militarism, Colonialism, and the Trafficking of Women: 'Comfort Women' Forced into Sexual Labor for Japanese Soldiers." *Bulletin of Concerned Asian Scholars* 26 (October-December).

Kessler, Suzanne J. 1990. "The Medical Construction of Gender: Case Management of Intersexed Infants." *Signs* 16:3-26.

―――. 1998. *Lessons from the Intersexed.* New Brunswick, NJ: Rutgers University Press.

Kimmel, Michael S., ed. 1990. *Men Confront Pornography.* New York: Meridian.

King, Donna. 1990. "Prostitutes as Pariah in the Age of AIDS: A Content Analysis of Coverage of Women Prostitutes in the *New York Times* and the *Washington Post* September 1985–April 1988." *Women and Health* 16:135-76.

Kinsey, A. C., W. B. Pomeroy, and C. E. Martin. 1948. *Sexual Behavior in the Human Male.* Philadelphia: W. B. Saunders.

Kinsey, A. C., W. B. Pomeroy, C. E. Martin, and P. H. Gebhard. 1953. *Sexual Behavior in the Human Female.* Philadelphia: W. B. Saunders.

Kitzinger, Celia. 1987. *The Social Construction of Lesbianism.* Newbury Park, CA: Sage.

Klein, Fritz, Barry Sepekoff, and Timothy J. Wolf. 1985. "Sexual Orientation: A Multi-variable Dynamic Process." *Journal of Homosexuality* 11, nos. 1-2:35-49.

Klein, Fritz, and Timothy J. Wolf, eds. 1985. *Two Lives to Lead: Bisexuality in Men and Women.* New York: Harrington Park.

Laqueur, Thomas. 1990. *Making Sex: Body and Gender from the Greeks to Freud.* Cambridge, MA: Harvard University Press.

Laumann, Edward O., John H. Gagnon, Robert T. Michael and Stuart Michaels. 1994. *The Social Organization of Sexuality: Sexual Practices in the United States.* Chicago: University of Chicago Press.

Lederer, Laura, ed. 1980. *Take Back the Night: Women on Pornography.* New York: Morrow.

Lefkowitz, Bernard. 1997. *Our Guys.* Berkeley: University of California Press.

Lorber, Judith. 1996. "Beyond the Binaries: Depolarizing the Categories of Sex, Sexuality, and Gender." *Sociological Inquiry* 66:143-59.

MacKinnon, Catharine A. 1987. *Feminism Unmodified: Discourses on Life and Law.* Cambridge, MA: Harvard University Press.

———. 1989. *Toward a Feminist Theory of the State*. Cambridge, MA: Harvard University Press.

Martin, Patricia Yancey and Robert A. Hummer. 1989. "Fraternities and Rape on Campus." *Gender & Society* 3:457-73.

McIntosh, Mary. 1993. "Queer Theory and the War of the Sexes." Pp.30-52 in *Activating Theory: Lesbian, Gay, and Bisexual Politics*, edited by Joseph Bristow and Angelia R. Wilson. London: Lawrence & Wishart.

McKinley, Jesse. 1998. "The Egg Woman." *New York Times*, May 17, City, pp. 1, 12.

Miller, Eleanor M. 1986. *Street Women*. Philadelphia: Temple University Press.

Millett, Kate. 1970. *Sexual Politics*. Garden City, NY: Doubleday.

Moers, Ellen. 1977. *Literary Women: The Great Writers*. Garden City, NY: Doubleday.

Moffatt, Michael. 1989. *Coming of Age in New Jersey: College and American Culture*. New Brunswick, NJ: Rutgers University Press.

Morris, Jan. 1975. *Conundrum*. New York: Signet.

Namaste, Ki. 1994. "The Politics of Inside/Out: Queer Theory, Poststructuralism, and a Sociological Approach to Sexuality." *Sociological Theory* 12:220-31.

Nanda, Serena. 1990. *Neither Man or Woman: The Hijiras of India*. Belmont, CA: Wadsworth.

Nardi, Peter M. and Beth E. Schneider, eds. 1998. "Kinsey: A 50th Anniversary Symposium." *Sexualities* 1:83-106.

Nead, Lynda. 1990. "The Female Nude: Pornography, Art, and Sexuality." *Signs* 15:323-35.

Nochlin, Linda. 1988. *Women, Art, and Power and Other Essays*. New York: Harper & Row.

Osmond, Marie Withers, K. G. Wambach, Diane Harrison, et al. 1993. "The Multiple Jeopardy of Race, Class, and Gender for AIDS Risk among Women." *Gender & Society* 7:99-120.

Overall, Christine. 1992. "What's Wrong with Prostitution? Evaluating Sex Work." *Signs* 17:705-24.

Padian, Nancy S., S. C. Shiboski, and N. P. Jewell. 1991. "Female-to-Male Transmission of Human Immunodeficiency Virus." *Journal of the American Medical Association* 266:1664-67.

Parlee, Mary Brown. 1996. "Situated Knowledges of Personal Embodiment: Transgender Activists' and Psychological Theorists' Perspectives on 'Sex' and 'Gender.' " *Theory and Psychology* 6:625-45.

Peña, Manuel. 1991. "Class, Gender, and Machismo: The 'Treacherous-Woman' Folklore of Mexican Male Workers." *Gender & Society* 5:30-46.

Person, Ethel Spector. 1980. "Sexuality as the Mainstay of Identity: Psychoanalytic Perspectives." *Signs* 5:605-30.

Putnam, Michael. Forthcoming. "Private 'I's: Investigating Men's Experiences of Pornographies." Ph.D. dissertation, City University of New York.

Raymond, Janice G. 1979. *The Transsexual Empire: The Making of the She-male.* Boston: Beacon.

Rich, Adrienne. 1980. "Compulsory Heterosexuality and Lesbian Existence." *Signs* 5:631-60.

Richardson, Diane, ed. 1996. *Theorizing Heterosexuality: Telling It Straight.* Buckingham: Open University Press.

Roiphe, Katie. 1993. *The Morning After: Sex, Fear and Feminism on Campus.* Boston: Little, Brown.

Rosen, Ruth. 1982. *The Lost Sisterhood: Prostitution in America, 1900-1918.* Baltimore: Johns Hopkins University Press.

Russell, Diana E. H. 1998. *Dangerous Relationships: Pornography, Misogyny, and Rape.* Thousand Oaks, CA: Sage.

Rust, Paula. 1992. "The Politics of Sexual Identity: Attraction and Behavior among Lesbian and Bisexual Women." *Social Problems* 39:366-86.

―――. 1993. " 'Coming Out' in the Age of Social Constructionism: Sexual Identity Formation among Lesbian and Bisexual Women." *Gender & Society* 7:50-77.

―――. 1995. *Bisexuality and the Challenge to Lesbian Politics: Sex, Loyalty, and Revolution.* New York: New York University Press.

Sanday, Peggy Reeves. 1981. "The Socio-cultural Context of Rape: A Cross-cultural Study." *Journal of Social Issues* 37:5-27.

―――. 1990. *Fraternity Gang Rape: Sex, Brotherhood and Privilege on Campus.* New York: New York University Press.

Scully, Diana. 1990. *Understanding Sexual Violence: A Study of Convicted Rapists.* Boston: Unwin Hyman.

Sedgwick, Eve Kosofsky. 1990. *Epistemology of the Closet.* Berkeley: University of California Press.

Segal, Lynne. 1994. *Straight Sex: Rethinking the Politics of Pleasure.* Berkeley: University of California Press.

―――. 1998. "Only the Literal: The Contradictions of Anti-pornography Feminism." *Sexualities* 1:43-62.

Shapiro, Judith. 1991. "Transsexualism: Reflections on the Persistence of Gender and the Mutability of Sex." Pp. 148-79 in *Body Guards: The Cultural Politics of Gender Ambiguity,* edited by Julia Epstein and Kristina Straus. New York: Routledge.

Snitow, Ann [Barr]. 1983. "Mass Market Romance: Pornography for Women Is Different." Pp. 245-63 in *Powers of Desire: The Politics of Sexuality,* edited by Ann Snitow, Christine Stansell, and Sharon Thompson. New York: Monthly Review Press.

Soble, Alan. 1986. *Pornography: Marxism, Feminism and the Future of Sexuality.* New Haven, CT: Yale University Press.

Specter, Michael. 1998. "Traffickers' New Cargo: Naive Slavic Women." *New York Times,* January 11, News, pp. 1, 6.

Stein, Edward, ed. 1992. *Forms of Desire: Sexual Orientation and the Social Constructionist Debate.* New York: Routledge.

Steinem, Gloria. 1978. "Erotica and Pornography: A Clear and Present Difference." *Ms.,* November, pp. 53-54, 75, 78.

Stoller, Robert J. 1985. *Presentations of Gender.* New Haven, CT: Yale University Press.

Stoltenberg, John. 1990. *Refusing to Be a Man: Essays on Sex and Justice.* New York: Meridian.

Stone, Sandy. 1991. "The *Empire* Strikes Back: A Posttranssexual Manifesto." Pp. 280-304 in *Body Guards: The Cultural Politics of Gender Ambiguity,* edited by Julia Epstein and Kristina Straus. New York: Routledge.

Strossen, Nadine. 1995. *Defending Pornography: Free Speech, Sex, and the Fight for Women's Rights.* New York: Scribner.

Taylor, Verta and Nancy E. Whittier. 1992. "Collective Identity in Social Movement Communities: Lesbian Feminist Mobilization." Pp. 104-29 in *Frontiers in Social Movement Theory,* edited by Aldon Morris and Carol McClurg Muellen. New Haven, CT: Yale University Press.

Tucker, Naomi, ed. 1995. *Bisexual Politics: Theories, Queries, and Visions.* New York: Harrington Park.

Valverde, Mariana. 1985. *Sex, Power and Pleasure.* Toronto: Women's Press.

Vance, Carole S., ed. 1984. *Pleasure and Danger: Exploring Female Sexuality.* Boston: Routledge & Kegan Paul.

Walkowitz, Judith R. 1980. *Prostitution and Victorian Society: Women, Class, and the State.* Cambridge: Cambridge University Press.

Walters, William W. A. and Michael W. Ross. 1986. *Transsexualism and Sex Reassignment.* Oxford: Oxford University Press.

Warner, Michael, ed. 1993. *Fear of a Queer Planet: Queer Politics and Social Theory.* Minneapolis: University of Minneapolis Press.

Weinberg, Martin S., Colin J. Williams, and Douglas W. Pryor. 1994. *Dual Attraction: Understanding Bisexuality.* New York: Oxford University Press.

Weston, Kathleen M. 1991. *Families We Choose: Lesbians, Gays, Kinship.* New York: Columbia University Press

Wheelwright, Julie. 1989. *Amazons and Military Maids: Women Who Cross-Dressed in Pursuit of Life, Liberty and Happiness.* London: Pandora.

Whisman, Vera. 1996. *Queer by Choice: Lesbians, Gay Men and the Politics of Difference.* New York: Routledge.

Wilkinson, Sue and Celia Kitzinger, eds. 1993. *Heterosexuality: A Feminism and Psychology Reader.* London: Sage.

Williams, Linda. 1989. *Hard Core: Power, Pleasure, and the "Frenzy of the Visible."* Berkeley: University of California Press.

Williams, Walter L. 1986. *The Spirit and the Flesh: Sexual Diversity in American Indian Culture.* Boston: Beacon.

Wilson, Elizabeth. 1993. "Is Transgression Transgressive?" Pp. 107-17 in *Activating Theory: Lesbian, Gay, and Bisexual Politics,* edited by Joseph Bristow and Angelia R. Wilson. London: Lawrence & Wishart.

Woodhouse, Annie. 1989. *Fantastic Women: Sex, Gender, and Transvestism.* New Brunswick, NJ: Rutgers University Press.

Zillmann, Dolf and Jennings Bryant. 1990. "Pornography, Sexual Callousness, and the Trivialization of Rape." Pp. 207-18 in *Men Confront Pornography,* edited by Michael S. Kimmel. New York: Meridian.

CHAPTER 16

Making Gendered People

Bodies, Identities, Sexualities

R. W. CONNELL

This chapter discusses the ways gender enters into our personal lives, bodily experience, sense of self, and sexuality. The discussion concerns what psychologists call *personality*, what philosophers call *subjectivity*, what sociologists used to call *socialization* and now more often discuss under the heading of *identity*. The issues that arise on this terrain cut across disciplinary boundaries and rapidly involve questions about the nature of gender itself.

Bodies

At the center of commonsense thinking about gender in contemporary Western culture is the idea of bodily difference between women and men. There are, it is usually assumed, two types of bodies, male and female, which are sharply distinct from each other—indeed, opposed to each other. These distinct bodies, it is assumed, give rise to two different kinds of person.

In English we talk easily of "the opposite sex." When pop psychologists inform us that men are from Mars and women are from Venus, or that our lives are ruled by "brain sex," or that women can't park cars and men can't keep houses tidy, these very silly ideas find an audience because viewers and readers are already accustomed to thinking that there are deep natural differences between women and men. We are also accustomed to thinking that these deep natural differences are the basis of sexual desire. We easily assume that "opposites attract," and that masculine-plus-feminine is the necessary basis of love, marriage, pleasure, and domesticity.

To a certain extent, any functioning member of a Western society must share these polarized categories, and experience life through them. We cannot enjoy pop songs or Hollywood movies, read love poetry, admire fashion, or go to a sporting event without participating as members in a gender-polarized world. So we are very likely to perceive our own and others' bodies in gender terms.

Yet even as we participate in these ways, disturbances are also likely. The body may not match the dichotomous imagination. Indeed, it generally does not. The image may be persistently displaced by contrary images. The most famous love poems in English, Shakespeare's sonnets, were quite possibly written to another man or to a boy; they were certainly dedicated to a man. Many people fall in love with members of the gender that is not "opposite"—that is, their own. Some people fall in love only with members of their own gender. It seems, then, that we need to look harder at the conception of dichotomy, and the place to start is the conception of distinct types of bodies.

Humans share with many other species, plants as well as animals, a method of reproduction that allows the combination of genetic material from two individuals rather than the cloning of one. Sexual reproduction in itself does not require bodies to be specialized by sex. For instance, among earthworms each individual is a hermaphrodite, producing both sperm and eggs. Thus every worm is able to perform what we think of as male and female functions. Among mammals, females carry fetuses in a womb (except for monotremes such as the platypus, which lay eggs) and feed infants with their milk. Among some mammal species, but not all, males have considerable extra bulk or carry extra equipment, such as antlers.

Humans are mammals with highly differentiated reproductive systems, but minor physical differences between sexes in other respects. We have no antlers. There are only small differences in average size or physical capacities between male and female humans; there is great overlap in physique and capacity between the two groups.

In Western popular thought, these minor differences are greatly amplified. The reproductive difference is assumed to be reflected in a whole range of other natural differences: in strength (women weaker), sexual interest (men stronger), physical skills (men, mechanical; women, fiddly work), recreational interests (men, sports; women, gossip), character (men, aggressive; women, nurturant), intellectual abilities (men, scientific genius; women, intuition), and so on.

The popular ideology of natural difference has been strongly reinforced by sociobiology, the revived attempt at an evolutionary explanation of human society that became fashionable in the 1970s. According to sociobiological theorists, men's and women's bodies are the bearers of traits produced by the evolutionary pressures that bore down upon the human stock in the remote past. Thus men are supposed to inherit, with the Y chromosome, tendencies toward aggression, family life, competitiveness, political power, hierarchy, territoriality, promiscuity, and bonding with each other by forming men's clubs. Women, conversely, are programmed to care for the men's offspring, ensuring the survival of the genes down through the generations.

According to Wilson (1978), the doyen of sociobiologists, "The physical and temperamental differences between men and women have been amplified by culture into universal male dominance." Others claim more precisely that current social arrangements are an outgrowth of the endocrine system: for instance, that patriarchy is based in a hormonal "aggression advantage" that men hold over women (Goldberg 1993).

Sociobiological speculation on gender is not well supported by evidence. Careful examinations of the research (Kemper 1990; Fausto-Sterling 1992) show that nothing like one-way determination of the social by the biological can be sustained. Social relations can and do shape biological processes, including the production of hormones; there is a constant interplay of social process with biological process. As Kemper (1990) bluntly concludes, "When racist and sexist ideologies sanction certain hierarchical social arrangements on the basis of biology, the biology is usually false" (p. 221). Biological explanations of social arrangements remain common because of the general prestige of "science" and because they broadly justify the status quo and the privileges of those who benefit from the status quo.

In the 1970s, feminist theorists proposed a sharp distinction between *sex* and *gender* that seemed to dispose of this problem. Sex was the biological fact, the difference between the male and the female human animal. Gender was the social fact, the difference between masculine and feminine roles, or men's and women's personalities.

To many at the time, this distinction was a conceptual breakthrough. It cut through the knot of natural difference, and showed why biology could not be used to justify women's subordination. The effects of biological difference were confined to the realm of biology itself. A broad realm of the social ("culture," "roles," and so on) remained, where most of the action took place—where gender as we experience it was constructed.

In this view, the social was above all a realm of freedom, where individuals or societies could *choose* the type of gender they wanted. As one very influential volume at that time concluded:

> We suggest that societies have the option of minimizing, rather than maximizing, sex differences through their socialization practices. A society could, for example, devote its energies more toward moderating male aggression than toward preparing women to submit to male aggression, or toward encouraging rather than discouraging male nurturance activities. (Maccoby and Jacklin 1975:374)

The concept of psychological "androgyny" put forward at this time by Bem (1974) and others was precisely an attempt to define an alternative gender pattern that an individual or a society could adopt.

In the 1970s this "two-realms" model of gender supported a sunny optimism about change. Oppressive gender arrangements, being the products of past social choices, could be abolished by fresh social choices. In the language of the time, sex-role expectations could be altered, and sex-role socialization would follow suit. Agendas of change were constructed around this principle. Among them were media reforms (to change sex-role models), educational reforms (to change the expectations transmitted to girls and boys), and new forms of psychotherapy (to help individuals make the change to new roles).

The two-realms model has, however, steadily eroded since the 1970s. Pringle (1992) shows that it ran into trouble on several fronts. The idea of gender as culturally chosen difference ("sex roles") was unable to explain why one side of the difference, the masculine, was consistently more highly valued. The tendency to marginalize biology ran counter to impulses in feminism that were placing more emphasis on bodies. For instance, radical feminism focused increasingly on men's violence and heterosexual desire, whose targets were not a feminine role but women's bodies. The growing influence of certain Parisian theorists—especially Foucault and Irigaray—highlighted bodies as the objects of social power and the sources of emotion and expression.

If the two realms could not be held strictly apart, perhaps they could be added together? A commonsense compromise would suggest that gender differences arise from *both* biology and social norms. This position was spelled out by Rossi (1985), once a feminist pioneer in American sociology, who became a critic of "cultural determinism" about gender. She claimed that there was a biological predisposition for women (but not men) to mother, that is, to learn how to care for infants, and actually to do the caring. Thus biology provided the basis of the gender division of labor in the family, in warfare, between family and workplace, and so on: "Gender differentiation is not simply a function of socialization, capitalist production, or patriarchy. It is grounded in a sex dimorphism that serves the fundamental purpose of reproducing the species" (p. 161).

There are difficulties in the additive conception of sex and gender, too. The two levels of analysis are not really being added, because they are not commensurate. As Rossi makes clear, the biological is "fundamental," it "grounds" the social. In the hierarchy of the sciences (a conception that goes back as far as Comte in the early nineteenth century), biology is routinely taken to be more basic than sociology. Its reality is somehow more real; its explanations explain more deeply.

But bodies are plural, and very diverse. There are not just two kinds. There are lots of kinds of bodies, and lots of differences among them. There are large bodies and small bodies; bodies permanently stained with soil or grease; bodies stooped from bending over a desk, and other bodies with spotless, manicured hands. Even in reproductive biology, human bodies are not strictly dimorphic. There is a complex group of intersex categories, such as people with extra or missing or damaged chromosomes. These categories have long fascinated sexologists; they do not correspond in any simple way to behavior or sense of identity.

Even when orthodox biologically, bodies may not fit comfortably into the places marked out for them by a given system of gender relations, as can be seen in sport. Elite sport is an important source of examples of hegemonic masculinity in the contemporary world (Messner and Sabo 1994). Yet elite sport can be remarkably destructive of the bodies engaged. As Messner puts it, "the body-as-weapon ultimately results in violence against one's own body." Playing hurt, accidents, drug use, and constant stress wear down even the fittest and strongest. Former athletes often live with damaged bodies and chronic pain, and tend to die early.

Some bodies are more than recalcitrant; they disrupt and subvert the social arrangements into which they are invited. The most striking example is gender switching ("transsexualism"), where bodies cross the most fundamental of lines in the modern social order. At the boundaries of gender categories, it seems, bodies may travel without passports granted by society. People who have made such journeys (e.g., Cummings 1992; Rubin forthcoming) speak of an undeniable need for change that is bodily as well as mental. The momentum may be so strong that body awareness is transformed, with awareness of the body being that of another sex—awareness sometimes temporary, sometimes permanent.

Bodies do not stand outside of, or prior to, history; they are open to change through social processes. In gender (as in other social structures) social practice draws bodies into a historical process in which bodies are materially transformed.

Some elements of this process are familiar: lengthening expectation of life, rising average height and weight (as nutrition and child health care improve), changing patterns of disease (e.g., polio declining, TB declining but now reviving). The transformation of bodies is structured, in part, on gender lines. The demographic indicators themselves show this. In the rich industrial countries, women's life expectancy has now reached 109 percent of men's. In India, women's life expectancy is 101 percent of men's. In Bangladesh and Nepal, men on average outlive women (United Nations Development Program 1994, table 9). The gendered industrial economy has a differential impact on men's and women's bodies. There are higher rates of industrial and vehicle accidents among men, who are the majority of workers in heavy industry and transport. There are higher rates of repetition strain injury among women, who are the majority of keyboard workers.

Practical transformations of the body include the disciplinary practices, such as gendered dress and deportment, where we present and decorate ourselves as gendered. Gender presentation often includes body modifications such as eyebrow plucking and diet, and increasingly involves the cosmetic use of drugs (e.g., diet pills for women who want to slim down, and steroids for men who want to bulk up) and cosmetic surgery, especially for women (though with a subspecialty of penis augmentation for men). Research in social psychology is a rich source of information about transformations of bodies. In *Body Politics*, Henley (1977) provides a comprehensive inventory of the "nonverbal communication" of gender messages, conveyed by the use of space, posture, demeanor in interaction, touch, gesture, eye contact, and so on. Each of these techniques is informally learned and may become a permanent part of one's repertoire of bodily practice.

Bodies are also transformed in formal learning. To learn skills—whether very widespread skills such as writing or highly specific occupational techniques such as using a lathe or playing a cello—is to transform the body's physical capacities. These transformations are often gendered. Technical education has long been the most segregated sector of education; few women are trained to use a lathe, few men are trained as secretaries. That this segregated practice is historically produced is made obvious in social emergencies when the pattern is abruptly reversed. During World War II, for instance, very large numbers of women were recruited into armaments factories and trained on presses, cranes, and rivet guns as well as lathes. At the same time (though this fact is less familiar), large numbers of men were doing clerical work inside the armed forces.

It is clear, then, that bodies do not produce simple dichotomies of experience or of action—though they are often subjected to social polarizations.

Identities

If the sense of being a gendered person does not arise simply from dichotomous bodies, we might seek to explain it in psychological terms. This is most often done by reference to "gender identity" (and sometimes "sexual identity").

The concept of "identity" has a long history in philosophy and literature, but took on its current meaning around the 1950s. The most influential formulation was that of the psychoanalyst Erikson ([1950] 1965), who interpreted a range of modern personal, social, and political problems as difficulties in achieving identity. "The study of identity, then, becomes as strategic in our time as the study of sexuality was in Freud's time" (p. 242).

Erikson's concept of personal identity was based on the Freudian insight that adult personality is formed by a long, conflict-ridden process of growth. Following Freud, Erikson saw personality as composed of several mental agencies, marked by conflicting impulses and repressions.

But where Freud had focused on conflicts involving the unconscious agencies (the "id" and the "superego"), Erikson emphasized issues about the conscious agency, the "ego." The ego is the mental agency involved in transactions with the outside world, the agency where the conscious sense of self is located. Personal identity, in Erikson's thought, meant the integration of the ego: the coherence of the psychological mechanisms by which the ego handles the pressures that impinge on it from the unconscious agencies, on the one side, and the outside world, on the other. This feat of balance, if successful, would be registered in a stable sense of self. Thus the question, "Who am I?" is, in principle, answered by the ego's success in mastering the trials and tribulations of psychological development.

Erikson picked up the Freudian idea that there were different stages in a child's psychosexual development and elaborated it into a model of the whole life cycle. Each of the eight stages Erikson named had its characteristic psychological conflict, which needed to be resolved before the individual could move on to the next. In one particular stage, conflict around identity was central: the stage of adolescence. This idea has led to a great deal of popular discussion of adolescence as a "search for identity."

The key application of the concept to gender issues, by the psychiatrist Stoller (1968), departed from Erikson's concept in two ways. First, the "core gender identity" that Stoller saw as the basis of adult personality was supposed to be formed very early in life—in the first two or three years—not in adolescence. Second, the concept of identity acquired a different frame of reference. Erikson's notion of identity referred to the integration of the ego as a whole, and philosophical and literary usages of the term referred to the continuity of selfhood for the person as a whole. Stoller's conception was much more specific. To talk of "gender identity" is to talk only of *one aspect* of the person—her or his involvement in gender relations or sexual practice.

To Stoller this narrower focus did not matter very much, because he assumed that the integration of the personality as a whole *was* largely focused on the sense of being a male or a female. But for any other view of personality and social process, an exclusive focus on gender is a problem. We can speak just as meaningfully of "racial identity," "generational identity," or "class identity." If we acknowledge the "constant interweaving" (Bottomley 1992) of these social relations, we *must* attend to these other forms of identity in order to understand gender identity. The concept of "identity" formulated by Stoller thus leads, with a plausible change of assumptions, toward a conception of identity as inherently *plural* rather than unitary.

A model of identity built on gender dichotomy was more easily accepted by the 1970s because of the growth of feminist research emphasizing gender differentiation in the rearing of children. The most influential statement of this point was Chodorow's *The Reproduction of Mothering* (1978). Chodorow's argument linked two dichotomies: a gender division of labor, which assigned the task of caring for babies and infants exclusively to women; and two paths of development, for girls and boys, respectively, which resulted from their different emotional situations in early childhood. Girls, brought up by a parent of their own gender, tend to have less distinct ego boundaries, and when they grow up have a stronger motivation for nurturing children. Boys, pushed toward separation from a mother responding to the gender distinction, tend to have an earlier discontinuity in development, more difficulty in establishing gender identity, and stronger boundaries to the self in adulthood.

The gender division of labor in child care is a fact. Though it has been well established that men *can* mother (Risman 1987), it is still the case that few of them do. But the reasons for this may have little to do with psychology; they certainly include the economic costs to families from the loss of a man's wage. In Norway, where these costs have been dramatically reduced by the introduction of a "father's quota" of paid parental leave, some 70 percent of eligible men currently take up their entitlement and are present as caregivers in the first month of their child's life (Gender Equality Ombudsman 1997). There has also been increasing recognition—by Chodorow (1994) among others—that a gender division of labor in child care does not necessarily produce dichotomous gender patterns in later life.

The outcomes of human development, indeed, seem curiously undichotomous. Given the popularity of quantitative "sex difference" research, the results of surveys such as Maccoby and Jacklin's (1975) are scandalous. Over much of the terrain psychologists have studied, there are no consistent differences between women and men (or girls and boys) at all. In those areas where differences persistently appear, they are small by comparison with the variation within each of the supposedly "dichotomous" groups.

Debate has raged about the interpretation of sex-difference research, with some proponents of meta-analysis (e.g., Eagly 1987) arguing that there are more differences than Maccoby and Jacklin's method could identify. Yet no reinterpretation can make the findings on the psychological characteristics of men and women look anything like a dichotomy.

Social researchers, too, have increasingly emphasized variation within the gender categories. This trend is noticeable in the growth of research and debate on masculinity. In contrast to the way "the male sex role" was discussed in the 1970s (with an emphasis on "the"), it has become common to speak of "masculinities." Research in the past two decades has shown great diversity among cultures in their constructions of gender for men (Cornwall and Lindisfarne 1994). There is also a considerable amount of research that documents multiple masculinities within given cultures, and even within particular institutions, peer groups, and workplaces (Connell 1995). A striking example is Foley's (1990) ethnography of a Texas high school, where the interplay of gender, class, and ethnicity constructs several versions of masculinity: the dominant group of Anglo jocks, antiauthoritarian Mexican American *vatos,* and the group Foley ironically calls the "silent majority."

Even the categories for our self-understanding, when carefully examined, appear quite complex. There is a whole spectrum of variations and fragments, painstakingly cataloged by Lorber (1994). She calculates that modern Western societies distinguish five sexes (based on genitalia), three sexual orientations, five gender displays, six types of relationships, and ten self-identifications. Leaving aside the five sexes, that makes, if my arithmetic is correct, 900 different situations one can be in. So much for dimorphism.

With the categories thus seeming more and more complex, the concept of identity has increasingly been used, not to name a box into which society puts us, but to name *claims made by individuals* about who or what they are. These claims are related to the dominance of "identity politics" since the decline of forms of radicalism that made universal claims. One becomes a member of a social movement by claiming the identity (as Black, as a woman, as lesbian, and so on) that the movement represents. "Queer" politics takes the process a step further, as queer activists have sought to disrupt taken-for-granted communities by insisting on their plurality: highlighting the presence of Black lesbians in White-dominated gay communities, for instance. At the extreme, the concept of identity becomes a way of naming one's uniqueness, rather than naming what is shared.

Sexualities

The paradox about identity is particularly sharp in relation to sexuality. Sexuality is precisely the realm of intimate contact where the strongest of bonds and solidarities are forged; yet on this very territory a trend toward fragmentation and multiplicity has emerged. The leading contemporary theorist of sexuality, Weeks (1986), argues that the

diversification of sexual practices, subcultures, and identities is characteristic of this moment in sexual history.

Sexual matters are dealt with in all cultures, but often in very
different terms. Ram (1991) notes how the language in which sexual
matters are spoken of among the Mukkuvar people of south India
makes women's sexuality inseparable from questions of auspicious-
ness, fertility, a kind of social prosperity. By contrast, Christianity long
valorized chastity within a classification of people as chaste or unchaste.
A vow of chastity was a basic part of monasticism. Chastity for priests,
imposed in Gregory VII's reform of the medieval church, separated
them further from the laity.

The current Western preoccupation with the homosexual/
heterosexual distinction is relatively recent. In medieval and early
modern European society, specific homosexual acts were often defined
as shameful or criminal, but were lumped together with other disrup-
tions of the religious or social order. Sodomy might be punished very
brutally, but enforcement was erratic and did not tend to define a
clear-cut social category (Greenberg 1988). Changed laws, in the late
nineteenth century, criminalized homosexual behavior generally and
led to regular police surveillance and arrests.

At about the same time, homosexuality was defined as a medical
condition. This was part of an extension of medical classifications to
include sexual behavior, crystallized in the Austrian doctor Krafft-
Ebing's famous book *Psychopathia Sexualis* ([1886] 1965), one of the
founding documents of modern sexology. There is debate among historians as to how far a sexual subculture had already created some kind
of identity. But there can be little doubt about the importance of legal
and medical discourses in shaping the modern category of "the homosexual" (Weeks 1977).

Sexuality, like gender, had often been treated as part of the realm of
nature; Darwin, for instance, theorized "sexual selection" as a key
mechanism of evolution. In the second half of the nineteenth century,
evolutionary biology displaced religion as the dominant framework for
understanding sex. At the turn of the century, Freud's "psychoanalysis," like Ellis's "psychology of sex," operated within this frame. Freud
understood the conflict and unhappiness in his cases to come from the
tragic incompatibility of natural impulse and the limits required by
social life.

This conception of a division between natural impulse and social
repression was directly adopted by the social critics who attempted to

combine Freud with Marx. The leading figures here were Reich and Marcuse, but they were far from isolated. A conception of an underlying natural impulse has been widespread in twentieth-century sexology. The pioneering ethnographers of sexuality, Malinowski and Mead, were acutely conscious of the diversity of social forms. They nevertheless presupposed a biological impulse that the social forms expressed. Even the arch-empiricist Kinsey, who replaced Freud's subtle analysis of desire with a mechanical analysis of physical performance, shared the notion of a robust, hedonistic, natural urge, which found varying expression according to social approval or prohibition (De Cecco 1990).

Conservative ideology, too, places sexuality at the boundary of the social, as the quintessence of what is irrational, uncontrollable, or animal in human life. Readings of sexuality as "natural" or beyond the social have provided both cultural feminism and New Age religion with images of women's sexuality outside of patriarchy.

The whole framework of "natural" urge and social superstructure was dramatically rejected in the 1970s. Similar stances were taken by the sociologists of the Kinsey Institute in the United States (Gagnon and Simon 1974), who developed the idea of sexual "scripts," and by the historian Foucault (1978) in France.

Gagnon and Simon's (1974) conception of sexual scripts is, essentially, an application to sexuality of the "role" notions that were very widespread in social psychology from the 1950s to the 1970s. The logic is like that of the "sex role" concept, and the descriptive detail in their model of the normative lifelong course of heterosexuality in the United States has a large overlap with the sex role literature of the day (Gagnon and Simon 1974:100-103).

Foucault's critique of the "repressive hypothesis" (addressed presumably to Freud and Reich) was more sophisticated, and the alternative he suggested more subtle. Foucault argued that society did not repress sexuality, which simply did not exist as an entity in nature. Rather, social discourses *constituted* sexuality as a cultural form, in the historical transition to modernity. This established a new form of power over bodies and their pleasures, a power exercised not only by law but also by medicine, psychotherapy, and sexology itself. Foucault's argument marked a decisive expansion of social constructionism, and has been followed by a flood of research on discourses of sexuality and the production of sexual identities that still shows little sign of abating.

Gender is, notoriously, absent from Foucault's theoretical universe. Gender has been present in scripting theory mainly in the very simplified form of "sex roles," or dichotomous sexual scripts. A well-recognized weakness of role theory is its difficulty in handling issues about social power. It is significant that those feminist approaches to sexuality that have most insisted on the importance of power—for instance, in campaigns against sexual violence—have been relatively receptive to a nonsocial, even biological-determinist, understanding of male sexuality.

Social constructionist accounts also seem to have difficulties understanding the bodily dimension of sexuality. It often seems to be bodily processes and products—arousal, orgasm, pregnancy and birth, menarche and menopause, tumescence and detumescence, semen, milk, and sweat—that underpin the biological-determinist sense of sex as a domain of eternal repetition.

Social constructionist approaches to sexuality, as Vance (1989) observes, risk drifting away from bodily experience altogether. There are ways of talking about the politics of AIDS, for instance, that treat the matter as a problem of language, the power of medical discourse to control debate about the issue (Gilder 1989). There is a strong tendency in poststructuralist theory to treat bodies as the surfaces on which social meanings are inscribed, that is, as a neutral substratum for the play of identity and signification.

It is important, then, to insist that the bodily processes and experiences conventionally taken to be outside history are indeed elements of social process. Sexual practice is body-recursive practice, focused on people's erotic and reproductive potentials. Bodies are in play in social relations, they are not surfaces or landscapes. We have no difficulty in accepting the social character of labor, which involves bodies as much as sexuality does. A sociology of bodies now exists that shows the varieties of ways bodies are drawn into social process and historical change. Glassner (1988), for instance, traces the rise of the body-culture industry and its connection to American moral ideologies. Theberge (1991) shows the many ways bodies are regulated and reconstructed in competitive sport. Sport itself undergoes constant institutional and cultural change, as shown in Gruneau and Whitson's (1993) striking analysis of the corporate and political interests that remade the obsessively masculine sport of ice hockey in Canada.

Survey research in the United States shows how the gender patterning of sexuality persists within historical change (Laumann et al. 1994;

Turner 1989). Comparison of surveys over time reveals two broad trends in heterosexual practice. One is a rising rate of sexual contact outside of marriage, most notably a greater number of partners in youth, for both genders. The other is a gradual but far from complete erosion of the double standard, with women's patterns becoming more like those of men. The convergence still has a long way to go. In the latest of these studies, women are less than half as likely as men to report coming to orgasm in heterosexual intercourse. And though the interpretation of the questions is tricky, it seems that women are more than five times as likely as men to report having been forced to do something sexual they did not want to do (Laumann et al. 1994:333-36).

Another pattern of change involves the historical production of new categories of sexuality and new erotic objects, a process emphasized by Weeks (1986). It is possible to trace in fine detail the construction of particular sexual subcultures, their venues, styles, leading personalities, economic and political histories, as Rubin (1991) does for a particular S/M venue in San Francisco. This kind of transformation affects heterosexuality as well. Studies of fashion (Wilson 1987) and conceptions of beauty (Banner 1983) chart historical changes in the object of heterosexual desire, and show how intricate are the social processes involved. Wilson (1987) is particularly interesting in showing a sustained interplay between feminism and fashion, long before the era of "lipstick lesbians" and power dressing.

Further evidence shows the contradictory and mutable character of this desire. The very recent creation of the "transsexual" as a category (King 1981) was the by-product of attempts to provide a surgical route from membership in one gender to membership in another. Some people were delayed en route, so to speak, and found they could survive in a gender-contradictory state, for instance, as specialized prostitutes (Perkins 1983). Their customers are not other transsexuals—this is not an erotic subculture in the sense of the S/M or leather scene—but straight men, excited by the gender contradiction embodied in the transsexual prostitute.

The most profound changes in sexuality at present are not, however, in the rich industrialized countries. As shown in ethnographies such as Clark's (1997) study of a highland community in Papua New Guinea, the more sweeping changes are the transformations of sexual categories and practices during dependent capitalist development in poor countries.

Murray's (1991) study of street traders and prostitutes in Jakarta traces this process in an urban setting. One type of prostitution in this case involves servicing the Westernized sexuality of businessmen by lower-class women, who use this trade as a way into the modernized sector of Javanese society. Another type involves middle-class house-wives, excluded from useful employment by the patriarchal policies of the Suharto dictatorship. Different class sexualities, as Murray puts it, are produced despite a homogenizing official ideology of womanhood.

The impact of global capitalism also affects sexuality among Java-nese men. Javanese society traditionally provided a space for *waria*, cross-dressing men who typically had sex with straight men. This pattern is now being displaced by a new sexual category, gay men, modeled on the gay sexuality of North American cities (Oetomo 1990). There is a striking parallel in Brazil. Here another pattern of male-to-male sexuality, this time involving a fundamental distinction between insertor and insertee (rather than cross-dressing), is also being reshaped by the development of gay sexuality on the North American model (Parker 1985).

Altman (1996) makes the important observation that such cases do not involve the simple substitution of a "Western" sexuality for a "traditional" sexuality. Globalization involves enormously complex interactions among sexual regimes that are in any case diverse and divided. The result is a spectrum of sexual practices and categories, formed in contexts of cultural disruption and massive economic in-equalities. Gender remains a key way in which sexuality is structured—but in a world in which gender relations themselves are being transformed.

Gendered People, Gendered Situations

Can we fit these complexities together into a coherent picture of gender in personal life and experience, including sexuality? I think we can, but the account will not much resemble the familiar old language of sex roles or biology versus society.

Our new model begins with the observation that human bodies are active players in social life. They are neither biological machines, pro-ducing social effects mechanically, nor blank pages on which cultural messages are written. Bodies are parties in social life, sharing in social agency, in generating and shaping courses of social conduct.

In gender practices, bodies are both agents and objects; the practices, thus, are body-reflexive. Such practices are not internal to the indi-vidual. Their circuits involve social relations and symbolism; they commonly encompass social institutions, even such large-scale institutions as states and markets. Particular versions of femininity and masculinity are constituted in their circuits as meaningful bodies and embodied meanings. Through body-reflexive practices, more than individual lives are formed: A social world is formed.

Through body-reflexive practices, bodies are addressed by social process and drawn into history, without ceasing to be bodies. They do not turn into symbols, signs, or positions in discourse. Their materiality (including material capacities to engender, to give birth, to give milk, to menstruate, to open, to penetrate, to ejaculate) is not erased. The *social* process of gender includes childbirth and child care, youth and aging, the pleasures of sport and sex, labor, injury, death from AIDS, and the struggle to live with AIDS.

Gender is the domain of social practice organized in relation to a *reproductive arena* constituted by the materiality of the body. The reproductive arena is the set of body-reflexive practices that respond to the reproductive division of humans into (mostly) males and females. To say that body-reflexive social practices *respond* to this bodily division is specifically to deny that biological reproduction *causes,* or even provides a template for, gender as practice (for debate on this point, see Hawkesworth 1997). Lesbian and gay sexualities, for instance, are gendered practices as much as heterosexuality is—they are sexualities organized with reference to women and men, respectively, as partners. Gender differentiations occur that have not the slightest logical connection to biological reproduction—for instance, the gender patterns in computer games. The connection with the reproductive arena is entirely a matter of the organization of social relations. Different societies do it differently, and they may stand on their heads with respect to each other, while still constituting gender. Thus early-eighteenth-century male Highlanders wore skirts into battle, whereas late-twentieth-century American men would not do such a thing in a pink fit. The Theban army in the fourth century B.C. required its shock troops (the "Sacred Band") to be homosexual couples; today's Americans would get thrown out of their army if they admitted even casual homosexual practice.

I speak of a "reproductive arena," not a "biological base," to emphasize that the concept is about a historical process that operates through and uses bodies, not about a fixed set of biological determinants. Gender is social practice that constantly refers to bodies and what bodies do; it is not social practice reduced to body functions.

Body-reflexive practices form—and are formed by—structures that have historical weight and solidity. When feminists first spoke of "patriarchy" as the master pattern in human history, the argument was overgeneralized. But the idea well captured the power and intractability of a massive structure of social relations: a structure that involves the state, the economy, culture, and communications, as well as kinship, child rearing, and sexuality.

The practices that construct femininity and masculinity are formative of reality. As body-reflexive practices, they constitute a world that has a bodily dimension, but is not biologically determined. Not being fixed by the physical logic of the body, this practice-made world may be hostile to bodies' physical well-being. Young men in the United States and Australia, enacting their fresh-minted masculinities on the roads, die in appalling numbers, at a rate four times as high as women. Young women in Southeast Asia, recruited into microprocessor assembly plants because of their supposed "natural" patience and delicacy, suffer irreversible bodily damage, which is completely determined by the labor system. Older women often suffer from chronic conditions that could be eased, or are regularly given unnecessary drugs, because there is no medical service available to them that takes their needs seriously. Older men sometimes die of diseases that could be cured, because they have learned it is unmanly to admit pain and request help.

Practice structured through the reproductive arena, generated as people and groups grapple with their historical situations, does not consist of isolated acts. Actions are configured in larger units, and when we speak of masculinity and femininity we are naming complex configurations of gender practice. As children grapple with their places in a gendered world, they are not primarily learning gender-specific behaviors or behavioral capacities (which, as noted above, are relatively rare). They are, much more importantly, learning how configurations work and how to navigate among them—what goes with what, who goes with whom, when and where one does this or that, what meanings are attached to things and acts, for what violations one is accountable.

Yet *configuration* is in many situations too static a term. Masculinity and femininity in the final analysis are *gender projects*. The idea of a "project" expresses the intentionality of social conduct and the way conduct is organized and coordinated through historical time, either by an individual person or by a collectivity. Gender projects configure gender practices through time, transforming their starting points in gender structures. They have, indeed, the capacity to transform the reproductive arena itself.

Sexuality is not the basis of the domain of gender, as classical psychoanalysis assumed, but it is a part of this domain. More exactly, sexual practice is strongly gender-structured, and the gender order includes social relations constituted through sexuality. The structure of these relations defines inequalities and gives rise to politics across a wide range of venues. Sexuality is not confined to the bedroom. What Hearn and Parkin (1987) call "organization sexuality" is a ubiquitous feature of life in offices and factories. In sexuality, the interplay between the body and the structure of social relations is unending. Henriksson (1995) gives one of the most dramatic and tragic examples. In the Swedish gay community he studied, there is more unsafe sex within committed relationships than in casual sex; so love, in his phrase, becomes an HIV/AIDS risk factor.

In much of the world, sexual social relations are constructed in conditions of gender inequality. Examples range from the Jakarta prostitutes interviewed by Murray (1991) to the London teenagers interviewed by Lees (1986). For both these groups, their disempowerment as women, and the social empowerment of men, is fundamental in the making of sexuality.

To change these patterns of sexuality requires not only material equality, but cultural resources, notably knowledge and social respect. For Lees's adolescent girls, the lack of respect shapes their sexuality under the threat of being discredited as "slags"—and behind that lies the threat of violence. Violence against women (Dobash and Dobash 1992) and violence against gays (Mason and Tomsen 1997) are key parts of current gender politics.

The personal and collective project of gender formation being undertaken within structures of inequality is likely to embed injustice within the very configurations of practice that constitute our experienced world of gender. Thus, the women's liberation and gay liberation movements spoke of "self-oppression." The project of gender formation may also give rise to struggles against injustice. The "speciation" of sexualities (Rubin 1984) within a hierarchy of power or legitimacy involves a politics of self-expression. This idea fits Young's (1990) analysis of justice, involving not only a struggle against domination but also a struggle against oppression. (By *domination* Young means the social conditions that prevent people from controlling their own actions, individually or collectively; by *oppression,* she means the social conditions that inhibit personal growth, self-expression, or communication with others.) Similarly, the hierarchy of masculinities (Connell 1995) involves a complex bundle of antagonisms and complicities. Think, for instance, of the middle-class White men who consume exemplary Black masculinities symbolically as television sports fans.

Domination may be constituted within intimate relations, including sexual practices. The most familiar cases are within heterosexuality, where the gendered object choice brings into play the structure of gender inequalities. Research on marital rape (Russell 1982), for instance, shows sexual violence by husbands occurring in a continuum of coercion, intimidation, claims of ownership, claims of right, claims of need, economic pressure, persuasion, and customary interpretations of marriage. That sexual violence is not just a local issue is shown by Laumann et al.'s (1994) finding, for a carefully constructed national sample in the United States, that the experience of forced sex is much more widespread among women than among men.

Intimate relations, it should never be forgotten, are addressed and to some extent shaped by large-scale institutions, particularly churches, corporations, and states. Governments introduce population policies directly regulating sexuality, and sometimes they work. The Chinese "one child" policy is the best-known current example. Governments also attempt public health measures, which often bear on gender and sexuality. A historical example is the intervention that created the modern sociolegal category of "the prostitute" (Walkowitz 1980), and a current one is the attempted regulation of homosexual practice through AIDS education. Governments, churches, and political movements may directly target intimate relations for regulation, as seen in contemporary struggles over abortion and contraception.

Governments and political movements, in turn, are only players on a wider stage of global markets, global communications, and international agencies. Here our concerns merge into other parts of this book, and this analysis must end. It is appropriate to end it with the relation between intimate life and society on the global scale. Gender analysis works best when it is insistent about connections.

References

Altman, Dennis. 1996. "Rupture or Continuity? The Internationalization of Gay Identities." *Social Text* 14, no. 3:77-94.

Banner, Lois. 1983. *American Beauty.* Chicago: University of Chicago Press.

Bem, Sandra L. 1974. "The Measurement of Psychological Androgyny." *Journal of Consulting and Clinical Psychology* 42:155-62.

Bottomley, Gillian. 1992. *From Another Place: Migration and the Politics of Culture*. Cambridge: Cambridge University Press.

Chodorow, Nancy. 1978. *The Reproduction of Mothering: Psychoanalysis and the Sociology of Gender*. Berkeley: University of California Press.

————. 1994. *Femininities, Masculinities, Sexualities: Freud and Beyond*. Lexington: University Press of Kentucky.

Clark, Jeffrey. 1997. "State of Desire: Transformations in Huli Sexuality." Pp. 191-211 in *Sites of Desire, Economies of Pleasure*, edited by Lenore Manderson and Margaret Jolly. Chicago: University of Chicago Press.

Connell, R. W. 1995. *Masculinities*. Berkeley: University of California Press.

Cornwall, Andrea and Nancy Lindisfarne, eds. 1994. *Dislocating Masculinity: Comparative Ethnographies*. London: Routledge.

Cummings, Katherine. 1992. *Katherine's Diary: The Story of a Transsexual*. Melbourne: Heinemann.

De Cecco, John P. 1990. "Sex and More Sex: A Critique of the Kinsey Conception of Human Sexuality." Pp. 367-86 in *Homosexuality/Heterosexuality: Concepts of Sexual Orientation*, edited by David P. McWhirter, June M. Reinisch, and Stephanie A. Sanders. New York: Oxford University Press.

Dobash, R. Emerson and Russell P. Dobash. 1992. *Women, Violence and Social Change*. London: Routledge.

Eagly, Alice H. 1987. *Sex Differences in Social Behavior: A Social Role Interpretation*. Hillsdale, NJ: Lawrence Erlbaum.

Erikson, Erik H. [1950] 1965. *Childhood and Society*. Harmondsworth: Penguin.

Fausto-Sterling, Anne. 1992. *Myths of Gender: Biological Theories about Women and Men*. 2d ed. New York: Basic Books.

Foley, Douglas E. 1990. *Learning Capitalist Culture: Deep in the Heart of Tejas*. Philadelphia: University of Pennsylvania Press.

Foucault, Michel. 1978. *The History of Sexuality*. Vol. 1, *An Introduction*. Translated by Robert Hurley. New York: Random House.

Gagnon, John H. and William Simon. 1974. *Sexual Conduct: The Social Sources of Human Sexuality*. London: Hutchinson.

Gender Equality Ombudsman. 1997. *The Father's Quota* (leaflet). Oslo: Gender Equality Ombudsman.

Gilder, Eric. 1989. "The Process of Political *Praxis*: Efforts of the Gay Community to Transform the Social Signification of AIDS." *Communication Quarterly* 37:27-38.

Glassner, Barry. 1988. *Bodies: Why We Look the Way We Do (and How We Feel About It)*. New York: Putnam.

Goldberg, Steven. 1993. *Why Men Rule: A Theory of Male Dominance.* Chicago: Open Court.

Greenberg, David F. 1988. *The Construction of Homosexuality.* Chicago: University of Chicago Press.

Gruneau, Richard and David Whitson. 1993. *Hockey Night in Canada: Sport, Identities and Cultural Politics.* Toronto: Garamond.

Hawkesworth, Mary. 1997. "Confounding Gender." *Signs* 22:649-85 (with comments and replies by McKenna and Kessler, Smith, Scott and Connell, pp. 687-713).

Hearn, Jeff and Wendy Parkin. 1987. *"Sex" at "Work": The Power and Paradox of Organisation Sexuality.* Brighton: Wheatsheaf.

Henley, Nancy M. 1977. *Body Politics: Power, Sex, and Nonverbal Communication.* Englewood Cliffs, NJ: Prentice Hall.

Henriksson, Benny. 1995. *Risk Factor Love: Homosexuality, Sexual Interaction and HIV-Prevention.* Göteborg: Göteborgs Universitet Institutionen für Socialt Arbete.

Kemper, Theodore D. 1990. *Social Structure and Testosterone: Explorations of the Socio-bio-social Chain.* New Brunswick, NJ: Rutgers University Press.

King, Dave. 1981. "Gender Confusions: Psychological and Psychiatric Conceptions of Transvestism and Transsexualism." Pp. 155-83 in *The Making of the Modern Homosexual,* edited by Kenneth Plummer. London: Hutchinson.

Krafft-Ebing, R. von. [1886] 1965. *Psychopathia Sexualis.* New York: Paperback Library.

Laumann, Edward O., John H. Gagnon, Robert T. Michael and Stuart Michaels. 1994. *The Social Organization of Sexuality: Sexual Practices in the United States.* Chicago: University of Chicago Press.

Lees, Sue. 1986. *Losing Out: Sexuality and Adolescent Girls.* London: Hutchinson.

Lorber, Judith. 1994. *Paradoxes of Gender.* New Haven, CT: Yale University Press.

Maccoby, Eleanor E. and Carol N. Jacklin. 1975. *The Psychology of Sex Differences.* Stanford, CA: Stanford University Press.

Mason, G. and S. Tomsen, eds. 1997. *Homophobic Violence.* Sydney: Federation.

Messner, Michael A. and Donald F. Sabo. 1994. *Sex, Violence and Power in Sports: Rethinking Masculinity.* Freedom, CA: Crossing Press.

Murray, Alison J. 1991. *No Money, No Honey: A Study of Street Traders and Prostitutes in Jakarta.* Singapore: Oxford University Press.

Oetomo, Dede. 1990. "Patterns of Bisexuality in Indonesia." Faculty of Social and Political Sciences, Universitas Airlangga. Unpublished manuscript.

Parker, Richard. 1985. "Masculinity, Femininity, and Homosexuality: On the Anthropological Interpretation of Sexual Meanings in Brazil." *Journal of Homosexuality* 11, nos. 3-4:155-63.

Perkins, Roberta. 1983. *The "Drag Queen" Scene: Transsexuals in King's Cross.* Sydney: Allen & Unwin.

Pringle, Rosemary. 1992. "Absolute Sex? Unpacking the Sexuality/Gender Relationship." In *Rethinking Sex: Social Theory and Sexuality Research,* edited by R. W. Connell and G. W. Dowsett. Melbourne: Melbourne University Press.

Ram, Kalpana. 1991. *Mukkuvar Women: Gender, Hegemony and Capitalist Transformation in a South Indian Fishing Community.* Sydney: Allen & Unwin.

Risman, Barbara J. 1987. "Intimate Relationships from a Microstructural Perspective: Men Who Mother." *Gender & Society* 1:6-32.

Rossi, Alice S. 1985. "Gender and Parenthood." Pp. 161-91 in *Gender and the Life Course,* edited by Alice S. Rossi. New York: Aldine.

Rubin, Gayle. 1984. "Thinking Sex: Notes for a Radical Theory of the Politics of Sexuality." Pp. 267-319 in *Pleasure and Danger: Exploring Female Sexuality,* edited by Carole S. Vance. Melbourne: Routledge & Kegan Paul.

———. 1991. "The Catacombs: A Temple of the Butthole." Pp. 119-41 in *Leatherfolk: Radical Sex, People, Politics, and Practice,* edited by Mark Thompson. Boston: Alyson.

Rubin, Henry. Forthcoming. *The Subject Matters: Transsexual Subjectivity and Embodiment.* Chicago: University of Chicago Press.

Russell, Diana E. H. 1982. *Rape in Marriage.* New York: Macmillan.

Stoller, Robert. 1968. *Sex and Gender: On the Development of Masculinity and Femininity.* New York: Science House.

Theberge, Nancy. 1991. "Reflections on the Body in the Sociology of Sport." *Quest* 43:123-34.

Turner, Charles F. 1989. "Research on Sexual Behaviors That Transmit HIV: Progress and Problems." *AIDS* 3, suppl. 1:63-69.

United Nations Development Program. 1994. *Human Development Report 1994.* New York: Oxford University Press.

Vance, Carole S. 1989. "Social Construction Theory: Problems in the History of Sexuality." Pp. 13-34 in *Homosexuality, Which Homosexuality?* edited by Dennis Altman et al. London: GMP.

Walkowitz, Judith R. 1980. *Prostitution and Victorian Society: Women, Class and the State.* Cambridge: Cambridge University Press.

Weeks, Jeffrey. 1977. *Coming Out: Homosexual Politics in Britain, from the Nineteenth Century to the Present.* London: Quartet.

———. 1986. *Sexuality.* London: Horwood & Tavistock.

Wilson, Edward O. 1978. *On Human Nature.* Cambridge, MA: Harvard University Press.

Wilson, Elizabeth. 1987. *Adorned in Dreams: Fashion and Modernity.* Berkeley: University of California Press.

Young, Iris Marion. 1990. *Justice and the Politics of Difference.* Princeton, NJ: Princeton University Press.

About the Contributors

Joan Acker is Professor Emerita in the Department of Sociology, University of Oregon. Her work includes feminist critiques of class and organizational theory and studies of gender and organization processes. She is currently finishing a study of gender and organizational change, a book on feminist sociology, and is in the beginning of a study of welfare reform.

Anette Borchorst received her doctorate in political science from Aalborg University, Denmark. She is currently Associate Professor at the Institute of Political Science at Aarhus University. Her research and publications have focused on gender issues at the intersection of economics and politics, including work on sex segregation of the labor market, gender differences in employment, family and child-care policies, and equal opportunity programs. Gender and the welfare state in comparative perspective, with special emphasis on Scandinavia and Western Europe, has been a major focus of her work. She is currently attached to the research program called Gender, Empowerment, and Politics (GEP), for which she has produced a monograph, *Research on Women in Political Decision Making in Denmark* (1997).

Lisa D. Brush, Assistant Professor of Sociology, is Principal Investigator of the Family Violence and Self-Sufficiency Project at the University of Pittsburgh. Current interests include issues of money, power, harm, and healing at the personal and institutional intersections of work, violence, stress, and welfare reform. Her work on such varied topics as gender, privatization, welfare state building, and violence against women has appeared in *Signs,* the *Berkeley Journal of Sociology,* and *Gender & Society,* where she currently serves on the editorial board. She is a contributor to *Violence Against Women: The Bloody Footprints,* edited by Pauline Bart and Eileen Moran (1993). She spent her postdoctoral year as the Warren Weaver Fellow in the Equal Opportunities Division of the Rockefeller Foundation. Along the way, she has also earned a black belt in traditional Japanese karate.

Patricia Hill Collins is Charles Phelps Taft Professor of Sociology at the Department of African-American Studies, University of Cincinnati.

Although her specialties in sociology include such diverse areas as sociology of knowledge, organizational theory, social stratification, and work and occupations, her research and scholarship have dealt primarily with issues of gender, race, and social class, specifically relating to African American women. She has published many articles in professional journals and edited volumes. Her first book, *Black Feminist Thought: Knowledge, Consciousness, and the Politics of Empowerment*, published in 1990, has won many awards. Her second book, *Race, Class, and Gender: An Anthology* (edited with Margaret Andersen), originally published in 1992, with second and third editions in 1995 and 1998, is widely used in undergraduate classrooms throughout the United States. Her latest book is *Fighting Words: Black Women and the Search for Justice* (1998). She has taught at several institutions, held editorial positions with professional journals, lectured widely in the United States and abroad, served in many capacities in professional organizations, and acted as consultant for a number of businesses and community organizations.

David L. Collinson is Senior Lecturer in Organizational Behaviour at the University of Warwick in the United Kingdom. He is the author of *Managing the Shopfloor: Subjectivity, Masculinity and Workplace Culture*, coauthor of *Managing to Discriminate*, and coeditor of *Job Redesign* and *Men as Managers, Managers as Men: Critical Perspectives on Men, Masculinities, and Managements*. He has conducted research and published papers on various aspects of gender and employment, including sex discrimination in selection, sexual harassment, men and masculinities, equal pay for work of equal value, time and space, managerial practices, and shop-floor culture. In addition, he has published research studies on workplace resistance, humor, stress, human resource management, and safety practices on North Sea oil installations. His theoretical interests center on the examination of power, culture, and subjectivity in the workplace. He is an Associate Editor of the journal *Gender, Work and Organization* and is an editorial board member of *Organizational Studies*.

R. W. Connell taught in three Australian universities and in four North American universities before coming to a Chair of Education at the University of Sydney. He has been President of the Sociological Association of Australia and New Zealand and a recipient of the American Sociological Association's award for distinguished contribution to the study of sex and gender, and has given keynote addresses at conferences in Brazil, Britain, Germany, Norway, and the United States, as well as Australia. His books include *Ruling Class, Ruling Culture; Class Structure in Australian History; Making the Difference; Gender and Power; Schools and Social Justice*, and *Masculinities*. His research interests have centered on social structure and the dynamics of change, the way personal lives are shaped within social contexts, and the interplay between education and social forces. His recent projects have concerned poverty and education, the making of masculinities, and the social theory of gender. His current research includes a study of the intellectual labor process and of intellectuals as a group on a world scale, including an examination of teachers in school and higher education.

Shari L. Dworkin is a PhD candidate in sociology at the University of Southern California. Her past research is on sports media coverage of male athletes with HIV / AIDS and appears in the *Journal of Sport and Social Issues* (1997), *Sociology of Sport Journal* (1998), and *Masculinities and Sport,* edited by Michael A. Messner, Don Sabo, and Jim McKay (forthcoming) (all co-authored with Faye Linda Wachs). Her dissertation is an ethnographic work on gendered and sexualized bodies among fitness participants and is entitled "The Glass Ceiling on Women's Muscular Strength: Gender Relations, the Body, and the Gym."

Myra Marx Ferree is Professor of Sociology and Women's Studies at the University of Connecticut. Among her recent publications are *Feminist Organizations: Harvest of the New Women's Movement,* coedited with Patricia Yancey Martin (1995), and various articles on gender, family, social movements, and feminism in the United States and Germany. She is currently working on a study of abortion discourse in Germany and the United States from 1970 to 1994.

Susan T. Fiske is Distinguished University Professor of Psychology at the University of Massachusetts, Amherst. She has authored more than 100 journal articles and book chapters, and has edited seven books and journal special issues, including *The Handbook of Social Psychology* (with Daniel Gilbert and Gardner Lindzey) and the *Annual Review of Psychology* (with Daniel Schacter and Carolyn Zahn-Waxler). Her graduate textbook, with Shelley Taylor, *Social Cognition* (1984, 1991), defined the subfield of how people think about and make sense of other people, and her research on cognition led to her expert testimony on segregation (cited in a U.S. Supreme Court decision), as well as testimony before President Clinton's Race Initiative Advisory Board in 1998. She received the 1991 American Psychological Association Award for Distinguished Contributions to Psychology in the Public Interest and, with Peter Glick, the 1995 Gordon Allport Intergroup Relations Award from the Society for the Psychological Study of Social Issues. In 1994, she served as President of the Society for Personality and Social Psychology. On campus, she teaches undergraduate courses on social psychology and on racism, in addition to serving on several diversity and multiculturalism committees.

Evelyn Nakano Glenn is Professor of Women's Studies and Comparative Ethnic Studies at the University of California, Berkeley. Her interests center on women's work, the political economy of households, and the intersection of race and gender. She has written extensively on a variety of topics within these broad areas, including racial ethnic women's labor, paid domestic work, impacts of changing technology on clerical labor processes, gender and immigration, and social constructions of mothering. She is the author of *Issei, Nisei, Warbride: Three Generations of Japanese American Women in Domestic Service* (1986) and coeditor (with Grace Chang and Linda Forcey) of *Mothering: Ideology, Experience, and Agency* (1994). Her current research focuses on raced and gendered constructions of labor and citizenship in three regions.

Peter Glick is Professor of Psychology at Lawrence University in Appleton, Wisconsin. He received his A.B. in psychology from Oberlin College in 1975 and his Ph.D. in social psychology from the University of Minnesota in 1984. Along with coauthor Susan T. Fiske, he received the 1995 Gordon Allport Intergroup Relations Prize, honoring the "best paper or article of the year on intergroup relations" for the "The Ambivalent Sexism Inventory: Differentiating Hostile and Benevolent Sexism." His research interests center on understanding intergroup and interpersonal relations between men and women, the ambivalent attitudes that each sex has about the other, and how the structure of intergroup relations influences the content of group stereotypes.

Beth B. Hess, Professor Emerita, County College of Morris, has published extensively in the areas of gender (with Myra Marx Ferree), social gerontology (with Elizabeth W. Markson), and introductory sociology (with Peter J. Stein and Elizabeth W. Markson). She has served as President of the Eastern Sociological Society, the Society for the Study of Social Problems, Sociologists for Women in Society, and the Association for Humanist Sociology, as well as Secretary of the American Sociological Association.

Judith Lorber is Professor Emerita of Sociology at Brooklyn College and the Graduate School, City University of New York, where she was first Coordinator of the Women's Studies Certificate Program. She is the author of *Gender Inequality: Feminist Theories and Politics* (1998), *Gender and the Social Construction of Illness* (1997), *Paradoxes of Gender* (1994), and *Women Physicians: Careers, Status and Power* (1984), as well as numerous articles on gender, women as health care workers and patients, and sociological aspects of the new procreative technologies. She was founding editor of *Gender & Society*, official publication of Sociologists for Women in Society, and, with Susan A. Farrell, coedited a collection of papers from that journal, *The Social Construction of Gender* (1991). She was Chair of the Sex and Gender Section of the American Sociological Association in 1993 and received the 1996 ASA Jessie Bernard Career Award. In 1997, she held the Marie Jahoda International Visiting Professorship of Feminist Studies at Ruhr University, Bochum, Germany.

Patricia Yancey Martin uses feminist principles to help her students question the *invisible* aspects of social life relative to gender, race, class, and sexuality. She is Professor of Sociology and Daisy Parker Flory Alumni Professor at Florida State University. Her areas of study are gender, organizations, and violence against women. She recently edited a collection of essays (with Myra Marx Ferree) on feminist organizations titled *Feminist Organizations: Harvest of the New Women's Movement* (1995). She is writing a monograph on the politics of rape processing work using data from 130 Florida organizations (rape crisis centers, police, prosecutors, judges, hospitals, and defense attorneys) as well as a textbook on gender and sexuality in organizations for the **Gender Lens** series. Her current research concerns men and masculinities at work, and gender in rape processing organizations (including rape crisis centers) that mobilize unobtrusively inside mainstream organizations.

Michael A. Messner is Associate Professor of Sociology and Gender Studies at the University of Southern California, where he teaches courses on sex and gender, men and masculinity, sexuality, and gender and sport. He is coeditor (with Donald F. Sabo) of *Sport, Men, and the Gender Order: Critical Feminist Perspectives* (1990), author of *Power at Play: Sports and the Problem of Masculinity* (1992), and coauthor (with Donald F. Sabo) of *Sex, Violence, and Power in Sports: Rethinking Masculinity* (1994). His most recent book is *Politics of Masculinities: Men in Movements* (1997).

Valentine M. Moghadam was born in Tehran, Iran, and received her PhD from American University. From 1990-1996 she was Senior Researcher and Coordinator of the Research Program on Women and Development at the WIDER Institute of the United Nations University, based in Helsinki, Finland. She was a member of the UN University delegation to the World Summit on Social Development (Copenhagen, March 1995) and the Fourth World Conference on Women (Beijing, September 1995). She has authored *Modernizing Women: Gender and Social Change in the Middle East* (1993) and *Women, Work, and Economic Reform in the Middle East and North Africa* (1998), and edited *Identity Politics and Women: Cultural Reassertions and Feminisms in International Perspective* (1994), and *Patriarchy and Development: Women's Positions at the End of the Twentieth Century* (1996). Since Fall 1996, she has been Director of Women's Studies and Associate Professor of Sociology at Illinois State University.

Anne R. Roschelle is Assistant Professor of Sociology, Director of the Women's Study Program, and a Faculty Associate at the Center for Latino Studies in the Americas at the University of San Francisco. Her teaching and research has focused on racial and ethnic minorities, gender inequality, and poverty. She is author of *No More Kin: Exploring Race, Class, and Gender in Family Networks* (1997), and is an affiliate at the Center for Critical Global Homeless Studies at San Francisco State University, and serves on the Editorial Board of *Race, Gender, and Class in the World Cultures*. She is also a member of the Bay Area Homeless Children's Network. Her current research is a qualitative analysis of homeless and formerly homeless families in the San Francisco Bay Area.

Barbara Katz Rothman is Professor of Sociology at the City University of New York. She is the author of *Genetic Maps and Human Imaginations: The Limits of Science in Understanding Who We Are* (1998), from which parts of her chapter in this volume are drawn. Her previous work includes *Recreating Motherhood* (recipient of the Jessie Bernard Award of the American Sociological Association), *The Tentative Pregnancy,* and *In Labor: Women and Power in the Workplace;* she is also coauthor, with Wendy Simonds, of *Centuries of Solace.*

Joan Wallach Scott is Professor of Social Science at the Institute for Advanced Study in Princeton, New Jersey. She is editor of *Feminism and History* (1996), and coeditor, with Judith Butler, of *Feminists Theorize the Political* (1992). She is the author of *Gender and the Politics of History* (1988) and, most recently, *Only Paradoxes to Offer: French Feminists and the Rights of Man* (1996).

Susan Starr Sered is Associate Professor of Anthropology at Bar Ilan University in Israel. Her research focuses on the intersection of gender and religion. She has carried out fieldwork in both Israel and Okinawa. Her publications include *Women as Ritual Experts: The Religious Lives of Jewish Women in Jerusalem* (1992), *Priestess, Mother, Sacred Sister: Religions Dominated by Women* (1994), and *Women of the Sacred Groves: Divine Priestesses of Okinawa* (1999). She is currently working on a project that examines situations of gendered religious conflict in Jewish communities in the United States and Israel.

Suzanna Danuta Walters is Associate Professor in the Department of Sociology at Georgetown University, where she also teaches in the Women's Studies Program. She is the author of numerous works in feminist cultural studies and lesbian and gay studies, including *Lives Together/Worlds Apart: Mothers and Daughters in Popular Culture* (1992), *Material Girls: Making Sense of Feminist Cultural Theory* (1995), and "From Here to Queer: Radical Feminism, Postmodernism, and the Lesbian Menace (or, Why Can't a Woman Be More Like a Fag?)" (*Signs,* summer 1996). She is currently working on two (popular and nonacademic) book projects. The first is a study of contemporary representations of lesbians and gay men in the popular imagination (*Visibly Unsettled: Pop Culture in the Gay 90s*), and the second is a book on feminist theory (*Feminism Is the Story of Our Lives: Feminist Theory for the 21st Century*). Both reckon with issues of identity politics in the postmodern age, the commodification of resistance, and the dangers of assimilation.